THE

HISTORY OF CIVILI.......

FROM THE FALL OF THE ROMAN EMPIRE
TO THE FRENCH REVOLUTION

F. GUIZOT

TRANSLATED BY WILLIAM HAZLITT

(the Registrar)

✻ SON OF William Hazlitt, the critic & essayist

IN THREE VOLUMES
VOL. I.

LONDON
GEORGE BELL & SONS
1898

The History of Civilzation, Volume I

F. Guizot

Recevez, Monsieur, l'assurance de ma Considération très distingué

Guizot

ADVERTISEMENT.

————

THE following Lectures were delivered by M. Guizot, in the years 1828, 1829, and 1830, at the Old Sorbonne, now the seat of the *Faculté des Lettres*, of Paris, on alternate days with MM. Cousin and Villemain, a triad of lecturers whose brilliant exhibitions, the crowds which thronged their lecture rooms, and the stir they excited in the active and aspiring minds so numerous among the French youth, the future historian will commemorate as among the remarkable appearances of that important era.

The first portion of these Lectures, those comprising the *General History of Civilization in Europe*, have already appeared amongst us; the *Lectures on the History of Civilization in France* are now for the first time introduced to English readers; a circumstance, from their high value, well calculated to surprise those who are not acquainted with the utter want of system in our adoption of the great productions of the continent; a want of system which has hitherto kept the English public in well-nigh total ignorance of the best works, of the best continental writers, and which it is one of the leading purposes of the EUROPEAN LIBRARY to obviate. Of these Lectures, it is most justly observed by the *Edinburgh Review:* " there is a consistency, a coherence, a comprehensiveness, and, what the Germans would term, many-sidedness, in the manner of M. Guizot's fulfilment of his task, that manifests him one to whom the whole subject is familiar; that exhibits a full possession of the facts which have any important bearing upon his conclusions; and a deliberateness, a matureness, an entire absence of haste or crudity, in his explanations of historical phenomena, which give evidence of a general scheme so well wrought out and digested beforehand, that the labours of research and of thought necessary for the whole work seem to have been performed before any part was committed to paper." The same writer laments that a knowledge of M. Guizot's writings is even now not a common possession in this country. It will be rendered such by the pages of the EUROPEAN LIBRARY.

W. HAZLITT

---

¹ The European Library in which this work first appeared was for the most part merged in BOHN'S STANDARD LIBRARY.

BIOGRAPHICAL NOTICE OF M. GUIZOT.

———

On the 8th of April, 1794, three days after the bloody victory of Robespierre over Danton, Camille Desmoulins, and the men of the Committee of Clemency, the scaffold was prepared at Nimes for a distinguished advocate, who was also suspected of resistance to the will of the terrible triumvirate, and desolation had seated itself at the fireside of one of the worthiest families of the country. A woman, all tears, was beseeching God for strength to support a fearful blow; for the executioner at that moment was rendering her a widow, and her two children orphans. The eldest of these, scarcely seven years old, already wore upon his contemplative countenance the stamp of precocious intellect. Misfortune is a species of hot-house; one grows rapidly within its influence. This child, who had no childhood, was François Pierre Guillaume Guizot.

Born a Protestant, on the 4th of October, 1787, under the sway of a legislation which refused to recognise the legal union of his parents and denied him a name and social rank, young Guizot saw the Revolution, with the same blow, restore him definitively to his rightful place in God's world, and make him pay for the benefit by the blood of his father. If we designed to write anything more than a biography, perhaps we might find in this concurrence of circumstances the first germ of that antipathy which the statesman afterwards manifested, almost equally for absolute monarchies and for democratic governments.

. After the fatal catastrophe just related, Madame Guizot

[1] Chiefly from the *Galerie des Contemporains Illustres*, 3rd edition. Paris, 1840.

b

left a city which was filled with such bitter recollections, and
went to seek at Geneva consolation in the bosom of her
family, and a solid education for her children. Young Guizot,
placed at the gymnasium of Geneva, devoted his whole soul
to study. His first and only playthings were books; and
at the end of four years, the advanced scholar was able to
read in their respective languages the works of Thucydides
and Demosthenes, of Cicero and Tacitus, of Dante and
Alfieri, of Schiller and Goethe, of Gibbon and Shakespere.
His last two years at college were especially consecrated to
historical and philosophical studies. Philosophy, in particular,
had powerful attractions for him. His mind, endowed by
nature with an especial degree of logical strength, was quite
at home, was peculiarly enabled to unfold and open in the
little Genevese republic, which has preserved something of
the learned and inflexible physiognomy of its patron, John
Calvin.

Having completed his collegiate studies with brilliant success, in 1805, M. Guizot proceeded to Paris to prepare himself
for the bar. It is well known that the law schools had disappeared amid the revolutionary whirlwind. Several private
establishments had been formed to supply the deficiency; but
M. Guizot, not caring for an imperfect knowledge of the profession, resolved upon mastering it in solitude. At once poor
and proud, austere and ambitious, the young man found himself cast into a world of intrigue, frivolity, and licentiousness.
The period between the Directory and the Empire was a
multiform, uncertain, dim epoch, like all periods of transition.
Violently agitated by the revolutionary blast, the social
current had not yet entirely resumed its course. Many of
the ideas which had been hurled to the ground were again
erect, but pale, enfeebled, tottering, and, as it were, stunned
by the terrible blow which had prostrated them. Some
superior minds were endeavouring to direct into a new path
the society which was rising from its ruins; but the mass,
long debarred from material enjoyments, only sought full use
of the days of repose which they feared to see too soon ended.
Hence that character of general over-excitement, that disso-
luteness of morals which well nigh brought back the times
of the Regency.

The serious and rigid nature of the Genevese scholar

sufficed to preserve him from the contagion. The first year
of his residence at Paris was one of sadness and isolation.
He fell back upon himself, like all men who, feeling themselves strong, want the means of making essay of their
strength.

The following year he became attached as tutor to the
household of M. Stapfer, minister for Switzerland at the
French court, where he experienced almost paternal kindness,
and had opened to him treasures of philosophical learning
well calculated to direct and promote his intellectual development. This connexion gave him admission to the salon of
M. Suard, where all the most distinguished minds of the
epoch were wont to assemble, and where he saw for the first
time the woman who was destined to exercise so noble and
beneficial an influence over his whole life.

The circumstance which brought about the marriage of M.
Guizot was somewhat tinged with romance. Born of a distinguished family, which had been ruined by the Revolution,
Mademoiselle Pauline de Meulan had found resources in an
education as solid as varied, and, to support her family, had
thrown herself into the trying career of journalism. At the
period in question, she was editing the *Publiciste*. A serious
malady, however, brought on by excess of toil, obliged her to
interrupt labours so essential to the happiness, the existence
of those she loved. Her situation threatened to become very
critical; she was almost in despair, when one day she received
an anonymous letter, entreating her to be tranquil, and offering to discharge her task during the continuance of her illness. The letter was accompanied by an article admirably
written, the ideas and the style of which, by a refinement of
delicacy, were exactly modelled upon her own. She accepted
this article, published it, and regularly received a similar con
tribution until her restoration to health. Profoundly affected
by such kindness, she related the affair in the salon of M.
Suard, exhausting her imagination in endeavours to discover
her unknown friend, and never thinking for a moment of a pale,
serious young man, with whom she was scarcely acquainted,
and who listened to her in silence, as she pursued her conjectures. Earnestly supplicated through the columns of the journal
to reveal himself, the generous incognito at last went in person to receive the well merited thanks. It was the young man

just alluded to, and five years afterwards Mademoiselle de Meulan took the name of Madame Guizot.

During the five years, M. Guizot was occupied with various literary labours. In 1809, he published his first work, the *Dictionnaire des Synonyme*, the introduction to which, a philosophical appreciation of the peculiar characteristics of the French language, displayed that spirit of precision and method which distinguishes M. Guizot. Next came the *Vies des Poetes Français;* then a translation of Gibbon, enriched with historical notes of the highest interest; and next, a translation of a work of Rehfus, *Spain in* 1808.

All these works were produced before the author had reached the age of twenty-five, a fact from which the character of his mind may be judged.

In 1812, his talents were sufficiently well known to induce M. de Fontanes to attach him to the university by appointing him assistant professor of history in the Faculty of Letters. Soon afterwards, he obtained complete possession of that Chair of Modern History, in connexion with which he has left such glorious recollections. There was formed his friendship with M. Royer-Collard, then professor of the history of philosophy —a friendship afterwards closely cemented by time.

This first portion of M. Guizot's life was exclusively literary. It has been attempted to make him out at this period an ardent legitimist, caballing and conspiring in secret to hasten the return of the Bourbons. We have discovered no fact that justifies the assertion. By his wife, by his literary relations, and by his tastes, he belonged, it is true, to a certain class, who retained, amid the roughness of the empire, traditions of the elegance and good taste of the aristocracy of the previous age. A sort of philosophical varnish was very much in fashion among the literati of that class, whom Napoleon used to denominate *idéologists*. They ideologized, in truth, a great deal; but they had little to do with politics. And it is well known, moreover, that it was requisite for the pen of the *Chantre des Martyrs* to devote itself entirely to the task of reviving the well nigh forgotten memory of the Bourbons in the heart of a generation which had not beheld their fall.

The events of 1814 found M. Guizot in his native town of Nimes, whither he had gone to visit his mother after a long separation. On his return, the young professor was indebted to the active friendship of Royer-Collard for his selection by the Abbé de Montesquiou, then Minister of the Interior, to fill the post of Secretary-General in his department. This was the first step of M. Guizot in the path of politics. Although he was placed in a secondary position, his great abilities exerted a considerable influence upon the administrative measures of the time. The partisans of the liberal cause reproached him especially with having, in conjunction with Royer-Collard, prepared that severe law against the press which was presented to the Chambers of 1814 by M. de Montesquiou, and also with having taken a seat in the committee of censorship, by the side of M. de Frayssinous. On the other hand, the ultra-royalist faction was indignant at hearing an insignificant plebeian, a professor, a protestant, employed in affairs of state, with a court abbé, talk of constitutional equilibrium, of balance of powers; to see him endeavouring to conciliate monarchical ideas with the new interests created by the Revolution. In the eyes of the one party, he did too little, in the eyes of the other, too much; Napoleon's return from Elba released him from his difficult position. After the departure of the Bourbons, he resumed his functions in the Faculty of Letters; and two months after, when the fall of the emperor became evident to all, he was charged by the constitutional royalists with a mission to Ghent, to plead the cause of the Charter before Louis XVIII., and to insist upon the absolute necessity of keeping M. de Blacas, the chief of the old regime party, from all participation in affairs. This is the statement of the affair given by his friends, and what seems to prove that it was in fact the object of M. Guizot's mission, is, that a month afterwards, on his return into France, the king dismissed M. de Blacas, and published the proclamation of Cambrai, in which he acknowledged the faults of his government, and added new guarantees to the Charter.

Every one knows what violent storms agitated the Chamber of 1815, composed of the most heterogeneous elements, and wherein the majority, more royalist than the king himself, constantly opposed every measure calculated to reconcile the country to the dynasty of the Bourbons. To say that M. Guizot then filled the office of Secretary-General, in the department of justice under the Marquis de Barbé-Marbois, is to say that, whilst he conceded much, too much, perhaps, to the demands of the victorious party, he endeavoured to arrest, as far as he could, the encroaching spirit of the partisans of absolute royalty.   His first political pamphlet, *Du Gouvernement Representatif, et de l'Etat actuel de la France*, which he published in refutation of a work by M. de Vitrolles, gave the criterion of his governmental ideas, and placed him in the ranks of the constitutional royalist minority, represented in the Chamber by Messrs. Royer-Collard, Pasquier, Camille Jourdain, and de Serres.   It was about this epoch, after the victory of the moderate party, the dissolution of the Chamber of 1815, and the accession of the ministry of the Duke Decazes, that a new word was introduced into the political language of France.   It has not been consecrated by the dictionary of the French Academy, for want, perhaps, of ability to give it a precise definition; but it appears to us desirable to furnish, if not its signification (which would be a difficult matter), at least its history.

It is well known that prior to 1789, the *Doctrinaires* were an educational body.   M. Royer-Collard had been educated in a college of *Doctrinaires*, and in the debates of the Chamber his logical and lofty understanding always impelling him to sum up the question in a dogmatical form, the word *doctrine* was often upon his lips, so that one day a wag of the royalist majority cried out, *Voilà bien les doctrinaires!*   The phrase took, and remained as a definition, if not clear, at all events absolute, of the political fraction directed by Royer-Collard.

Let us now explain the origin of that famous *canapé de la doctrine*, which awakens ideas as vague as the divan of the Sublime Porte.   One day, Count Beugnot, a *doctrinaire*, was asked to enumerate the forces of his party.   "Our party," he replied, " could all be accommodated on this canapé (sofa)."   This phrase also was successful, and the changes were rung on it to such a degree that the multitude came to regard the *doctrinaires* as a collection of individuals, half-jesuits, half-epicureans, seated like Turks, upon downy cushions, and pedantically discoursing about public affairs.

The reaction consequent upon the assassination of the Duke de Berri is not yet forgotten.   The Decazes ministry fell, and the firmest supporters of the constitutional party were driven from office. Messrs. Royer-Collard, Camille Jourdain, and de Barante left the council of state; M. Guizot accompanied them, and from that moment until the accession of the Martignac cabinet, of 1828, his political life was an incessant struggle against the administration of Villèle. Whilst the national interests of France had eloquent defenders in the Chambers, M. Guizot, who was still too young to be permitted to ascend the tribune, sustained the same cause in writings, the success of which was universal. We cannot here analyze the entire series of the occasional productions of M. Guizot from 1820 to 1822. In one he defends the system of the Duke Decazes, trampled upon as revolutionary by the counter revolution; in another he investigates the cause of those daily conspiracies which appear to him to be insidiously provoked by the agents of government for the overthrow of constitutional institutions. Elsewhere, in his work, entitled *La Peine de Mort Matière Politique*, without pretending to erase completely from our laws the punishment of death, even for political crimes, he demonstrates, in a grave and elevated style, that power has a deep interest in keeping within its scabbard the terrible weapon which transforms into persecutors those who brandish it, and into martyrs those whom it smites.

Among these political lucubrations, there is one which strikes us as worthy, in many respects, of special mention. In his treatise upon *Des Moyens d'Opposition et de Gouvernement dans l'Etat actuel de la France*, published in 1821, M. Guizot completely lays bare the nature of his political individuality, and furnishes both an explanation of his past, and the secret of his future career. It was not an ordinary opposition, that of M. Guizot. He defends the public liberties, but he defends them in his own way, which is not that of all the world. He may be said to march alone in his path, and if he is severe towards the men whom he combats, he is not less so towards those who are fighting with him.

In his view, the capital crime of the Villèle ministry was not the abuse of power in itself, but rather the consequences of that abuse which placed in peril the principle of authority by exposing it to a fatal conflict.

Unlike other polemical writings, which are usually altogether negative and dissolving, those of M. Guizot are
eminently affirmative, governmental, and constituent. When
the word *right* comes from his pen, you may be sure that the
word *duty* is not far off; and never does he put his finger on
an evil without indicating at once what seems to him a
remedy.

At the height of his strife with the ministry, M. Guizot
was engaged in developing, from his professional chair, amid
the applause of a youthful and numerous audience, the various phases of representative government in Europe, since
the fall of the Roman empire, in the course of lectures given
in the following pages. The minister revenged himself upon
the professor for the assaults of the publicist: the lectures were
interdicted in 1825. Retiring into private life, after having
passed through high political functions, M. Guizot was still
poor; but his pen remained to him. Renouncing the in-
flammatory questions of the moment, he undertook a series
of great historical works, which the biographer may confi-
dently praise; for his merits as an historian have never been
denied. Then were successively published, the *Collection des
Memoires relatifs à la Revolution d'Angleterre;* the *Histoire
de la Revolution d'Angleterre, en* 1640; which forms one of
the previous volumes of the European Library; a *Collection
des Memoires relatifs à l'Histoire de France;* and, finally, *Essais
sur l'Histoire de France,* a work by which he carried light
into the dark recesses of the national origin. At the same
time he presented the public with historical essays upon
Shakespere and upon Calvin, a revised translation of the works
of the great English dramatist, and a considerable number of
political articles of a high order in the *Revue Française.*

In 1827, death deprived him of the companion of his
labours—that beloved wife, whose lofty intelligence and
moral strength had sustained him amid the agitations of his
career. It was sad, though calm, philosophical, Christian, that
parting scene between the husband and the dying wife, and
their young son, soon about to follow his mother to the tomb.
Though born and bred a catholic, Madame Guizot had just
before this joined the faith of her husband; that husband
now soothed the last moments of his beloved partner by

reading to her, in his grave, solemn, impressive tones, one of the finest productions of Bossuet, his funeral oration upon the Queen of England.[1]

Some time afterwards, M. Guizot became one of the most active members of the society *Aide-toi, le ciel t'aidera*, the object of which was to defend, in all legal modes, the freedom of elections against the influence of power. The Villèle ministry fell, and that of Martignac restored M. Guizot to his professorial chair and to the circle of admiring students, whom he proceeded to delight with his lectures on the History of Civilization in France. A short time after the formation of the Polignac cabinet, he was elected deputy for Lisieux, and voted for the address of the 221, adding to his vote these words: "'Truth has already trouble enough in penetrating to the council of kings; let us not send it there pale and feeble; let it be no more possible to mistake it than to doubt the loyalty of our sentiments." He wished to oblige power to live, but power was determined to die. On the 26th of July he returned from Nîmes to Paris; on the 27th he drew up the protest of the deputies against the ordinances—a protest more respectful than hostile, manifesting a conservative spirit, dreading rather than desiring a revolution. Power deemed it seditious; the people pronounced it feeble and timid: events proved the people were right.

In the meeting at M. Lafitte's, on the 29th, when all minds were intoxicated with triumph, M. Guizot, ever exclusively occupied with the immediate necessity of regulating the revolution, rose and insisted upon the urgency of at once constituting a municipal commission whose especial duty should be the re-establishment and maintenance of order. On the 30th, this commission appointed him provisional minister of public instruction; on the 31st, he read in the chamber the proclamation conferring the lieutenant-generalship of the kingdom on the Duke of Orleans. During the period preceding the ceremony of the 9th of August, he was busied with the general recomposition of the administration of public affairs, and the revision of the charter, his organizing activity

[1] M. Guizot, in 1828, married Mademoiselle Eliza Dillon, the niece of his first wife, according, it is said, to the earnest entreaties of the latter previous to her death.

having caused him to be transferred to the then most difficult post, the ministry of the interior. In a few days, seventy-six prefects, one hundred and seventy-six sub-prefects, thirty-eight secretaries-general, were removed and replaced. In the draft of the new charter, he endeavoured, but without success, to lower to twenty-five years the age required for eligibility as a representative.

The first ministry of July, formed in a moment of enthusiasm, was as ephemeral as the excitement of the three days. Personal differences, for a time effaced by great events and a common interest, re-appeared more marked than ever, when it became necessary to consolidate the work so rapidly effected. The impulse was still too strong, too near its source, to be guided. The principle of order was compelled to yield to that of liberty; M. Guizot retired.

The history of the Lafitte cabinet is well known. After its dissolution on the 13th of March, the conservative element, at first trampled under foot, raised itself erect, potent, imperious, in the person of Casimir Perier. For the first time since July, a compact, resolute and durable majority was formed in the Chambers. This governmental army, hitherto undisciplined and confused, was divided into three distinct corps manœuvring with unanimity and harmony, under the orders of the fiery minister—the left wing, composed of a goodly fraction of the old liberal opposition of the Restoration, was commanded by M. Thiers, the brilliant deserter from the camp of M. Lafitte; the right wing, formed of the old constitutional monarchists, marched under the banner of M. Guizot, the man of inflexible and conservative will; as to the centre, an aggregation of the undecided and wavering of all sides, it was astonished to find for the first time in M. Dupin, the most eccentric and restive of men, a chief obedient to the word of command and eager for the fray.

Supported by this triple phalanx, the ministry of the 13th was able to make head against opposition in the Chambers, to overcome insurrection in the streets, force the gates of Ancona, and consolidate the system established in July by rescuing it from the exaggeration of its principle.

After the death of Casimir Périer, his captains for some time disputed among themselves the command; M. Thiers and M. Guizot shook hands, and the cabinet of the 11th of

October, 1832 was formed. Upon the proceedings of their administration, M. Guizot exercised a sustained and often preponderant influence.

Whatever may be thought of their acts, there was one exclusively appertaining to the department of M. Guizot— that of public instruction—so glorious, that all parties, the most hostile to the man, have emblazoned it with unqualified approbation. The great and noble law of the 28th of June, 1833, as to primary instruction, conceived, prepared, sustained and executed by M. Guizot, will ever remain one of the grandest creations of our time: the principle of popular education, adopted and proclaimed by the Revolution of '89, but arrested by the social tumults of the last fifty years, at last received its full development beneath the auspices of M. Guizot. Eleven thousand parishes, that is to say, one-fourth of France, previously destitute of that primary instruction which makes the honest man and the good citizen, have seen erected by the side of the humble parish church, the modest school-house, where the children of the poor resort for knowledge, that other bread of the soul which is to support them through the rough trials of life. Volumes might be formed of the detailed instructions addressed by M. Guizot, in reference to this law, to prefects, rectors, mayors, and committees of examination; they are models of precision and clearness. The finest of these productions is undoubtedly the circular to the teachers of the parishes. In its few pages there is, perhaps, as much true eloquence, as much poetry of style and of thought, as in the most admirable works of the epoch. With what touching familiarity does the minister stretch forth his hand to the poor, obscure village preceptor! how he elevates him in the eyes of all, and especially in his own! how he fills him with the importance of his mission! He is almost his friend, his colleague, his equal! For both are striving, each in his sphere, to secure the repose and glory of the country. And then with what paternal solicitude does the statesman, from the recesses of his cabinet, enter into the most insignificant details of the relations of the teacher with children, parents, the mayor, and the curate! "No sectarian or party spirit," he exclaims, "in your school; the teacher must rise above the fleeting quarrels which agitate society! Faith in Providence, the sanctity of duty, submission to parental authority, respect for the laws, the prince, the rights of all, such are the sentiments he must seek to develop." Can there be anything more affecting than the following simple picture of the painful duties of the teacher and the consolations he must find within himself: "There is no fortune to be made, there is little renown to be gained in the painful obligations which the teacher fulfils. Destined to see his life pass away in a monotonous occupation, sometimes even to experience the injustice or ingratitude of ignorance, he would often be saddened, and perhaps would succumb, if he derived courage and strength from no other sources then the prospect of immediate or merely personal reward. He must be sustained and animated by a profound sense of the moral importance of his labours; the grave happiness of having served his fellow-creatures, and obscurely contributed to the public welfare, must be his compensation, and this his conscience alone can give. It is his glory not to aspire to aught beyond his obscure and laborious condition, to exhaust himself in sacrifices scarcely noticed by those whom they benefit, to toil, in short, for man, and to expect his recompence only from God."

Couple these pages of patriarchal gentleness with the pitiless language of M. Guizot in presence of a revolt; hear him thundering from the tribune against the *wicked tail of the Revolution;* behold him reading Bossuet to his dying wife, or throwing with stoic hand the first piece of earth on the coffin of his son; and say, if there be not something strange, grand, immense, in this individuality, in which we find at once the fiery zeal of Luther, the unctuous mildness of Melancthon, the impassibility of Epictetus, the simple kindliness of Fenelon, and the inflexible severity of Richelieu.

After an existence of four years, the cabinet of the 11th of October was dissolved by two causes, one external, the other internal. The public perils at an end, it was deemed too repressive by the Chambers; the majority which had supported it was enfeebled and dislocated, whilst dissensions broke out in its councils between M. Guizot and M. Thiers. The former retired, but did not enter into open hostilities until the formation of the Molé ministry, on the 15th of April, 1838, the policy of which he thus severely denounced: "It is a policy without principle and without banner, made up of expedients and pretexts, ever tottering, leaning on

every side for support, and advancing, in reality, towards
no object; which tampers with, foments, aggravates that uncertainty of men's minds, that relaxation of heart, that want
of faith, consistency, perseverance, energy, which cause disquiet to the country, and weakness to power." To fortify
power, M. Guizot threw himself into the coalition. Many
think that he failed in his purpose. We will not decide the question; it is certain that the governmental car was for an instant
stopped, and the cause dear to M. Guizot brought into peril.

Called upon by the Soult ministry of May 12, 1839, to
replace Marshal Sebastiani, as the representative of France at
the court of St. James's, retained in that office by the
ministry of the 1st March following, and charged with the
defence of the interests of France, in the stormy question of
the East, M. Guizot appeared at first in London under the
most favourable auspices. His literary reputation, his calm,
grave dignity, his thorough knowledge of English manners,
language, and literature, his protestantism, all these features
combined to conciliate for him the suffrages of the haughtiest
and most fastidious of all aristocracies. His society was
universally sought; no French ambassador, since Chateau-
briand, had created so great a sensation. At the Foreign
office, too, everything seemed to be smoothed for him, and
arrangements of a satisfactory nature appeared to be on the
eve of completion, when the Syrian insurrection broke out,
and M. Guizot's position was changed.

The results of the treaty of the 15th July are well known;
there is no need for us to go into a detail of the circumstances under which the ministry of the 1st March fell, and
M. Guizot was called upon to form the Soult-Guizot cabinet
of the 29th Oct. 1840, himself accepting the office of
Minister of Foreign Affairs, which he has ever since retained.

M. Guizot may be considered in four points of view—as a
private individual, as a writer, as an historian, as an orator
and politician.

The virtue of the man has never been called in question.
"The morals of M. Guizot," says one of his most violent
political foes, "are rigid, and pure, and he is worthy, by the
lofty virtue of his life and sentiments, of the esteem of all
good men."

As a writer, his style is one that may be recognised among
a thousand. With his pen in his hand, he takes a firm,

decided tone, goes straight to his object, is not exempt from a species of stiffness, and particularly affects abstract terminology; the form in which he envelopes his thoughts is a little obscure, but the thought is so clear, so brilliant, that it always shines through.

As an historian, he has rendered eminent service to science. He is one of the chiefs of that modern historical school which has taught us to emerge from the present to go and examine the past, and no longer to measure the men and things of former times by our standards of to-day.

As an orator, his manner is dignified and severe. Small and frail in person, he is lofty and proud in bearing; his voice is imposing and sonorous; his language, whether calm or vehement, is always pure and chastened; it has more energy than grace, it convinces rather than moves. When he ascends the tribune, friends and enemies all open their ears; there is no more talking, little coughing, and nobody goes to sleep.

Much has been said of the political versatility of M. Guizot, of his sudden changes, of his former opposition and his present servility; but, from his words, his writings, and his acts at every epoch, we have derived the profound conviction, that, save a few trifling exceptions of detail, his general and distinctive characteristic as a politician is tenacity and consistency; such as he was under the Decazes ministry, or in the opposition to Villèle, such he appears to us to be now. Let us explain our idea without flattery and without enmity.

Providence has imposed upon society an eternal problem, the solution of which it has reserved to itself. There has been, and there always will be, a conflict between two opposite principles, *right* and *duty*, *power* and *liberty*. In presence of these two hostile elements, which the eminent minds of all ages have essayed to conciliate, no one can remain perfectly calm, perfectly impartial. Mathematical truths belong to the head; people do not become excited about them; political truths act upon both the head and the heart; and no one can guard himself from an involuntary movement of attraction or repulsion in relation to them, according to his nature, to the bent of his mind, to his individuality. Some are especially inclined to liberty, others are more disposed to power; some would play the minister, others the tribune; these have the instinct of authority, those the sentiment of independence. Now, M. Guizot is essentially one of the latter; his is an elevated and progressive intellect, but domineering by nature, and governmental by conviction. In his eyes, the France of our day, founded upon two great victories of the principle of liberty, is naturally prone to abuse its triumph, and of the two elements equally necessary for social life, the feeblest at present, the vanquished one, is power.

Setting out from this idea, M. Guizot seeks to re-establish the equilibrium between the two bases of the edifice, giving to the one what the other has too much of, and combining this arrangement of forces within certain limits, with certain measures, the details of which are too long and too complicated to be gone into here.

If we read with attention the political writings of M. Guizot, during the period of the Restoration, we shall soon discover, through all his attacks upon the agents of power, a real sympathy for power itself. Legitimacy exaggerates its rights. Pushed on by imprudent friends and insidious enemies, it drives full sail upon a rock: from the heigh where he has placed himself, M. Guizot sees the danger rebukes those who manage the vessel, and even after it has struck, continues to exclaim, " 'Bout ship!"

The Revolution of July discomposed, perhaps, for an instant, but did not discourage M. Guizot; thus, on the 29th, when the principle which is the object of his solicitude had fallen beneath the popular assault, we behold him earnest to raise it by degrees, and revive its strength, and at length urging it boldly in the direction which he wished it to take before its fall.

What, in short is M. Guizot?

He is, above all, a man of power and of government, and at the same time the most independent of men—submissive to the yoke of self-imposed principles, but bearing his head erect in all questions as to persons; a politician of great worth, and estimating himself at that worth; more convinced than enthusiastic; more proud of the approbation of his conscience than of the homage of the crowd; gifted in a supreme degree with that strength of will and perseverance which make the statesman, a mortal foe to all that resembles disorder, and capable, if things were to come to their worst, of throwing himself, without hesitation, into the arms of despotism, which he does not love, rather than undergo the anarchy which he abhors

[M. Guizot's history, since the above sketch was written, in 1840, includes his career as minister of Louis Philippe, ending with the Revolution of 1848, which dethroned that king and drove him and his minister into exile in England. M. Guizot's story, indeed, from 1840 to 1848 is simply that of France itself.

Soon after the establishment of the Second Empire in 1851, M. Guizot ventured to return to France ; and thenceforward, having settled himself down upon his estate at Val Richer, in Normandy, he devoted himself exclusively to literature, and to the concerns of the French Protestant Church, of which to the day of his death he was looked up to as the head. Many additional works, and many contributions to the journals and reviews, emanated from the pen of the retired statesman, including his *Memoirs*, the *History of Oliver Cromwell, Meditations on Christianity*, etc.

M. Guizot died at Val Richer on September 12th, 1874, and was buried in the neighbouring cemetery of St. Ouen le Pin, the Vicomte d'Harcourt, representing the French Republic, the Duc de Broglie, and Dean Stanley being among the crowd of eminent personages attending his funeral.]

CONTENTS

HISTORY OF CIVILIZATION IN EUROPE.

FIRST LECTURE

SECOND LECTURE.

THIRD LECTURE.

a

FOURTH LECTURE.

FIFTH LECTURE.

SIXTH LECTURE.

SEVENTH LECTURE.

EIGHTH LECTURE.

NINTH LECTURE.

TENTH LECTURE.

ELEVENTH LECTURE.

TWELFTH LECTURE.

THIRTEENTH LECTURE.

FOURTEENTH LECTURE.

HISTORY OF CIVILIZATION IN FRANCE.

———

FIRST LECTURE.

SECOND LECTURE.

THIRD LECTURE.

FOURTH LECTURE.

FIFTH LECTURE.

SIXTH LECTURE.

SEVENTH LECTURE.

EIGHTH LECTURE.

NINTH LECTURE.

TENTH LECTURE.

HISTORY

OF

CIVILIZATION IN EUROPE.

LECTURE THE FIRST.

Object of the course—History of European civilization—Part taken by France in the civilization of Europe—Civilization a fit subject for narrative—It is the most general fact in history—The ordinary and popular meaning of the word *civilization*—Two leading facts constitute civilization: 1. The development of society; 2. The development of the individual—Demonstration—These two facts are necessarily connected the one with the other, and, sooner or later, produce the one the other—Is the destiny of man limited wholly within his actual social condition?—The history of civilization may be exhibited and considered under two points of view—Remarks on the plan of the course—The present state of men's minds, and the prospects of civilization.

GENTLEMEN,

I AM deeply affected by the reception you give me, and which, you will permit me to say, I accept as a pledge of the sympathy which has not ceased to exist between us, notwithstanding so long a separation—Alas! I speak as though you, whom I see around me, were the same who, seven years ago, used to assemble within these walls, to participate in my then labours; because I myself am here again, it seems as if all my former hearers should be here also; whereas, since that period, a change, a mighty change, has come over all things. Seven years ago we repaired hither depressed with anxious doubts and fears, weighed down with sad thoughts and anticipations; we saw ourselves surrounded with difficulty and danger; we felt ourselves dragged on towards an evil which we essayed to

B

avert by calm, grave, cautious reserve, but in vain. Now, we meet together, full of confidence and hope, the heart at peace, thought free.   There is but one way in which we can worthily manifest our gratitude for this happy change; it is by bringing to our present meetings, our new studies, the same calm tranquillity of mind, the same firm purpose, which guided our conduct when, seven years ago, we looked, from day to day, to have our studies placed under rigorous supervision, or, indeed, to be arbitrarily suspended.   Good fortune is delicate, frail, uncertain; we must keep measures with hope as with fear; convalescence requires well nigh the same care, the same caution, as the approaches of illness.   This care, this caution, this moderation, I am sure you will exhibit.   The same sympathy, the same intimate conformity of opinions, of sentiments, of ideas, which united us in times of difficulty and danger, and which at least saved us from grave faults, will equally unite us in more auspicious days, and enable us to gather all their fruits.   I rely with confidence upon your co-operation, and I need nothing more.

The time between this our first meeting and the close of the year is very limited; that which I myself have had, wherein to meditate upon the Lectures I am about to deliver, has been infinitely more limited still.   One great point, therefore, was the selection of a subject, the consideration of which might best be brought within the bounds of the few months which remain to us of this year, within that of the few days I have had for preparation; and it appeared to me, that a general review of the modern history of Europe, considered with reference to the development of civilization—a general sketch, in fact, of the history of European civilization, of its origin, its progress, its aim, its character, might suitably occupy the time at our disposal.   This, accordingly, is the subject of which I propose to treat.

I have used the term European civilization, because it is evident that there is an European civilization; that a certain unity pervades the civilization of the various European states; that, notwithstanding infinite diversities of time, place, and circumstance, this civilization takes its first rise in facts almost wholly similar, proceeds everywhere upon the same principles, and tends to produce well nigh everywhere analogous results. There is, then, an European civilization, and it is to the subject of this aggregate civilization that I will request your attention.

Again, it is evident that this civilization cannot be traced back, that its history cannot be derived from the history of any single European state. If, on the one hand, it is manifestly characterized by brevity, on the other, its variety is no less prodigious; it has not developed itself with completeness, in any one particular country. The features of its physiognomy are wide-spread; we must seek the elements of its history, now in France, now in England, now in Germany, now in Spain.

We of France occupy a favourable position for pursuing the study of European civilization. Flattery of individuals, even of our country, should be at all times avoided: it is without vanity, I think, we may say that France has been the centre, the focus of European civilization. I do not pretend, it were monstrous to do so, that she has always, and in every direction, marched at the head of nations. At different epochs, Italy has taken the lead of her, in the arts; England, in political institutions; and there may be other respects under which, at particular periods, other European nations have manifested a superiority to her; but it is impossible to deny, that whenever France has seen herself thus outstripped in the career of civilization, she has called up fresh vigour, has sprung forward with a new impulse, and has soon found herself abreast with, or in advance of, all the rest. And not only has this been the peculiar fortune of France, but we have seen that when the civilizing ideas and institutions which have taken their rise in other lands, have sought to extend their sphere, to become fertile and general, to operate for the common benefit of European civilization, they have been necessitated to undergo, to a certain extent, a new preparation in France; and it has been from France, as from a second native country, that they have gone forth to the conquest of Europe. There is scarcely any great idea, any great principle of civilization, which, prior to its diffusion, has not passed in this way through France.

And for this reason: there is in the French character something sociable, something sympathetic, something which makes its way with greater facility and effect than does the national genius of any other people; whether from our language, whether from the turn of our mind, of our manners, certain it is that our ideas are more popular than those of other people, present themselves more clearly and intelligibly to the masses, and penetrate among them more readily; in a word, perspicuity, sociability, sympathy, are the peculiar characteristics of France, of her civilization, and it is these qualities which rendered her eminently fit to march at the very head of European civilization.

In entering, therefore, upon the study of this great fact, it is no arbitrary or conventional choice to take France as the centre of this study; we must needs do so if we would place ourselves, as it were, in the very heart of civilization, in the very heart of the fact we are about to consider.

I use the term *fact*, and I do so purposely; civilization is a fact like any other—a fact susceptible, like any other, of being studied, described, narrated.

For some time past, there has been much talk of the necessity of limiting history to the narration of facts: nothing can be more just; but we must always bear in mind that there are far more facts to narrate, and that the facts themselves are far more various in their nature, than people are at first disposed to believe; there are material, visible facts, such as wars, battles, the official acts of governments; there are moral facts, none the less real that they do not appear on the surface; there are individual facts which have denominations of their own; there are general facts, without any particular designation, to which it is impossible to assign any precise date, which it is impossible to bring within strict limits, but which are yet no less facts than the rest, historical facts, facts which we cannot exclude from history without mutilating history.

The very portion of history which we are accustomed to call its philosophy, the relation of events to each other, the connexion which unites them, their causes and their effects,—these are all facts, these are all history, just as much as the narratives of battles, and of other material and visible events. Facts of this class it is doubtless more difficult to disentangle and explain; we are more liable to error in giving an account of them, and it is no easy thing to give them life and animation, to exhibit them in clear and vivid colours; but this difficulty in no degree changes their nature; they are none the less an essential element of history.

Civilization is one of these facts; a general, hidden, complex fact; very difficult, I allow, to describe, to relate, but which none the less for that exists, which, none the less for that, has a right to be described and related. We may raise as to this fact a great number of questions; we may ask, it has been asked, whether it is a good or an evil? Some bitterly deplore it; others rejoice at it. We may ask, whether it is an universal fact, whether there is an universal civilization of the human species, a destiny of humanity; whether the nations have handed down from age to age, something which has never been lost, which must increase, form a larger and larger mass, and thus pass on to the end of time? For my own part, I am convinced that there is, in reality, a general destiny of humanity, a transmission of the aggregate of civilization; and, consequently, an universal history of civilization to be written. But without raising questions so great, so difficult to solve, if we restrict ourselves to a definite limit of time and space, if we confine ourselves to the history of a certain number of centuries, of a certain people, it is evident that within these bounds, civilization is a fact which can be described, related—which is history. I will at once add, that this history is the greatest of all, that it includes all.

And, indeed, does it not seem to yourselves that the fact civilization is the fact *par excellence*—the general and definitive fact, in which all the others terminate, into which they all resolve themselves? Take all the facts which compose the history of a nation, and which we are accustomed to regard as the elements of its life; take its institutions, its commerce, its industry, its wars, all the details of its government: when we would consider these facts in their aggregate, in their connexion, when we would estimate them, judge them, we ask in what they have contributed to the civilization of that nation, what part they have taken in it, what influence they have exercised over it. It is in this way that we not only form a complete idea of them, but measure and appreciate their true value; they are, as it were, rivers, of which we ask what quantity of water it is they contribute to the ocean? For civilization is a sort of ocean, constituting the wealth of a people, and on whose bosom all the elements of the life of that people, all the powers supporting its existence, assemble and unite. This is so true, that even facts, which from their nature are odious, pernicious, which weigh painfully upon nations, despotism, for example, and anarchy, if they have contributed in some way to civilization, if they have enabled it to make an onward stride, up to a certain point we pardon them, we overlook their wrongs, their evil nature; in a word, wherever we recognise civilization, whatever the facts which have created it, we are tempted to forget the price it has cost.

There are, moreover, facts which, properly speaking, we cannot call social; individual facts, which seem to interest the human soul rather than the public life: such are religious creeds and philosophical ideas, sciences, letters, arts. These facts appear to address themselves to man with a view to his moral perfection, his intellectual gratification; to have for their object his internal amelioration, his mental pleasure, rather than his social condition. But, here again, it is with reference to civilization that these very facts are often considered, and claim to be considered.

At all times, in all countries, religion has assumed the glory of having civilized the people; sciences, letters, arts, all the intellectual and moral pleasures, have claimed a share in this glory; and we have deemed it a praise and an honour to them, when we have recognised this claim on their part. Thus, facts the most important and sublime in themselves, independently of all external result, and simply in their relations with the soul of man, increase in importance, rise in sublimity from their affinity with civilization. Such is the value of this general fact, that it gives value to everything it touches. And not only does it give value; there are even occasions when the facts of which we speak, religious creeds, philosophical ideas, letters, arts, are especially considered and judged of with reference to their influence upon civilization; an influence which becomes, up to a certain point and during a certain time, the conclusive measure of their merit, of their value.

What, then, I will ask, before undertaking its history, what, considered only in itself, what is this so grave, so vast, so precious fact, which seems the sum, the expression of the whole life of nations?

I shall take care here not to fall into pure philosophy; not to lay down some ratiocinative principle, and then deduce from it the nature of civilization as a result; there would be many chances of error in this method. And here, again, we have a fact to verify and describe.

For a long period, and in many countries, the word *civilization* has been in use; people have attached to the word ideas more or less clear, more or less comprehensive; but there it is in use, and those who use it, attach some meaning or other to it. It is the general, human, popular meaning of this word that we must study. There is almost always in the usual acceptation of the most general terms, more accuracy than in the definitions, apparently more strict, more precise, of science. It is common sense which gives to words their ordinary signification, and common sense is the characteristic of humanity. The ordinary signification of a word is formed by gradual progress, and in the constant presence of facts; so that when a fact presents itself which seems to come within the meaning of a known term, it is received into it, as it were, naturally; the signification of the term extends itself, expands, and by degrees, the various facts, the various ideas which from the nature of the things themselves men should include under this word, are included.

When the meaning of a word, on the other hand, is determined by science, this determination, the work of one individual, or of a small number of individuals, takes place under the influence of some particular fact which has struck upon the mind. Thus scientific definitions are, in general, much more narrow, and, hence, much less accurate, much less true, at bottom, than the popular meanings of the terms. In studying as a fact the meaning of the word civilization, in investigating all the ideas which are comprised within it, according to the common sense of mankind, we shall make a much greater progress towards a knowledge of the fact itself, than by attempting to give it ourselves a scientific definition, however more clear and precise the latter might appear at first.

I will commence this investigation by endeavouring to place before you some hypotheses: I will describe a certain number of states of society, and we will then inquire whether general instinct would recognise in them the condition of a people civilising itself; whether we recognise in them the meaning which mankind attaches to the word civilization?

First, suppose a people whose external life is easy, is full of physical comfort; they pay few taxes, they are free from suffering; justice is well administered in their private relations —in a word, material existence is for them altogether happy, and happily regulated. But at the same time, the intellectual and moral existence of this people is studiously kept in a state of torpor and inactivity; of, I will not say, oppression, for they do not understand the feeling, but of compression. We are not without instances of this state of things. There has been a great number of small aristocratic republics in which the people have been thus treated like flocks of sheep, well kept and materially happy, but without moral and intellectual activity. Is this civilization? Is this a people civilizing itself?

Another hypothesis: here is a people whose material existence is less easy, less comfortable, but still supportable. On the other hand, moral and intellectual wants have not been neglected, a certain amount of mental pasture has been served out to them; elevated, pure sentiments are cultivated in them; their religious and moral views have attained a certain degree of development; but great care is taken to stifle in them the principle of liberty; the intellectual and moral wants, as in the former case the material wants, are satisfied; each man has meted out to him his portion of truth; no one is permitted to seek it for himself. Immobility is the characteristic of moral life; it is the state into which have fallen most of the populations of Asia; wherever theocratic dominations keep humanity in check; it is the state of the Hindoos, for example. I ask the same question here as before; is this a people civilizing itself?

I change altogether the nature of the hypothesis: here is a people among whom is a great display of individual liberties, but where disorder and inequality are excessive: it is the empire of force and of chance; every man, if he is not strong, is oppressed, suffers, perishes; violence is the predominant feature of the social state. No one is ignorant that Europe has passed through this state. Is this a civilized state? It may, doubtless, contain principles of civilization which will develop themselves by successive degrees; but the fact which dominates in such a society is, assuredly, not that which the common sense of mankind call civilization.

I take a fourth and last hypothesis: the liberty of each individual is very great, inequality amongst them is rare, and at all events, very transient. Every man does very nearly just what he pleases, and differs little in power from his neighbour; but there are very few general interests, very few public ideas, very little society,—in a word, the faculties and existence of individuals appear and then pass away, wholly apart and without acting upon each other, or leaving any trace behind them; the successive generations leave society at the same point at which they found it: this is the state of savage tribes; liberty and equality are there, but assuredly not civilization.

I might multiply these hypotheses, but I think we have before us enough to explain what is the popular and natural meaning of the word *civilization*.

It is clear that none of the states I have sketched corresponds, according to the natural good sense of mankind, to this term. Why? It appears to me that the first fact comprised in the word civilization (and this results from the different examples I have rapidly placed before you), is the fact of progress, of development; it presents at once the idea of a people marching onward, not to change its place, but to change its condition; of a people whose culture is condition itself, and ameliorating itself. The idea of progress, of development, appears to me the fundamental idea contained in the word, *civilization*. What is this progress? what this development? Herein is the greatest difficulty of all.

The etymology of the word would seem to answer in a clear and satisfactory manner: it says that it is the perfecting of civil life, the development of society, properly so called, of the relations of men among themselves.

Such is, in fact, the first idea which presents itself to the understanding when the word civilization is pronounced; we at once figure forth to ourselves the extension, the greatest activity, the best organization of the social relations : on the one hand, an increasing production of the means of giving strength and happiness to society; on the other a more equitable distribution, amongst individuals, of the strength

Is this all? Have we here exhausted all the natural, ordinary meaning of the word civilization? Does the fact contain nothing more than this?

It is almost as if we asked: is the human species after all a mere ant-hill, a society in which all that is required is order and physical happiness, in which the greater the amount of labour, and the more equitable the division of the fruits of labour, the more surely is the object attained, the progress accomplished.

Our instinct at once feels repugnant to so narrow a definition of human destiny. It feels at the first glance, that the word, civilization, comprehends something more extensive, more complex, something superior to the simple perfection of the social relations, of social power and happiness.

Fact, public opinion, the generally received meaning of the term, are in accordance with this instinct.

Take Rome in the palmy days of the republic, after the second Punic war, at the time of its greatest virtues, when it was marching to the empire of the world, when its social state was evidently in progress. Then take Rome under Augustus, at the epoch when her decline began, when, at all events, the progressive movement of society was arrested, when evil principles were on the eve of prevailing: yet there is no one who does not think and say that the Rome of Augustus was more civilized than the Rome of Fabricius or of Cincinnatus.

Let us transport ourselves beyond the Alps: let us take the France of the seventeenth and eighteenth centuries: it is evident that, in a social point of view, considering the actual amount and distribution of happiness amongst individuals, the France of the seventeenth and eighteenth centuries was inferior to some other countries of Europe, to Holland and to England, for example. I believe that in Holland and in England the social activity was greater, was increasing more rapidly, distributing its fruit more fully, than in France, yet ask general good sense, and it will say that the France of the seventeenth and eighteenth centuries was the most civilized country in Europe. Europe has not hesitated in her affirmative reply to the question: traces of this public opinion, as to France, are found in all the monuments of European literature.

We might point out many other states in which the prosperity is greater, is of more rapid growth, is better distributed amongst individuals than elsewhere, and in which, nevertheless, by the spontaneous instinct, the general good sense of men, the civilization is judged inferior to that of countries not so well portioned out in a purely social sense.

What does this mean? what advantages do these latter countries possess? What is it gives them, in the character of civilized countries, this privilege? what so largely compensates in the opinion of mankind for what they so lack in other respects?

A development other than that of social life has been gloriously manifested by them; the development of the individual, internal life, the development of man himself, of his faculties, his sentiments, his ideas. If society with them be less perfect than elsewhere, humanity stands forth in more grandeur and power. There remain, no doubt, many social conquests to be made ; but immense intellectual and moral conquests are accomplished ; worldly goods, social rights, are wanting to many men ; but many great men live and shine in the eyes of the world. Letters, sciences, the arts, display all their splendour. Wherever mankind beholds these great signs, these signs glorified by human nature, wherever it sees created these treasures of sublime enjoyment, it there recognises and names civilization.

Two facts, then, are comprehended in this great fact; it subsists on two conditions, and manifests itself by two symptoms: the development of social activity, and that of individual activity; the progress of society and the progress of humanity. Wherever the external condition of man extends itself, vivifies, ameliorates itself; wherever the internal nature of man displays itself with lustre, with grandeur; at these two signs, and often despite the profound imperfection of the social state, mankind with loud applause proclaims civilization.

Such, if I do not deceive myself, is the result of simple and purely common-sense examination, of the general opinion of mankind. If we interrogate history, properly so-called, if we examine what is the nature of the great crises of civilization, of those facts which, by universal consent, have propelled it onward, we shall constantly recognise one or other of the two elements I have just described.   They are always crises of individual or social development, facts which have changed the internal man, his creed, his manners, or his external condition, his position in his relation with his fellows. Christianity, for example, not merely on its first appearance, but during the first stages of its existence, Christianity in no degree addressed itself to the social state; it announced aloud, that it would not meddle with the social state; it ordered the slave to obey his master; it attacked none of the great evils, the great wrongs of the society of that period.   Yet who will deny that Christianity was a great crisis of civilization? Why was it so?   Because it changed the internal man, creeds, sentiments; because it regenerated the moral man, the intellectual man.

We have seen a crisis of another nature, a crisis which addressed itself, not to the internal man, but to his external condition; one which changed and regenerated society.   This also was assuredly one of the decisive crises of civilization. Look through all history, you will find everywhere the same result; you will meet with no important fact instrumental in the development of civilization, which has not exercised one or other of the two sorts of influence I have spoken of.

Such, if I mistake not, is the natural and popular meaning of the term ; you have here the fact, I will not say defined, but described, verified almost completely, or, at all events, in its general features.   We have before us the two elements of civilization.   Now comes the question, would one of these two suffice to constitute it; would the development of the social state, the development of the individual man, separately presented, be civilization?   Would the human race recognise it as such? or have the two facts so intimate and necessary a relation between them, that if they are not simultaneously produced, they are notwithstanding inseparable, and sooner or later one brings on the other.

We might, as it appears to me, approach this question on three several sides.   We might examine the nature itself of the two elements of civilization, and ask ourselves whether by that alone, they are or are not closely united with, and necessary to each other.   We might inquire of history whether they had manifested themselves isolately, apart the one from the other, or whether they had invariably produced the one the other. We may, lastly, consult upon this question the common opinion of mankind—common sense. I will address myself first to common sense.

When a great change is accomplished in the state of a country, when there is operated in it a large development of wealth and power, a revolution in the distribution of the social means, this new fact encounters adversaries, undergoes opposition; this is inevitable. What is the general cry of the adversaries of the change? They say that this progress of the social state does not ameliorate, does not regenerate, in like manner, in a like degree, the moral, the internal state of man; that it is a false, delusive progress, the result of which is detrimental to morality, to man. The friends of social development energetically repel this attack; they maintain, on the contrary, that the progress of society necessarily involves and carries with it the progress of morality; that when the external life is better regulated, the internal life is refined and purified. Thus stands the question between the adversaries and partisans of the new state.

Reverse the hypothesis: suppose the moral development in progress: what do the labourers in this progress generally promise? What, in the origin of societies, have promised the religious rulers, the sages, the poets, who have laboured to soften and to regulate men's manners? They have promised the amelioration of the social condition, the more equitable distribution of the social means. What, then, I ask you, is involved in these disputes, these promises? What do they mean? What do they imply?

They imply that in the spontaneous, instinctive conviction of mankind, the two elements of civilization, the social development and the moral development, are closely connected together; that at sight of the one, man at once looks forward to the other. It is to this natural instinctive conviction that those who are maintaining or combating one or other of the two developments address themselves, when they affirm or deny their union. It is well understood, that if we can persuade mankind that the amelioration of the social state will be adverse to the internal progress of individuals, we shall have succeeded in decrying and enfeebling the revolution in operation throughout society. On the other hand, when we promise mankind the amelioration of society by means of the

amelioration of the individual, it is well understood that the
tendency is to place faith in these promises, and it is accordingly made use of with success. It is evidently, therefore,
the instinctive belief of humanity, that the movements of
civilization are connected the one with the other, and reciprocally produce the one the other.

If we address ourselves to the history of the world, we
shall receive the same answer. We shall find that all the
great developments of the internal man have turned to the
profit of society; all the great developments of the social state
to the profit of individual man. We find the one or other of
the two facts predominating, manifesting itself with striking
effect, and impressing upon the movement in progress a distinctive character. It is, sometimes, only after a very long
interval of time, after a thousand obstacles, a thousand transformations, that the second fact, developing itself, comes to
complete the civilization which the first had commenced. But
if you examine them closely, you will soon perceive the bond
which unites them. The march of Providence is not restricted to narrow limits; it is not bound, and it does not
trouble itself, to follow out to-day the consequences of the
principle which it laid down yesterday. The consequences
will come in due course, when the hour for them has arrived,
perhaps not till hundreds of years have passed away; though
its reasoning may appear to us slow, its logic is none the less
true and sound. To Providence, time is as nothing; it strides
through time as the gods of Homer through space : it makes
but one step, and ages have vanished behind it. How many
centuries, what infinite events passed away before the regene
ration of the moral man by Christianity exercised upon the
regeneration of the social state its great and legitimate influence. Yet who will deny that it any the less succeeded?

If from history we extend our inquiries to the nature itself
of the two facts which constitute civilization, we are infallibly
led to the same result. There is no one who has not experienced this in his own case. When a moral change is operated in man, when he acquires an idea, or a virtue, or a
faculty, more than he had before—in a word, when he develops himself individually, what is the desire, what the want,
which at the same moment takes possession of him? It
is the desire, the want, to communicate the new senti-

ment to the world about him, to give realization to his thoughts externally. As soon as a man acquires anything, as soon as his being takes in his own conviction a new development, assumes an additional value, forthwith he attaches to this new development, this fresh value, the idea of possession; he feels himself impelled, compelled, by his instinct, by an inward voice, to extend to others the change, the amelioration, which has been accomplished in his own person. We owe the great reformers solely to this cause; the mighty men who have changed the face of the world, after having changed themselves, were urged onward, were guided on their course, by no other want than this. So much for the alteration which is operated in the internal man; now to the other. A revolution is accomplished in the state of society; it is better regulated, rights and property are more equitably distributed among its members—that is to say, the aspect of the world becomes purer and more beautiful, the action of government, the conduct of men in their mutual relations, more just, more benevolent. Do you suppose that this improved aspect of the world, this amelioration of external facts, does not re-act upon the interior of man, upon humanity? All that is said as to the authority of examples, of customs, of noble models, is founded upon this only: that an external fact, good, well-regulated, leads sooner or later, more or less completely, to an internal fact of the same nature, the same merit; that a world better regulated, a world more just, renders man himself more just; that the inward is reformed by the outward, as the outward by the inward; that the two elements of civilization are closely connected the one with the other; that centuries, that obstacles of all sorts, may interpose between them; that it is possible they may have to undergo a thousand transformations, in order to regain each other; but sooner or later they will rejoin each other: this is the law of their nature, the general fact of history, the instinctive faith of the human race.

I think I have thus—not exhausted the subject, very far from it—but, exhibited in a well-nigh complete, though cursory manner, the fact of civilization; I think I have described it, settled its limits, and stated the principal, the fundamental questions to which it gives rise. I might stop here; but I cannot help touching upon a question which meets me at this point; one of those questions which are not historical question*, properly so called; which are questions, I will not call them hypothetical, but conjectural; questions of which man holds but one end, the other end being permanently beyond his reach; questions of which he cannot make the circuit, nor view on more than one side; and yet questions not the less real, not the less calling upon him for thought; for they present themselves before him, despite of himself, at every moment.

Of those two developments of which we have spoken, and which constitute the fact of civilization, the development of society on the one hand and of humanity on the other, which is the end, which is the means? Is it to perfect his social condition, to ameliorate his existence on earth, that man develops himself, his faculties, sentiments, ideas, his whole being?—or rather, is not the amelioration of the social condition, the progress of society, society itself, the theatre, the occasion, the *mobile*, of the development of the individual, in a word, is society made to serve the individual, or the individual to serve society? On the answer to this question inevitably depends that whether the destiny of man is purely social; whether society drains up and exhausts the whole man; or whether he bears within him something extrinsic—something superior to his existence on earth.

A man, whom I am proud to call my friend, a man who has passed through meetings like our own to assume the first place in assemblies less peaceable and more powerful; a man, all whose words are engraven on the hearts of those who bear them, M. Royer-Collard, has solved this question according, to his own conviction at least, in his speech on the Sacrilege Bill. I find in that speech these two sentences: " Human societies are born, live, and die, on the earth; it is there their destinies are accomplished. . . . . . But they contain not the whole man. After he has engaged himself to society, there remains to him the noblest part of himself, those high faculties by which he elevates himself to God, to a future life, to unknown felicity in an invisible world. . . . . . We, persons individual and identical, veritable beings endowed with immortality, we have a different destiny from that of states."[1]

I will add nothing to this; I will not undertake to treat the

---

[1] Opinion de M. Royer-Collard sur le Projet de Loi relatif au Sacrilège. pp 7, 17

question itself; I content myself with stating it. It is met with at the history of civilization: when the history of civilization is completed, when there is nothing more to say as to our present existence, man inevitably asks himself whether all is exhausted, whether he has reached the end of all things? This, then, is the last, the highest of all those problems to which the history of civilization can lead. It is sufficient for me to have indicated its position and its grandeur.

From all I have said, it is evident that the history of civilization might be treated in two methods, drawn from two sources, considered under two different aspects. The historian might place himself in the heart of the human mind for a given period, a series of ages, or among a determinate people; he might study, describe, relate, all the events, all the transformations, all the revolutions, which had been accomplished in the internal man; and when he should arrive at the end, he would have a history of civilization amongst the people, and in the period he had selected. He may proceed in another manner: instead of penetrating the internal man, he may take his stand—he may place himself in the midst of the world; instead of describing the vicissitudes of the ideas, the sentiments, of the individual being, he may describe external facts, the events, the changes of the social state. These two portions, these two histories of civilization, are closely connected with each other; they are the reflection, the image of each other. Yet, they may be separated; perhaps, indeed, they ought to be so, at least at the onset, in order that both the one and the other may be treated of in detail, and with perspicuity. For my part, I do not propose to study with you the history of civilization in the interior of the human soul; it is the history of external events, of the visible and social world that I shall occupy myself with. I had wished, indeed, to exhibit to you the whole fact of civilization, such as I can conceive it in all its complexity and extent, to set forth before you all the high questions which may arise from it. At present, I restrict myself; mark out my field of inquiry within narrower limits; it is only the history of the social state that I purpose investigating.

We shall begin by seeking all the elements of European civilization in its cradle, at the fall of the Roman empire;

c

we will study with attention society, such as it was, in the midst of those famous ruins. We will endeavour, not to resuscitate, but to place its elements side by side; and when we have done so, we will endeavour to make them move, and follow them in their developments through the fifteen centuries which have elapsed since that epoch.

I believe that when we have got but a very little way into this study, we shall acquire the conviction that civilization is as yet very young; that the world has by no means as yet measured the whole of its career. Assuredly human thought is at this time very far from being all that it is capable of becoming; we are very far from comprehending the whole future of humanity: let each of us descend into his own mind, let him interrogate himself as to the utmost possible good he has formed a conception of and hopes for; let him then compare his idea with what actually exists in the world; he will be convinced that society and civilization are very young; that notwithstanding the length of the road they have come, they have incomparably further to go. This will lessen nothing of the pleasure that we shall take in the contemplation of our actual condition. As I endeavour to place before you the great crises in the history of civilization in Europe during the last fifteen centuries, you will see to what a degree, even up to our own days, the condition of man has been laborious, stormy, not only in the outward and social state, but inwardly, in the life of the soul. During all those ages, the human mind has had to suffer as much as the human race; you will see that in modern times, for the first time, perhaps, the human mind has attained a state, as yet very imperfect, but still a state in which reigns some peace, some harmony. It is the same with society; it has evidently made immense progress; the human condition is easy and just, compared with what it was previously; we may almost, when thinking of our ancestors, apply to ourselves the verses of Lucretius:—

> " Suave mari magno, turbantibus æquora ventis,
> E terrâ magnum alterius spectare laborem."[1]

---

[1] " 'Tis pleasant, in a great storm, to contemplate, from a safe position on shore, the perils of some ships tossed about by the furious winds and the stormy ocean."

We may say of ourselves, without too much pride, as Sthe-nelus in Homer:—

Ἡμεῖς τοὶ γ ετερων μεγ' ἀμείνονες εὐχόμεθ' εἶναι.[1]

Let us be careful, however, not to give ourselves up too much to the idea of our happiness and amelioration, or we may fall into two grave dangers, pride and indolence; we may conceive an over-confidence in the power and success of the human mind, in our own enlightenment, and, at the same time, suffer ourselves to become enervated by the luxurious ease of our condition. It appears to me that we are constantly fluctuating between a tendency to complain upon light grounds, on the one hand, and to be content without reason, on the other. We have a susceptibility of spirit, a craving, an unlimited ambition in the thought, in our desire, in the movement of the imagination; but when it comes to the practical work of life, when we are called upon to give ourselves any trouble, to make any sacrifices, to use any efforts to attain the object, our arms fall down listlessly by our sides, and we give the matter up in despair, with a facility equalled only by the impatience with which we had previously desired its attainment. We must beware how we allow ourselves to yield to either of these defects. Let us accustom ourselves duly to estimate beforehand the extent of our force, our capacity, our knowledge; and let us aim at nothing which we feel we cannot attain legitimately, justly, regularly, and with unfailing regard to the principles upon which our civilization itself rests. We seem at times tempted to adopt the very principles which, as a general rule, we assail and hold up to scorn—the principles, the right of the strongest of barbarian Europe; the brute force, the violence, the downright lying which were matters of course, of daily occurrence, four or five hundred years ago. But when we yield for a moment to this desire, we find in ourselves neither the perseverance nor the savage energy of the men of that period, who, suffering greatly from their condition, were naturally anxious, and incessantly essaying, to emancipate themselves from it. We, of the present day, are content with our

[1] " Thank Heaven, we are infinitely better than those who went before us."

c 2

condition; let us not expose it to danger by indulging in
vague desires, the time for realizing which has not come.
Much has been given to us, much will be required of us; we
must render to posterity a strict account of our conduct; the
public, the government, all are now subjected to discussion,
examination, responsibility.   Let us attach ourselves firmly,
faithfully, undeviatingly, to the principles of our civiliza
tion — justice, legality, publicity, liberty; and let us never
forget, that while we ourselves require, and with reason,
that all things shall be open to our inspection and inquiry
we ourselves are under the eye of the world, and shall, in our
turn, be discussed, be judged.

SECOND LECTURE

Purpose of the lecture—Unity of ancient civilization—Variety of modern
  civilization—Its superiority—Condition of Europe at the fall of the
  Roman empire—Preponderance of the towns—Attempt at political reform
  by the emperors—Rescript of Honorius and of Theodosius II.—Power
  of the name of the Empire—The Christian church—The various stages
  through which it had passed at the fifth century—The clergy exercising
  municipal functions—Good and evil influence of the church—The barbarians—They introduce into the modern world the sentiments of personal independence, and the devotion of man to man—Summary of the
  different elements of civilization in the beginning of the fifth century.

In meditating the plan of the course with which I propose
to present you, I am fearful lest my lectures should possess
the double inconvenience of being very long, by reason of the
necessity of condensing much matter into little space, and,
at the same time, of being too concise.

I dread yet another difficulty, originating in the same
cause: the necessity, namely, of sometimes making affirmations
without proving them.   This is also the result of the narrow
space to which I find myself confined.   There will occur
ideas and assertions of which the confirmation must be postponed.   I hope you will pardon me for sometimes placing
you under the necessity of believing me upon my bare word.
I come even now to an occasion of imposing upon you this
necessity.

I have endeavoured, in the preceding lecture, to explain
the fact of civilization in general, without speaking of any
particular civilization, without regarding circumstance of time
and place, considering the fact in itself, and under a purely

philosophical point of view. I come, to-day, to the history
of European civilization; but before entering upon the narrative itself, I wish to make you acquainted, in a general
manner, with the particular physiognomy of this civilization;
I desire to characterize it so clearly to you, that it may appear
to you perfectly distinct from all other civilizations which
have developed themselves in the world. This I am going to
attempt, more than which I dare not say; but I can only
affirm it, unless I could succeed in depicting European society
with such faithfulness, that you should instantly recognise it
as a portrait. But of this I dare not flatter myself.

When we regard the civilizations which have preceded that
of modern Europe, whether in Asia or elsewhere, including
even Greek and Roman civilization, it is impossible to help
being struck with the unity which pervades them. They
seem to have emanated from a single fact, from a single idea;
one might say that society has attached itself to a solitary
dominant principle, which has determined its institutions, its
customs, its creeds, in one word, all its developments.

In Egypt, for instance, it was the theocratic principle which
pervaded the entire community; it reproduced itself in the
customs, in the monuments, and in all that remains to us of
Egyptian civilization. In India, you will discover the same
fact; there is still the almost exclusive dominion of the theocratic principle. Elsewhere you will meet with another
organizing principle—the domination of a victorious caste;
the principle of force will here alone possess society, imposing
thereupon its laws and its character. Elsewhere, society will
be the expression of the democratic principle; it has been
thus with the commercial republics which have covered the
coasts of Asia Minor and of Syria, in Ionia, in Phenicia.
In short, when we contemplate ancient civilizations, we find
them stamped with a singular character of unity in their
institutions, their ideas, and their manners; a sole, or, at
least, a strongly preponderating force governs and deter
mines all.

I do not mean to say that this unity of principle and form
in the civilization of these states has always prevailed therein.
When we go back to their earlier history, we find that the
various powers which may develop themselves in the heart

of a society, have often contended for empire. Among the Egyptians, the Etruscans, the Greeks themselves, &c., the order of warriors, for example, has struggled against that of the priests; elsewhere, the spirit of clanship has struggled against that of free association; the aristocratic against the popular system, &c. But it has generally been in ante-historical times that such struggles have occurred; and thus only a vague recollection has remained of them.

The struggle has sometimes reproduced itself in the course of the existence of nations; but, almost invariably, it has soon been terminated; one of the powers that disputed for empire has soon gained it, and taken sole possession of the society. The war has always terminated by the, if not exclusive, at least largely preponderating, domination of some particular principle. The co-existence and the combat of different principles have never, in the history of these peoples, been more than a transitory crisis, an accident.

The result of this has been a remarkable simplicity in the majority of ancient civilizations. This simplicity has produced different consequences. Sometimes, as in Greece, the simplicity of the social principle has led to a wonderfully rapid development; never has any people unfolded itself in so short a period, with such brilliant effect. But after this astonishing flight, Greece seemed suddenly exhausted; its decay, if it was not so rapid as its rise, was nevertheless strangely prompt. It seems that the creative force of the principle of Greek civilization was exhausted; no other has come to renew it.

Elsewhere, in Egypt and in India, for instance, the unity of the principle of civilization has had a different effect; society has fallen into a stationary condition. Simplicity has brought monotony; the country has not been destroyed, society has continued to exist, but motionless, and as if frozen.

It is to the same cause that we must attribute the character of tyranny which appeared in the name of principle and under the most various forms, among all the ancient civilizations. Society belonged to an exclusive power, which would allow of the existence of none other. Every differing tendency was proscribed and hunted down. Never has the ruling principle chosen to admit beside it the manifestation and action of a different principle.

This character of unity of civilization is equally stamped upon literature and the works of the mind. Who is unacquainted with the monuments of Indian literature, which have lately been distributed over Europe? It is impossible not to see that they are all cast in the same mould; they seem all to be the result of the same fact, the expression of the same idea; works of religion or morals, historical traditions, dramatic and epic poetry, everywhere the same character is stamped; the productions of the mind bear the same character of simplicity and of monotony which appears in events and institutions. Even in Greece, in the centre of all the riches of the human intellect, a singular uniformity reigns in literature and in the arts.

It has been wholly otherwise with the civilization of modern Europe. Without entering into details, look upon it, gather together your recollections: it will immediately appear to you varied, confused, stormy; all forms, all principles of social organization coexist therein; powers spiritual and temporal; elements theocratic, monarchical, aristocratic, democratic; all orders, all social arrangements mingle and press upon one another; there are infinite degrees of liberty, wealth, and influence. These various forces are in a state of continual struggle among themselves, yet no one succeeds in stifling the others, and taking possession of society. In ancient times, at every great epoch, all societies seemed cast in the same mould: it is sometimes pure monarchy, sometimes theocracy or democracy, that prevails; but each, in its turn, prevails completely. Modern Europe presents us with examples of all systems, of all experiments of social organization; pure or mixed monarchies, theocracies, republics, more or less aristocratic, have thus thrived simultaneously, one beside the other; and, notwithstanding their diversity, they have all a certain resemblance, a certain family likeness, which it is impossible to mistake.

In the ideas and sentiments of Europe there is the same variety, the same struggle. The theocratic, monarchic, aristocratic, and popular creeds, cross, combat, limit, and modify each other. Open the boldest writings of the middle

ages; never there is an idea followed out to its last consequences. The partisans of absolute power recoil suddenly
and unconsciously before the results of their own doctrine;
they perceive around them ideas and influences which arrest
them, and prevent them from going to extremities. The
democrats obey the same law. On neither part exists that
imperturbable audacity, that blind determination of logic,
which show themselves in ancient civilizations. The sentiments offer the same contrasts, the same variety; an energetic
love of independence, side by side with a great facility of
submission; a singular faithfulness of man to man, and, at the
same time, an uncontrollable wish to exert free will, to shake
off every yoke, and to live for oneself, without caring for
any other. The souls of men are as different, as agitated as
society.

The same character discovers itself in modern literatures. We cannot but agree that, as regards artistic form
and beauty, they are very much inferior to ancient literature;
but, as regards depth of sentiment and of ideas, they are far
more rich and vigorous. We see that the human soul has
been moved upon a greater number of points, and to a greater
depth. Imperfection of form results from this very cause.
The richer and more numerous the materials, the more difficult it is to reduce them to a pure and simple form. That
which constitutes the beauty of a composition, of that which
we call form, in works of art, is clearness, simplicity, and a
symbolic unity of workmanship. With the prodigious diversity of the ideas and sentiments of European civilization, it
has been much more difficult to arrive at this simplicity, this
clearness.

On all sides, then, this predominant character of modern
civilization discovers itself. It has, no doubt, had this disad-
vantage, that, when we consider separately such or such a
particular development of the human mind in letters, in the
arts, in all directions in which it can advance, we usually
find it inferior to the corresponding development in ancient
civilizations; but, on the other hand, when we regard it in
the aggregate, European civilization shows itself incomparably
richer than any other; it has displayed, at one and the same
time, many more different developments. Consequently, you

find that it has existed fifteen centuries, and yet is still in a state of continuous progression; it has not advanced nearly so rapidly as the Greek civilization, but its progress has never ceased to grow. It catches a glimpse of the vast career which lies before it, and day after day it shoots forward more rapidly, because more and more of freedom attends its movements. Whilst, in other civilizations, the exclusive, or, at least, the excessively preponderating dominion of a single principle, of a single form, has been the cause of tyranny, in modern Europe, the diversity of elements, which constitute the social order, the impossibility under which they have been placed of excluding each other, have given birth to the freedom which prevails in the present day. Not having been able to exterminate each other, it has become necessary that various principles should exist together,—that they should make between them a sort of compact. Each has agreed to undertake that portion of the development which may fall to its share; and whilst elsewhere the predominance of a principle produced tyranny, in Europe liberty has been the result of the variety of the elements of civilization, and of the state of struggle in which they have constantly existed.

This constitutes a real and an immense superiority; and if we investigate yet further, if we penetrate beyond external facts into the nature of things, we shall discover that this superiority is legitimate, and acknowledged by reason as well as proclaimed by facts. Forgetting for a moment European civilization, let us turn our attention to the world in general, on the general course of terrestrial things. What character do we find? How goes the world? It moves precisely with this diversity and variety of elements, a prey to this constant struggle which we have remarked in European civilization. Evidently it has not been permitted to any single principle, to any particular organization, to any single idea, or to any special force, that it should possess itself of the world, moulding it once for all, destroying all other influences to reign therein itself exclusively.

Various powers, principles, and systems mingle, limit each other, and struggle without ceasing, in turn predominating, or predominated over, never entirely conquered or conquering. A variety of forms, of ideas, and of principles, their, struggles, their efforts after a certain unity, a certain ideal which perhaps can never be attained, but to which the human race tends by freedom and work; these constitute the general condition of the world. European civilization is, therefore, the faithful image of the world: like the course of things in the world, it is neither narrow, exclusive, nor stationary. For the first time, I believe, the character of specialty has vanished from civilization; for the first time it is developed as variously, as richly, as laboriously, as the great drama of the universe.

European civilization has entered, if we may so speak, into the eternal truth, into the plan of Providence; it progresses according to the intentions of God. This is the rational account of its superiority.

I am desirous that this fundamental and distinguishing character of European civilization should continue present to your minds during the course of our labours. At present I can only make the affirmation: the development of facts must furnish the proof. It will, nevertheless, you will agree, be a strong confirmation of my assertion, if we find, even in the cradle of our civilization, the causes and the elements of the character which I have just attributed to it; if, at the moment of its birth, at the moment of the fall of the Roman empire, we recognise in the state of the world. in the facts that, from the earliest times, have concurred to form European civilization, the principle of this agitated but fruitful diversity which distinguishes it. I am about to attempt this investigation. I shall examine the condition of Europe at the fall of the Roman empire, and seek to discover, from institutions, creeds, ideas, and sentiments, what were the elements bequeathed by the ancient to the modern world. If, in these elements, we shall already find impressed the character which I have just described, it will have acquired with you, from this time forth, a high degree of probability.

First of all, we must clearly represent to ourselves the ature of the Roman empire, and how it was formed.

Rome was, in its origin, only a municipality, a corporation. The government of Rome was merely the aggregate of the institutions which were suited to a population confined

within the walls of a city: these were municipal institutions,
—that is their distinguishing character.

This was not the case with Rome only. If we turn our
attention to Italy, at this period, we find around Rome
nothing but towns. That which was then called a people
was simply a confederation of towns. The Latin people was
a confederation of Latin towns. The Etruscans, the Samnites,
the Sabines, the people of Græcia Magna, may all be described
in the same terms.

There was, at this time, no country—that is to say, the
country was wholly unlike that which at present exists; it
was cultivated, as was necessary, but it was uninhabited.
The proprietors of lands were the inhabitants of the towns.
They went forth to superintend their country properties, and
often took with them a certain number of slaves; but that
which we at present call the country, that thin population—
sometimes in isolated habitations, sometimes in villages—
which everywhere covers the soil, was a fact almost unknown
in ancient Italy.

When Rome extended itself, what did she do? Follow
history, and you will see that she conquered or founded
towns; it was against towns that she fought, with towns that
she contracted alliances; it was also into towns that she sent
colonies. The history of the conquest of the world by Rome
is the history of the conquest and foundation of a great
number of towns. In the East, the extension of Roman
dominion does not carry altogether this aspect: the population there was otherwise distributed than in the West—it was
much less concentrated in towns. But as we have to do here
with the European population, what occurred in the East is
of little interest to us.

Confining ourselves to the West, we everywhere discover
the fact to which I have directed your attention. In Gaul,
in Spain, you meet with nothing but towns. At a distance from the towns, the territory is covered with marshes
and forests. Examine the character of the Roman monuments, of the Roman roads. You have great roads, which
reach from one city to another; the multiplicity of minor
roads, which now cross the country in all directions, was
then unknown; you have nothing resembling that countless

number of villages, country seats, and churches, which have
been scattered over the country since the middle ages. Rome
has left us nothing but immense monuments, stamped with
the municipal character, and destined for a numerous population collected upon one spot.   Under whatever point of
view you consider the Roman world, you will find this almost
exclusive preponderance of towns, and the social non-exist-
ence of the country.

This municipal character of the Roman world evidently
rendered unity, the social bond of a great state, extremely
difficult to establish and maintain.   A municipality like
Rome had been able to conquer the world, but it was much
less easy to govern and organize it.   Thus, when the work
appeared completed, when all the West, and a great part of
the East, had fallen under Roman dominion, you behold this
prodigious number of cities, of little states, made for isolation
and independence, disunite, detach themselves, and escape, so
to speak, in all directions.   This was one of the causes which
rendered necessary the Empire, a form of government more
concentrated, more capable of holding together elements so
slightly coherent.   The Empire endeavoured to introduce
unity and combination into this scattered society.   It succeeded up to a certain point.   It was between the reigns
of Augustus and Diocletian that, at the same time that civil
legislation developed itself, there became established the vast
system of administrative despotism which spread over the
Roman world a network of functionaries, hierarchically distributed, well linked together, both among themselves and with
the imperial court, and solely applied to rendering effective
in society the will of power, and in transferring to power the
tributes and energies of society.

And not only did this system succeed in rallying and
in holding together the elements of the Roman world, but
the idea of despotism, of central power, penetrated minds
with a singular facility.   We are astonished to behold rapidly
prevailing throughout this ill-united assemblage of petty republics, this association of municipalities, a reverence for the
imperial majesty alone, august and sacred.   The necessity of
establishing some bond between all these portions of the
Roman world must have been very pressing, to ensure so

easy an access to the mind for the faith and almost the
sentiments of despotism.

It was with these creeds, with this administrative organization, and with the military organization which was combined
with it, that the Roman empire struggled against the dissolution at work inwardly, and against the invasion of the
barbarians from without. It struggled for a long time, in a
continual state of decay, but always defending itself. At last
a moment came in which dissolution prevailed: neither the
skill of despotism nor the indifference of servitude sufficed to
support this huge body. In the fourth century it everywhere
disunited and dismembered itself; the barbarians entered on
all sides; the provinces no longer resisted, no longer troubled
themselves concerning the general destiny. At this time, a
singular idea suggested itself to some of the emperors: they
desired to try whether hopes of general liberty, a confederation—a system analogous to that which, in the present day,
we call representative government—would not better defend
the unity of the Roman empire than despotic administration.
Here is a rescript of Honorius and Theodosius the younger,
addressed, in the year 418, to the prefect of Gaul, the only
purpose of which was to attempt to establish in the south of
Gaul a sort of representative government, and, with its aid,
to maintain the unity of the empire.

  " Rescript of the emperors Honorius and Theodosius the
      younger, addressed, in the year 418, to the prefect of
      the Gauls, sitting in the town of Arles.

  " Honorius and Theodosius, Augusti, to Agricola, prefect
      of the Gauls:

  " Upon the satisfactory statement that your Magnificence
has made to us, among other information palpably advantageous to the state, we decree the force of law in perpetuity
to the following ordinances, to which the inhabitants of our
seven provinces will owe obedience, they being such that
they themselves might have desired and demanded them.
Seeing that persons in office, or special deputies, from motives
of public or private utility, not only from each of the provinces, but also from every town, often present themselves
before your Magnificence, either to render accounts or to

treat of things relative to the interest of proprietors, we have judged that it would be a seasonable and profitable thing that, from the date of the present year, there should be annually, at a fixed time, an assemblage held in the metropolis—that is, in the town of Arles, for the inhabitants of the seven provinces. By this institution we have in view to provide equally for general and particular interests. In the first place, by the meeting of the most notable of the inhabitants in the illustrious presence of the prefect, if motives of public order have not called him elsewhere, the best possible information may be gained upon every subject under deliberation. Nothing of that which will have been treated of and decided upon, after a ripe consideration, will escape the knowledge of any of the provinces, and those who shall not have been present at the assembly will be bound to follow the same rules of justice and equity. Moreover, in ordaining that an annual assembly be held in the city of Constantine,[1] we believe that we are doing a thing not only advantageous to the public good, but also adapted to multiply social relations. Indeed, the city is so advantageously situated, strangers come there in such numbers, and it enjoys such an extensive commerce, that everything finds its way there which grows or is manufactured in other places. All admirable things that the rich East, perfumed Arabia, delicate Assyria, fertile Africa, beautiful Spain, valiant Gaul produce, abound in this place with such profusion, that whatever is esteemed magnificent in the various parts of the world seems there the produce of the soil. Besides, the junction of the Rhone with the Tuscan sea approximates and renders almost neighbours those countries which the first traverses, and the second bathes in its windings. Thus, since the entire earth places at the service of this city all that it has most worthy—since the peculiar productions of all countries are transported hither by land, by sea, and by the course of rivers, by help of sails, of oars, and of waggons—how can our Gaul do otherwise than behold a benefit in the command which we give to convoke a public assembly in a city, wherein are united, as it were, by the gift of God, all the enjoyments of life, and all the facilities of commerce?

---

[1] Constantine the Great had a singular liking for the town of Arles. It was he who established there the seat of the Gaulish prefecture; he desired also that it should bear his name, but custom prevailed against his wish.

"The illustrious prefect Petronius,[1] through a laudable and reasonable motive, formerly commanded that this custom should be observed; but as the practice thereof was interrupted by the confusion of the times, and by the reign of usurpers, we have resolved to revive it in vigour by the authority of our wisdom. Thus, then, dear and beloved cousin Agricola, your illustrious Magnificence, conforming yourself to our present ordinance, and to the custom established by your predecessors, will cause to be observed throughout the provinces the following rules:

"'Let all persons, who are honoured with public functions, or who are proprietors of domains, and all judges of provinces, be informed that, each year, they are to assemble in council in the city of Arles, between the ides of August and those of September, the days of convocation and of sitting being determined at their pleasure.

"'Novem Populinia and the second Aquitaine, being the most distant provinces, should their judges be detained by indispensable occupations, may send deputies in their place, according to custom.

"'Those who shall neglect to appear at the place assigned and at the time appointed, shall pay a fine, which, for the judges, shall be five pounds of gold, and three pounds for the members of the *curiæ*[2] and other dignitaries.'

"We propose, by this means, to confer great advantages and favour on the inhabitants of our provinces. We feel, also, assured of adding to the ornaments of the city of Arles, to the fidelity of which we are so much indebted, according to our brother and patrician.[3]

"Given on the 15th of the calends of May; received a' Arles on the 10th of the calends of June."

The provinces and the towns refused the benefit; no one would nominate the deputies, no one would go to Arles. Centralization and unity were contrary to the primitive character of that society; the local and munificent spirit reappeared everywhere, and the impossibility of reconstituting

---

[1] Petronius was prefect of the Gauls between the years 402 and 408.

[2] The municipal bodies of Roman towns were called *curiæ*, and the members of those bodies, who were very numerous, were called *curiales*.

[3] Constantine, the second husband of Placidius, whom Honorius had chosen for colleague in 421.

a general society or country became evident. The towns confined themselves, each to its own walls and its own affairs, and the empire fell because none wished to be of the empire, because citizens desired to be only of their own city. Thus we again discover, at the fall of the Roman empire, the same fact which we have detected in the cradle of Rome, namely, the predominance of the municipal form and spirit. The Roman world had returned to its first condition; towns had constituted it; it dissolved; and towns remained.

In the municipal system we see what ancient Roman civilization has bequeathed to modern Europe; that system was very irregular, much weakened, and far inferior, no doubt, to what it had been in earlier times; but, nevertheless, the only real, the only constituted system which had outlived all the elements of the Roman world.

When I say *alone*, I make a mistake. Another fact, another idea equally survived: the idea of the empire, the name of emperor, the idea of imperial majesty, of an absolute and sacred power attached to the name of emperor. These are the elements which Roman has transmitted to European civilization; upon one hand, the municipal system, its habits, rules, precedents, the principle of freedom; on the other, a general and uniform civil legislation, the idea of absolute power, of sacred majesty, of the emperor, the principle of order and subjection.

But there was formed at the same time, in the heart of the Roman society, a society of a very different nature, founded upon totally different principles, animated by different sentiments, a society which was about to infuse into modern European society elements of a character wholly different; I speak of the *Christian church*. I say, the Christian church, and not Christianity. At the end of the fourth and at the beginning of the fifth century, Christianity was no longer merely an individual belief, it was an institution; it was constituted; it had its government, a clergy, an hierarchy calculated for the different functions of the clergy, revenues, means of independent action, rallying points suited for a great society, provincial, national, and general councils, and the custom of debating in common upon the affairs of the society. In a word, Christianity, at this epoch, was not only a religion, it was also a church.

D

Had it not been a church, I cannot say what might have happened to it amid the fall of the Roman empire. I confine myself to simply human considerations; I put aside every element which is foreign to the natural consequences of natural facts: had Christianity been, as in the earlier times, no more than a belief, a sentiment, an individual conviction, we may believe that it would have sunk amidst the dissolution of the empire, and the invasion of the barbarians. In later times, in Asia and in all the north of Africa, it sunk under an invasion of the same nature, under the invasion of the Moslem barbarians; it sunk then, although it subsisted in the form of an institution, or constituted church. With much more reason might the same thing have happened at the moment of the fall of the Roman empire. There existed, at that time, none of those means by which, in the present day. moral influences establish themselves or offer resistance, independently of institutions; none of those means whereby a pure truth, a pure idea obtains a great empire over minds, governs actions, and determines events. Nothing of the kind existed in the fourth century to give a like authority to ideas and to personal sentiments. It is clear that a society strongly organized and strongly governed, was indispensable to struggle against such a disaster, and to issue victorious from such a storm. I do not think that I say more than the truth in affirming that at the end of the fourth and the commencement of the fifth centuries it was the Christian church that saved Christianity; it was the church with its institutions, its magistrates, and its power, that vigorously resisted the internal dissolution of the empire and barbarism; that conquered the barbarians and became the bond, the medium, and the principle of civilization between the Roman and barbarian worlds. It is, then, the condition of the church rather than that of religion, properly so called, that we must look to, in order to discover what Christianity has, since then, added to modern civilization, and what new elements it has introduced therein. What was the Christian church at that period?

When we consider, always under a purely human point of view, the various revolutions which have accomplished themselves during the development of Christianity, from the time of its origin up to the fifth century; if, I repeat, we consider it simply as a community and not as a religious creed, we find that it passed through three essentially different states.

In the very earliest period, the Christian society presents itself as a simple association of a common creed and common sentiments; the first Christians united to enjoy together the same emotions, and the same religious convictions. We find among them no system of determinate doctrines, no rules, no discipline, no body of magistrates.

Of course, no society, however newly born, however weakly constituted it may be, exists without a moral power which animates and directs it. In the various Christian congregations there were men who preached, taught, and morally governed the congregation, but there was no formal magistrate, no recognised discipline; a simple association caused by a community of creed and sentiments was the primitive condition of the Christian society.

In proportion as it advanced—and very speedily, since traces are visible in the earliest monuments—a body of doctrines, of rules, of discipline, and of magistrates, began to appear: one kind of magistrates were called πρεσβυτεροι, or *ancients*, who became the priests; another, επισκοποι, or inspectors, or superintendents, who became bishops; a third διακονοι, or deacons, who were charged with the care of the poor, and with the distribution of alms.

It is scarcely possible to determine what were the precise functions of these various magistrates; the line of demarcation was probably very vague and variable, but what is clear is that an establishment was organized. Still, a peculiar character prevails in this second period: the preponderance and rule belonged to the body of the faithful. It was the body of the faithful which prevailed, both as to the choice of functionaries, and as to the adoption of discipline, and even doctrine. The church government and the Christian people were not as yet separated. They did not exist apart from, and independently of, one another; and the Christian people exercised the principal influence in the society.

In the third period all was different. A clergy existed who were distinct from the people, a body of priests who had their own riches, jurisdiction, and peculiar constitution; in a word, an entire government, which in itself was a complete society, a society provided with all the means of ex-

D 2

istence, independently of the society to which it had reference, and over which it extended its influence. Such was the
third stage of the constitution of the Christian church; such
was the form in which it appeared at the beginning of the
fifth century. The government was not completely separated
from the people; there has never been a parallel kind of
government, and less in religious matters than in any others;
but in the relations of the clergy to the faithful, the clergy
ruled almost without control.

The Christian clergy had moreover another and very different source of influence. The bishops and the priests
became the principal municipal magistrates. You have seen,
that of the Roman empire there remained, properly speaking,
nothing but the municipal system. It had happened, from
the vexations of despotism and the ruin of the towns, that
the *curiales*, or members of the municipal bodies, had become
discouraged and apathetic; on the contrary, the bishops, and
the body of priests, full of life and zeal, offered themselves
naturally for the superintendence and direction of all matters.
We should be wrong to reproach them for this, to tax them
with usurpation; it was all in the natural course of things;
the clergy alone were morally strong and animated; they
became everywhere powerful. Such is the law of the universe.

The marks of this revolution are visible in all the legislation of the emperors at this period. If you open the code,
either of Theodosius or of Justinian, you will find numerous
regulations which remit municipal affairs to the clergy and
the bishops. Here are some of them:

" *Cod. Just. I.* 1. *tit. IV., de episcopali audientiâ.* § 26.—
With respect to the yearly affairs of cities, whether they
concern the ordinary revenues of the city, either from funds
arising from the property of the city, or from private gifts or
legacies, or from any other source; whether public works, or
depôts of provisions, or aqueducts, or the maintenance of
baths, or ports, or the construction of walls or towers, or the
repairing of bridges or roads, or trials in which the city may
be engaged in reference to public or private interests, we ordain
as follows:—The very pious bishop, and three notables chosen
from amongst the first men of the city, shall meet together;
they shall, each year, examine the works done; they shall take

care that those who conduct them, or who have conducted them, shall regulate them with precision, render their accounts, and show that they have duly performed their engagements in the administration, whether of the public monuments, or of the sums appointed for provisions or baths, or of expenses in the maintenance of roads, aqueducts, or any other work.

"*Ibid.* § 30.—With regard to the guardianship of young persons of the first or second age, and of all those for whom the law appoints guardians, if their fortune does not exceed 500 *aurei*, we ordain that the nomination of the president of the province shall not be waited for. as this gives rise to great expenses, particularly if the said president do not reside in the city in which it is necessary to provide the guardianship. The nomination of guardians shall in such case be made by the magistrate of the city......in concert with the very pious bishop and other person or persons invested with public offices, if there be more than one.

" *Ibid. I.* 1, *tit. LV., de defensoribus,* § 8.—We desire that the defenders of the cities, being well instructed in the holy mysteries of the orthodox faith, be chosen and instituted by the venerable bishops, the priests, the notables, the proprietors, and the *curiales.* As regards their installation, it shall be referred to the glorious power of the pretorian prefect, in order that their authority may have infused into it more solidity and vigour from the letters of admission of his Magnificence."

I might cite a great number of other laws, and you would everywhere meet with the fact which I have mentioned: between the municipal system of the Romans, and that of the middle ages, the municipal-ecclesiastic system interposed; the preponderance of the clergy in the affairs of the city succeeded that of the ancient municipal magistrates, and preceded the organization of the modern municipal corporations.

You perceive what prodigious power was thus obtained by the Christian church, as well by its own constitution, as by its influence upon the Christian people, and by the part which it took in civil affairs. Thus, from that epoch, it powerfully assisted in forming the character and furthering the development of modern civilization. Let us endeavour to sum up the elements which it from that time introduced into it.

And first of all there was an immense advantage in the presence of a moral influence, of a moral power, of a power which reposed solely upon convictions and upon moral creeds and sentiments, amidst the deluge of material power which at this time inundated society. Had the Christian church not existed, the whole world must have been abandoned to purely material force. The church alone exercised a moral power. It did more: it sustained, it spread abroad the idea of a rule, of a law superior to all human laws. It proposed, for the salvation of humanity, the fundamental belief, that there exists, above all human laws, a law which is denominated, according to periods and customs, sometimes reason, sometimes the divine law, but which, everywhere and always, is the same law under different names.

In short, with the church originated a great fact, the separation of spiritual and temporal power. This separation is the source of liberty of conscience; it is founded upon no other principle but that which is the foundation of the most perfect and extended freedom of conscience. The separation of temporal and spiritual power is based upon the idea that physical force has neither right nor influence over souls, over conviction, over truth. It flows from the distinction established between the world of thought and the world of action, between the world of internal and that of external facts. Thus this principle of liberty of conscience for which Europe has struggled so much, and suffered so much, this principle which prevailed so late, and often, in its progress, against the inclination of the clergy, was enunciated, under the name of the separation of temporal and spiritual power, in the very cradle of European civilization; and it was the Christian church which, from the necessity imposed by its situation of defending itself against barbarism, introduced and maintained it.

The presence, then, of a moral influence, the maintenance of a divine law, and the separation of the temporal and spiritual powers, are the three grand benefits which the Christian church in the fifth century conferred upon the European world.

Even at that time, however, all its influences were not equally salutary. Already, in the fifth century, there appeared in the church certain unwholesome principles, which have played a great part in the development of our civilization. Thus, at this period, there prevailed within it the separation of governors and the governed, the attempt to establish the independence of governors as regards the governed, to impose laws upon the governed, to possess their mind, their life, without the free consent of their reason and of their will. The church, moreover, endeavoured to render the theocratic principle predominant in society, to usurp the temporal power, to reign exclusively. And when it could not succeed in obtaining temporal dominion, in inducing the prevalence of the theocratic principle, it allied itself with temporal princes, and, in order to share, supported their absolute power, at the expense of the liberty of the people.

Such were the principles of civilization which Europe in the fifth century derived from the church and from the Empire. It was in this condition that the barbarians found the Roman world, and came to take possession of it. In order to fully understand all the elements which met and mixed in the cradle of our civilization, it only remains for us to study the barbarians.

When I speak of the barbarians, you understand that we have nothing to do here with their history; narrative is not our present business. You know that at this period, the conquerors of the Empire were nearly all of the same race; they were all Germans, except some Sclavonic tribes, the Alani, for example. We know also that they were all in pretty nearly the same stage of civilization. Some difference, indeed, might have existed between them in this respect, according to the greater or less degree of connexion which the different tribes had had with the Roman world. Thus no doubt the Goths were more advanced, possessed milder manners than the Franks. But in considering matters under a general point of view, and in their results as regards ourselves, this original difference of civilization among the barbarous people is of no importance.

It is the general condition of society among the barbarians that we need to understand. But this is a subject with which, at the present day, it is very difficult to make ourselves acquainted. We obtain without much difficulty a comprehension of the Roman municipal system, of the Christian church; their influence has been continued up to our own days. We find traces of it in numerous institutions and actual facts; we have a thousand means of recognising and explaining them. But the customs and social condition of the barbarians have completely perished. We are compelled to make them out either from the earliest historical monuments, or by an effort of the imagination.

There is a sentiment, a fact, which, before all things, it is necessary that we should well understand, in order to represent faithfully to oneself the barbaric character: the pleasure of individual independence; the pleasure of enjoying oneself with vigour and liberty, amidst the chances of the world and of life; the delights of activity without labour; the taste for an adventurous career, full of uncertainty, inequality, and peril. Such was the predominating sentiment of the barbarous state, the moral want which put in motion these masses of human beings. In the present day, locked up as we are in so regular a society, it is difficult to realize this sentiment to oneself with all the power which it exercised over the barbarians of the fourth and fifth centuries. There is only one work, which, in my opinion, contains this characteristic of barbarism, stamped in all its energy: "The History of the Conquest of England by the Normans," of M. Thierry, the only book wherein the motives, tendencies, and impulses which actuate men in a social condition, bordering on barbarism, are felt and reproduced with a really Homeric faithfulness. Nowhere else do we see so well the nature of a barbarian and of the life of a barbarian. Something of this sort is also found, though, in my opinion, in a much lower degree, with much less simplicity, much less truth, in Cooper's romances upon the savages of America. There is something in the life of the American savages, in the relations and the sentiments they bear with them in the middle of the woods, that recals, up to a certain point, the manners of the ancient Germans. No doubt these pictures are somewhat idealised, somewhat poetic; the dark side of the barbaric manners and life is not presented to us in all its grossness. I speak not only of the evils induced by these manners upon the social state, but of the internal and individual condition of the barbarian himself. There was, within this passionate want of personal independence, something more gross and more material than one would be led to conceive from the work of M. Thierry; there was a degree of brutality and of apathy which is not always exactly conveyed by his recitals. Nevertheless, when we look to the bottom of the question, notwithstanding this alloy of brutality, of materialism, of dull, stupid selfishness, the love of independence is a noble and a moral sentiment, which draws its power from the moral nature of man; it is the pleasure of feeling oneself a man, the sentiment of personality, of human spontaneity in its free development.

It was through the German barbarians that this sentiment was introduced into European civilization; it was unknown in the Roman world, unknown in the Christian church, and unknown in almost all the ancient civilizations. When you find liberty in ancient civilizations, it is political liberty, the liberty of the citizen: man strove not for his personal liberty, but for his liberty as a citizen: he belonged to an association, he was devoted to an association, he was ready to sacrifice himself to an association. It was the same with the Christian church: a sentiment of strong attachment to the Christian corporation, of devotion to its laws, and a lively desire to extend its empire; or rather, the religious sentiment induced a reaction of man upon himself, upon his soul, an internal effort to subdue his own liberty, and to submit himself to the will of his faith. But the sentiment of personal independence, a love of liberty displaying itself at all risks, without any other motive but that of satisfying itself; this sentiment, I repeat, was unknown to the Roman and to the Christian society. It was by the barbarians that it was brought in and deposited in the cradle of modern civilization, wherein it has played so conspicuous a part, has produced such worthy results, that it is impossible to help reckoning it as one of its fundamental elements.

There is a second fact, a second element of civilization, for which we are equally indebted to the barbarians: this is military clientship; the bond which established itself between individuals, between warriors, and which, without destroying the liberty of each, without even in the beginning destroying, beyond a certain point, the equality which almost completely existed between them, nevertheless founded an hierarchical subordination, and gave birth to that aristocratical organisation, which afterwards became feudalism. The foundation of this relation was the attachment of man to man,

the fidelity of individual to individual, without external necessity, and without obligation based upon the general principles
of society. In the ancient republics you see no man attached
freely and especially to any other man; they were all attached
to the city. Among the barbarians it was between individuals that the social bond was formed; first by the relation of
the chief to his companion, when they lived in the condition
of a band wandering over Europe; and, later, by the relation
of suzerain to vassal. This second principle, which has
played so great a part in the history of modern civilization,
this devotion of man to man, came to us from the barbarians;
it is from their manners that it has passed into ours.

I ask you, was I wrong in saying at the beginning,
that modern civilization, even in its cradle, had been as
varied, as agitated, and as confused as I have endeavoured to
describe it to you in the general picture I have given
you of it? Is it not true that we have now discovered, at the
fall of the Roman empire, almost all the elements which
unite in the progressive development of our civilization?
We have found, at that time, three wholly different societies:
the municipal society, the last remains of the Roman empire;
the Christian society; and the Barbaric society. We find
these societies very variously organized, founded upon totally
different principles, inspiring men with wholly different sentiments; we find the craving after the most absolute independence side by side with the most complete submission; military
patronage side by side with ecclesiastical dominion; the
spiritual and temporal powers everywhere present; the canons
of the church, the learned legislation of the Romans, the
almost unwritten customs of the barbarians; everywhere the
mixture, or rather the coexistence of the most diverse races,
languages, social situations, manners, ideas, and impressions.
Herein I think we have a sufficient proof of the faithfulness
of the general character under which I have endeavoured to
present our civilization to you.

No doubt, this confusion, this diversity, this struggle,
have cost us very dear; these have been the cause of the slow
progress of Europe, of the storms and sufferings to which
she has been a prey. Nevertheless, I do not think we need
regret them. To people, as well as to individuals, the chance
of the most complete and varied development, the chance

of an almost unlimited progress in all directions, compensates of itself alone for all that it may cost to obtain the right of casting for it. And, all things considered, this state, so agitated, so toilsome, so violent, has availed much more than the simplicity with which other civilizations present themselves; the human race has gained thereby more than it has suffered.

We are now acquainted with the general features of the condition in which the fall of the Roman empire left the world; we are acquainted with the different elements which were agitated and became mingled, in order to give birth to European civilization. Henceforth we shall see them advancing and acting under our eyes. In the next lecture I shall endeavour to show what they became, and what they effected in the epoch which we are accustomed to call the times of barbarism; that is to say, while the chaos of invasion yet existed

THIRD LECTURE.

Object of the lecture—All the various systems pretend to be legitimate—What is political legitimacy?—Co-existence of all systems of government in the fifth century—Instability in the condition of persons properties, and institutions—There were two causes of this, one material, the continuation of the invasion; the other moral, the selfish sentiment of individuality peculiar to the barbarians—The germs of civilization have been the necessity for order, the recollections of the Roman empire, the Christian church, and the barbarians—Attempts at organization by the barbarians, by the towns, by the church of Spain, by Charlemagne, and Alfred—The German and Arabian invasions cease—The feudal system begins.

I HAVE placed before you the fundamental elements of European civilization, tracing them to its very cradle, at the moment of the fall of the Roman empire. I have endeavoured to give you a glimpse beforehand of their diversity, and their constant struggle, and to show you that no one of them succeeded in reigning over our society, or at least in reigning over it so completely as to enslave or expel the others. We have seen that this was the distinguishing character of European civilization. We now come to its history at its commencement, in the ages which it is customary to call the barbarous.

At the first glance we cast upon this epoch, it is impossible not to be struck with a fact which seems to contradict what we have lately said. When you examine certain notions which are accredited concerning the antiquities of modern Europe, you will perceive that the various elements of our civilization, the monarchical, theocratical, aristocratical, and democratical principles, all pretend that European society originally belonged to them, and that they have only lost the sole dominion by the usurpations of contrary principles. Question all that has been written, all that has been said upon this subject, and you will see that all the systems whereby our beginnings are sought to be represented or explained, maintain the exclusive predominance of one or other of the elements of European civilization.

Thus there is a school of feudal publicists, of whom the most celebrated is M. de Boulainvilliers, who pretend that, after the fall of the Roman empire, it was the conquering nation, subsequently become the nobility, which possessed all powers and rights; that society was its domain; that kings and peoples have despoiled it of this domain; that aristocratic organization was the primitive and true form of Europe.

Beside this school, you will find that of the monarchists, the abbé Dubos, for instance, who maintain, on the contrary, that it was to royalty European society belonged. The German kings, say they, inherited all the rights of the Roman emperors; they had even been called in by the ancient nations, the Gauls among others; they alone ruled legitimately; all the acquisitions of the aristocracy were only encroachments upon monarchy.

A third party presents itself, that of the liberal publicists, republicans, democrats, or whatever you like to call them. Consult the abbé de Mably; according to him, it is to the system of free institutions, to the association of free men, to the people properly so called, that the government of society devolved from the period of the fifth century: nobles and kings enriched themselves with the spoils of primitive freedom; it sank beneath their attacks, indeed, but it reigned before them.

And above all these monarchical, aristocratical, and popular pretensions, rises the theocratical pretension of the church, who affirms, that in virtue of her very mission, of her divine title, society belonged to her; that she alone had the right to govern it; that she alone was the legitimate queen of the European world, won over by her labours to civilization and to truth.

See then the position in which we are placed! We fancied we had shown that no one of the elements of European civilization had exclusively ruled in the course of its history; that those elements had existed in a constant state of vicinity,

of amalgamation, of combat, and of compromise; and yet, at
our very first step, we meet with the directly contrary
opinion, that, even in its cradle, in the bosom of barbaric
Europe, it was such or such a one of their elements which
alone possessed society.   And it is not only in a single country, but in all the countries of Europe, that, beneath slightly
different forms, at different periods, the various principles of
our civilization have manifested these irreconcilable pretensions.   The historical schools we have just characterized, are
to be met with everywhere.

   This is an important fact,—important not in itself, but
because it reveals other facts which hold a conspicuous
place in our history.   From this simultaneous setting forth
of the most opposite pretensions to the exclusive possession of power in the first age of modern Europe, two
remarkable facts become apparent.   The first the principle,
the idea of political legitimacy; an idea which has played a
great part in the course of European civilization.   The second
the veritable and peculiar character of the condition of barbaric Europe, of that epoch with which we are at present
especially concerned.

   I shall endeavour to demonstrate these two facts, to deduce them successively from this combat of primitive pretensions which I have just described.

   What do the various elements of European civilization,
the theocratical, monarchical, aristocratical, and popular
elements pretend to, when they wish to appear the first
who possessed society in Europe?   Do they not thus pretend to have been alone legitimate?   Political legitimacy is
evidently a right founded upon antiquity, upon duration;
priority in time is appealed to as the source of the right, as
the proof of the legitimacy of power.   And observe, i pray
you, that this pretension is not peculiar to any one system, to
any one element of our civilization; it extends to all.   In
modern times we are accustomed to consider the idea of
legitimacy as existing in only one system, the monarchical.
In this we are mistaken; it is discoverable in all.   You have
already seen that all the elements of our civilization have
equally desired to appropriate it.   If we enter into the subsequent history of Europe, we shall find the most different
social forms and governments equally in possession of their

character of legitimacy.   The Italian and Swiss aristocracies and democracies, the republic of San Marino, as well as the greatest monarchies of Europe, have called themselves, and have been regarded as legitimate; the former, like the latter, have founded their pretension to legitimacy upon the antiquity of their institutions, and upon the historical priority and perpetuity of their system of government.

If you leave Europe and direct your attention to other times and other countries, you everywhere meet with this idea of political legitimacy; you find it attaching itself everywhere to some portion of the government, to some institution, form, or maxim.   There has been no country, and no time, in which there has not existed a certain portion of the social system, public powers; which has not attributed to itself, and in which has not been recognised this character of legitimacy, derived from antiquity and long duration.

What is this principle? what are its elements? how has it introduced itself into European civilization?

At the origin of all powers, I say of all without any distinction, we meet with physical force.   I do not mean to state that force alone has founded them all, or that if, in their origin, they had not had other titles than that of force, they would have been established.   Other titles are manifestly necessary; powers have become established in consequence of certain social expediences, of certain references to the state of society, manners, and opinions.   But it is impossible to avoid perceiving that physical force has stained the origin of all the powers of the world, whatever may have been their character and form.

Yet none will have anything to say to this origin; all powers, whatever they may be, reject it; none will admit themselves the offspring of force.   An unconquerable instinct warns governments that force does not found right, and that if force was their origin, their right could never be established.   This, then, is the reason why, when we go back to early times, and there find the various systems and powers a prey to violence, all exclaim, " I was anterior to all this, I existed previously, in virtue of other titles; society belonged to me before this state of violence and struggle in which you meet with me; I was legitimate, but others contested and seized my rights."

This fact alone proves that the idea of force is not the foundation of political legitimacy, but that it reposes upon a totally different basis. What, indeed, is done by all these systems in thus formally disavowing force? They themselves proclaim that there is another kind of legitimacy, the true foundation of all others, the legitimacy of reason, justice, and right; and this is the origin with which they desire to connect themselves. It is because they wish it not to be supposed that they are the offspring of force, that they pretend to be invested in the name of their antiquity, with a different title. The first characteristic, then, of political legitimacy, is to reject physical force as a source of power, and to connect it with a moral idea, with a moral force, with the idea of right, of justice, and of reason. This is the fundamental element from which the principle of political legitimacy has issued. It has issued thence by the help of antiquity and long duration. And in this manner:

After physical force has presided at the birth of all governments, of all societies, time progresses; it alters the works of force, it corrects them, corrects them by the very fact that a society endures, and is composed of men. Man carries within himself certain notions of order, justice, and reason, a certain desire to induce their prevalence, to introduce them into the circumstances among which he lives; he labours unceasingly at this task; and if the social condition in which he is placed continues, he labours always with a certain effect. Man places reason, morality, and legitimacy in the world in which he lives.

Independently of the work of man, by a law of Providence which it is impossible to mistake, a law analogous to that which regulates the material world, there is a certain measure of order, reason, and justice, which is absolutely necessary to the duration of a society. From the single fact of its duration, we may conclude that a society is not wholly absurd, insensate, and iniquitous; that it is not utterly deprived of that element of reason, truth, and justice, which alone gives life to societies. If, moreover, the society develops itself, if it becomes more vigorous and more powerful, if the social condition from day to day, is accepted by a greater number of men, it is because it gathers by the action of time more reason, justice, and right; because circumstances regulate themselves, step by step, according to true legitimacy.

Thus the idea of political legitimacy penetrates the world, and men's minds, from the world. It has for its foundation and first origin, in a certain measure at least, moral legitimacy, justice, reason, and truth, and afterwards the sanction of time, which gives cause for believing that reason has won entrance into facts, and that true legitimacy has been introduced into the external world. At the epoch which we are about to study, we shall find force and falsehood hovering over the cradle of royalty, of aristocracy, of democracy, and of the church herself; you will everywhere behold force and falsehood reforming themselves, little by little, under the hand of time, right and truth taking their places in civilization. It is this introduction of right and truth into the social state, which has developed, step by step, the idea of political legitimacy; it is thus that it has been established in modern civilization.

When, therefore, attempts have at different times been made to raise this idea as the banner of absolute power, it has been perverted from its true origin. So far is it from being the banner of absolute power, that it is only in the name of right and justice that it has penetrated and taken root in the world. It is not exclusive; it belongs to no one in particular, but springs up wherever right develops itself. Political legitimacy attaches itself to liberty as well as to power; to individual rights, as well as to the forms according to which public functions are exercised. We shall meet with it, in our way, in the most contrary systems; in the feudal system, in the municipalities of Flanders and Germany, in the Italian republics, no less than in monarchy. It is a character spread over the various elements of modern civilization, and which it is necessary to understand thoroughly on entering upon its history.

The second fact which clearly reveals itself in the simultaneous pretensions of which I spoke in the beginning, is the true character of the so called barbarian epoch. All the elements of European civilization pretend at this time to have possessed Europe; it follows that neither of them predominated. When a social form predominates in the world, it is not so difficult to recognise it. On coming to the tenth century we shall recognise, without hesitation, the predominance of the feudal system; in the seventeenth century we shall not hesitate to affirm that the monarchical system pre-

vails; if we look to the municipalities of Flanders, to the
Italian republics, we shall immediately declare the empire of
the democratic principle. When there is really any predominating principle in society, it is impossible to mistake it.

The dispute which has arisen between the various systems
that have had a share in European civilization, upon the
question, which predominated at its origin, proves, then,
that they all co-existed, without any one of them prevailing
generally enough, or certainly enough to give to society its
form and its name.

Such, then, is the character of the barbarian epoch; it was
the chaos of all elements, the infancy of all systems, an universal turmoil, in which even strife was not permanent or
systematic. By examining all the aspects of the social state
at this period, I might show you that it is impossible anywhere to discover a single fact, or a single principle, which
was anything like general or established. I shall confine
myself to two essential points: the condition of individuals,
and the condition of institutions. That will be enough to
paint the entire society.

At this period we meet with four classes of persons—
1. The free men; that is to say, those who depended upon no
superior, upon no patron, and who possessed their property
and regulated their life in complete liberty, without any bond
of obligation to any other man. 2. The *leudes*, *fideles*,
anstrustions, &c., bound at first by the relation of companion
to chief, and afterwards by that of vassal to suzerain, to another man, towards whom, on account of a grant of lands, or
other gifts, they had contracted the obligation of service.
3. The freedman. 4. The slaves.

But were these various classes fixed? Did men, when
once they were inclosed in their limits, remain there? Had
the relations of the various classes anything of regularity and
permanence? By no means. You constantly behold freemen who leave their position to place themselves in the service of some one, receiving from him some gift or other, and
passing into the class of *leudes*; others you see who fall into
the class of slaves. Elsewhere *leudes* are seen struggling to
separate themselves from their patrons, to again become independent, to re-enter the class of freemen. Everywhere you
behold a movement, a continual passage of one class into

another; an uncertainty, a general instability in the relations of the classes; no man remaining in his position, no position remaining the same.

Landed properties were in the same condition. You know that these were distinguished as allodial, or wholly free, and beneficiary, or subject to certain obligations with regard to a superior: you know how an attempt has been made to establish, in this last class of properties, a precise and defined system; it has been said that the benefices were at first given for a certain determinate number of years, afterwards for life, and that finally they became hereditary. A vain attempt! All these kinds of tenure existed without order and simultaneously; we meet, at the same moment, with benefices for a fixed time, for life, and hereditary; the same lands, indeed, passed in a few years through these different states. There was nothing more stable in the condition of lands than in that of individuals. On all sides was felt the laborious transition of the wandering to the sedentary life, of personal relations to the combined relations of men and properties, or to real relations. During this transition all is confused, local, and disordered.

In the institutions we find the same instability, the same chaos. Three systems of institutions co-existed: royalty; aristocratic institutions, or the dependence of men and lands, one upon another; and free institutions, that is to say, the assemblies of free men deliberating in common. Neither of these systems was in possession of society; neither of them prevailed over the others. Free institutions existed, but the men who should have taken part in the assemblies rarely attended them. The signorial jurisdiction was not more regularly exercised. Royalty, which is the simplest of institutions, and the easiest to determine, had no fixed character; it was partly elective, partly hereditary. Sometimes the son succeeded the father; sometimes a selection was made from the family; sometimes it was a simple election of a distant relation, or of a stranger. In no system will you find anything fixed; all institutions, as well as all social situations, existed together, became confounded, and were continually changing.

In states the same fluctuation prevailed: they were erected and suppressed, united and divided; there were no boundaries,

E 2

no governments, no distinct people; but a general confusion of situations, principles, facts, races, and languages: such was barbarous Europe.

Within what limits is this strange period bounded? Its origin is well marked; it begins with the fall of the Roman empire. But when did it conclude? In order to answer this question, we must learn to what this condition of society is to be attributed, what were the causes of this barbarism.

I think I can perceive two principal causes: the one material, arising from without, in the course of events; the other moral, originating from within, from man himself.

The material cause was the continuation of the invasion. We must not fancy that the invasion of the barbarians ceased in the fifth century; we must not think that, because Rome was fallen, we shall immediately find the barbaric kingdoms founded upon its ruins, or that the movement was at an end. This movement lasted long after the fall of the empire; the proofs of this are manifest.

See the Frank kings, even of the first race, called continually to make war beyond the Rhine; Clotaire, Dagobert constantly engaged in expeditions into Germany, fighting against the Thuringians, Danes, and Saxons, who occupied the right bank of the Rhine. Wherefore? Because these nations wished to cross the river, to come and take their share of the spoils of the empire. Whence, about the same time, those great invasions of Italy by the Franks established in Gaul, and principally by the Eastern or Austrasian Franks? They attacked Switzerland; passed the Alps; entered Italy. Why? Because they were pressed, on the north-east, by new populations; their expeditions were not merely forays for pillage, they were matters of necessity; they were disturbed in their settlements, and went elsewhere to seek their fortune. A new Germanic nation appeared upon the stage, and founded in Italy the kingdom of the Lombards. In Gaul, the Frank dynasty changed; the Carlovingians succeeded the Merovingians. It is now acknowledged that this change of dynasty was, to say the truth, a fresh invasion of Gaul by the Franks, a movement of nations, which substituted the eastern for the western Franks. The change was completed; the second race now governed. Charlemagne commenced against the Saxons what the Merovingians had done against the

Thuringians; he was incessantly engaged in war against the nations beyond the Rhine. Who urged these on? The Obotrites, the Wiltzes, the Sorabes, the Bohemians, the entire Sclavonic race which pressed upon the Germanic, and from the sixth to the ninth century compelled it to advance towards the west. Everywhere to the north-east the movement of invasion continued and determined events.

In the south, a movement of the same nature exhibited itself: the Moslem Arabs appeared. While the Germanic and Sclavonic people pressed on along the Rhine and Danube, the Arabs began their expeditions and conquests upon all the coasts of the Mediterranean.

The invasion of the Arabs had a peculiar character. The spirit of conquest and the spirit of proselytism were united. The invasion was to conquer a territory and disseminate a faith. There was a great difference between this movement and that of the Germans. In the Christian world, the spiritual and temporal powers were distinct. The desire of propagating a creed and making a conquest, did not co-exist in the same men. The Germans, when they became converted, preserved their manners, sentiments, and tastes; terrestrial passions and interests continued to rule them; they became Christians, but not missionaries. The Arabs, on the contrary, were both conquerors and missionaries; the power of the sword and that of the word, with them, were in the same hands. At a later period, this character determined the unfortunate turn taken by Mussulman civilization; it is in the combination of the spiritual and temporal powers, in the confusion of moral and material authority, that the tyranny which seems inherent in this civilization originated. This I conceive to be the cause of the stationary condition into which that civilization is everywhere fallen. But the fact did not make its appearance at first; on the contrary, it added prodigious force to the Arab invasion. Undertaken with moral passions and ideas, it immediately obtained a splendour and a greatness which was wanting to the German invasion; it exhibited far more energy and enthusiasm, and far differently influenced the minds of men.

Such was the state of Europe, from the fifth to the ninth century: pressed on the south by the Mahometans, on the north by the Germans and the Sclavonic tribes, it

was scarcely possible that the reaction of this double invasion
should do other than hold the interior of Europe in continual
disorder.   The populations were constantly being displaced,
and forced one upon the other; nothing of a fixed character
could be established; the wandering life recommenced on all
sides.   There was, no doubt, some difference in this respect
in the different states : the chaos was greater in Germany
than in the rest of Europe, Germany being the focus of the
movement; France was more agitated than Italy.   But in no
place could society settle or regulate itself ; barbarism continued on all sides, from the same cause that had originated it.

So much for the material cause, that which arose from the
course of events.   I now come to the moral cause, which
sprang from the internal condition of man, and which was no
less powerful.

After all, whatever external events may be, it is man himself who makes the world; it is in proportion to the ideas,
sentiments, and dispositions, moral and intellectual, of man,
that the world becomes regulated and progressive; it is upon
the internal condition of man that the visible condition of
society depends.

What is required to enable men to found a society with
anything of durability and regularity?   It is evidently necessary that they should have a certain number of ideas sufficiently extended to suit that society, to apply to its wants, to
its relations.   It is necessary, moreover, that these ideas should
be common to the greater number of the members of the
society; finally, that they should exercise a certain empire
over their wills and actions.

It is clear, that if men have no ideas extending beyond
their own existence, if their intellectual horizon is confined
to themselves, if they are abandoned to the tempest of their
passions and their wills, if they have not among them a certain number of notions and sentiments in common, around
which to rally, it is clear, I say, that between them no
society is possible, and that each individual must be a principle of disturbance and dissolution to any association which
he may enter.

Wherever individuality predominates almost exclusively,
wherever man considers no one but himself, and his ideas
do not extend beyond himself, and he obeys nothing but

his own passions, society (I mean a society somewhat extended and permanent) becomes for him almost impossible. Such, however, was the moral condition of the con querors of Europe, at the time upon which we are now occupied. I remarked in my last lecture that we are indebted to the Germans for an energetic sentiment of individual liberty, of human individuality. But in a state of extreme barbarism and ignorance, this sentiment becomes selfishness in all its brutality, in all its insociability. From the fifth to the eighth century it was at this point among the Germans. They cared only for their own interests, their own passions, their own will: how could they be reconciled to a condition even approximating to the social? Attempts were made to prevail upon them to enter it; they attempted to do so themselves. But they immediately abandoned it by some act of carelessness, some burst of passion, some want of intelligence. Constantly did society attempt to form itself; constantly was it destroyed by the act of man, by the absence of the moral conditions under which alone it can exist.

Such were the two determining causes of the barbarous state. So long as these were prolonged, barbarism endured. Let us see how and when they at last terminated.

Europe laboured to escape from this condition. It is in the nature of man, even when he has been plunged into such a condition by his own fault, not to desire to remain in it. However rude, however ignorant, however devoted to his own interests and to his own passions he may be, there is within him a voice and an instinct, which tells him that he was made for better things, that he has other powers, another destiny. In the midst of disorder, the love of order and of progress pursues and harasses him. The need of justice, foresight, development, agitates him even under the yoke of the most brutal selfishness. He feels himself impelled to reform the material world, and society, and himself; and he labours to do this, though unaware of the nature of the want which urges him. The barbarians aspired after civilization, while totally incapable of it, nay more, detesting it from the instant that they became acquainted with its law.

There remained, moreover, considerable wrecks of the Roman civilization. The name of the Empire, the recollection of that great and glorious society, disturbed the memories of men, particularly of the senators of towns, of bishops, priests, and all those who had had their origin in the Roman world.:

Among the barbarians themselves, or their barbaric ancestors, many had been witnesses of the grandeur of the Empire; they had served in its armies, they had conquered it. The image and name of Roman civilization had an imposing influence upon them, and they experienced the desire of imitating, of reproducing, of preserving something of it. This was another cause which urged them to quit the condition of barbarism I have described.

. There was a third cause which suggests itself to every mind; I mean the Christian church. The church was a society regularly constituted, having its principles, its rules, and its discipline, and experiencing an ardent desire to extend its influence and conquer its conquerors. Among the Christians of this period, among the Christian clergy, there were men who had thought upon all moral and political questions, who had decided opinions and energetic sentiments upon all subjects, and a vivid desire to propagate and give them empire. Never has any other society made such efforts to influence the surrounding world, and to stamp thereon its own likeness, as were made by the Christian church between the fifth and the tenth centuries. When we come to study its particular history, we shall see all that it has done. It attacked barbarism, as it were, at every point, in order to civilize by ruling over it.

Finally, there was a fourth cause of civilization, a cause which it is impossible fitly to appreciate, but which is not therefore the less real, and this is the appearance of great men. No one can say why a great man appears at a certain epoch, and what he adds to the development of the world; that is a secret of Providence: but the fact is not therefore less certain. There are men whom the spectacle of anarchy and social stagnation strikes and revolts, who are intellectually shocked therewith as with a fact which ought not to exist, and are possessed with an unconquerable desire of changing it, a desire of giving some rule, somewhat of the general, regular, and permanent to the world before them. A terrible and often tyrannical power, which commits a thousand crimes, a thousand errors, for human weakness attends it; a power, nevertheless, glorious and salutary, for it gives to humanity, and with the hand of man, a vigorous impulse forward, a mighty movement.

These different causes and forces led, between the fifth and ninth century, to various attempts at extricating European society from barbarism.

The first attempt, which, although but slightly effective, must not be overlooked, since it emanated from the barbarians themselves, was the drawing up of the barbaric laws: between the sixth and eighth centuries the laws of almost all the barbarous people were written. Before this they had not been written; the barbarians had been governed simply by customs, until they established themselves upon the ruins of the Roman empire. We may reckon the laws of the Burgundians, of the Salian and Ripuarian Franks, of the Visigoths, of the Lombards, the Saxons, the Frisons, the Bavarians, the Alemanni, &c. Here was manifestly a beginning of civilization; an endeavour to bring society under general and regular principles. The success of this attempt could not be great: it was writing the laws of a society which no longer existed, the laws of the social state of the barbarians before their establishment upon the Roman territory, before they had exchanged the wandering for the sedentary life, the condition of nomade warriors for that of proprietors. We find, indeed, here and there, some articles concerning the lands which the barbarians had conquered, and concerning their relations with the ancient inhabitants of the country; but the foundation of the greater part of their laws is the ancient mode of life, the ancient German condition; they were inapplicable to the new society, and occupied only a trifling place in its development.

At the same time, another kind of attempt was made in Italy and the South of Gaul. Roman society had not so completely perished there as elsewhere; a little more order and life remained in the cities. There civilization attempted to lift again its head. If, for example, we look to the kingdom of the Ostrogoths in Italy under Theodoric, we see even under the dominion of a barbarous king and nation the municipal system, taking breath, so to speak, and influencing the general course of events. Roman society had acted upon the Goths, and had to a certain degree impressed them with its likeness. The same fact is visible in the south of Gaul.

It was at the commencement of the sixth century that a Visigoth king of Toulouse, Alaric, caused the Roman laws to be collected, and published a code for his Roman subjects under the name of the *Breviarium Aniani.*

In Spain it was another power—namely that of the church, which tried to revive civilization. In place of the ancient German assemblies, the assemblies of warriors, it was the council of Toledo which prevailed in Spain; and although distinguished laymen attended this council, the bishops had dominion there. Look at the law of the Visigoths; you will see that it is not a barbarous law; it was evidently compiled by the philosophers of the time, the clergy. It abounds in general ideas, in theories, theories wholly foreign to barbarous manners. Thus: you know that the legislation of the barbarians was a personal legislation—that is to say, that the same law applied only to men of the same race. The Roman law governed the Romans, the Frank law governed the Franks; each people had its law, although they were united under the same government and inhabited the same territory. This is what is called the system of personal legislation, in opposition to that of real legislation fixed upon the territory. Well, the legislation of the Visigoths was not personal, but fixed upon the territory. All the inhabitants of Spain, Visigoths and Romans, were subject to the same law. Continue your investigation, and you will find yet more evident traces of philosophy. Among the barbarians, men had, according to their relative situations, a determinate value; the barbarian, the Roman, the freeman, the vassal, &c., were not held at the same price, there was a tariff of their lives. The principle of the equal value of men in the eye of the law was established in the law of the Visigoths. Look to the system of procedure, and you find, in place of the oath of *compurgatores,* or the judicial combat, the proof by witnesses, and a rational investigation of the matter in question, such as might be prosecuted in a civilized society. In short, the whole Visigoth law bears a wise, systematic, and social character. We may perceive herein the work of the same clergy who prevailed in the councils of Toledo, and so powerfully influenced the government of the country.

In Spain, then, up to the great invasion of the Arabs, it

was the theocratic principle which attempted the revival of civilization.

In France the same endeavour was the work of a different power; it came from the great men, above all from Charlemagne. Examine his reign under its various aspects; you will see that his predominating idea was the design of civilizing his people. First, let us consider his wars. He was constantly in the field, from the south to the north-east, from the Ebro to the Elbe or the Weser. Can you believe that these were mere wilful expeditions, arising simply from the desire of conquest? By no means. I do not mean to say that all that he did is to be fully explained, or that there existed much diplomacy or strategetic skill in his plans; but he obeyed a great necessity—a strong desire of suppressing barbarism. He was engaged during the whole of his reign in arresting the double invasion—the Mussulman invasion on the south, and the German and Sclavonic invasion on the north. This is the military character of the reign of Charlemagne; his expedition against the Saxons had no other origin and no other purpose.

If you turn from his wars to his internal government, you will there meet with a fact of the same nature—the attempt to introduce order and unity into the administration of all the countries which he possessed. I do not wish to employ the word *kingdom* nor the word *state;* for these expressions convey too regular a notion, and suggest ideas which are little in harmony with the society over which Charlemagne presided. But this is certain, that being master of an immense territory, he felt indignant at seeing all things incoherent, anarchical, and rude, and desired to alter their hideous condition. First of all he wrought by means of his *missi dominici,* whom he dispatched into the various parts of his territory, in order that they might observe circumstances and reform them, or give an account of them to him. He afterwards worked by means of general assemblies, which he held with much more regularity than his predecessors had done. At these assemblies he caused all the most considerable persons of the territory to be present. They were not free assemblies, nor did they at all resemble the kind of deliberations with which we are acquainted; they were merely a means taken by Charlemagne of being well informed of facts, and of introducing some order and unity among his disorderly populations.

Under whatever point of view you consider the reign of Charlemagne, you will always find in it the same character, namely, warfare against the barbarous state, the spirit of civilization; this is what appears in his eagerness to establish schools, in his taste for learned men, in the favour with which he regarded ecclesiastical influence, and in all that he thought proper to do, whether as regarded the entire society or individual man.

An attempt of the same kind was made somewhat later in England by king Alfred.

Thus the different causes to which I have directed attention, as tending to put an end to barbarism, were in action in some part or other of Europe from the fifth to the ninth century.

None succeeded. Charlemagne was unable to found his great empire, and the system of government which he desired to establish therein. In Spain, the church succeeded no better in establishing the theocratic principle. In Italy and in the south of Gaul, although Roman civilization often attempted to rise again, it was not till afterwards, towards the end of the tenth century, that it really re-acquired any vigour. Up to that time all efforts to terminate barbarism proved abortive; they supposed that men were more advanced than they truly were; they all desired, under various forms, a society more extended or more regular than was compatible with the distribution of power and the condition of men's minds. Nevertheless, they had not been wholly useless. At the beginning of the tenth century, neither the great empire of Charlemagne nor the glorious councils of Toledo were any longer spoken of; but barbarism had not the less arrived at its extreme term— two great results had been obtained.

I. The movement of the invasions on the north and south had been arrested: after the dismemberment of the empire of Charlemagne, the states established on the right bank of the Rhine opposed a powerful barrier to the tribes who continued to urge their way westward. The Normans prove this incontestably: up to this period, if we except the tribes which cast themselves upon England, the movement of maritime invasions had not been very considerable. It was during the ninth century that it became constant and general. And this was because invasions by land were become very difficult, society having, on this side, acquired more fixed and certain frontiers. That portion of the wandering population which could not be driven back, was constrained to turn aside and carry on its roving life upon the sea. Whatever evils were done in the west by Norman expeditions, they were far less fatal than invasions by land; they disturbed dawning society far less generally.

In the south, the same fact declared itself. The Arabs were quartered in Spain; warfare continued between them and the Christians, but it no longer entailed the displacement of the population. Saracenic bands still, from time to time, infested the coasts of the Mediterranean; but the grand progress of Islamism had evidently ceased.

II. At this period we see the wandering life ceasing, in its turn, throughout the interior of Europe; populations established themselves; property became fixed; and the relations of men no longer varied from day to day, at the will of violence or chance. The internal and moral condition of man himself began to change; his ideas and sentiments, like his life, acquired fixedness; he attached himself to the places which he inhabited, to the relations which he had contracted there, to those domains which he began to promise himself that he would bequeath to his children, to that dwelling which one day he will call his castle, to that miserable collection of colonists and slaves which will one day become a village. Everywhere little societies, little states, cut, so to speak, to the measure of the ideas and the wisdom of man, formed themselves. Between these societies was gradually introduced the bond, of which the customs of barbarism contained the germ, the bond of a confederation which did not annihilate individual independence. On the one hand, every considerable person established himself in his domains, alone with his family and servitors; on the other hand, a certain hierarchy of services and rights became established between these warlike proprietors scattered over the land. What was this? The feudal system rising definitively from the bosom of barbarism. Of the various elements of our civilization, it was natural that the Germanic element should first prevail; it had strength on its side, it had con-

quered Europe; from it Europe was to receive its earliest
social form and organization. This is what happened. Feudalism, its character, and the part played by it in the history
of European civilization, will be the subject-matter of my
next lecture; and, in the bosom of that victorious feudal
system, we shall meet, at every step, with the other elements of
our civilization—royalty, the church, municipal corporations;
and we shall foresee without difficulty that they are not
destined to sink beneath this feudal form, to which they
become assimilated, while struggling against it, and while
waiting the hour when victory shall visit them in their turn.

FOURTH LECTURE.

Object of the lecture—Necessary alliance between facts and doctrines—Preponderance of the country over the towns—Organization of a small feudal society—Influence of feudalism upon the character of the possessor of the fief, and upon the spirit of family—Hatred of the people towards the feudal system—The priest could do little for the serfs—Impossibility of regularly organizing feudalism: 1. No powerful authority; 2. No public power; 3. Difficulty of the federative system—The idea of the right of resistance inherent in feudalism—Influence of feudalism favourable to the development of the individual, unfavourable to social order.

WE have studied the condition of Europe after the fall of the Roman empire, in the first period of modern history, the barbarous. We have seen that, at the end of this epoch, and at the commencement of the tenth century, the first principle, the first system that developed itself and took possession of European society, was the feudal system; we have seen that feudalism was the first-born of barbarism. It is, then, the feudal system which must now be the object of our study.

I scarcely think it necessary to remind you that it is not the history of events, properly speaking, which we are considering. It is not my business to recount to you the destinies of feudalism. That which occupies us is the history of civilization; this is the general and hidden fact which we seek under all the external facts which envelop it.

Thus events, social crises, the various states through which society has passed, interest us only in their relations to the development of civilization; we inquire of them solely in what respects they have opposed or assisted it, what they have given to it, and what they have refused it. It is only under this point of view that we are to consider the feudal system.

In the commencement of these lectures we defined the nature of civilization; we attempted to investigate its elements; we saw that it consisted, on the one hand, in the development of man himself, of the individual, of humanity; on the other hand, in that of his external condition, in the development of society. Whenever we find ourselves in the presence of an event, of a system, or of a general condition of the world, we have this double question to ask of it, what has it done for or against the development of man, for or against the development of society?

You understand beforehand, that, during our investigations, it is impossible that we should not meet upon our way most important questions of moral philosophy. When we desire to know in what an event or a system has contributed to the development of man and of society, it is absolutely needful that we should be acquainted with the nature of the true development of society and of man; that we should know what developments are false and illegitimate, perverting instead of ameliorating, causing a retrogressive instead of a progressive movement.

We shall not seek to escape from this necessity. Not only should we thereby mutilate and lower our ideas and the facts, but the actual state of the world imposes upon us the necessity of freely accepting this inevitable alliance of philosophy and history. This is precisely one of the characteristics, perhaps the essential characteristic of our epoch. We are called upon to consider, to cause to progress together, science and reality, theory and practice, right and fact. Up to our times, these two powers have existed separately; the world has been accustomed to behold science and practice following different roads, without recognising each other, or, at least, without meeting. And when doctrines and general ideas have desired to amalgamate with events and influence the world, they have only succeeded under the form and by means of the arm of fanaticism. The empire of human societies, and the direction of their affairs, have hitherto been shared between two kinds of influences: upon one hand, the believers, the men of general ideas and principles, the fanatics; on the other, men strangers to all rational principles, who govern themselves merely according to circumstances, practicians, freethinkers, as the seventeenth century called them. This condition of things is now ceasing; neither fanatics nor free-thinkers will any longer have dominion. In order now to govern and prevail with men, it is necessary to be acquainted with general ideas and circumstances; it is necessary to know how to value principles and facts, to respect virtue and necessity, to preserve oneself from the pride of fanatics, and the not less blind scorn of free-thinkers. To this point have we been conducted by the development of the human mind and the social state: upon one hand, the human mind, exalted and freed, better comprehends the connexion of things, knows how to look around on all sides, and makes use of all things in its combinations; on the other hand, society has perfected itself to that degree, that it can be compared with the truth; that facts can be brought into juxta-position with principles, and yet, in spite of their still great imperfections, not inspire by the comparison invincible discouragement or distaste. I shall thus obey the natural tendency, convenience, and the necessity of our times, in constantly passing from the examination of circumstances to that of ideas, from an exposition of facts to a question of doctrines. Perhaps, even, there is in the actual disposition of men's minds, another reason in favour of this method. For some time past a confirmed taste, I might say a sort of predilection, has manifested itself among us, for facts, for practical views, for the positive aspect of human affairs. We have been to such an extent a prey to the despotism of general ideas, of theories; they have, in some respects, cost us so dear, that they are become the objects of a certain degree of distrust. We like better to carry ourselves back to facts, to special circumstances, to applications. This is not to be regretted; it is a new progress, a great step in knowledge, and towards the empire of truth ; provided always that we do not allow ourselves to be prejudiced and carried away by this disposition; that we do not forget that truth alone has a right to reign in the world; that facts have no value except as they tend to explain, and to assimilate themselves more and more to the truth; that all true greatness is of thought; and that all fruitfulness belongs to it. The civilization of our country has this peculiar character, that it has never wanted intellectual greatness; it has always been rich in ideas; the power of the human mind has always been great in French

F

society; greater, perhaps, than in any other. We must not lose this high privilege; we must not fall into the somewhat subordinate and material state which characterizes other societies. Intelligence and doctrines must occupy in the France of the present day, at least the place which they have occupied there hitherto.

We shall, then, by no means avoid general and philosophical questions; we shall not wander in search of them, but where facts lead us to them, we shall meet them without hesitation or embarrassment. An occasion of doing so will more than once present itself, during the consideration of the feudal system in its relations to the history of European civilization.

A good proof that, in the tenth century, the feudal system was necessary, was the only possible social state, is the universality of its establishment. Wherever barbarism ceased, everything took the feudal form. At the first moment, men saw in it only the triumph of chaos; all unity, all general civilization vanished; on all sides they beheld society dismembering itself; and, in its stead, they beheld a number of minor, obscure, isolated, and incoherent societies erect themselves. To contemporaries, this appeared the dissolution of all things, universal anarchy. Consult the poets and the chroniclers of the time; they all believed themselves at the end of the world. It was, nevertheless, the beginning of a new and real society, the feudal, so necessary, so inevitable, so truly the only possible consequence of the anterior state, that all things entered into it and assumed its form. Elements, the most foreign to this system, the church, municipalities, royalty, were compelled to accommodate themselves to it; the churches became suzerains and vassals, cities had lords and vassals, royalty disguised itself under the form of suzerainship. All things were given in fief, not only lands, but certain rights, the right, for instance, of felling in forests, and of fishing. the churches gave in fief their perquisites, from their revenues from baptisms, the churchings of women. Water and money were given in fief. Just as all the general elements of society entered into the feudal frame, so the smallest details, and the most trifling facts of common life, became a part of feudalism.

In beholding the feudal form thus taking possession of all things, we are tempted to believe, at first, that the essential and vital principle of feudalism everywhere prevailed. But this is a mistake. In borrowing the feudal form, the elements and institutions of society which were not analogous to the feudal system, did not renounce their own nature or peculiar principles. The feudal church did not cease to be animated and governed, at bottom, by the theocratic principle; and it laboured unceasingly, sometimes in concert with the royal power, sometimes with the pope, and sometimes with the people, to destroy this system, of which, so to speak, it wore the livery. It was the same with royalty and with the corporations; in the one the monarchical, in the other the democratical principle, continued, at bottom, to predominate. Notwithstanding their feudal livery, these various elements of European society constantly laboured to deliver themselves from a form which was foreign to their true nature, and to assume that which corresponded to their peculiar and vital principle.

Having shown the universality of the feudal form, it becomes very necessary to be on our guard against concluding from this the universality of the feudal principle, and against studying feudalism indifferently, whenever we meet with its physiognomy. In order to know and comprehend this system thoroughly, to unravel and judge of its effects in reference to modern civilization, we must examine it where the form and principle are in harmony; we must study it in the hierarchy of lay possessors of fiefs, in the association of the conquerors of the European territory. There truly resided feudal society; thereupon we are now to enter.

I spoke just now of the importance of moral questions, and of the necessity of not avoiding them. But there is a totally opposite kind of considerations, which has generally been too much neglected; I mean the material condition of society, the material changes introduced into mankind's method of existing, by a new fact, by a revolution, by a new social state. We have not always sufficiently considered these things; we have not always sufficiently inquired into the modifications introduced by these great crises of the world, into the material existence of men, into the material aspect of their relations. These modifications have more influence upon the entire society than is supposed. Who does not know how much the influence of climates has been studied. and how much im-

portance was attached to it by Montesquieu. If we regard
the immediate influence of climate upon men, perhaps it is
not so extensive as has been supposed; it is, at all events,
very vague and difficult to be appreciated. But the indirect
influence of climate, that which, for example, results from
the fact, that, in a warm country, men live in the open air,
while, in a cold country, they shut themselves up in their
houses, that, in one case, they nourish themselves in one
manner, in the other, in another, these are facts of great importance, facts which by the simple difference of material
life, act powerfully upon civilization. All great revolutions
lead to modifications of this sort in the social state, and these
are very necessary to be considered.

The establishment of the feudal system produced one of
these modifications, of unmistakeable importance; it altered
the distribution of the population over the face of the
land. Hitherto the masters of the soil, the sovereign population, had lived united in more or less numerous masses
of men, whether sedentarily in cities, or wandering in bands
through the country. In consequence of the feudal system, these same men lived isolated, each in his own habitation, and at great distances from one another. You will
immediately perceive how much influence this change was
calculated to exercise upon the character and course of civilization. The social preponderance, the government of society,
passed suddenly from the towns to the country; private property became of more importance than public property;
private life than public life. Such was the first and purely
material effect of the triumph of feudal society. The further
we examine into it, the more will the consequence of this
single fact be unfolded to our eyes.

Let us investigate this society in itself, and see what
part it has played in the history of civilization. First of all,
let us take feudalism in its most simple, primitive, and fundamental element; let us consider a single possessor of a fief in
his domain, and let us see what will become of all those who
form the little society around him.

He establishes himself upon an isolated and elevated spot,
which he takes care to render safe and strong: there he
constructs what he will call his castle. With whom does he
establish himself? With his wife and children; perhaps some

freemen, who have not become proprietors, attach themselves to his person, and continue to live with him, at his table. These are the inhabitants of the interior of the castle. Around and at its foot, a little population of colonists and serfs gather together, who cultivate the domains of the possessor of the fief. In the centre of this lower population religion plants a church; it brings hither a priest. In the early period of the feudal system, this priest was commonly at the same time the chaplain of the castle and the pastor of the village; by and bye these two characters separated; the village had its own pastor, who lived there, beside his church. This, then, was the elementary feudal society, the feudal molecule, so to speak. It is this element that we have first of all to examine. We will demand of it the double question which should be asked of all our facts: What has resulted from it in favour of the development, 1. of man himself, 2. of society?

We are perfectly justified in addressing this double question to the little society which I have just described, and in placing faith in its replies; for it was the type and faithful image of the entire feudal society. The lord, the people on his domains, and the priest; such is feudalism upon the great as well as the small scale, when we have taken from it royalty and the towns, which are distinct and foreign elements.

The first fact that strikes us in contemplating this little society, is the prodigious importance which the possessor of the fief must have had, both in his own eyes, and in the eyes of those who surrounded him. The sentiment of personality, of individual liberty, predominated in the barbaric life. But here it was wholly different; it was no longer only the liberty of the man, of the warrior; it was the importance of the pro-prietor, of the head of the family, of the master, that came to be considered. From this situation an impression of immense superiority must have resulted; a superiority quite peculiar, and very different from everything that we meet with in the career of other civilizations. I will give the proof of this. I take in the ancient world some great aristocratical position, a Roman patrician, for instance: like the feudal lord, the Roman patrician was head of a family, master, superior. He was, moreover, the religious magistrate, the pontiff in the interior of his family. Now, his importance as a religious magistrate came to him from without; it was not a purely

personal and individual importance; he received it from on
high; he was the delegate of the Divinity; the interpreter of
the religious creed.   The Roman patrician was, besides,
the member of a corporation which lived united on the
same spot, a member of the senate; this again was an
importance which came to him from without, from his
corporation, a received, a borrowed importance.   The
greatness of the ancient aristocrats, associated as it was
with a religious and political character, belonged to the
situation, to the corporation in general, rather than to the
individual.   That of the possessor of the fief was purely
individual; it was not derived from any one; all his rights,
all his power, came to him from himself.   He was not a
religious magistrate; he took no part in a senate; it was in
his person that all his importance resided; all that he was, he
was of himself, and in his own name.   What a mighty influence must such a situation have exerted on its occupant!
What individual haughtiness, what prodigious pride—let us
say the word—what insolence, must have arisen in his soul!
Above himself there was no superior of whom he was the
representative or interpreter; there was no equal near him;
no powerful and general law which weighed upon him; no
external rule which influenced his will; he knew no curb
but the limits of his strength and the presence of danger.
Such was the necessary moral result of this situation upon
the character of man.

I now proceed to a second consequence, mighty also, and
too little noticed, namely, the particular turn taken by the
feudal family spirit.

Let us cast a glance over the various family systems. Take
first of all the patriarchal system of which the Bible and oriental
records offer the model.   The family was very numerous; it
was a tribe. The chief, the patriarch, lived therein in common
with his children, his near relations, the various generations
which united themselves around him, all his kindred, all his
servants; and not only did he live with them all, but he had
the same interests, the same occupations, and he led the same
life.   Was not this the condition of Abraham, of the patriarchs, and of the chiefs of the Arab tribes, who still reproduce
the image of the patriarchal life?

Another family system presents itself, namely, the *clan*, a petty society, whose type we must seek for in Scotland or Ireland. Through this system, very probably, a large portion of the European family has passed. This is no longer the patriarchal family. There is here a great difference between the situation of the chief and that of the rest of the population. They did not lead the same life: the greater portion tilled and served; the chief was idle and warlike. But they had a common origin; they all bore the same name; and their relations of kindred, ancient traditions, the same recollections, the same affections, established a moral tie, a sort of equality between all the members of the clan.

These are the two principal types of the family society presented by history. But have we here the feudal family? Obviously not. It seems, at first, that the feudal family bears some relation to the clan; but the difference is much greater than the resemblance. The population which surrounded the possessor of the fief were totally unconnected with him; they did not bear his name; between them and him there was no kindred, no bond, moral or historical. Neither did it resemble the patriarchal family. The possessor of the fief led not the same life, nor did he engage in the same occupations with those who surrounded him; he was an idler and a warrior, whilst the others were labourers. The feudal family was not numerous; it was not a tribe; it reduced itself to the family, properly so called, namely, to the wife and children; it lived separated from the rest of the population, shut up in the castle. The colonists and serfs made no part of it; the origin of the members of this society was different, the inequality of their situation immense. Five or six individuals, in a situation at once superior to and estranged from the rest of the society, that was the feudal family. It was of course invested with a peculiar character. It was narrow, concentrated, and constantly called upon to defend itself against, to distrust, and, at least, to isolate itself from, even its retainers. The interior life, domestic manners, were sure to become predominant in such a system. I am aware that the brutality of the passions of a chief, his habit of spending his time in warfare or the chase, were a great obstacle to the development of domestic manners. But this would be conquered; the chief necessarily returned home habitually; he always found there his wife and children, and

these well nigh only; these would alone constitute his permanent
society—they would alone share his interests, his destiny.
Domestic life necessarily, therefore, acquired great sway.
Proofs of this abound.   Was it not within the bosom of the
feudal family that the importance of women developed itself?
In all the ancient societies, I do not speak of those where
the family spirit did not exist, but of those wherein it was
very powerful in the patriarchal life, for instance, women
did not hold at all so considerable a place as they acquired
in Europe under the feudal system.   It was to the development and necessary preponderance of domestic manners in
feudalism, that they chiefly owed this change, this progress in
their condition.   Some have desired to trace the cause to the
peculiar manners of the ancient Germans; to a national respect which, it is said, they bore towards women amidst their
forests.   Upon a sentence of Tacitus, German patriotism has
built I know not what superiority, what primitive and un-
eradicable purity of German manners, as regards the relations of the two sexes. Mere fancies! Phrases similar to that
of Tacitus, concerning sentiments and usages analogous to
those of the ancient Germans, are to be found in the recitals
of a crowd of observers of savage or barbarous people. There
is nothing primitive therein, nothing peculiar to any particular race.   It was in the effects of a strongly marked social
position, in the progress and preponderance of domestic manners, that the importance of women in Europe originated;
and the preponderance of domestic manners became, very
early, an essential characteristic of the feudal system.

A second fact, another proof of the empire of domestic life,
equally characterises the feudal family: I mean the hereditary
spirit, the spirit of perpetuation, which evidently predominated therein.   The hereditary spirit is inherent in the family
spirit; but nowhere has it so strongly developed itself as
under the feudal system. This resulted from the nature of the
property with which the family was incorporated.   The fief
was   unlike   other   properties: it   constantly   demanded   a
possessor to defend it, serve it, acquit himself of the
obligations inherent in the domain, and thus maintain it in
its rank amidst the general association of the masters of the
soil.   Thence resulted a sort of identification between the
actual possessor of the fief and the fief itself, and all the series
of its future possessors.

This circumstance greatly contributed to fortify and make closer the family ties, already so powerful by the very nature of the feudal family.

I now issue from the seignorial dwelling, and descend amidst the petty population that surrounds it. Here all things wear a different aspect. The nature of man is so good and fruitful, that when a social situation endures for any length of time, a certain moral tie, sentiments of protection, benevolence, and affection, inevitably establish themselves among those who are thus approximated to one another, whatever may be the conditions of approximation. It happened thus with feudalism. No doubt, after a certain time, some moral relations, some habits of affection, became contracted between the colonists and the possessor of the fief. But this happened in spite of their relative position, and not by reason of its influence. Considered in itself, the position was radically wrong. There was nothing morally in common between the possessor of the fief and the colonists; they constituted part of his domain; they were his property; and under this name, property, were included all the rights which, in the present day, are called rights of public sovereignty, as well as the rights of private property, the right of imposing laws, of taxing, and punishing, as well as that of disposing of and selling. As far as it is possible that such should be the case where men are in presence of men, between the lord and the cultivators of his lands there existed no rights, no guarantees, no society.

Hence, I conceive, the truly prodigious and invincible hatred with which the people at all times have regarded the feudal system, its recollections, its very name. It is not a case without example for men to have submitted to oppressive despotisms, and to have become accustomed to them; nay, to have willingly accepted them. Theocratic and monarchical despotisms have more than once obtained the consent, almost the affections, of the population subjected to them. But feudal despotism has always been repulsive and odious; it has oppressed the destinies, but never reigned over the souls of men. The reason is, that in theocracy and monarchy, power is exercised in virtue of certain words which are common to the master and to the subject; it is the representative, the minister of another power superior to all human

power; it speaks and acts in the name of the Divinity or of
a general idea, and not in the name of man himself, of man
alone. Feudal despotism was altogether different; it was the
power of the individual over the individual; the dominion of
the personal and capricious will of a man. This is, perhaps,
the only tyranny of which, to his eternal honour, man will
never willingly accept. Whenever, in his master, he beholds
a mere man, from the moment that the will which oppresses
him appears a merely human and individual will, like his
own, he becomes indignant, and supports the yoke wrathfully.
Such was the true and distinguishing character of feudal
power; and such was also the origin of the antipathy which
it has ever inspired.

The religious element which was associated with it was
little calculated to ease the burden. I do not conceive that
the influence of the priest, in the little society which I have
just described, was very great, nor that he succeeded much
in legitimating the relations of the inferior population with
the lord. The church has exerted a very great influence
upon European civilization, but this it has done by proceedings of a general character, by changing, for instance, the
general dispositions of men. When we enter closely
into the petty feudal society, properly so called, we find that
the influence of the priest, between the colonists and the
lord, scarcely amounted to anything. Most frequently he
was himself rude and subordinate as a serf, and very
little in condition or disposition to combat the arrogance of
the lord. No doubt, called, as he was, to sustain and develop
somewhat of moral life in the inferior population, he was dear
and useful to it on this account; he spread through it somewhat
of consolation and of life; but, I conceive, he could and did
very little to alleviate its destiny.

I have examined the elementary feudal society; I have placed
before you the principal consequences which necessarily flowed
from it, whether to the possessor of the fief himself, or his
family, or the population congregated around him. Let us now
go forth from this narrow inclosure. The population of the fief
was not alone upon the land; there were other societies,
analogous or different, with which it bore relation. What
influence did the general society to which that population
belonged, necessarily exercise upon civilization?

I will make a brief remark, before answering this question: It is true that the possessor of the fief and the priest belonged, one and the other, to a general society; they had, at a distance, numerous and frequent relations. It was not the same with the colonists, the serfs: every time that, in order to designate the population of the country at this period, we make use of a general word, which seems to imply one and the same society, the word *people*, for example, we do not convey the truth. There was for this population no general society; its existence was purely local. Beyond the territory which they inhabited, the colonists had no connexion with any thing or person. For them there was no common destiny, no common country; they did not form a people. When we speak of the feudal association as a whole, it is only the possessors of the fiefs that are concerned.

Let us see what were the relations of the petty feudal society with the general society with which it was connected, and to what consequences these relations necessarily led as regards the development of civilization.

You are acquainted with the nature of the ties which united the possessors of the fiefs among themselves, with the obligations of service, on the one hand, of protection on the other. I shall not enter into a detail of these obligations; it suffices that you have a general idea of their character. From these obligations there necessarily arose within the mind of each possessor of a fief, a certain number of moral ideas and sentiments, ideas of duty, sentiments of affection. The fact is evident that the principle of fidelity, of devotion, of loyalty to engagements, and all sentiments connected therewith, were developed and sustained by the relations of the possessors of the fiefs between themselves.

These obligations, duties, and sentiments, endeavoured to convert themselves into rights and institutions. Every one knows that feudalism desired legally to determine what were the services due from the possessor of the fief towards his suzerain; what were the services which he might expect in return; in what cases the vassal owed pecuniary or military aid to his suzerain; in what forms the suzerain ought to obtain the consent of his vassals, for services to which they were not compelled by the simple tenure of their fiefs. Attempts were made to place all their rights under the guarantee of institutions, which aimed at insuring their being respected. Thus, the seignorial jurisdictions were destined to render justice between the possessors of the fiefs, upon claims carried before their common suzerain. Thus, also, each lord who was of any consideration assembled his vassals in a parliament, in order to treat with them concerning matters which required their consent or their concurrence. In short, there existed a collection of political, judicial, and military means, with which attempts were made to organise the feudal system, converting the relations between the possessors of fiefs into rights and institutions.

But these rights and these institutions had no reality, no guarantee.

If one is asked, what is meant by a guarantee, a political guarantee, one is led to perceive that its fundamental character is the constant presence, in the midst of the society, of a will, of a power disposed and in a condition to impose a law upon particular wills and powers, to make them observe the common rule, and respect the general right.

There are only two systems of political guarantees possible: it is either necessary there should be a particular will and power so superior to all others, that none should be able to resist it, and that all should be compelled to submit to it as soon as it interferes; or else that there should be a public will and power, which is the result of agreement, of the development of particular wills, and which, once gone forth from them, is in a condition to impose itself upon, and to make itself respected equally by all.

Such are the two possible systems of political guarantees : the despotism of one or of a body, or free government. When we pass systems in review, we find that all of them come under one or other of these heads.

Well, neither one nor the other existed, nor could exist under the feudal system.

No doubt the possessors of the fiefs were not all equal among themselves ; there were many of superior power, many powerful enough to oppress the weaker. But there was no one, beginning from the first of .the suzerains, the king, who was in condition to impose law upon all the others, and make himself obeyed. Observe that all the permanent means of power and action were wanting: there were no permanent troops, no permanent taxes, no permanent tribunals. The social powers and institutions had, after a manner, to recommence and create themselves anew every time they were required. A tribunal was obliged to be constructed for every process, an army whenever there was a war to be made, a revenue whenever money was wanted; everything was occasional, accidental, and special; there was no means of central, permanent, and independent government. It is plain that, in such a system, no individual was in a condition to impose his will upon others, or to cause the general rights to be respected by all.

On the other hand, resistance was as easy as repression was difficult. Shut up in his castle, having to do only with a small number of enemies, easily finding, among vassals of his own condition, the means of coalition, and of assistance, the possessor of the fief defended himself with the greatest facility.

Thus, then, we see that the first system of guarantees, the system which places them in the intervention of the strongest, was not possible under feudalism.

The other system, that of a free government, a public power, was equally impracticable; it could never have arisen in the bosom of feudalism. The reason is sufficiently simple. When we speak, in the present day, of a public power, of that which we call the rights of sovereignty, the right of giving laws, taxing, and punishing, we all think that those rights belong to no one, that no one has, on his own account, a right to punish others, and to impose upon them a charge, a law. Those are rights which belong only to society in the mass, rights which are exercised in its name, which it holds not of itself, but receives from the Highest. Thus, when an individual comes before the powers invested with these rights, the sentiment which, perhaps without his consciousness, reigns in him is, that he is in the presence of a public and legitimate power, which possesses a mission for commanding him, and he is submissive beforehand and internally. But it was wholly otherwise under feudalism. The possessor of the fief, in his domain, was invested with all the rights of sovereignty over those who inhabited it; they were inherent to the domain, and a part of his private property. What are at present public rights were then private rights; what is now public power was then private power. When the possessor of a fief, after having exercised sovereignty in his own name, as a proprietor over all tn. population amidst which he lived, presented himself at an assembly, a parliament held before his suzerain, a parliament not very numerous, and composed in general of men who were his equals, or nearly so, he did not bring with him, nor did he carry away the idea of a public power. This idea was in contradiction to all his existence, to all that he had been in the habit of doing in the interior of his own domains. He saw there only men who were invested with the same rights as himself, who were in the same situation, and, like him, acted in the name of their personal will. Nothing in the most elevated department of the government, in what we call public institutions, conveyed to him, or forced him to recognise this character of superiority and generality, which is inherent to the idea that we form to ourselves of public powers. And if he was dissatisfied with the decision, he refused to agree with it, or appealed to force for resistance.

Under the feudal system, force was the true and habitual guarantee of right, if, indeed, we may call force a guarantee. All rights had perpetual recourse to force to make themselves recognised or obeyed. No institution succeeded in doing this; and this was so generally felt that institutions were rarely appealed to. If the seignorial courts and parliaments of vassals had been capable of influence, we should have met with them in history more frequently than we do, and found them exerting more activity; their rarity proves their invalidity.

At this we must not be astonished; there is a reason for it more decisive and deeply seated than those which I have described.

Of all systems of government and political guarantee, the federative system is certainly the most difficult to establish and to render prevalent; a system which consists in leaving in each locality and each particular society all that portion of the government which can remain there, and in taking from it only that portion which is indispensable to the maintenance of the general society, and carrying this to the centre of that society, there to constitute of it a central government. The federative system, logically the most simple, is, in fact, the most complex. In order to reconcile the degree of local independence and liberty which it allows to remain, with the degree of general order and submission which it demands and supposes in certain cases, a very advanced degree of civilization is evidently requisite; it is necessary that the will of man, that individual liberty should concur in the establishment and maintenance of this system, much more than in that of any other, for its means of coercion are far less than those of any other.

The federative system, then, is that which evidently requires the greatest development of reason, morality, and civilization, in the society to which it is applied. Well, this, nevertheless, was the system which feudalism endeavoured to establish; the idea of general feudalism, in fact, was that of a federation. It reposed upon the same principles on which are founded, in our day, the federation of the United States of America, for example. It aimed at leaving in the hands of each lord all that portion of government and sovereignty which could remain there, and to carry to the suzerain, or to the general assembly of barons, only the least possible portion of power, and that only in cases of absolute necessity. You perceive the impossibility of establishing such a system amidst ignorance, amidst brutal passions—in short, in a moral state so imperfect as that of man under feudalism. The very nature of government was contradictory to the ideas and manners of the very men to whom it was attempted to be applied. Who can be astonished at the ill success of these endeavours at organization?

We have considered feudal society, first, in its most simple and fundamental element, then in its entirety. We have examined, under these two points of view, that which it necessarily did, that which naturally flowed from it, as to its influence upon the course of civilization. I conceive that we have arrived at this double result:

First, federalism has exerted a great, and, on the whole, a salutary influence upon the internal development of the individual; it has awakened in men's minds ideas, energetic sentiments, moral requirements, fine developments of character and passion.

Secondly, under the social point of view, it was unable to establish either legal order or political guarantees; it was indispensable to the revival in Europe of society, which had been so entirely dissolved by barbarism, that it was incapable of a more regular and more extended form; but the feudal form, radically bad in itself, could neither regulate nor extend itself. The only political right which the feudal system caused to assert itself in European society was the right of resistance,—I do not say legal resistance, that could not have place in a society so little advanced. The progress of society consists precisely in substituting, on the one hand, public powers for particular wills; on the other, legal, for individual resistance. In this consists the grand aim, the principal perfection of the social order; much latitude is left to personal liberty; then, when that liberty fails, when it becomes necessary to demand from it an account of itself, appeal is made to public reason alone, to determine the process instituted against the liberty of the individual. Such is the system of legal order and of legal resistance. You perceive, without difficulty, that under feudalism there existed nothing of this sort. The right of resistance which the feudal system maintained and practised was the right of personal resistance—a terrible, unsocial right, since it appeals to force and to war, which is the destruction of society itself; a right which, nevertheless, should never be abolished from the heart of man, for its abolition is the acceptation of servitude. The sentiment of the right of resistance had perished in the disgrace of Roman society, and could not rise anew from its wreck; it could not come more naturally, in my opinion, from the principle of the Christian society. To feudalism we are indebted for its re-introduction into the manners of Europe. It is the boast of civilization to render it always useless and inactive; it is the boast of the feudal system to have constantly professed and defended it.

Such, if I do not deceive myself, is the result of an examination of feudal society, considered in itself, in its general elements, and independently of historical development. If we pass on to facts, to history, we shall see that has happened which might have been looked for; that the feudal system has done what it was fitted to do; that its destiny has been in conformity with its nature. Events may be adduced in proof of all the conjectures and inferences which I have drawn from the very nature of this system.

Cast a glance upon the general history of feudalism between the tenth and thirteenth centuries; it is impossible to mistake the great and salutary influence exerted by it upon the development of sentiments, characters, and ideas. We cannot look into the history of this period without meeting with a crowd of noble sentiments, great actions, fine displays of humanity, born evidently in the bosom of feudal manners. Chivalry, it is true, does not resemble feudalism—nevertheless, it is its daughter: from feudalism issued this ideal of elevated, generous, loyal sentiments. It says much in favour of its parentage.

Turn your eyes to another quarter: the first bursts of European imagination, the first attempts of poetry and of literature, the first intellectual pleasures tasted by Europe on its quitting barbarism, under the shelter, under the wings of feudalism, in the interior of the feudal castles, that all these were born. This kind of development of humanity requires a movement in the soul, in life, leisure, a thousand conditions which are not to be met with in the laborious, melancholy, coarse, hard existence of the common people. In France, in England, in Germany, it is with the feudal times that the first literary recollections, the first intellectual enjoyments of Europe connect themselves.

On the other, if we consult history upon the social influence of feudalism, its answers will always be in harmony with our conjectures; it will reply that the feudal system has been as much opposed to the establishment of general order as to the extension of general liberty. Under whatever point of view you consider the progress of society, you find the feudal system acting as an obstacle. Therefore, from the earliest existence of feudalism, the two forces which have been the grand motive powers of the development of order and liberty—on one hand the monarchical power, the popular power on the other; royalty, and the people—have attacked and struggled against it unceasingly. Some attempts have, at different times, been made to regulate it, and construct out of it a state somewhat legal and general: in England, such attempts were made by William the Conqueror and his sons; in France, by St. Louis; in Germany, by many of the emperors. All attempts, all efforts have failed. The very nature of feudal society was repugnant to order and legality. In modern ages, some men of intellect have attempted to re-establish feudalism as a social system; they have desired to discover therein a legal, regulated, and

G

progressive state; they have made of it an age of gold.
But ask them to assign the age of gold to some particular place
or time, and they can do no such thing : it is an Utopia
without a date, a drama for which we find, in past times,
neither theatre nor actors.   The cause of this error is easy to
discover, and it equally explains the mistake of those who
cannot pronounce the name of feudalism without cursing it.
Neither one party nor the other has taken the pains to consider the double aspect under which feudalism presents itself;
to distinguish, on the one hand, its influence upon the individual development of man, upon sentiments, characters,
and passions, and, on the other, its influence upon the social
state.   The one party has not been able to persuade itself
that a social system, in which so many beautiful sentiments,
so many virtues are found—in which they behold the birth of
all literatures, and in which manners assume a certain elevation and nobility—can have been so bad and fatal as it is pretended.   The other party has only seen the wrong done by
feudalism to the mass of the population, the obstacles opposed
by it to the establishment of order and liberty; and this
party has not been able to believe that fine characters, great
virtues, and any progress, can have resulted from it.   Both
have mistaken the double element of civilization; they have
not understood that it consists of two developments, of which
the one may, in time, produce itself independently of the
other; although, after the course of centuries, and by means
of a long series of circumstances, they must reciprocally call
forth and lead to each other.

    For the rest, that which feudalism was in theory it was in
fact; that to which theory pointed as likely to result from it,
has resulted from it.   Individuality and energy of personal
existence, such was the predominating trait among the conquerors of the Roman world; the development of individuality
necessarily resulted, before all things, from the social system
which was founded by and for themselves.   That which man
himself brings to a social system, at the moment of his
entrance, his internal and moral qualities, powerfully influence
the situation in which he establishes himself.   The situation,
in turn, re-acts upon these qualities, and strengthens and
develops them.   The individual predominated in the German
society; it was for the benefit of the development of the in-

dividual that feudal society, the daughter of German society, exerted its influence.   We shall again find the same fact in the different elements of civilization ; they have remained faithful to their principle; they have advanced and urged on the world in the direction which they first entered.   In our next lecture, the history of the church and of its influence, from the fifth to the twelfth century, upon European civilization, will furnish us with another and a striking illustration of this fact.

FIFTH LECTURE.

Object of the lecture—Religion is a principle of association —Constraint
is not of the essence of government—Conditions of the legitimacy of a
government: 1. The power must be in the hands of the most worthy :
2. The liberty of the governed must be respected—The church being
a corporation, and not a caste, fulfilled the first of these conditions—Of
the various methods of nomination and election that existed therein—It
wanted the other condition, on account of the illegitimate extension of
authority, and on account of the abusive employment of force—Movement and liberty of spirit in the bosom of the church—Relations of the
church with princes—The independence of spiritual power laid down as
a principle—Pretensions and efforts of the church to usurp the tem
poral power.

WE have examined the nature and influence of the feudal
system; it is with the Christian church, from the fifth to the
twelfth century, that we are now to occupy ourselves: I
say, with the *church*; and I have already laid this emphasis,
because it is not with Christianity properly speaking, with
Christianity as a religious system, but with the church as an
ecclesiastical society, with the Christian clergy, that I propose
to engage your attention.

In the fifth century, this society was almost completely
organized; not that it has not since then undergone many
and important changes; but we may say that, at that time,
the church, considered as a corporation, as a government of
Christian people, had attained a complete and independent
existence.

One glance is enough to show us an immense difference
between the state of the church and that of the other elements
of European civilization in the fifth century. I have mentioned, as the fundamental elements of our civilization, the

municipal and feudal systems, royalty, and the church. The municipal system, in the fifth century, was no more than the wreck of the Roman empire, a shadow without life or determinate form. The feudal system had not yet issued from the chaos. Royalty existed only in name. All the civil elements of modern society were either in decay or infancy. The church alone was, at the same time, young and constituted; it alone had acquired a definite form, and preserved all the vigour of early age; it alone possessed, at once, movement and order, energy and regularity, that is to say, the two great means of influence. Is it not, let me ask you, by moral life, by internal movement, on the one hand, and by order and discipline on the other, that institutions take possession of society? The church, moreover, had mooted all the great questions which interest man; it busied itself with all the problems of his nature, and with all the chances of his destiny. Thus its influence upon modern civilization has been very great, greater, perhaps, than even its most ardent adversaries, or its most zealous defenders have supposed. Occupied with rendering it services, or with combating it, they have regarded it only in a polemical point of view, and have therefore, I conceive, been unable either to judge it with equity, or to measure it in all its extent.

The Christian church in the fifth century presents itself as an independent and constituted society, interposed between the masters of the world, the sovereigns, the possessors of the temporal power on the one hand, and the people on the other, serving as a bond between them, and influencing all.

In order completely to know and comprehend its action, we must therefore consider it under three aspects: first of all we must regard it in itself, make an estimate of what it was, of its internal constitution, of the principles which predominated in it, and of its nature; we must then examine it in its relation to the temporal sovereignties, kings, lords, and others; lastly, in its relations to the people. And when from this triple examination we shall have deduced a complete picture of the church, of its principles, its situation, and the influence which it necessarily exercised, we shall verify our assertions by an appeal to history; we shall find out whether the facts and events, properly so called, from the fifth to the twelfth century, are in harmony with the results to which we have been led by the study of the nature of the church, and of its relations, both with the masters of the world and with the people.

First of all, let us occupy ourselves with the church in itself, with its internal condition, and its nature.

The first fact which strikes us, and perhaps the most important, is its very existence, the existence of a religious government, of a clergy, of an ecclesiastical corporation, of a priesthood, of a religion in the sacerdotal state.

With many enlightened men, these very words, a body of priesthood, a religious government, appear to determine the question. They think that a religion which ends in a body of priests, a legally constituted clergy, in short, a governed religion, must be, taking all things together, more injurious than useful. In their opinion, religion is a purely individual relation of man to God; and that whenever the relation loses this character, whenever an external authority comes between the individual and the object of religious creeds, —namely, God—religion is deteriorated, and society in danger.

We cannot dispense with an examination of this question. In order to ascertain what has been the influence of the Christian church, we must know what ought to be, by the very nature of the institution, the influence of a church and of a clergy. In order to appreciate this influence, we must find out, first of all, whether religion is, in truth, purely individual, whether it does not provoke and give birth to something more than merely a private relation between each man and God; or whether it necessarily becomes a source of new relations between men, from which a religious society and a government of that society necessarily flow.

If we reduce religion to the religious sentiment properly so called, to that sentiment which is very real, though somewhat vague and uncertain as to its object, and which we can scarcely characterize otherwise than by naming it,—to this sentiment which addresses itself sometimes to external nature, sometimes to the innermost recesses of the soul, to-day to poetry, to-morrow to the mysteries of the future, which, in a word, wanders everywhere, seeking everywhere to satisfy itself, and fixing itself nowhere,—if we reduce religion to this sentiment, it seems evident to me that it should remain purely individual. Such a sentiment may provoke a momentary

association between men; it can, it even ought to take pleasure in sympathy, nourishing and strengthening itself thereby.
But by reason of its fluctuating and doubtful character, it
refuses to become the principle of a permanent and extensive
association, to adapt itself to any system of precepts, practices,
and forms; in short, to give birth to a religious society and
government.

But either I deceive myself strangely, or this religious
sentiment is not the complete expression of the religious
nature of man. Religion, I conceive, is a different thing,
and much more than this.

In human nature and in human destiny there are problems
of which the solution lies beyond this world, which are connected with a class of things foreign to the visible world, and
which inveterately torment the soul of man, who is fixedly
intent upon solving them. The solution of these problems,
creeds, dogmas, which contain that solution, or, at least,
flatter themselves that they do, these constitute the first object
and the first source of religion.

Another path leads men to religion. To those among you
who have prosecuted somewhat extended philosophical studies,
it is, I conceive, sufficiently evident at present that morality
exists independently of religious ideas; that the distinction of
moral good and evil, the obligation to shun the evil, and
to do the good, are laws, which, like the laws of logic, man
discovers in his own nature, and which have their principle
in himself, as they have their application in his actual
life. But these facts being decided, the independence of
morality being admitted, a question arises in the human
mind—Whence comes morality? To what does it lead? Is
this obligation to do good, which subsists of itself, an isolated
fact, without author and aim? Does it not conceal from, or
rather, does it not reveal to man a destiny which is beyond
this world? This is a spontaneous and inevitable question,
by which morality, in its turn, leads man to the door of
religion, and discovers to him a sphere from which he had
not borrowed morality.

Thus, in the problems of our nature, upon one hand, and
in the necessity of discovering a sanction, origin, and aim for
morality, on the other, we find assured and fruitful sources of
religion, which thus presents itself under aspects very different

from that of a mere instrument, as it has been described; it
presents itself as a collection—1st, of doctrines called forth by
problems which man discovers within himself; and, of precepts which correspond to those doctrines, and give to natural
morality a meaning and a sanction; 3rd, of promises which
address themselves to the hopes of humanity in the future.
This is what truly constitutes religion; this is what it is at
bottom, and not a mere form of sensibility, a flight of the
imagination, a species of poetry.

Reduced in this manner to its true elements and to its
essence, religion no longer appears as a purely individual
fact, but as a powerful and fruitful principle of association.
Consider it as a system of creeds and dogmas: truth belongs
to no one; it is universal, absolute; men must seek and profess it in common.   Consider the precepts that associate
themselves with doctrines: an obligatory law for one is such
for all; it must be promulgated, it must bring all men under
its empire.   It is the same with the promises made by
religion in the name of its creeds and precepts: they must be
spread abroad, and all men must be called to gather the
fruits of them.   From the essential elements of religion, then,
you see that the religious society is born; indeed, it flows
therefrom so infallibly that the word which expresses the most
energetic social sentiment, the most imperious necessity of
propagating ideas and extending a society, is the word proselytism, a word which applies above all to religious creeds,
and, indeed, seems to be almost exclusively consecrated to
them.

The religious society being once born, when a certain
number of men become united in common religious creeds,
under the law of common religious precepts, and in common
religious hopes, that society must have a government.   There
is no society which can survive a week, an hour, without a
government.   At the very instant in which the society forms
itself, and even by the very fact of its formation, it calls a
government, which proclaims the common truth, the bond of
the society, and promulgates and supports the precepts which
originate in that truth.   The necessity for a power, for a
government over the religious society, as over every other,
is implied in the fact of the existence of that society.   And
not only is government necessary, but it naturally forms

itself. I must not pause for any time to explain how government originates and establishes itself in society in general. I shall confine myself to saying that, when things follow their natural laws, when external force does not mix itself up with them, power always flies to the most capable, to the best, to those who will lead society towards its aim. In a warlike expedition, the bravest obtain the power. Is research or skilful enterprise the object of an association? the most capable will be at the head of it. In all things, when the world is left to its natural course, the natural inequality of men freely displays itself, and each takes the place which he is capable of occupying. Well, as regards religion, men are no more equal in talents, faculties, and power, than in the other cases; such a one will be better able than any other to expound religious doctrines, and to cause them to be generally adopted; some other bears about him more authority to induce the observance of religious precepts; a third will excel in sustaining and animating religious emotions and hopes in the souls of men. The same inequality of faculties and influence which gives rise to power in civil society, originates it equally in religious society. Missionaries arise and declare themselves like generals. Thus, as, on one hand, religious government necessarily flows from the nature of religious society, so, on the other, it naturally develops itself therein by the mere effect of the human faculties and their unequal partition. Therefore, from the moment at which religion is born in man, religious society develops itself; and from the moment at which religious society appears, it gives rise to its government.

But now a fundamental objection arises: there is nothing in this case to ordain or impose; nothing coercive. There is no room for government, since unlimited liberty is required to exist.

It is, I conceive, a very rude and petty idea of government in general, to suppose that it resides solely, or even principally, in the force which it exerts to make itself obeyed in its coercive element.

I leave the religious point of view; I take civil government. I pray you follow with me the simple course of facts. The society exists: there is something to be done, no matter what, in its interest and name; there is a law to make, a

measure to take, a judgment to pronounce. Assuredly there
is likewise a worthy manner of fulfilling these social wants;
a good law to make, a good measure to take, a good judgment
to pronounce. Whatever may be the matter in hand, whatever may be the interest in question, there is in every case
a truth that must be known, a truth which must decide the
conduct of the question.

The first business of government is to seek this truth, to
discover what is just, reasonable, and adapted to society.
When it has found it, it proclaims it. It becomes then necessary that it should impress it upon men's minds; that the
government should make itself approved of by those upon
whom it acts; that it should persuade them of its reasonableness. Is there anything coercive in this? Assuredly
not. Now, suppose that the truth which ought to decide
concerning the affair, no matter what, suppose, I say, that
this truth once discovered and proclaimed, immediately all
understandings are convinced, all wills determined, that all
recognise the reasonableness of the government, and spontaneously obey it; there is still no coercion, there is no room
for the employment of force. Is it that the government did
not exist? is it that, in all this, there was no government?
Evidently there was a government, and it fulfilled its task.
Coercion comes then only when the resistance of individual
will occurs, when the idea, the proceeding which the government has adopted, does not obtain the approbation and voluntary submission of all.   The government then employs force
to make itself obeyed; this is the necessary result of human
imperfection, an imperfection which resides at once in the
governing power and in the society. There will never be
any way of completely avoiding it; civil governments will
ever be compelled to have recourse, to a certain extent, to
coercion. But governments are evidently not constituted by
coercion: whenever they can dispense with it, they do, and to
the great profit of all: indeed, their highest perfection is to
dispense with it, and to confine themselves to methods purely
moral, to the action which they exert upon the understanding;
so that the more the government dispenses with coercion,
the more faithful it is to its true nature, the better it fulfils
its mission. It is not thereby reduced in power or contracted, as is vulgarly supposed; it acts only in another man-

ner, and in a manner which is infinitely more general and powerful. Those governments which make the greatest use of coercion, succeed not nearly so well as those which employ it scarcely at all.

In addressing itself to the understanding, in determining the will, in acting by purely intellectual means, the government, instead of reducing, extends and elevates itself; it is then that it accomplishes the most and the greatest things. On the contrary, when it is obliged incessantly to employ coercion, it contracts and lessens itself, and effects very little, and that little very ill.

Thus the essence of government does not reside in coercion, in the employment of force; but that which above all things constitutes it, is a system of means and powers, conceived with the design of arriving at the discovery of what is applicable to each occasion; at the discovery of truth, which has a right to rule society, in order that afterwards the minds of men may be brought to open themselves to it, and adopt it voluntarily and freely. The necessity for, and the actual existence of a government are thus perfectly conceivable, when there is no occasion for coercion, when even it is absolutely interdicted.

Well, such is the government of the religious society. Undoubtedly, coercion is interdicted to it; undoubtedly, the employment of force by it is illegitimate, whatever may be its aim, for the single reason that its exclusive territory is the human conscience: but not the less, therefore, does it subsist; not the less has it to accomplish all the acts I have mentioned. It must discover what are the religious doctrines which solve the problems of the human destiny; or, if there exists already a general system of creeds whereby those problems are solved, it must discover and exhibit the consequences of that system, as regards each particular case; *it* must promulgate and maintain the precepts which correspond to its doctrines; it must preach and teach them, in order that, when the society wanders from them, it may bring it back. There must be no coercion; the duties of this government are, examining, preaching, and teaching religious virtues; and, at need, admonishing or censuring. Suppress coercion as completely as you will, you will yet behold all the essential questions of the organisation of a government arise and claim solutions. For example, the question whether a body of religious magistrates is necessary, or whether it is possible to trust to the religious inspiration of individuals (a question which is debated between the majority of religious societies and the Quakers), will always exist, it will always be necessary to discuss it. In like manner, the question, whether, when it has been agreed that a body of religious magistrates is necessary, we should prefer a system of equality, of religious ministers equal among themselves, and deliberating in common, to an hierarchical constitution, with various degrees of power; this question will never come to an end, because you deny all coercive power to ecclesiastical magistrates, whosoever they may be. Instead, then, of dissolving religious society in order that we may have the right of destroying religious government, we must rather recognise that the religious society forms itself naturally, that the religious government flows as naturally from the religious society, and that the problem to be solved is to ascertain under what conditions this government should exist, what are its foundations, principles, and conditions of legitimacy. This is the real investigation which is imposed by the necessary existence of a religious government as of all others.

The conditions of legitimacy are the same for the government of a religious society as for that of any other; they may be reduced to two: the first, that the power should attach itself to and remain constantly in the hands of the best and most capable, as far, at least, as human imperfection will allow of its doing so; that the truly superior people who exist dispersed among the society should be sought for there, brought to light, and called upon to unfold the social law, and to exercise power: the second, that the power legitimately constituted, should respect the legitimate liberties of those over whom it exercises itself. In these two conditions, a good system of forming and organizing power, and a good system of guarantees of liberty, consists the worth of government in general, whether religious or civil; all governments ought to be judged according to this criterion.

Instead, then, of taunting the church, or the government of the Christian world, with its existence, we should find out how it was constituted. and whether its principles corresponded with the two essential conditions of all good government. Let us examine the church in this twofold view.

As regards the formation and transmission of power in the church, there is a word which is often used in speaking of the Christian clergy, and which I wish to discard; it is the word *caste*. The body of ecclesiastical magistrates has often been called a caste. Look round the world; take any country in which castes have been produced, in India or Egypt; you will see everywhere that the caste is essentially hereditary; it is the transmission of the same position, and the same power, from father to son. Wherever there is no inheritance, there is no caste, there is a corporation; the spirit of a corporation has its inconveniences, but it is very different from the spirit of the caste. The word *caste*, cannot be applied to the Christian church. The celibacy of the priests prevents the Christian church from ever becoming a caste.

You already see, to a certain extent, the consequences of this difference. To the system of caste, to the fact of inheritance, monopoly is inevitably attached. This results from the very definition of the word caste. When the same functions and the same powers become hereditary in the same families, it is evident that privilege must have been attached to them, and that no one could have acquired them independently of his origin. In fact, this was what happened; wherever the religious government fell into the hands of a caste, it became a matter of privilege; no one entered into it but those who belonged to the families of the caste. Nothing resembling this is met with in the Christian church; and not only is there no resemblance found, but the church has continually maintained the principle of the equal admissibility of all men to all her duties and dignities, whatever may have been their origin The ecclesiastical career, particularly from the fifth to the twelfth century, was open to all. The church recruited herself from all ranks, alike from the inferior as well as the superior; more often indeed from the inferior. Around her all was disposed of under the system of privilege; she alone maintained the principle of equality and competition; she alone called all who were possessed of legitimate superiority to the possession of power. This was the first great consequence which naturally resulted from her being a body, and not a caste.

Again, there is an inherent spirit in castes, the spirit
of immobility. This assertion needs no proof. Open any
history, and you will see the spirit of immobility imprinted
upon all societies, whether political or religious, where the
system of castes dominated. The fear of progress, it is true,
was introduced at a certain epoch, and up to a certain point,
in the Christian church. But we cannot say that it has
dominated there; we cannot say that the Christian church has
remained immovable and stationary; for many long ages she
has been in movement and progress; sometimes provoked by
the attacks of an external opposition, sometimes impelled from
within, by desires of reform and internal development. Upon
the whole, it is a society which has continually changed and
marched onwards, and which has a varied and progressive
history. There can be no doubt that the equal admission of
all men to the ecclesiastical functions, that the continual recruiting of the church according to principles of equality, has
powerfully contributed to maintain, and incessantly reanimate
within it, its life and movement, to prevent the triumph of
the spirit of immobility.

How could the church who thus admitted all men to
power assure herself of their right to it? How could she
discover and bring to light, from the heart of society, the
legitimate superiorities which were to share the government?

Two principles were in vigour in the church: first, the
election of the inferior by the superior—the choice. the nomination; secondly, the election of the superior by the subordinates—that is, an election properly so called, what we
understand as such in the present day.

The ordination of priests, for instance, the power of making
a man a priest, belonged to the superior alone. The choice
was exercised by the superior over the inferior. So, in the collation of certain ecclesiastical benefices, among others, benefices
attached to the feudal concessions, it was the superior—king,
pope, or lord—who nominated the incumbent; in other cases,
the principle of election, properly so called, was in force.
The bishops had long been, and at the epoch which occupies
us were still very often, elected by the body of the clergy
sometimes even the congregations interfered. In the interior of monasteries, the abbot was elected by the monks. At
Rome, the popes were elected by the college of cardinals, and

at one time even the whole of the Roman clergy took part in the election. You thus see the two principles—the choice of the inferior by the superior, and the election of the superior by the subordinate—acknowledged and acted upon in the church, especially at the epoch under consideration. It was by one or other of these means that she nominated the men called upon to exercise a portion of the ecclesiastical power.

Not only were these two principles co-existent, but being essentially different, there was a struggle between them. After many centuries and many vicissitudes, the nomination of the inferior by the superior gained the mastery in the Christian church; but as a general thing, from the fifth to the twelfth century, it was the other principle, the choice of the superior by the subordinate, which still prevailed. And do not be surprised at the co-existence of two principles so dissimilar. Regard society in general, the natural course of the world, the manner in which power is transmitted in it, you will see that this transmission is brought into force sometimes according to one of these principles and sometimes according to the other. The church did not originate them; she found them in the providential government of human things, and thence she borrowed them. There is truth and utility in each of them; their combination will often be the best means of discovering the legitimate power. It is a great misfortune, in my opinion, that one of these two, the choice of the inferior by the superior, should have gained the mastery in the church; the second, however, has never entirely prevailed; and under various names, with more or less success, it has been reproduced in all epochs, so as at all events to enter protest and interrupt prescription.

The Christian church derived, at the epoch which occupies us, immense strength from its respect for equality and legitimate superiorities. It was the most popular society, the most accessible and open to all kinds of talent, to all the noble ambitions of human nature. Thence arose its power, much more than from its riches, or from the illegitimate means which it has too often employed.

As regards the second condition of a good government, respect for liberty, there was much to wish for in the church.

Two evil principles met in it; the one avowed, and, as it were, incorporated in the doctrines of the church; the other introduced into it by human weakness, and not as a legitimate consequence of doctrines.

The first was the denial of the right of individual reason, the pretension to transmit creeds down through the whole religious society, without any one having the right to judge for himself. It was easier to lay down this principle than to make it actually prevail. A conviction does not enter into the human intellect unless the intellect admits it; it must make itself acceptable. In whatever form it presents itself, and whatever name it evokes, reason weighs it; and if the creed prevail, it is from being accepted by reason. Thus, under whatever form they may be concealed, the action of the individual reason is always exerted upon the ideas which are sought to be imposed upon it. It is very true that reason may be altered; it may to a certain extent abdicate and mutilate itself; it may be induced to make an ill use of its faculties, or not to put in force all the use of them to which it has a right; such, indeed, has been the consequence of the ill principle admitted by the church; but as regards the pure and complete influence of this principle, it never has been, and never can be, put into full force.

The second evil principle is, the right of constraint which the church arrogates to herself,—a right contrary to the very nature of religious society, to the very origin of the church, and her primitive maxims,—a right which has been disputed by many of the most illustrious fathers, St. Ambrose, St. Hilary, St. Martin, but which has, notwithstanding, prevailed and become a dominant fact. The pretension of forcing to believe, if two such words can stand in juxta-position, or of physically punishing belief, the persecution of heresy, contempt for the legitimate liberty of human thought, this is an error which was introduced into the church even before the fifth century; and dearly has it cost her.

If, then, we consider the church in relation to the liberty of her members, we perceive that her principles in this respect were less legitimate and less salutary than those which presided at the formation of the ecclesiastical power. It must not be supposed, however, that an evil principle radically vitiates an institution, nor even that it is the cause of all the evil which it carries in its breast. Nothing more falsifies history than logic: when the human mind rests upon an idea, it draws from it every possible consequence, makes it produce all the effect it is capable of producing, and then pictures it in history with the whole retinue. But things do not happen in this way; events are not so prompt in their deductions as the human mind. There is in all things a mixture of good and evil so profound and invincible, that wherever you penetrate, when you descend into the most hidden elements of society or the soul, you find there these two orders of existent facts developing them-selves side by side, combating without exterminating one another. Human nature never goes to the extremity either of evil or good; it passes incessantly from one to the other, erecting itself at the moment when it seems most likely to fall, and weakening at the moment when its walk seems firmest. We shall find here that character of discordance, variety, and strife, which I have remarked as being the fundamental characteristic of European civilization. There is still another general fact which characterizes the government of the church, and of which it is necessary to take notice.

At the present day, when the idea of government presents itself to us, whatever it may be, we know that there is no pretension of governing other than the external actions of man— the civil relations of men among themselves; governments profess to apply themselves to nothing more. With regard to human thought, human conscience, and morality, properly so called, with regard to individual opinions and private manners, they do not interfere; these fall within the domain of liberty.

The Christian church did or wished to do directly the contrary; she undertook to govern the liberty, private manners, and opinions of individuals. She did not make a code like ours, to define only actions at once morally culpable and socially dangerous, and only punishing them in proportion as they bore this two-fold character. She made a catalogue of all actions morally culpable, and under the name of sins she punished all with the intention of repressing all: in a word, the government of the church did not address itself, like modern governments, to the external man, to the purely civil relations of men among themselves; it addressed itself to the internal man, to the thought and conscience, that is to say, to all that

H

ıs most private to him, most free and rebellious against constraint. The church, then, from the very nature of her
enterprise, together with the nature of some of the principles
upon which she founded her government, was in danger of
becoming tyrannical, and of employing illegitimate force.
But at the same time the force encountered a resistance which
it could not vanquish. However little movement and space
are left them, human thought and liberty energetically re-act
against all attempts to subdue them, and at every moment
compel the very despotism which they endure to abdicate.
Thus it happened in the bosom of the Christian church.
You have seen the proscription of heresy, the condemnation
of the right of inquiry, the contempt for individual reason,
and the principle of the imperative transmission of doctrines
upon authority. Well! show one society in which individual
reason has been more boldly developed than in the church!
What are sects and heresies, if they are not the fruit of
individual opinions? Sects and heresies, all the party of
opposition in the church, are the incontestable proof of the
moral life and activity which reigned in it; a life tempestuous
and painful, overspread with perils, errors, crimes, but noble
and powerful, and one that has given rise to the finest developments of mind and intellect. Leave the opposition,
look into the ecclesiastical government itself; you will find
it constituted and acting in a manner very different from
what some of its principles seem to indicate. It denied the
right of inquiry, and wished to deprive individual reason of
its liberty; and yet it is to reason that it incessantly appeals,
and liberty is its dominant fact. What are its institutions
and means of action? provincial councils, national councils,
general councils, a continual correspondence, the incessant
publication of letters, admonitions, and writings. Never did
a government proceed to such an extent by discussion and
common deliberation. We might suppose ourselves in the heart
of the Greek schools of philosophy; and yet it was no mere
discussion, or seeking for truth that was at issue; it involved
questions of authority, of adopting measures, of promulgating decrees; in fine, of a government. But such in the very
heart of this government was the energy of intellectual life,
that it became the dominant and universal fact, to which all

others gave way; and what shone forth on all sides, was the exercise of reason and liberty.

I am far from inferring that these bad principles which I have attempted to set forth, and which, in my opinion, existed in the system of the church, remained in it without effect. At the epoch which now occupies us, they already bore but too bitter fruit, and were destined at a later period to bear fruit still more bitter: but they have not accomplished all the evil of which they were capable, they have not stifled all the good which grew in the same soil. Such was the church, considered in itself, in its internal construction and nature. I now pass to its relations with the sovereigns, the masters of temporal power. This is the second point of view under which I promised to consider it.

When the Empire fell—when, instead of the ancient Roman system, the government, in the midst of which the church had taken birth, with which she had arisen, and had habits in common, and ancient ties, she found herself exposed to those barbarian kings and chiefs who wandered over the land, or remained fixed in their castles, and to whom neither traditions, creeds, nor sentiments, could unite her; her danger was great, and as great was her terror.

A single idea became dominant in the church: this was to take possession of the new comers, to convert them. The relations between the church and the barbarians had, at first, scarcely any other aim. In influencing the barbarians, it was necessary that their senses and their imagination should be appealed to. We therefore find at this epoch a great augmentation in the number, pomp, and variety of the ceremonies of worship. The chronicles prove that this was the chief means by which the church acted upon the barbarians; she converted them by splendid spectacles. When they were established and converted, and when there existed some ties between them and the church, she did not cease to run many dangers on their part. The brutality and recklessness of the barbarians were such, that the new creeds and sentiments with which they were inspired exercised but little empire over them. Violence soon reassumed the upper hand, and the church, like the rest of society, was its victim. For her defence she proclaimed a principle formerly laid down under

H 2

the Empire, although more vaguely,—this was the separation
of the spiritual from the temporal power, and their reciprocal
independence. It was by the aid of this principle that the church
lived freely in connexion with the barbarians; she maintained
that force could not act upon the system of creeds, hopes, and
religious promises; that the spiritual world and the temporal
world were entirely distinct. You may at once see the salutary consequences resulting from this principle. Independently of its temporal utility to the church, it had this ines-
timable effect, of bringing about, on the foundation of right,
the separation of powers, and of controlling them by means of
each other. Moreover, in sustaining the independence of
the intellectual world, as a general thing, in its whole extent,
the church prepared the way for the independence of the
individual intellectual world,—the independence of thought.
The church said that the system of religious creeds could not
fall under the yoke of force; and each individual was led to
apply to his own case the language of the church. The
principle of free inquiry, of liberty of individual thought, is
exactly the same as that of the independence of general
spiritual authority, with regard to temporal power.

Unhappily, it is easy to pass from the desire for liberty to
the lust for domination. It thus happened within the bosom
of the church; by the natural development of ambition and
human pride, the church attempted to establish, not only the
independence of spiritual power, but also its domination over
temporal power. But it must not be supposed that this pretension had no other source than in the weaknesses of human
nature; there were other more profound sources which it is
of importance to know.

When liberty reigns in the intellectual world; when thought
and human conscience are not subjected to a power which
disputes their right to debate and decide, or employs force
against them; when there is no visible and constituted spiritual government, claiming and exercising the right to dictate
opinions; then the idea of the domination of the spiritual over
the temporal order is impossible. Nearly such is the present state of the world. But when there exists, as there did
exist in the tenth century, a government of the spiritual
order; when thought and conscience come under laws, institutions, and powers, which arrogate to themselves the right

of commanding and constraining them; in a word, when spiritual power is constituted, when it actually takes possession of human reason and conscience, in the name of right and force, it is natural that it should be led to assume the domination over the temporal order, that it should say:— "How! I have right and influence over that which is most elevated and independent in man; over his thought, his internal will, and his conscience, and shall I not have right over his exterior, material, and passing interests! I am the interpreter of justice and truth, and am I not allowed to regulate worldly affairs according to justice and truth?" In very virtue of this reasoning, the spiritual order was sure to attempt the usurpation of the temporal order. And this was the more certain from the fact that the spiritual order embraced every development of human thought at that time; there was but one science, and that was theology; but one spiritual order, the theological; all other sciences, rhetoric, arithmetic, even music, all was comprised in theology.

The spiritual power, thus finding itself at the head of all the activity of human thought, naturally arrogated to itself the government of the world. A second cause tended as powerfully to this end—the frightful state of the temporal order, the violence and iniquity which prevailed in the government of temporal societies.

We, for many centuries, have spoken at our ease of the rights of temporal power; but at the epoch under consideration, the temporal was mere force, ungovernable brigandage. The church, however imperfect her notions still were concerning morality and justice, was infinitely superior to such a temporal government as this; the cries of the people continually pressed her to take its place. When a pope, or the bishops, proclaimed that a prince had forfeited his rights, and that his subjects were absolved from their oath of fidelity, this intervention, without doubt subject to various abuses, was often, in particular cases, legitimate and salutary. In general, when liberty has failed mankind, it is religion that has had the charge of replacing it. In the tenth century, the people were not in a state to defend themselves, and so make their rights available against civil violence: religion, in the name of Heaven, interfered. This is one of the causes which have most contributed to the victories of the theocratical principle.

There is a third, which I think is too seldom remarked: the complexity of situation of the heads of the church, the variety of aspects under which they have presented themselves in society.   On one hand, they were prelates, members of the ecclesiastical order, and part of the spiritual power, and by this title independent; on the other, they were vassals, and, as such, engaged in the bonds of civil feudalism.   This is not all; besides being vassals, they were subjects; some portion of the ancient relations between the Roman emperors, and the bishops, and the clergy, had now passed into those between the clergy and the barbarian sovereigns.   By a series of causes which it would be too tedious to develop, the bishops had been led to regard, up to a certain point, the barbarian sovereigns as the successors of the Roman emperors, and to attribute to them all their prerogatives.   The chiefs of the clergy, then, had a three-fold character: an ecclesiastical character, and as such, an independent one; a feudal character, one, as such, bound to certain duties, and holding by certain services; and, lastly, the character of a simple subject, and as such, bound to obey an absolute sovereign.   Now mark the result.   The temporal sovereigns, who were not less covetous and ambitious than the bishops, availed themselves of their rights as lords or sovereigns, to encroach upon the spiritual independence, and to seize upon the collation of benefices, the nomination of bishops, &c.   The bishops, on their side, often entrenched themselves in their spiritual independence, in order to escape their obligations as vassals or subjects; so that, on either hand, there was an almost inevitable tendency which led the sovereigns to destroy spiritual independence, and the heads of the church to make spiritual independence a means of universal domination.

The result has been shown in facts of which no one is ignorant: in the quarrels concerning investitures, and in the struggle between the priesthood and the empire.   The various situations of the heads of the church, and the difficulty or reconciling them, were the real sources of the uncertainty and contest of these pretensions.

Lastly, the church had a third relation with the sovereigns, which was for her the least favourable and the most unfortunate of them all.   She laid claim to coaction, to the right of restraining and punishing heresy; but she had no means of doing this; she had not at her disposal a physical force; when she had condemned the heretic, she had no means of executing judgment upon him. What could she do? She invoked the aid of what was called the secular arm; she borrowed the force of civil power, as a means of coaction. And she thereby placed herself, in regard to civil power, in a situation of dependence and inferiority. A deplorable necessity to which she was reduced by the adoption of the evil principle of coaction and persecution.

It remains for me to make you acquainted with the relations of the church with the people; what principles were prevalent in them, and what consequences have thence resulted to civilization in general. I shall afterwards attempt to verify the inductions we have here drawn from the nature of its institutions and principles, by means of history, facts, and the vicissitudes of the destiny of the church from the fifth to the twelfth century.

SIXTH LECTURE.

Object of the lecture—Separation of the governing and the governed party
    in the church—Indirect influence of the laity upon the clergy—The
    clergy recruited from all conditions of society—Influence of the church
    upon the public order and upon legislation—The penitential system—
    The development of the human mind is entirely theological—The church
    usually ranges itself on the side of power—Not to be wondered at; the
    aim of religions is to regulate human liberty—Different states of the
    church, from the fifth to the twelfth century—1st. The imperial church
    —2nd. The barbaric church; development of the separating principle
    of the two powers; the monastic order—3rd. The feudal church; at-
    tempts at organization; want of reform; Gregory VII.—The theocratical
    church—Regeneration of the spirit of inquiry; Abailard—Movement
    of the boroughs—No connexion between these two facts.

WE were unable, at our last meeting, to terminate the inquiry
into the state of the church from the fifth to the twelfth
century. After having decided that it should be considered
under three principal aspects,—first, in itself alone, in its
internal constitution, and in its nature as a distinct and independent society; next, in its relations to the sovereign and
the temporal power; and lastly, in its relations with the
people,—we have only accomplished the two first divisions of
this task. It now remains for me to make you acquainted
with the church in its relations with the people. I shall
afterwards endeavour to draw from this three-fold inquiry a
general idea of the influence of the church upon European
civilization from the fifth to the twelfth century. And lastly,
we will verify our assertions by an examination of the facts,
by the history of the church itself at that epoch.

You will easily understand that, in speaking of the relations
of the church with the people, I am forced to confine myself

to very general terms. I cannot enter into a detail of the practices of the church, or of the daily relations of the clergy with the faithful. It is the dominant principles and grand effects of the system and of the conduct of the church towards the Christian people, that I have to place before you.

The characteristic fact, and, it must so be called, the radical vice of the relations of the church with the people, is the separation of the governing and the governed, the non-influence of the governed in their government, the independence of the Christian clergy with regard to the faithful.

This evil must have been provoked by the state of man and of society, for we find it introduced into the Christian church at a very early period. The separation of the clergy and the Christian people was not entirely consummated at the epoch under consideration; there was, on certain occasions, in the election of bishops for instance, at least in some cases, a direct intervention of the Christian people in its government. But this intervention became by degrees more weak, and of more rare occurrence; it was from the second century of our era that it began visibly and rapidly to decline. The tendency to the isolation and independence of the clergy is, in a measure, the history of the church itself, from its very cradle. From thence, it cannot be denied, arose the greater portion of those abuses which, at this epoch, and still more at a later period, have cost so dear to the church. We must not, however, impute them solely to this, nor regard this tendency to isolation as peculiar to the Christian clergy. There is in the very nature of religious society a strong inclination to raise the governing far above the governed, to attribute to the former something distinct and divine. This is the effect of the very mission with which they are charged, and of the character under which they present themselves to the eyes of people, and such an effect is more grievous in the religious society than in any other. What is it that is at stake with the governed? Their reason, their conscience, their future destiny, that is to say, all that is most near to them, most individual, and most free. We can conceive, to a certain point, that although great evil may result therefrom, a man may abandon to an external authority the direction of his material interests, and his temporal destiny. We can understand the philosopher, who, when they came to tell him that his house was on fire, answered, "Go and inform my wife; I do not meddle in the household affairs." But, when it extends to the conscience, the thought, and the internal existence, to the abdication of self-government, to the delivering oneself to a foreign power, it is truly a moral suicide, a servitude a hundred-fold worse than that of the body, or than that of the soil. Such, however, was the evil which, without prevailing entirely, as I shall immediately show, gradually usurped the Christian church in its relations with the faithful. You have already seen that, for the clergy themselves, and in the very heart of the church, there was no guarantee for liberty. It was far worse beyond the church, and among the laity. Among ecclesiastics, there was, at least, discussion, deliberation, and a display of individual faculties; there the excitement of contest supplied, in some measure, the want of liberty. There was none of this between the clergy and the people. The laity took part in the government of the church as mere spectators. Thus we see springing up and prevailing at a very early period, the idea that theology and religious questions and affairs, are the privileged domain of the clergy; that the clergy alone have the right, not only of deciding, but of taking part therein at all; that in any case the laity can have no kind of right to interfere. At the period under consideration, this theory was already in full power; centuries, and terrible revolutions were necessary to conquer it, to bring back within the public domain, religious questions and science.

In principle, then, as well as in fact, the legal separation of the clergy and the Christian people was almost consummated before the twelfth century.

I would not have you suppose, however, that even at this epoch the Christian people were entirely without influence in its government. The legal intervention was wanting, but not influence—that is almost impossible in any government, still more so in a government founded upon a belief common both to the governing and the governed. Wherever this community of ideas is developed, or wherever a similar intellectual movement prevails with the government and the people, there must necessarily exist a connexion between them, which no vice in the organization can entirely destroy

To explain myself clearly, I will take an example near to us, and from the political order: at no epoch in the history of France has the French people had less legal influence on its government, by means of institutions, than in the seventeenth and eighteenth centuries, under Louis XIV. and Louis XV.

No one is ignorant that at this period nearly all official and direct influence of the country in the exercise of authority had perished; yet there can be no doubt that the people and the country then exercised upon the government far more influence than in other times—in the times, for instance, when the states-general were so often convoked, when the parliament took so important a part in politics, and when the legal participation of the people in power was much greater.

It is because there is a force which cannot be inclosed by laws, which, when need is, can dispense with institutions: it is the force of ideas, of the public mind and opinion. In France, in the seventeenth and eighteenth centuries, there was a public opinion which was much more powerful than at any other epoch. Although deprived of the means of acting legally upon the government, it acted indirectly by the empire of ideas, which were common alike to the governing and the governed, and by the impossibility which the governing felt of taking no note of the opinion of the governed. A similar fact happened in the Christian church from the fifth to the twelfth century; the Christian people, it is true, were deficient in legal action, but there was a great movement of mind in religious matters—this movement brought the laity and the ecclesiastics into conjunction, and by this means the people influenced the clergy.

In all cases in the study of history, it is necessary to hold, as highly valuable, indirect influences; they are much more efficacious, and sometimes more salutary, than is generally supposed. It is natural that men should wish their actions to be prompt and evident, should desire the pleasure of participating in their success, power, and triumph. This is not always possible, not always even useful. There are times and situations in which indirect and unseen influences are alone desirable and practicable. I will take another example from the political order. More than once, especially in 1641,

the English parliament, like many other assemblies in similar
crises, has claimed the right of nominating directly the chief
officers of the crown, the ministers, councillors of state, &c.;
it regarded this direct action in the government as an
immense and valuable guarantee. It has sometimes exercised this prerogative, and always with bad success. The
selections were ill concerted, and affairs ill governed. But
how is it in England at the present day? Is it not the influence of parliament which decides the formation of the
ministry, and the nomination of all the great officers of
the crown? Certainly; but then it is an indirect and general
influence, instead of a special intervention. The end at
which England has long aimed is gained, but by different
means; the first means which were tried had never acted
beneficially.

There is a reason for this, concerning which I ask your
permission to detain you for a moment. Direct action
supposes, in those to whom it is confided, far more enlightenment, reason, and prudence: as they are to attain the
end at once, and without delay, it is necessary that they
should be certain of not missing that end. Indirect influences, on the contrary, are only exercised through
obstacles, and after tests which restrain and rectify them;
before prospering, they are condemned to undergo discussion,
and to see themselves opposed and controlled; they triumph
but slowly, and, in a measure, conditionally. For this reason,
when minds are not sufficiently advanced and ripened to
guarantee their direct action being taken with safety, indirect influences, although often insufficient, are still preferable. It was thus that the Christian people influenced their
government, very incompletely, in much too limited an extent,
I am convinced—but still they influenced it.

There was also another cause of approximation between the
church and the people; this was the dispersion, so to speak,
of the Christian clergy amongst all social conditions. Almost
everywhere, when a church has been constituted independently of the people whom it governed, the body of priests
has been formed of men nearly in the same situation; not
that great inequalities have not existed among them, but, upon
the whole, the government has appertained to colleges of
priests living in common, and governing, from the depths of

the temple, the people under their law. The Christian church was quite differently organized. From the miserable habitation of the serf, at the foot of the feudal castle, to the king's palace itself, everywhere there was a priest, a member of the clergy. The clergy was associated with all human conditions. This diversity in the situation of the Christian priests, this participation in all fortunes, has been a grand principle of union between the clergy and the laity, a principle which has been wanting in most churches invested with power. The bishops and chiefs of the Christian clergy were, moreover, as you have seen, engaged in the feudal organization, and were members, at one and the same time, of a civil and of an ecclesiastical hierarchy. Hence it was that the same interests, habits, and manners, became common to both the civil and religious orders. There has been much complaint, and with good reason, of bishops who have gone to war, of priests who have led the life of laymen. Of a verity, it was a great abuse, but still an abuse far less grievous than was, elsewhere, the existence of those priests who never left the temple, and whose life was totally separated from that of the community. Bishops, in some way mixed up in civil discords, were far more serviceable than priests who were total strangers to the population, to all its affairs and its manners. Under this connexion, there was established between the clergy and the Christian people a parity of destiny and situation, which, if it did not correct, at least lessened the evil of the separation between the governing and the governed.

This separation being once admitted, and its limits determined (the attainment of which object I have just attempted) let us investigate the manner in which the Christian church was governed, and in what way it acted upon the people under its command. On the one hand, how it tended to the development of man, and the internal progress of the individual; and on the other how it tended to the amelioration of the social condition.

As regards the development of the individual, I do not think, correctly speaking, that, at the epoch under consideration, the church troubled itself much in the matter; it endeavoured to inspire the powerful of the world with milder sentiments, and with more justice in their relations with the weak; it maintained in the weak a moral life, together with sentiments and desires of a more elevated order than those to which their daily destiny condemned them. Still, for the development of the individual, properly so called, and for increasing the worth of man's personal nature, I do not think that at this period the church did much, at all events not among the laity. What it did effect was confined to the ecclesiastical society; it concerned itself much with the development of the clergy, and the instruction of the priests it had for them schools, and all the institutions which the deplorable state of society permitted. But they were ecclesiastical schools destined only for the instruction of the clergy, beyond this, the church acted only indirectly and by very dilatory means upon the progress of ideas and manners. It doubtless provoked general activity of mind, by the career which it opened to all those whom it judged capable of serving it; but this was all that it did at this period towards the intellectual development of the laity.

It worked more, I believe, and that in a more efficacious manner, towards the amelioration of social society. There can be no doubt that it struggled resolutely against the great vices of the social state, against slavery, for instance. It has often been repeated, that the abolition of slavery among modern people is entirely due to Christians. That I think is saying too much: slavery existed for a long period in the heart of Christian society, without it being particularly astonished or irritated. A multitude of causes, and a great development in other ideas and principles of civilization, were necessary for the abolition of this iniquity of all iniquities. It cannot be doubted, however, that the church exerted its influence to restrain it. We have an undeniable proof of this. The greater part of the forms of enfranchisement, at various epochs, were based upon religious principles: it is in the name of religious ideas, upon hopes of the future, and upon the religious equality of mankind, that enfranchisement has almost always been pronounced.

The church worked equally for the suppression of a crowd of barbarous customs, and for the amelioration of the criminal and civil legislation. You know how monstrous and absurd this legislation then was, despite some principles of liberty in it; you also know what ridiculous proofs, such as judicial combat, and even the simple oaths of a few men, were considered as the only means of arriving at the truth. The church endeavoured to substitute in their stead more rational and legitimate means. I have already spoken of the difference which may be observed between the laws of the Visigoths, issued chiefly from the councils of Toledo, and other barbarous laws. It is impossible to compare them without being struck by the immense superiority of the ideas of the church in matters of legislation, justice, and in all that interests the search for truth and the destiny of mankind. Doubtless many of these ideas were borrowed from the Roman legislation; but had not the church preserved and defended them, if it had not worked their propagation, they would, doubtless, have perished. For example, as regards the employment of the oath in legal procedure; open the law of the Visigoths, and you will see with what wisdom it is used :

"Let the judge, that he may understand the cause, first interrogate the witnesses, and afterwards examine the writings, to the end that the truth may be discovered with more certainty, and that the oath may not be needlessly administered. The search for truth requires that the writings on either side be carefully examined, and that the necessity for the oath, suspended over the heads of the parties, arrive unexpectedly. Let the oath be administered only in those cases when the judge can discover no writings, proof, or other certain evidence of the truth." (*For. Jud.* l. ii. tit. i. 21.)

In criminal matters, the relation between the punishments and the offences is determined according to philosophical and moral notions, which are very just. One may there recognise the efforts of an enlightened legislator struggling against the violence and want of reflection of barbarous manners. The chapter, *De cæde et morte hominum*, compared with laws corresponding thereto in other nations, is a very remarkable example. Elsewhere, it is the damage done which seems to constitute the crime, and the punishment is sought in the material reparation of pecuniary composition. Here the crime is reduced to its true, veritable, and moral element, the intention. The various shades of criminality, absolutely involuntary homicide, homicide by inadvertency, provoked homicide, homicide with or without premeditation, are distinguished and defined nearly as correctly as in our codes, and the punish

ments vary in just proportion. The justice of the legislator
went still further. He has attempted, if not to abolish, at
least to lessen the diversity of legal value, established among
men by the laws of barbarism. The only distinction which he
kept up, was that of the free man and the slave. As regards
free men, the punishment varies neither according to the
origin nor the rank of the deceased, but solely according to
the various degrees of moral culpability of the murderer.
With regard to slaves, although not daring to deprive the
master of all right to life and death, he at least attempted
to restrain it, by subjecting it to a public and regular procedure. The text of the law deserves citation.

"If no malefactor or accomplice in a crime, should go un-
punished, with how much more reason should we condemn
those who have committed homicide lightly and maliciously!
Therefore, as masters, in their pride, often put their slaves to
death, without fault on their part, it is right that this licence
should be entirely extirpated, and we ordain that the present
law be perpetually observed by all. No master or mistress
can put to death without public trial any of their male or
female slaves, nor any person dependent upon them. If a
slave, or any other servant, shall commit any crime which
will render him liable to capital punishment, his master, or
accuser, shall immediately inform the judge, or the count, or the
duke, of the place where the crime was committed. After an
investigation into the affair, if the crime be proved, let the
culprit undergo, either through the judge or his own master,
the sentence of death which he merits: provided, however,
that if the judge will not put the accused to death, he shall
draw up a capital sentence against him in writing; and then
it shall be in the power of the master either to kill him or
spare his life. At the same time, if the slave by a fatal
audacity, resisting his master, shall strike, or attempt to strike,
him with a weapon or stone, and if the master, while defending himself, should kill the slave in his rage, the master shall
not receive the punishment due to a homicide; but it must be
proved that this really was the fact, and that, by the testimony
or oath of the slaves, male or female, who may have been
present, and by the oath of the author of the deed himself.
Whoever in pure malice, whether with his own hand or
by that of another, shall kill his slave without public

judgment, shall be reckoned infamous, and declared incapable of bearing testimony, and shall pass the remainder of his life in exile or penitence, and his goods shall fall to his nearest heir, to whom the law accords the inheritance." (For. Jud. l. vi. tit. v. l. 12.)

There is one fact in the institutions of the church, which is generally not sufficiently remarked: it is the penitential system, a system so much the more curious to study in the present day, from its being, as regards the principles and applications of the penal law, exactly in accordance with the ideas of modern philosophy. If you study the nature of the punishments of the church, and the public penances which were its principal mode of chastisement, you will see that the chief object is to excite repentance in the soul of the culprit, and moral terror in the beholders, by the example. There was also another idea mixed with it, that of expiation. I know not, as a general thing, if it be possible to separate the idea of expiation from that of punishment, and whether there is not in all punishment, independently of the necessity of provoking repentance in the culprit, and of deterring those who might be tempted to become so, a secret and imperious want to expiate the wrong committed. But, leaving aside this question, it is evident that repentance and example are the ends proposed by the church in its whole penitential system. Is not this, also, the end of a truly philosophical legislation? Is it not in the name of these principles, that the most enlightened jurists of this and the past century have advocated the reform of the European penal legislation? Open their works, those of Bentham for instance, and you will be surprised by all the resemblances which you will meet with between the penal means therein proposed, and those employed by the church. They certainly did not borrow them from her, nor could she have foreseen that one day her example would be invoked to aid the plans of the least devout of philosophers. Lastly, she strove by all sorts of means to restrain violence and continual warfare in society. Every one knows what was the *truce of God*, and numerous measures of a similar kind, by which the church struggled against the employment of force, and strove to introduce more order and gentleness into society. These facts are so well known that it is needless for me to enter into details. Such

I

are the principal points which I have to place before you concerning the relations between the church and the people. We
have considered it under the three aspects which I first announced; and have gained an inward and outward knowledge
of it, both in its internal constitution and its twofold position.   It now remains for us to deduct from our knowledge,
by means of induction and conjecture, its general influence
upon European civilization.   This, if I mistake not, is a work
almost completed, or at least far advanced; the simple an-
nouncement of the dominant facts and principles in the church,
show and explain its influence; the results have, in some
measure, already passed before your eyes with the causes. If,
however, we attempt to recapitulate them, we shall, I think,
be led to two general assertions.

The first is, that the church must have exercised a very
great influence upon the moral and intellectual orders in
modern Europe, upon public ideas, sentiments and manners.

The fact is evident; the moral and intellectual development
of Europe has been essentially theological.   Survey history
from the fifth to the twelfth centuries; it is theology that possessed and directed the human spirit; all opinions are impressed by theology; philosophical, political, and historical
questions, are all considered under a theological point of view.
So all powerful is the church in the intellectual order, that
even the mathematical and physical sciences are held in submission to its doctrines.   The theological spirit is, in a manner, the blood which ran in the veins of the European world,
down to Bacon and Descartes.   For the first time, Bacon in
England, and Descartes in France, carried intelligence beyond
the path of theology.

The same fact is evident in all branches of literature ;
theological habits, sentiments, and language, are manifest at
every step.

Upon the whole, this influence has been salutary; not only
has it sustained and fertilized the intellectual movement in
Europe, but the system of doctrines and precepts, under the
name of which it implanted the movement, was far superior
to anything with which the ancient world was acquainted.
There was at the same time movement and progress.

The situation of the church, moreover, gave an extent and
a variety to the development of the human mind in the

modern world, which it had not possessed previously. In the east, intellect is entirely religious; in Greek society, it is exclusively human; in the one, humanity, properly so called, that is, its actual nature and destiny, vanishes; in the other, it is man himself, his actual passions, sentiments, and interests which occupy the whole stage. In the modern world, the religious spirit is mixed up with everything, but it excludes nothing. Modern intellect has at once the stamp of humanity and of divinity. Human sentiments and interests occupy an important place in our literature; and yet the religious character of man, that portion of his existence which links him to another world, appears in every step; so that the two great sources of man's development, humanity and religion, have flowed at one time, and that abundantly; and despite all the evil and abuses with which it is mixed, despite many acts of tyranny, regarded in an intellectual point of view, the influence of the church has tended more to develop than compress, more to extend than to confine.

Under a political point of view, it is otherwise. There can be no doubt that in softening sentiments and manners, in crying down and exploding numerous barbarous customs, the church has powerfully contributed to the amelioration of the social state; but in the political order, properly so called, as regards the relations between the government and the subject, between power and liberty, I do not think that, upon the whole, her influence has been beneficial. Under this relation, the church has always presented itself as the interpreter and defender of two systems, the theocratic or the Roman imperial system, that is, of despotism, sometimes under a religious, and sometimes under a civil form. Take all her institutions, and all her legislation; take her canons and procedure; and you will always find, as the dominant principle, theocracy or the empire. If weak, the church sheltered herself under the absolute power of the emperors; if strong, she claimed the same absolutism on her own account, in the name of her spiritual power. We must not confine ourselves to particular facts or special instances. The church has, doubtless, often invoked the rights of the people against the bad government of the sovereigns; and often even approved of, and provoked insurrection; has often maintained, in face of the sovereign, the rights and interests of the people. But when the question of political guarantees has arisen between power and liberty, when the question was of establishing a system of permanent institutions, which might truly place liberty beyond the invasions of power, the church has generally ranged upon the side of despotism.

One need not be much astonished at this, nor charge the clergy with too great a degree of human weakness, nor suppose it a vice peculiar to the Christian church. There is a more profound and powerful cause. What does a religion pretend to? It pretends to govern the human passions and the human will. All religion is a restraint, a power, a government. It comes in the name of divine law, for the purpose of subduing human nature. It is human liberty, then, with which it chiefly concerns itself; it is human liberty which resists it, and which it wishes to overcome. Such is the enterprise of religion, such its mission and its hope.

It is true, that although human liberty is what religions concern themselves with, although they aspire to the reformation of the will of man, they have no moral means of acting upon him but through himself, by his own will. When they act by external means, by force, seduction, or any means, in fact, which are foreign to the free concurrence of man, when they treat him as they would water or wind, as a material power, they do not attain their end, they neither reach nor govern the human will. For religions to accomplish what they attempt, they must make themselves acceptable to liberty itself; it is needful that man should submit, but he must do so voluntarily and freely, and must preserve his liberty in the very heart of his submission. This is the double problem which religions are called upon to solve.

This they have too often overlooked; they have considered liberty as an obstacle, not as a means; they have forgotten the nature of the force to which they address themselves, and have treated the human soul as they would a material force. It is in following this error that they have almost always been led to range themselves on the side of power and despotism against human liberty, regarding it only as an adversary, and taking more pains to subdue than to secure it. If religions had turned their means of action to good account, if they had not allowed themselves to be carried away by a natural but deceitful inclination, they would have seen tnat it is necessary to guarantee liberty in order to regulate it morally; that religion cannot, nor ought to act except by moral means; they would have respected the will of man in applying themselves to govern it. This they have too often forgotten, and religious power has ended in itself suffering as much as liberty.

I will go no further in the examination of the general con sequence of the influence of the church upon European civilization. I have recapitulated them in this twofold result; a great and salutary influence upon the social and moral order, an influence rather unfortunate than beneficial on the political order, properly so called. We have now to verify our assertions by facts, to verify by history that which we have deduced from the mere nature and situation of the ecclesiastical society. Let us see what was the fate of the Christian church from the fifth to the twelfth century, and whether the principles which I have placed before you, and the results which I have attempted to draw from them, were really developed, as I have ventured to describe.

You should be careful not to suppose that these principles and consequences have appeared at the same periods, and with the same distinctness that I have represented them. It is a great and too common an error, when considering the past at the distance of many centuries, to forget the moral chronology, to forget (singular obliviousness!) that history is essentially successive. Take the life of a man, of Cromwell, Gustavus Adolphus, or cardinal Richelieu. He enters upon his career, he moves and progresses; he influences great events, and he in his turn is influenced by them; he arrives at the goal. We then know him; but it is in his whole, it is, as it were, such as he has issued after much labour from the workshop of Providence. But at starting he was not what he has thus become; he has never been complete and finished at any single period of his life; he has been formed progressively. Men are formed morally as physically; they change daily; their being modifies itself without ceasing; the Cromwell of 1650 was not the Cromwell of 1640. There is always a groundwork of individuality; it is always the same man who perseveres; but how changed are his ideas, sentiments, and will! What things has he lost and acquired! At whatever moment we look upon the life of man, there is no time when it has been what we shall see it when its term is attained.

It is here, however, that most historians have fallen into error; because they have gained one complete idea of man, they see him such throughout the whole course of his career. For them, it is the same Cromwell who enters parliament in 1628, and who dies thirty years afterwards in the palace of Whitehall. And with regard to institutions and general influences, they incessantly commit the same error. Let us guard against it; I have represented to you the principles of the church in their entirety, and the development of the consequences. But remember that historically the picture is not correct; all has been partial and successive, cast here and there over space and time. We must not expect to find this uniformity, this prompt and systematic connexion, in the recital of facts. Here we shall see one principle springing up, there another; all will be incomplete, unequal, and dispersed. We must come to modern times, to the end of the career, before we shall find the entire result. I shall now place before you the various states through which the church passed between the fifth and the twelfth century. We can not collect an entire demonstration of the assertions which I have placed before you, but we shall see sufficient to enable us to presume they are legitimate.

The first condition in which the church appears at the fifth century is the imperial state, the church of the Roman empire. When the Roman empire was on the decline, the church thought herself at the term of her career, and that her triumph was accomplished. It is true, she had completely vanquished paganism. The last emperor who took the rank of sovereign pontiff, which was a pagan dignity, was the emperor Gratian, who died at the end of the fourth century. Gratian was called sovereign pontiff, like Augustus and Tiberius. The church likewise thought herself at the end of her struggle with the heretics, especially with the Arians, the chief heretics of the day. The emperor Theodosius, towards the end of the fourth century, instituted against them a complete and severe legislation. The church then enjoyed the government and the victory over its two most formidable enemies. It was at this moment that she saw the Roman empire fail her, and found herself in the presence other pagans and heretics, in the presence of the barbarians, Goths, Vandals, Burgundians, and Franks. The fall was immense. You may easily conceive the lively attachment for the empire which must have been preserved in the bosom of the church. Thus we see her strongly adhering to what remained of it—to the municipal system and to absolute power. And when she had converted the barbarians, she attempted to resuscitate the empire; she addressed herself to the barbarous kings, conjured them to become Roman emperors, to take all the rights belonging to them, and enter into the same relations with the church as that which she had maintained with the Roman empire. This was the work of the bishops between the fifth and the sixth centuries, the general state of the church.

This attempt could not be successful; there were no means of re-forming the Roman society with barbarians. Like the civil world, the church herself fell into barbarism. This was its second state. When one compares the writings of the ecclesiastical chroniclers of the eighth century with those of preceding ages, the difference is immense. Every wreck of Roman civilization had disappeared, even the language; everything felt itself, as it were, cast into barbarism. On the one hand, barbarians entered the clerical order, and became priests and bishops; and on the other hand, the bishops adopted a life of barbarism, and without quitting their bishoprics, placed themselves at the head of bands, overrunning the country, pillaging, and making war, like the companions of Clovis. You will find in Gregory of Tours mention of several bishops, among others Salonus and Sagittarius, who thus passed their lives.

Two important facts developed themselves in the bosom of this barbarous church. The first is, the separation of spiritual and temporal power. This principle took its rise at this epoch. Nothing could be more natural. The church not having succeeded in resuscitating the absolute power of the Roman empire, and sharing it herself, was forced to seek safety in independence. It was necessary that she should defend herself on all sides, for she was continually threatened. Each bishop and priest saw his barbarous neighbours incessantly interfering in the affairs of the church, to usurp her riches, lands, and power; her only means of defence was to say, " The spiritual order is totally separate from the temporal; you have not the right to interfere in its affairs." This principle, above all others, became the defensive arm of the church against barbarism.

A second important fact belonged to this epoch, the development of the monastic order in the west. It is known that at the commencement of the sixth century, St. Benedict instituted his order among the monks of the west, who were then trifling in number, but who have since prodigiously increased. The monks at this epoch were not members of the clergy, they were still regarded as laymen. No doubt priests, or even bishops, were sought for among them; but it was only at the end of the fifth and beginning of the sixth century, that the monks, in general, were considered as forming a part of the clergy, properly so called. We then find that priests and bishops became monks, believing that by so doing they made a fresh progress in religious life. Thus the monastic order in Europe took all at once a great development. The monks struck the fancy of the barbarians far more than the secular clergy. Their number was as imposing as their singularity of life. The secular clergy, the bishop or simple priest, were common to the imagination of the barbarians, who were accustomed to see, maltreat, and rob them. It was a much more serious affair to attack a monastery, where so many holy men were congregated in one holy place. The monasteries, during the barbaric epoch, were an asylum for the church, as the church was for the laity. Pious men there found a refuge, as in the east they sheltered themselves in the Thebaid, to escape a worldly life and the temptations of Constantinople.

Such are the two great facts in the history of the church, which belong to the barbaric epoch; on one side, the development of the principle of separation between the spiritual and temporal power; on the other, the development of the monastic system in the west.

Towards the end of the barbaric epoch, there was a new attempt to resuscitate the Roman empire made by Charlemagne. The church and the civil sovereign again contracted a close alliance. This was an epoch of great docility, and hence one of great progress for papacy. The attempt again failed, and the empire of Charlemagne fell; but the advantages which the church had gained from his alliance still remained with

her. Papacy found herself definitively at the head of Chris
tianity.

On the death of Charlemagne, chaos recommenced; the
church again fell into it as well as civil society, and only left
it to enter the frame of feudalism. This was its third state.
By the dissolution of the empire of Charlemagne, there happened almost the same thing in the ecclesiastical order as in
the civil order; all unity disappeared, all became local, partial, and individual. There then commenced in the situation
of the clergy a struggle which it had never experienced
before. This was the struggle between the sentiments and
.nterests of the fief-holder, and the sentiments and interests of the priest. The chiefs of the church were placed
between these two positions, each tended to overcome the
other; the ecclesiastical spirit was no longer so powerful
or so universal; individual interest became more influential,
and the desire for independence and the habits of a feudal
life, loosened the ties of the ecclesiastical hierarchy. There
was then made in the bosom of the church an attempt to
remedy the effects of this relaxation. They sought in
various quarters, by a system of federation, and by communal
assemblies and deliberations, to organise national churches.
It is at this epoch, and under the feudal system, that we find
the greatest number of councils, convocations, and ecclesiastical assemblies, both provincial and national. It was in
France, more especially, that this attempt at unity seemed
followed with the greatest ardour. Hincmar, archbishop of
Rheims, may perhaps be considered as the representative of
this idea. His constant care was to organise the French
church; he sought and put in force all the means of correspondence and union which might bring back some unity into
the feudal church. We find Hincmar maintaining on the
one side the independence of the church with regard to its
temporal power, and on the other its independence with
regard to papacy; it was he who, knowing that the pope
wished to come into France, and threatened the bishops with
excommunication, said, *Si excommunicaturus venerit, excom-
municatus abibit.* But this attempt to organise the feudal
church succeeded no better than the attempt to organise the
imperial church had done. There were no means of establishing unity in this church. Its dissolution was always in-

creasing. Each bishop, prelate, and abbot, isolated himself more and more within his diocese or his monastery. The disorder increased from the same cause. This was the time of the greatest abuses of simony, of the entirely arbitrary disposition of ecclesiastical benefices, and of the greatest looseness of manners among the priests. This disorder greatly shocked the people and the better portion of the clergy. We thence see at an early time, a certain spirit of reform appear in the church, and the desire to seek some authority which could rally all these elements, and impose law upon them. Claude, bishop of Turin, and Agobard, archbishop of Lyons, originated in their dioceses some attempts of this nature; but they were not in a condition to accomplish such a work. There was within the whole church but one force adequate to it, and that was the court of Rome, the papacy. It was, therefore, not long ere it prevailed. The church passed during the course of the eleventh century into its fourth state, that of the theocratical or monastical church. The creator of this new form of church, in so far as a man can create, was Gregory VII.

We are accustomed, to represent to ourselves Gregory VII. as a man who wished to render all things immoveable, as an adversary to intellectual development and social progress, and as a man who strove to maintain the world in a stationary or retrograding system. Nothing can be so false. Gregory VII. was a reformer upon the plan of despotism, as were Charlemagne and Peter the Great. He, in the ecclesiastical order, was almost what Charlemagne in France, and Peter the Great in Russia were in the civil order. He wished to reform the church, and through the church to reform society, to introduce therein more morality, more justice, and more law—he wished to effect this through the holy see, and to its profit.

At the same time that he strove to subject the civil world to the church, and the church to papacy, with an aim of reform and progress, and not one of immobility or retrogression, an attempt of the same kind, and a similar movement, was produced in the heart of monasteries. The desire for order, discipline, and moral strictness, was zealously shown. It was at this period that Robert de Molême introduced a severe order at Citeaux. This was the age of St.

Norbert and the reform of the prebendaries, of the reform of Cluni; and lastly, of the great reform of St. Bernard. A general ferment reigned in the monasteries; the old monks defended themselves, declared it to be an injurious thing, said that their liberty was in danger, that the manners of the times must be complied with, that it was impossible to return to the primitive church, and treated all the reformers as madmen, dreamers, and tyrants. Open the history of Normandy, by Orderic Vital, and you will continually meet with these complaints.

All therefore seemed tending to the advantage of the church, to its unity and power. While papacy sought to seize upon the government of the world, and while monasteries reformed themselves in a moral point of view, some powerful though isolated men claimed for human reason its right to be considered as something in man, and its right to interfere in his opinions. The greater part of them did not attack received doctrines nor religious creeds; they only said that reason had a right to test them, and that it did not suffice that they should be affirmed upon authority. John Erigena, Roscelin, and Abailard were the interpreters through whom reason once more began to claim her inheritance; these were the first authors of the movement of liberty which is associated with the movement of reform of Hildebrand and St. Bernard. When we seek the dominant character of this movement, we find that it is not a change of opinion, or a revolt against the system of public creeds—it is simply the right of reasoning claimed on the behalf of reason. The pupils of Abailard asked him, as he himself tells us in his *Introduction to Theology*, "for philosophical argument calculated to satisfy the reason, supplicating him to instruct them, not to repeat what he taught them, but to understand it; because nothing can be believed without being understood, and it is ridiculous to preach things which neither he who professes, nor those whom he teaches, can understand. . . . . To what purpose were the study of philosophy, if not to lead to the study of God, to whom all things should be referred? With what view are the faithful permitted to read the writings which treat of the age and the books of the Gentiles, unless to prepare them for understanding the Holy Scriptures, and the necessary capacity for defending them? In this view, it is especially necessary to be aided with all the force of reason, so as to prevent, upon questions so difficult and complicated as are those which form the object of the Christian faith, the subtleties of its enemies from easily contriving to adulterate the purity of our faith."

The importance of this first attempt at liberty, this regeneration of the spirit of inquiry, was soon felt. Although occupied in reforming herself, the church did not the less take the alarm. She immediately declared war against these new reformers, whose methods menaced her more than their doctrines.

This is the great fact which shone forth at the end of the eleventh and beginning of the twelfth century, at the time when the state of the church was that of the theocratical or monastic. At this epoch, for the first time, there arose a struggle between the clergy and the freethinkers. The quarrels of Abailard and St. Bernard, the councils of Soissons and Sens, where Abailard was condemned, are nothing but the expression of this fact, which holds so important a position in the history of modern civilization. It was the principal circumstance in the state of the church at the twelfth century, at the point at which we shall now leave it.

At the same time, a movement of a different nature was produced, the movement for the enfranchisement of the boroughs. Singular inconsistency of rude and ignorant manners! If it had been said to the citizens who conquered their liberty with so much passion, that there were men who claimed the rights of human reason, the right of free inquiry —men whom the church treated as heretics—they would have instantly stoned or burnt them. More than once did Abailard and his friends run this risk. On the other hand, those very writers who claimed the rights of human reason, spoke of the efforts for the enfranchisement of the boroughs as of an abominable disorder, and overthrow of society. Between the philosophical and the communal movement, between the political and the rational enfranchisement, war seemed to be declared. Centuries were necessary to effect the reconciliation of these two great powers, and to make them understand that their interests were in common. At the twelfth century, they had nothing in common.

SEVENTH LECTURE.

Object of the Lecture—Comparative picture of the state of the boroughs at the twelfth and the eighteenth century—Double question—1st. The enfranchisement of the boroughs—State of the towns from the fifth to the tenth century—Their decay and regeneration—Communal insurrection—Charters—Social and moral effects of the enfranchisement of the boroughs—2nd. Internal government of the boroughs—Assemblies of the people—Magistrates—High and low burghership—Diversity of the state of the boroughs in the different countries of Europe.

WE have conducted, down to the twelfth century, the history of the two great elements of civilization, the feudal system and the church. It is the third of these fundamental elements, I mean the boroughs, which we now have to trace likewise down to the twelfth century, confining ourselves to the same limits which we have observed in the other two.

We shall find ourselves differently situated with regard to the boroughs, from what we were with regard to the church or the feudal system. From the fifth to the twelfth century, the feudal system and the church, although at a later period they experienced new developments, showed themselves almost complete, and in a definitive state; we have watched their birth, increase, and maturity. It is not so with the boroughs. It was only at the end of the epoch which now occupies us, in the eleventh and twelfth centuries, that they take up any position in history; not but that before then they had a history which was deserving of study; nor is it that there were not long before this epoch traces of their existence; but it was only at the eleventh century that they became evidently visible upon the great scene of the world, and as an important element of modern civilization. Thus, in the feudal system and the church, from the fifth to the twelfth century, we have

seen the effects born and developed from the causes. Whenever, by way of induction or conjecture, we have deduced certain principles and results, we have been able to verify them by
an inquiry into the facts themselves. As regards the boroughs,
this facility fails us; we are present only at their birth. At
present I must confine myself to causes and origins. What
I say concerning the effects of the existence of the boroughs,
and their influence in the course of European civilization, I
shall say in some measure by way of anticipation. I cannot
invoke the testimony of contemporaneous and known facts.
It is at a later period, from the twelfth to the fifteenth century,
that we shall see the boroughs taking their development, the
institution bearing all its fruit, and history proving our assertions. I dwell upon this difference of situation in order to
anticipate your objections against the incompleteness and pre-
maturity of the picture which I am about to offer you. I will
suppose, that in 1789, at the time of the commencement of
the terrible regeneration of France, a burgher of the twelfth
century had suddenly appeared among us, and that he had
been given to read, provided he knew how, one of the
pamphlets which so powerfully agitated mind; for example,
the pamphlet of M. Sieyes—"Who is the third estate?"
His eyes fall upon this sentence, which is the foundation of the pamphlet: "The third estate is the French
nation, less the nobility and the clergy." I ask you, what
would be the effect of such a phrase upon the mind of such a
man? Do you suppose he would understand it? No, he
could not understand the words, *the French nation*, because
they would represent to him no fact with which he was
acquainted, no fact of his age; and if he understood the
phrase, if he clearly saw in it this sovereignty attributed to
the third estate above all society, of a verity it would appear
to him mad, impious, such would be its contradiction to all
that he had seen, to all his ideas and sentiments.

Now, ask this astonished burgher to follow you; lead him
to one of the French boroughs of this epoch, to Rheims,
Beauvais, Laon, or Noyon; a different kind of astonishment
would seize him: he enters a town; he sees neither towers,
nor ramparts, nor burgher militia; no means of defence;
all is open, all exposed to the first comer, and the first occupant. The burgher would doubt the safety of this borough;

he would think it weak and ill-secured. He penetrates into the interior, and inquires what is passing, in what manner it is governed, and what are its inhabitants. They tell him, that beyond the walls there is a power which taxes them at pleasure, without their consent; which convokes their militia, and sends it to war, without their voice in the matter. He speaks to them of magistrates, of the mayor, and of the aldermen; and he hears that the burghers do not nominate them. He learns that the affairs of the borough are not decided in the borough; but that a man belonging to the king, an intendant, administers them, alone and at a distance. Furthermore, they will tell him that the inhabitants have not the right of assembling and deliberating in common upon matters which concern them; that they are never summoned to the public place by the bell of their church. The burgher of the twelfth century would be confounded. First, he was stupified and dismayed at the grandeur and importance that the communal nation, the third estate, attributed to itself; and now he finds it on its own hearthstone, in a state of servitude, weakness, and nonentity, far worse than anything which he had experienced. He passes from one spectacle to another utterly different, from the view of a sovereign burghership to that of one entirely powerless. How would you have him comprehend this,—reconcile it, so that his mind be not overcome.

Let us, burghers of the nineteenth century, go back to the twelfth, and be present at an exactly corresponding double spectacle. Whenever we regard the general affairs of a country, its state, government, the whole society, we shall see no burghers, hear speak of none; they interfere in nothing, and are quite unimportant. And not only have they no importance in the state, but if we would know what they think of their situation, and how they speak of it, and what their position in regard to their relation with the government of France in general is in their own eyes, we shall find in their language an extraordinary timidity and humility. Their ancient masters, the lords, from whom they forced their franchises, treat them, at least in words, with a haughtiness which confounds us; but it neither astonishes nor irritates them.

Let us enter into the borough itself; let us see what passes there. The scene changes; we are in a kind of fortified place defended by armed burghers: these burghers tax themselves, elect their magistrates, judge and punish, and assemble for the purpose of deliberating upon their affairs. All come to these assemblies; they make war on their own account against their lord; and they have a militia. In a word, they govern themselves; they are sovereigns. This is the same contrast which, in the France of the eighteenth century, so much astonished the burgher of the twelfth; it is only the parts that are changed. In the latter, the burgher nation is all, the borough nothing; in the former, the burghership is nothing, the borough everything.

Assuredly, between the twelfth and the eighteenth century, many things must have passed—many extraordinary events, and many revolutions have been accomplished, to bring about, in the existence of a social class, so enormous a change. Despite this change, there can be no doubt but that the third estate of 1789 was, politically speaking, the descendant and heir of the corporations of the twelfth century. This French nation, so haughty and ambitious, which raises its pretensions so high, which so loudly proclaims its sovereignty, which pretends not only to regenerate and govern itself, but to govern and regenerate the world, undoubtedly descends, principally at least, from the burghers who obscurely though courageously revolted in the twelfth century, with the sole end of escaping in some corner of the land from the obscure tyranny of the lords.

Most assuredly it is not in the state of the boroughs in the twelfth century that we shall find the explanation of such a metamorphosis: it was accomplished and had its causes in the events which succeeded it from the twelfth to the eighteenth century; it is there that we shall meet it in its progression. Still the origin of the third estate has played an important part in its history; although we shall not find there the secret of its destiny, we shall, at least, find its germ: for what it was at first is again found in what it has become, perhaps, even to a greater extent than appearances would allow of our presuming. A picture, even an incomplete one, of the state of the boroughs in the twelfth century, will, I think, leave you convinced of this.

The better to understand this state, it is necessary to consider the boroughs from two principal points of view. There are two great questions to resolve: the first, that of the enfranchisement of the boroughs itself—the question how the revolution was operated, and from what causes—what change it brought into the situation of the burghers, what effect it has had upon society in general, upon the other classes, and upon the state. The second question relates only to the government of the boroughs, the internal condition of the enfranchised towns, the relations of the burghers among themselves, and the principles, forms, and manners which dominated in the cities.

It is from these two sources, on the one hand, from the change introduced into the social condition of the burghers, and on the other, from their internal government and their communal condition, that all their influence upon modern civilization originated. There are no facts produced by this influence, but which should be referred to one or other of these causes. When, therefore, we shall have summed them up, when we thoroughly understand, on one side, the enfranchisement of the boroughs, and on the other, the government of the boroughs, we shall be in possession, so to speak, of the two keys to their history.

Lastly, I shall say a word concerning the various state of the boroughs throughout Europe. The facts which I am about to place before you do not apply indifferently to all the boroughs of the twelfth century, to the boroughs of Italy, Spain, England, or France; there are certainly some which belong to all, but the differences are great and important. I shall point them out in passing; we shall again encounter them in a later period of civilization, and we will then investigate them more closely.

To understand the enfranchisement of the boroughs, it is necessary to recal to your minds what was the state of the towns from the fifth to the eleventh century—from the fall of the Roman empire down to the commencement of the communal revolution. Here, I repeat, the differences were very great; the state of the towns varied prodigiously in the various countries of Europe; still there are general facts which may be affirmed of almost all towns; and I shall try to confine myself to them. When I depart from this restriction, what I say more especially will apply to the

x

boroughs of France, and particularly to the boroughs of the
north of France, beyond the Rhone and the Loire. These
will be the prominent points in the picture which I shall
attempt to trace.

After the fall of the Roman empire, from the fifth to the
tenth century, the condition of the towns was one neither
of servitude nor liberty. One runs the same risk in the
employment of words, that I spoke of the other day in the
painting of men and events. When a society and a language
has long existed, the words take a complete, determined,
and precise sense, a legal and official sense, in a manner.
Time has introduced into the sense of each term a multitude
of ideas, which arise the moment that it is pronounced, and
which, not belonging to the same date, are not applicable
alike to all times. For example, the words *servitude* and
liberty call to our minds in the present day ideas infinitely
more precise and complete than the corresponding facts of
the eighth, ninth, or tenth centuries. If we say that, at the
eighth century, the towns were in a state of liberty, we say
far too much; in the present day we attach a sense to the
word *liberty*, which does not represent the fact of the eighth
century. We shall fall into the same error if we say that
the towns were in a state of servitude, because the word
implies an entirely different thing from the municipal facts of
that period.

I repeat that, at that time, the towns were neither in a state
of servitude nor liberty; they suffered all the ills which accompany weakness; they were a prey to the violence and continual depredations of the strong; but yet, despite all these
fearful disorders, despite their impoverishment and depopulation, the towns had preserved, and did still preserve a
certain importance: in most of them there was a clergy, a
bishop, who by the great exercise of power and his influence
upon the population, served as a connecting link between
them and their conquerors, and thus maintained the town in
a kind of independence, and covered it with the shield of
religion. Moreover, there remained in the towns many
wrecks of Roman institutions. One meets at this epoch (and
many facts of this nature have been collected by M.M. de
Savigny and Hullman, Mademoiselle de Lézardiére, &c.)
with frequent convocations of the senate, of the curia; there

is mention made of public assemblies and municipal magistrates. The affairs of the civil order, wills, grants, and a multitude of acts of civil life, were legalised in the curia by its magistrates, as was the case in the Roman municipality. The remains of urban activity and liberty, it is true, gradually disappeared. Barbarism, disorder, and always increasing misfortunes, accelerated the depopulation. The establishment of the masters of the land in the rural districts, and the growing preponderance of agricultural life, were new causes of decay to the towns. The bishops themselves, when they had entered the frame of feudalism, placed less importance on their municipal existence. Finally, when feudalism had completely triumphed, the towns, without falling into the servitude of serfs, found themselves entirely in the hands of a lord, inclosed within some fief, and robbed of all the independence which had been left to them, even in the most barbarous times, in the first ages of the invasion. So that from the fifth century, down to the time of the complete organization of feudalism, the condition of the towns was always upon the decline.

When once feudalism was thoroughly established, when each man had taken his place, and was settled upon his land, when the wandering life had ceased, after some time the towns again began to acquire some importance, and to display anew some activity. It is, as you know, with human activity as with the fecundity of the earth; from the time that commotion ceases, it reappears and makes everything germinate and flourish. With the least glimpse of order and peace, man takes hope, and with hope goes to work. It was thus with the towns; the moment that feudalism was a little fixed, new wants sprang up among the fief-holders, a certain taste for progress and amelioration; to supply this want, a little commerce and industry reappeared in the towns of their domain; riches and population returned to them; slowly, it is true, but still they returned. Among the circumstances which contributed thereto, one, I think, is too little regarded; this is the right of sanctuary in the churches. Before the boroughs had established themselves, before their strength and their ramparts enabled them to offer an asylum to the afflicted population of the country, when as yet they had no safety but that afforded by the church, this sufficed to draw

x 2

into the towns many unhappy fugitives. They came to
shelter themselves in or around the church; and it was not
only the case with the inferior class, with serfs and boors, who
sought safety, but often with men of importance, rich outlaws.
The chronicles of the time are filled with examples of this
nature. One sees men, formerly powerful themselves, pursued
by a more powerful neighbour, or even by the king himself,
who abandon their domains, carrying with them all they can,
shut themselves up within a town, and putting themselves
under the protection of the church, become citizens. These
kind of refugees have not been, I think, without their influence upon the progress of the towns; they introduced into
them riches, and elements of a superior population to the
mass of their inhabitants. Besides. who knows not, that
when once an association is in part formed, men flock to
it, both because they find more safety, and also for the mere
sake of that sociability which never leaves them?

By the concurrence of all these causes, after the feudal
government was in some manner regulated, the towns regained
a little strength. Their security, however, did not return to
them in the same proportion. The wandering life had ceased,
it is true, but the wandering life had been for the conquerors,
for the new proprietors of the soil, a principal means of satisfying their passions. When they had wished to pillage, they
made an excursion, they went to a distance to seek another
fortune, another domain. When each was nearly established,
when it became necessary to renounce this conquering va-
grancy, there was no cessation of their avidity, their inordinate
wants, nor their violent desires. Their weight, then, fell on
the people nearest at hand, upon the towns. Instead of going
to a distance to pillage, they pillaged at home. The extor-
tions of the nobility upon the burgesses were redoubled from
the commencement of the tenth century. Whenever the proprietor of a domain in which a town was situated had any fit
of avarice to satisfy, it was upon the burgesses that he exercised his violence. This, above all, was the epoch in which
the complaints of the burgesses against the absolute want of
security of commerce, burst forth. The merchants, after
having made their journeys, were not permitted to enter their
towns in peace; the roads and approaches were incessantly
beset by the lord and his followers. The time at which

industry was recommencing, was exactly that in which security was most wanting. Nothing can irritate a man more than being thus interfered with in his work, and despoiled of the fruits which he had promised himself from it. He is far more annoyed and enraged than when harassed in an existence which has been some time fixed and monotonous, when that which is carried from him has not been the result of his own activity, has not excited in his bosom all the pleasures of hope. There is, in the progressive movement towards fortune of a man or a population, a principle of resistance against injustice and violence far more energetic than in any other situation.

This, then, was the position of the towns during the tenth century; they had more strength, more importance, more riches, and more interests to defend. At the same time, it was more than ever necessary to defend them, because this strength, these interests, these riches, became an object of envy to the lords. The danger and evil increased with the means of resisting them. Moreover, the feudal system gave to all those who participated in it the example of continued resistance; it never presented to the mind the idea of an organised government, capable of ruling and quelling all by imposing its single intervention. It offered, on the contrary, the continuous spectacle of the individual will refusing submission. Such, for the most part, was the position of the possessors of fiefs towards their superiors, of the lesser lords towards the greater; so that at the moment when the towns were tormented and oppressed, when they had new and most important interests to sustain, at that moment they had before their eyes a continual lesson of insurrection. The feudal system has rendered one service to humanity, that of incessantly showing to men the individual will in the full display of its energy. The lesson prospered: in spite of their weakness, in spite of the infinite inequality of condition between them and their lords, the towns arose in insurrection on all sides.

It is difficult to assign an exact date to this event. It is generally said, that the enfranchisement of the commons commenced in the eleventh century; but, in all great events, how many unhappy and unknown efforts occur, before the one which succeeds! In all things, to accomplish its designs, Providence lavishly expends courage, virtues, sacrifices, in a word, man himself; and it is only after an unknown number of unrecorded labours, after a host of noble hearts have succumbed in discouragement, convinced that their cause is lost, it is only then that the cause triumphs. It doubtless happened thus with the commons. Doubtless, in the eighth, ninth, and tenth centuries, there were many attempts at resistance, and movements towards enfranchisement, which not only were unsuccessful, but of which the memory remained alike without glory or success. It is true, however, that these attempts have influenced posterior events; they reanimated and sustained the spirit of liberty, and prepared the way for the great insurrection of the eleventh century.

I say designedly, insurrection. The enfranchisement of the commons in the eleventh century was the fruit of a veritable insurrection, and a veritable war, a war declared by the population of the towns against their lords. The first fact which is always met with in such histories, is the rising of the burgesses, who arm themselves with the first thing that comes to hand; the expulsion of the followers of the lord who have come to put in force some extortion; or it is an enterprise against the castle; these are always the characteristics of the war. If the insurrection fails, what is done by the conqueror? He orders the destruction of the fortifications raised by the citizens, not only round the town but round each house. One sees at the time of the confederation, after having promised to act in common, and after taking the oath of mutual aid, the first act of the citizen is to fortify himself within his house. Some boroughs, of which at this day the name is entirely obscure, as, for example, the little borough of Vezelay in Nivernois, maintained a very long and energetic struggle against their lord. Victory fell to the abbot of Vezelay; he immediately enjoined the demolition of the fortifications of the citizen's houses; the names of many are preserved, whose fortified houses were thus immediately destroyed.

Let us enter the interior of the habitations of our ancestors; let us study the mode of their construction and the kind of life which they suggest; all is devoted to war, all has the character of war.

This is the construction of a citizen's house in the twelfth century, as far as we can follow it out: there were generally three floors, with one room upon each floor; the room on the ground floor was the common room, where the family took their meals; the first floor was very high up, by way of security ; this is the most remarkable characteristic of the construction.   On this floor was the room which the citizen and his wife inhabited.   The house was almost always flanked by a tower at the angle, generally of a square form; another symptom of war, a means of defence.   On the second floor was a room, the use of which is doubtful, but which probably served for the children, and the rest of the family.   Above, very often, was a small platform, evidently intended for a place of observation.   The whole construction of the house suggests war.   This was the evident character, the true name of the movement which produced the enfranchisement of the commons.

When war has lasted a certain time, whoever may be the belligerent powers, it necessarily leads to peace.   The treaties of peace between the commons and their adversaries were the charters.   The borough charters are mere treaties of peace between the burgesses and their lord.

The insurrection was general.   When I say *general*, I do not mean that there was union or coalition between all the citizens in a country: far from it.   The situation of the commons was almost everywhere the same; they were everywhere a prey to the same danger, afflicted with the same evil. Having acquired almost the same means of resistance and defence, they employed them at nearly the same epoch.   Example, too, may have done something, and the success of one or two boroughs may have been contagious.   The charters seem sometimes to have been drawn after the same pattern; that of Noyon, for example, served as a model for those of Beauvais, St. Quentin, &c.   I doubt, however, whether example had so much influence as has been supposed.   Communications were difficult and rare, and hearsay vague and transient; it is more likely that the insurrection was the result of a similar situation, and of a general and spontaneous movement.   When I say, general, I mean to say that it took place almost everywhere; for, I repeat, that the movement was not unanimous and concerted, all was special and local : each borough was insurgent against its lord upon its own account; all passed in its own locality.

The vicissitudes of the struggle were great.   Not only did

success alternate, but even when peace seemed established, after the charter had been sworn to by each party, it was violated and eluded in every way. The kings played a great part in the alternations of this struggle. Of this I shall speak in detail when I treat of royalty itself. Its influence in the movement of communal enfranchisement has been sometimes praised, perhaps too highly; sometimes, I think, too much undervalued, and sometimes denied. I shall confine myself at present to saying that it frequently interfered, sometimes invoked by the boroughs and sometimes by the lords; that it has often played contrary parts; that it has acted sometimes on one principle, sometimes on another; that it has unceasingly changed its intentions, designs, and conduct; but that, upon the whole, it has done much, and with more of good than of evil effect.

Despite these vicissitudes, despite the continual violations of the charters, the enfranchisement of the boroughs was consummated in the twelfth century. All Europe, and especially France, which for a century had been covered with insurrections, was covered with charters more or less favourable; the corporations enjoyed them with more or less security, but still they enjoyed them. The fact prevailed, and the right was established.

Let us now attempt to discover the immediate results of this great fact, and what changes it introduced into the condition of the burgesses, in the midst of society.

In the first place, it changed nothing, at least not in the commencement, in the relations of the burgesses with the general government of the country—with what we of the present day call the state; they interfered no more in it than heretofore: all remained local, inclosed within the limits of the fief.

One circumstance, however, should modify this assertion: a bond now began to be established between the citizens and the king. At times, the burgesses had invoked the aid of the king against their lord, or his guarantee, when the charter was promised or sworn to. At other times, the lords had invoked the judgment of the king between themselves and the citizens. At the demand of either one or other of the parties in a multitude of different causes, royalty had interfered in the quarrel; from thence resulted a frequent relation, and sometimes a rather intimate one, between the burgesses and the king. It was by this relation that the burgesses approached the centre of the state, and began to have a connexion with the general government.

Notwithstanding that all remained local, a new and general class was created by the enfranchisement. No coalition had existed between the citizens; they had, as a class, no common and public existence. But the country was filled with men in the same situation, having the same interests, and the same manners, between whom a certain bond and unity could not fail of being gradually established, which should give rise to the *bourgeoisie*. The formation of a great social class, the bourgeoisie, was the necessary result of the local enfranchisement of the burghers.

It must not be imagined that this class was at this time that which it has since become. Not only has its situation changed, but its elements were entirely different: in the twelfth century it consisted almost entirely of merchants, traders carrying on a petty commerce, and of small proprietors either of land or houses, who had taken up their residence in the town. Three centuries after, the bourgeoisie comprehended besides, advocates, physicians, learned men of all sorts, and all the local magistrates. The bourgeoisie was formed gradually, and of very different elements; as a general thing, in its history no account is given of its succession or diversity. Wherever the bourgeoisie is spoken of, it seems to be supposed that at all epochs it was composed of the same elements. This is an absurd supposition. It is perhaps in the diversity of its composition at different epochs of history that we should look for the secret of its destiny. So long as it did not include magistrates nor men of letters, so long as it was not what it became in the sixteenth century, it possessed neither the same importance nor the same character in the state. To comprehend the vicissitudes of its fortune and power, it is necessary to observe in its bosom the successive rise of new professions, new moral positions, and a new intellectual state. In the twelfth century, I repeat, it was composed of only the small merchants, who retired into the towns after having made their purchases and sales, and of the proprietors of houses and small domains who had fixed their residence there. Here we see the European burgher class in its first elements.

The third great consequence of the enfranchisement of the

commons was the contest of classes, a contest which constitutes the fact itself, and which fills modern history. Modern
Europe was born from the struggle of the various classes of
society.   Elsewhere, as I have already observed, this struggle
led to very different results: in Asia, for example, one class
completely triumphed, and the government of castes succeeded
to that of classes, and society sunk into immobility. Thank
God, none of this has happened in Europe.   Neither of the
classes has been able to conquer or subdue the others; the
struggle, instead of becoming a principle of immobility, has
been a cause of progress; the relations of the principal classes
among themselves, the necessity under which they found
themselves of combating and yielding by turns; the variety of
their interests and passions, the desire to conquer without the
power to satisfy it; from all this has arisen perhaps the most
energetic and fertile principle of the development of European
civilization.   The classes have incessantly struggled; they
detested each other; an utter diversity of situation, of
interests, and of manners, produced between them a profound
moral hostility: and yet they have progressively approached
nearer, come to an understanding, and assimilated; every
European nation has seen the birth and development in its
bosom of a certain universal spirit, a certain community of
interests, ideas, and sentiments, which have triumphed over
diversity and war.   In France, for example, in the seventeenth and eighteenth centuries, the social and moral separation of the classes was still very profound; yet the fusion
was advancing; still, without doubt, at that time there was a
veritable French nation, not an exclusive class, but which
embraced them all, and in which all were animated by a
certain sentiment in common, having a common social existence, strongly impressed, in a word, with nationality. Thus,
from the bosom of variety, enmity, and war, has arisen in
modern Europe the national unity so striking in the present
day, and which tends to develop and refine itself, from day
to day, with still greater brilliancy.

   Such are the great external, apparent, and social effects of
the revolution which at present occupies us.   Let us investigate its moral effects, what changes it brought about in the
soul of the citizens themselves, what they became, what, in
fact, they necessarily became morally in their new situation.

There is a fact by which it is impossible not to be struck while contemplating the relation of the burghers towards the state in general, the government of the state, and the general interests of the country, not only in the twelfth century, but also in subsequent ages; I mean the prodigious timidity of the citizens, their humility, the excessive modesty of their pretensions as to the government of the country, and the facility with which they contented themselves. Nothing is seen among them of the true political spirit, which aspires to influence, reform, and govern; nothing which gives proof or boldness of thought, or grandeur of ambition: one might call sensible-minded, honest, freed men.

There are but two sources in the sphere of politics from which greatness of ambition or firmness of thought can arise. It is necessary to have either the feeling of immense importance, of great power exercised upon the destiny of others, and in a vast extent—or else it is necessary to bear within oneself a feeling of complete individual independence, a confidence in one's own liberty, a conviction of a destiny foreign to all will but that of the man himself. To one or other of these two conditions seem to belong boldness of thought, greatness of ambition, the desire of acting in an enlarged sphere, and of obtaining great results.

Neither one nor the other of these conditions entered into the condition of the burghers of the middle ages. These, as you have just seen, were only important to themselves; they exercised no sensible influence beyond their own town, or upon the state in general. Nor could they have any great sentiment of individual independence. It was in vain that they conquered, in vain that they obtained a charter. The citizen of a town, in comparing himself with the inferior lord who dwelt near him, and who had just been conquered, was not the less sensible of his extreme inferiority; he was not filled with the haughty sentiment of independence which animated the proprietor of the fief; he held not his portion of liberty from himself alone, but from his association with others; a difficult and precarious succour. Hence that character of reserve, of timidity of spirit, of retiring modesty, and humility of language, even in conjunction with a firmness of conduct, which is so deeply imprinted in the life of the citizens, not only in the twelfth century, but even of their

descendants. They had no taste for great enterprises; and
when fate forced them among them, they were uneasy and
embarrassed; the responsibility annoyed them; they felt that
they were out of their sphere of action, and wished to return
to it; they therefore treated on moderate terms. Thus one
finds in the course of European history, especially of France,
that the bourgeoisie has been esteemed, considered, flattered,
and even respected, but rarely feared; it has rarely produced
upon its adversaries an impression of a great and haughty
power, of a truly political power. There is nothing to be
surprised at in this weakness of the modern bourgeoisie;
its principal cause lay in its very origin, and in the circumstances of its enfranchisement, which I have just placed
before you. A high ambition, independently of social conditions, enlargement and firmness of political thought, the
desire to participate in the affairs of the country, the full
consciousness of the greatness of man as man, and of the
power which belongs to him, if he is capable of exercising it,
these are in Europe sentiments and dispositions entirely
modern, the fruit of modern civilization, the fruit of that
glorious and powerful universality which characterizes it, and
which cannot fail of insuring to the public an influence
and weight in the government of the country, which were
always wanting, and necessarily so, to the burghers our
ancestors.

On the other hand, they acquired and displayed, in the
struggle of local interests which they had to maintain in
their narrow stage, a degree of energy, devotedness, perseverance, and patience, which has never been surpassed. The
difficulty of the enterprise was such, and such the perils
which they had to strive against, that a display of unex-
ampled courage was necessary. In the present day, a very
false idea is formed of the life of the burghers in the twelfth
and thirteenth centuries. You have read in one of the novels
of Walter Scott, *Quentin Durward*, the representation he
has given of the burgomaster of Liege; he has made of him
a regular burgher in a comedy, fat, indolent, without experience or boldness, and wholly occupied in passing his life
easily. Whereas, the burghers of this period always had a
coat of mail upon their breast, a pike in their hand; their life
was as tempestuous, as warlike, and as hardy, as that of the

lords with whom they fought. It was in these continual perils, in struggling against all the difficulties of practical life, that they acquired that manly character, and that obstinate energy, which is, in a measure, lost in the soft activity of modern times.

None of these social or moral effects of the enfranchisement of the boroughs had attained their development in the twelfth century; it is in the following centuries that they distinctly appeared, and are easily discernible. It is certain, however, that the germ was laid in the original situation of the boroughs, in the manner of their enfranchisement, and the place then taken by the burghers in society. I was, therefore, right in placing them before you alone. Let us now investigate the interior of the borough of the twelfth century; let us see how it was governed, what principles and facts dominated in the relations of the citizens among themselves.

You will recollect that in speaking of the municipal system, bequeathed by the Roman empire to the modern world, I told you that the Roman empire was a great coalition of municipalities, formerly sovereign municipalities like Rome itself. Each of these towns had originally possessed the same existence as Rome, had once been a small independent republic, making peace and war, and governing itself as it thought proper. In proportion as they became incorporated with the Roman empire, the rights which constitute sovereignty, the right of peace and war, the right of legislation, the right of taxation, &c., left each town and centred in Rome. There remained but one sovereign municipality, Rome, reigning over a large number of municipalities which had now only a civil existence. The municipal system changed its character; and instead of being a political government and a system of sovereignty, it became a mode of administration.

This was the great revolution which was consummated under the Roman empire. The municipal system became a mode of administration, was reduced to the government of local affairs, and the civic interests of the city. This was the condition in which the towns and their institutions were left at the fall of the Roman empire. In the midst of the chaos of barbarism, all ideas, as well as facts, were in utter confusion; all the attributes of sovereignty and of the administration were confounded. These distinctions were no

longer attended to.   Affairs were abandoned to the course of
necessity.   There was a sovereign or an administrator, in each
locality, according to circumstances.   When the towns rose
in insurrection, to recover some security, they took upon
themselves the sovereignty.   It was not, in any way, for the
purpose of following out a political theory, nor from a feeling
of their dignity; it was that they might have the means of
resisting the lords against whom they rebelled that they
appropriated to themselves the right of levying militia, of
taxation for the purposes of war, of themselves nominating
their chiefs and magistrates; in a word, of governing themselves.   The government in the interior of the towns was
the means of defence and security.   Thus sovereignty re-
entered the municipal system, from which it had been eradi-
cated by the conquests of Rome.   The boroughs again became
sovereign.   We have here the political character of their
enfranchisement.

It does not follow that this sovereignty was complete.   It
always retained some trace of external sovereignty: sometimes the lord preserved to himself the right of sending
a magistrate into the town, who took for his assessors the
municipal magistrates; sometimes he possessed the right of
receiving certain revenues; elsewhere, a tribute was secured
to him.   Sometimes the external sovereignty of the community lay in the hands of the king.

The boroughs themselves having entered within the frame
of feudalism, had vassals, became suzerains, and by virtue
of this title partly possessed themselves of the sovereignty
which was inherent in the lord paramount.   This caused a
confusion between the rights which they had from their
feudal position, and those which they had conquered by their
insurrections; and under this double title the sovereignty
belonged to them.

Thus we see, as far as can be judged from very deficient
monuments, how government was administered, at least in the
early ages, in the interior of a borough.   The totality of the
inhabitants formed the assembly of the borough; all those who
had sworn the borough oath (and whoever lived within the
walls was obliged to do so) were convoked by the ringing of
a bell to the general assembly.   It was there that they
nominated the magistrates.   The number and form of the

magistracy were very various. The magistrates being once nominated, the assembly was dissolved, and the magistrates governed almost alone, somewhat arbitrarily, and without any other responsibility than that of the new elections, or popular riots, which were the chief mode of responsibility in those times.

You see that the internal organization of boroughs reduced itself to two very simple elements; the general assembly of the inhabitants, and a government invested with an almost arbitrary power, under the responsibility of insurrections and riots. It was impossible, principally from the state of manners, to establish a regular government, with veritable guarantees for order and duration. The greater portion of the population of the boroughs was in a state of ignorance, brutality, and ferocity, which it would have been very difficult to govern. After a short time, there was almost as little security in the interior of the borough as there had formerly been in the relations between the burgher and the lord. There was formed, however, very quickly a superior bourgeoisie. You easily comprehend the causes. The state of ideas and of social relations led to the establishment of industrial professions, legally constituted corporations. The system of privilege was introduced into the interior of boroughs, and from this a great inequality ensued. There was shortly everywhere a certain number of rich and important burghers, and a working population more or less numerous, which, in spite of its inferiority, had an important influence in the affairs of the borough. The boroughs were then divided into a high bourgeoisie, and a population subject to all the errors and vices of a populace. The superior bourgeoisie found itself pressed between the immense difficulty of governing the inferior population, and the incessant attempts of the ancient master of the borough, who sought to re-establish his power. Such was its situation, not only in France but in all Europe, down to the sixteenth century. This perhaps has been the chief means of preventing the corporations, in most European nations, and especially in France, from possessing all the important political influence which they might otherwise have had. Two principles carried on incessant warfare within them; in the inferior population, a blind, unbridled, and ferocious spirit of democracy; and, as a consequence, in the superior population, a spirit of timidity at making agreements, an excessive facility of con ciliation, whether in regard to the king, the ancient lords, or in re-establishing some peace and order in the interior of the borough. Each of these principles could not but tend to deprive the corporation of any great influence in the state.

All these effects were not visible in the twelfth century; still, however, one might foresee them in the very character of the insurrection, in the manner of its commencement, and in the condition of the various elements of the communal population.

Such, if I mistake not, are the principal characteristics and the general results of the enfranchisement of the boroughs and of their internal government. I forewarn you, that these facts were neither so uniform nor so universal as I have broadly represented them. There is great diversity in the history of boroughs in Europe. For example, in Italy and in the south of France, the Roman municipal system dominated; there was not nearly so much diversity and inequality here as in the north, and the communal organization was much better, either by reason of the Roman traditions, or from the superior condition of the population. In the north, the feudal system prevailed in the communal existence; there, all was subordinate to the struggle against the lords. The boroughs of the south were more occupied with their internal organization, amelioration, and pro gress; they thought only of becoming independent republics. The destiny of the northern boroughs, in France particu larly, showed themselves more and more incomplete, and destined for less fine developments. If we glance at the boroughs of Germany, Spain, and England, we shall find in them other differences. I shall not enter into these details; we shall remark some of them as we advance in the history of civilization. In their origin, all things are nearly confounded under one physiognomy; it is only by successive developments that variety shows itself. Then commences a new development which urges society towards free and high unity, the glorious end of all the efforts and wishes of the human race.

EIGHTH LECTURE.

Object of the lecture—Glance at the general history of European civilization—Its distinctive and fundamental character—Epoch at which that
character began to appear—State of Europe from the twelfth to the
sixteenth century—Character of the crusades—Their moral and social
causes—These causes no longer existed at the end of the thirteenth
century—Effects of the crusades upon civilization.

I HAVE not as yet explained to you the complete plan of my
course. I commenced by indicating its object; I then passed in
review European civilization without considering it as a whole,
without indicating to you at one and the same time the point
of departure, the route, and the port, the commencement, the
middle, and the end. We have now, however, arrived at an
epoch when this entire view, this general sketch of the region
which we survey, has become necessary. The times which
have hitherto occupied us in some measure explain themselves, or are explained by immediate and evident results.
Those upon which we are about to enter would not be understood, nor even would they excite any lively interest, unless
they are connected with even the most indirect and distant
of their consequences.

In so extensive a study, moments occur when we can no
longer consent to proceed, while all before us is unknown
and dark; we wish not only to know whence we have come
and where we are, but also to what point we tend. This is
what we now feel. The epoch to which we are approaching
is not intelligible, nor can its importance be appreciated
except by the relations which unite it to modern times. Its
true meaning is not evident until a later period.

We are in possession of almost all the essential elements
of European civilization. I say almost, because as yet I have

L

not spoken to you of royalty. The decisive crisis of the development of royalty did not take place until the twelfth or even thirteenth century; it was not until then that the institution was really constituted, and that it began to occupy a definite place in modern society. I have, therefore, not treated of it earlier; it will form the subject of my next lecture. With this exception, I repeat, we have before us all the great elements of European civilization: you have beheld the birth of feudal aristocracy, of the church, the boroughs; you have seen the institutions which should correspond to these facts; and not only the institutions, but also the principles and ideas which these facts should raise up in the mind. Thus, while treating of feudalism, you were present at the cradle of the modern family, at the hearth of domestic life; you have comprehended, in all its energy, the sentiment of individual independence, and the place which it has held in our civilization. With regard to the church, you have seen the purely religious society rise up, its relations with the civil society, the theocratical principle, the separation of the spiritual and temporal powers, the first blows of persecutions, and the first cries of the liberty of conscience. The rising boroughs have shown you glimpses of an association founded upon altogether other principles than those of feudalism and the church, the diversity of the social classes, their struggles, the first and profound characteristics of modern burgher manners, timidity of spirit side by side with energy of soul, the demagogue spirit side by side with the legal spirit. In a word, all the elements which have contributed to the formation of European society, all that it has been, and, so to speak, all that it has suggested, have already met your view.

Let us now transport ourselves to the heart of modern Europe: I speak not of existing Europe, after the prodigious metamorphoses which we have witnessed, but of Europe in the seventeenth and eighteenth centuries. I ask you, do you recognise the society which we have just seen in the twelfth century? What a wonderful difference! I have already dwelt upon this difference as regards the boroughs: I afterwards tried to make you sensible of how little the third estate of the eighteenth century resembled that of the twelfth. If we make the same essay upon feudalism and the church, we shall be struck with the same metamorphosis. There was no more resemblance between the nobility of the court of Louis XV. and the feudal aristocracy, or between the church of cardinal de Bernis and that of the abbot Suger, than between the third estate of the eighteenth century and the bourgeoisie of the twelfth century. Between these two epochs, although already in possession of all its elements, society was entirely transformed.

I wish to establish clearly the general and essential character of this transformation. From the fifth to the twelfth century, society contained all that I have described. It possessed kings, a lay aristocracy, a clergy, burghers, labourers, religious and civil powers—in a word, the germs of every-- thing which is necessary to form a nation and a government, and yet there was neither government nor nation. Throughout the epoch upon which we are occupied, there was nothing bearing a resemblance to a people, properly so called, nor to a veritable government, in the sense which the words have for us in the present day. We have encountered a multitude of particular forces, of special facts, and local institutions; but nothing general or public; no policy, properly so called, nor no true nationality.

Let us regard, on the contrary, the Europe of the seventeenth and eighteenth centuries; we shall everywhere see two leading figures present themselves upon the scene of the world, the government, and the people. The action of a universal power upon the whole country, and the influence of the country upon the power which governs it, this is society, this is history: the relations of the two great forces, their alliance, or their struggle, this is what history discovers and relates. The nobility, the clergy, and the burghers, all these particular classes and forces, now only appear in a secondary rank, almost like shadows effaced by those two great bodies, the people and its government.

This, if I mistake not, is the essential feature which distinguishes modern from primitive Europe; this is the metamorphosis which was accomplished from the thirteenth to the sixteenth centuries.

It is, then, from the thirteenth to the sixteenth century, that is to say, in the period which we are about to enter upon, that the secret of this must be sought for; it is the distinctive cha-

L 2

racter of this epoch that it was employed in converting primitive Europe into modern Europe; and hence its historical importance and interest. If it is not considered from this point of
view, and unless we everywhere seek what has arisen from it,
not only will it not be understood, but we shall soon be
weary of, and annoyed by it. Indeed, viewed in itself, and
apart from its results, it is a period without character, a period
when confusion continues to increase, without our being able
to discover its causes, a period of movement without direction,
and of agitation without result. Royalty, nobility, clergy,
bourgeoisie, all the elements of social order seem to turn
in the same circle, equally incapable of progress or repose.
They make attempts of all kinds, but all fail; they attempt
to settle governments, and to establish public liberties; they
even attempt religious reforms, but nothing is accomplished
—nothing perfected. If ever the human race has been
abandoned to a destiny, agitated and yet stationary, to labour
incessant, yet barren of effect, it was between the thirteenth
and the fifteenth centuries that such was the physiognomy of
its condition and its history.

I know of but one work in which this physiognomy is
truly shown; the *Histoire des ducs de Bourgogne*, by M. de
Barante. I do not speak of the truth which sparkles in the
descriptions of manners, or in the detailed recital of facts, but
of that universal truth which makes the entire book a faithful
image, a sincere mirror of the whole epoch, of which it at
the same time shows the movement and the monotony.

Considered, on the contrary, in its relation to that which
follows, as the transition from the primitive to the modern
Europe, this epoch brightens and becomes animated; we discover in it a totality, a direction, and a progress; its unity
and interest consist in the slow and secret work which is
accomplished in it.

The history of European civilization may then be summed
up into three grand periods:—1st, A period which I shall
call the period of origins, of formation—a time when the
various elements of our society freed themselves from the
chaos, took being, and showed themselves under their native
forms with the principles which animated them. This period
extended nearly to the twelfth century. 2nd, The second
period is a time of essay, of trial, of groping; the various

elements of the social order drew near each other, combined, and, as it were, felt each other, without the power to bring forth anything general, regular, or durable. This state was not ended, properly speaking, till the sixteenth century. 3rd, The period of development, properly so called, when society in Europe took a definite form, followed a determined tendency, and progressed rapidly and universally towards a clear and precise end. This commenced at the sixteenth century, and now pursues its course.

Such appears to me to be the spectacle of European civilization in its whole, and such I shall endeavour to represent it to you. It is the second period that we enter upon now. We have to seek in it the great crises and determinative causes of the social transformation which has been the result of it.

The crusades constitute the first great event which presents itself to us, which, as it were, opens the epoch of which we speak. They commenced at the eleventh century, and extended over the twelfth and thirteenth. Of a surety, a great event; for since it was completed, it has not ceased to occupy philosophic historians; even before reading the account of it, all have foreseen that it was one of those events which change the condition of the people, and which it is absolutely necessary to study in order to comprehend the general course of facts.

The first characteristic of the crusades is their universality; the whole of Europe joined in them—they were the first European event. Previously to the crusades, Europe had never been excited by one sentiment, or acted in one cause; there was no Europe. The crusades revealed Christian Europe. The French formed the vans of the first army of crusaders; but there were also Germans, Italians, Spaniards, and English. Observe the second, the third crusade; all the Christian nations engaged in it. Nothing like it had yet been seen.

This is not all: just as the crusades form an European event, so in each country do they form a national event. All classes of society were animated with the same impression, obeyed the same idea, abandoned themselves to the same impulse. Kings, lords, priests, burghers, countrymen, all took the same part, the same interest in the crusades. The

moral unity of nations was shown—a fact as novel as the
European unity.

When such events happen in the infancy of a people, at a
time when men act freely and spontaneously, without premeditation, without political intention or combination, one
recognises therein what history calls heroic events—the heroic
age of nations. In fact, the crusades constitute the heroic
event of modern Europe—a movement at once individual
and general, national, and yet unregulated.

That such was really their primitive character is verified
by all documents, proved by all facts. Who were the first
crusaders that put themselves in motion? Crowds of the
populace, who set out under the guidance of Peter the Hermit,
without preparation, without guides, and without chiefs, followed rather than guided by a few obscure knights; they
traversed Germany, the Greek empire, and dispersed or
perished in Asia Minor.

The superior class, the feudal nobility, in their turn became
eager in the cause of the crusade. Under the command of
Godefroi de Bouillon, the lords and their followers set out full
of ardour. When they had traversed Asia Minor, a fit of indifference and weariness seized the chiefs of the crusaders. They
cared not to continue their route; they united to make conquests
and establish themselves. The common people of the army
rebelled; they wished to go to Jerusalem—the deliverance of
Jerusalem was the aim of the crusade; it was not to gain
principalities for Raimond de Toulouse, nor for Bohemond,
nor for any other, that the crusaders came. The popular,
national, and European impulsion was superior to all individual wishes; the chiefs had not sufficient ascendancy over the
masses to subdue them to their interests. The sovereigns,
who had remained strangers to the first crusade, were at last
carried away by the movement, like the people. The great
crusades of the twelfth century were commanded by kings.

I pass at once to the end of the thirteenth century. People
still spoke in Europe of the crusades, they even preached
them with ardour. The popes excited the sovereigns and
the people—they held councils in recommendation of the Holy
Land; but no one went there—it was no longer cared for.
Something had passed into the European spirit and European
society that put an end to the crusades. There were still

some private expeditions. A few lords, a few bands, still set out for Jerusalem; but the general movement was evidently stopped; and yet it does not appear that either the necessity or the facility of continuing it had disappeared. The Moslems triumphed more and more in Asia. The Christian kingdom founded at Jerusalem had fallen into their hands. It was necessary to reconquer it; there were greater means of success than they had at the commencement of the crusades; a large number of Christians were established, and still powerful, in Asia Minor, Syria, and Palestine. They were better acquainted with the means of travelling and acting. Still nothing could revive the crusades. It was clear that the two great forces of society—the sovereigns on one side and the people on the other—were averse to it.

It has often been said that this was lassitude—that Europe was tired of thus falling upon Asia. We must come to an understanding upon this word *lassitude*, which is so often used upon similar occasions; it is strangely inexact. It is not possible that human generations can be weary with what they have never taken part in; weary of the fatigues undergone by their forefathers. Weariness is personal, it cannot be transmitted like a heritage. Men in the thirteenth century were not fatigued by the crusades of the twelfth: they were influenced by another cause. A great change had taken place in ideas, sentiments, and social conditions. There were no longer the same wants and desires. They no longer thought or wished the same things. It is these political or moral metamorphoses, and not weariness, which explain the different conduct of successive generations. The pretended lassitude which is attributed to them is a false metaphor.

Two great causes, one moral and the other social, threw Europe into the crusades. The moral cause, as you know, was the impulsion of religious sentiment and creeds. Since the end of the seventh century, Christianity had been struggling against Mahommedanism; it had conquered it in Europe after being dangerously menaced; it had succeeded in confining it to Spain. Thence also it still constantly strove to expel it. The crusades have been represented as a kind of accident, as an event unforeseen, unheard of, born solely of the recitals of pilgrims on their return from Jerusalem, and of the preachings of Peter the Hermit. It was nothing of the kind.

The crusades were the continuation, the zenith of the grand struggle which had been going on for four centuries between Christianity and Mahommedanism. The theatre of this struggle had been hitherto in Europe; it was now transported into Asia. If I put any value upon those comparisons and parallels, into which some people delight at times to press, suitably, or not, historical facts, I might show you Christianity running precisely the same career in Asia, and undergoing the same destiny as Mahommedanism in Europe. Mahommedanism was established in Spain, and had there conquered and founded a kingdom and principalities. The Christians did the same in Asia. They there found themselves, with regard to Mahommedans, in the same situation as the latter in Spain with regard to the Christians. The kingdom of Jerusalem and the kingdom of Grenada correspond to each other. But these similitudes are of little importance. The great fact is the struggle of the two social and religious systems; and of this the crusades was the chief crisis. In that lies their historical character, the connecting link which attaches them to the totality of facts.

There was another cause, the social state of Europe in the eleventh century, which no less contributed to their outburst. I have been careful to explain why, between the fifth and the eleventh century, nothing general could be established in Europe. I have attempted to show how everything had become local, how States, existences, minds, were confined within a very limited horizon. It was thus feudalism had prevailed. After some time, an horizon so restricted did not suffice; human thought and activity desired to pass beyond the circle in which they had been confined. The wandering life had ceased, but not the inclination for its excitement and adventures. The people rushed into the crusades as into a new existence, more enlarged and varied, which at one time recalled the ancient liberty of barbarism, at others opened out the perspective of a vast future.

Such, I believe, were the two determinating causes of the crusades of the twelfth century. At the end of the thirteenth century, neither of these causes existed. Men and society were so much changed, that neither the moral impulsion nor the social need which had precipitated Europe upon Asia, was any longer felt. I do not know if many of you have read the original historians of the crusades, or whether it has ever occurred to you to compare the contemporaneous chroniclers of the first crusades, with those at the end of the twelfth and thirteenth centuries; for example, Albert d'Aix, Robert the Monk, and Raymond d'Agiles, who took part in the first crusade, with William of Tyre and James de Vitry. When we compare these two classes of writers, it is impossible not to be struck by the distance which separates them. The first are animated chroniclers, full of vivid imagination, who recount the events of the crusades with passion. But they are, at the same time, men of very narrow minds, without an idea beyond the little sphere in which they have lived; strangers to all science, full of prejudices, and incapable of forming any judgment whatever upon what passes around them, or upon the events which they relate. Open, on the contrary, the history of the crusades by William of Tyre: you will be surprised to find almost an historian of modern times, a mind developed, extensive and free, a rare political understanding of events, completeness of views, a judgment bearing upon causes and effects. James de Vitry affords an example of a different kind of development; he is a scholar, who not only concerns himself with what has reference to the crusades, but also occupies himself with manners, geography, ethnography, natural history; who observes and describes the country. In a word, between the chroniclers of the first crusades and the historians of the last, there is an immense interval, which indicates a veritable revolution in mind.

This revolution is above all seen in the manner in which each speaks of the Mahommedans. To the first chroniclers, and consequently to the first crusaders, of whom the first chroniclers are but the expression, the Mahommedans are only an object of hatred. It is evident that they knew nothing of them, that they weighed them not, considered them not, except under the point of view of the religious hostility which existed between them; we discover no trace of any social relation; they detested and fought them, and that was all. William of Tyre, James de Vitry, and Bernard the Treasurer, speak quite differently of the Mussulmans: one feels that, although fighting them, they do not look upon them as mere monsters; that to a certain point they have entered into their ideas; that they have lived with them, that there is a sort of relation, and

even a kind of sympathy established between them. William
of Tyre warmly eulogises Noureddin—Bernard the Treasurer, Saladin. They even go so far as to compare the manners and conduct of the Mussulmans with those of the Christians; they take advantage of the Mussulmans to satirize the
Christians, as Tacitus painted the manners of the Germans
in contrast with the manners of the Romans. You see how
enormous the change between the two epochs must have
been, when you find in the last, with regard to the enemies
of the Christians, to those against whom the crusades were
directed, a liberty and impartiality of spirit which would have
filled the first crusaders with surprise and indignation.

This, then, was the first and principal effect of the crusades,
a great step towards the enfranchisement of mind, a great
progress towards more extensive and liberal ideas. Commenced
in the name and under the influence of religious creeds, the
crusades removed from religious ideas, I will not say their
legitimate influence, but the exclusive and despotic possession
of the human mind. This result, doubtless altogether unforeseen, was born of many causes. The first is evidently the
novelty, extension, and variety of the spectacle which was
opened to the view of the crusaders. It happened with them
as with travellers. It is a common saying that the mind of
travellers becomes enlarged; that the habit of observing various
nations and manners, and different opinions, extends the ideas,
and frees the judgment from old prejudices. The same fact
was accomplished among these travelling nations who were
called crusaders: their minds were opened and elevated, by
seeing a multitude of different things, and by observing other
manners than their own. They also found themselves in
juxtaposition with two civilizations, not only different from
their own, but more advanced; the Greek on the one hand,
and the Mahommedan on the other. There can be no doubt
that the Greek society, although enervated, perverted, and
falling into decay, had upon the crusaders the effect of a more
advanced, polished, and enlightened society than their own.
The Mahommedan society afforded them a spectacle of the
same nature. It is curious to observe in the old chronicles
the impression which the crusaders made upon the Mussul
mans; these latter regarded them at first as barbarians, as
the rudest, most ferocious, and most stupid class of men they

had ever seen. The crusaders, on their part, were struck with the riches and elegance of manners of the Mussulmans. To this first impression succeeded frequent relations between the two people. These extended and became much more important than is generally supposed. Not only had the Christians of the east habitual relations with the Mussulmans, but the west and the east became acquainted, visited and mixed with each other. It is not long since that one of those scholars who honour France in the eyes of Europe, M. Abel Remusat, discovered the existence of relations between the Mongol emperors and the Christian kings. Mongol ambassadors were sent to the Frank kings, to Saint Louis among others, to treat for an alliance with them, and to recommence the crusades in the common interest of the Mongols and the Christians against the Turks. And not only were diplomatic and official relations thus established between the sovereigns; frequent and various national relations were formed. I quote the words of M. Abel Remusat.[1]

"Many Italian, French, and Flemish monks, were charged with diplomatic missions to the Great Khan. Mongols of distinction came to Rome, Barcelona, Valentia, Lyons, Paris, London, Northampton; and a Franciscan of the kingdom of Naples was archbishop of Pekin. His successor was a professor of theology of the faculty of Paris. But how many others, less known, were drawn after these, either as slaves, or attracted by the desire for gain, or guided by curiosity into countries till then unknown! Chance has preserved the names of some: the first who came to visit the king of Hungary, on the part of the Tartars, was an Englishman, banished from his country for certain crimes, and who, after wandering all over Asia, ended by taking service among the Mongols. A Flemish shoemaker met in the depths of Tartary a woman from Metz, named Paquette, who had been carried off from Hungary; a Parisian goldsmith, whose brother was established at Paris, upon the great bridge; and a young man from the environs of Rouen, who had been at the taking of Belgrade. He saw, also, Russians, Hungarians, and Flemings. A chorister, named Robert, after having travelled over

---

[1] *Mémoires sur les Relations Politiques des Princes Chrétiens avec les Empereurs Mongols.* Deuxième Mémoire, pp. 154—157.

Eastern Asia, returned to finish his days in the cathedral of Chartres. A Tartar was purveyor of helmets in the army of Philip the Handsome; John de Plancarpin found near Gayouk a Russian gentleman, whom he calls Temer, who was serving as an interpreter; many merchants of Breslaw, Poland, and Austria, accompanied him in his journey to Tartary. Others returned with him by way of Russia; these were Genoese, Pisans, and Venetians. Two merchants, whom chance had led to Bokhara, consented to follow a Mongol ambassador sent by Koulagou to Khoubilai. They sojourned several years both in China and Tartary, returned with letters from the Great Khan to the pope; again returned to the Great Khan, taking with them the son of one of them, the celebrated Marco Polo, and again quitted the court of Khoubilai to return to Venice. Travels of this kind were not less frequent in the following century. Among the number are those of Sir John Mandeville, an English physician, of Oderic of Friuli, of Pegoletti, of William de Bouldeselle, and several others; and we may suppose, that those whose memorials are preserved, form but the least part of what were undertaken, and that there were at this period more persons capable of executing long journeys than of writing an account of them. Many of these adventurers remained and died in the countries which they visited. Others returned to their country as obscure as when they left it; but with an imagination filled with what they had seen, relating it to their family, exaggerating, no doubt, but leaving around them, amidst absurd fables, useful remembrances and traditions capable of bearing fruit. Thus in Germany, Italy, and France, in the monasteries, in the castles of the lords, and even down to the lowest ranks of society, were deposited precious seeds destined before long to germinate. All these unknown travellers carried the arts of their native land into the most distant countries, brought back other knowledge no less precious, and thus made, without being aware of it, more advantageous exchanges than all those of commerce. By these means, not only the trade in silk, porcelain, and Indian commodities was extended and facilitated—new routes opened to commercial industry and activity —but, what was of much more importance, foreign manners, unknown nations, extraordinary productions, offered themselves in crowds to the minds of the Europeans, confined, since the fall of the Roman empire, within too narrow a circle. They began to know the value of the most beautiful, the most populous, and the most anciently civilized of the four quarters of the globe. They began to study the arts, creeds, and idioms of its inhabitants, and there was even talk of establishing a professorship of the Tartar language in the university of Paris. Romantic narrative, when duly discussed and investigated, spread on all sides more just and varied notions. The world seemed to open on the side of the east; geography took a great stride, and the desire for discovery became the new form which clothed the adventurous spirit of the Europeans. The idea of another hemisphere ceased to present itself as a paradox void of all probability, when our own became better known; and it was in searching for the Zipangri of Marco Polo that Christopher Columbus discovered the New World."

You see, by the facts which led to the impulsion of the crusades, what, at the thirteenth and fourteenth centuries, was the new and vast world which was thrown open to the European mind. There can be no doubt but that this was one of the most powerful causes of development, and of the freedom of mind which shone forth at the end of this great event.

There is another cause which merits observation. Down to the time of the crusades, the court of Rome, the centre of the church, had never been in communication with the laity, except through the medium of ecclesiastics, whether legates sent from the court of Rome, or the bishops and the entire clergy. There had always been some laymen in direct relation with Rome; but, taken all together, it was through the ecclesiastics that she communicated with the people. During the crusades, on the contrary, Rome became a place of passage to the greater part of the crusaders, both in going and in returning. Numbers of the laity viewed her policy and manners, and could see how much of personal interest influenced religious controversy. Doubtless this new knowledge inspired many minds with a hardihood till then unknown.

When we consider the state of minds in general, at the end of the crusades, and particularly in ecclesiastical matters, it is impossible not to be struck by one singular fact: religious ideas experienced no change; they had not been replaced by contrary or even different opinions. Yet minds were in finitely more free; religious creeds were no longer the only sphere in which it was brought into play; without abandoning them, it began to separate itself from them, and carry itself elsewhere. Thus, at the end of the thirteenth century, the moral cause which had determined the crusades, which at least was its most energetic principle, had vanished; the moral state of Europe was profoundly modified.

The social state had undergone an analogous change. Much investigation has been expended upon what was the influence of the crusades in this respect; it has been shown how they reduced a large number of fief-holders to the necessity of selling them to their sovereigns, or of selling charters to the boroughs in order to procure the means of following the crusade. It has been shown that by their mere absence, many of the lords must have lost the greater portion of their power. Without entering into the details of this inquiry, we may, I think, resolve into a few general facts, the influence of the crusades upon the social state.

They greatly diminished the number of petty fiefs and small domains, of inferior fief-holders; and they concentred property and power in a smaller number of hands. It is with the commencement of the crusades that we see the formation and augmentation of large fiefs, and great feudal existences.

I have often regretted that there is no map of France divided into fiefs, as there is of its division into departments, arrondissements, cantons, and parishes, in which all the fiefs should be marked, with their extent and successive relations and changes. If we were to compare, with the aid of such a map, the state of France before and after the crusades, we should see how many fiefs had vanished, and to what a degree the great and middle fiefs had increased. This was one of the most important facts to which the crusades led.

Even where the petty proprietors preserved their fiefs, they no longer lived as isolated as formerly. The great fief-holders became so many centres, around which the smaller ones converged, and near to which they passed their lives It had become necessary, during the crusades, for them to put themselves in the train of the richest and most powerful, to receive succour from him; they had lived with him, partaken of his fortune, gone through the same adventures,

When the crusaders returned home, this sociability, this habit of living near to the superior lord, remained fixed in their manners. Thus as we see the augmentation of the great fiefs after the crusades, so we see the holders of those fiefs holding a much more considerable court in the interior of their castles, having near them a larger number of gentlemen who still preserved their small domains, but did not shut themselves up within them.

The extension of the great fiefs and the creation of a certain number of centres of society, in place of the dispersion which formerly existed, are the two principal effects brought about by the crusades in the heart of feudalism.

As to the burghers, a result of the same nature is easily perceptible. The crusades created the great boroughs. Petty commerce and industry did not suffice to create boroughs such as the great towns of Italy and Flanders were. It was commerce on a great scale, maritime commerce, and especially that of the east, which gave rise to them; it was the crusades which gave to maritime commerce the most powerful impulsion it had ever received.

Upon the whole, when we regard the state of society at the end of the crusades, we find that this movement of dissolution, of the dispersion of existences and influences, this movement of universal localization, if such a phrase be permitted, which had preceded this epoch, had ceased, by a movement with an exactly contrary tendency, by a movement of centralization. All now tended to approximation. The lesser existences were either absorbed in the greater, or were grouped around them. It was in this direction that society advanced, that all its progress was made.

You now see, why, towards the end of the thirteenth and fourteenth centuries, neither people nor sovereigns any longer desired the crusades; they had no longer either the need or desire for them; they had been cast into them by the impulsion of the religious spirit, and by the exclusive domination of religious ideas upon the whole existence; this domination had lost its energy. They had sought, too, in the crusades a new life, more extensive and more varied; they now began to find it in Europe itself, in the progress of social relations. It was at this epoch the career of political aggrandizement opened itself to kings. Wherefore seek kingdoms

in Asia, when they had them to conquer at their own doors?
Philip Augustus went to the crusades against his will: what
could be more natural? He had to make himself king of
France. It was the same with the people. The career of
riches opened before their eyes; they renounced adventures
for work. For the sovereigns, the place of adventures was
supplied by policy; for the people, by work on a great scale.
One single class of society still had a taste for adventure:
this was that portion of feudal nobility who, not being in a
condition to think of political aggrandizement, and not liking
work, preserved their ancient condition and manners. They
therefore continued to rush to the crusades, and attempted
their revival.

Such, in my opinion, are the great and true effects of the
crusades: on one side, the extension of ideas, the enfranchisement of mind; on the other, the aggrandizement of
existences, and a large sphere opened to activity of all kind:
they produced at once a greater degree of individual liberty,
and of political unity. They aided the independence of man
and the centralization of society. Much has been asked as
to the means of civilization—which they directly imported
from the east; it has been said that the chief portion of the
great discoveries which, in the fourteenth and fifteenth centuries, called forth the development of European civilization—
the compass, printing, gunpowder—were known in the east,
and that the crusaders may have brought them thence.
This, to a certain point, is true. But some of these assertions
are disputable. That which is not disputable is this influence,
this general effect of the crusades upon the mind on one
hand, and upon society on the other hand; they drew European
society from a very straightened track, and led it into new
and infinitely more extensive paths; they commenced that
transformation of the various elements of European society
into governments and peoples, which is the character of
modern civilization. About the same time, royalty, one of
those institutions which have most powerfully contributed to
this great result, developed itself. Its history, from the birth
of modern states down to the thirteenth century, will form
the subject of my next lecture.

NINTH LECTURE.

Object of the lecture—Important part taken by royalty in the history of
Europe, and in the history of the world—True causes of this importance
—Two-fold point of view under which the institution of royalty should
be considered—1st. Its true and permanent nature—It is the personification of the sovereignty of right—With what limits—2nd. Its flexibility
and diversity—European royalty seems to be the result of various kinds
of royalty—Of barbarian royalty—Of imperial royalty—Of religious
royalty—Of feudal royalty—Of modern royalty, properly so called, and
of its true character.

In our last lecture, I attempted to determine the essential
and distinctive character of modern European society, as
compared with primitive European society; I believe that
we discovered in this fact, that all the elements of the
social state, at first numerous and various, reduce themselves
to two: on one hand the government, and on the other, the
people. Instead of encountering the feudal nobility, the
clergy, the kings, burghers, and serfs, as the dominant powers
and chief actors in history, we find in modern Europe but
two great figures which alone occupy the historic scene, the
government and the country.

If such is the fact in which European civilization terminates,
such also is the end to which we should tend, and to which
our researches should conduct us. It is necessary that we
should see this grand result take birth, and progressively
develop and strengthen itself. We are entered upon the
epoch in which we may arrive at its origin: it was, as you
have seen, between the twelfth and the sixteenth century that
the slow and concealed work operated in Europe which has
led our society to this new form and definitive state. We

M

have likewise studied the first great event, which, in my opinion, evidently and powerfully impelled Europe in this direction, that is, the crusades.

About the same epoch, almost at the moment that the crusades broke out, that institution commenced its aggrandizement, which has, perhaps, contributed more than anything to the formation of modern society, and to that fusion of all the social elements into two powers, the government and the people; royalty.

It is evident that royalty has played a prodigious part in the history of European civilization; a single glance at facts suffices to convince one of it; we see the development of royalty marching with the same step, so to speak, at least for a long period, as that of society itself; the progress is mutual.

And not only is the progress mutual, but whenever society advances towards its modern and definitive character, royalty seems to extend and prosper; so that when the work is consummated, when there is no longer any, or scarcely any other important or decisive influence in the great states of Europe, than that of the government and the public, royalty is the government.

And it has thus happened, not only in France, where the fact is evident, but also in the greater portion of European countries: a little earlier or a little later, under somewhat different forms, the same result is offered us in the history of society in England, Spain, and Germany. In England, for example, it was under the Tudors, that the ancient, peculiar and local elements of English society were perverted and dissolved, and gave place to the system of public powers; this also was the time of the greatest influence of royalty. It was the same in Germany, Spain, and all the great European states.

If we leave Europe, and if we turn our view upon the rest of the world, we shall be struck by an analogous fact; we shall everywhere find royalty occupying an important position, appearing as, perhaps, the most general and permanent of institutions, the most difficult to prevent, where it did not formerly exist, and the most difficult to root out where it had existed. From time immemorial it has possessed Asia. At the discovery of America, all the great states there were found with different combinations, subject to the monarchical system. When we penetrate into the interior of Africa, wherever we meet with nations in any way extensive, this is the prevailing system. And not only has royalty penetrated everywhere, but it has accommodated itself to the most diverse situations, to civilization and to barbarism, to manners the most pacific, as in China, for example, and to those in which war, in which the military spirit dominate. It has alike established itself in the heart of the system of castes, in the most rigorously classified societies, and in the midst of a system of equality, in societies which are utter strangers to all legal and permanent classification. Here despotic and oppressive, there favourable to civilization and even to liberty, it seems like a head which may be placed upon a multitude of different bodies, a fruit that will spring from the most dissimilar germs.

In this fact, we may discover many curious and important consequences. I will take only two. The first is, that it is impossible such a result should be the fruit of mere chance, of force or usurpation alone; it is impossible but that there should be a profound and powerful analogy between the nature of royalty, considered as an institution, and the nature, whether of individual man, or of human society. Doubtless, force is intermixed with the origin of the institution; doubtless, force has taken an important part in its progress; but when we meet with such a result as this, when we see a great event developing and reproducing itself during the course of many centuries, and in the midst of such different situations, we cannot attribute it to force. Force plays a great part, and an incessant one, in human affairs; but it is not their principle, their *primum mobile*; above force and the part which it plays, there hovers a moral cause which decides the totality of things. It is with force in the history of societies, as with the body in the history of man. The body surely holds a high place in the life of man, but still it is not the principle of life. Life circulates within it, but it does not emanate from it. So it is with human societies; whatever part force takes therein, it is not force which governs them, and which presides supremely over their destinies; it is ideas and moral influences, which conceal themselves under the accidents of force, and regulate the course of the society. It is a cause of this kind, and not force, which gave success to royalty.

M 2

A second fact, and one which is no less worthy of remark, is the flexibility of the institution, its faculty of modifying, and adapting itself to a multitude of different circumstances. Mark the contrast: its form is unique, permanent, and simple; it does not offer that prodigious variety of combinations which we see in other institutions, and yet it applies itself to societies which the least resemble it. It must evidently allow of great diversity, and must attach itself, whether in man himself or in society, to many different elements and principles.

It is from not having considered the institution of royalty in its whole extent; from not having on the one hand penetrated to its peculiar and fixed principle, which, whatever may be the circumstances to which it applies itself, is its very essence and being—and on the other, from not having estimated all the varieties to which it lends itself, and all the principles with which it may enter into alliance; it is, I say, from not having considered royalty under this vast and twofold point of view, that the part taken by it in the history of the world has not been always comprehended, that its nature and effects have often been misconstrued.

This is the work which I wish to go through with you, and in such a manner as to take an exact and complete estimate of the effects of this institution in modern Europe, whether they have flowed from its own peculiar principles or the modifications which it has undergone.

There can be no doubt that the force of royalty, that moral power which is its true principle, does not reside in the sole and personal will of the man momentarily king; there can be no doubt that the people, in accepting it as an institution, philosophers in maintaining it as a system, have not intended or consented to accept the empire of the will of a man, essentially narrow, arbitrary, capricious, and ignorant.

Royalty is quite a distinct thing from the will of a man, although it presents itself in that form; it is the personification of the sovereignty of right, of that will, essentially reasonable, enlightened, just, and impartial, foreign and superior to all individual wills, and which in virtue of this title has a right to govern them. Such is the meaning of royalty in the minds of nations, such the motive for their adhesion.

Is it true that there is a sovereignty of right, a will which

possesses the right of governing men? It is quite certain
that they believe so; because they seek, and constantly have
sought, and indeed cannot but seek, to place themselves
under its empire. Conceive to yourselves the smallest
assembly of men, I will not say a people : conceive that
assembly under the submission to a sovereign who is only
so *de facto*, under a force which has no right except that
of force, which governs neither according to reason, justice,
nor truth ; human nature revolts at such a supposition—
it must have right to believe in. It is the supremacy of
right which it seeks, that is the only power to which man
consents to submit. What is history but the demonstration of this universal fact ? What are the greater portion of the struggles which take place in the life of nations,
but an ardent effort towards the sovereignty of right, so
that they may place themselves under its empire ? And
not only nations but philosophers believe in its existence, and
incessantly seek it. What are all the systems of political
philosophy, but the search for the sovereign of right ?
What is it that they treat of, but the question of knowing
who has a right to govern society ? Take the theocratical,
monarchical, aristocratical, or democratical systems, all of
them boast of having discovered wherein the sovereignty of
right resides; all promise to society that they will place it
under the rule of its legitimate master. I repeat, this is the
end alike of all the works of philosophers, of all efforts of
nations.

How should they but believe in the sovereignty of right?
How should they but be constantly in search of it? Take the
most simple suppositions; let there be something to accomplish, some influence to exercise, whether upon society in
its whole, or upon a number of its members, or upon a
single individual; there is evidently always a rule for this
action, a legitimate will to follow and apply. Whether
you penetrate into the smallest details of social life, or whether you elevate yourselves to the greatest events, you will
everywhere encounter a truth to be proved, or a just and
reasonable idea to be passed into reality. This is the
sovereign of right, towards which philosophers and nations
have never ceased and never can cease to aspire.

Up to what point can the sovereignty of right be represented

in a general and permanent manner by a terrestrial force or
by a human will? How far is such a supposition necessarily
false and dangerous? What should be thought in particular of the personification of the sovereignty of right under
the image of royalty? Upon what conditions, within what
limits is this personification admissible? Great questions,
which I have not to treat of here, but which I could
not resist pointing out, and upon which I shall say a word
in passing.

I affirm, and the merest common sense will acknowledge,
that the sovereignty of right completely and permanently can
appertain to no one; that all attribution of the sovereignty of
right to any human power whatsoever, is radically false and
dangerous. Hence arises the necessity for the limitation of
all powers, whatever their names or forms may be; hence
the radical illegitimacy of all absolute power, whether its
origin be from conquest, inheritance, or election. People
may differ as to the best means of seeking the sovereign of
right; they may vary as to place and times; but in no place,
no time, can any legitimate power be the independent possessor of this sovereignty.

This principle being laid down, it is no less certain that
royalty, in whatever system it is considered, presents itself as
the personification of the sovereign of right. Listen to the
theocratical system: it will tell you that kings are the image
of God upon earth; this is only saying that they are the personification of sovereign justice, truth, and goodness. Address
yourself to the jurisconsults; they will tell you that the king
is the living law; that is to say, the king is the personification
of the sovereign of right, of the just law, which has the
right of governing society. Ask royalty itself, in the system
of pure monarchy; it will tell you that it is the personification
of the State, of the general interest. In whatever alliance
and in whatever situation you consider it, you will always find
it summing itself up in the pretension of representing and
reproducing the sovereign of right, alone capable of legitimately governing society.

There is no occasion for astonishment in all this. What
are the characteristics of the sovereign of right, the characteristics derivable from his very nature? In the first place
he is unique; since there is but one truth, one justice, there

can be but one sovereign of right. He is permanent, always the same; truth never changes. He is placed in a superior situation, a stranger to all the vicissitudes and changes of this world; his part in the world is, as it were, that of a spectator and judge. Well! it is royalty which externally reproduces, under the most simple form, that which appears its most faithful image, these rational and natural characteristics of the sovereign of right. Open the work in which M. Benjamin Constant has so ingeniously represented royalty as a neutral and moderating power, raised above the accidents and struggles of social life, and only interfering at great crises. Is not this, so to speak, the attitude of the sovereign of right in the government of human things? There must be something in this idea well calculated to impress the mind, for it has passed with singular rapidity from books to facts. One sovereign made it in the constitution of Brazil the very foundation of his throne; there royalty is represented as a moderating power, raised above all active powers, as a spectator and judge.

Under whatever point of view you regard this institution, as compared with the sovereign of right, you will find that there is a great external resemblance, and that it is natural for it to have struck the minds of men. Accordingly, whenever their reflection or imagination turned with preference towards the contemplation or study of the nature of the sovereign of right, and his essential characteristics, they have inclined towards royalty. As, in the time of the preponderance of religious ideas, the habitual contemplation of the nature of God led mankind towards the monarchical system, so when the jurisconsults dominated in society, the habit of studying, under the name of the law, the nature of the sovereign of right, was favourable to the dogma of his personification in royalty. The attentive application of the human mind to the contemplation of the nature of the sovereignty of right when no other causes have interfered to destroy the effect, has always given force and credit to royalty, which presents its image.

Moreover, there are times peculiarly favourable to this personification: these are the times when individual powers display themselves in the world with all their risks and caprices; times when egotism dominates in individuals, whether

from ignorance and brutality, or from corruption. Then
society, abandoned to the contests of personal wills, and unable
to raise itself by their free concurrence to a common and
universal will, passionately long for a sovereign to whom all
individuals may be forced to submit; and the moment any
institution, bearing any one of the characteristics of the
sovereignty of right, presented itself, and promised its empire
to society, society rallied round it with eager earnestness, like
outlaws taking refuge in the asylum of a church. This is
what has been seen in the disorderly youth of nations, such as
we have surveyed. Royalty is admirably adapted to epochs
of vigorous and fruitful anarchy, so to speak, when society
desires to form and regulate itself, without knowing how to
do so by the free concord of individual wills. There are other
times when, from directly opposite causes, it has the same
recommendation. Why did the Roman empire, so nearly in
a state of dissolution at the end of the republic, subsist for
nearly fifteen centuries afterwards, under the name of that
empire, which, after all, was but a continual decay, a lengthened agony? Royalty alone could produce such an effect; that
alone could hold together a society which selfishness incessantly tended to destroy. The imperial power struggled for
fifteen centuries against the ruin of the Roman world.

Thus there are times when royalty alone can retard the
dissolution of society, and times when it alone accelerates its
formation. And in both these cases, it is because it represents
more clearly and powerfully than any other form the sovereignty of right, that it exercises this power upon events.

From whatever point of view you may consider this institution, and at whatever epoch, you will acknowledge then that
its essential characteristic, its moral principle, its true and
inmost meaning is the image, the personification, the presumed interpreter of this unique, superior, and essentially
legitimate will, which alone has the right of governing society.

Let us now regard royalty from the second point of view,
that is to say, in its flexibility, in the variety of parts which
it has played, and the effects which it has produced; it is
necessary that we should give the reason of these features,
and determine their causes.

Here we have an advantage; we can immediately enter
upon history, and upon our own history. By a concourse of

singular circumstances, it has happened, that in modern Europe royalty has assumed every character under which it has shown itself in the history of the world. If I may be allowed to use an arithmetical expression, European royalty is the sum total of all possible species of royalty. I will run over its history from the fifth to the twelfth century; you will see how various are the aspects under which it presents itself, and to what an extent we shall everywhere find this character of variety, complication, and conflict which belongs to all European civilization.

In the fifth century, at the time of the great German invasion, two royalties are present; the barbarian and the imperial royalty, that of Clovis and that of Constantine; both differing essentially in principles and effects. Barbaric royalty is essentially elective; the German kings were elected, although their election did not take place with the same forms which we are accustomed to attach to the idea; they were military chiefs, who were bound to make their power freely acceptable to a large number of companions who obeyed them as being the most brave and the most able among them. Election is the true source of barbaric royalty, its primitive and essential characteristic.

Not that this characteristic in the fifth century was not already a little modified, or that different elements had not been introduced into royalty. The various tribes had had their chiefs for a certain time; some families had raised themselves to more trust, consideration, and riches than others. Hence a commencement of inheritance; the chief was now mostly elected out of these families. This was the first differing principle which became associated with the dominant principle of election.

Another idea, another element, had also already penetrated into barbaric royalty: this was the religious element. We find among some of the barbarous nations, among the Goths, for example, that the families of their kings descended from the families of their gods, or from those heroes of whom they had made gods, such as Odin. This is the situation of the kings of Homer, who sprang from gods or demi-gods, and by reason of this title were the objects of a kind of religious veneration, despite their limited power.

Such, in the fifth century, was barbaric royalty, already

varying and fluctuating, although its primitive principle still dominated.

I take imperial, Roman royalty; this is a totally different thing; it is the personification of the state, the heir of the sovereignty and majesty of the Roman people. Consider the royalty of Augustus and Tiberius; the emperor is the representative of the senate, the comitia, and the whole republic; he succeeded them, and they are summed up in his person. Who would not recognise this in the modesty of language of the first emperors; of those, at least, who were men of sense, and understood their situation? They felt themselves in the presence of the late sovereign people who had abdicated in their favour; they addressed them as their representatives and ministers. But, in fact, they exercised the whole power of the people, and that with the most formidable intensity. It is easy for us to understand such a transformation; we have ourselves witnessed it; we have seen the sovereignty pass from the people to a man; that is the history of Napoleon. He also was the personification of the sovereign people; he unceasingly repeated to it, " Who like me has been elected by eighteen millions of men ? Who like me is the representative of the people *Republique Française !*" And when upon one side of his coinage we read, *The French Republic*, and upon the other, *Napoleon, Empereur*, what does this mean, if not the fact which I have described, the people become king?

Such was the fundamental character of imperial royalty, which it preserved for the three first centuries of the empire· it was not till Diocletian that it took its definitive and complete form. It was then, however, upon the point of undergoing a great change; a new royalty had almost appeared. Christianity laboured for three centuries to introduce the religious element into society. It was under Constantine that it met with success, not in making it the prevalent fact, but in making it play an important part. Here royalty presents itself under a different aspect; its origin is not earthly; the prince is not the representative of the public sovereignty; he is the image of God, his representative and delegate. Power came down to him from above, while in imperial royalty it came from below. These are two utterly different situations, and have entirely different results. The rights of liberty, political guarantees are difficult to combine with the principle of religious royalty; but the principle itself is elevated, moral, and salutary. Let us see the idea which was formed of the prince in the seventh century, in the system of religious royalty. I take it from the canons of the councils of Toledo.

"The king is called king (*rex*,) because he governs justly, (*rectè*). If he act with justice (*recte*), he legitimately possesses the name of king; if he act with injustice, he miserably loses it. Our fathers, therefore, said, with good reason: *Rex ejus, eris si recta facis, si autem non facis, non eris.* The two principal royal virtues are justice and truth, (science of the reason).

"The royal power is bound, like the people, to respect the laws . . . . Obedience to the will of Heaven, gives to us and to our subjects wise laws, which our greatness and that of our successors is bound to obey, as well as the whole population of our kingdom. . . .

"God, the creator of all things, in disposing the structure of the human body, has raised the head on high, and has willed that the nerves of all the members should proceed therefrom. And he has placed in the head the torch of the eyes, to the end that from thence may be viewed all things that might be prejudicial. He has established the power of intellect, charging it to govern all the members, and wisely to regulate their action. . . . It is first necessary, then, to regulate what relates to princes, to watch over their safety, and to protect their life, and then to order what relates to the people; so that in guaranteeing, as is fitting, the safety of kings, they at the same time guarantee, and more effectually, that of the people."[1]

But, in the system of religious royalty, another element, quite different from that of royalty itself, almost always introduced itself. A new power took its place by the side of it, a power nearer to God, to the source whence royalty emanates, than royalty itself: this was the clergy, the ecclesiastical power which interposed itself between God and kings, and between kings and the people; so that royalty, the image of divinity, ran a chance of falling to the rank of an instrument

---

[1] *Forum Judicum*, i. lib. 2; tit. i. l. 2, l. 4.

of the human interpreters of the divine will. This was a new
cause of diversity in the destinies and effects of the institution.

Here, then, we see, what in the fifth century were the
various royalties which manifested themselves upon the ruins
of the Roman empire: the barbaric royalty, the imperial
royalty, and the rising religious royalty. Their fortunes were
as various as their principles.

In France, under the first race, barbaric royalty prevailed;
there were many attempts of the clergy to impress upon it the
imperial or religious character; but election in the royal
family, with some mixture of inheritance and religious ideas,
remained dominant. In Italy, among the Ostrogoths, imperial
royalty superseded the barbarian customs. Theodoric asserted
himself the successor of the emperors. You need only read
Cassiodorus, to acknowledge this character of his government.

In Spain, royalty appeared more religious than elsewhere;
as the councils of Toledo were, I will not say the masters, but
the influencing power, the religious character dominated, if
not in the government, properly so called, of the Visigoth
kings, at least, in the laws with which the clergy inspired
them, and the language which it made them speak.

In England, among the Saxons, barbarian manners subsisted
almost entire. The kingdoms of the heptarchy were merely the
domains of various bands, having each its chief. The military
election is more evident there than elsewhere. Anglo
Saxon royalty is the most perfect type of barbaric royalty.

Thus from the fifth to the twelfth century, three kinds of
royalty manifested themselves at the same time, in general
facts; one or other of them prevailed, according to circum
stances, in each of the different states of Europe.

The chaos was such at this epoch, that nothing universal
or permanent could be established; and, from one vicissitude
to another, we arrive at the eighth century, without royalty
having anywhere taken a definitive character. Towards the
middle of the eighth century, with the triumph of the second
race of the Frank kings, events generalized themselves and
became clearer; as they were accomplished upon a greater
scale, they were better understood, and led to more results.
You will shortly see the different royalties distinctly succeed
and combine with each other.

At the time when the Carlovingians replace the Merovingians, a return of barbaric royalty is visible; election again appears. Pepin causes himself to be elected at Soissons. When the first Carlovingians give the kingdoms to their sons they take care to have them accepted by the chief persons in the states assigned them; when they make a partition, they wish it to be sanctioned in the national assemblies. In a word, the elective principle, under the form of public acceptation, reassumes some reality. You bear in mind, that this change of dynasty was like a new invasion of the Germans in the west of Europe, and brought back some shadow of their ancient institutions and manners.

At the same time we see the religious principle introduced more clearly into royalty, and playing therein a more important part. Pepin was acknowledged and crowned by the pope. He had need of religious sanction; it had already a great power, and he courted it. Charlemagne took the same precaution; religious royalty was developing. Still under Charlemagne this character did not dominate; imperial royalty was evidently what he attempted to resuscitate. Although he closely allied himself to the clergy, and made use of them, he was not their instrument. The idea of a great state, of a great political unity, the resurrection of the Roman empire, was the favourite idea, the dream of Charlemagne's reign. He died, and was succeeded by Louis le Debonnaire. Every one knows what character the royal power instantly assumed; the king fell into the hands of the clergy, who censured, deposed, re-established, and governed him; religious royalty, late subordinate, seemed on the point of being established.

Thus, from the middle of the eighth to the middle of the ninth century, the diversity of three kinds of royalty manifested itself in important, closely connected, and palpable events.

After the death of Louis le Debonnaire, in the dissolution into which Europe fell, the three species of royalty disappeared almost simultaneously; all became confusion. After some time, when the feudal system prevailed, a fourth royalty presented itself, different from any that we have yet seen; this was feudal royalty. This is confused, and very difficult to define. It has been said that the king

in the feudal system was sovereign of sovereigns, lord of
lords, that he held by sure ties, from one class to another,
the entire society; that in calling around him his vassals,
then the vassals of his vassals, he called the whole nation,
and truly showed himself a king. I do not deny that this
was the theory of feudal royalty; but it is a mere theory,
which has never governed facts. That general influence of
the king by the means of an hierarchical organization, those
ties which united royalty to the entire feudal society, are the
dreams of publicists. In fact, the greater part of the feudal
lords were at this epoch entirely independent of royalty; a
large number scarcely knew the name, and had little or no
connexion with it. All the sovereignties were local and
independent: the title of king, borne by one of the feudal
lords, expressed rather a remembrance than a fact.

This was the state of royalty during the course of the
tenth and eleventh centuries. In the twelfth, with the reign
of Louis le Gros, the aspect of things began to change. We
more often find the king spoken of; his influence penetrated
into places where hitherto he had never made way; his part
in society became more active. If we seek by what title, we
shall recognise none of the titles of which royalty had
hitherto been accustomed to avail itself. It was not as the
heir of the emperors, or by the title of imperial royalty, that
it aggrandized itself and assumed more coherence; nor was
it in virtue of election, nor as the emanation of divine
power. All trace of election had disappeared, the hereditary
principle of succession had become definitively established;
and although religion sanctioned the accession of kings, the
minds of men did not appear at all engrossed with the religious character of the royalty of Louis le Gros. A new
element, a character hitherto unknown, produced itself in
royalty; a new royalty commenced.

I need not repeat that society was at this epoch in a
prodigious disorder, a prey to unceasing violence. So
ciety had in itself no means of striving against this deplorable state, of regaining any regularity or unity. The feudal
institutions, those parliaments of barons, those seigneurial
courts, all those forms under which, in modern times, feudalism has been represented as a systematic and organised
regime, all this was devoid of reality, of power; there was

nothing there which could re-establish order or justice; so that, amidst this social desolation, none knew to whom to have recourse for the reparation of any great injustice, or to remedy any great evil, or in any way to constitute anything resembling a state. The name of king remained; a lord bore it, and some few addressed themselves to him. The various titles under which royalty had hitherto presented itself, although they did not exercise any great control, were still present to many minds, and on some occasions were recognised. It sometimes happened that they had recourse to the king to repress any scandalous violence, or to re-establish something like order in any place near to his residence, or to terminate any difference which had long existed; he was sometimes called upon to interfere in matters not strictly within his jurisdiction; he interfered as the protector of public order, as arbitrator and redresser of wrongs. The moral authority which remained attached to his name, by degrees attracted to him this power.

Such is the character which royalty began to take under Louis le Gros, and under the administration of Suger. Then, for the first time, we see in the minds of men the idea, although very incomplete, confused, and weak, of a public power, foreign to the powers which possessed society, called to render justice to those who were unable to obtain it by ordinary means, capable of establishing, or, at least, of commanding order; the idea of a great magistrate, whose essential character was that of maintaining or re-establishing peace, of protecting the weak, and of ending differences which none others could decide. This is the entirely new character under which, dating from the twelfth century, royalty presented itself in Europe, and especially in France. It was neither as a barbarous royalty, a religious royalty, nor as an imperial royalty, that it exercised its empire; it possessed only a limited, incomplete, and accidental power the power, as it were, (I know of no expression more exact, of a great justice of peace for the whole nation.

This is the true origin of modern royalty; this, so to speak, is its vital principle; that which has been developed in the course of its career, and which, I do not hesitate in saying, has brought about its success. At the different epochs of history, we see the different characters of royalty reappear;

we see the various royalties which I have described attempting by turns to regain the preponderance. Thus the clergy
has always preached religious royalty; jurisconsults laboured
to resuscitate imperial royalty; and the nobles have sometimes wished to revive elective royalty, or the feudal. And
not only have the clergy, jurisconsults, and nobility, striven
to make dominant in royalty such or such a character; it
has itself made them all subservient to the aggrandizement of
its power; kings have sometimes represented themselves as
the delegates of God, sometimes as the successors of the
emperors, according to the need or inclination of the moment;
they have illegitimately availed themselves of these various
titles, but none of them has been the veritable title of
modern royalty, or the source of its preponderating influence.
It is, I repeat, as the depositary and protector of public
order, of universal justice, and common interest—it is under
the aspect of a great magistracy, the centre and union of
society—that it has shown itself to the eyes of the people, and
has appropriated their strength by obtaining their adhesion.

You will see, as we advance, this characteristic of modern
European royalty, which commenced at the twelfth century,
under the reign of Louis le Gros, strengthen and develop
itself, and became, so to speak, its political physiognomy.
It is through it that royalty has contributed to the great
result which characterizes European societies in the present
day, namely, the reduction of all social elements into two,
the government and the country.

Thus, at the termination of the crusades, Europe entered
the path which was to conduct it to its present state; and
royalty took its appropriate part in the great transformation.
In our next lecture we shall study the different attempts
made at political organization, from the twelfth to the sixteenth century, with a view to maintain, by regulating it,
the order, then almost in ruin. We shall consider the efforts
of feudalism, of the church, and even of the boroughs, to
constitute society after its ancient principles, and under its
primitive forms, and thus defend themselves against the
general metamorphosis which was in preparation.

TENTH LECTURE.

I WISH to determine correctly, and at the outset, the object of this lecture.

You will recollect, that one of the first facts which struck us in the elements of ancient European society, was their diversity, separation, and independence. The feudal nobility, clergy, and boroughs, had a situation, laws, and manners, all entirely different; they were so many societies which governed themselves, each upon its own account, and by its own rules and power. They stood in relation and came in contact, but there was no true union; they did not form, properly speaking, a nation, a State.

The fusion of all these societies into one has been accomplished; it is precisely, as you have seen, the distinctive fact, the essential character of modern society. The ancient social elements are reduced to two, the government and the people; that is to say, the diversity has ceased, that similitude has led to union. But before this result was consum-

M

mated, and even with a view to its prevention, many efforts
were tried to make all particular societies live and act in
common, without destroying their diversity or independence.
It was not wished to strike a blow in any way prejudicial to
their situation, privileges, or special nature, and yet to unite
them in a single State, to form of them one nation, to rally
them under one and the same government.

All these attempts failed. The result which I have just
mentioned, the unity of modern society, proves their ill success. Even in those European countries where some traces
of the ancient diversity of social elements, in Germany, for
example, where there is still a true feudal nobility and a
bourgeoisie; in England, where a national church is in possession of special revenues and a particular jurisdiction, it is
clear that this pretended distinct existence is but an appearance, an illusion; that these special societies are politically
confounded with the general society, absorbed in the State,
governed by the public powers, in subjection to the same
system, and carried away in the current of the same ideas, and
the same manners. I repeat that, where even the form of it
still subsists, the independence of the ancient social elements
has no reality.

Still these attempts to make them co-ordinate without
transforming them, to attach them to a national unity without
abolishing their diversity, have held an important place in
the history of Europe; they partly fill the epoch which now
occupies our attention, that epoch which separates primitive
from modern Europe, and in which the metamorphosis of
European society was accomplished. And not only has it
occupied an important place therein, but it has also greatly
influenced posterior events, and the manner in which the
reduction of all social elements into two, the government
and the public, has been brought about. It is, therefore, of
consequence to properly estimate and thoroughly understand
all the essays at political organization which were made from
the twelfth to the sixteenth century, to create nations and
governments, without destroying the diversity of the secondary societies placed side by side. Such will be our business
in this lecture.

It is a difficult and even a painful task. These attempts at political organization have not all been conceived and directed with a good intention; many of them have had no other views but those of selfishness and tyranny. More than one, however, has been pure and disinterested; more than one has really had for its object the moral and social good of mankind. The state of incoherence, violence, and iniquity in which society was then placed, shocked great minds and elevated souls, and they incessantly sought the means of escaping from it. Still, even the best of these noble essays have failed; and so much courage and virtue, so many sacrifices and efforts, have been lost : is it not a heart-rending spectacle? There is even one thing still more painful, the source of a sadness still more bitter: not only have these attempts at social amelioration failed, but an enormous mass of error and evil has been mixed up therein. Despite the good intention, the greater part were absurd, and indicated a profound ignorance of reason, justice, the rights of humanity, and the foundations of the social state; so that not only has success been wanting to mankind, but they have merited their failures. We here, then, have the spectacle, not only of the hard destiny of humanity, but also of its weakness. One may here see how the merest instalment of truth suffices so to occupy the greatest minds, that they entirely forget all the rest, and become blind to everything which does not come within the straightened horizon of their ideas; how a mere glimpse of justice in a cause suffices to make them lose sight of all the injustice which it involves and permits. This outburst of the vices and imperfection of man, is, in my opinion, a contemplation even more melancholy than the misery of his condition; his faults weigh more heavily upon me than his sufferings. The attempts which I have to describe, exhibit each of these spectacles. It is necessary to go through with them, and to be just towards those men, those ages, who have so often gone astray, and have so cruelly failed, and who, notwithstanding, have displayed such high virtues, made such noble efforts, merited so much glory!

The attempts at political organization formed from the twelfth to the sixteenth century, are of two kinds: the object of the one was to bring about the predominance of a particular social element, whether the clergy, the feudal nobility, or the boroughs; to make all the others subordinate to this, and on these terms to establish unity. The other proposed to itself to reconcile all the particular societies, and make them act in common, leaving to each its liberty, and guaranteeing its share of influence. The first class of these attempts is much more liable to the suspicion of selfishness and tyranny than the second. They have, in fact, oftener been tainted with these vices; they are indeed, by their very nature, essentially tyrannical in their means of action. Some of them, however, may have been—in fact, have been—conceived with pure views for the good and progress of humanity.

The first which presents itself is the attempt at a theocratical organization—that is to say, the design of subduing the various classes of society to the principles and empire of the ecclesiastical society. You will call to mind what I have said concerning the history of the church. I have endeavoured to show what principles have been developed within it, what was the share of legitimacy of each, how they were born of the natural course of events, what services they have rendered, and what evil they have brought about. I have characterized the various states into which the church passed from the eighth to the twelfth century; I have shown the state of the imperial church, the barbarian, the feudal, and lastly, the theocratical church. I suppose these recollections to be present to your minds; I shall now endeavour to indicate what the clergy did to dominate in Europe, and why they failed.

The attempt at theocratical organization appeared at a very early period, whether in the acts of the court of Rome, or in those of the clergy in general; it naturally resulted from the political and moral superiority of the church, but we shall find that it encountered, from the first, obstacles which, even in its greatest vigour, it did not succeed in removing.

The first was the very nature of Christianity. Wholly different in this respect from the greater number of religious creeds, Christianity was established by persuasion alone, by simply moral means; it was never, from the time of its birth, armed with force. In the early ages, it conquered by the Word alone, and it only conquered souls. Hence it happened, that even after its triumph when the church was

in possession of great riches and consideration, we never find
her invested with the direct government of society. Her
origin, purely moral, and merely by means of persuasion, was
found impressed in her condition. She had much influence,
but she had no power. She insinuated herself into the
municipal magistracies, she acted powerfully upon the emperors and their agents, but she had not the positive administration of public affairs, the government, properly so called.
Now a system of government—the theocratical, or any other—
cannot be established in an indirect manner by mere force of
influence; it is necessary to administer, command, receive
taxes, dispose of revenues, govern, in a word, actually to
take possession of society. When nations and governments
are acted upon by persuasion, much may be effected, and a
great empire exercised; but there would be no government,
no system would be founded, the future could not be provided
for. Such has been, from its very origin, the situation of
the Christian church; she has always been at the side of the
government of society, but she has never removed it, and
taken its place : a great obstacle which the attempt at theocratical organization could not surmount.

She met, at a very early period, with a second obstacle.
The Roman empire once fallen, and the barbarian states
founded, the church found herself among the conquered.
The first thing necessary was to escape this situation ;
the work she had to commence by converting the conquerors, and thus raising herself to their rank. When
this task was accomplished, and the church aspired to domination, she encountered the pride and resistance of the
feudal nobility. This was a great service rendered to
Europe by the feudal laity: in the eleventh century, nations
were almost entirely subjected to the church—sovereigns
were scarce able to defend themselves; the feudal nobility
alone never received the yoke of the clergy, never humbled
themselves before it. One need only recal the general
physiognomy of the middle ages to be struck by the singular
mixture of haughtiness and submission, of blind credulity and
freedom of mind, in the relations between the lay lords and
the priests: we there see some wreck of their primitive condition. You will call to mind how I endeavoured to represent to you the origin of feudalism, its first elements, and the

manner in which the elementary feudal society was formed
around the habitation of the fief-holder. I remarked how,
in that society, the priest was below the lord. Well, there
always remained in the heart of the feudal nobility a recollection and feeling of this situation; it always regarded itself,
not only as independent of the church, but as superior
to it, as alone called to possess and really govern the country; it was always willing to live in concord with the
clergy, but so as to guard its own interests, and not to give
in to those of the clergy. During many centuries, it was the
lay aristocracy which maintained the independence of society
with regard to the church—that haughtily defended it when
kings and people were subdued. It was the first to oppose,
and perhaps contributed more than any other power to the
failure of the attempt at, a theocratical organization of society.

A third obstacle was likewise opposed, of which, in general,
but little account has been held, and often even its effects
been misconstrued.

Wherever a clergy has seized upon society, and subjected it
to a theocratical organization, it is upon a married clergy that
this empire has devolved, upon a body of priests recruiting
themselves from their own bosom, and bringing up their
children from their very birth in and for the same situation.
Examine history: look at Asia, Egypt; all the great theocracies are the work of a clergy which is a complete society
in itself, which suffices for its own wants, and borrows
nothing from without.

By the celibacy of priests, the Christian clergy was in
an entirely different position; it was obliged, in order to its
perpetuation, to have continual recourse to the laity; to seek
from abroad, in all social positions and professions, the means
of duration. In vain did the *esprit-de-corps* labour afterwards to assimilate these foreign elements; something of the
origin of the new comers always remained; burghers or nobles,
they always preserved some trace of their ancient spirit,
their former condition. Doubtless celibacy, in placing the
Catholic clergy in an entirely special situation, foreign to the
interests and common life of mankind, has been to it a chief
cause of isolation; but it has thus unceasingly forced it into
connexion with lay society, in order to recruit and renew
itself therefrom, to receive and undergo some part of the

moral revolutions which were accomplished in it; and I do not
hesitate to say that this necessity, constantly renewing, has
been much more prejudicial to the success of the attempt at
theocratical organization, than the *esprit-de-corps*, strongly
maintained by celibacy, has been able to promote it.

The church finally encountered, within her own bosom,
powerful adversaries to this attempt. Much has been said
concerning the unity of the church; and it is true she has
constantly aspired to it, and in some respects has happily
attained it. But let us not be deceived by the pomp of words,
nor by that of partial facts. What society has presented
more civil dissensions, or undergone more dismemberment
than the clergy? What nation has been more divided, more
disordered, more unfixed than the ecclesiastical nation? The
national churches of the majority of European countries
almost incessantly struggled against the court of Rome;
councils struggled against popes; heresies have been innumerable and constantly renewing, schism always in readiness ; nowhere has there been such diversity of opinions,
such fury in contest, such parcelling out of power. The
internal life of the church, the divisions which have broken
out in it, the revolutions which have agitated it, have,
perhaps, been the greatest obstacles to the triumph of that
organization which she has attempted to impose upon society.

All these obstacles were in action and visible in the very
cradle of the great attempt which we have in review. They
did not, however, prevent its following its course, nor its being
in progress for many centuries. Its most glorious time, its day
of crisis, so to speak, was in the reign of Gregory VII., at the
end of the eleventh century. You have already seen that the
dominant idea of Gregory VII. was to subjugate the world to
the clergy, the clergy to the papal power, and Europe to a
vast and regular theocracy. In this design, as far as it may be
permitted us to judge of events at such a distance, this great
man committed, in my opinion, two great faults; one the
fault of a theorist, the other of a revolutionist. The first was
that of ostentatiously displaying his plan, of systematically
proclaiming his principles on the nature and rights of spiritual
power, of drawing from them beforehand, like an intractable
logician, the most distant consequences. He thus menaced
and attacked all the lay sovereignties of Europe, before being

assured of the means of conquering them. Success in human
affairs is neither obtained by such absolute proceedings, not
in the name of philosophical argument.   Moreover, Gregory
VII. fell into the common error of revolutionists, that of
attempting more than they can execute, and not taking the
possible as the measure and limit of their efforts. In order to
hasten the domination of his ideas, he engaged in contest with
the Empire, with all the sovereigns, and with the clergy itself.
He hesitated at no consequence, nor cared for any interest,
but haughtily proclaimed that he willed to reign over all
kingdoms as well as over all minds, and thus raised against
him, on one side, all the temporal powers, who saw themselves
in pressing danger, and on the other, the free-thinkers, who
began to appear, and who already dreaded the tyranny over
thought. Upon the whole, Gregory perhaps compromised
more than he advanced the cause he wished to serve.

It, however, continued to prosper during the whole of the
twelfth and down to the middle of the thirteenth century.
This is the time of the greatest power and brilliancy of the
church, though I do not think it can be strictly said that she
made any great progress in that epoch. Down to the end of
the reign of Innocent III. she rather cultivated than extended
her glory and power. It was at the moment of her greatest
apparent success that a popular reaction declared itself against
her, in a large portion of Europe. In the south of France,
the heresy of the Albigenses broke forth, which took possession of an entire, numerous, and powerful community. Almost
at the same time, in the north, in Flanders, ideas and desires
of the same nature appeared. A little later, in England,
Wickliff attacked with talent the power of the church, and
founded a sect which will never perish. Sovereigns did not
long delay entering the same path as the people. It was at
the commencement of the thirteenth century that the most
powerful and the ablest sovereigns of Europe, the emperors
of the house of Hohenstaufen, succumbed in their struggle
with the papacy. During this century, Saint Louis, the most
pious of kings, proclaimed the independence of the temporal
power, and published the first Pragmatic Sanction, which has
been the basis of all others. At the commencement of the
fourteenth century, the quarrel broke out between Philip le
Bel and Boniface VIII.; the king of England, Edward I.

was not more docile towards Rome. At this epoch, it is clear, the attempt at a theocratical organization has failed; the church, henceforth, will be on the defensive; she will ne longer undertake to impose her system upon Europe; her only thought will be to preserve what she has conquered. It is from the end of the thirteenth century that the emancipation of the European lay society really dates; it was then that the church ceased to pretend to the possession of it.

She had long before renounced this claim, in the very sphere in which she seemed to have had the best chance of success. Long since, upon the very threshold of the church, around her very throne in Italy, theocracy had completely failed, and given place to an entirely different system—to that attempt at a democratical organization, of which the Italian republics are the type, and which, from the eleventh to the sixteenth cen tury, played so brilliant a part in Europe.

You recollect what I have already related of the history of the boroughs, and the manner in which they were formed. In Italy, their destiny was more precocious and powerful than anywhere else; the towns there were much more numerous and wealthy than in Gaul, Britain, or Spain; the Roman municipal system remained more full of life and regular there.

The country parts of Italy, also, were much less fit to become the habitation of their new masters, than those of the rest of Europe. They had everywhere been cleared, drained, and cultivated; they were not clothed with forests; here the barbarians were unable to follow the hazards of the chase, or to lead an analogous life to that of Germany. Moreover, one part of this territory did not belong to them. The south of Italy, the Campagna di Roma, and Ravenna, continued to depend upon the Greek emperors. Favoured by its distance from the sovereign and the vicissitudes of war, the republican system, at an early period, gained strength and developed itself in this part of the country. And not only the whole of Italy was not in the power of the barbarians, but even where the Barbarians did conquer it, they did not remain in tranquil and definitive possession. The Ostrogoths were destroyed and driven out by Belisarius and Narses. The kingdom of the Lombards succeeded no better in establishing itself. The Franks destroyed it; and, without destroying the Lombard population, Pepin and Charlemagne judged it expedient to form an alliance with the ancient Italian population, in order to struggle against the recently conquered Lombards. The barbarians, then, were not in Italy, as elsewhere, the exclusive and undisturbed masters of the land and of society. Hence it was, that beyond the Alps, only a very weak, thin, and scattered feudalism was established. The preponderance, instead of passing into the inhabitants of the country parts, as had happened in Gaul, for example, continued to appertain to the towns. When this result became evident, a large portion of the fief-holders, either from free-will or necessity, ceased to inhabit the country, and settled in the cities. Barbarian nobles became burghers. You may imagine what power and superiority this single fact gave the Italian towns as compared with the other boroughs of Europe. What we have remarked in these latter, was the inferiority and timidity of the population. The burghers appeared to us like courageous freed men painfully struggling against a master who was always at their gates. The burghers of Italy were very different; the conquering and the conquered population mixed within the same walls: the towns had not to defend themselves from a neighbouring master; their inhabitants were citizens, from all time free, at least the majority of them, who defended their independence and their rights against distant and foreign sovereigns, at one time against the Frank kings, at another against the emperors of Germany. Hence, the immense and early superiority of the towns of Italy: while elsewhere even the poorest boroughs were formed with infinite trouble, here we see republics, States arise.

Thus is explained the success of the attempt at republican organization in this part of Europe. It subdued feudalism at a very early period, and became the dominant form of society. But it was little calculated to spread or perpetuate itself; it contained but few germs of amelioration, the necessary condition to extension and duration.

When we examine the history of the republics of Italy, from the eleventh to the fifteenth century, we are struck with two apparently contradictory yet incontestable facts. We find an admirable development of courage, activity, and genius, and in consequence great prosperity; there is there a movement and liberty which is wanting to the rest of

Europe. Let us ask, what was the real condition of the inhabitants, how their life was passed, what was their share of
happiness? Here the aspect changes; no history can be
more melancholy and gloomy. There is, perhaps, no epoch
or country in which the position of man appears to have
been more agitated, subject to more deplorable mischances,
or where we meet with more dissensions, crimes, and misfortunes. Another fact is manifest at the same time; in the
political system of the greater part of the republics liberty
continually diminished. The want of security was such,
that the factions were inevitably forced to seek refuge in a
system less tempestuous though less popular than that with
which the state had commenced. Take the history of Florence,
Venice, Genoa, Milan, Pisa; you will everywhere see that
the general course of events, instead of developing liberty,
and enlarging the circle of institutions, tends to contract
it, and to concentre the power within the hands of a small
number of men. In a word, in these republics, so energetic,
brilliant, and wealthy, two things were wanting: security of
life, the first condition of a social state, and the progress of
institutions.

Thence a new evil, which did not allow of the extension
of the attempt at republican organization. It was from
without, from foreign sovereigns, that the greatest danger
was threatened to Italy. Yet this danger had never the
effect of reconciling these republics and making them act
in concert; they would never resist in common a common
enemy. Many of the most enlightened Italians, accordingly, the best patriots of our time, deplore the republican system of Italy in the middle ages as the real cause of
its never having become a nation. It was parcelled out, they
say, into a multitude of petty people, too much under the
control of their passions to allow of their confederating, or
constituting themselves a state. They regret that their
country, like the rest of Europe, has not passed through a
despotic centralization, which would have formed it into a
nation, and have rendered it independent of foreigners.
It seems, then, that the republican organization, even under
the most favourable circumstances, did not contain within
itself, at this epoch, the principle of progress, of duration,
extension—that it had no future. Up to a certain point, one

may compare the organization of Italy in the middle ages to
that of ancient Greece.   Greece also was a country full of
petty republics, always rivals and often enemies, and sometimes rallying towards a common end.   The advantage in
this comparison is entirely with Greece.   There can be no
doubt that, although history gives us many instances of
iniquity in them, too, there was more order, security, and
justice, in the interior of Athens, Lacedæmon, Thebes, than
in the Italian republics.   Yet how short was the political
existence of Greece!   What a principle of weakness existed
in that parcelling out of power and territory!   When Greece
came in contact with great neighbouring states, with Mace-
donia and Rome, she at once succumbed.   These small
republics, so glorious and still so flourishing, could not form
a coalition for defence   How much stronger was the reason
for the same result happening in Italy, where society and
human reason had been so much less developed and less firm
than among the Greeks.

If the attempt at republican organization had so little
chance of duration in Italy, where it had triumphed, where
the feudal system had been vanquished, you may easily conceive that it would much sooner succumb in the other parts
of Europe.

I will rapidly place its destinies before you.

There was one portion of Europe which bore a great
resemblance to Italy; this was the South of France and the
neighbouring Spanish provinces, Catalonia, Navarre, and
Biscay.   There likewise the towns had gained great development, importance, and wealth.   Many of the petty lords
were allied with the burghers; a portion of the clergy had
likewise embraced their cause; in a word, the country was in
a situation remarkably analogous to that of Italy.   Accordingly, in the course of the eleventh century, and at the commencement of the twelfth, the towns of Provence, Languedoc,
and Aquitaine, aimed at a political flight, at forming themselves into independent republics, just like those beyond the
Alps.   But the south of France was in contact with a very
strong feudalism, that of the north.   At this time occurred
the heresy of the Albigenses, and war broke out between feudal
and municipal France.   You know the history of the
crusade against the Albigenses, under Simon de Montfort.

This was the contest of the feudalism of the north against the attempt at democratical organization of the south. Despite the southern patriotism, the north carried the day; political unity was wanting in the south, and civilization was not sufficiently advanced for men to supply its place by concert. The attempt at republican organization was put down, and the crusade re-established the feudal system in the south of France.

At a later period, the republican attempt met with better success in the mountains of Switzerland. There the theatre was very straitened: they had only to struggle against a foreign sovereign, who, although of a superior force to the Swiss, was by no means among the most formidable sovereigns of Europe. The struggle was courageously sustained. The Swiss feudal nobility allied themselves in a great measure with the towns; a powerful succour, which, however, altered the nature of the revolution which it aided, and imprinted upon it a more aristocratic and less progressive character than it seemed at first intended to bear.

I now pass to the north of France, to the boroughs of Flanders, the banks of the Rhine, and the Hanseatic league. There the democratical organization triumphed fully in the interior of the towns; yet we perceive, from its outset, that it was not destined to extend itself, or to take entire possession of society. The boroughs of the north were surrounded and oppressed by feudalism, by lords and sovereigns, so that they were constantly on the defensive. It is clear that all they did was to defend themselves as well as they could, they essayed no conquests. They preserved their privileges, but remained shut up within their own walls. There the democratical organization was confined and stopped short; if we go elsewhere, into the country, we do not find it.

You see what was the state of the republican attempt; triumphant in Italy, but with little chance of success or progress; vanquished in the south of Gaul; victorious on a small scale, in the mountains of Switzerland; in the north, in the boroughs of Flanders, the Rhine, and the Hanseatic league, condemned never to pass beyond the town walls. Still, in this position, evidently inferior in force to the other elements of society, it inspired the feudal nobility with a prodigious terror. The lords were jealous of the wealth of the boroughs, and feared their power; the democratical spirit penetrated into the rural districts; the insurrections of the peasants became more frequent and obstinate. A great coalition was formed among the feudal nobility against the boroughs, almost throughout Europe. The party was unequal; the boroughs were isolated; there was no understanding or communication between them; all was local. There existed, indeed, a certain sympathy between the burghers of various countries; the successes or reverses of the towns in Flanders in the struggles with the dukes of Burgundy, certainly excited a lively emotion in the French towns; but this emotion was transitory and without result; no tie, no real union, was established; nor did the boroughs lend strength to one another. Feudalism, then, had immense advantages over them. But, itself divided and incoherent, it did not succeed in destroying them. When the struggle had lasted a certain time, when they had acquired the conviction that a complete victory was impossible, it became necessary to acknowledge the petty republican burghers, to treat with them, and to receive them as members of the state. Then a new order commenced, a new attempt at political organization, that of mixed organization, the object of which was to reconcile all the elements of society, the feudal nobility, the boroughs, clergy, and sovereigns, and to make them live and act together, in spite of their profound hostility.

All of you know what are the States-general in France, the Cortes in Spain and Portugal, the Parliament in England, and the Diets in Germany. You know, likewise, what were the elements of these various assemblies; the feudal nobility, the clergy, and the boroughs, collected at them with a view to unite themselves into a single society, into one state, under one law and one power. They all, under various names, have the same tendency and design.

I shall take, as the type of this attempt, the fact which is the most interesting and the best known to us, namely, the States-general in France. I say the best known to us; yet I am convinced that the name of States-general awakens in your minds only vague and incomplete ideas. None of you can say what there was fixed or regular in the States-general of France, what was the number of their members, what the subjects of deliberation, or what the periods of convocation and the duration of sessions; nothing is known of these things; it is impossible to draw from history any clear, general, or universal results as to this subject. When we examine closely the character of these assemblies in the history of France, they look like mere accidents, political last resource alike for people and kings; as a last resource for kings when they had no money, and knew not how to escape from their embarrassments; and as a last resource for the people when the evil became so great that they knew not what remedy to apply. The nobility were present in the States-general; the clergy likewise took part in them; but they came full of indifference, for they knew that this was not their great means of action, that they could not promote by it the real part they took in the government. The burghers themselves were scarcely more eager about it; it was not a right which they took an interest in exercising, but a necessity which they tolerated. Thus may be seen the character of the political activity of these assemblies. They were sometimes utterly insignificant, and sometimes terrible. If the king was the strongest, their humility and docility were carried to an extreme; if the situation of the crown was unfortunate, if it had absolute need of the States, they fell into faction, and became the instruments of some aristocratical intrigue, or some ambitious leaders. In a word, they were sometimes mere assemblies of notables, sometimes regular conventions. Thus their works almost always died with them; they promised and attempted much, and did nothing. None of the great measures which have really acted upon society in France, no important reform in the government, the legislation, or the administration, has emanated from the States-general. It must not, however, be supposed that they were without utility or effect; they have had a moral effect, of which too little account is generally taken; they have been, from one epoch to another, a protest against political servitude, a violent proclamation of certain tutelary principles; for example, that the country has the right to impose taxes, to interfere in its own affairs, and to impose a responsibility upon the agents of power.

That these maxims have never perished in France, is to be attributed to the States-general, and it is no small service to render to a people, to maintain in its manners, and renew in its thoughts, the remembrances and rights of liberty. The

States-general have possessed this virtue, but they have never
been a means of government; they have never entered into
the political organization; they have never attained the end
for which they were formed, that is to say, the fusion into
a single body of the various societies which divided the
country.

The Cortes of Spain and Portugal offer us the same result.
In a thousand circumstances, however, they are different.
The importance of the Cortes varies according to place
and time; in Aragon, and Biscay, amidst the debates concerning the succession to the crown, or the struggles against
the Moors, they were more frequently convoked and more
powerful. In certain Cortes, for example, in those of Castile,
in 1370 and 1373, the nobles and the clergy were not called.
There is a crowd of details which it is necessary should be
taken into account, if we look closely into events. But in
the general view to which I am obliged to confine myself, it
may be said of the Cortes, as of the States-general of France,
that they have been an accident in history, and never a system, political organization, or a regular means of government.

The destiny of England was different. I shall not now
enter upon this subject in detail. I propose to devote one
lecture especially to the political life of England; I shall
now merely say a few words upon the causes which have
imparted to it a direction entirely different from that of the
continent.

And first, there were no great vassals in England, no subject in a condition to strive personally against royalty. The
English barons and great lords were obliged to coalesce in
order to resist in common. Thus have prevailed, in the high
aristocracy, the principle of association and true political
manners. Moreover, English feudalism, the petty fief-holders,
have been gradually led, by a series of events which I cannot
enumerate at present, to unite themselves with the burghers,
to sit with them in the House of Commons, which thus possessed a power superior to that of the continental assemblies,
a force truly capable of influencing the government of the
country. Let us see what was the state of the British parliament in the fourteenth century. The House of Lords was
the great council of the king, a council actively associated in
the exercise of power. The House of Commons, composed

of the deputies of the petty fief-holders, and of burghers, took
scarcely any part in the government, properly so called, but
it established rights, and very energetically defended private
and local interests. The parliament, considered as a whole,
did not yet govern, but it was already a regular institution,
a means of government adopted in principle, and often, in
fact, indispensable. Thus the attempt at junction and alliance
between the various elements of society, with a view to form
of them a single political body, a regular State, was successful in England, while it had failed everywhere on the continent.

I shall say but a few words as to Germany, and those
only to indicate the dominant character of its history.
There, the attempts at fusion, unity, and general political
organization, were followed with little ardour. The various
social elements remained much more distinct and independent
than in the rest of Europe. If a proof is wanted, one may
be found in modern times. Germany is the only country
in which the feudal election long took part in the creation
of royalty. I do not speak of Poland, nor the Sclavonian
nations, which entered at so late an age into the system of
European civilization. Germany is likewise the only country of Europe where ecclesiastical sovereigns remained; which
preserved free towns, having a true political existence and
sovereignty. It is clear that the attempt to combine in a
single society the elements of primitive European society, has
there had much less activity and effect than elsewhere.

I have now placed before you the great essays at political
organization in Europe down to the end of the fourteenth
century and the beginning of the fifteenth. You have seen
them all fail. I have endeavoured to indicate in passing,
the causes of this ill success; indeed, truly speaking, they are
reduceable to one. Society was not sufficiently advanced for
unity; everything was as yet too local, too special, too narrow
too various in existence, and in men's minds. There were
neither general interests nor general opinions capable of controlling particular interests and opinions. The most elevated
and vigorous minds had no idea of administration, nor of true
political justice. It was evidently necessary that a more active
and vigorous civilization should first mix, assimilate, and, so
to speak, grind together all these incoherent elements; it was

o

first necessary that a powerful centralization of interest, laws, manners, and ideas, should be brought about; in a word, it was necessary that a public power and public opinion should arise. We have arrived at the epoch when this great work was consummated. Its first symptoms, the state of mind and manners during the course of the fifteenth century, the tendency towards the formation of a central government, and a public opinion, will form the subject of our next lecture.

ELEVENTH LECTURE.

Object of the lecture—Special character of the fifteenth century—Progressive centralization of nations and governments—1st. Of France—Formation of the national French spirit—Government of Louis XI.—2nd.
Of Spain—3rd. Of Germany—4th. Of England—5th. Of Italy—Origin
of the external relations of states and of diplomacy—Movement in religious ideas—Attempt at aristocratical reform—Council of Constance
and Basle—Attempt at popular reform—John Huss—Regeneration of
literature—Admiration for antiquity—Classical school, or free-thinkers
—General activity—Voyages, discoveries, inventions—Conclusion.

WE touch the threshold of modern history, properly so
called—the threshold of that society which is our own, of
which the institutions, opinions, and manners were, forty
years ago, those of France, are still those of Europe, and still
exercise so powerful an influence upon us, despite the metamorphosis brought about by our revolution. It was with
the sixteenth century, as I have already said, that modern society really commenced. Before entering upon it,
recal to your minds, I pray you, the roads over which
we have passed. We have discovered, amidst the ruins
of the Roman empire, all the essential elements of the Europe of the present day; we have seen them distinguish
and aggrandize themselves, each on its own account, and
independently. We recognised, during the first epoch of
history, the constant tendency of these elements to separation, isolation, and a local and special existence. Scarcely
was this end obtained—scarcely had feudalism, the boroughs,
and the clergy each taken its distinct form and place, than
we see them tending to approach each other, to reunite, and
form themselves into a general society, into a nation and

o 2

a government. In order to arrive at this result, the various
countries of Europe addressed themselves to all the different systems which co-existed in its bosom; they demanded
the principle of social unity, the political and moral tie,
from theocracy, aristocracy, democracy, and royalty. Hitherto,
all these attempts had failed; no system or influence had
known how to seize upon society, and by its empire to insure
it a truly public destiny. We have found the cause of this
ill success in the absence of universal interests and ideas.
We have seen that all was, as yet, too special, individual,
and local; that a long and powerful labour of centralization was necessary to enable society to extend and cement
itself at the same time, to become at once great and regular—an end to which it necessarily aspired. This was the
state in which we left Europe at the end of the fourteenth
century.

She was far from understanding her position, such as I
have endeavoured to place it before you. She did not know
distinctly what she wanted or what she sought; still she applied herself to the search, as if she knew. The fourteenth cen
tury closed. Europe entered naturally, and, as it were, instinctively, the path which led to centralization. It is the characteristic of the fifteenth century to have constantly tended to
this result; to have laboured to create universal interests and
ideas, to make the spirit of speciality and locality disappear,
to reunite and elevate existences and minds; in fine, to
create, what had hitherto never existed on a large scale,
nations and governments. The outbreak of this fact belongs
to the sixteenth and seventeenth centuries; it was in the
fifteenth that it was preparing. It is this preparation which
we have to investigate at present—this silent and concealed
work of centralization, whether in social relations or ideas, a
work accomplished by the natural course of events, without
premeditation or design.

Thus man advances in the execution of a plan which he
has not himself conceived, or which, perhaps, he does not
even understand. He is the intelligent and free artificer
of a work which does not belong to him. He does not recognise or comprehend it until a later period, when it mani
fests itself outwardly and in realities; and even then he
understands it but very incompletely. Yet it is by him, it is

by the development of his intellect and his liberty that it is accomplished. Conceive a great machine, of which the idea resides in a single mind, and of which the different pieces are confided to different workmen, who are scattered, and are strangers to one another; none of them knowing the work as a whole, or the definitive and general result to which it concurs, yet each executing with intelligence and liberty, by rational and voluntary acts, that of which he has the charge. So is the plan of Providence upon the world executed by the hand of mankind; thus do the two facts which manifest themselves in the history of civilization co-exist; on the one hand, its fatality, that which escapes science and the human will—and on the other, the part played therein by the liberty and intellect of man, that which he infuses of his own will by his own thought and inclination.

In order properly to comprehend the fifteenth century—to obtain a clear and exact idea of this prelude, as it were, of modern society—we will distinguish the different classes of facts. We will first examine the political facts, the changes which have tended to form both nations and governments. Thence we will pass to moral facts; we will observe the changes which have been produced in ideas and manners, and we will thence deduce what general opinions were in preparation. As regards political facts, in order to proceed simply and quickly, I will run over all the great countries of Europe, and show you what the fifteenth century made of them—in what state it found and left them.

I shall commence with France. The last half of the fourteenth century and the first half of the fifteenth were, as you know, the times of great national wars—the wars against the English. It was the epoch of the struggle for the independence of France and the French name against a foreign dominion. A glance at history will show with what ardour, despite a multitude of dissensions and treasons, all classes of society in France concurred in this struggle; what patriotism took possession of the feudal nobility, the burghers, and even the peasants. If there were nothing else to show the popular character of the event than the history of Joan of Arc, it would be a more than sufficient proof. Joan of Arc sprang from the people. It was by the sentiments, creed, and passions of the people that she was inspired and sustained. She was looked upon with distrust, scorn, and even enmity, by the people of the court and the chiefs of the army; but she had the soldiers and the people ever on her side. It was the peasants of Lorraine who sent her to the succour of the burghers of Orleans. No event has more strikingly shown the popular character of this war, and the feeling with which the whole country regarded it.

Thus began the formation of French nationality. Up to the reign of the Valois, it was the feudal character which dominated in France; the French nation, the French mind, French patriotism, did not as yet exist. With the Valois commenced France, properly so called. It was in the course of their wars, through the phases of their destiny, that the nobility, the burghers, and the peasants, were for the first time united by a moral tie, by the tie of a common name, a common honour, and a common desire to conquer the enemy. But expect not to find there as yet any true political spirit, nor any great purpose of unity in the government and institutions, such as we conceive them in the present day. Unity, in the France of this epoch, resided in its name, its national honour, and in the existence of a national royalty, whatever it might be, provided the foreigner did not appear therein. It is in this way that the struggle against the English powerfully contributed to the formation of the French nation, to impel it towards unity. At the same time that France was thus morally forming herself, and the national spirit was being developed, she was also forming herself materially, so to speak—that is to say, her territory was being regulated, extended, strengthened. This was the period of the incorporation of the greater part of the provinces which have become *France*. Under Charles VII., after the expulsion of the English, almost all the provinces which they had occupied, Normandy, Angoumois, Touraine, Poitou, Saintonge, &c., became definitively French. Under Louis XI., ten provinces, three of which were afterwards lost and regained, were united to France; namely, Roussillon and Cerdagne, Burgundy, Franche-Comté, Picardy, Artois, Provence, Maine, Anjou, and Perche. Under Charles VIII and Louis XII., the successive marriages of Anne with these two kings brought us Brittany. Thus, at the same epoch, and during the course of the same events, the national territory and mind were forming together; moral and material France conjointly acquired strength and unity.

. Let us pass from the nation to the government; we shall see the accomplishment of similar facts, shall move towards the same result. Never had the French government been more devoid of unity, connexion, and strength, than under the reign of Charles VI. and during the first part of that of Charles VII. At the end of this latter reign, the aspect of all things changed. There was evidently a strengthening, extending, and organizing of power; all the great means of government—taxes, military force, law,—were created upon a great scale, and with some uniformity. This was the time of the formation of standing armies—free companies, cavalry—and free archers, infantry. By these companies Charles VII. re-established some order in those provinces which had been desolated by the disorders and exactions of the soldiery, even after war had ceased. All contemporary historians speak with astonishment of the marvellous effects of the free companies. It was at the same epoch that the poll-tax, one of the principal revenues of the kingdom, became perpetual; a serious blow to the liberty of the people, but which powerfully contributed to the regularity and strength of the government. At this time, too, the great instrument of power, the administration of justice, was extended and organized; parliaments multiplied. There were five new parliaments constituted within a very short period of time: under Louis XI., the parliament of Grenoble (in 1451), of Bordeaux (in 1462), and of Dijon (1477); under Louis XII., the parliaments of Rouen (in 1499) and of Aix (in 1501). The parliament of Paris, also, at this time greatly increased in importance and firmness, both as regards the administration of justice, and as charged with the policy of its jurisdiction.

Thus, as regards military force, taxation, and justice, that is, in what constitutes its very essence, government in France, in the fifteenth century, acquired a character of permanence and regularity hitherto unknown; public power definitively took the place of the feudal powers.

At the same time another and far different change was

brought about; a change which was less visible, and which
has less impressed itself upon historians, but which was perhaps of still more importance—namely, the change which
Louis XI. effected in the manner of governing.

Much has been said concerning the struggle of Louis XI.
against the high nobles of the kingdom, of their abasement,
and of his favour towards the burghers and the lower classes.
There is truth in this, although much of it is exaggerated; it
is also true, that the conduct of Louis XI. towards the
different classes oftener troubled than served the state.   But
he did something much more important.   Up to this time,
the government had proceeded almost entirely by force and
by material means.   Persuasion, address, the managing men's
minds, and leading them to particular views, in a word,
policy—policy, doubtless, of falsehood and imposition, but
also of management and prudence, had hitherto been but
little attended to.   Louis XI. substituted in the government
intellectual in place of material means, artifice instead of
force, the Italian policy in place of the feudal.   Look at the
two men whose rivalry occupies this epoch of our history,
Charles le Téméraire and Louis XI.   Charles was the representative of the ancient form of governing; he proceeded
by violence alone, he appealed incessantly to war, he was
incapable of exercising patience, or of addressing himself to
the minds of men in order to make them instruments to his
success.   It was, on the contrary, the pleasure of Louis XI.
to avoid the use of force, and take possession of men individually by conversation, and the skilful handling of interests
and minds.   He changed neither the institutions nor the external system, but only the secret proceedings, the tactics or
power.   It was left for modern times to attempt a still greater
revolution, by labouring to introduce, alike into political
means as into political ends, justice instead of selfishness, and
publicity in place of lying fraud.   It is not less true, however,
that there was great indication of progress in renouncing the
continual employment of force, in invoking chiefly intellectual
superiority, in governing through mind, and not by the ruin
of existences.   It was this that Louis XI. commenced, by
force of his high intellect alone, amidst all his crimes and
faults, despite his bad nature.

From France I pass to Spain; there I find events of the same nature; it was thus that the national unity of Spain was formed in the fifteenth century; at that time, by the conquest of the kingdom of Grenada, the lengthened struggle between the Christians and the Arabs was put an end to. Then, also, the country was centralized; by the marriage of Ferdinand the Catholic and Isabella, the two principal kingdoms of Castile and Aragon were united under one power. As in France, royalty was here extended and strengthened; sterner institutions, and which bore a more mournful name, served as its fulcrum; instead of parliament, the inquisition arose. It contained in germ what it was to be, but it was not then the same as in its maturer age. It was at first rather political than religious, and intended rather to maintain order, than to defend the faith. The analogy extends beyond institutions, it is found even in the persons. With less artifice, mental movement, and restless and busy activity, the character and government of Ferdinand the Catholic resemble that of Louis XI. I hold as unimportant all arbitrary comparisons and fanciful parallels; but here the analogy is profound, and visible alike in general facts and in details.

We find the same in Germany. It was in the middle of the fifteenth century, in 1438, that the house of Austria returned to the Empire, and with it the imperial power acquired a permanence which it had never possessed before; election afterwards did little more than consecrate the hereditary successor. At the end of the fifteenth century, Maximilian I. definitively founded the preponderance of his house, and the regular exercise of central authority; Charles VII. first created in France a standing army, for the maintenance of order; Maximilian was also the first, in his hereditary states, to attain the same end by the same means. Louis XI. established the post-office in France; and Maximilian introduced it into Germany. Everywhere the same progressions of civilization were similarly cultivated for the good of central power.

The history of England in the fifteenth century consists of two great events; without, the struggle against the French, and within, that of the two Roses, the foreign and the civil war. These two so dissimilar wars led to the same result. The struggle against the French was sustained by the English people with

an ardour which profited only royalty.   This nation, already
more skilful and firm than any other in keeping back its forces
and supplies, at this epoch abandoned them to its kings without foresight or limit.   It was under the reign of Henry V.
that a considerable tax, the customs, was granted to the king
from the commencement of his reign, until his death. When the
foreign war was ended, or almost so, the civil war, which had
York been associated with it, continued alone; the houses of
at first and Lancaster disputed for the throne.   When they
came to the end of their bloody contests, the high English
aristocracy found itself ruined, decimated, and incapable of
preserving the power which it had hitherto exercised.   The
coalition of the great barons could no longer influence the
throne.   The Tudors ascended it, and with Henry VII. in
1485, commenced the epoch of political centralization, and
the triumph of royalty.

Royalty was not established in Italy, at least not under that
name; but this matters little as regards the result.   It was in
the fifteenth century that the republics fell; even where the
name remained, the power was concentred in the hands of
one or more families; republican life was extinct.   In the
north of Italy, almost all the Lombard republics were absorbed
in the duchy of Milan.   In 1434, Florence fell under the
domination of the Medicis; in 1464, Genoa became subject
to the Milanese.   The greater portion of the republics, great
and small, gave place to sovereign houses.   The pretensions
of foreign sovereigns were soon put forth upon the north
and south of Italy, upon the Milanese on one side, and on the
kingdom of Naples on the other.

Upon whatever country of Europe we turn our eyes, and
whatever portion of its history we may consider, whether it
has reference to the nations themselves, or to their governments, to the institutions or the countries, we shall everywhere see the ancient elements and forms of society on the
point of disappearing.   The traditional liberties perish, and
new and more concentrated and regular powers arise.   There
is something profoundly sad in the fall of the old European
liberties; at the time, it inspired the bitterest feelings.   In
France, Germany, and, above all, in Italy, the patriots of
the fifteenth century contested with ardour, and deplored
with despair, this revolution, which, on all sides, was bringing

about what might justly be called despotism. One cannot help admiring their courage and commiserating their sorrow; but, at the same time, it must be understood that this revolution was not only inevitable, but beneficial also. The primitive system of Europe, the old feudal and communal liberties, had failed in the organization of society. What constitutes social life is security and progress. Any system which does not procure present order and future progress, is vicious, and soon abandoned. Such was the fate of the ancient political forms, the old European liberties, in the fifteenth century. They could give to society neither security nor progress. These were sought elsewhere, from other principles and other means. This is the meaning of all the facts which I have just placed before you.

From the same epoch dates another fact, which has held an important place in the political history of Europe. It was in the fifteenth century that the relations of governments between themselves began to be frequent, regular, permanent. It was then, for the first time, that those great alliances were formed, whether for peace or war, which at a later period produced the system of equilibrium. Diplomacy in Europe dates from the fifteenth century. Towards the end of this century you see the principal powers of Continental Europe, the popes, the dukes of Milan, the Venetians, the emperors of Germany, and the kings of Spain and of France, form connexions, negotiate, unite, balance each other. Thus, at the time that Charles VII. formed his expedition to conquer the kingdom of Naples, a great league was formed against him, between Spain, the pope, and the Venetians. The league of Cambrai was formed some years later, (in 1508,) against the Venetians. The holy league, directed against Louis XII, succeeded in 1511 to the league of Cambrai. All these alliances arose from Italian policy, from the desire of various sovereigns to possess Italy, and from the fear that some one of them, by seizing it exclusively, should acquire an overpowering preponderance. This new order of facts was highly favourable to the development of royalty. On the one hand, from the nature of the external relations of states, they can only be conducted by a single person or a small number of persons, and exact a certain secrecy; on the other, the people had so little foresight, that the consequences of an alliance of this kind escaped them; it was not, for them, of any internal or direct interest; they cared little about it, and left such events to the discretion of the central power. Thus diplomacy, at its birth, fell into the hands of the kings, and the idea that it belonged exclusively to them, that the country, although free, and having the right of voting its taxes and interfering in its affairs, was not called upon to mix itself in external matters—this idea, I say, was established in almost all European minds, as an accepted principle, a maxim of common law. Open English history at the sixteenth and seventeenth centuries, you will see what power this idea exercised, and what obstacles it opposed to English liberties under the reigns of Elizabeth, James I., and Charles I. It was always under the name of this principle that peace and war, commercial relations, and all external affairs, appertained to the royal prerogative; and it was by this that absolute power defended itself against the rights of the country. Nations have been excessively timid in contesting this part of prerogative; and this timidity has cost them the more dear, since, from the epoch upon which we are now entering, that is to say, the sixteenth century, the history of Europe is essentially diplomatic. External relations, during nearly three centuries, are the important fact of history. Within, nations became regulated, the internal government, upon the continent, at least, led to no more violent agitations, nor absorbed public activity. It is external relations, wars, negotiations, and alliances, which attract attention, and fill the pages of history, so that the greater portion of the destiny of nations has been abandoned to the royal prerogative and to central power.

Indeed, it was hardly possible it should be otherwise. A very great progress in civilization, and a great development of intellect and political skill are necessary, before the public can interfere with any success in affairs of this kind. From the sixteenth to the eighteenth century, the people were very far from being thus qualified. See what took place under James I. in England, at the commencement of the seventeenth century: his son-in-law, the elector-palatine, elected king of Bohemia, lost his crown; he was even robbed of his hereditary states, the palatinate. The whole of protestantism was interested in his cause, and for that reason England testified a lively interest towards him. There was a powerful ebullition of public opinion to force king James to take the part of his son-in-law, and regain for him the palatinate. Parliament furiously demanded war, promising all the means for carrying it on. James was unwilling; he eluded the matter, made some attempts at negotiation, sent some troops to Germany, and then came to tell parliament that £900,000 sterling were necessary to maintain the contest with any chance of success. It is not said, nor indeed does it appear to have been the case, that his calculation was exaggerated. But the parliament recoiled with surprise and terror at the prospect of such a charge, and it unwillingly voted £70,000 sterling to re-establish a prince, and reconquer a country three hundred leagues from England. Such was the political ignorance and incapacity of the public in matters of this kind; it acted without knowledge of facts, and without troubling itself with any responsibility. It was not, then, in a condition to interfere in a regular or efficacious manner. This is the principal cause of the external relations falling into the hands of the central power; that alone was in a condition to direct them, I do not say for the public interest, for it was far from being always consulted, but with any continuity or good sense.

You see, under whatever point of view the political history of Europe at this epoch is presented to us, whether we turn our eyes upon the internal state of nations, or upon the relations of nations with each other, whether we consider the administration of war, justice, or taxation, we everywhere find the same character; everywhere we see the same tendency to the centralization, unity, formation, and preponderance of general interests and public powers. This was the secret work of the fifteenth century, a work which did not as yet lead to any very prominent result, nor any revolution, properly so called, in society, but which prepared the way for all of them. I shall immediately place before you facts of another nature, moral facts, facts which relate to the development of the human mind, and universal ideas. There also we shall acknowledge the same phenomenon, and arrive at the same result.

I shall commence with a class of facts which has often occupied us, and which, under the most various forms, has

always held an important place in the history of Europe,
namely, facts relative to the church.   Down to the fifteenth
century we have seen in Europe no universal and powerful
ideas acting truly upon the masses, except those of a religious
nature.   We have seen the church alone invested with the
power of regulating, promulgating, and prescribing them.
Often, it is true, attempts at independence, even separation, were formed, and the church had much to do to overcome them.   But hitherto she had conquered them; creeds
repudiated by the church had taken no general and permanent possession of the minds of the people; the Albigenses
themselves were crushed.   Dissension and contest were of
incessant occurrence in the heart of the church, but without
any decisive or eminent result.   At the beginning of the fifteenth century, an entirely different fact announced itself;
new ideas, a public and avowed want of change and reform,
agitated the church herself.   The end of the fourteenth and
commencement of the fifteenth century were marked by the
great schism of the west, the result of the translation of the
holy see to Avignon, and of the creation of two popes, one at
Avignon, the other at Rome.   The struggle between these
two papacies is what is called the great schism of the west.
It commenced in 1378.   In 1409, the council of Pisa wishing
to end it, deposed both popes, and nominated a third, Alexander V.   So far from being appeased, the schism became
warmer; there were three popes instead of two.   The disorder and abuses continued to increase.   In 1414, the
council of Constance assembled, at the summons of the
emperor Sigismond.   It proposed to itself a work very different from nominating a new pope; it undertook the reform
of the church.   It first proclaimed the indissolubility of the
general council, and its superiority over the papal power; it
undertook to make these principles prevalent in the church,
and to reform the abuses which had crept into it, above all
the exactions by which the court of Rome had procured supplies.   For the attainment of this end, the council nominated
what we will call a commission of inquiry, that is to say, a
college of reform, composed of deputies of the council taken
from different nations; it was the duty of this college to seek
what were the abuses which disgraced the church, and how
they might best be remedied, and to make a report to the

council, which would consult upon the means of execution.
But while the council was occupied in this work, the question was mooted as to whether they could proceed in the reformation of abuses, without the visible participation of the
chief of the church, without the sanction of the pope.   The
negative was passed by the influence of the Romanist party,
supported by honest, but timid men; the council elected
a new pope, Martin V., in 1417.   The pope was desired to
present on his part a plan of reform in the church.   This
plan was not approved, and the council separated.   In 1431
a new council assembled at Basle with the same view.   It
resumed and continued the work of reform of the council of
Constance, and met with no better success.   Schism broke
out in the interior of the assembly, the same as in Christianity.
The pope transferred the council of Basle to Ferrara, and
afterwards to Florence.   Part of the prelates refused to obey
the pope, and remained at Basle; and as formerly there had
been two popes, so there were now two councils.   That of
Basle continued its projects of reform, and nominated its
pope, Felix V.   After a certain time, it transported itself to
Lausanne; and in 1449 dissolved itself, without having
effected anything.

* Thus papacy carried the day, and remained in possession
of the field of battle and the government of the church.   The
council could not accomplish what it had undertaken; but
it effected things which it had not undertaken, and which
survived it.   At the time that the council of Basle failed in
its attempts at reform, sovereigns seized upon the ideas which
it proclaimed, and the institutions which it suggested.   In
France, upon the foundation of the decrees of the council of
Basle, Charles V. formed the Pragmatic Sanction, which he
issued at Bourges in 1438; it enunciated the election of
bishops, the suppression of first fruits, and the reform of the
principal abuses which had been introduced into the church.
The Pragmatic Sanction was declared in France the law of the
state.   In Germany, the diet of Mayence adopted it in 1439,
and likewise made it a law of the German empire.   What
the spiritual power had unsuccessfully attempted, the temporal power seemed destined to accomplish.

New reverses sprang up for the projects of reform.   As
the council had failed, so did the Pragmatic Sanction.   In

Germany it perished very abruptly. The diet abandoned it in 1448, in consequence of a negotiation with Nicholas V. In 1516, Francis I. likewise abandoned it, and in its place substituted his Concordat with Leo X. The princes' reform did not succeed any better than that of the clergy. But it must not be supposed that it entirely perished. As the council effected things which survived it, so also the Pragmatic Sanction had consequences which it left behind, and which played an important part in modern history. The principles of the council of Basle were powerful and fertile. Superior men, and men of energetic character, have adopted and supported them. John of Paris, D'Ailly, Gerson, and many distinguished men of the fifteenth century, devoted themselves to their defence. In vain was the council dissolved; in vain was the Pragmatic Sanction abandoned; its general doctrines upon the government of the church, and upon the reforms necessary to be carried out, had taken root in France; they were perpetuated; they passed into the parliaments, and became a powerful opinion. They gave rise first to the Jansenists, and afterwards to the Gallicans. All this series of maxims and efforts tending to reform the church, which commenced with the council of Constance, and terminated with the four propositions of Bossuet, emanated from the same source, and were directed towards the same end; it was the same fact successively transformed. It was in vain that the attempt at legal reform in the fifteenth century failed; not the less has it taken its place in the course of civilization —not the less has it indirectly exercised an enormous influence.

The councils were right in pursuing a legal reform, for that alone could prevent a revolution. Almost at the moment when the council of Pisa undertook to bring the great schism of the west to a termination, and the council of Constance to reform the church, the first essays at popular religious reform violently burst forth in Bohemia. The predictions and progress of John Huss date from 1404, at which period he began to teach at Prague. Here, then, are two reforms marching side by side; the one in the very heart of the church, attempted by the ecclesiastical aristocracy itself—a wise, but embarrassed and timid reform; the other, outside and against the church, violent and passionate. A contest arose between these two powers and designs. The council summoned John Huss and Jerome of Prague to Constance, and condemned them as heretics and revolutionists. These events are perfectly intelligible to us at the present day. We can very well understand this simultaneousness of separate reforms—enterprises undertaken, one by the governments, the other by the people, opposed to one another, and yet emanating from the same cause and tending to the same end, and, in fine, although at war with each other, still concurring to the same result. This is what occurred in the fifteenth century. The popular reform of John Huss was for the instant stifled; the war of the Hussites broke forth three or four years after the death of the irmaster. It lasted long, and was violent, but the Empire finally triumphed. But as the reform of the councils had failed, as the end which they pursued had not been attained, the popular reform ceased not to ferment. It watched the first opportunity, and found it at the commencement of the sixteenth century. If the reform undertaken by the councils had been well carried out, the Reformation might have been prevented. But one or the other must have succeeded; their coincidence shows a necessity.

This, then, is the state in which Europe was left by the fifteenth century with regard to religious matters—an aristocratical reform unsuccessfully attempted, and a popular reform commenced, stifled, and always ready to re-appear. But it was not to the sphere of religious creeds that the fermentation of the human mind at this epoch was confined. It was in the course of the fourteenth century, as you all know, that Greek and Roman antiquity were, so to speak, restored in Europe. You know with what eagerness Dante, Petrarch, Boccaccio, and all their contemporaries sought for the Greek and Latin manuscripts, and published and promulgated them, and what noise and transports the least discovery of this kind excited.

In the midst of this excitement, a school was commenced in Europe which has played a very much more important part in the development of the human mind than has generally been attributed to it: this was the classical school. Let me warn you from attaching the same sense to this word which we give to it in the present day; it was then a very different thing from a literary system or contest. The classical school of that period was inflamed with admiration, not only

P

for the writings of the ancients, for Virgil and Homer, but for the whole of ancient society, for its institutions, opinions, and philosophy, as well as for its literature. It must be confessed that antiquity, under the heads of politics, philosophy, and literature, was far superior to the Europe of the fourteenth and fifteenth centuries. It cannot therefore be wondered at that it should exercise so great a sway, or that for the most part elevated, active, refined, and fastidious minds, should take a disgust at the coarse manners, confused ideas, and barbarous forms of their own times, and that they should devote themselves with enthusiasm to the study, and almost to the worship of a society at once more regular and developed. Thus was formed that school of free thinkers which appeared at the commencement of the fifteenth century, and in which prelates, jurisconsults, and scholars, met together.

Amidst this excitement happened the taking of Constantinople by the Turks, the fall of the Eastern empire, and the flight into Italy of the Greek fugitives. They brought with them a higher knowledge of antiquity, numerous manuscripts, and a thousand new means of studying ancient civilization. The redoubled admiration and ardour with which the classical school was animated may easily be imagined. This was the time of the most brilliant development of the high clergy, particularly in Italy, not as regards political power, properly speaking, but in point of luxury and wealth; they abandoned themselves with pride to all the pleasures of a voluptuous, indolent, elegant, and licentious civilization—to the taste for letters and arts, and for social and material enjoyments. Look at the kind of life led by the men who played a great political and literary part at this epoch—by Cardinal Bembo, for instance; you will be surprised at the mixture of sybaritism and intellectual development, of effeminate manners and hardihood of mind. One would think, indeed, when we glance over this epoch, when we are present at the spectacle of its ideas and the state of its moral relations, one would think we were living in France in the midst of the eighteenth century. There is the same taste for intellectual excitement, for new ideas, for an easy, agreeable life; the same effeminateness and licentiousness; the same deficiency in political energy and moral faith, with a singular sincerity and activity of mind. The literati of the fifteenth century were, with regard to the prelates of the high church, in the same relation as men of letters and philosophers of the eighteenth century with the high aristocracy; they all had the same opinions and the same manners, lived harmoniously together, and did not trouble themselves about the commotions that were in preparation around them. The prelates of the fifteenth century, commencing with Cardinal Bembo, most certainly no more foresaw Luther and Calvin than the people of the court foresaw the French revolution. The position, however, was analogous.

Three great facts, then, present themselves at this epoch in the moral order: first, an ecclesiastical reform attempted by the church herself; secondly, a popular religious reform; and finally an intellectual reform, which gave rise to a school of free thinkers. And all these metamorphoses were in preparation amidst the greatest political change which had taken place in Europe, amidst the work of centralization of people and governments.

This was not all. This also was the time of the greatest external activity of mankind; it was a period of voyages, enterprises, discoveries, and inventions of all kinds. This was the time of the great expeditions of the Portuguese along the coast of Africa, of the discovery of the passage of the Cape of Good Hope by Vasco de Gama, of the discovery of America by Christopher Columbus, and of the wonderful extension of European commerce. A thousand new inventions came forth; others already known, but only within a narrow sphere, became popular and of common use. Gunpowder changed the system of war, the compass changed the system of navigation. The art of oil painting developed itself, and covered Europe with masterpieces of art: engraving on copper, invented in 1460, multiplied and promulgated them. Linen paper became common; and lastly, from 1436 to 1452, printing was invented; printing, the theme of so much declamation and so many common-places, but the merit and effects of which no common-place nor any declamation can ever exhaust.

You see what was the greatness and activity of this century—a greatness still only partially apparent, an activity, the results of which have not yet been fully developed.

P 2

Violent reforms seem unsuccessful, governments strengthened,
and nations pacified.   It might be thought that society was
preparing to enjoy a better order of things, amidst a more
rapid progress.   But the powerful revolutions of the sixteenth century were impending: the fifteenth had been preparing them.   They will be the subject of my next lecture.

TWELFTH LECTURE.

Object of the lecture—Difficulty of distinguishing general facts in modern history—Picture of Europe in the sixteenth century—Danger of precipitate generalization—Various causes assigned to the Reformation—Its dominant character was the insurrection of the human mind against absolute power in the intellectual order—Evidences of this fact—Fate of the Reformation in different countries—Weak side of the Reformation—The Jesuits—Analogy between the revolutions of religious society and those of civil society.

WE have often deplored the disorder and chaos of European society; we have complained of the difficulty of understanding and describing a society thus scattered, incoherent, and broken up; we have longed for, and patiently invoked, the epoch of general interests, order, and social unity. We have now arrived at it; we are entering upon the epoch when all is general facts and general ideas, the epoch of order and unity. We shall here encounter a difficulty of another kind. Hitherto we have had much trouble in connecting facts with one another, in making them co-ordinate, in perceiving whatever they may possess in common, and distinguishing some completeness. Everything reverses itself in modern Europe; all the elements and incidents of social life modify themselves, and act and react on one another; the relations of men among themselves become much more numerous and complicated. It is the same in their relations with the government of the state, the same in the relations of the states among themselves, the same in ideas and in the works of the human mind. In the times which we have gone through, a large number of facts passed away isolated, foreign to one another, and without reciprocal influence.

We shall now no longer find this isolation; all things touch, commingle, and modify as they meet. Is there anything more difficult than to seize the true unity amid such diversity, to determine the direction of a movement so extended and complex, to recapitulate this prodigious number of various elements so clearly connected with one another; in fine, to ascertain the general dominant fact, which sums up a long series of facts, which characterizes an epoch, and is the faithful expression of its influence and its share in the history of civilization? You will measure with a glance this difficulty, in the great event which now occupies our attention. We encountered, in the twelfth century, an event which was religious in its origin if not in its nature, I mean the crusades. Despite the greatness of this event, despite its long duration and the variety of incidents to which it led, we found it difficult enough to distinguish its general character, and to determine with any precision its unity and its influence. We have now to consider the religious revolution of the sixteenth century, usually called the Reformation. Permit me to say, in passing, that I shall use the word *reformation* as a simple and understood term, as synonymous with *religious revolution*, and without implying any judgment of it. You see, at the very commencement, how difficult it is to recognise the true character of this great crisis, to say in a general manner what it was and what it effected.

It is between the commencement of the sixteenth and the middle of the seventeenth century that we must look for the Reformation; for that period comprises, so to speak, the life of the event, its origin and end. All historical events have, so to speak, a limited career; their consequences are prolonged to infinity; they have a hold upon all the past and all the future; but it is not the less true that they have a particular and limited existence, that they are born, that they increase, that they fill with their development a certain duration of time, and then decrease and retire from the scene in order to make room for some new event.

The precise date assigned to the origin of the Reformation is of little importance; we may take the year 1520, when Luther publicly burnt, at Wittemberg, the bull of Leo X.

which condemned him, and thus formally separated him-self from the Roman church. It was between this epoch and the middle of the seventeenth century, the year 1648, the date of the treaty of Westphalia, that the life of the Reforma-tion was comprised. Here is the proof of it. The first and greatest effect of the religious revolution was to create in Europe two classes of states, the Catholic states and the Pro-testant states, to place them opposite each other, and open the contest between them. With many vicissitudes, this struggle lasted from the commencement of the sixteenth century down to the middle of the seventeenth. It was by the treaty of Westphalia, in 1648, that the Catholic and Pro-testant states at last acknowledged one another; agreed to, then, a mutual existence, and promised to live in society and peace, independently of the diversity of religion. Dating from 1648, diversity in religion ceased to be the dominant principle of the classification of states, of their external policy, their relations, and alliances. Up to this epoch, in spite of great variations, Europe was essentially divided into a Catholic and a Protestant league. After the treaty of West-phalia, this distinction vanished; states were either allied or divided upon other considerations than religious creeds. At that point, then, the preponderance, that is to say, the career, of the Reformation stopped, although its consequences did not then cease to develop themselves. Let us now glance hastily over this career; and without doing more than naming events and men, let us indicate what it contains. You will see by this mere indication, by this dry and incom-plete nomenclature, what must be the difficulty of recapitu-lating a series of facts so varied and so complex—of recapitu-lating them, I say, in one general fact; of determining what was the true character of the religious revolution of the six-teenth century, and of assigning its part in the history of our civilization. At the moment when the Reformation broke forth, it fell, so to speak, into the midst of a great political event, the struggle between Francis I. and Charles V., between France and Spain; a contest, first for the pos-session of Italy, afterwards for that of the empire of Ger-many, and, lastly, for the preponderance in Europe. It was then the house of Austria elevated itself, and became dominant in Europe. It was then, also, that England, under

Henry VIII., interfered in continental politics with more
regularity, permanence, and to a greater extent than she had
hitherto done.

Let us follow the course of the sixteenth century in France.
It was filled by the great religious wars of the Protestants and
Catholics, the means and the occasion of a new attempt of
the great lords to regain the power they had lost. This
is the political purport of our religious wars, of the League,
of the struggle of the Guises against the Valois, a struggle
which ended by the accession of Henry IV.

In Spain, during the reign of Philip II., the revolution of
the United Provinces broke out. The inquisition and civil
and religious liberty waged war under the names of the duke
of Alva and the prince of Orange. While liberty triumphed
in Holland by force of perseverance and good sense, she
perished in the interior of Spain, where absolute power prevailed, both lay and ecclesiastical.

In England, during this period, Mary and Elizabeth
reigned; there was the contest of Elizabeth, the head of Protestantism, against Philip II. Accession of James Stuart to
the throne of England; commencement of the great quarrels
between royalty and the English people.

About the same time, new powers were created in the
north. Sweden was reinstated by Gustavus Vasa, in 1523.
Prussia was created by the secularising of the Teutonic order.
The powers of the north then took in European politics a
place which they had never hitherto occupied, the importance
of which was soon to be shown in the thirty years war.

I return to France. The reign of Louis XIII.; Cardinal
Richelieu changed the internal administration of France, entered into relations with Germany, and lent aid to the Protestant party. In Germany, during the last part of the sixteenth century, the contest took place against the Turks;
and at the commencement of the seventeenth century the
thirty years war, the greatest event of modern Eastern
Europe. At this time flourished Gustavus Adolphus, Wallen-
stein, Tilly, the duke of Brunswick, and the duke of Weimar,
the greatest names that Germany has yet to pronounce.

At the same epoch, in France, Louis XIV. ascended the
throne; the Fronde commenced. In England, the revolution which dethroned Charles I., broke out.

I only take the leading events of history, events whose name every one knows; you see their number, variety, and importance. If we seek events of another nature, events which are less apparent, and which are less summed up in names, we shall find this epoch equally full. This is the period of the greatest changes in the political institutions of almost all nations, the time when pure monarchy prevailed in the majority of great states, whilst in Holland the most powerful republic in Europe was created, and in England constitutional monarchy triumphed definitively, or nearly so. In the church, this was the period when the ancient monastic orders lost almost all political power, and were replaced by a new order of another character, and the importance of which, perhaps erroneously, is held as far superior to theirs, the Jesuits. At this epoch, the council of Trent effaced what might still remain of the influence of the councils of Constance and Basle, and secured the definitive triumph of the court of Rome in the ecclesiastical order. Let us leave the church, and cast a glance upon philosophy, upon the free career of the human mind; two men present themselves, Bacon and Descartes, the authors of the greatest philosophical revolution which the modern world has undergone, the chiefs of the two schools which disputed its empire. This also was the period of the brilliancy of Italian literature, and of the commencement of French and of English literature. And lastly, it was the time of the foundation of great colonies and the most active developments of the commercial system. Thus, under whatever point of view you consider this epoch, its political, ecclesiastical, philosophical, and literary events are in greater number, and more varied and important, than in any century preceding it. The activity of the human mind manifested itself in every way, in the relations of men between themselves, in their relations with power, in the relations of states, and in purely intellectual labours; in a word, it was a time for great men and for great things. And in the midst of this period, the religious revolution which occupies our attention is the greatest event of all; it is the dominant fact of this epoch, the fact which gives to it its name, and determines its character. Among so many powerful causes which have played so important a part, the Reformation is the most power-

ful, that in which all the others ended, which modified
them all, or was by them modified. So that what we have to
do at present is to truly characterise and accurately sum up
the event which in a period of the greatest events dominated
over all, the cause which effected more than all others in a
time of the most influential causes.

You will easily comprehend the difficulty of reducing facts
so various, so important, and so closely united, to a true
historical unity. It is, however, necessary to do this. When
events are once consummated, when they have become history,
what are most important, and what man seeks above all things,
are general facts, the connexion of causes and effects. These,
so to speak, are the immortal part of history, that to which all
generations must refer in order to understand the past, and
to understand themselves. The necessity for generalisation
and rational result, is the most powerful and the most
glorious of all intellectual wants; but we should be careful
not to be contented with incomplete and precipitate gene-
ralisations. Nothing can be more tempting than to give
way to the pleasure of assigning immediately and at the
first view, the general character and permanent results of an
epoch or event. The human mind is like the will, always
urgent for action, impatient of obstacles, and eager for
liberty and conclusions; it willingly forgets facts which im-
pede and cramp it; but in forgetting, it does not destroy
them; they subsist to condemn it some day and convict it of
error. There is but one means for the human mind to escape
this danger; that is, courageously and patiently to exhaust
the study of facts before generalising and concluding. Facts
are to the mind what rules of morality are to the will. It
is bound to know them and to bear their weight; and it is
only when it has fulfilled this duty, when it has viewed and
measured their whole extent, it is then only that it is permitted
to unfold its wings, and take flight to the high region where
it will see all things in their totality and their results. If it
attempt to mount too quickly, and without having gained a
knowledge of all the territory which it will have to contemplate from thence, the chance of error and failure is very
great. It is the same as in an arithmetical calculation,
where one error leads to others, *ad infinitum*. So in history,
if in the first labour we do not attend to all the facts, if we

give ourselves up to the taste for precipitate generalisation, it is impossible to say to what mistakes we may be led.

I am warning you in a measure against myself. I have only made, and, indeed, could only make, attempts at generalisation, general recapitulations of facts which we have not studied closely and at large. But having arrived at an epoch when this undertaking is much more difficult than at any other, and when the chances of error are much greater, I have thought it a duty thus to warn you. That done, I shall now proceed and attempt as to the Reformation what I have done as to other events; I shall endeavour to distinguish its dominant fact, to describe its general character, to say, in a word, what is the place and the share of this great event in European civilization.

You will call to mind how we left Europe at the end of the fifteenth century. We have seen, in its course, two great attempts at religious revolution and reform: an attempt at legal reform by the councils, and an attempt at revolutionary reform in Bohemia by the Hussites; we have seen them stifled and failing one after the other; but still we have seen that it was impossible the event should be prevented, that it must be reproduced under one form or another; that what the fifteenth century had attempted, the sixteenth would inevitably accomplish. I shall not recount in any way the details of the religious revolution of the sixteenth century: I take it for granted that they are almost universally known. I attend only to its general influence upon the destinies of the human race.

When the causes which determined this great event have been investigated, the adversaries of the Reformation have imputed it to accidents, to misfortunes in the course of civilization; for example, to the sale of indulgences having been confided to the Dominicans, which made the Augustines jealous: Luther was an Augustin, and, therefore, was the determining cause of the Reformation. Others have attributed it to the ambition of sovereigns, to their rivalry with the ecclesiastical power, and to the cupidity of the lay nobles, who wished to seize upon the property of the church. They have thus sought to explain the religious revolution merely from the ill side of men and human affairs, by suggestions of private interests and personal passions.

On the other hand, the partisans and friends of the Reformation have endeavoured to explain it merely by the necessity for reform in the existing abuses of the church; they have represented it as a redressing of religious grievances, as an attempt conceived and executed with the sole design of reconstituting a pure and primitive church. Neither of these explanations seems to me sound. The second has more truth in it than the first; at least it is more noble, more in unison with the extent and importance of the event; still I do not think it correct. In my opinion, the Reformation was neither an accident, the result of some great chance, of personal interest, nor a mere aim at religious amelioration, the fruit of an Utopia of humanity and truth. It had a far more powerful cause than all this, and which dominates over all particular causes. It was a great movement of the liberty of the human mind, a new necessity for freely thinking and judging, on its own account, and with its own powers, of facts and ideas which hitherto Europe had received, or was held bound to receive, from the hands of authority. It was a grand attempt at the enfranchisement of the human mind; and, to call things by their proper names, an insurrection of the human mind against absolute power in the spiritual order. Such I believe to be the true, general, and dominant character of the Reformation.

When we consider the state, at this epoch, of the human mind on the one hand, and on the other, that of the church which governed the human mind, we are struck by this twofold fact: on the part of the human mind there was much more activity, and much more thirst for development and empire than it had ever felt. This new activity was the result of various causes, but which had been accumulating for ages. For example, there had been ages when heresies took birth, occupied some space of time, fell, and were replaced by others; and ages when philosophical opinions had run the same course as the heresies. The labour of the human mind, whether in the religious or in the philosophical sphere, had accumulated from the eleventh to the sixteenth century: and at last the moment had arrived when it was necessary that the result should appear. Moreover, all the means of instruction, created or encouraged in the very bosom of the church, bore their fruits. Schools had been instituted: from these schools had issued men with some knowledge, and their number was daily augmented. These men wished at last to think for themselves, and on their own account, for they felt stronger than they had ever yet done. Finally arrived that renewal and regeneration of the human mind by the restoration of antiquity, the progress and effects of which I have described to you.

The union of all these causes at the commencement of the sixteenth century, impressed upon the mind a highly energetic movement, an imperative necessity for progress.

The situation of the government of the human mind, the spiritual power, was quite different; it, on the contrary, had fallen into a state of indolence and immobility. The political credit of the Church, of the court of Rome, had very much diminished; European society no longer belonged to it; it had passed into the dominion of lay governments. Still the spiritual power preserved all its pretensions, all its splendour and external importance. It happened with it, as it has more than once done with old governments. The greater part of the complaints urged against it were no longer applied. It is not true that the court of Rome in the sixteenth century was very tyrannical; nor is it true that its abuses, properly so called, were more numerous, or more crying than they had been in other times. On the contrary, perhaps ecclesiastical government had never been more easy and tolerant, more disposed to let all things take their course, provided they did not put itself in question, provided it was so far acknowledged as to be left in the enjoyment of the rights which it had hitherto possessed, that it was secured the same existence, and paid the same tributes. It would willingly have left the human mind in tranquillity, if the human mind would have done the same towards it. But it is precisely when governments are least held in consideration, when they are the least powerful, and do the least evil, that they are attacked, because then they can be attacked, and formerly they could not be.

It is evident, then, by the mere examination of the state of the human mind, and that of its government at this epoch, that the character of the Reformation must have been a new impulse of liberty, a great insurrection of the human intellect. Do not doubt but this was the dominant cause, the cause which rose above all the others—a cause superior to all interests, whether of nations or sovereigns—superior also to any mere necessity for reform, or the necessity for redressing of griev-ances which were then complained of.

I will suppose that after the first years of the Reformation, when it had displayed all its pretensions, set forth all its grievances, the spiritual power had suddenly fallen in with its views, and had said—"Well, so be it. I will reform every-thing; I will return to a more legal and religious order; I will suppress all vexations, arbitrariness, and tributes; even in doctrinal matters, I will modify, explain, and return to the primitive meaning. But when all grievances are thus re-dressed, I will preserve my position—I will be as formerly, the government of the human mind, with the same power and the same rights." Do you suppose that on these conditions the religious revolution would have been content, and would have stopped its progress? I do not think it. I firmly believe that it would have continued its career, and that after having demanded reformation, it would have demanded liberty. The crisis of the sixteenth century was not merely a reforming one, it was essentially revolutionary. It is impossible to take from it this character, its merits and its vices; it had all the effects of this character.

Let us cast a glance upon the destinies of the Reformation; let us see, especially and before all, what it effected in the different countries where it was developed. Observe that it was developed in very various situations, and amidst very un-equal chances. If we find that in spite of the diversity of situations, and the inequality of chances, it everywhere pur-sued a certain end, obtained a certain result, and preserved a certain character, it will be evident that this character, which surmounted all diversities of situation, and all inequalities of chances, must have been the fundamental character of the event—that this result must have been its essential aim.

Well, wherever the religious revolution of the sixteenth century prevailed, if it did not effect the entire enfranchise-ment of the human mind, it procured for it new and very great increase of liberty. It doubtless often left the mind to all the chances of the liberty or servitude of political institu-tion; but it abolished or disarmed the spiritual power, the systematic and formidable government of thought. This is the result which the Reformation attained amidst the most various combinations. In Germany, there was no political liberty; nor did the Reformation introduce it. It fortified rather than weakened the power of princes. It was more against the free institutions of the middle ages than favourable to their development. Nevertheless, it resuscitated and maintained in Germany a liberty of thought greater, perhaps, than anywhere else.

In Denmark, a country where absolute power dominated, where it penetrated into the municipal institutions, as well as into the general institutions of the state, there also, by the influence of the Reformation, thought was enfranchised and freely exercised in all directions.

In Holland, in the midst of a republic, and in England, under constitutional monarchy, and despite a religious tyranny of long duration, the emancipation of the human mind was likewise accomplished. And, lastly, in France, in a situation which seemed the least favourable to the effects of the religious revolution, in a country where it had been conquered, there even it was a principle of intellectual independence and liberty. Down to 1685, that is to say, until the revocation of the edict of Nantes, the Reformation had a legal existence in France. During this lengthened period it wrote and discussed, and provoked its adversaries to write and discuss with it. This single fact, this war of pamphlets and conferences between the old and new opinions, spread in France a liberty far more real and active than is commonly believed—a liberty which tended to the profit of science, the honour of the French clergy, as well as to the profit of thought in general. Take a glance at the conferences of Bossuet with Claude upon all the religious polemics of that period, and ask yourselves whether Louis XIV. would have allowed a similar degree of liberty upon any other subject. It was between the Reformation and the opposite party that there existed the greatest degree of liberty in France during the seventeenth century. Religious thought was then far more bold, and treated questions with more freedom than the political spirit of Fénélon himself in *Telemachus*. This state of things did not cease until the revocation of the edict of Nantes. Now, from 1685 to the outburst of the human mind in the eighteenth century, there were not forty years; and the influ-

ence of the religious revolution in favour of intellectual
liberty had scarcely ceased, when that of the philosophical
revolution commenced.

You see that wherever the Reformation penetrated, wherever it played an important part, victorious or vanquished,
it had as a general, dominant, and constant result, an immense
progress in the activity and liberty of thought, and towards
the emancipation of the human mind.

And not only had the Reformation this result, but with
this it was satisfied; wherever it obtained that it sought, for
nothing further, so much was it the foundation of the event,
its primitive and fundamental character. Thus, in Germany
it accepted, I will not say political servitude, but, at least,
the absence of liberty. In England, it consented to the con
stitutional hierarchy of the clergy, and the presence of a
church with quite as many abuses as there had ever been in
the Romish church, and far more servile.

Why should the Reformation, so passionate and stubborn
in some respects, show itself in this so easy and pliant? It was
because it had obtained the general fact to which it tended,
the abolition of spiritual power, the enfranchisement of the
human mind. I repeat, that wherever it attained this end,
it accommodated itself to all systems and all situations.

Let us now take the counter-proof of this inquiry; let us
see what happened in countries into which the religious revolution had not penetrated, where it had been stifled in the
beginning, where it had never been developed. History
shows that there the human mind has not been enfranchised;
two great countries, Spain and Italy, will prove this. Whilst
in those European countries where the Reformation had taken
an important place, the human mind, during the three last
centuries, has gained an activity and a freedom before unknown, in those where it has not penetrated it has fallen,
during the same period, into effeminacy and indolence; so
that the proof and counter-proof have been made, so to speak,
simultaneously, and given the same result.

Impulse of thought, and the abolition of absolute power in
the spiritual order, are therefore the essential character of the
Reformation, the most general result of its influence, and the
dominant fact of its destiny

I designedly say, the *fact*. The emancipation of the human mind was in reality, in the course of the Reformation, a fact rather than a principle, a result rather than an intention. In this respect, I think the Reformation executed more than it had undertaken; more perhaps than it had even desired. Contrary to most other revolutions, which have remained far behind their wishes, of which the event is far inferior to the thought, the consequences of the revolution surpassed its views; it is greater as an event than as a plan; what it effected it did not fully foresee, nor fully avow.

What were the reproaches with which its adversaries constantly upbraid the Reformation? Which of its results did they in a manner cast in its teeth to reduce it to silence?

Two principal ones. 1st. The multiplicity of sects, the prodigious licence allowed to mind, the dissolution of the religious society as a whole. 2nd. Tyranny and persecution. " You provoke licence," said they to the reformers; " you even produce it; and when you have created it, you wish to restrain and repress it. And how do you repress it? By the most severe and violent means. You yourselves persecute heresy, and by virtue of an illegitimate authority."

Survey and sum up all the great attacks directed against the Reformation, discarding the purely dogmatical questions; these are the two fundamental reproaches to which they always reduce themselves.

The reformed party was greatly embarrassed by them. When they imputed to it the multiplicity of sects, instead of avowing them, and maintaining the legitimacy of their development, it anathematized them, deplored their existence, and denied them. Taxed with persecution, it defended itself with the same embarrassment; it alleged the necessity; it had, it said, the right to repress and punish error, because it was in the possession of truth; its creed and institutions alone were legitimate; and if the Roman church had not the right to punish the reformers, it was because she was in the wrong as against them.

And when the reproach of persecution was addressed to the dominant party in the Reformation, not by its enemies, but by its own offspring, when the sects which it anathematized said to it, " We only do what you have done; we only separate ourselves, as you separated yourselves," it was still

Q

more embarrassed for an answer, and often only replied by redoubled rigour.

In fact, while labouring for the destruction of absolute power in the spiritual order, the revolution of the sixteenth century was ignorant of the true principles of intellectual liberty; it enfranchised the human mind, and yet pretended to govern it by the law; in practice it was giving prevalence to free inquiry, and in theory it was only substituting a legitimate in place of an illegitimate power. It did not elevate itself to the first cause, nor descend to the last consequences of its work. Thus it fell into a double fault; on the one hand, it neither knew nor respected all the rights of human thought; at the moment that it clamoured for them on its own account, it violated them with regard to others; on the other hand, it knew not how to measure the rights of authority in the intellectual order; I do not speak of coercive authority, which in such matters should possess none, but of purely moral authority, acting upon the mind alone, and simply by way of influence. Something is wanting in most of the reformed countries, to the good organization of the intellectual society, and to the regular action of ancient and general opinions. They could not reconcile the rights and wants of tradition with those of liberty; and the cause doubtless lay in this fact, that the Reformation did not fully comprehend and receive its own principles and effects.

Hence, also, it had a certain air of inconsistency and narrow-mindedness, which often gave a hold and advantage over it to its adversaries. These last knew perfectly well what they did, and what they wished to do; they went back to the principles of their conduct, and avowed all the consequences of it. There was never a government more consistent and systematic than that of the Roman church. In practice the court of Rome has greatly yielded and given way, much more so than the Reformation; in theory, it has much more completely adopted its peculiar system, and kept to a much more coherent conduct. This is a great power, this full knowledge of what one does and wishes, this complete and rational adoption of a doctrine and a design. The religious revolution of the sixteenth century presented in its course a striking example of it. Every one knows that the chief power instituted to struggle against it was the order of Jesuits.

Throw a glance upon their history; they have everywhere failed. Wherever they have interfered to any extent, they have carried misfortune into the cause with which they mixed. In England they ruined kings; in Spain, the people. The general course of events, the development of modern civilization, the liberty of the human mind, all these powers against which the Jesuits were called upon to contest, fought and conquered them. And not only have they failed, but call to mind the means they have been obliged to employ. No splendour or grandeur; they brought about no great events, nor put in motion powerful masses of men; they have acted only by underhanded, obscure, and subordinate means; by ways which are nothing suited to strike the imagination, to conciliate that public interest which attaches to great things, whatever may be their principle or end. The party against which it struggled, on the contrary, not only conquered, but conquered with splendour; it did great things, and by great means; it aroused the people, it gave to Europe great men, and changed, in the face of day, the fashion and form of states. In a word, everything was against the Jesuits, both fortune and appearances; neither good sense which desires success, nor imagination which requires splendour, were satisfied by their career. And yet nothing can be more certain than that they have had grandeur; that a great idea is attached to their name, their influence, and their history. How so?

It is because they knew what they were doing, and what they desired to do; because they had a full and clear acquaintance with the principles upon which they acted, and the aim to which they tended; that is to say, they had greatness of thought and greatness of will, and this saved them from the ridicule which attaches itself to constant reverses and contemptible means. Where, on the contrary, the event was greater than the thought, where the actors appeared to want a knowledge of the first principles and last results of their action, there remained something incomplete, inconsistent, and narrow, which placed the conquerors themselves in a sort of rational and philosophical inferiority, of which the influence has been sometimes felt in events. This was, I conceive, in the struggle of the old against the new spiritual order, the weak side of the Reformation, the circum-

stance which often embarrassed it, and hindered it from defending itself as it ought to have done.

We might consider the religious revolution of the sixteenth
century under many other aspects.   I have said nothing, and
have nothing to say, concerning its dogmas, concerning its
effect on religion, and in regard to the relations of the human
soul with God and the eternal future; but I might exhibit
it to you in the diversity of its relations with the social order,
bringing on, in all directions, results of mighty importance.
For instance, it awoke religion amidst the laity, and in the
world of the faithful.   Up to that time, religion had been,
so to speak, the exclusive domain of the clergy, of the
ecclesiastical order, who distributed the fruits, but disposed
themselves of the tree, and had almost alone the right to
speak of it.   The Reformation caused a general circulation
of religious creeds; it opened to believers the field of faith,
which hitherto they had had no right to enter.   It had, at
the same time, a second result—it banished, or nearly
banished, religion from politics; it restored the independence of the temporal power.   At the very moment when, so
to speak, religion came again to the possession of the faithful,
it quitted the government of society.   In the reformed countries, notwithstanding the diversity of ecclesiastical constitutions, even in England, where that constitution is nearer to
the ancient order of things, the spiritual power no longer
makes any serious pretensions to the direction of the temporal
power.

I might enumerate many other consequences of the Reformation, but I must check myself, and rest content with
having placed before you its principal character, the emancipation of the human mind, and the abolition of absolute
power in the spiritual order—an abolition which, no doubt,
was not complete, but nevertheless formed the greatest step
that has, up to our days, been taken in this direction.

Before concluding, I must pray you to remark the striking
similarity of destiny which, in the history of modern Europe,
presents itself as existing between the civil and religious
societies, in the revolutions to which they have been subject.

The Christian society, as we saw when I spoke of the
church, began by being a perfectly free society, and formed

solely in virtue of a common creed, without institutions or
government, properly so called, and regulated only by moral
powers, varying according to the necessity of the moment.
Civil society commenced in like manner in Europe, or partially at least, with bands of barbarians; a society perfectly
free, each one remaining in it because he thought proper,
without laws or constituted powers. At the close of this
state, which could not co-exist with any considerable development, religious society placed itself under an essentially
aristocratic government; it was the body of the clergy, the
bishops, councils, and ecclesiastical aristocracy, which governed
it. A fact of the same kind happened in civil society at the
termination of barbarism; it was the lay aristocracy, the lay
feudal chiefs, by which it was governed. Religious society
left the aristocratic form to assume that of pure monarchy;
that is the meaning of the triumph of the court of Rome over
the councils and over the European ecclesiastical aristocracy.
The same revolution accomplished itself in civil society:
it was by the destruction of aristocratical power that royalty
prevailed and took possession of the European world. In the
sixteenth century, in the bosom of religious society, an insurrection burst forth against the system of pure monarchy,
against absolute power in the spiritual order. This revolution brought on, consecrated, and established free inquiry in
Europe. In our own days we have seen the same event
occurring in the civil order. Absolute temporal power was
attacked and conquered. Thus you have seen that the
two societies have undergone the same vicissitudes, have
been subject to the same revolutions; only religious society
has always been the foremost in this career.

We are now in possession of one of the great facts of
modern society, namely, free inquiry, the liberty of the human
mind. We have seen that, at the same time, political centralization almost everywhere prevailed. In my next lecture
I shall treat of the English revolution; that is to say, of the
event in which free inquiry and pure monarchy, both results
of the progress of civilization, found themselves for the first
time in conflict.

THIRTEENTH LECTURE

Object of the lecture—General character of the English revolution—Its
principal causes—It was more political than religious—The three great
parties in it: 1. The party of legal reform; 2. The party of the political revolution; 3. The party of the social revolution—They all fail
—Cromwell—The restoration of the Stuarts—The legal ministry—The
profligate ministry—The revolution of 1688 in England and Europe.

You have seen that during the sixteenth century all the elements and features that had belonged to former European
society resolved themselves into two great facts, free inquiry,
and the centralization of power.   The first prevailed among
the clergy, the second among the laity.   There simultaneously
triumphed in Europe the emancipation of the human mind,
and the establishment of pure monarchy.

It was scarcely to be expected but that sooner or later
a struggle should arise between these two principles; for
they were contradictory; the one was the overthrow of
absolute power in the spiritual order, the other was its
victory in the temporal; the first paved the way for the
decay of the ancient ecclesiastical monarchy, the last perfected
the ruin of the ancient feudal and communal liberties.   The
fact of their advent being simultaneous, arose, as you have
seen, from the revolution in religious society advancing
with a more rapid step than that in the civil society: the one
occurred exactly at the time of the enfranchisement of the
individual mind, the other not until the moment of the centralization of universal power under one head.   The coincidence of these two facts, so far from springing out of their
similitude, did not prevent their inconsistency.   They were

each advances in the course of civilization, but they were advances arising from dissimilar situations, and of a different moral date, if I may be allowed the expression, although cotemporary. That they should run against one another before they came to an understanding was inevitable.

Their first collision was in England. In the struggle of free inquiry, the fruit of the Reformation, against the ruin of political liberty, the fruit of the triumph of pure monarchy; and in the effort to abolish absolute power both in the temporal and spiritual orders, we have the purport of the English revolution, its share in the course of our civilization.

The question arises, why should this struggle take place in England sooner than elsewhere? wherefore should the revolutions in the political order have coincided more closely with those in the moral order, in that country, than on the continent?

Royalty in England has undergone the same vicissitudes as on the continent: under the Tudors, it attained to a concentration and energy which it has never known since. It does not follow that the despotism of the Tudors was more violent, or that it cost dearer to England than that of their predecessors. I believe that there were at least as many acts of tyranny and instances of vexation and injustice, under the Plantagenets, as under the Tudors, perhaps even more. And I believe, likewise, that at this era the government of pure monarchy was more harsh and arbitrary on the continent than in England. The new feature under the Tudors was, that absolute power became systematic; royalty assumed a primitive and independent sovereignty; it adopted a style hitherto unknown. The theoretical pretensions of Henry VIII., of Elizabeth, of James I., or of Charles I., are entirely different to those of Edward I. or Edward III.; though the power of these two last kings was neither less arbitrary nor less extensive. I repeat, that it was the principle, the rational system of monarchy, rather than its practical power, which experienced a mutation in England during the sixteenth century: royalty assumed absolute power, and pretended to be superior to all laws, to those even which it had declared should be respected.

Again, the religious revolution was not accomplished in

England in the same manner as on the continent; here it was the work of the kings themselves. Not but that in this country, as elsewhere, there had long been the germs of, and even attempts at a popular reformation, which would probably, ere long, have been carried out. But Henry VIII. took the initiative; power became revolutionary. The result was that, in its origin at least, as a redress of ecclesiastical tyranny and abuse, and as the emancipation of the human mind, the Reformation was far less complete in England than on the continent. It consulted, and very naturally, the interest of its authors. The king and the retained episcopacy shared the riches and power, the spoils of the preceding government, of the papacy. It was not long before the consequence was felt. It was said that the Reformation was finished; yet most of the motives which had made it neces-sary still existed. It reappeared under a popular form; it ex-claimed against the bishops as it had done against the court of Rome; it accused them of being so many popes. As often as the general character of the religious reformation was compromised, whenever there was question of a struggle with the ancient church, all portions of the reformed party rallied, and made head against the common enemy; but the danger passed, the interior struggle recommenced; popular reform again attacked regal and aristocratical reform, de-nounced its abuses, complained of its tyranny, called upon it for a fulfilment of its promises, and not again to establish the power which it had dethroned.

There was, about the same time, a movement of enfran-chisement manifested in civil society, a need for political freedom, till then unknown, or at least powerless. During the sixteenth century, the commercial prosperity of England in-creased with excessive rapidity; at the same time, terri-torial wealth, landed property, in a great measure changed hands. The division of land in England in the sixteenth century, consequent on the ruin of the feudal aristocracy and other causes, too many for present enumeration, is a fact de-serving more attention than has yet been given to it. All documents show us the number of landed proprietors in-creasing to an immense extent, and the larger portion of the lands passing into the hands of the *gentry*, or inferior nobility, and the citizens. The upper house, the higher nobility, was not nearly so rich at the commencement of the seventeenth century as the House of Commons. There was then at the same time a great development of commercial wealth, and a great mutation in landed property. Amidst these two influences came a third—the new movement in the minds of men. The reign of Elizabeth is, perhaps, the greatest period of English history for literary and philosophical activity, the era of lofty and fertile imaginations; the puritans without hesitation followed out all the consequences of a vigorous although narrow doctrine; the opposite class of minds, less moral and more free, strangers to any principle or method, received with enthusiasm everything which promised to satisfy their curiosity or feed their excitement. Wherever the impulse of intelligence brings with it a lively pleasure, liberty will soon become a want, and will quickly pass from the public mind into the government.

There was on the Continent, in some of those countries where the Reformation had gone forth, a manifestation of a similar feeling, a certain want for political liberty; but the means of satisfying it were wanting; they knew not where to look for it; no aid for it could be found either in the institutions or in manners; they remained vague and uncertain, seeking in vain to satisfy their want. In England, it was very different: there the spirit of political freedom, which reappeared in the sixteenth century, following the Reformation, found its fulcrum and the means of action in the ancient institutions and social conditions.

Every one knows the origin of the free institutions of England; it is universally known how the union of the great barons in 1215, forced *Magna Charta* from King John. What is not so generally known is, that the great charter was from time to time recalled and again confirmed by most of the succeeding kings. There were more than thirty confirmations of it between the thirteenth and the sixteenth century. And not only was the charter confirmed, but new statutes were introduced for the purpose of maintaining and developing it. It therefore lived, as it were, without interval or interruption. At the same time, the House of Commons was formed, and took its place among the supreme institutions of the country. It was under the Plantagenets that it truly struck root; not that it took any great part in the state during that period; the government did not, properly speaking, belong to it, even in the way of influence; it only interfered therein at the call of the king, and then always reluctantly and hesitatingly, as if it was more fearful of engaging and compromising itself than desirous of augmenting its power. But when the matter in hand was the defence of private rights, the families or fortune of the citizens, in a word, the liberties of the individual, the House of Commons acquitted itself of its duty with much energy and perseverance, and founded all those principles which have become the basis of the English constitution.

After the Plantagenets, and especially under the Tudors, the House of Commons, or rather the entire parliament, presented itself under a different aspect. It no longer defended the individual liberties, as under the Plantagenets. Arbitrary detentions, the violation of private rights, now become much more frequent, are often passed over in silence. On the other hand, the parliament took a much more active part in the general government of the state. In changing the religion and in regulating the order of succession, Henry VIII. had need of some medium, some public instrument, and in this want he was supplied by the parliament, and especially by the House of Commons. Under the Plantagenets it had been an instrument of resistance, the guardian of private rights; under the Tudors it became an instrument of government and general policy; so that at the end of the sixteenth century, although it had undergone almost every species of tyranny, its importance was much augmented, its great power began, that power upon which the representative government depends

When we glance at the state of the free institutions of England at the end of the sixteenth century, we find first, fundamental rules and principles of liberty, of which neither the country nor the legislature had ever lost sight, second, precedents, examples of liberty, a good deal mixed, it is true, with inconsistent examples and precedents, but sufficing to legalize and sustain the claims, and to support the defenders of liberty in any struggle against tyranny or despotism; third, special and local institutions, replete with germs of liberty; the jury, the right of assembling, and of being armed; the independence of municipal administrations and jurisdictions; fourth, and last, the parliament and its power, of which the crown had more need than ever, since it had lavished away the greater part of its independent revenues, domains, feudal rights, &c., and was dependent for its very support upon the national vote.

The political condition of England, therefore, in the sixteenth century was wholly different from that of the continent. In spite of the tyranny of the Tudors, and systematic triumph of pure monarchy, there was still a fixed fulcrum, a sure means of action for the new spirit of liberty.

There were, then, two national wants in England at this period: on one side was the need of religious revolution and liberty in the heart of the reformation already commenced; and on the other, was required political liberty in the heart of the pure monarchy then in progress; and in the course of their progress these two wants were able to invoke all that had already been done in either direction. They combined. The party who wished to pursue religious reformation, invoked political liberty to the assistance of its faith and conscience against the king and the bishops. The friends of political liberty again sought the aid of the popular reformation. The two parties united to struggle against absolute power in the temporal and in the spiritual orders, a power now concentrated in the hands of the king. This is the origin and purport of the English revolution.

It was thus essentially devoted to the defence or achievement of liberty. For the religious party it was a means, and for the political party an end; but with both, liberty was the question, and they were obliged to pursue it in common. There was no real religious quarrel between the episcopal and the puritan party; little dispute upon dogmas, or concerning faith; not but that there existed real differences of opinion between them, differences of great importance; but this was not the principal point. Practical liberty was what the puritans wished to force from the episcopal party: it was for this that they strove. There was also another religious party who had to found a system, to establish its dogmas, ecclesiastical constitution, and discipline; this was the presbyterian party: but although it worked to the utmost of its power, it did not in this point progress in proportion to its desire. Placed on the defensive, oppressed by the bishops, unable to act without

the assent of the political reformers, its allies and chief supporters, its dominant aim was liberty, the general interest
and common aim of all the parties, whatever their diversity, who concurred in the movement. Taking everything
together, the English revolution was essentially political; it
was brought about in the midst of a religious people and in a
religious age; religious thoughts and passions were its instruments; but its chief design and definite aim were political, were devoted to liberty, and the abolition of all absolute
power.

I shall now glance at the different phases of this revolution,
and its great parties; I shall then connect it with the general
course of European civilization; I shall mark its place and
influence therein; and show you by a detail of the facts, as at
the first view, that it was the first blow which had been
struck in the cause of free inquiry and pure monarchy, the
first manifestation of a struggle between these two great
powers.

. Three principal parties sprang up in this great crisis, three
revolutions in a manner were comprised in it, and successively
appeared upon the scene. In each party, and in each revolution, two parties are allied, and work conjointly, a political
and a religious party; the first at the head, the second followed, but each necessary to the other; so that the twofold
character of the event is impressed upon all its phases

The first party which appeared was the party of legal reform, under whose banner all the others at first ranged
themselves. When the English revolution commenced,
when the long parliament was assembled in 1640, it was
universally said, and by many sincerely believed, that the
legal reform would suffice for all things; that in the ancient
laws and customs of the country, there was that which would
remedy all abuses, and which would re-establish a system of
government entirely conformable to the public wishes. This
party loudly censured, and sincerely wished to prevent the
illegal collecting of taxes, arbitrary imprisonments, in a word,
all acts disallowed by the known laws of the country. At
the root of its ideas was the belief in the king's sovereignty,
—that is, in absolute power. A secret instinct warned it,
indeed, there was something false and dangerous therein;
it wished, therefore, to say nothing of it; pushed to the

extremity, however, and forced to explain itself, it admitted
in royalty a power superior to all human origin, and above
all control, and, when need was, defended it. It believed at
the same time that this sovereignty, absolute in theory, was
bound to observe certain forms and rules; that it could not
extend beyond certain limits; and that these rules, forms,
and limits, were sufficiently established and guaranteed in
the great charter, in the confirmatory statutes, and in the
ancient laws of the country. Such was its political idea.
In religious matters, the legal party thought that the episcopal power was excessive; that the bishops had too much
political power, that their jurisdiction was too extensive,
and that it was necessary to overlook and restrain its exercise. Still it firmly supported the episcopacy, not only as
an ecclesiastical institution, and as a system of church
government, but as a necessary support for the royal prerogative, as a means of defending and maintaining the
supremacy of the king in religious matters. The sovereignty
of the king in the political order being exercised according to
known forms, and within the limits of acknowledged rules,
royalty in the religious order should be sustained by the
episcopacy; such was the two-fold system of the legal party,
of which the chiefs were Clarendon, Colepepper, Lord Capel,
and Lord Falkland himself, although an ardent advocate of
public liberty, and a man who numbered in his ranks almost
all the high nobility who were not servilely devoted to the
court.

Behind these followed a second party, which I shall call the
party of the political revolution: these were of opinion that
the ancient guarantees and legal barriers had been and still
were insufficient; that a great change, a regular revolution
was necessary, not in the forms, but in the realities of government: that it was necessary to withdraw from the king and
his council the independence of their power, and to place the
political preponderance in the House of Commons; that the
government, properly so called, should belong to this assembly
and its chiefs. This party did not give an account of their
ideas and intentions as clearly and systematically as I have
done; but this was the essence of its doctrines, of its political tendencies. Instead of the sovereignty of the king,
pure monarchy, it believed in the sovereignty of the House

of Commons as the representative of the country. Under this idea was hidden that of the sovereignty of the people, an idea, the bearing of which, and its consequences, the party was very far from contemplating, but which presented itself, and was received under the form of the sovereignty of the House of Commons.

A religious party, that of the presbyterians, was closely united with the party of the political revolution. The presbyterians wished to bring about in the church a revolution analogous to that meditated by their allies in the state. They wished to govern the church by assemblies, giving the religious power to an hierarchy of assemblages agreeing one with the other, as their allies had invested the House of Commons with the political power. But the presbyterian revolution was more vigorous and complete, for it tended to change the form as well as the principle of the government of the church, while the political party wished only to moderate the influences and preponderating power of institutions, did not meditate an overthrow of the form of the institutions themselves.

But the chiefs of the political party were not all of them favourable to the presbyterian organization of the church. Many of them, as for instance, Hampden and Holles, would have preferred, it seems, a moderate episcopacy, confined to purely ecclesiastical duties, and more freedom of conscience. But they resigned themselves to it, being unable to do without their fanatical allies.

A third party was yet more exorbitant in its demands: this party asserted that an entire change was necessary, not only in the form of government, but in government itself; that the whole political constitution was bad. This party repudiated the past ages of England, renounced the national institutions and memories, with the intention of founding a new government, according to a pure theory, or what it supposed to be such. It was not a mere reform in the government, but a social revolution which this party wished to bring about. The party of which I just now spoke, that of the political revolution, wished to introduce important changes in the relations between the parliament and the crown; it wished to extend the power of parliament, particularly that of the House of Commons, giving them the nomination to high public offices, and the supreme direction in general affairs; but its projects of reform extended very little further than this. For instance, it had no idea of changing the electoral, judicial, or municipal and administrative systems of the country. The republican party meditated all these changes, and proclaimed their necessity; and, in a word, wished to reform, not only the public administration, but also the social relations and the distribution of private rights.

This party, like that which preceded it, was partly religious and partly political. The political portion included the republicans, properly so called, the theorists, Ludlow, Harrington, Milton, &c. On that side were ranged the republicans from interest, the chief officers of the army, Ireton, Cromwell, and Lambert, who, more or less sincere at the onset, were soon swayed and guided by interested views and the necessities of their situations. Around these collected the religious republican party, which included all those enthusiasts who acknowledged no legitimate power except that of Jesus Christ, and who, while waiting for his advent, wished to be governed by his elect. And, lastly, the party was followed by a large number of inferior freethinkers, and fantastical dreamers, the one set in hope of licence, the others of equality of property and universal suffrage.

In 1653, after a struggle of twelve years, all these parties had successively failed, at least, they had reason to believe they had failed, and the public was convinced of their failure. The legal party, which quickly disappeared, had seen the ancient laws and constitution disdained and trodden under foot, and innovation visible upon every side. The party of political reform saw parliamentary forms perish under the new use which they wished to make of them; they saw the House of Commons, after a sway of twelve years, reduced, by the successive expulsion of the royalists and the presbyterians, to a very trifling number of members, and those looked upon by the public with contempt and detestation, and incapable of governing. The republican party seemed to have succeeded better: it remained, to all appearance, master of the field of battle, of power; the House of Commons reckoned no more than from fifty to sixty members, and all of these were republicans. They might fairly deem themselves and declare themselves masters of the country. But the country

absolutely rejected them; they could nowhere carry their
resolutions into effect; they exercised no practical influence
either over the army or over the people.   There no longer
subsisted any social tie, any social security; justice was no
longer administered, or, if it was, it was no longer justice,
but the arbitrary rendering of decrees at the dictation of
passion, prejudice, party.   And not only was there an entire
disappearance of security from the social relations of men,
there was none whatever on the highways, which were
covered with thieves and robbers; material anarchy as well
as moral anarchy, manifested itself in every direction, and
the House of Commons and the Republican Council were
wholly incapable of repressing either the one or the other.

The three great parties of the revolution had thus been
called successively to conduct it, to govern the country according to their knowledge and will, and they had not been able
to do it; they had all three of them completely failed; they
could do nothing more.   " It was then," says Bossuet, " that
a man was found who left nothing to fortune which he could
take from it by council or foresight;" an expression full of
error, and controverted by all history.   Never did man leave
more to fortune than Cromwell; never has man hazarded
more, gone on with more temerity, without design or aim,
but determined to go as far as fate should carry him.   An
unlimited ambition, an admirable faculty of extracting from
every day and circumstance some new means of progress, the
art of turning chance to profit, without pretending to rule it,
all these were Cromwell's.   It was with Cromwell as perhaps
it has been with no other man in his circumstances; he sufficed
for all the most various phases of the revolution; he was a
man for its first and latest epochs; first of all, he was the
leader of insurrection, the abettor of anarchy, the most fiery
of the English revolutionists; afterwards the man for the
anti-revolutionary reaction, for the re-establishment of order,
and for social organization; thus performing singly all the
parts which, in the course of revolutions, are divided among
the greatest actors.   One can hardly say that Cromwell was
a Mirabeau; he wanted eloquence, and although very active,
did not make any show during the first years of the Long
Parliament.   But he was successively a Danton and a Buona-
parte.   He, more than any others, had contributed to the

overthrow of power; and he raised it up again because none but he knew how to assume and manage it; some one must govern; all had failed, and he succeeded. That constituted his title. Once master of the government, this man, whose ambition had shown itself so bold and insatiable, who, in his progress, had always driven fortune before him, determined never to stop, now displayed a good sense, prudence, and knowledge of the possible, which dominated all his most violent passions. He had, no doubt, a great love for absolute power, and a strong desire to place the crown on his own head, and establish it in his family. He renounced this last design, the danger of which he saw in time; and as to the absolute power, although, in fact, he exercised it, he always knew that the tendency of his age was against it; that the revolution in which he had co-operated, and which he had followed through all its phases, had been directed against despotism, and that the imperishable desire of England was to be governed by a parliament, and in parliamentary forms. Therefore he himself, a despot by inclination and in fact, undertook to have a parliament and to govern in a parliamentary manner. He addressed himself unceasingly to all parties; he endeavoured to form a parliament of religious enthusiasts, of republicans, of presbyterians, of officers of the army. He attempted all means to constitute a parliament which could and would co-operate with him. He tried in vain: all parties, once seated in Westminster, wished to snatch from him the power which he exercised, and rule in their turn. I do not say that his own interest and personal passion were not first in his thoughts; but it is not therefore the less certain that, if he had abandoned power, he would have been obliged to take it up again the next day. Neither puritans nor royalists, republicans nor officers, none, besides Cromwell, was in condition to govern with any degree of order or justice. The proof had been shown. It was impossible to allow the parliament, that is to say, the parties sitting in parliament, to take the empire which they could not keep. Such, then, was the situation of Cromwell; he governed according to a system which he knew very well was not that of the country; he exercised a power acknowledged as necessary, but accepted by no one. No party regarded his dominion as a definitive government. The royalists, the presbyterians, the republi-

R

cans, the army itself, the party which seemed most devoted to
Cromwell, all were convinced that he was but a transitory
master. At bottom, he never reigned over men's minds; he
was never anything but a make-shift, a necessity of the
moment. The protector, the absolute master of England, was
all his life obliged to employ force in order to protect his
power; no party could govern like him, but no party wished
him for governor: he was constantly attacked by all parties
at once.

At his death the republicans alone were in a condition to
seize upon power; they did so, and succeeded no better than
they had done before. This was not for want of confidence,
at least as regards the fanatics of the party. A pamphlet of Milton, published at this period, and full of talent
and enthusiasm, is entitled, "A ready and easy way to establish a free commonwealth." You see what was the blindness
of these men. They very soon fell again into that impossibility of governing which they had already experienced.
Monk undertook the conduct of the event which all England
looked for. The restoration was accomplished.

The restoration of the Stuarts in England was a deeply
national event. It presented itself with the advantages at
once of an ancient government, of a government which rests
upon its traditions, upon the recollections of the country, and
with the advantages of a new government, of which no recent
trial has been made, and of which the faults and weight have
not been experienced. The ancient monarchy was the only
species of government which for the last twenty years had
not been despised for its incapacity and ill-success in the administration of the country. These two causes rendered the
restoration popular; it had nothing to oppose it but the remnants of violent parties; and the public rallied around it
heartily. It was, in the opinion of the country, the only
means of legal government; that is to say, of that which the
country most ardently desired. This was also what the
restoration promised, and it was careful to present itself
under the aspect of a legal government.

The first royalist party which, at the return of Charles II.,
undertook the management of affairs was, in fact, the legal
party, represented by its most able chief, the chancellor
Clarendon. You are aware that, from 1660 to 1667, Cla-

rendon was prime minister, and the truly predominating influence in England. Clarendon and his friends reappeared with their ancient system, the absolute sovereignty of the king, kept within legal limits, and restrained, in matters of taxation, by parliament, and in matters of private rights and individual liberties, by the tribunals; but possessing, as regards government properly so called, an almost complete independence, the most decisive preponderance, to the exclusion, or even against the wishes, of the majority in parliament, especially in the House of Commons. As to the rest, they had a due respect for legal order, a sufficient solicitude for the interests of the country, a noble sentiment of its dignity, and a grave and honourable moral tone: such was the character of Clarendon's administration of seven years.

But the fundamental ideas upon which this administration rested, the absolute sovereignty of the king, and the government placed beyond the influence of the preponderating opinion of parliament, these ideas, I say, were obsolete, impotent. In spite of the reaction of the first moments of the restoration, twenty years of parliamentary rule, in opposition to royalty, had irremediably ruined them. A new element soon burst forth in the centre of the royalist party: freethinkers, rakes, and libertines, who participated in the ideas of the time, conceived that power was vested in the Commons, and, caring very little for legal order or the absolute sovereignty of the king, troubled themselves only for their own success, and sought it whenever they caught a glimpse of any means of influence or power. These formed a party which became allied with the national discontented party, and Clarendon was overthrown.

Thus arose a new system of government, namely, that of that portion of the royalist party which I have now described: profligates and libertines formed the ministry, which is called the ministry of the Cabal, and many other administrations which succeeded it. This was their character: no care for principles, laws, or rights; as little for justice and for truth; they sought upon each occasion to discover the means of succeeding: if success depended upon the influence of the Commons, they chimed in with their opinions; if it seemed expedient to flout the House of Commons, they did so, and begged its pardon on the morrow. Corruption was

R 2

tried one day, flattery of the national spirit, another; there
was no regard paid to the general interests of the country, to
its dignity, or to its honour; in a word, their government
was profoundly selfish and immoral, a stranger to all public
doctrine or views; but, at bottom, and in the practical administration of affairs, very intelligent and liberal. Such was the
character of the Cabal, of the ministry of the earl of Danby,
and of the entire English government, from 1667 to 1679.
Notwithstanding its immorality, notwithstanding its contempt
of the principles and the true interests of the country, this
government was less odious and less unpopular than the ministry of Clarendon had been: and why? because it was
much better adapted to the times, and because it better understood the sentiments of the people, even in mocking
them. It was not antiquated and foreign to them, like that of
Clarendon; and though it did the country much more harm,
the country found it more agreeable. Nevertheless, there
came a moment when corruption, servility, and contempt or
rights and public honour were pushed to such a point that
the people could no longer remain resigned. There was a
general rising against the government of the profligates. A
national and patriotic party had formed itself in the bosom of
the House of Commons. The king decided upon calling its
chiefs to the council. Then came to the direction of affairs
lord Essex, the son of him who had commanded the first
parliamentary armies during the civil war, lord Russell, and
a man who, without having any of their virtues, was far
superior to them in political ability, lord Shaftesbury.
Brought thus to the management of affairs, the national
party showed itself incompetent; it knew not how to possess
itself of the moral force of the country; it knew not how to
treat the interests either of the king, the court, or of any of
those with whom it had to do. It gave to no one, neither to
the people nor to the king, any great notion of its ability and
energy. After remaining a short time in power, it failed.
The virtue of its chiefs, their generous courage, the nobleness
of their deaths, have exalted them in history, and have justly
placed them in the highest rank; but their political capacity
did not answer to their virtue, and they knew not how to
wield the power which could not corrupt them, nor to secure
the triumph of the cause for the sake of which they knew
how to die.

This attempt having failed, you perceive the condition of the English restoration; it had, after a manner, and like the revolution, tried all parties and all ministries, the legal ministry, the corrupted ministry, and the national ministry; but none had succeeded. The country and the court found themselves in much the same situation as that of England in 1653, at the end of the revolutionary tempest. Recourse was had to the same expedient; what Cromwell had done for the good of the revolution, Charles II. did for the good of his crown: he entered the career of absolute power.

James II. succeeded his brother. Then a second question was added to that of absolute power; namely, the question of religion. James II. desired to bring about the triumph of popery as well as that of despotism. Here, then, as at the beginning of the revolution, we have a religious and a political warfare, both directed against the government. It has often been asked, what would have happened had William III. never existed, or had he not come with his Hollanders to put an end to the quarrel which had arisen between James II. and the English nation? I firmly believe that the same event would have been accomplished. All England, except a very small party, had rallied, at this epoch, against James, and, under one form or another, it would have accomplished the revolution of 1688. But this crisis was produced by other and higher causes than the internal state of England. It was European as well as English. It is here that the English revolution connects itself by facts themselves, and independently of the influence which its example may have had, with the general course of European civilization.

While this struggle, which I have sketched in outline, this struggle of absolute power against civil and religious liberty, was taking place in England, a struggle of the same kind was going on upon the continent, very different, indeed, as regards the actors, forms, and theatre, but at bottom the same, and originated by the same cause. The pure monarchy of Louis XIV. endeavoured to become an universal monarchy; at least it gave reason for the fear that such was the case; and in fact, Europe did fear that it was. A league was made in Europe, between various political parties, in order to resist this attempt, and the chief of this league was the chief of the party in favour of civil and religious liberty upon the continent,

William, prince of Orange.   The protestant republic of
Holland, with William at its head, undertook to resist the
pure monarchy represented and conducted by Louis XIV.
It was not civil and religious liberty in the interior of the
states, but their external independence which was apparently
the question.   Louis XIV. and his adversaries did not
imagine that, in fact, they were contesting between them the
question which was being contested in England.   This
struggle went on, not between parties, but between states; it
proceeded by war and diplomacy, not by political movements
and by revolutions.   But, at bottom, one and the same question was at issue.

When, therefore, James II. resumed in England the contest
between absolute power and liberty, this contest occurred just
in the midst of the general struggle which was going on in
Europe between Louis XIV. and the prince of Orange, the
representatives, severally, of the two great systems at war upon
the banks of the Scheldt, as well as on those of the Thames.
The league was so powerful against Louis XIV. that, openly,
or in a hidden but very real manner, sovereigns were seen
to enter it, who were assuredly very far from being interested in favour of civil and religious liberty.   The emperor
of Germany and pope Innocent XI. supported William III.
against Louis XIV.   William passed into England, less
in order to serve the internal interests of the country than
to draw it completely into the struggle against Louis XIV.
He took this new kingdom as a new power of which he was
in want, and of which his opponent had, up to that time,
made use against him.   While Charles II. and James II.
reigned, England belonged to Louis XIV.; he had directed
its external relations, and had constantly opposed it to Holland.   England was now snatched from the party of pure
and universal monarchy, in order to become the instrument
and strongest support of the party of religious liberty.   This
is the European aspect of the revolution of 1688; it was
thus that it occupied a place in the total result of the
events of Europe, independently of the part which it played
by means of its example, and the influence which it exercised
upon minds in the following century.

Thus you see that, as I told you in the beginning, the
true meaning and essential character of this revolution was

the attempt to abolish absolute power in temporal as well as spiritual things. This act discovers itself in all the phases of the revolution—in its first period up to the restoration, in the second up to the crisis of 1688—and whether we consider it in its internal development or in its relations with Europe in general.

It now remains for us to study the same great event upon the continent, the struggle of pure monarchy and free inquiry, or, at least, its causes and approaches. This will be the subject of our next lecture

FOURTEENTH LECTURE.

In my last lecture I endeavoured to determine the true
character and political meaning of the English revolution.
We have seen that it was the first shock of the two great
facts to which all the civilization of primitive Europe reduced
itself in the course of the sixteenth century, namely, pure
monarchy, on one hand, and free inquiry on the other; those
two powers came to strife for the first time in England.
Attempts have been made to infer from this fact the existence
of a radical difference between the social state of England
and that of the continent; some have pretended that no comparison was possible between countries of destinies so different; they have affirmed that the English people had
existed in a kind of moral isolation analogous to its material
situation.

It is true that there had been an important difference
between English civilization, and the civilization of the continental states,—a difference which we are bound to calculate.
You have already, in the course of my lectures, been enabled
to catch a glimpse of it. The development of the different
principles and elements of society occurred in England simul-

taneously, and, as it were, abreast; at least, far more so than upon the continent. When I attempted to determine the peculiar physiognomy of European civilization as compared with the ancient and Asiatic civilizations, I showed you the first varied, rich, and complex; that it never fell under the dominion of an exclusive principle; that therein the various elements of the social state were modified, combined, and struggled with each other, and had been constantly compelled to agree and live in common. This fact, the general characteristic of European civilization, has above all characterized the English civilization; it was in England that this character developed itself with the most continuity and obviousness; it was there that the civil and religious orders, aristocracy, democracy, royalty, local and central institutions, moral and political developments, progressed and increased together, pell-mell, so to speak, and if not with an equal rapidity, at least always within a short distance of each other. Under the reign of the Tudors, for instance, in the midst of the most brilliant progress of pure monarchy, we see the democratical principle, the popular power, arising and strengthening itself at the same time. The revolution of the seventeenth century burst forth; it was at the same time religious and political. The feudal aristocracy appeared here in a very weakened condition, and with all the symptoms of decline: nevertheless, it was ever in a position to preserve a place and play an important part therein, and to take its share in the results. It is the same with the entire course of English history: never has any ancient element completely perished; never has any new element wholly triumphed, or any special principle attained to an exclusive preponderance. There has always been a simultaneous development of different forces, a compromise between their pretensions and their interests.

Upon the continent, the progress of civilization has been much less complex and complete. The various elements of society—the religious and civil orders —monarchy, aristocracy, and democracy, have developed themselves, not together and abreast, but in succession. Each principle, each system has had, after a certain manner, its turn. Such a century belongs, I will not say exclusively, which would be saying too much, but with a very marked preponderance, to feudal aristocracy, for example; another belongs to the monarchical principle; a third to the democratical system.

Compare the French with the English middle ages, the eleventh, twelfth, and thirteenth centuries of our history with the corresponding centuries beyond the channel; you will find that at this period, in France, feudalism was almost absolutely sovereign, while royalty and the democratical principle were next to nullities. Look to England: it is, indeed, the feudal aristocracy which predominates; but royalty and democracy were nevertheless powerful and important.

Royalty triumphed in England under Elizabeth, as in France under Louis XIV.; but how many precautions was it obliged to take; to how many restrictions—now from the aristocracy, now from the democracy, did it submit! In England, also, each system and each principle has had its day of power and success; but never so completely, so exclusively as upon the continent; the conqueror has always been compelled to tolerate the presence of his rivals, and to allow each his share.

With the differences in the progress of the two civilizations, are connected advantages and disadvantages, which manifest themselves, in fact, in the history of the two countries. There can be no doubt, for instance, but that this simultaneous development of the different social elements greatly contributed to carry England, more rapidly than any other of the continental states, to the final aim of all society—namely, the establishment of a government at once regular and free. It is precisely the nature of a government to concern itself for all interests and all powers, to reconcile them, and to induce them to live and prosper in common; now, such, beforehand, by the concurrence of a multitude of causes, was the disposition and relation of the different elements of English society: a general and somewhat regular government had therefore less difficulty in becoming constituted there. So, the essence of liberty is the manifestation and simultaneous action of all interests, rights, powers, and social elements. England was therefore much nearer to its possession than the majority of other states. For the same reasons, national good sense, the comprehension of public affairs, necessarily formed themselves there more rapidly than elsewhere; political good sense consists in knowing how to estimate all facts, to appreciate them, and render to each its share of consideration; this, in England, was a necessity of the social state, a natural result of the course of civilization.

On the other hand, in the continental states, each system, each principle having had its turn, having predominated after a more complete and more exclusive manner, its development was wrought upon a larger scale, and with more grandeur and brilliancy. Royalty and feudal aristocracy, for instance, came upon the continental stage with far greater boldness, extension, and freedom. Our political experiments, so to speak, have been broader and more finished: the result of this has been that political ideas (I speak of general ideas, and not of good sense applied to the conduct of affairs) and political doctrines have risen higher, and displayed themselves with much more rational vigour. Each system having, in some measure, presented itself alone, and having remained a long time upon the stage, men have been enabled to consider it in its entirety, to mount up to its first principles, to follow it out into its last consequences, and fully to unfold its theory. Whoever attentively observes the English character, must be struck with a twofold fact—on the one hand, with the soundness of its good sense and its practical ability; on the other, with its lack of general ideas, and its pride as to theoretical questions. Whether we open a work upon English history, upon jurisprudence, or any other subject, it is rarely that we find the grand reason of things, the fundamental reason. In all things, and especially in the political sciences, pure doctrine, philosophy, and science, properly so called, have prospered much better on the Continent than in England; their flights have, at least, been far more powerful and bold; and we cannot doubt but that the different developments of civilization in the two countries have greatly contributed to this result.

For the rest, whatever we may think of the advantages or disadvantages which this difference has entailed, it is a real and incontestable fact, the fact which most deeply distinguishes England from the continent. But it does not follow, because the different principles and social elements have been there developed more simultaneously, here more successively, that, at bottom, the path and the goal have not been one and

the same. Considered in their entirety, the continent and
England have traversed the same grand phases of civilization;
events have, in either, followed the same course, and the
same causes have led to the same effects. You have been
enabled to convince yourselves of this fact from the picture
which I have placed before you of civilization up to the sixteenth century, and you will equally recognise it in studying
the seventeenth and eighteenth centuries. The development
of free inquiry, and that of pure monarchy, almost simultaneous in England, accomplished themselves upon the continent at long intervals; but they did accomplish themselves,
and the two powers, after having successively preponderated
with splendour, came equally, at last, to blows. The general
path of societies, considering all things, has thus been the
same, and though the points of difference are real, those of
resemblance are more deeply seated. A rapid sketch of
modern times will leave you in no doubt upon this subject.

Glancing over the history of Europe in the seventeenth
and eighteenth centuries, it is impossible not to perceive that
France has advanced at the head of European civilization.
At the beginning of this work I have already insisted upon
this fact, and I have endeavoured to point out its cause.
We shall now find it more striking than ever.

The principle of pure monarchy, of absolute royalty, predominated in Spain under Charles V. and Philip II., before
developing itself in France under Louis XIV. In the same
manner the principle of free inquiry had reigned in England
in the seventeenth century, before developing itself in France
in the eighteenth. Nevertheless, pure monarchy and free
inquiry came not from Spain and England to take possession of the world. The two principles, the two systems
remained, in a manner, confined to the countries in which
they had arisen. It was necessary that they should pass
through France in order that they might extend their conquests; it was necessary that pure monarchy and free inquiry
should become French in order to become European. This
communicative character of French civilization, this social
genius of France, which has displayed itself at all periods,
was thus more than ever manifest at the period with which we
now occupy ourselves. I will not further insist upon this
fact; it has been developed to you with as much reason of

brilliancy in other lectures wherein you have been called upon to observe the influence of French literature and philosophy in the eighteenth century. You have seen that philosophic France possessed more authority over Europe, in regard to liberty, than even free England. You have seen that French civilization showed itself far more active and contagious than that of any other country. I need not, therefore, pause upon the details of this fact, which I mention only in order to rest upon it my right to confine my picture of modern European civilization to France alone. Between the civilization of France and that of the other states of Europe at this period, there have, no doubt, been differences, which it would have been necessary to bear in mind, if my present purpose had been a full and faithful exposition of the history of those civilizations; but I must go on so rapidly that I am compelled to omit entire nations and ages, so to speak. I choose rather to concentrate your attention for a moment upon the course of French civilization, an image, though imperfect, of the general course of things in Europe.

The influence of France in Europe, during the seventeenth and eighteenth centuries, presents itself under very different aspects. In the former, it was French government that acted upon Europe, and advanced at the head of general civilization. In the latter it was no longer to the government, but France herself, that the preponderance belonged. In the first case, it was Louis XIV. and his court, afterwards France and her opinion, that governed minds and attracted attention. In the seventeenth century there were peoples who, as peoples, appeared more prominently upon the scene, and took a greater part in events, than the French people. Thus during the thirty years war, the German nation, in the English revolution, the English people, played, in their own destinies, a much greater part than was played, at this period, by the French, in theirs. So, also, in the eighteenth century, there were governments stronger, of greater consideration, and more to be dreaded, than the French government. No doubt Frederick II., Catherine II., and Maria Theresa, had more influence and weight in Europe than Louis XV.; nevertheless, at both periods, it was France that was at the head of European civilization, placed

there, first, by its government, afterwards, by itself; now by
the political action of its masters, now by its peculiar intellectual development.

In order to fully understand the predominant influence in
the course of civilization in France, and therefore in Europe,
we must study, in the seventeenth century, French government, in the eighteenth, French society. We must change
the plan and the drama according as time alters the stage
and the actors.

When we occupy ourselves with the government of Louis
XIV., when we endeavour to appreciate the causes of his
power and influence in Europe, we scarcely think of anything but his renown, his conquests, his magnificence, and
the literary glory of his time. It is to external causes that
we apply ourselves, and attribute the European preponderance of the French government. But I conceive that
this preponderance had deeper and more serious foundations. We must not believe that it was simply by means of
victories, *fêtes*, or even master-works of genius, that Louis
XIV. and his government, at this epoch, played the part
which it is impossible to deny them.

Many of you may remember, and all of you have heard
speak of the effect which the consular government produced
in France twenty-nine years ago, and of the condition in
which it found our country. Without, was impending
foreign invasion, and continual disasters were occurring in
our armies; within, was an almost complete dissolution of
power and of the people; there were no revenues, no public
order; in a word, society was prostrate, humiliated, and disorganised: such was France on the advent of the consulate
government. Who does not recal the prodigious and feli-
citous activity of this government, that activity which, in a
little time, secured the independence of the land, revived
national honour, reorganized the administration, remodelled
the legislation, and, after a manner, regenerated society under
:he hand of power?

Well, the government of Louis XIV., when it commenced,
did something analogous to this for France; with great difference of times, proceedings, and forms, it pursued and
attained nearly the same results.

Recal to your memory the state into which France was

fallen after the government of cardinal Richelieu, and during the minority of Louis XIV. : the Spanish armies always on the frontiers, sometimes in the interior; continual danger of an invasion; internal dissensions urged to extremity, civil war, the government weak and discredited at home and abroad. Society was perhaps in a less violent, but still sufficiently analogous state to ours, prior to the eighteenth *Brumaire*. It was from this state that the government of Louis XIV. extricated France. His first victories had the effect of the victory of Marengo: they secured the country, and retrieved the national honour. I am about to consider this government under its principal aspects—in its wars, in its external relations, in its administration, and in its legislation; and you will see, I imagine, that the comparison of which I speak, and to which I attach no puerile importance (for I think very little of the value of historical parallels), you will see, I say, that this comparison has a real foundation, and that I have a right to employ it.

First of all let us speak of the wars of Louis XIV. The wars of Europe have originated, as you know, and as I have often taken occasion to remind you, in great popular movements. Urged by necessity, caprice, or any other cause, entire populations, sometimes numerous, sometimes in simple bands, have transported themselves from one territory to another. This was the general character of European wars until after the crusades, at the end of the thirteenth century.

At that time began a species of wars scarcely less different from modern wars than the above. These were the distant wars, undertaken no longer by the people, but by governments, which went at the head of their armies to seek states and adventures afar off. They quitted their countries, abandoned their own territories, and plunged, some into Germany, others into Italy, and others into Africa, with no other motives than personal caprice. Almost all the wars of the fifteenth and even of a part of the sixteenth century were of this description. What interest — I speak not of a legitimate interest — but what possible motive had France that Charles VIII. should possess the kingdom of Naples? This evidently was a war dictated by no political consideration: the king conceived that he had a personal right to the kingdom of Naples, and with a personal aim and

to satisfy his personal desire, he undertook the conquest of a
distant country, which was in no way adapted for annexation
to his kingdom; which, on the contrary, did nothing but
compromise his power externally, and internally, his repose.
It was the same with the expedition of Charles the Fifth to
Africa. The latest war of this kind was the expedition of
Charles XII. against Russia. The wars of Louis XIV. had
no such character; they were the wars of a regular government, fixed in the centre of its states, and labouring to make
conquests around it, to extend or consolidate its territory; in
a word, they were political wars.

They may have been just or unjust; they may have cost
France too dearly; there are a thousand reasons which might
be adduced against their morality and their excess; but they
bear a character incomparably more rational than the antece-
dent wars: they were no longer undertaken for whim or adventure; they were dictated by some serious motive; it was
some natural limit that it seemed desirable to attain; some
population speaking the same language that they aimed at
annexing; some point of defence against a neighbouring
power, which it was thought necessary to acquire. No doubt
personal ambition had a share in these wars; but examine one
after another of the wars of Louis XIV., particularly those of
the first part of his reign, and you will find that they had truly
political motives; and that they were conceived for the interest
of France, for obtaining power, and for the country's safety.

The results are proofs of the fact. France of the present day
is still, in many respects, what the wars of Louis XIV. have
made it. The provinces which he conquered, Franche-Comté,
Flanders, and Alsace, remain yet incorporated with France.
There are sensible as well as senseless conquests: those of
Louis XIV. were of the former species; his enterprises have
not the unreasonable and capricious character which, up to
his time, was so general; a skilful, if not always just and wise
policy, presided over them.

Leaving the wars of Louis XIV., and passing to the consideration of his relations with foreign states, of his diplomacy,
properly so called, I find an analogous result. I have insisted
upon the occurrence of the birth of diplomacy in Europe at the
end of the fifteenth century. I have endeavoured to show how
the relations of governments and states between themselves

up to that time accidental, rare, and transitory, became at
this period more regular and enduring; how they took a
character of great public interest; how, in a word, at the end
of the fifteenth, and during the first half of the sixteenth century, diplomacy came to play an immense part in events.
Nevertheless, up to the seventeenth century, it had not been,
truly speaking, systematic; it had not led to long alliances,
or to great, and above all, durable combinations, directed,
according to fixed principles, towards a constant aim, with
that spirit of continuity which is the true character of established governments.   During the course of the religious
revolution, the external relations of states were almost completely under the power of the religious interest; the Pro ·
testant and Catholic leagues divided Europe.   It was in the
seventeenth century, after the treaty of Westphalia, and under
the influence of the government of Louis XIV., that diplomacy changed its character.   It then escaped from the exclusive influences of the religious principle; alliances and
political combinations were formed upon other considerations.
At the same time it became much more systematic, regular,
and constantly directed towards a certain aim, according to
permanent principles.   The regular origin of this system of
balance in Europe belongs to this period.   It was under
the government of Louis XIV. that the system, together
with all the considerations attached to it, truly took possession of European policy.   When we investigate what was the
general idea in regard to this subject, what was the predominating principle of the policy of Louis XIV., I believe that
the following is what we discover:

I have spoken of the great struggle between the pure
monarchy of Louis XIV., aspiring to become universal
monarchy, and civil and religious liberty, and the independence of states, under the direction of the prince of
Orange, William III.   You have seen that the great fact of
this period was the division of the powers under these two
banners.   But this fact was not then estimated as we estimate
it now; it was hidden and unknown even to those who accomplished it; the suppression of the system of pure monarchy
and the consecration of civil and religious liberty was, at
bottom, the necessary result of the resistance of Holland and
its allies to Louis XIV.; but the question was not thus

s

openly enunciated between absolute power and liberty.
It has been often said that the propagation of absolute
power was the predominant principle of the diplomacy of
Louis XIV.; but I do not believe it. This consideration
played no very great part in his policy, until latterly, in his
old age. The power of France, its preponderance in Europe,
the humbling of rival powers, in a word, the political interest
and strength of the state, was the aim which Louis XIV.
constantly pursued, whether in fighting against Spain, the
emperor of Germany, or England; he acted far less with a
view to the propagation of absolute power than from a desire
for the power and aggrandizement of France and of its
government. Among many proofs, I will adduce one which
emanates from Louis XIV. himself. In his Memoirs, under
the year 1666, if I remember right, we find a note nearly
in these words:—

"I have had, this morning, a conversation with Mr. Sidney,
an English gentleman, who maintained to me the possibility
of reanimating the republican party in England. Mr. Sidney
demanded from me, for that purpose, 400,000 livres. I told
him that I could give no more than 200,000. He induced
me to summon from Switzerland another English gentleman, named Ludlow, and to converse with him of the same
design."

And, accordingly, we find among the Memoirs of Ludlow,
about the same date, a paragraph to this effect :—

"I have received from the French government an invitation to go to Paris, in order to speak of the affairs of my
country; but I am distrustful of that government."

And Ludlow remained in Switzerland.

You see that the diminution of the royal power in England
was, at this time, the aim of Louis XIV. He fomented
internal dissensions, and laboured to resuscitate the repub
lican party, to prevent Charles II. from becoming too powerful in his country. During the embassy of Barillon in
England, the same fact constantly reappears. Whenever
the authority of Charles seemed to obtain the advantage, and
the national party seemed on the point of being crushed, the
French ambassador directed his influence to this side, gave
money to the chiefs of the opposition, and fought, in a word,
against absolute power, when that became a means of

weakening a rival power to France. Whenever you attentively consider the conduct of external relations under Louis XIV., it is with this fact that you will be the most struck.

You will also be struck with the capacity and skill of French diplomacy at this period. The names of M.M. de Torcy, d'Avaux, de Bonrepos, are known to all well-informed persons. When we compare the despatches, the memoirs, the skill and conduct of these counsellors of Louis XIV. with those of Spanish, Portuguese, and German negotiators, we must be struck with the superiority of the French ministers; not only as regards their earnest activity and their application to affairs, but also as regards their liberty of spirit. These courtiers of an absolute king judged of external events, of parties, of the requirements of liberty, and of popular revolutions, much better even than the majority of the English ministers themselves at this period. There was no diplomacy in Europe, in the seventeenth century, which appears equal to the French, except the Dutch. The ministers of John de Witt and of William of Orange, those illustrious chiefs of the party of civil and religious liberty, were the only ministers who seemed in condition to wrestle with the servants of the great and absolute king.

You see, then, that whether we consider the wars of Louis XIV., or his diplomatical relations, we arrive at the same results. We can easily conceive that a government which conducted its wars and negotiations in this manner, should have assumed a high standing in Europe, and presented itself therein, not only as dreadworthy, but as skilful and imposing.

Let us now consider the interior of France, the administration and legislation of Louis XIV.; we shall there discern new explanations of the power and splendour of his government.

It is difficult to determine with any degree of precision, what we ought to understand by *administration* in the government of a state. Nevertheless, when we endeavour to investigate this fact, we discover, I believe, that, under the most general point of view, administration consists in an aggregate of means destined to propel, as promptly and certainly as possible, the will of the central power through all parts of

s 2

society, and to make the force of society, whether consisting
of men or money, return again, under the same conditions,
to the central power.   This, if I mistake not, is the true aim,
the predominant characteristic of administration.   Accordingly we find that in times when it is above all things needful
to establish unity and order in society, administration is the
chief means of attaining this end, of bringing together, of
cementing, and of uniting incoherent and scattered elements.
Such, in fact, was the work of the administration of Louis XIV.
Up to this time, there had been nothing so difficult, in France
as in the rest of Europe, as to effect the penetration of the
action of the central power into all parts of society, and to
gather into the bosom of the central power the means of force
existing in society.   To this end Louis XIV. laboured, and
succeeded, up to a certain point; incomparably better, at least,
than preceding governments had done.   I cannot enter into
details: just run over, in thought, all kinds of public services, taxes, roads, industry, military administration, all the
establishments which belong to whatsoever branch of administration; there is scarcely one of which you do not find either
the origin, development, or great amelioration under Louis
XIV.   It was as administrators that the greatest men of his
time, Colbert and Louvois, displayed their genius and exercised their ministry.   It was by the excellence of its administration that his government acquired a generality, decision,
and consistency which were wanting to all the European
governments around him.

Under the legislative point of view, this reign presents to
you the same fact.   I return to the comparison which I have
already made use of, to the legislative activity of the consular
government, to its prodigious work of revising and generally
recasting the laws.   A work of the same nature took place
under Louis XIV.   The great ordinances which he promulgated, the criminal ordinance, the ordinances of procedure,
commerce, the marine, waters, and woods, are true codes,
which were constructed in the same manner as our codes,
discussed in the council of state, some of them under the
presidency of Lamoignon.   There are men whose glory consists in having taken part in this labour and this discussion,
M. Pussort, for instance.   If we were to consider it in
itself, we should have much to say against the legislation of

Louis XIV.; it was full of vices, which now fully declare themselves, and which no one can deny; it was not conceived in the interest of true justice and of liberty, but in the interest of public order, and for giving more regularity and firmness to the laws. But even that was a great progress; and we cannot doubt but that the ordinances of Louis XIV., so very superior to anything preceding them, powerfully contributed to advance French society in the career of civilization.

You see that under whatever point of view we regard this government, we very soon discover the source of its power and influence. It was the first government that presented itself to the eyes of Europe as a power sure of its position, which had not to dispute its existence with internal enemies —tranquil as to its dominions and the people, and intent only on governing. Up to that time, all European governments had been unceasingly thrown into wars, which deprived them of security as well as leisure, or had been so beset with parties and internal enemies, that they were compelled to spend their time in fighting for their lives. The government of Louis XIV. appeared as the first which applied itself solely to the conduct of affairs, as a power at once definitive and progressive; which was not afraid of innovating, because it could count upon the future. There have, in fact, existed very few governments of such an innovating spirit. Compare it with a government of the same nature, with the pure monarchy of Philip II. in Spain; it was more absolute than that of Louis XIV., and yet far less regular and less tranquil. But how did Philip II. succeed in establishing absolute power in Spain? By stifling the activity of the country, by refusing to it every species of amelioration, by rendering the condition of Spain completely stationary. The government of Louis XIV., on the contrary, showed itself active in all kinds of innovations, favourable to the progress of letters, of arts, of riches, and, in a word, of civilization. These are the true causes of its preponderance in Europe; a preponderance such that it became upon the continent, during the whole of the seventeenth century, the type of government, not only for sovereigns, but even for nations.

And now we inquire—and it is impossible to help doing

so—how it happened that a power, thus brilliant, and, judging from the facts which I have placed before you, thus well established, so rapidly fell into decline? how, after having played such a part in Europe, it became, in the next century, so inconsistent, weak, and inconsiderable? The fact is incontestable. In the seventeenth century the French government was at the head of European civilization; in the eighteenth century it disappeared; and it was French society, separated from its government, often even opposed to it, that now preceded and guided the European world in its progress.

It is here that we discover the incorrigible evil and the infallible effect of absolute power. I will not go into any detail concerning the faults of the government of Louis XIV.; he committed many: I will speak neither of the war of the Spanish succession, nor of the revocation of the edict of Nantes, nor of excessive expenses, nor of many other of the fatal measures that compromised his fortunes. I will take the merits of the government as I have described them. I will agree that perhaps there has never existed an absolute power more fully recognised by its age and nation, nor one which has rendered more real services to the civilization of its country and of Europe in general. But, by the very fact that this government had no other principle than absolute power, and reposed upon no other base than this, its decline became sudden and well merited. What France, under Louis XIV., essentially wanted, was political institutions and forces, independent, subsisting of themselves, and, in a word, capable of spontaneous action and resistance. The ancient French institutions, if they merited that name, no longer existed: Louis XIV. completed their ruin. He took no care to endeavour to replace them by new institutions; they would have cramped him, and he did not choose to be cramped. All that appeared conspicuous at that period was will, and the action of central power. The government of Louis XIV. was a great fact, a fact powerful and splendid, but without roots. Free institutions are a guarantee, not only of the wisdom of governments, but also of their duration. No system can endure except by means of institutions. When absolute power has endured, it has been supported by true institutions, sometimes by the division of society into strongly distinct castes, sometimes by a system of religious institutions. Under the reign

of Louis XIV. institutions were wanting to power as well as
to liberty. In France, at this period, nothing guaranteed
either the country against the illegitimate actions of the
government, or the government itself against the inevitable
action of time. Thus we see the government helping on
its own decay. It was not Louis XIV. alone who was be
coming aged and weak at the end of his reign: it was the
whole absolute power. Pure monarchy was as much worn
out in 1712 as was the monarch himself: and the evil was so
much the more grave, as Louis XIV. had abolished political
morals as well as political institutions. There are no political
morals without independence. He alone who feels that he
has a strength of his own is always capable either of serving
or opposing power. Energetic characters disappear with independent situations, and dignity of soul alone gives birth to
security of rights.

This, then, is the state in which Louis XIV. left France
and power: a society in full development of riches,
power, and all kinds of intellectual activity; and, side by
side with this progressive society, a government essentially stationary, having no means of renewing itself, of
adapting itself to the movement of its people; devoted, after
half a century of the greatest splendour, to immobility and
weakness, and already, during the life of its founder, fallen
into a decline which seemed like dissolution. Such was the
condition of France at the conclusion of the seventeenth century, a condition which impressed the epoch that followed with
a direction and a character so different.

I need hardly say that the onward impulse of the human
mind, that free inquiry was the predominating feature, the
essential fact of the eighteenth century. You have already
heard much concerning this fact from this chair; already you
have heard that powerful epoch characterised by a philosophical orator, and by that of an eloquent philosopher. I
cannot pretend, in the short space of time which remains to
me, to trace all the phases of the great moral revolution
which then accomplished itself. I would, nevertheless, fain
not leave you without calling your attention to some cha·
racteristics which have been too little remarked upon.

The first,—one which strikes me most, and which I have
already mentioned, is the, so to speak, almost complete disap

pearance of the government in the course of the eighteenth
century, and the appearance of the human mind as the principal and almost the only actor.

Except in that which is connected with external relations under the ministry of the duc de Choiseul, and in certain great concessions made to the general tendency of
opinion, for instance, in the American war; except, I say,
in some events of this nature, perhaps there has scarcely ever
been so inactive, apathetic, and inert a government as was the
French government of this period. Instead of the energetic,
ambitious government of Louis XIV., which appeared everywhere, and put itself at the head of everything, you have
a government which laboured only to hide itself, to keep itself
in the background, so weak and compromised did it feel itself
to be. Activity and ambition had passed over wholly to
the people. It was the nation, which, by its opinion and its
intellectual movement, mingled itself with all things, interfered in all, and, in short, alone possessed moral authority,
which is the only true authority.

A second characteristic which strikes me, in the condition
of the human mind in the eighteenth century, is the universality of free inquiry. Up to that time, and particularly in
the seventeenth century, free inquiry had been exercised
within a limited and partial field; it had had for its object
sometimes religious questions, sometimes religious and political questions together, but it did not extend its pretensions
to all subjects. In the eighteenth century, on the contrary, the
character of free inquiry is universality; religion, politics, pure
philosophy, man and society, moral and material nature, all
at the same time became the object of study, doubt, and system; ancient sciences were overturned, new sciences were
called into existence. The movement extended itself in all
directions, although it had emanated from one and the same
impulse.

This movement, moreover, had a peculiar character;
one which, perhaps, is not to be met elsewhere in the
history of the world: it was purely speculative. Up to that
time, in all great human revolutions, action had commingled
itself with speculation. Thus, in the sixteenth century, the
religious revolution began with ideas, with purely intellectual
discussions, but it very soon terminated in events. The heads

of intellectual parties soon became the heads of political parties; the realities of life were mixed with the labour of the understanding. Thus, too, it happened in the seventeenth century, in the English revolution. But in France, in the eighteenth century, you find the human spirit exercising itself upon all things, upon ideas which, connecting themselves with the real interests of life, seemed calculated to have the most prompt and powerful influence upon facts. Nevertheless, the leaders and actors of these great discussions remained strangers to all species of practical activity—mere spectators, who observed, judged, and spoke, without ever interfering in events. At no other time has the government of facts, of external realities, been so completely distinct from the government of minds. The separation of the spiritual and temporal orders was never completely real in Europe until the eighteenth century. For the first time, perhaps, the spiritual order developed itself wholly apart from the temporal order: an important fact, and one which exercised a prodigious influence upon the course of events. It gave to the ideas of the time a singular character of ambition and inexperience; never before had philosophy aspired so strongly to rule the world, never had philosophy been so little acquainted with the world. It became obvious that a day must arrive for coming to facts; for the intellectual movement to pass into external events; and as they had been totally separated, their meeting was the more difficult, the shock far more violent.

How can we now be surprised with another character of the condition of the human mind at this epoch, I mean its prodigious boldness? Up to that time its greatest activity had always been confined by certain barriers; the mind of man had always existed amidst facts, whereof some inspired it with caution, and, to a certain extent, checked its movements. In the eighteenth century, I should be at a loss to say what external facts the human mind respected, or what external facts exercised any empire over it: it hated or despised the entire social state. It concluded, therefore, that it was called upon to reform all things; it came to consider itself a sort of creator; institutions, opinions, manners, society, and man himself, all seemed to require reform, and human reason charged itself with the enterprise. What audacity equal to this had ever before been imagined by it!

Such was the power which, in the course of the
eighteenth century, confronted what still remained of the
government of Louis XIV. You perceive that it was impossible to avoid the occurrence of a shock between these
two so unequal forces. The predominant fact of the English
revolution, the struggle between free inquiry and pure
monarchy, was now also to burst forth in France. No doubt
the differences were great, and these necessarily perpetuated
themselves in the results; but, at bottom, the general conditions were similar, and the definitive event had the same
meaning.

I do not pretend to exhibit the infinite consequences of
this struggle. The time for concluding this course of lectures
has arrived; I must check myself. I merely desire, before
leaving you, to call your attention to the most grave, and, in
my opinion, the most instructive fact which was revealed to us
by this great struggle. This is the danger, the evil, and
the insurmountable vice of absolute power, whatever form,
whatever name it may bear, and towards whatever aim it
may direct itself. You have seen that the government of
Louis XIV. perished by almost this cause only. Well, the
power which succeeded it, the human mind, the true sovereign of the eighteenth century, suffered the same fate; in
its turn, it possessed an almost absolute power; it, in its turn,
placed an excessive confidence in itself. Its onward impulse was beautiful, good, most useful; and were it necessary that I should express a definitive opinion, I should
say that the eighteenth century appears to me to have been
one of the greatest ages of history, that which, perhaps, has
done the greatest services for humanity, that which has in
the greatest degree aided its progress, and rendered that
progress of the most general character: were I asked to
pronounce upon it as a public administration, I should
pronounce in its favour. But it is not the less true that,
at this epoch, the human mind. possessed of absolute
power, became corrupted and misled by it; holding established facts and former ideas in an illegitimate disdain
and aversion; an aversion which carried it into error and
tyranny. The share of error and tyranny, indeed, which
mingled itself with the triumph of human reason, at the end
of this century. a portion which we cannot conceal from our-

selves, was very great, and which we must proclaim and not deny; this portion of error and tyranny was chiefly the result of the extravagance into which the mind of man had been thrown, at this period, by the extension of his power.

It is the duty, and, I believe, it will be the peculiar merit of our times, to know that all power, whether intellectual or temporal, whether belonging to governments or peoples, to philosophers or ministers, whether exercising itself in one cause or in another, bears within itself a natural vice, a principle of weakness and of abuse which ought to render it limited. Now nothing but the general freedom of all rights, all interests, and all opinions, the free manifestation and legal coexistence of all these forces, can ever restrain each force and each power within its legitimate limits, prevent it from encroaching on the rest, and, in a word, cause the real and generally profitable existence of free inquiry. Herein consists for us the grand lesson of the struggle which occurred at the end of the eighteenth century, between absolute temporal power and absolute spiritual power.

I have now arrived at the term which I proposed to myself. You remember that my object, in commencing this course, was to present you with a general picture of the development of European civilization, from the fall of the Roman empire to our own days. I have traversed this career very rapidly, and without being able to inform you, far from it, of all that was important, or to bring proofs of all that I have said. I have been compelled to omit much, and often to request you to believe me upon my word. I hope, nevertheless, that I have attained my aim, which was to mark the grand crises in the development of modern society. Allow me yet one word more.

I endeavoured, in the beginning, to define civilization, and to describe the fact which bears this name. Civilization seemed to me to consist of two principal facts: the development of human society, and that of man himself; on the one hand, political and social development; on the other, internal and moral development. I have confined myself so far to the history of society. I have presented civilization only under the social point of view; and have said nothing of the development of man himself. I have not endeavoured to unfold to you the history of opinions, of the moral progress of humanity. I propose, when we meet again, to confine myself especially to France, to study with you the history of French civilization, to study it in detail, and under its various aspects. I shall endeavour to make you acquainted, not only with the history of society in France, but also with that of man: to be present with you at the progress of institutions, of opinions, and of intellectual works of all kinds; and to arrive thus at a complete understanding of the development of our glorious country, in its entirety. In the past as well as in the future, our country may well lay claim to our tenderest affections.

END OF THE HISTORY OF CIVILIZATION IN EUROPE.

HISTORY

OF

CIVILIZATION IN FRANCE.

From the Fall of the Roman Empire.

––––––

LECTURE THE FIRST.

Object of the course—Two methods of studying in detail the history of
European civilization—Reasons for preferring the study of the history
of the civilization of a particular country—Reasons for studying that
of France—Of the essential facts which constitute the perfection of
civilization — Comparison of the great European nations under this
point of view—Of civilization in England—Germany—Italy—Spain—
France—French civilization is the most complete, and offers the most
faithful representation of civilization in general—That the student has
other things to bear in mind besides the mere study—Of the present
prevailing tendencies in the intellectual order — Of the prevailing
tendencies in the social order—Two problems resulting therefrom—
Their apparent contradiction—Our times are called upon to solve them
—A third and purely moral problem, rendered equally important by the
present state of civilization—The unjust reproaches of which it is the
object—The necessity of meeting them—All science, in the present
day, exerts a social influence—All power should tend to the moral perfection of the individual, as well as to the improvement of society in
general.

MANY of you will call to mind the nature and aim of
a course of lectures which were brought to a close some
months since. That course was cursory and of a general
nature. I then attempted, in a very short period of time, to
place before you an historical view of European civilization.

I hastened, as it were, from point to point, confining myself
strictly to general facts and assertions, at the risk of being
sometimes misunderstood and perhaps discredited.

Necessity, as you know, imposed this method upon me; but
in spite of this necessity I should have been much pained by
the inconveniences which arose from it, had I not foreseen that
in a future course I should be enabled to remedy it; and
had I not proposed to myself, at the time, to complete, at
some future period, the outline which I then traced, and of
leading you to the general results which I placed before
you, by the same path which I myself had followed, an
attentive and complete study of the facts. Such is the end
at which I now aim.

Two methods offer themselves as tending to the attainment
of the proposed end. I might either recommence the course
of last summer, and review the general history of European
civilization in its whole extent, by giving in detail that which
it was impossible to give in mass, and by again passing
over with more leisurely steps that ground which before was
gone over in almost breathless haste. Or I might study the
history of civilization in a single great country, in one of the
principal European nations in which it has been developed,
and thus, by confining the field of my researches, be the
better enabled thoroughly to explore it.

The first method seemed to offer serious inconveniences.
It would be very difficult, if not impossible, to maintain any
unity in a history with so extensive a range, and which, at
the same time should be perfect in all its details. We discovered last summer, that there was a true unity running
through European civilization; but this unity is only visible
in general actions and grand results. We must ascend the
highest mountain before the petty inequalities and diversities of the surface will become invisible, and before we can
discover the general aspect, and the true and essential nature
of the entire country. When we quit general facts and wish
to look into particulars, the unity vanishes, the diversities
again appear, and in the variety of occurrences one loses
sight of both causes and effects; so that to give a detailed
history, and still to preserve some harmony, it is absolutely
necessary to narrow the field of inquiry.

There is also another great objection to this method, in the immense extent and diversity of knowledge which it presupposes and requires both in the speaker and his audience. Those who wish to trace with moderate accuracy the course of European civilization should have a sufficiently intimate acquaintance, not only with the events which have passed among each people, with their history, but likewise with their language, literature, and philosophy, in short, with all phases of their career; a work which is evidently almost impossible, and certainly so in the time which we could spend upon it.

It appears to me, that by studying the history of civilization in one great European nation, I shall arrive more quickly at the desired result. The unity of the narrative will then, indeed, be compatible with details; there is in every country a certain national harmony, which is the result of the community of manners, laws, language, and events, and this harmony is imprinted in the civilization. We may pass from fact to fact without losing sight of the whole picture. And lastly, though I will not say that it can easily be done, it is yet possible to combine the knowledge necessary for such a work.

I have therefore decided upon this second method, upon that of abandoning the general history of European civilization, in all the nations which have contributed thereto, and confining myself to the civilization of one country, which, if we note the differences between it and other countries, may become, for our purpose, an image of the whole destiny of Europe.

The choice of method being once made, that of a nation easily follows; I have taken the history and civilization of France. I shall certainly not deny having experienced a sensation of pleasure while making this choice. No one will deny that the emotions of patriotism are legitimate, provided they be sanctioned by truth and reason. Some there are, in the present day, who seem to fear that patriotism suffers much from the enlargement of ideas and sentiments, arising from the actual state of European civilization; they predict that it will become enervated, and lose itself in cosmopolitism. I cannot share such fears. In the present day, it will be with patriotism as with all human actions, feelings and opinions. It is condemned, I admit, incessantly to undergo the test of publicity, of inquiry and discussion; it is condemned no longer to remain a mere prejudice, habit, or a blind and exclusive passion; it must give a reason for itself. It will be oppressed by this necessity no more than any natural and legitimate feelings are; on the contrary, it will become refined and elevated. These are the tests to which it must submit, and it will soar above them. I can truly say, if any other history in Europe had appeared to me greater, more instructive, or better suited to represent the general course of civilization than that of France, I should have chosen it. But I have reasons for selecting France; independently of the special interest which its history has for us, France has long since been proclaimed by all Europe the most civilized of its nations. Whenever the opinion of the struggle has not been between the national all-love, when one seeks the true and disinterested opinion of people in the ideas and actions wherein it manifests itself indirectly, without taking the form of a controversy, we find that France is acknowledged to be the country in which civilization has appeared in its most complete form, where it has been most communicative, and where it has most forcibly struck the European imagination.

And we must not suppose, that the superiority of this country is solely attributable to the amenity of our social relations, to the gentleness of our manners, or to that easy and animated life which people so often come to seek among us. There can be no doubt that it partly arises from these attributes; but the fact of which I speak has more profound and universal causes: it is not a fashion, as might have been supposed when the question was concerning the civilization of the age of Louis XIV., neither is it a popular ebullition, as a view of our own times would lead us to suppose. The preference which the disinterested opinion of Europe accords to French civilization is philosophically just; it is the result of an instinctive judgment, doubtless in some measure confused, but well based, upon the essential elements and general nature of civilization.

You will call to mind the definition of civilization I attempted to give in the commencement of the former course of lectures. I there sought to discover what ideas attach themselves to this word in the common sense of men. It appeared to me, on a reference to general opinion, that civilization essentially consists of two principles; the improvement of the exterior and general condition of man, and that of his inward and personal nature; in a word, in the improvement both of society and of humanity.

And it is not these two principles of themselves, which constitute civilization; to bring it to perfection, their intimate and rapid union, simultaneousness, and reciprocal action, are absolutely necessary. I showed that if they do not always arrive conjointly—that if, at one time, the improvement of society, and at another, that of individual man, progresses more quickly or extends further, they are not the less necessary the one to the other; they excite each other, and sooner or later will amalgamate. When one progresses for any length of time without the other, and when their union is long interrupted, a feeling of regret, and of a painful hiatus and incompleteness, seizes the spectators. If an important social improvement, a great progress in material well being is manifested among a people without being accompanied by intellectual improvement, or an analogous progression in mind; the social improvement seems precarious, inexplicable, and almost unjust. One asks what general ideas have produced and justified it, or to what principles it attaches itself. One wishes to assure oneself that it will not be limited to particular generations, to a single country; but that it will spread and communicate itself, and that it will fill every nation. And how can social improvement spread and communicate itself but by ideas, upon the wings of doctrines? Ideas alone mock at distance, pass over oceans, and everywhere make themselves received and comprehended. Besides, such is the noble nature of humanity, that it cannot see a great improvement in material strength, without aspiring to the moral strength which should be joined with it and direct it; something subordinate remains imprinted on social improvement, as long as it bears no fruit but mere physical prosperity, as long as it does not raise the mind of man to the level of his condition.

So, on the other hand, if any great intellectual improvement appears, unaccompanied by a social progress, one feels uneasy and surprised. It seems as if we saw a beautiful tree

T

devoid of fruit, or a sun bringing with it neither heat nor fertility.   One feels a kind of disdain for ideas thus barren and not seizing upon the external world.   And not only do we feel a disdain for them, but in the end we doubt their reasonable legitimacy and truth; one is tempted to believe them chimerical, when they show themselves powerless and incapable of governing human condition.   So powerfully is man impressed with the feeling that his business upon earth is to transform the ideal into the actual, to reform and regulate the world which he inhabits according to the truth he conceives; so closely are the two great elements of civilization, social and intellectual development, bound to one another; so true is it that its perfection consists, not only in their union, but in their simultaneousness, and in the extent, facility, and rapidity with which they mutually evoke and produce themselves.

Let us now endeavour to regard from this point of view the several nations of Europe: let us investigate the particular characteristics of the civilization in each particular case, and inquire how far these characteristics coincide with that essential, fundamental, and sublime fact which now constitutes for us the perfection of civilization.   We shall thus discover which of the various kinds of European civilization is the most complete, and the most conformable to the general type of civilization, and, consequently, which possesses the best right to our attention, and best represents the history of Europe.

I begin with England.   English civilization has been especially directed towards social perfection; towards the amelioration of the external and public condition of men; towards the amelioration, not only of their material but also of their moral condition; towards the introduction of more justice, more prosperity into society; towards the development of right as well as of happiness.

Nevertheless, all things considered, in England the development of society has been more extensive and more glorious than that of humanity; social interests and social facts have, in England, maintained a more conspicuous place, and have exercised more power than general ideas: the nation seems greater than the individual.   This is so true, that even the philosophers of England, men who seem devoted by their profession to the development of pure intelligence—as Bacon,

Locke, and the Scotch philosophers—belong to what one may call the practical school of philosophy; they concern themselves, above all things, with direct and positive results; they trust themselves neither to the flights of the imagination, nor to the deductions of logic: theirs is the genius of common sense. I turn to the periods of England's greatest intellectual activity, the periods when ideas and mental movements occupied the most conspicuous place in her history: I take the political and religious crisis of the sixteenth and seventeenth centuries. No man is ignorant of the mighty movement which was going on at that time in England. Can any one, however, tell me of any great philosophical system, of any great general doctrines since become law in Europe, which were born of this movement? It has had immense and admirable results; it has established rights, manners; it has not only powerfully influenced social relations, it has influenced the souls of men; it has made sects and enthusiasts, but it has hardly exalted or extended — at all events, directly — the horizon of the human mind; it has not ignited one of those great intellectual torches which illuminate an entire epoch. Perhaps in no country have religious creeds possessed, nor at the present day do they possess more power than in England; but they are, above all things, practical; they exert a great influence over the conduct, happiness, and sentiments of individuals; but they have few general and mental results, results which address themselves to the whole of the human race. Under whatever point of view you regard this civilization, you will discover this essentially practical and social character. I might investigate this development in a more extended degree; I might review every class of English society, and I should everywhere be struck with the same fact. In literature, for instance, practical merit still predominates. There is no one who will say that the English are skilful at composing a book, the artistical and rational arrangement of the whole, in the distribution of the parts, in executing, so as to strike the imagination of the reader with that perfection of art and form, which, above all things, gratifies the understanding. This purely intellectual aim in works of genius is the weak point of English writers, whilst they excel in the power of persuasion by the lucidity of their expositions, by frequently returning to the same ideas, by the

T 2

evidence of good sense, in short, by all the ways of leading to
practical effects.

The same character is seen, even in the English language.
It is not a language rationally, uniformly, and systematically
constructed; it borrows words on all sides, from the most
various sources, without troubling itself about maintaining
any symmetry or harmony.   Its essential want is that logical
beauty which is seen in the Greek and Latin languages: it
has an appearance of coarseness and incoherence.   But it
is rich, flexible, fitted for general adaptation, and capable of
supplying all the wants of man in the external course of life.
Everywhere the principle of utility and application dominates
in England, and constitutes at once the physiognomy and the
force of its civilization.

From England I shall pass to Germany.   The development of civilization has here been slow and tardy; the
brutality of German manners has been proverbial throughout Europe for centuries.   Still when, under this apparent
grossness, one seeks the comparative progress of the two
fundamental elements of civilization, we find that, in Germany,
intellectual development has always surpassed and left behind
social development, that the human spirit has there prospered
much more than the human condition.

Compare the intellectual state of the German reformers at
the sixteenth century—Luther, Melancthon, Bucer, and many
others—compare, I say, the development of mind which is
shown in their works with the contemporaneous manners of
the country.   What a disparity!   In the seventeenth century,
place the ideas of Leibnitz, the studies of his disciples, and
the German universities, by the side of the manners which
prevailed, not only among the people, but also among the
superior classes; read, on one side, the writings of the
philosophers, and, on the other, the memoirs which paint
the court of the elector of Brandenburg or Bavaria.   What
a contrast!   When we arrive at our own times, this contrast
is yet more striking.   It is a common saying in the present
day, that beyond the Rhine, ideas and facts, the intellectual
and the real orders, are almost entirely separated.   No
one is ignorant of what has been the activity of spirit in
Germany for the last fifty years; in all classes, in philosophy,
history, general literature, or poetry, it has advanced very far.
It may be said that it has not always followed the best path ;

one may contest part of the results at which it has arrived; yet concerning its energy and extensive development it is impossible to dispute. But assuredly the social state and public condition have not advanced at the same pace. Without doubt, there also progress and amelioration have been made; but it is impossible to draw a comparison between the two facts. Thus, the peculiar character of all works in Germany, in poetry, philosophy, or history, is a non-acquaintance with the external world, the absence of the feeling of reality. One perceives, in reading them, that life and facts have exercised but little influence upon the authors, that they have not pre-occupied their imagination; they have lived retired within themselves, by turns enthusiasts or logicians. Just as the practical genius everywhere shows itself in England, so the pure intellectual activity is the dominant feature of German civilization.

In Italy we shall find neither one nor the other of these characters. Italian civilization has been neither essentially practical as that of England, nor almost exclusively speculative as that of Germany; in Italy, neither great development of individual intelligence, nor social skill and ability have been wanting; the Italians have flourished and excelled at one and the same time in the pure sciences, the arts and philosophy, as well as in practical affairs and life. For some time, it is true, Italy seems to have stopped in both of these progressions; society and the human mind seem enervated and paralysed; but one feels, upon looking closely, that this is not the effect of an inward and national incapacity; it is from without that Italy is weighed down and impeded; she resembles a beautiful flower that wishes to blossom, but is compressed in every part by a cold and rude hand. Neither intellectual nor political capacity has perished in Italy; it wants that which it has always wanted, and which is everywhere one of the vital conditions of civilization,—it wants faith, the faith in truth. I wish to make myself correctly understood, and not to have attributed to my words a different sense from that which I intend to convey. I mean here, by faith, that confidence in truth, which not only causes it to be held as truth, and which satisfies the mind, but which gives men a confidence in right to reign over the world, to govern facts, and in its power to succeed. It is by this feeling that, once having possession of truth, man feels called upon to introduce it into external facts, to reform them, and to regulate them according to reason. Well, it is this which is almost universally wanted in Italy; she has been fertile in great minds, and in universal ideas; she has been thronged with men of rare practical ability, versed in the knowledge of all conditions of external life, and in the art of conducting and managing society; but these two classes of men and facts have remained strangers to each other. The men of universal ideas, the speculative spirits, have not believed in the duty, perhaps not even in the right, of influencing society; although confident in the truth of their principles, they have doubted their power. Men of action, on the other hand, the masters of society, have held small account of universal ideas; they have scarcely ever felt a desire to regulate, according to fixed principles, the facts which came under their dominion. Both have acted as if it was desirable merely to know the truth, but as if it had no further influence, and demanded nothing more. It is this, alike in the fifteenth century and in later times, that has been the weak side of civilization in Italy; it is this which has struck with a kind of barrenness both its speculative genius and its practical ability; here the two powers have not lived in reciprocal confidence, in correspondence, in continual action and reaction.

There is another great country of which, indeed, I speak more out of consideration and respect for a noble and unhappy nation, than from necessity; I mean Spain. Neither great minds nor great events have been wanting in Spain; understanding and human society have at times appeared there in all their glory; but these are isolated facts, cast here and there throughout Spanish history, like palm-trees on a desert. The fundamental character of civilization, its continued and universal progress, seems denied in Spain, as much to the human mind as to society. There has been either solemn immobility, or fruitless revolutions. Seek one great idea, or social amelioration, one philosophical system or fertile institution, which Spain has given to Europe; there are none such: this nation has remained isolated in Europe; it has received as little from it as it has contributed to it. I should have reproached myself, had I wholly omitted its name; but its civilization is of small importance in the history of the civilization of Europe.

You see that the fundamental principle, the sublime fact of

general civilization, the intimate and rapid union, and the harmonious development of ideas and facts, in the intellectual and real orders, has been produced in neither of the great countries at which we have glanced. Something is essentially wanting in all of them to complete civilization; neither of them offers us the complete image, the pure type of civilization in all its conditions, and with all its great characteristics.

In France it is different. In France, the intellectual and social development have never failed each other. Here society and man have always progressed and improved, I will not say abreast and equally, but within a short distance of each other. By the side of great events, revolutions, and public ameliorations, we always find in this country universal ideas and corresponding doctrines. Nothing has passed in the real world, but the understanding has immediately seized it, and thence derived new riches; nothing within the dominion of understanding, which has not had in the real world, and that almost always immediately, its echo and result. Indeed, as a general thing, in France, ideas have preceded and impelled the progress of the social order; they have been prepared in doctrines, before being accomplished in things, and in the march of civilization mind has always taken the lead. This two-fold character of intellectual activity and practical ability, of meditation and application, is shown in all the great events of French history, and in all the great classes of French society, and gives them an aspect which we do not find elsewhere.

At the commencement of the twelfth century, for example, burst forth the great movement for the enfranchisement of the Commons, a great step in social condition; at the same time was manifested a vivid aspiration after freedom of thought. Abailard was contemporary with the citizens of Laon and Vezelay. The first great struggle of free-thought against absolute power in the intellectual order, is contemporaneous with the struggle of the citizens for public liberty. These two movements, it is true, were apparently foreign to each other; the philosophers had a very ill opinion of the insurgent citizens, whom they treated as barbarians; and the citizens, in their turn, when they heard them spoken of, regarded the philosophers as heretics. But the double progress is not the less simultaneous.

Quit the twelfth century; take one of the establishments
which have played the most conspicuous part in the history
of mind in France, the University of Paris.   No one is
ignorant of what have been its scientific labours, dating from
the thirteenth century; it was the first establishment of the
kind in Europe.   There was no other in the same age which
had so important and active a political existence.   The University of Paris is associated with the policy of kings, and
with all the struggles of the French clergy against the court
of Rome, and those of the clergy against the temporal power;
ideas developed themselves, and doctrines were established in
its bosom; and it strove almost immediately to propagate
them in the external world.   It was the principles of the
University of Paris which served as the standard of the
reformers at the councils of Constance and Basle; which were
the origin of, and sustained the Pragmatic Sanction of
Charles VII.

Intellectual activity and positive influence have for centuries been inseparable in this great school.   Let us pass to
the sixteenth century, and glance at the history of the
Reformation in France; it has here a distinguishing character; it was more learned, or, at least, as learned as elsewhere,
and more moderate and reasonable.   The principal struggle
of erudition and doctrine against the Catholic church was
sustained by the French Reformers; it was either in France
or Holland, and always in French, that so many philosophical,
historical, and polemical works were written in this cause;
it is certain, that at this epoch, neither in Germany nor in
England, was there so much spirit and learning employed;
the French Reformation, too, was a stranger to the flights
of the German anabaptists and the English sectarians; it was
seldom it was wanting in practical prudence, and yet one
cannot doubt the energy and sincerity of its creed, since for
so long a period it withstood the most severe reverses.

In modern times, in the seventeenth and eighteenth centuries, the intimate and rapid union of ideas with facts, and
the development both of society and of man as an individual,
are so evident, that it is needless to insist upon them.

We see, then, four or five great epochs, and four or five
grand events, in which the particular character of French
civilization is shown.   Let us take the various classes of our

society; let us regard their manners and physiognomy, and we shall be struck with the same fact. The clergy of France is both learned and active, it is connected with all intellectual works and all worldly affairs as reasoner, scholar, administrator; it is, as it were, neither exclusively devoted to religion, science, nor politics, but is constantly occupied in combining and conciliating them all. The French philosophers also present a rare mixture of speculation and practical knowledge; they meditate profoundly and boldly; they seek the pure truth, without any view to its application; but they always keep up a sympathy with the external world, and with the facts in the midst of which they live; they elevate themselves to the greatest height, but without ever losing sight of the earth. Montaigne, Descartes, Pascal, Bayle, almost all the great French philosophers, are neither pure logicians nor enthusiasts. Last summer, in this place, you heard their eloquent interpreter[1] characterize the genius of Descartes, who was at the same time a man of science and a man of the world. "Clear, firm, resolved, and daring, he thought in his study with the same intrepidity with which he fought under the walls of Prague;" having an inclination alike for the movement of life and for the activity of thought. Our philosophers have not all of them possessed the same genius, nor experienced the same adventurous destiny as Descartes; but almost all of them, at the same time that they sought truth, have comprehended the world. They were alike capable of observing and of meditating.

Finally, in the history of France, what is the particular trait which characterizes the only class of men who have there taken a truly public part, the only men who have attempted to thoroughly bring the country within its administration, and to give a legal government to the nation, the French magistracy and the bar, the parliaments and all that surrounds them? Is it not essentially this mixture of learning and practical wisdom, this respect for ideas and facts, for science and its application? Wherever pure knowledge is exercised, in erudition, philosophy, literature, or history, everywhere you encounter the parliaments and the French bar; they take part, at the same time, in all affairs, both public and private; and they have had a hand in all the real and positive interests of society

[1] M. Villemain.

From whatever point of view we regard France, we shall
discover this two-fold character. The two essential prin
ciples of civilization are there developed in a strict correspondence. There man has never been wanting in individual
greatness; nor has his individual greatness been devoid of
public importance and utility. Much has been said, especially
latterly, of good sense as a distinguishing trait of French
genius. This is true; but it is not a purely practical good
sense, merely calculated to succeed in its enterprises; it is an
elevated and philosophical good sense, which penetrates to
the roots of ideas, and comprehends and judges them in all
their bearings, while at the same time it attends to external
facts. This good sense is reason; the French mind is at the
same time reasoning and reasonable.

To France, then, must be ascribed this honour, that her
civilization has reproduced more faithfully than any other
the general type and fundamental idea of civilization. It is
the most complete, the most veritable, and, so to speak, the
most civilized of civilizations. This it is has given her the
first rank in the disinterested opinion of Europe. France
has proved herself at once intelligent and powerful, rich in
ideas, and in the means of giving effect to those ideas. She
has addressed herself at once to the intellect of the nations,
and to their desire for social amelioration; she has aroused at
once imagination and ambition; she has manifested a capability
of discovering the truth, and of making it prevail. By this
double title, she has rendered herself popular, for this is the
double want of humanity.

We are, then, fully entitled to regard civilization in France
as having the first claim on our attention, as being the most
important in itself, the most fruitful of consequences. In
studying it, we must earnestly regard it under the double
aspect I have indicated, of social development and of intellectual development; we must closely watch the progress
of ideas, of mind, of the interior individual man, and of his
exterior and general condition. Considering it upon this
principle, there is not in the general history of Europe any
great event, any great question which we shall not meet with
in our own. We shall thus attain the historical and scientific
object which we proposed to ourselves; we shall be constantly
present at the spectacle of European civilization, without

being ourselves lost in the number and variety of the scenes and actors.

But we have before us, as I conceive, something more, and something more important than a spectacle, or even than study; unless I am altogether mistaken, we seek something beyond mere information. The course of civilization, and in particular that of the civilization of France, has raised a great problem, a problem peculiar to our own time, in which all futurity is interested, not only our own future but that of humanity at large, and which we, we of the present generation, are, perhaps, especially called upon to solve.

What is the spirit which now prevails in the intellectual world, which presides over the search after truth, in whatever direction truth is sought? A spirit of rigorous reserve, of strict, cautious prudence, a scientific spirit, a philosophical spirit pursuing a philosophical method. It is a spirit which carefully observes facts, and only admits generalization slowly, progressively, concurrently with the ascertainment of facts. This spirit has, for more than a half century past, manifestly prevailed in the conduct of the sciences which occupy themselves in the material world; it has been the cause of their progress, the source of their glory; and now, every day it infuses itself more and more deeply into the sciences of the moral world, into politics, history, philosophy. In every direction the scientific method is extending and establishing itself; in every direction the necessity is more and more felt of taking facts as the basis and rule of our proceedings; and we all fully understand that facts constitute the subject matter of science, and that no general idea can be of any real value, unless it be founded upon, and supported throughout its progress by facts. Facts are now in the intellectual order, the power in authority.

In the real order, in the social world, in the government, in the public administration, in political economy, we perceive a different tendency; there prevails the empire of ideas, of reasoning, of general principles, of what is called theory. Such is evidently the feature of the great revolution which has developed itself in our time, of all the labours of the eighteenth century; and the feature is not merely one characterizing a crisis, a period of transient agitation; it is the permanent, regular, calm characteristic of the social state which is now establishing, or, at all events, announcing itself in every direction—a social state, which has its basis on discussion and publicity, that is to say, on the empire of public reason, on the empire of doctrines, of convictions common to all the members of the society. On the one hand, then, never before have facts held so large a place in science; on the other, never before have ideas played so leading a part in the outer world.

Matters were very different a hundred years ago: then, in the intellectual order, in science properly so called, facts were but slightly consulted, but little respected; reason and imagination gave themselves full career, and men yielded without hesitation to the wildest impulses of hypothesis, dashing on recklessly, with no other guide than the thread of deduction. In the political order, on the contrary, in the real world, facts were all powerful, were admitted without a doubt or a murmur, as the authority alike *de jure* and *de facto*. Men complained, indeed, of particular facts, but scarcely ever ventured to contest them; sedition itself was more common in those times than freedom of thought. He who should have claimed for an idea, though in the name of truth itself, any place in the affairs of this world, would have had reason to repent of his temerity.

The course of civilization, then, has reversed the former order of things: it has established the empire of facts where once the free movement of mind dominated, and raised ideas to the throne once filled exclusively by facts.

This proposition is so true, that the result stated forms a marked feature in the reproaches of which modern civilization is made the object. Whenever the adversaries of that civilization speak of the actual condition of the human mind, of the direction of its labours, they charge it with being hard, dry, narrow. This rigorous positive method, this scientific spirit, cramps, say they, the ideas, freezes up the imagination, takes from the understanding its breadth, its freedom, confines, materialises it. When the question turns upon the actual state of societies, upon what societies are attempting, are effecting, these same men exclaim: "Out upon chimeras! Place no faith in theories: it is facts alone which should be studied, respected, valued; it is experience alone which should be believed." So that modern civilization is accused at once of dryness and of dreamy reverie, of hesitation and of precipitation, of timidity and of temerity. As philosophers, we creep along the earth; as politicians, we essay the enterprise of Icarus, and we shall undergo the same fate.

It is this double reproach, or rather this double danger, which we have to repel. We are called upon, in fact, to solve the problem which has occasioned it. We are called upon to confirm, more and more, in the intellectual order, the empire of facts—in the social order, the empire of ideas; to govern our reason more and more according to reality, and reality according to our reason; to maintain at once the strictness of the scientific method, and the legitimate empire of the intellect. There is nothing incongruous or inconsistent in this, far from it; it is, on the contrary, the natural, necessary result of the position of man, as a spectator of the world, and of his mission as an actor in its mighty drama. I take nothing for granted here, I make no comment; I merely describe what I see before me. We are thrown into the midst of a world which we neither invented nor created; we find it before us, we look at it, we study it: we must needs take it as a fact, for it subsists out of us, independently of us; it is with facts our mind exercises itself; it has only facts for materials; and when it comes to the general laws resulting from them, the general laws themselves are facts like any others. So much for our position as spectators. As actors, we proceed in a different way: when we have observed external facts, our acquaintance with these develops in us ideas which are of a nature superior to them; we feel ourselves called upon to reform, to perfectionate, to regulate that which is; we feel ourselves capable of acting upon the world, of extending therein the glorious empire of reason. This is the mission of man: as spectator, he is subject to facts; as actor, he takes possession of them, and impresses upon them a more regular, a more perfect form. I was justified, then, in saying that there is nothing incongruous, nothing self-contradictory in the problem which we have to solve. It is quite true, however, that there is a double danger involved in this double task: it is quite true, that in studying facts, the understanding may be overwhelmed by them; that it may become depressed, confined, materialized; it may conceive that there are no other facts than those which strike us at first glance, which present themselves directly, obviously before us, which make themselves palpable to the senses; a great and grievous error: there are facts, facts so remote as to be obscure, facts vast, sublime, most difficult to compass, to observe, to describe, but which are none the less facts, and facts which man is, none the less, absolutely called upon to study and to know. If he fail to make himself acquainted with them, if he forget them the character of his thought will be inevitably and prodigiously lowered, and all the learning which he may possess will bear the impress of that abasement. On the other hand, it is quite possible for intellectual ambition, in its action upon the real world, to be carried away, to become excessive, chimerical; to lose itself in its eagerness to extend too far and too rapidly the empire of its ideas over external things. But this double danger itself proves the double mission whence it originates; and this mission must be accomplished, the problem must be solved, for the actual condition of civilization lays it down with perfect clearness, and will not permit it to be lost sight of. Henceforth, whosoever, in the search after truth, shall depart from the scientific method, will not be in a position to take the study of facts as the basis of intellectual development; and whosoever, in administering the affairs of society, shall refuse the guidance of general principles and ideas, of doctrines, will assuredly achieve no permanent success, will find himself without any real power; for power and success, whether rational or social, now wholly depend upon the conformity of our labours with these two laws of human activity, with these two tendencies of civilization.

This is not all; we have still a far different problem to solve. Of the two which I have laid down, the one is scientific and the other social; the one concerns pure intelligence, the study of truth; the other applies the results of this study to the external world. There is a third, which arises equally from the present state of civilization, and the solution of which is equally prescribed to us; a moral problem which refers not to science, not to society, but to the internal development of each of us to the merit, the worth of the individual man.

In addition to the other reproaches of which, as I have said, our civilization is made the object, it is accused of exercising a baleful effect upon our moral nature. Its opponents say, that by its everlastingly disputative spirit, by its mania for discussing and weighing everything, for reducing everything to a precise and definite value, it infrigidates, dries up. concentres the human soul; that the result of its setting up a pretension to universal infallibility, of its assumption of a superiority to all illusion, all impulse of the thought, of its affecting to know the real value of all things, will be that man will become severally disgusted with all the rest of the world, will become absorbed in self. Further, it is said, that owing to the tranquil ease of life in our times, to the facility and amenity of social relations, to the security which prevails throughout society, men's minds become effeminate, enervated; and that thus, at the same time that we acquire the habit of looking only to oneself, one acquires also a habit of requiring all things for oneself, a disposition to dispense with nothing, to sacrifice nothing, to suffer nothing. In a word, it is asserted that selfishness on the one hand, and captious effeminacy on the other, the dry hardness of manners, and their puerile enervation, are the natural matter-of-course results of the actual condition of civilization; that high-souled devotion and energy, at once the two great powers and the two great virtues of man, are wanting, and will be more and more wanting, in the periods which we call civilized, and more especially in our own.

It were easy, I think, to repel this double reproach, and to establish: 1, the general proposition, that the actual condition of civilization, considered thoroughly and as a whole, by no means as a matter of moral probability, induces as its results selfishness and effeminacy; 2, the fact that neither devotion nor energy have been found to be wanting, in time of need, to the civilized members of modern times. But this were a question which would carry us too far. It is true, the actual state of civilization imposes upon moral devotion and energy, as upon patriotism, as upon all the noble thoughts and feelings of man, an additional difficulty. These great faculties of our nature have hitherto often manifested themselves somewhat fortuitously, in a manner characterized by no reflection, by no reference to motives; so to speak, at random. Henceforth they will be bound to proceed only upon the basis of reason; legitimacy of motives, and utility of results will be required of them. Doubtless, this is an additional weight for nature to raise up ere she can manifest her-

self in all her grandeur; but she will raise it up. Never
yet has human nature been wanting to herself, never has
she failed of that which circumstances have required at her
hands; the more has been asked of her, the more she has
given. Her revenue ever more than keeps pace with her
expenditure. Energy and devotion will derive from other
sources, will manifest themselves under other forms. Doubtless, we possess not fully as yet those general ideas, those
innate convictions which must inspire the qualities I speak
of; the faith which corresponds with our manners is as yet
weak, shadowy, tottering; the principles of devotion and
energy which were in action in past times are now without
effect, for they have lost our confidence. It must be our
task to seek out until we discover principles of a character
to take strong hold of us, to convince our minds and to move
our hearts at one and the same time. These will inspire
devotion and energy; these will keep our minds in that state
of disinterested activity, of simple, unsophisticated stedfast-
ness which constitutes moral health. The same progress of
events which imposes the necessity of doing this upon us,
will supply us with the means of doing it.

In the study, then, upon which we are about to enter, we
have to aim at far more than the mere acquisition of knowledge; intellectual development cannot, may not remain an
isolated fact. We are imperatively called upon to derive
from it, for our country, new materials of civilization; for
ourselves, a moral regeneration. Science is a beautiful
thing, undoubtedly, and of itself well worth all the labour
that man may bestow upon it; but it becomes a thousand
times grander and more beautiful when it becomes a power;
when it becomes the parent of virtue. This, then, is what
we have to do in the course of these lectures: to discover the
truth; to realise it out of ourselves in external facts, for the
benefit of society; in ourselves, to convert it into a faith
capable of inspiring us with disinterestedness and moral
energy, the force and dignity of man in this world. This is
our triple task; this the aim and object of our labour; a
labour difficult of execution and slow of progress, and which
uccess, instead of terminating, only extends. But in nothing,
        s, is it given to man ever to arrive at the goal he has
        to himself; his glory is in advancing towards it.

SECOND LECTURE.

Necessity of reading a general history of France before we study that of civilization — M. de Sismondi's work—Why we should study the political state of a country before its moral state, the history of society before that of man—The social state of Gaul in the 5th century—Original monuments and modern works descriptive of that subject—Difference between the civil and religious society of that period—Imperial government of Gaul—The provincial governors—Their official establishments — Their salaries—Benefits and defects of the administration—Fall of the Roman empire—Gaulish society : 1. The senators; 2. The *curiales ;* 3. The people ; 4. The slaves — Public relations of these various classes—Decline and helplessness of Gaulish civil society—Causes of this—The people attach themselves to the religious community.

BEFORE entering upon the history of French civilization, I would engage those among you who propose to make a serious study of the subject, to read with attention one of the larger histories of France, which may serve, as it were, for a frame in which to place the facts and ideas we shall together collect. For I do not propose to relate to you the course of what are more especially called events, which yet it is indispensable for you to know. Of all the histories of France I could point out to you, the best beyond any question is that of M. de Sismondi. It is no part of my intention to enter here into a discussion of the merits and defects of that work, but I will, in a few words, indicate to you what you will more peculiarly find there, and what I advise you more peculiarly to seek there. Considered as a critical exposition of the institutions, the political development, the government of France, the *Histoire des Français* of M. de Sismondi is incomplete,[1] leaving

---

[1] M. Guizot speaks of the first twelve volumes of the Paris edition.

U

in my opinion something to be desired. Speaking of the volumes already published, I should say that its account of the two epochs most important for the political destiny of France, the reign of Charlemagne and that of St. Louis, is, perhaps, among the feeblest portions of the work. As a history of intellectual development of ideas, it is deficient, to a certain extent, in depth of research, and in exactness as to results. But, as a narrative of events, as a picture of the revolutions and vicissitudes of the social state, of the mutual relations of the various classes of society at different periods, of the progressive formation of the French nation, it is a work of the highest order, a work whence instruction of the most valuable kind is to be derived. You may, perhaps, find occasion to desire in it somewhat more impartiality, somewhat greater freedom of imagination; you may, perhaps, detect in it, at times, too much of the influence upon the writer's mind of contemporary events and opinions; but, nevertheless, it is a prodigious, a splendid work, infinitely superior to all those which preceded it, and one which, read with attention, will admirably prepare you for the studies we are about to pursue.

It is part of my plan, whenever we approach a particular epoch, or a crisis of French society, to point out to you the original literary monuments which are extant with respect to it, and the principal modern works which have treated of the subject. You will thus be enabled to test for yourselves, in the crucible of your own studies, the results which I shall endeavour to lay before you.

You will remember that I proposed to consider civilization in its aggregate, as a social development, and as a moral development, in the history of the mutual relations of man, and in that of ideas; I shall accordingly examine each epoch under this double aspect. I shall commence in every case with the study of the social state. I am quite aware that in so doing, I shall not begin with the beginning: the social state derives, among a number of other causes, from the moral state of nations; creeds, feelings, ideas, manners, precede the external condition, the social relations, the political institutions; society, saving a necessary and powerful reaction, is that which men make it. Conformably with true chronology, with the internal and moral chronology, we ought to study man before society. But the true historic

order, the order in which facts succeed one another, and re ·
ciprocally create each other, differs essentially from the scientific order, from the order in which it is proper to study them.
In reality, facts develop themselves, so to speak, from within
to without; causes inward produce effects outward. Study, on
the contrary—study, science, proceed, and properly proceed,
from without to within. It is with the outward that its attention is first occupied; it is the outward which it first seizes
upon, and following which, it advances, penetrates on and on,
until by degrees it arrives within.

And here we come to the great question, the question so
often and so well treated, but not as yet, perhaps, exhausted,
the question between the two methods of analysis and synthesis; the latter, the primitive method, the method of creation; the other, the method of the second period, the scientific method. If science desired to proceed according to the
method of creation, if it sought to take facts in the order according to which they reproduce each other, it would run a
great risk, to say the least, of missing the full, pure source of
things, of not embracing the whole broad principle, of arriving
at only one of the causes whence effects have sprung; and thus
involved in a narrow, tortuous, fallacious path, it would wander
more and more remote from the right direction; and instead
of arriving at the veritable creation, instead of finding the
facts such as they really are, such as they really produce one
the other, it would give birth to mere valueless chimeras,
grand, indeed, in appearance, but in reality, notwithstanding
the amount of intellectual wealth expended in their pursuit,
utterly frivolous and of no account.

On the other hand, were science, in proceeding from without to within, according to its own proper method, to forget
that this is not the primitive productive method, that facts
in themselves subsist and develop themselves in another
order than that in which it views them, it might in time also
forget that it was preceded by facts, it might exclude from its
remembrance the very foundation of things, it might be
dazzled with itself, it might fancy that it was reality; and it
would thus speedily become a mere combination of appearances and terms, as vain, as fallacious as the hypothesis and
deductions of the contrary method.

It is highly important not to lose sight of this distinction

u 2

and its consequences; we shall meet with them again more than once on our way.

In a former lecture, on seeking in the cradle of European civilization for its primitive and essential elements, I found, on the one side, the Roman world, on the other, the barbarians. In commencing, therefore, in any quarter of Europe, the study of modern civilization, we must first investigate the state of Roman society there, at the moment when the Roman empire fell, that is to say, about the close of the fourth and the opening of the fifth century. This investigation is peculiarly necessary in the case of France. The whole of Gaul was subject to the Empire, and its civilization, more especially in its southern portions, was thoroughly Roman. In the histories of England and of Germany, Rome occupies a less prominent position; the civilization of these countries, in its origin, was not Roman, but Germanic; it was not until a later period of their career that they really underwent the influence of the laws, the ideas, the traditions of Rome. The case with our civilization was different; it was Roman from its very outset. It is characterised, moreover, by this peculiar feature, that it drew nourishment from both the sources of general European civilization. Gaul was situated upon the limits of the Roman world and of the Germanic world. The south of Gaul was essentially Roman, the north essentially Germanic. Germanic manners, institutions, influences, prevailed in the north of Gaul; Roman manners, institutions, influences, in the south. And here we already recognise that distinctive character of French civilization, which I endeavoured to demonstrate in my first lecture, namely, that it is the most complete, the most faithful image of European civilization in the aggregate. The civilization of England and of Germany is especially Germanic; that of Spain and Italy especially Roman; that of France is the only one which participates almost equally of the two origins, which has reproduced, from its outset, the complexity, the variety of the elements of modern society.

The social state of Gaul, then, towards the end of the fourth and the commencement of the fifth century, is the first object of our studies. Before entering upon it, I will mention what are the great original monuments, and what the principal modern works on the subject which I would advise you to consult.

Of the original monuments, the most important, beyond all doubt, is the Theodosian code. Montesquieu, though he does not exactly say so, is evidently[1] of opinion that this code constituted, in the fifth century, the whole Roman law, the entire body of Roman legislation. It constitutes nothing of the sort. The Theodosian code is a collection of the constitutions of the emperors, from Constantine to Theodosius the younger, and was published by the latter in 438. Independently of these constitutions, the ancient Senatus Consulta, the ancient Plebiscita, the law of the Twelve Tables, the Pretorian Edicts, and the opinions of the jurisconsults, constituted a part of the Roman law. Just previously, by a decree of Valentinian III. in 426, the opinions of five of the great lawyers, Papinian, Ulpian, Paul, Gaius, and Modestinus, had expressly been invested with the force of law. It were, however, quite accurate to say that, in a practical point of view, the Theodosian code was the most important law book of the Empire; it is, moreover, the literary monument which diffuses the greatest light over this period.[2]

The second original document to which I would invite your attention, is the *Notitia Imperii Romani*, that genuine imperial almanac of the fifth century, giving lists of all the functionaries of the empire, and presenting a complete review of the whole of its administration, of all the relations between the government and its subjects.[3] The *Notitia* has been illustrated with the greatest learning by the jurisconsult Pancirolus; I know of no work which contains so many remarkable and curious facts as to the interior of Roman society.

I will refer you, for a third original source, to the great collections of the acts of the councils. Of these there are two; the collections of the councils held in Gaul, which were published by Père Sirmond,[4] with a supplementary volume compiled by Lalande,[5] and the general collection of councils, compiled by the Père Labbe.[6]

---

[1] *Esprit des Loix*, xxvii. chap. 4.

[2] Six vols folio, *avec les Commentaires de J. Godefroy*. Ritter, Leipsig, 1738.

[3] The best edition is that printed in the 7th vol. of the *Thesaurus Antiquitatum Romanarum* of Grævius.

[4] Three vols. folio. Paris, 1629.   [5] One vol. folio. Paris, 1660.

[6] Eighteen vols. folio. Paris, 1672.

Of modern works connected with the subject, I will first mention those French productions which I think you may consult with great advantage.

1. There is the *Theorie des Lois politiques de la Monarchie Française*, a work very little known, published at the commencement of the revolution.[1] It was compiled by a woman, Mademoiselle de Lezardiére, and consists of very little more than original texts, legislative and historical, illustrating the condition, the manners, the constitutions, of the Franks and Gauls from the third to the ninth century; but these texts are selected, arranged, and translated with a skill and exactness rarely to be met with.

2. You will permit me to point out to you, in the second place, the *Essais sur l'Histoire de France* that I myself have published,[2] inasmuch as in them I have more especially applied myself to retracing, under its different aspects, the state of society in Gaul, immediately before and immediately after the fall of the Roman empire.

As to ecclesiastical history, Fleury's appears to me the best.

Those who are acquainted with the German, will do well to read,

1. The *History of the Roman Law in the Middle Ages*, by M. de Savigny,[3] a work the purpose of which is to show that the Roman law has never perished in Europe, but is to be met with throughout the period extending from the fifth to the thirteenth centuries, in a multitude of institutions, laws, and customs. The moral state of society is not always accurately appreciated in this work, nor represented with fidelity; but as to facts, its learning and critical acumen are of a superior character.

2. The *General History of the Christian Church*, by M. Henke;[4] a work incompletely developed, and which leaves much to be desired in reference to the knowledge and appreciation of facts, but learned and judicious in the criticisms it furnishes, and characterized by an independence of spirit too seldom met with in works of this nature.

3. The *Manual of Ecclesiastical History* of M. Giesclor,

---

[1] In 1792; eight vols. 8vo. Paris   [2] One vol. 8vo. Paris.
[3] Six vols. 8vo.   [4] Six vols. 8vo. 4th ed. Brunswick, 1800.

the latest and most complete, upon this subject, of those learned summaries so extensively diffused in Germany, and which serve as guides when we are desirous of entering upon any particular study.

You have probably remarked that I point out here two classes of works; the one relating to civil, the other to ecclesiastical history. I do so for this reason; that at the period we speak of, there existed in the Roman world two very different societies—the civil society and the religious society. They differed not only in their object, not only in that they were governed by principles and by institutions entirely dissimilar, not only in that the one was old and the other young; there existed between them a diversity far more profound, far more important. The civil society, to all outward appearances, seemed Christian, equally with the religious society. The great majority of the European kings and nations had embraced Christianity; but, at bottom, the civil society was pagan. Its institutions, its laws, its manners, were all essentially pagan. It was entirely a society formed by paganism; not at all a society formed by Christianity. Christian civil society did not develop itself till a later period, till after the invasion of the barbarians; it belongs, in point of time, to modern history. In the fifth century, whatever outward appearances may say to the contrary, there existed between civil society and religious society incoherence, contradiction, contest; for they were essentially different both in their origin and in their nature.

I would pray you never to lose sight of this diversity; it is a diversity which alone enables us to comprehend the real condition of the Roman world at this period.

What then was this civil society, nominally Christian, but in reality the pagan?

Let us first consider it in its outward, most obvious aspect, in its government, in its institutions, its administration.

The empire of the west was divided, in the fifth century, into two prefectures, that of Gaul and that of Italy. The prefecture of Gaul comprised three dioceses—that of Gaul, that of Spain, and that of Britain. At the head of the prefecture was a pretorian-prefect; at the head of each diocese a vice-prefect.

The pretorian-prefect of Gaul resided at Trèves. Gaul

was divided into seventeen provinces, the affairs of each of which were administered by a governor of its own, under the general orders of the prefect. Of these provinces, six were governed by *consulares*,[1] the other eleven by presidents.[2]

As to the mode of administration, there existed no important distinction between these two classes of governors; they exercised in reality the same power, differing only in rank and title.

In Gaul, as elsewhere, the governors had two kinds of functions:

1st. They were the emperor's immediate representatives, charged, throughout the whole extent of the Empire, with the interests of the central government, with the collection of taxes, with the management of the public domains, the direction of the imperial posts, the levy and regulation of the armies—in a word, with the fulfilment of all the relations between the emperor and his subjects.

2nd. They had the administration of justice between the subjects themselves. The whole civil and criminal jurisdiction was in their hands, with two exceptions. Certain towns of Gaul possessed what was called *jus Italicum*—the Italian law. In the municipia of Italy, the right of administering justice to the citizens, at least in civil matters and in the first instance, appertained to certain municipal magistrates, *Duumviri, Quatuorviri, Quinquenvales, Ædiles, Prætores*, &c. It has been often stated that the case was the same out of Italy, in all the provinces as a rule, but this is a mistake: it was only in a limited number of these towns assimilated to the Italian municipia, that the municipal magistrates exercised any real jurisdiction; and this in every instance subject to an appeal to the governor.

There was also, subsequent to the middle of the fourth century, in almost all the towns, a special magistrate, called *defensor*, elected not merely by the curia or municipal body, but by the population at large, whose duty it was to defend

---

[1] Viennensis, Lugdunensis 1ma; Germania Superior, Germania Inferior, Belgica 1ma and 2nda.

[2] Alpes Maritimæ, Alpes Penninæ, Sequanensis 1ma; Aquitanica 1ma and 2nda; Novempopulonia, Narbonensis 1ma and 2nda; Lugdunensis 2nda and 3ma; Lugdunensis Senonensis

the interests of the people, even against the governor himself, if need were. The *defensor* exercised in such matters the jurisdiction in the first instance; he also acted as judge in that class of cases, which we now term police cases.

With these two exceptions, the governors alone adjudicated all suits; and there was no appeal from them except direct to the emperor.

This jurisdiction of theirs was exercised in the following manner:—In the first ages of the Empire, conformably with ancient custom, he to whom the jurisdiction appertained, prætor, provincial governor, or municipal magistrate, on a case being submitted to him, merely determined the rule of law, the legal principle according to which it ought to be adjudged. He decided, that is to say, the question of law involved in the case, and then appointed a private citizen, called the *judex*, the veritable juror, to examine and decide upon the question of fact. The legal principle laid down by the magistrate was applied to the fact found by the *judex*, and so the case was determined.

By degrees, in proportion as imperial despotism established itself, and the ancient liberties of the people disappeared, the intervention of the *judex* became less regular. The magistrates decided, without any reference to this officer, certain matters which were called *extraordinariæ cognitiones*. Diocletian formally abolished the institution in the provinces; it no longer appeared but as an exception; and Justinian testifies, that in his time it had fallen completely into desuetude. The entire jurisdiction in all cases then appertained to the governors—agents and representatives of the emperor in all things, and masters of the lives and fortunes of the citizens, with no appeal from their judgments but to the emperor in person.

In order to give you an idea of the extent of their power, and of the manner in which it was exercised, I have drawn up from the *Notitia Imperii Romani*—a list of the officers of a provincial governor; a list exactly similar to that which we might at the present day derive from the *Almanach Royal*, of the official establishment of a government office, or a prefecture. They are the officers of the pretorian prefect whom I am about to introduce to you, but the governors subordinate to the pretorian prefect, the *consulares, correctores, præ-*

sides, exercised, under his superintendence, the same powers with himself; and their establishments were almost entirely the same as his, only on a smaller scale.

The principal officers of a prætorian prefect were:

1. *Princeps,* or *primiscrinius officii.* He cited before the tribunal of the prefect those who had business there: he drew up the judgments: it was upon his order that accused persons were taken into custody. His principal business, however, was the collection of taxes. He enjoyed various privileges.

2. *Cornicularius.*—He made public the ordinances, edicts, and judgments of the governor. His post was one of very great antiquity; the tribunes of the people had their *cornicularius,* (Val. Maximus, I., vi. c. 11.) He was so entitled because he carried with him, as a distinctive badge, a horn, of which he made use, in all probability, to impose silence on the crowd when he was about to perform his official duty. The *præco,* or herald, was under his direction, and he had a large establishment of clerks. His period of office was only a year. He was a species of recorder.

3. *Adjutor,* a supplementary officer, whose services appear to have been due to all the other functionaries, when required; his specific business was to arrest accused persons, to superintend the infliction of the torture, &c. He had an office of his own.

4. *Commentariensis,* the director of prisons, an officer higher in rank than our gaolers, but having the same functions; he had the internal regulation of the prisons, conducted the prisoners before the tribunals, furnished them with provisions when they were destitute, had the torture administered to them, &c.

5. *Actuarii vel ab actis.*—These officers drew up contracts for the citizens, and all such deeds as the law required to bear a legal character, such as wills, grants, &c. They were the predecessors of our notaries. As the *actuarii* attached to the office of the pretorian prefect or of the *præses,* could not be everywhere, the decemvirs and other municipal magistrates were authorised to act as their deputies.

6. *Numerarii.*—These were the keepers of the accounts. The ordinary governors had two, called *tabularii;* the prætorian prefects four:—1. The *Numerarius Bonorum,* who

kept an account of the funds appertaining to the exchequer, the revenues of which went to the *comes rerum privatarum;* 2. The *numerarius tributorum,* who was intrusted with the account of the public revenues, which went to the *ærarium,* and to the account of the sacred donatives; 3. The *numerarius auri,* who received the gold drawn from the provinces, had the silver money he received changed into gold, and kept the accounts of the gold mines within his district; 4. The *numerarius operum publicorum,* who kept the accounts of the various public works, such as forts, walls, aqueducts, baths, &c., all of which were maintained by a third of the revenues of the cities, and by a land tax levied on and according to occasion. These *numerarii* had under their orders a large body of clerks.

7. *Sub-adjuva;* an assistant to the *adjutor.*

8. *Curator epistolarum.*—This was the secretary who had charge of the correspondence; he had a number of subordinates, called *epistolares.*

9 *Regerendarius.*—The officer charged to transmit to the prefect the petitions of the subject, and to write the answers.

10. *Exceptores.*—They wrote out all the documents relating to the judgments given by the prefects, and read them before his tribunal; they were under the direction of a *primicerius.* They may be assimilated to our registrars.

11. *Singularii,* or *Singulares, Ducenarii, Centenarii, &c.*—Officers commanding a sort of military police attached to the service of the provincial governors. The *singulares* attended these functionaries as a guard, executed their orders in the province, arrested accused parties, and conducted them to prison. They acted as collectors of the taxes; the office of the ducenarii, (captains of two hundred men, or *cohortales,*) of the *centenarii,* the *sexagenarii,* was the same.

12. *Primilipus.*—The chief officer of these *cohortales;* it was his especial charge to superintend the distribution of provisions to the soldiers, in the name of the pretorian prefect, and to inspect the provisions previous to delivery.

It is obvious that only the more prominent employments are indicated here, and that these officers must have had a great many others under their direction. In the offices of the prætor of Africa, there were 398 persons employed, in those of the count of the East, 600. Independently of their number,

you perceive, from the nature of their functions, that the
jurisdiction of the provincial governors comprehended all
things, all classes, that the whole society had to do with them,
and they with the whole of society.

I will now direct your attention, for a moment, to the
salaries which these officers received; you may derive from
this information some rather curious illustrations of the social
state of the period.

Under Alexander Severus, according to a passage in his
biographer Lampridius,[1] the governors of a province received
twenty pounds of silver and one hundred pieces of gold,[2] six
pitchers (phialas) of wine, two mules, and two horses, two
state suits, (vestes forsenes), and one ordinary suit (vestes
domesticas), a bathing tub, a cook, a muleteer, and, lastly, (I
have to solicit your pardon for this detail, but it is too characteristic to be omitted,) when they were not married, a con-
cubine, *quod sine his esse non possent*, says the text. When
they quitted office, they were obliged to return the mules, the
horses, the muleteer, and the cook. If the emperor was
satisfied with their administration, they were allowed to retain
the other gifts he had bestowed upon them; if he was dissatisfied, they were compelled to give him four times the value of
what they had received. Under Constantine, the part pay-
ment in goods still subsisted; we find the governors of two
great provinces, *Asiana* and *Pontus*, receiving an allowance
of oil for four lamps. It was not until the reign of Theodosius II., in the first half of the fifth century, that this mode
of paying the governors was altogether discontinued. The
subordinate *employés*, however, continued, down to the time
of Justinian, to receive in the eastern empire a portion of
their salaries in provisions and other goods. I dwell upon
this circumstance because it furnishes a striking idea of the
inactive state of commercial relations, and of the imperfect
circulating medium of the Empire.

The facts I have stated, which are perfectly clear, make
equally evident the nature of the government under our consideration; an utter absence of independence on the part of
the various functionaries; all of them subordinate one to the
other, up to the emperor, who absolutely disposes and decides

the fate of them all. No appeal for the subject from the functionary, but to the emperor; nothing like co-ordinate co-equal powers, destined to control and limit one another, is to be met with. All proceeds straight upwards or downwards, on the principle of a sole, strict hierarchy. It is a pure, unmitigated, administrative despotism.

Do not, however, conclude from what I have stated, that this system of government, this administrative machinery, was instituted for the sole behoof of absolute power, that it never aimed at or produced any other effect than that of promoting the views of despotism. In order to appreciate the matter fairly, we must present to our minds a just idea of the state of the provinces, and more especially of Gaul, at the moment preceding that when the empire took the place of the republic. There were two powers in authority, that of the Roman proconsul, sent to administer, for a temporary period, such or such a province, and that of the old national chiefs, the governors whom the country obeyed before it passed under the Roman yoke. These two powers were, upon the whole, more iniquitous, in my opinion, and more noxious in their operation, than the imperial administration which superseded them. I can conceive no affliction more fearful for a province than the government of a Roman proconsul, a greedy tyrant, coming there for a greater or less period, in the sole view of making his fortune, and giving unchecked way for a time to all the impulses of grasping self-interest, to all the caprices of absolute power. I do not mean to say that these proconsuls were every one a Verres or a Piso, but the great crimes of a period enable us in their history to estimate the measure of iniquity in that period; and if it required a Verres to arouse the indignation of Rome, we may fairly judge how far a proconsul might go, so that he kept within the limits outstepped by the more daring monster denounced by Cicero. As to the ancient chiefs of the country, theirs was, I have no doubt, a government altogether irregular, oppressive, barbarous. The civilization of Gaul, when it was conquered by the Romans, was very inferior to that of Rome: the two powers which held sway there were, on the one hand, that of the priests, the Druids; on the other, that of the chiefs, whom we may assimilate with the more modern chiefs of clans. The ancient social organization of the country part of Gaul, had, in point of fact, a close resemblance to that of Ireland or of the High-lands of Scotland in later times; the population clustered round the more considerable personages, round the great landed proprietors: Vercingetorix, for example, was probably a chief of this description, the leader of a multitude of peasantry and of petty landholders connected by personal considerations with his domains, with his family, with his interests. This system may doubtless give birth to lofty and honourable senti-ments, it may inspire those who live under it with powerfully marked habits and associations, with strong mutual attach-ments; but it is, on the whole, far from favourable to the progress of civilization. There is nothing regular, nothing comprehensive in it; the ruder passions have full and unchecked sway; private warfare is incessant; manners make no advance; the decision of all questions is entirely a matter of individual or local interest; every feature in the system is an obstacle to the increase of prosperity, to the extension of ideas, to the rich and rapid development of man and of society. When therefore the imperial administration came into operation in Gaul, however bitter may have been the resentment and regret which naturally filled patriotic minds, we can entertain no doubt that it was more enlightened, more impartial, more guided by general views and by considerations of really public interests, than the old national government had been. It was neither mixed up with jealousies of family, city, or tribe, nor fettered to savage and stagnant ideas and manners by preju-dices of religion or birth. On the other hand, the new governors, invested with more permanent functions, con-trolled, up to a certain point, by the imperial authority, were less grasping, less violent, less oppressive than the proconsuls of the senate had been. We accordingly observe with the progress of the first, second, and even the third centuries, a pro-gress in the prosperity and civilization of Gaul. The towns grew rich, and extended themselves; the freemen became more and more numerous. It had been, amongst the ancient Gauls, a custom, or rather a necessity, for the individual free-men to place themselves under the protection of some great man, to enrol themselves under the banner of a patron, as the only mode of effecting security for themselves. This cus-tom, without entirely disappearing, abated in the first ages of imperial administration; the freemen assumed a more independent existence, which proves that their existence was better secured by the general operation of the laws, by the public power. There was greater equality introduced among the various classes, none of whom were now arbitrarily excluded from the attainment of fortune and power. Manners were softened, ideas expanded, the country became covered with roads and buildings. Everything indicated a society in cours of development, a civilization in progress.

But the benefits of despotism are shortlived; it poisons the very springs which it lays open. If it display a merit, it is an exceptional one; if a virtue, it is created of circumstances; and once this better hour has passed away, all the vices of its nature break forth with redoubled violence, and weigh down society in every direction.

In proportion as the Empire, or more properly speaking, the power of the emperor, grew weaker, in proportion as it found itself a prey to external and internal dangers, its wants grew greater and more urgent; it required more money, more men, more means of action of every description; it demanded more and more at the hands of the subject nations, and at the same time did less and less for them in return. The larger reinforcements of troops were sent to the frontiers to resist the barbarians, the fewer of course remained to maintain order in the interior. The more money there was spent at Constantinople or at Rome to purchase the services of auxiliaries, or to bribe dangerous courtiers, the less had the emperor to expend upon the due administration of the provinces. Despotism thus found itself at once more exacting and more feeble, necessitated to take more from the people, and incapable of protecting for them the little it left them. This double evil had fully developed itself at the close of the fourth century. Not only at this epoch had all social progress ceased, but a retrograde movement was sensibly felt; the empire was invaded in every direction, and its interior swept and devastated by bodies of barbarians; the population fell off, more especially in the provinces; in the towns, all public works were put a stop to, all embellishments suspended; the free men once more went in crowds to solicit the protection of some powerful chief. Such are the incessant complaints of the Gaulish writers of the fourth and fifth centuries, of Salvienus, for example, in his work *De Gubernatione Dei*, perhaps the most vivid and most interesting picture that we have of the period. In a word, in every direction we see manifesting themselves unequivocal symptoms of the decline of the government, of the desolation of the land.

At length the evil grew so great, that the Roman empire found itself unable to go on; it began by recalling its troops; it said to the provinces, to Britain, to Gaul: "I can no longer defend you: you must take care of yourselves." Ere long it ceased to govern them, as it had ceased to protect them: its administrative officers withdrew as its armies had done. This was the fact which was accomplished in the middle of the fifth century. The Roman empire fell back in every direction, and abandoned, either to the barbarians or to themselves, the provinces which it had taken so much pains to conquer.

What, more especially in Gaul, was the society thus left to itself, thus compelled to provide for itself? How was it constituted? What means, what strength had it with which to protect itself?

Four classes of persons, four different social conditions existed at this period in Gaul. 1. The senators; 2. the *curiales*; 3. the people, properly so called; 4. the slaves.

The distinct existence of the senatorial families is attested by all the monuments of the period. We meet with the designation at every step, in the legislative documents, and in the historians. Did it indicate families whose members belonged or had belonged to the Roman senate, or did it merely refer to the municipal senators of the Gaulish towns? This is a legitimate question, since the senate of each town, the municipal body known under the name of *curia*, often also called itself *senate*.

There can be little doubt, I think, that it meant families which had belonged to the Roman senate. The emperors, who filled up that senate just as they pleased, used to recruit it from the provinces with members of the most distinguished families in the principal cities. Those who had occupied high local offices, who had acted, for instance, as provincial governors, were entitled to expect a seat in the Roman senate; at a later period, the same favour was granted to persons who had been nominated to certain honorary charges; and ultimately the possession of a mere title, that of *clarissimus*, which was conferred in the same way that the title of baron or count is now, was sufficient to give its holder a seat in the senate.

This quality gave certain privileges which raised the senators to a position superior to that of the other citizens. 1, the title itself; 2, the right to be tried by a special tribunal: when a senator had to be tried for a capital offence, the magistrate was obliged to associate with himself five assessors drawn by lot; 3, exemption from torture; 4, exemption from filling municipal offices, which at this time had become a very serious burden.

Such was the condition of the senatorial families. It were, perhaps, extravagant to say that they formed a class of citizens essentially distinct from the rest, for the senators were taken from all classes of the population; we find even freedmen among them—and the emperor could at any time deprive them, or any of them, of the privileges he had conferred. But, at the same time, as these privileges were real and substantial, and, moreover, hereditary, at least in reference to children born after the elevation of the father to the senatorial dignity, we may fairly point to them as creating an essential distinction in social relations, as manifesting the principle, or at all events, the very decided appearance of a political aristocracy.

The second class of citizens was that of the *curiales* or *decuriones*, men of easy circumstances, members, not of the Roman senate, but of the *curia* or municipal body of their own city. I have in my *Essai sur l'Histoire de France* drawn up a summary of laws and facts relative to the curiales; and in order to give an exact picture of their condition, I will, with your permission, introduce this summary here:

The class of curiales comprised all such inhabitants of towns, whether natives (*municipes*) or settlers (*incolæ*) as possessed landed property to the extent of not less than twenty-five acres (*jugera*), and were not included in any way among the privileged persons exempt from curial functions.

Persons belonged to this class either by origin or by nomination.

Every son of a curialis was himself a curialis, and bound to fulfil all the duties inherent in that quality.

x

Every inhabitant of a town, trader or otherwise, who acquired landed property to the extent of twenty-five acres and upwards, was liable to be claimed by the *curia*, and could not refuse to join it.

No curialis was allowed by any personal and voluntary act to relinquish his condition. They were prohibited from living in the country, from entering the army, from accepting offices which would relieve them from municipal functions, until they had exercised all these functions, from that of simple member of the curia up to that of first magistrate of the city. Then, and not till then, were they permitted to become soldiers, public functionaries, and senators. The children born to them before their elevation remained in the class of curiales.

They were not allowed to become priests unless they transferred their property to some one who was willing to become a curialis in their place, or to the curia itself.

The curiales were constantly endeavouring to relinquish their condition, and we accordingly find a multitude of laws prescribing the rigorous pursuit of all such as had fled, or surreptitiously entered the army, or the order of priests, or the senate, or into public functions, and ordering them, when discovered, to be compelled to return to their curia.

The functions and duties of the curiales thus forcibly confined within their curia, were as follow:—

1. To administer the affairs of the municipium, its revenue and its expenditure, either deliberatively as a private member of the curia, or executively as a municipal magistrate. In this double situation, the curiales were not only responsible for their own individual conduct, but they were called upon to provide for the wants of the town out of their own means, if the civic revenue was insufficient.

2. To collect the public taxes. Here also they were themselves responsible if they failed to levy the full amount imposed. Any lands subject to the land-tax which were abandoned by their possessors reverted to the curia, who were bound to pay the tax in respect of them, until some one was found who was willing to take the land and its liabilities upon himself. If no such person appeared, the tax continued to be made up amongst the other proprietors.

3. No curialis could sell, without the permission of the

provincial governor, the property in respect of which he was a curialis.

4. Heirs of curiales, not themselves members of the curia, and the widow or inheriting daughter of a curialis who married a man not a curialis, were obliged to resign a fourth of their property to the curia.

5. Curiales without children could only dispose by will of a fourth of their property. The other three-fourths went to the curia.

6. They were not allowed to absent themselves from the municipium, even for a limited time, without the permission of the provincial governor.

7. If they quitted their curia without such permission, and could not, after a certain interval, be found, their property was confiscated for the benefit of the curia.

8. The burden of the impost designated *Aurum Coronarium*, which was a tribute paid to the prince on certain solemn occasions, fell solely upon the curiales.

By way of compensating the curiales for these heavy incumbrances, they were:—

1. Exempt from the torture, except in very grave cases.

2. Exempt from certain corporeal and ignominious punishments, which were reserved for the lower classes.

3. After having gone through the whole series of municipal offices, those who had managed to escape the ruinous risks which had presented themselves at every stage of their progress, were exempt from serving any municipal office for the future, enjoyed certain honours, and not unfrequently received the title of *comes*.

4. Decayed decuriones were maintained at the expense of the town.

I need not point out to you how hard and oppressive this condition was—into what a state it necessarily tended to reduce the burgher class in all the towns. We accordingly find every indication that this class became, day after day, less numerous. There are no documents from which we can form any satisfactory idea of the number of curiales. A list of the members of each curia, *album curiæ*, was, indeed, drawn up every year; but these lists have disappeared. M. de Savigny cites one, after Fabretti, the *album* of Canusium, (Canosa,) a small town of Italy. It is for the year 223, and

x 2

sets down the number of the curiales of that town at a hundred
and forty-eight.   Judging from their extent and comparative
importance, the larger towns of Gaul, Arles, Narbonne,
Toulouse, Lyons, Nismes, had far more than this number.
There can be no doubt, indeed, that such was the case in the
earlier periods; but as I have said, the *curiales* became constantly fewer and fewer, and at the epoch on which we are
now engaged, there were scarcely more than a hundred o,
them in the very largest cities.

The third class of the Gaulish community consisted of the
people, especially so called,—the *plebs*.   This class comprehended, on the one hand, the petty landholders, whose property was not sufficient to qualify them for the curia; on the
other, the small tradespeople and the free artisans.   I have
no observations to make with reference to the petty landholders in this class; they were probably very few in number;
but with reference to the free artisans, it is necessary to
enter into some explanations.

You are all aware that under the republic and in the earlier
years of the empire, operative industry was a domestic profession, carried on by the slaves for the benefit of their masters.   Every proprietor of slaves had whatever mechanical
production he required manufactured in his own house; he
had slave-blacksmiths, slave-shoemakers, slave-carpenters,
slave-ironworkers, &c.   And he not only employed them in
making things for himself, but he sold the products of their
industry to freemen, his clients and others, who had no slaves
of their own.

By one of those revolutions which work on slowly and unseen until they become accomplished and manifest at a particular epoch, whose course we have not followed, and whose
origin we never trace back, it happened that industry threw off
the domestic menial character it had so long worn, and that
instead of slave artisans, the world saw free artisans, who
worked, not for a master, but for the public, and for their
own profit and benefit.   This was an immense change in
the state of society, a change pregnant with incalculable results.   When and how it was operated in the Roman world,
I know not, nor has any one else, I believe, identified its precise date; but at the period we are now considering, at the
commencement of the fifth century it was in full action; there

were in all the large towns of Gaul a numerous class of free artisans, already erected into corporations, into bodies formally represented by some of their own members. The majority of these trade-corporations, the origin of which is usually assigned to the middle ages, may readily be traced back, more especially in the south of Gaul and in Italy, to the Roman world. Ever since the fifth century, we come upon indications of them, more or less direct, at every epoch of history; already, at that period, they constituted in many towns one of the principal, one of the most important portions of the popular community.

The fourth class was that of slaves; of these there were two kinds. We are too much in the habit of attaching to the word *slave*, one bare single idea,—of connecting with the term one sole condition; this is an entire misconception. We must carefully distinguish, at the period now under our consideration, between the domestic slaves and the predial or rural slaves. As to the former, their condition was everywhere very nearly the same; but as to those who cultivated the soil, we find them designated by a multitude of different names. *coloni, inquilini, rustici, agricolæ, aratores, tributarii, originarii, adscriptitii,* each name, well nigh, indicating a difference of condition. Some were domestic slaves, sent to a man's country estate, to labour in the fields there, instead of working indoors, at his town-house. Others were regular serfs of the soil, who could not be sold except with the domain itself; others were farmers, who cultivated the ground, in consideration of receiving half the produce; others, farmers of a higher class, who paid a regular money rent; others, a sort of comparatively free labourers, farm-servants, who worked for wages. Sometimes, moreover, these very different conditions seem mixed up together under the general denomination of *coloni,* sometimes they are designated under various names.

Thus, judging from appearances, and from existing terms, a political nobility, an upper burgher class or municipal nobility, the people especially so called, domestic or rural slaves, in their different conditions, constituted Gaulish society, constituted the strength which subsisted in Gaul, after the withdrawal of Rome.

But what is the real value to be attached to these appearances? What was the real strength of this strength? What

living and powerful society could the concurrences of these
various classes form?

We are in the habit of giving to every privileged class the
name of aristocracy. I do not conceive that this name pro
perly appertains to the senatorial families of which I have
just spoken. It was an hierarchical collection of functionaries, but not an aristocracy. Neither privilege, nor wealth,
nor even with these the possession of power, are sufficient to
constitute an aristocracy. Permit me to call your attention
for a moment, to the true meaning of this term; I shall not go
far in search of it; I will consult, for the history of the word,
the language whence we have derived it.

In the more ancient Greek authors, the word αρειων, αριστος, generally means the strongest, the person possessing the
superiority in personal, physical, material strength. We find
the term thus employed in Homer, Hesiod, and even in some
of the choruses of Sophocles; it came, perhaps, from the word
which designated the God Mars, the God of Strength, Αρης.

As we advance in the progress of Greek civilization, as we
approach the period when social development gave effect to
other causes of superiority than physical force, the word
αριστος designates the great, powerful, the most considerable,
the most wealthy; it is the title assigned to the principal
citizens, whatever the sources of their power and influence.

Going a little further, we come to the philosophers, to the
men whose work it was to elevate and purify ideas; with them
the word αριστος is often used to convey a meaning of a far
more moral character; it indicates the best, the most virtuous,
the most able man; intellectual superiority. In the eyes of
these definers, the aristocratic government was the government of the best, that is to say, the ideal of governments.

Thus, then, physical force, social preponderance, moral
superiority—thus, so to speak, and judging from the vicissitudes in the meanings of the words, thus have these been the
gradations of aristocracy, the various states through which it
has had to pass.

And, indeed, for an aristocracy to be real, for it to merit
its name, it must possess, and possess of itself, one or the
other of these characteristics; it must have either a force of its
own, a force which it borrows from no one, and which none
can wrest from it, or a force admitted, proclaimed by the
men over whom it exercises this force. It must have either

independence or popularity. It must either have power, in its mere personal right, as was the case with the feudal aristocracy, or it must receive power by national and free election, as is the case in representative governments. Nothing resembling either of these characteristics is to be met with in the senatorial aristocracy of Gaul; it possessed neither independence nor popularity. Power, wealth, privilege, all it had and exercised, was borrowed and precarious. Undoubtedly the senatorial families occupied a position in society and in the eyes of the people, for they were rich, and had filled public offices; but they were incapable of any great effort, incapable of carrying the people with them, or using them either to defend or to govern the country.

Let us now turn to the second class, the curiales, and examine what the real extent of their strength was. Judging from appearances, these had something beyond what the preceding class possessed; among them, the presence of principles of liberty is evident. I have already endeavoured to explain these in the following manner, in my *Essai sur le regime Municipal Romain au V. Siecle:*

1. Every inhabitant of a town, possessor of a fortune sufficient to secure his independence and the development of his understanding, is a curialis, and as such called upon to take part in the administration of civic affairs.

The right of curialship, then, is attached to the presumed capacity of filling it, and not to any privilege of birth, and without any limit as to numbers; and this right is not a mere right of election, but a right to deliberate upon and to participate directly in the administration of affairs, a right to discuss matters and interests, the comprehension of which, and the ability to discuss which, it may reasonably be supposed that all persons above the very lowest in the scale of existence possess. The *curia* is not a limited and select town council, but an assembly of all such inhabitants as come within the curial qualification.

2. An assembly cannot act administratively; there must be magistrates to do this. Such magistrates are all elected by the curia, for a very limited period, and are responsible with their fortunes for the integrity of their administration.

3. In great emergencies, when the fate of a city is in question, or when it is proposed to elect a magistrate invested with uncertain and more arbitrary powers, the curia itself

does not suffice; the whole population is summoned to concur in these solemn acts.

Who, at the aspect of such rights existing, would not imagine he recognised a petty republic, in which the municipal life and the political life were mixed up and confounded together, in which democracy of the most unequivocal description prevailed? Who would imagine, for one instant, that a town so governed formed part of a great empire, and was connected by strict and necessary bonds with a distant and sovereign central power? Who would not expect to find here all the impulsive manifestations of liberty, all the agitation, all the faction and cabal, all the violence, all the disorder, which invariably characterize small societies, inclosed and self-governed within their own walls?

Nothing of the sort was the fact; all these apparent principles were without life, and there were others existent, which absolutely precluded their reanimation.

1. Such are the effects, such the exigences of the central despotism, that the quality of curialis becomes not a right recognised in all those who are capable of exercising it, but a burden imposed upon all who are capable of bearing it. On the one hand, the central government has relieved itself of the duty of providing for any branch of the public service in which it is not immediately interested, throwing this duty upon the class of citizens in question; on the other hand, it employs this class of citizens in collecting the taxes which it imposes on its own peculiar account, and makes them responsible for the full amount. It ruins the curiales, in order to pay its functionaries and its soldiers; it grants its functionaries and its soldiers all sorts of practical advantages and privileges, as inducements to them to aid it in preventing the curiales from saving themselves from ruin. Completely null as citizens, the curiales only live to be stripped of all they gain as men of labour and industry.

2. The magistrates elected by the *curiæ* are, in point of fact, merely the imperial agents of despotism, for whose benefit they despoil their fellow-citizens, until some opportunity or other occurs to them of getting rid of this hard obligation.

3. Their election itself is valueless, for the imperial representative in the province may annul it; a favour which they

have the greatest desire to obtain at his hands; another circumstance putting them more firmly in his power.

4. Their authority is not real, for they cannot enforce it. No effective jurisdiction is placed in their hands; they take no step which may not be annulled. Nay, more: despotism, perceiving more and more clearly their ill-will to the task, or their inability to execute it, encroaches more and more, by itself or its immediate representatives, into the sphere of their functions. The business of the curia gradually disappears with its powers, and a day will come when the municipal system may be abolished at a single blow, in the still subsisting empire, " because," as the legislator will say, " all these laws wander, as it were, vainly and without object around the legal soil."[1]

Thus, then, it is seen, force, real life, were equally wanting to the curiales, as to the senatorial families; equally with the senatorial families, they were incapable of defending or of governing the society.

As to the people, I need not dwell upon their situation; it is obvious that they were in no condition to save and regene rate the Roman world. Yet we must not think them altogether so powerless, so utterly null, as is ordinarily supposed. They were tolerably numerous, more especially in the south of Gaul, both from the development of industrial activity during the three first ages of Christianity, and from the circumstance of a portion of the rural population taking refuge in the towns from the devastation of the barbarians. Besides, with the progress of disorder in the higher ranks, the popular influence had a tendency to increase. In times of regularity, when the administration, its functionaries, and its troops were on the spot, ere the curia had become altogether ruined and powerless, the people remained in their ordinary state of inaction, or passive dependence. But when all the various masters of the society had fallen away or disappeared, when the dissolution of things became general, the people, in their turn, grew to be something, and assumed, at all events, a certain degree of activity and importance.

I have nothing to say about the slaves; they were nothing

[1] Nov. 46, rendered by the Emperor of the East, Leo the Philosopher towards the close of the ninth century.

for themselves; how, then, could they do anything for society? It was, moreover, the coloni who underwent well nigh all the disasters of invasion; it was they whom the barbarians pillaged, hunted, carried away captive, pell-mell with their cattle. I may remark, however, incidentally, that under the Empire the condition of the slaves was greatly improved; this is clear from its legislation.

Let us now collect all these scattered features of Gaulish civil society in the fifth century, and form a collective idea, as near the fact as we can, of its aggregate.

Its government was monarchical, even despotic; and yet all the monarchical institutions and powers were falling, were themselves abandoning their post. Its internal organization seemed aristocratic; but it was an aristocracy without strength, without coherence, incapable of playing a public part. A democratic element, municipalities, free burghers, were still visible; but democracy was as enervated, as powerless, as aristocracy and monarchy. The whole of society was in a state of dissolution, was dying.

And here we see the radical vice of the Roman society, and of every society where slavery exists on a large scale, where a few masters rule over whole herds of people. In all countries, at all times, whatever the political system which prevails, after an interval more or less long, by the sole effect of the enjoyment of power, of wealth, of the intellectual development, of the various social advantages they enjoy, the higher classes wear themselves out, become enervated, unless they are constantly excited by emulation, and refreshed by the immigration of the classes who live and labour below them. See what has taken place in modern Europe. There has been in it a prodigious variety of social conditions, infinite gradations in wealth, liberty, enlightenment, influence, civilization. And up all the steps of this long ladder, an ascending movement has constantly impelled each class and all classes, the one by the other, towards greater development, to which none was allowed to remain a stranger. Hence the fecundity, the immortality, so to speak, of modern civilization, thus incessantly recruited and renewed.

Nothing at all resembling this existed in the Roman society; there, men were divided off into two great classes, separated from each other by an immense interval; there was no variety, no ascending movement, no genuine democracy; it was, as it were, a society of officers, who did not know whence to recruit their numbers, and did not, in point of fact, recruit them. There was, indeed, from the first to the third century, as I have just now said, a progressive movement on the part of the lower classes of the people; they increased in liberty, in number, in activity. But the movement was far too slow, far too limited, to enable the people by re-integrating in time the superior classes, to save them from their decline and fall.

Besides these, there became formed another society, young, energetic, fruitful of results,—the ecclesiastical society. It was around this society that the people rallied; no powerful bond united them to the senators, nor, perhaps, to the curiales; they assembled, therefore, around the priests and bishops. Alien to pagan civil society, whose chiefs created therein no place for it, the mass of the population entered with ardour into the Christian society, whose leaders opened their arms to it. The senatorial and curial aristocracy was a mere phantom; the clergy became the real aristocracy; there was no Roman people; a Christian people arose. It is with them we shall occupy ourselves in the next lecture.

THIRD LECTURE.

THE subject which is now about to occupy our attention, is
the state of religious society in the fifth century.   I need not
remind you of the great part it has played in the history of
modern civilization; that is a fact perfectly well understood.
Nor is it in modern history that this fact first manifested
itself; the world has seen more than one striking example of
the power of the religious society, of its ideas, its institutions,
its government.   But there is a fundamental difference to be
remarked.   In Asia, in Africa, in antiquity, everywhere
before the organization of Europe, religious society presents
itself under a general and simple form; this is the clear prevalence of a system, the domination of a principle: sometimes
the society is subordinate; it is the temporal power which
exercises the spiritual functions and directs the worship, and
even the faith: sometimes it occupies the chief place; it is
the spiritual power which rules the civil order.   In both the
one case and the other, the position and organization of the

religious society are clear, simple, stable. In modern Europe, on the contrary, it presents every possible variety of system; we find in it every possible principle; it seems made up of samples of all the forms under which it has appeared elsewhere.

Let us endeavour, for the sake of greater perspicuity, to disintricate and classify the different principles, the different systems which have been, in various measure, adopted into European religious society, the different constitutions it has received.

Two great questions here present themselves: on the one hand, the exterior situation of the religious society, its position with reference to civil society, the relations, that is to say, of church with state; and on the other, its interior organization, its internal government.

With both the one and the other of these questions, we must connect the modifications of which religious society has been the object in the particular respect.

I will first consider its external situation, its relations with the state.

Four systems, essentially differing from one another, have been maintained on this subject:

1. The state is subordinate to the church; in the moral point of view, in the chronological order itself, the church precedes the state; the church is the first society, superior, eternal; civil society is nothing more than the consequence, than an application of its principles; it is to the spiritual power that sovereignty belongs of right; the temporal power should merely act as its instrument.

2. It is not the state which is in the church, but the church which is in the state: it is the state which rules the land, which makes war, levies taxes, governs the external destiny of the citizens. It is for the state to give to the religious society the form and constitution which best accord with the interests of general society. Whenever creeds cease to be individual, whenever they give birth to associations, these come within the cognizance and authority of the temporal power, the only veritable power in a state.

3. The church ought to be independent, unnoticed in the state; the state has nothing to do with her; the temporal power ought to take no cognizance of religious creeds; it

should let them approximate or separate, let them go on and
govern themselves as they think best; it has no right, no
occasion, to interfere in their affairs.

4. The church and the state are distinct societies, it is
true; but they are at the same time close neighbours, and
are nearly interested in one another: let them live separate,
but not estranged; let them keep up an alliance on certain
conditions, each living to itself, but each making sacrifices
for the other, in case of need, each lending the other its
support.

In the internal organization of the religious society, the
diversity of principles and forms is even still greater.

And first, we see before us two leading systems: in the
one, power is concentrated in the hands of the clergy; the
priests alone form a constituted body; the ecclesiastical society governs the religious society: in the other, the religious
society governs itself, or at least participates in the administration of its affairs; the social organization comprehends the
body of the faithful, as well as the priests.

Government in the hands of the ecclesiastical society solely
may be constituted in various ways. 1. Under the form of
pure monarchy; there are several examples of this in the
history of the world. 2. Under the form of an aristocracy;
where the bishops, for instance, each in his own diocese,
or in a collective assembly, govern the church in their
own right, without the concurrence of the inferior clergy.
3. Under a democratic form, where, for instance, the government of the church belongs to the whole body of the clergy, to
assemblies of priests all equal among themselves.

In cases where the society governs itself, the diversity of
forms is equally great. 1. The body of the faithful, the
laity, sit with the priests in the assemblies charged with the
general government of the church. 2. There is no general
government of the church; each congregation forms a several
local, independent church, which governs itself; whose members select their own spiritual chief, according to their particular views and purposes. 3. There is no distinct and permanent spiritual government at all; no clergy, no priests;
teaching, preaching, all the spiritual functions are exercised
by the body of the faithful themselves, according to circumstances, according to inspiration; there is constant change,
constant agitation.

I might combine in an infinity of ways these various forms, mixing their elements together in various proportions, and thus create a host of other diversified forms, but with my utmost ingenuity I could devise no combination which has not already been exhibited to the world.

And not only have all these principles been professed, not only have all these systems been maintained each as the only true and legitimate system, but all of them have been brought into practical operation, all of them have existed.

Every one knows that in the twelfth and thirteenth centuries the spiritual power claimed as its right, sometimes the direct exercise, sometimes the indirect nomination of the temporal power. Every one sees that in England, where Parliament has disposed of the faith as of the crown of the country, the church is subordinate to the state. What are popery, Erastianism,[1] episcopacy, presbyterianism, the independents, the quakers, but applications of the doctrines I have pointed out. All doctrines have become facts: there are examples of all systems, and of all the so varied combinations of systems. And not only have all systems been realised, but they have, every one of them, set up a claim to historical as well as to rational legitimacy; they have, every one of them, referred their origin to the earliest age of the Christian church; they have, every one of them, claimed ancient facts for their own, as their own peculiar foundation and justification.

Nor are they wholly wrongs any of them; we find in the first ages of the age, facts with which all of them are entitled to claim a connexion. I do not mean to say that they are all alike true, rationally, all alike authentic, historically, nor that they all represent a series of different facts, through which the church has necessarily passed. What I mean is simply, that there is in each of these systems a greater or less proportion of moral truth and of historical reality. They have all played a part, have occupied a place, in the history of modern religious history: they have all, in various measure, contributed to the work of its formation.

I will view them successively in the first ages of the church; we shall have no difficulty in tracing them there.

---

[1] The system in which the church is governed by the state, so named from Erastus, a German theologian and physician of the 16th century, who first maintained this principle with any distinguished effect.

Let us first consider the external situation of the church, and its relations with civil society.

As to the system of a church, independent, unnoticed in the state, existing and governing itself without the intervention of the temporal power, this is evidently the primitive situation of the Christian church. So long as it was confined within a limited space, or disseminated only in small and isolated congregations, the Roman government took no notice of it, and allowed it to exist and regulate its affairs as it thought proper.

This state of things terminated: the Roman empire took cognizance of the Christian society; I do not refer to the period when it took notice of it in the way of persecution, but to that when the Roman world became Christian, when Christianity ascended the throne with Constantine. The position of the church with reference to the state underwent a great change at this epoch. It were incorrect to say that it fell at this period under the government of the church, that the system of its subordination to power then came into operation. In general, the emperors did not pretend to regulate the faith; they took the doctrines of the church as they found them. The majority of the questions which at a later period excited the rivalship of the two powers had not as yet arisen. Still, even at this period, we meet with a great number of facts wherein the system of the sovereignty of the state over the church might have sought, and has, indeed, sought its origin. Towards the close of the third and the commencement of the fourth century, for instance, the bishops observed an extremely humble and submissive tone with the emperors; they were incessantly exalting the imperial majesty. Doubtless, had it attempted to assail the independence of their faith, they would have defended themselves, as, in point of fact, they often did defend themselves, with energy; but they were greatly in need of the emperors' protection so recently extended to them. But just recognised and adopted by the temporal power, they were anxious to treat it with the utmost respect and consideration. Besides, they could do nothing of themselves; the religious society, or rather its government, had at this epoch no means of carrying its will into execution; it had no institutions, no rules, no system; it was constantly obliged to have recourse to the intervention of the civil government, the ancient and only organized authority. This continual necessity for a foreign sanction, gave religious society an air of subordination and dependence, more apparent than real; at bottom, its independence and even its power were considerable, but still, in almost all its affairs, in all matters affecting the interest of the church, the emperor interfered; his consent and approbation were invariably solicited. The councils were generally assembled by his order; and not only did he convene them, but he presided over them, either in person or by deputy, and decided what subjects should be discussed by them. Thus Constantine was present in person at the council of Arles, in 314, and at the council of Nicea, in 325, and, apparently at least, superintended the deliberations. I say apparently; for the mere presence of the emperor at a council was a triumph for the church, a proof of victory far more than of subjection. But however this may have been, the forms, at all events, were those of respectful subordination; the church availed herself of the power of the Empire, covered herself with its majesty; and Erastianism, independently of the national grounds upon which it proceeds, has found, in the history of this epoch, facts which have served as its justification.

As to the opposite system, the general and absolute sovereignty of the church, it is clear that it cannot be met with in the cradle of a religious society; it necessarily belongs to the period of its greatest power, of its fullest development. Yet one may already detect glimpses of it, and very distinct glimpses, in the fifth century. The superiority of spiritual over temporal interests, of the destiny of the believer as compared with that of the mere citizen, the principle enunciated by the religious society, was already recognised and admitted by the civil society.

We accordingly find the language of the heads of the spiritual society, erewhile so gentle, so reserved, so modest, now becoming confident, bold, often even haughty; whilst, on the other hand, that of the chiefs of the civil society, of the superiors themselves, despite the pomp still clinging round its forms, is in reality mild and submissive. At this period, indeed, the whole framework of temporal power was in a state of rapid decay; the Empire was expiring; the imperial power was day by day more and more nearly approaching

Y

the condition of an utter, of a ridiculous nonentity. The spiritual power, on the contrary, grew stronger and stronger, and penetrated more deeply and widely into civil society; the church became more wealthy, her jurisdiction more extended; she was visibly progressing towards domination. The complete fall of the Empire in the west, and the rise of the barbarous monarchies, contributed greatly to the exaltation of her pretensions and of her power. The church had long been under the emperors, obscure, feeble, a mere child, so to speak; she had thence acquired a sort of reserve in her intercourse with them; a habit of respect for their ancient power, their name; and it is quite possible that had the Empire continued to exist, the church would never have completely emancipated herself from this custom of her youth. What corroborates this supposition is the fact that such has been the case in the eastern empire; that Empire lived on for twelve centuries in a state of gradual decay; the imperial power became little more than nominal. Yet the church there never attained, never even sought to attain the sovereignty. The Greek church remained, with the eastern emperors, in nearly the same relation in which the Romish church stood with the Roman emperors. In the west, the Empire fell; kings covered with furs took the place of princes clothed in purple; the church yielded not to these new comers the same consideration, the same respect which she had paid to their predecessors. Moreover, to contend successfully against their barbarism, she found herself under the necessity of stretching to its utmost bent the spring of spiritual power: the exaltation of popular feeling in this direction, was her means of safety and of action. Hence the so rapid progress now of those pretensions of hers to the sovereignty, which in the fifth century were scarce perceptible.

As to the system of alliance between the two distinct and independent societies, it is not difficult to recognise it at this period; there was nothing precise or fixed in the conditions of the alliance; the two powers never continued long upon equal terms under them; they kept each in its own sphere, and treated together whenever they happened to come in contact.

We find, then, from the first to the fifth century, in germ and in development all the systems according to which the relations between church and state may be regulated; they all of them derive their origin from facts dating from the cradle of religious society.   Let us pass on to the interior organization of this society, to the internal government of the church; we shall arrive at the same result.

It is clear that this last form cannot be that of an infant church: no moral association begins with the *inertia* of the mass of those associated, with the separation of the people and the government.   It is certain, accordingly, that at the outset of Christianity, the body of the faithful participated in the administration of the affairs of the society.   The presbyterian system, that is to say, the government of the church by its spiritual chiefs, assisted by the leading members of the body, was the primitive system.   There may be many questions raised as to the titles, functions, and mutual relations of these lay and ecclesiastical chiefs of the rising congregations; but as to the fact of their concurrence in the regulation of their common affairs, there can be no doubt.

Equally unquestionable is it that at this period the separate societies, the Christian congregations in each town, were far more independent of each other than they have been at any subsequent time; there is no doubt that they governed themselves, perhaps not completely, but almost so, each for itself, and apart from the rest.   Hence the system of the *Independents*, who insist that the religious society should have no general government, but that each local congregation should be an entire and sovereign society in itself.

No doubt, again, that in these petty Christian societies of early date, unconnected with one another, and often without the means of preaching and teaching, no doubt that in the absence of a spiritual leader instituted by the original founder of the faith, it often occurred that, under the influence of an inward impulse, some individual member of the body, of strong mind, and endowed with the gift of acting upon his fellows, arose and preached the word to the association to which he belonged.   Hence the system of the Quakers, the system of spontaneous individual preaching, without any order of priests, of regular and permanent clergy.

These are some of the principles, some of the forms of the religious societies in the first age of the Christian church. It comprehended many others; perhaps, indeed, those which

Y 2

I have mentioned were not the most powerful in their influence.

In the first place, it is incontestable that the first founders, or, more correctly speaking, the first instruments in the foundation of Christianity, the apostles, regarded themselves as invested with a special mission received from on high, and that they in turn transmitted to their disciples by the laying on of hands, or in some other form, the right to teach and to preach. Ordination is a primitive fact in the Christian church, hence an order of priests, a distinct permanent clergy, invested with peculiar functions, duties, and rights.

Let us turn to another primitive fact. The particular congregations were, it is true, isolated; but the tendency of them all was to unite, to live under one common discipline as under one common faith; it was the tendency, the aim, natural to every society in progress of self-formation; it is the necessary condition of its extension, of its firm establishment.

Approximation, assimilation of the various elements, movement towards unity, such is the regular course of creation. The first propagators of Christianity, the apostles or their disciples, preserved, moreover, over the most distant congregations a certain amount of authority, a remote but efficacious superintendence. They took care to form and to maintain ties not only of moral brotherhood, but of organizations between the particular churches. Hence a constant tendency towards a general government of the churches, an identical and permanent constitution.

It appears to me perfectly clear that in the minds of the first Christians, in their common and simple feeling, the apostles were regarded as superior to their disciples, and the immediate disciples of the apostles as superior to their successors; a superiority purely moral, not established as an institution, but real and admitted. In it we have the first germ, the religious germ of the episcopal system. That system derives also from another source. The towns into which Christianity had made its way, were very unequal in population, in wealth, in importance; and the inequality in intellectual development, in moral power, was as great as the material inequality. There was, consequently, an inequality, likewise, in the distribution of influence among the spiritual heads of the congregations. The chiefs of the more important, of the more enlightened towns, naturally took the lead and exercised an authority, at first moral, then institutional, over the minor congregations within a certain circle around them. This was the political germ of the episcopal system.

Thus, at the same time that we recognise in the primitive state of the religious society the association of lay-members with the priests in the government, that is to say, the Presbyterian system; the isolation of the particular congregations, that is to say, the system of the Independents; free, spontaneous, casual preaching, that is to say, the system of the Quakers: on the other hand, we see rising up in opposition to the system of the Quakers, an order of priests, a permanent clergy; in opposition to the system of the Independents, a general government of the church; in opposition to the Presbyterian system, the principle of inequality among the priests themselves, the Episcopal system.

How have these principles, so various, so contrary to each other, become developed? To what causes have been owing the abasement of one, the elevation of another. And, first, how was the transition from a government, shared by the body of the faithful, to a government vested in the clergy alone, accomplished? By what progress did the religious society pass under the empire of the ecclesiastical society?

In the revolution by which this change was effected, the ambition of the clergy, personal interests, human passions, had a large share. I do not seek to under-estimate its proportion. It is quite undeniable that all these causes contributed to the result which now occupies our attention; but yet, had there been only these causes at work, the result would never have been realised. I have already observed, and it is a remark I repeat on all available occasions, that no great event is accomplished by causes altogether illegitimate. Beneath these, or at their side, there are always legitimate causes in operation, good and sound reasons why an important fact should be accomplished. We have here a fresh example of this.

It is, I believe, a clear principle—a principle generally established—that participation in power presupposes the moral capacity to exercise it; where the capacity is wanting, participation in power comes to an end, as a matter of course.

The right to exercise it continues virtually to reside in human nature; but it slumbers, or rather rests only in germ, in perspective, until the capacity needed develops itself, and then it awakens and develops itself with the capacity.

You will remember what I said in our last lecture, as to the state of Roman civil society in the fifth century. I endeavoured to describe its profound decay. You saw the aristocratic classes perishing away, their numbers immensely reduced, their influence gone—their virtue gone.

Whosoever amongst them possessed any energy, any moral activity, entered into the body of the Christian clergy. There remained, in point of fact, only the mere populace, the *plebs romana*, who rallied around the priests and the bishops, and formed the Christian people.

Between this people and its new chiefs, between religious society and ecclesiastical society, the inequality was extremely great: an inequality not only in wealth, in influence, in social situation, but in information, in intellectual and moral development. And the more Christianity, by the mere fact of its continuous duration, developed itself, extended itself, elevated itself, the more this inequality increased and manifested itself. The questions of faith and doctrine became, year after year, more complex and more difficult of solution; the rules of church discipline, her relations with civil society, in like manner grew more extensive and complicated; so that in order to take part in the administration of its affairs, there was requisite, from epoch to epoch, a greater and still greater development of mind, of learning, of character; in a word, moral conditions more and more elevated, more and more difficult to be met with; and yet, such was the general disorder in society, such the universal calamity of the period, that the moral condition of the people, instead of growing better, and of a higher character, fell lower and lower every day.

We have here, after having made every allowance for the part taken in the change by human passions and personal interests, we have here, I say, the true cause which transferred religious society to the empire of ecclesiastical society, which took all power from the body of the faithful and gave it to the clergy alone.

Let us inquire how this second revolution, of which we

have seen the origin, was worked out. How, in the very bosom of ecclesiastical society, power passed from the priests to the bishops.

We have here an important distinction to observe: the position of the bishops in their diocese, and in relation to the general government of the church, was, in the fifth century, no longer what it had been. Within his diocese, the bishop did not govern by his sole authority; he required the concurrence and assent of his clergy. This, indeed, was not an absolute institution: the fact was not regulated in any fixed manner, nor according to permanent forms; but the existence of the fact is manifested by every document connected with urban or diocesan administration. The words *cum assensu clericorum*, constantly recur in the monuments of the period. In questions, however, concerning the general government, whether of the ecclesiastical province, or of the church at large, the case was different; the bishops alone attended the councils, as representatives of this government; when simple priests appeared there it was as delegates of their bishops. The general government of the church at this period was entirely episcopal.

You must not, however, attach to the words which have just occurred, the meaning which they assumed at a later period: you must not imagine that each bishop went to the councils solely on his own account, in virtue of his own right. He went there as the representative of his clergy. The idea that the bishop, the natural chief of his priests, should speak and act everywhere on their behalf, and in their name, was at this period prevalent in all minds, in the minds of the bishops themselves, and limited their power, while it practically served as a ladder whereby they ascended higher and higher, and gradually emancipated themselves from control.

Another cause, and one perhaps still more decisive, limited the councils to the bishops alone: this was the small number of priests, and the consequent inconvenience which would have arisen from their too frequent absence from their posts. To judge merely from the great part which they play, and, permit me the expression, from the noise which they make in the fifth century, one is disposed to imagine the priests a very numerous body. Such was not at all the case: we have positive indications, historical proofs, which show the con-

trary. In the commencement of the fifth century, for in
stance, we meet with a question as to the number of the
priests at Rome; and we find it mentioned, as an illustration
of the peculiar wealth and importance of that city, that she
possessed eighty churches and seventy-seven priests.

The indirect proofs we have supply the same conclusions;
the acts of the councils of the fourth and fifth centuries are
full of canons prohibiting a simple clerk from going into any
other diocese than his own to be ordained; a priest from quitting his diocese to perform duty elsewhere, or even from
travelling at all without the consent of his bishop.[1] All sorts
of means were adopted for keeping the priests in their own
immediate district; they were watched with a care amounting
to the oppressive, so limited was their number, so anxious
were the other bishops to get possession of them. After the
establishment of the barbarian monarchies, the Frank or Burgundian kings, the rich and more notable chiefs, were constantly endeavouring to seduce from each other those companions, those *leudes*, those *anstrustions*, who constituted their
immediate train, their select guard: the barbarian laws are full
of enactments intended to check these attempts. We find the
kings constantly undertaking, in their mutual treaties, not to
invite to their courts, nor even to receive, their respective
leudes. The ecclesiastical legislation of the fourth and fifth
centuries exhibits similar regulations with respect to the
priests, doubtless, on the same grounds.

It was therefore a very serious affair for a priest to quit on
a distant mission the church to which he was attached; it was
difficult to replace him—the service of religion suffered in his
absence. The establishment of the representative system, in
church as in state, presupposes a sufficient body of men to
admit of one easily supplying the place of another upon occasion, and of their moving about without inconvenience to
themselves or to the society. Such was not the case in the
fifth century; and in order to have procured the attendance at
councils of the priests, indemnification and coercive measures
might perhaps have been necessary, as they were for a long
time necessary in England, to bring the citizens to parliament.

---

[1] See the canons of the councils of Arles, in 314, of Turin, in 397, of
Arles in 450, of Tours, in 461.

Everything, therefore, tended to transfer the government of the church to the bishops; and, accordingly, in the fifth century, the episcopal system was almost in full operation.

As to the system of pure monarchy, the only one upon which we have not as yet remarked, because it is a system which facts have not as yet presented to us, it was very far from dominating at this epoch, or even from claiming to dominate; and the most practised sagacity, the most ardent aspirations of personal ambition, could not then have foreseen its future destinies. Not but that we see, even thus early, the papacy increasing daily in consideration and influence; it is impossible to read with impartiality the monuments of the period, without perceiving that, from every part of Europe, applications were constantly being made to the bishop of Rome for his opinion, nay, his decision, in matters of faith, of discipline, in the trials of bishops, in a word, upon all the great occasions wherein the church is interested. Very often, indeed, it was merely an opinion for which he was asked: and when he had given it, those of the interested parties who disapproved of his judgment, refused to abide by it; but, on the other hand, it was supported by a more or less powerful party, and, as a general result, his preponderance became more and more decided after every one of these appeals. There were two causes which more especially contributed to produce these references to the bishop of Rome: on the one hand, the patriarchate principle still held sway in the church; above bishops and archbishops, with privileges more nominal than real, but still generally admitted in theory, there was a patriarch presiding. The east had several patriarchs, the patriarch of Jerusalem, the patriarch of Antioch, the patriarch of Constantinople, of Alexandria. In the west there was but one patriarch, the bishop of Rome; and this circumstance had a great share in the exclusive elevation of the papacy. The tradition, moreover, that St. Peter had been bishop of Rome, and the idea that the popes were his successors, already strongly possessed the minds of the western Christians.

We thus clearly trace, in the first five ages, the historical foundations of all the systems which have been cited or applied, both as to the internal organization, and as to the external position of the religious society These systems are

far from being of the same importance; some of them have
only appeared, in passing, as mere transitory, accidental
circumstances; the others have remained for a long time in
germ, have developed themselves slowly and deliberately;
they are of different dates, and, as I have said, of very various
importance; but they are all connected with some fact, they
can all cite some authority.

When we seek what principles prevailed amidst this variety
of principles, what great results were accomplished in the
fifth century, we discover the following facts:—

1. The separation of the religious society and of the ecclesiastical society: a result more especially due to the extreme
intellectual and social inequality which existed between the
people and the Christian clergy.

2. The predominance of the aristocratic system in the interior organization of the ecclesiastical society: the intervention of simple priests in the government of the church became
less and less frequent, less and less influential; power concentrated itself more and more in the hands of the bishops.

3. Finally, as to the relations of the religious society with
the civil society of the church, with the state, the system in
force was that of alliance, of intercourse between powers
distinct, but in perpetual contact with each other.

These are the three great features which characterize the
state of the church at the commencement of the fifth century.
At the bare statement of them, in their general appearance
alone, it is impossible not to perceive the germs of danger,
on the one hand, in the bosom of the religious society, to the
liberty of the body of the faithful, and in the bosom of the
ecclesiastical society to the liberty of the body of the clergy.
The almost exclusive predominance of the priests over the
faithful, and of the bishops over the priests, gave clear pre-
sage of the abuses of power and of the disorders of revolutions. The men of the fifth century, however, though they
might well have conceived such fears, had no notion whatever of them; the Christian society of that period was wholly
absorbed in regulating itself, in constituting itself a fixed and
determinate body; it required, beyond all things, order, law,
government; and despite the dangerous tendency of some of
the principles which then prevailed, the liberties, both of the
people in the religious society, and of the simple priests in

the ecclesiastical society, were not without reality and security.

The first consisted in the election of the bishops, a fact which I need not seek to establish, for it is perfectly self-evident to any one who but glances over the monuments of the period. This election was conducted neither according to general rules, nor with permanent forms; it was altogether irregular, various, and influenced by fortuitous circumstances. In 374, the bishop of Milan, Auxentius, an Arian in his opinions, being dead, his successor was about to be elected in the cathedral.

The people, the clergy, the bishops of the province, were all there, and all very animated; the two parties, the orthodox and the Arians, each wished to nominate a bishop. The tumult ended in a violent confusion. A governor had just arrived at Milan, in the name of the emperor; he was a young man named Ambrose. Informed of the tumult, he repaired to the church in order to quiet it; his words, his air, were pleasing to the people. He had a good reputation: a voice arose in the midst of the church—according to tradition, the voice of a child; it cried, "Let Ambrose be nominated bishop!" And, forthwith, Ambrose was nominated bishop; he afterwards became Saint Ambrose.

This is an example of the manner in which episcopal elections were still made at the end of the fourth century. It is true they were not all so disorderly and sudden; but these characteristics did not shock or astonish any one, and the day following his elevation, Saint Ambrose was acknowledged by all to be properly elected. Would you wish that we should look to a posterior epoch, to the end of the fifth century, for example? I open the collection of the letters of Sidonius Apollinarius, the most curious, and, at the same time, the most authentic monument of the manners of that time, especially the manners of religious society; Sidonius was bishop of Clermont; he himself collected and revised his letters; what we find there written is exactly what he wished to bequeath to posterity. Here is a letter which he addressed to his friend Domnulus.

"SIDONIUS TO HIS DEAR DOMNULUS; HEALTH.[1]

"Since you desire to know what our father in Christ.

[1] Book IV., Letter 25.

the pontiff Patient,[1] with his customary piety and firmness, has done at Châlons, I can no longer delay causing you to share our great joy. He arrived in this town, partly preceded and partly followed by the bishops of the province, assembled, in order to give a chief to the church of this city so troubled and unsteady in its discipline since the retir ment and death of bishop Paul.

"The assembly found various factions in the town, all those private intrigues which can never be formed but to the detri- ment of public welfare, and which were excited by a trium virate of competitors. One of them, destitute of all virtue made a parade of his antique race; another, like a new Apicius, got himself supported by the applause and clamours of noisy parasites, gained by the agency of his kitchen; a third engaged himself by a secret bargain, if he attained the object of his ambition, to abandon the domains of the church to the pillage of his partisans. Saint Patient and Saint Euphronius,[2] who, setting aside all aversion and all favour, were the first to maintain firmly and rigidly the most sound views, were not long in learning the state of things. Before manifesting anything in public, they first held counsel in secret with the bishops their colleagues; then, braving the cries of a mob of furies, they suddenly nominated, without his having formed any desire or having any idea of being elected, a pious man named John, commendable from his honesty, charity, and mildness. John had first been a reader, and had served at the altar from his infancy; after much time and labour, he became an archdeacon.... He was, therefore, a priest only of the second order, and amidst these furious factions no one exalted by his praise a man who asked nothing; but neither did any one dare to accuse a man who merited only eulogies. Our bishops have proclaimed him their colleague, to the great astonishment of the intriguers, to the extreme confusion of the wicked, but with the acclamations of good men, and without any person daring or wishing to oppose him."

Just now we were at a popular election; here is one equally irregular and unforeseen, brought about at once, in the midst of the people, by two pious bishops. Here is a third, if pos-

---

[1] Bishop of Lyons   [2] Bishop ot Autun.

sible, still more singular. Sidonius himself is at once the narrator and actor of it.

The bishop of Bourges was dead: such was the ardour of the competitors and their factions, that the town was thrown into disorder by them, and could find no means of coming to a decision. The inhabitants of Bourges thought of addressing themselves to Sidonius, illustrious throughout Gaul for his birth, wealth, eloquence, and knowledge, long since invested with the highest civil functions, and recently nominated bishop of Clermont. They begged him to choose them a bishop, almost in the same way as, in the infancy of the Greek republics, the people, tired of civil storms and its own powerlessness, sought a foreign sage to give them laws. Sidonius, rather surprised at first, nevertheless consented, assured himself of the concurrence of the bishops, who would have to ordain the person whom he alone had the charge of electing, and repairing to Bourges, assembled the people in the cathedral. I will cite the letter in which he gives an account of the whole affair to Perpetuus, bishop of Tours, and sends him the discourse which he pronounced in this assembly, they are both rather lengthy; but this mixture of rhetoric and religion, these literary puerilities amidst the most animated scenes of real life, this confusion of the *bel esprit* and of the bishop, make this singular society better known than all the dissertations in the world; this society at once old and young, in decline and in progress: I shall only here and there omit a passage without interest.

"SIDONIUS TO THE LORD POPE PERPETUUS; HEALTH.[1]

"In your zeal for spiritual reading, you go so far as to wish to become acquainted with writings which are not in any way worthy of your attention, or of exercising your judgment. You thus ask me to send you the discourse which I delivered in the church to the people of Bourges, a discourse to which neither the divisions of rhetoric, nor the movements of the oratorical art, nor grammatical figures, have lent fitting elegance or regularity; for on this occasion I was unable to combine, according to the general usage of orators, the grave testimonies of history, the fictions of poets, the flashes of controversy. The seditions, cabals, and differences

[1] Book VII., Letter 9.

of parties, hurried me away; and if the occasion furnished
me with ample materials, affairs did not allow me time to
meditate upon them. There was such a crowd of competitors,
that two benches could not accommodate all the candidates
for a single see; all were pleasing to themselves, and each
displeasing to the rest. We could not even have done anything for the common good, if the people, more calm, had
not renounced its own judgment in order to submit itself to
that of the bishops. A few priests whispered in a corner,
but in public not a sound of disapprobation was heard from
them; for the greater part dreaded their own order no less
than the other orders.... Accept, then, this sheet: I have
dictated it, Christ is witness, in two watches of a summer
night; but I much fear that in reading it you will think more
of it than I propose.

" THE DISCOURSE.

"Dearly beloved, profane history reports that a certain
philosopher taught his disciples patience in keeping silence,
before he disclosed to them the art of speaking, and that for this
purpose all novices observed a rigorous silence for five years,
amid the discussions of their co-disciples; so that the most
prompt minds could not be praised until a suitable time
had elapsed for them to be understood. With regard to myself, my weakness is reserved for a very different condition, I
who, before having filled with any man the more humble function of disciple, see myself obliged to undertake with you
the task of doctor.[1] ... But since it is your pleasure in your
error, to wish that I, devoid of wisdom, should seek for
you, with the aid of Christ, a bishop full of wisdom, and
in whose person all kinds of virtues are to be united, know
that your agreement in this desire, while it does me great
honour, also imposes upon me a great burden. ...

"And first, it is necessary that you should know what
torrents of injuries await me, and to what bayings of human
voices the crowd of pretenders will give way against you...
If I should nominate one from among the monks, if he
were even comparable with Paul, with Auton, Hilarius, or
Macarius, already do I feel resounding round my ears the

---

[1] Sidonius had just been nominated bishop; towards the end of 471.

noisy murmurs of an ignoble crowd of pigmies who complain, saying: 'he they have nominated, fills the functions, not of a bishop, but of an abbot; he is far more fitted to intercede for souls with the celestial judge, than for bodies before the judges upon earth.' Who will not be profoundly irritated, at seeing the most sincere virtues represented as vices? If we select an humble man, they will call him abject; if we select one of a proud character they will treat him as haughty; if we propose a man with but little enlightenment, his ignorance will bring ridicule upon him; if, on the contrary, he is a scholar, his learning will be called puffed up pride; if he be austere, they will hate him as cruel; if he be indulgent, they will accuse him of too great facility; if simple, they will disdain him as a beast; if full of penetration, they will reject him as cunning; if he be exact, they will call him peddling; if easy, they will call him negligent; if he has an astute mind, they will declare he is ambitious; if tranquil in his manner, they will reckon him lazy; if sober, they will take him to be avaricious; if he eat in order to nourish himself, they will accuse him of gormandising; if he fast regularly, they will tax him with ostentation. . Thus, in whatever manner one lives, good conduct, and good qualities will always be abandoned to the keen tongues of slander, which resemble hooks with two barbs. And, moreover, the people in its stubbornness, the priests in their indocility, are with difficulty brought under monastic discipline.

"If I nominate a priest, those who have been ordained after him will be jealous, those who have been ordained before him will defame him; for among them there are some (and be it said without offence to others) who think that the length of the duration of priesthood is the only measure of merit, and who consequently wish, that in the election of a prelate, we should proceed not with a view to the common welfare, but according to age . . .

"If, by chance, I were to point out to you a man who had filled military offices, I should soon hear these words: 'Sidonius, because he has passed from the secular functions to the spiritual, will not take a man from the religious order for a bishop; proud of his birth, raised to the first rank by the insignia of his dignities, he scorns the poor in Christ.' It is for this reason that I at once make the declaration which I owe, not so much to the charity of good people, as to the suspicions of the wicked. In the name of the Holy Spirit, our Almighty God, who, by the voice of Peter, condemned Simon the magician, for having thought that the grace of the Holy Ghost could be bought with gold, I declare that in the choice of the man whom I believed most worthy, I have not been influenced by either money or favour; and that after having examined, as much and even more than was necessary, the individual, the time, the province, and the town, I have judged that he who was the best suited to be given to you, is the man whose life I shall review in a few words.

" Simplicius, blessed of God, answers to the wishes of the two orders both by his conduct and profession; the republic may find in him much to admire, the church much to cherish. If we would bear respect to birth, (and the Evangelist himself has proved to us that this consideration must not be neglected, for Luke, in beginning the eulogy of John, reckons it a great advantage that he descended from a sacerdotal race), the relations of Simplicius have presided in the church and in the tribunals; his family has been illustrious in bishops and prelates; so that his ancestors have always been in possession of the power of carrying out the laws, both human and divine.... If we look to his age, he has at once all the activity of youth and the prudence of age .... If charity be desired, he has shown it in profusion to the citizen, the priest, and the pilgrim, to the common people as to the great; and his bread has been more frequently and the rather tasted by him who gave nothing in return. If the fulfilment of a mission be necessary, more than once has Simplicius presented himself for your town, before kings covered with ermine and before princes adorned with purple. ... I had almost forgotten to speak of a thing which, notwithstanding, should not be omitted. Formerly, in those ancient times of Moses, according to the Psalmist, when it was necessary to elevate the ark of the covenant, all Israel, in the desert, heaped the produce of its offerings at the feet of Beseleel. Afterwards, Solomon, in order to construct the temple of Jerusalem, put in motion the whole force of the people, although he had united the gifts of the queen of the southern country of Saba to the riches of Palestine, and to the tributes of the neighbouring kings. Simplicius, young, a soldier, unaided, still under the paternal roof, though already a father, has also constructed you a church; he was arrested in his pious work, neither by the attachment of old men to their property, nor by consideration for his young children; and still his modesty is such that he has kept silence upon this subject. And in fact, if I do not deceive myself, this man is a stranger to all popular ambition; he seeks not the favour of all, but only that of good men; he does not lower him. self to an imprudent familiarity, but he attaches a high value to solid friendships. . . . Lastly, he should especially be desired for a bishop, because he is not in the least desirous of it; he labours not to obtain the priesthood, but to deserve it.

"Some one will, perhaps, say to me, But how, in so short a time, have you learned so much concerning this man? I will answer him: I knew the inhabitants of Bourges before knowing the town. I have learnt much of them on my road, in the military service, in the relations of money and affairs, in their travels and mine. One also learns much of things from public opinion, for nature does not confine fame to the narrow limits of a particular country.

"The wife of Simplicius descends from the family of the Palladii, who have occupied professorships of letters and served altars, with the approbation of their order; and as the character of a matron should only be called back succinctly and with modesty, I shall content myself with affirming that this lady worthily responds to the merit and honours of the two families, whether of that where she was born and has grown up, or of that into which she has passed by an honourable choice. Both bring up their sons worthily and with all wisdom, and the father, in comparing them with himself, finds a new subject of happiness that his children already surpass himself.

"And since you have sworn to acknowledge and accept my declaration upon the subject of this election, in the name of the Father, the Son and the Holy Ghost, Simplicius is he whom I declare bishop of our province, and sovereign pontiff of your town. With regard to yourselves, if you adopt my decision concerning the man whom I have been speaking of, approve it conformably to your first engagements."

It is needless to add more; these three examples are fully sufficient thoroughly to explain what the election of bishops

was in the fifth century. Without doubt, it possessed none
of the characteristics of a veritable constitution; devoid of
rules, of permanent and legal forms, abandoned to the chance
of circumstances and passions, it was not one of those powerful
liberties before which a long future opens itself, but, for the
time being, it was a genuine reality; it led to a great
movement in the interior of cities; it was an efficacious
guarantee.

There was a second, the frequent holding of councils.
The general government of the church, at this epoch, was
completely in the hands of the councils—general, national,
provincial councils. They there discussed questions of faith
and discipline, the actions of bishops, all the great or difficult affairs of the church. In the course of the fourth
century, we find fifteen councils, and in the fifth century,
twenty-five;[1] and these are only the principal councils, those
of which written notices have been left; there were certainly
besides a large number of local councils, of short duration,
which have left no monument, of which even the recollection is lost.

An indirect evidence shows the importance of councils at
this epoch. Every one knows that, in England, in the origin

[1] *List of the principal Councils of the Fourth Century.*

Date.	Place.	Present.
314	Arles	{ 33 bishops, 14 priests, 25 deacons, 8 readers or exorcists.
346	Cologne	14 bishops, 10 delegate priests.
353	Arles	
355	Poitiers	The bishops of Gaul.
356	Beziers	
358	Vaison	Ibid.
358	Place unknown .	Ibid.
360	Place unknown .	Ibid.
362	Paris	Ibid.
374	Valencia	21 bishops.
385	Bordeaux . . .	
386	Tréves	
386	Place unknown . .	The bishops of Gaul.
387	Nimes	
397	Turin	
15		

of representative government, at the time of the formation of
the House of Commons, many statutes were made, prescribing the regular and frequent holding of parliaments
The same fact appears, at the fifth century, with regard to
councils. Many canons—among others, those of the council
of Orange, held in 441—enact that a council shall never
separate without indicating the following council, and that
if the misfortunes of the times prevent them from holding a
council twice a year, according to the canons, all possible
precautions shall be taken to insure that no long period
shall elapse without one.

Thus the two great guarantees of liberty in society,
election and discussion, existed, in fact, in the ecclesiastical

List of the principal Councils of the Fifth Century.

Date.	Place.	Present.
406	Toulouse	The bishops of Gaul.
419	Valencia	Ibid.
429	Place uncertain . .	
439	Riez	13 bishops, 1 delegate priest.
441	Orange	16 bishops, 1 priest.
442	Vaison	
444	Place uncertain . .	
451	Place uncertain . .	
452	Arles	44 bishops.
452	Narbonne . . .	The bishops of Narbonnensis prima.
453	Angers	8 bishops.
454	Bourges . . .	The bishops of Gaul.
455	Arles	13 bishops.
460	Lyons	
461	Tours	8 bishops, 1 delegate priest.
		1 bishop, subscribed afterwards.
463	Arles	19 bishops.
465	Vannes	6 bishops.
470	Châlons-sur-Saône	The bishops of the Lyonnese.
472	Bourges .	
474	Vienne . .	
475	Arles	30 bishops.
475	Lyons	
495	Lyons	
496	Reims . . .	
499	Lyons	8 bishops.
25		

z 2

society of the fifth century—disordered, it is true, incomplete,
precarious, as after times have clearly proved, but, for the time
being, real and powerful, at once the cause and the evidence
of the movement and ardour of mind.

Now, let us put this state of the religious society by
the side of the civil society which I endeavoured to picture
in our last meeting. I shall not stay to deduce the consequences of this comparison; they hasten before the eyes, and
already must be recognised. I shall recapitulate them thus:

In the civil society, there is no people nor government;
the imperial administration is fallen, the senatorial aristocracy
is fallen, the municipal aristocracy is fallen; everywhere
there is dissolution; power and liberty are struck by the
same sterility, the same nullity. In religious society, on the
contrary, a very animated people and a very active government show themselves. The causes of anarchy and tyranny
are numerous, but liberty is real, and power also. Everywhere, the germs of a very energetic popular activity, and a
very strong government, develop themselves. It is, in a
word, a society replete with the future, a stormy future,
charged with good and with evil, but powerful and fertile.

Do you wish that we should prosecute this comparison any
further? We have hitherto considered only general facts,
the public life, so to speak, of the two societies. Do you
wish that we should penetrate into the domestic life, into the
interior of houses? that we should seek how, on the one side,
men of note in civil society, and on the other the chiefs o.
the religious society, are employed, how they pass their time?
It is worth while to address this question to the fifth century,
because its answer cannot but be instructive.

At the end of the fourth and in the fifth century, there
was in Gaul a large number of important and honoured men,
long invested with the great charges of the state, semi-
pagans, semi-Christians,—that is, having taken no part, and
not wishing to take any part in religious matters;
men of mind, literati, philosophers, full of desire for study
and intellectual pursuits; rich, and living in magnificence.
Such, at the end of the fourth century, was the poet Ausonius,
count of the imperial palace, questor, pretorian-prefect, consul,
and who possessed much beautiful property in Saintonge
and near Bourdeaux; such, at the end of the fifth century,

was Tonance Ferrèol, prefect of Gaul, in great credit with the kings of the Visigoths, and whose domains were situated in Languedoc and Rouergue, upon the borders of the Gardon, and near Milhau; Eutropius, also prefect of the Gauls, a platonist by profession, who lived in Auvergne; Consencius, of Narbonne, one of the richest citizens of the south, and whose country house, called *Octaviana*, situated upon the road to Beziers, passed for the most magnificent in the province. These were the great lords of Roman Gaul; after having occupied the superior posts of the country, they lived upon their estates far from the mass of the population, passing their time in the chase, or fishing, in amusements of all kinds; they had fine libraries, often a theatre, where they played the dramas of some Rhetor, their client: the rhetorician, Paul, had his comedy, the *Delirus*, played at the house of Ausonius, composed himself the music for the interludes, and presided at the representation. At these entertainments were combined intellectual discussions, literary conversation; the merits of the ancient authors were canvassed; their works examined, commented upon; the guests made verses upon all the petty incidents of life. In this way passed time, agreeable, smooth, varied, but enervated, egoistical, sterile; stranger to all serious occupation, to all powerful and general interest. And I speak here of the most honourable remnant of the Roman society, of men who were neither corrupt, profligate, nor debased, who cultivated their intellect, and who were disgusted with the servile manners and the decay of their age.

See what was the life of a bishop; for example, of Saint Hilary, bishop of Arles, and of Saint Loup, bishop of Troyes, at the commencement of the fifth century.

Saint Hilary arose very early in the morning: he always dwelt in the town; from the time that he arose, any one who wished to see him was received. He heard complaints, adjusted differences, performed the office of a justice of the peace. He afterwards repaired to the church, performed service, preached, taught, sometimes many hours consecutively. Returned home, he took his repast, and while this lasted he heard some pious reading; or else he dictated, and the people often entered freely, and listened. He also performed manual labour, sometimes spinning for the poor, sometimes cultivating the fields of his church. Thus passed his day, in the midst of the people, in grave useful occupations, of a public interest, which, every hour, had some result.

The life of Saint Loup was not exactly the same; his manners were more austere, his activity less varied; he lived severely; and the rigidity of his conduct, the assiduity of his prayers, were incessantly celebrated by his contemporaries. Thus he exercised more ascendancy by his general example than by his actions in detail. He struck the imagination of men to such a point, that according to a tradition, the truth of which is of little importance—true or false, it equally shows contemporaneous opinion—Attila, in quitting Gaul, carried Saint Loup with him to the banks of the Rhine, supposing that so sainted a man would protect his army. Saint Loup was besides of a cultivated mind, and took an active interest in intellectual development. He was solicitous in his diocese about schools and pious reading; and when it was necessary to go and contend against the doctrines of Pelagius in Britain, it was upon his eloquence, as well as that of Saint Germain d'Auxerre, that the council of 429 confided for success.

What more need be said? the facts speak clearly; between the great lords of the Roman society and the bishops, it is not difficult to say where the power was, to whom the future belonged.

I will add one fact, indispensable to the completion of this picture of Gaulish society in the fifth century, and of its singular state.

The two classes of men, the two kinds of activity which I have just placed before your eyes, were not always as distinct, as separate as one would be tempted to believe, and as their difference might cause it to be supposed. Great lords, scarcely Christians, ex-prefects of Gaul, men of the world and of pleasure, often became bishops. They ended, even, by being obliged so to do, if they wished to take any part in the moral movement of the epoch, to preserve any real importance, to exercise any active influence. This is what happened to Sidonius Apollinaris, as to many others. But, in becoming bishops, they did not completely lay aside thei habits, their tastes; the rhetorician, the grammarian, th man of wit, the man of the world and of pleasure, did not always vanish under the episcopal mantle; and the two societies, the two kinds of manners sometimes showed themselves singularly mixed up together. Here is a letter from Sidonius, a curious example and monument of this strange alliance. He writes to his friend Eriphius:

"SIDONIUS TO HIS DEAR ERIPHIUS; HEALTH.

" You are always the same, my dear Eriphius; neither the chase, the town, nor the fields attract you so strongly, that the love of letters cannot still detain you. You direct me to send you the verses which I made at the request of your father-in-law,[1] that respectable man who, in the society of his equals, was equally ready to command or to obey. But as you desire to know in what place and upon what occasion those verses were made, to the end better to understand this valueless production, lay the blame only on yourself if the preface be longer than the work.

"We were met at the sepulchre of Saint Just,[2] illness preventing you from joining us. Before day, the annual procession was made, amidst an immense populace of both sexes, that could not be contained in the church and the crypt, although surrounded by immense porticoes; after the monks and priests had performed morning service, alternately singing the psalms with great sweetness. each retired—not very far, however—to the end that all might be ready for tierce, when the priests should celebrate the divine sacrifice. The narrow dimensions of the place, the crowd which pressed around us, and the large quantity of lights, had choked us; the oppressive vapour of a night still bordering upon summer, although cooled by the first freshness of an autumnal dawn, made this inclosure still warmer. While the various classes of society dispersed on all sides, the chief citizens assembled round the tomb of the consul Syagrius, which was not at the distance of an arrow-shot.

"Some were seated under the shade of an arbour formed of stakes covered with the branches of the vine; we were

---

[1] Philimathius.

[2] Bishop of Lyons, towards the end of the fourth century. His fête is celebrated on the 2nd of September.

stretched upon the green turf embalmed with the perfume
of flowers. The conversation was sweet, cheerful, pleasant;
moreover (and this was far more agreeable), there was
no question either of powers or tributes; no word which
could compromise, nor person who could be compromised.
Whosoever could in good terms relate an interesting history,
was sure to be listened to with earnestness. Nevertheless,
no continuous narration was made, because gaiety frequently interrupted the discourse. Tired at length of this
long repose, we desired to do something else. We soon
separated into two bands, according to ages, one party loudly
demanded the game of tennis, the others a table and dice.
For myself, I was the first to give the signal for tennis,
because I love it, as you know, as much as books. On the other
side, my brother Dominicius, a man full of kindness and cheer-
fulness, seized the dice, shook them, and struck with his dice-
box, as if he had sounded a trumpet, to call players to him.
As to us, we played a good deal with the crowd of scholars,
so as to reanimate by this salutary exercise the vigour of
our limbs stiffened by too long repose. The illustrious Philimathius himself, as says the poet of Mantua,

" Ausus et ipse manu juvenum tentare laborem,"

constantly mixed with the players at tennis. He succeeded very
well at it when he was younger, but now, as he was often driven
from the middle, where people were standing, by the shock or
some running player; as at other times, if he entered the
arena, he could neither make way nor avoid the ball, and as
frequently overthrown, he only raised himself with pain from
the unlucky fall, he was the first to leave the scene of the
game, heaving sighs, and very much heated: this exercise had
swollen the fibres of the liver, and he experienced poignant
pains. I left off at once, charitably to cease at the same time
as he, and thus save our brother from feeling embarrassed at
his fatigue. We then seated ourselves again, and soon he
was forced to ask for water to bathe his face; they brought
him some, and at the same time a napkin covered with hair
which had been washed and was by chance suspended from a
cord, held by a pulley before the folding door of the house
of the porter. While he leisurely dried his cheeks, he
said to me: ' I wish you would dictate for me a quatrain

upon the cloth that has rendered me this office.' 'Be it so,' I answered. 'But,' added he, 'let my name be contained in these verses.' I replied, that what he asked was feasible. 'Well!' he replied, 'dictate them.' I then said to him with a smile; 'Know, however, that the muses will soon be irritated if I attempt to meddle with their choir amidst so many witnesses.' He then answered very briskly, and yet with politeness (for he is of great readiness of imagination and an inexhaustible fund of wit): 'Rather take care, lord Solius, that Apollo does not become far more irritated, if you attempt to seduce his dear pupils in secret and alone.' You may imagine the applause excited by this prompt and well turned answer. Then, and without further delay, I called his secretary, who was there already, tablets in hand, and I dictated to him a quatrain to this effect:

" 'Another morning, whether in going out of the hot-bath, or when the chase has heated his brow, may the handsome Philimathius still find this linen to dry his dripping face, so that the water may pass from his forehead into this fleece as into the throat of a drinker !'

"Scarcely had your Epiphanius written these verses when they announced to us that the hour was come when the bishop came forth, and we immediately arose."

Sidonius was then bishop, and doubtless many of those who accompanied him to the tomb of Saint Just and to that of the consul Syagrius, who participated with him in the celebration of divine service, and at the game of tennis, in the chaunting of the psalms, and in the taste for trifling verses, were bishops like him.

We are now at the end of the first question which we laid down: we have considered the social state of civil and religious, Roman and Christian Gaul, at the fifth century. It remains for us to study the moral state of the same epoch, the ideas, the doctrines, the sentiments which agitated it; in a word, the internal and intellectual life of men. This will form the subject of the next lecture.

FOURTH LECTURE.

Object of the lecture—What must be understood by the moral state of a
society—Reciprocal influence of the social state upon the moral state,
and of the moral state upon the social state—At the fourth century, civil
Gaulish society alone possessed institutions favourable to intellectual development—Gaulish schools—Legal situation of the professors — Religious society has no other mediums of development and influence than its
ideas—Still one languishes, and the other prospers—Decline of the civil
schools—Activity of the Christian society—Saint Jerome, Saint Augustin,
and Saint Paulin of Nola—Their correspondence with Gaul—Foundation and character of monasteries in Gaul—Causes of the difference of
the moral state of the two societies—Comparative view of the civil literature and the Christian literature in the fourth and fifth centuries—
Inequality of the liberty of mind in the two societies—Necessity for
religion lending its aid to studies and letters.

BEFORE entering into the examination of the moral state of
Gaulish society at the end of the fourth and at the commencement of the fifth century, I must be allowed to say a few words
as to the nature of this part of my task. These words,
moral state, have, in the eyes of some people, a somewhat
vague appearance. I would wish to determine their meaning
with precision. Moral sciences, now-a-days, are accused of a
want of exactitude, of perspicuity, of certainty; they are reproached as not being sciences. They should, they may be
sciences, just the same as physical sciences, for they also
exercise themselves upon facts. Moral facts are not less
real than others: man has not invented them: he discovered and named them; he takes note of them every moment of his life; he studies them as he studies all that
surrounds him, all that comes to his intelligence by the

interposition of his senses.   Moral sciences have, if the expression be allowed, the same matter as other sciences; they are, then, not by any means condemned by their nature to be less precise or less certain.   It is more difficult, I grant, for them to arrive at exactitude, perspicuity, precision.   Moral facts are, on the one hand, more extended and more exact, and, on the other, more profoundly concealed, than physical facts; they are at once more complex in their development, and more simple in their origin.   Hence arises a much greater difficulty of observing them, classifying them, and reducing them to a science.   This is the true source of the reproaches of which the moral sciences have often been the subject. Mark their singular fate: they are evidently the first upon which the human race occupied itself; when we go back to the cradle of societies, we everywhere encounter moral facts, which, under the cloak of religion or of poetry, attracted the attention, and excited the thought of men.   And yet, in order to succeed in thoroughly knowing them, scientifically knowing them, all the skill, all the penetration, and all the prudence of the most practised reason is necessary.   Such, therefore, is the state of moral sciences, that they are at once the first and the last in the chronological order; the first, the necessity which works upon the human mind; the last, that it succeeds in elevating to the precision, clearness, and certainty, which is the scientific character.   We must not, therefore, be astonished nor affrighted by the reproaches which they have incurred; they are natural and legitimate: let it be known that neither the certainty nor the value of the moral sciences are in the least affected by them; and thence let this useful lesson be drawn, that, in their study, in the observation and description of moral facts, it is necessary, if possible, to be still more nice, exact, attentive, and strict than in anything else.   Profiting by the lesson, I commence by determining with precision, what I intend to convey by these words—the *moral state* of society.

We have hitherto been occupied with the social state of Gaul, that is, the relations of men among themselves, and their external and natural condition.   This done, the social relations described, are the facts, whose aggregate constitutes the life of an epoch, exhausted?   Certainly not: there remains to be studied the internal, the personal state of men,

the state of souls, that is, on one side, the ideas, doctrines,
the whole intellectual life of man; on the other, the relations
which connect ideas with actions, creeds with the determi-
nations of the will, thought with human liberty.

This is the twofold fact which constitutes, in my opinion,
the moral state of a society, and which we have to study in
the Gaulish society of the fifth century.

According to a very general opinion, I might dispense with
insisting long upon this inquiry. It has often been said that
the moral state depends upon the social state, that the relations of men between themselves, the principles or customs
which preside in these relations, decide their ideas, their sentiments, their internal life; that governments and institutions make the people. This was a dominant idea in the
last century, and was produced, under different forms, by
the most illustrious writers of the age, Montesquieu, Voltaire,
the economists, the publicists, &c. Nothing is more simple:
the revolution that the last century brought forth was a
social revolution; it was far more occupied in changing the
respective situation of men, than their internal and personal
disposition; it desired rather to reform society than the individual. Who will be surprised that it was everywhere
preoccupied with what it sought, with what it did—that it
was too much taken up with the social state? Yet there
were circumstances which might have served to have warned
it: it laboured to change the relations, the external condition
of men; but what were the instruments, the fulcrum of its
work? ideas, sentiments, internal and individual dispositions:
it was by the aid of the moral state that it undertook the reform of the social state. The moral state, then, must be
acknowledged to be, not only distinct from, but, to a certain
point, independent of the social state; it should be seen that
situations, institutions are not all, nor do they decide all, in
the life of nations; that other causes may modify, contend
with, even surmount these; and that if the external world
acts upon man, man in his turn acts upon the world. I
would not, that it should be thought I reject the idea
which I combat; far from it; its share of legitimacy is
great: no doubt but that the social state exercised a powerful
influence upon the moral state. I do not so much as wish
that this doctrine should be exclusive; the influence is shared

and reciprocal: if it be correct to say that governments make nations, it is no less true that nations make governments. The question which is here encountered is higher and greater than it appears: it is a question whether events, the life of the social world, are, as the physical world, under the empire of external and necessary causes, or whether man himself, his thought, his will, concur to produce and govern them; a question what is the share of fatality and that of liberty in the lot of the human race. A question of immense interest, and which I shall one day perhaps have occasion to treat in the manner which it merits; at present, I can only assign it its place, and I content myself by claiming for liberty, for man himself, a place, a great place, among the authors of events in the creation of history.

I return to the inquiry into the moral state of civil society and religious society in Gaul, in the fourth and fifth centuries.

If institutions could do all, if laws supplied and the means furnished to society could do everything, the intellectual state of Gaulish civil society at this epoch would have been far superior to that of the religious society. The first, in fact, alone possessed all the institutions proper to second the development of mind, the progress and empire of ideas. Roman Gaul was covered with large schools. The principal were those of Trèves, Bordeaux, Autun, Toulouse, Poitiers, Lyons, Narbonne, Arles, Marseilles, Vienne, Besançon, &c. Some were very ancient; those of Marseilles and of Autun, for example, dated from the first century. They there taught philosophy, medicine, jurisprudence, literature, grammar, astrology, all the sciences of the age. In the greater part of these schools, indeed, they at first taught only rhetoric and grammar; but towards the fourth century, professors of philosophy and law were everywhere introduced.

Not only were these schools numerous, and provided with many chairs, but the emperors continually took the professors of new measures into favour. Their interests are, from Constantine to Theodosius the younger, the subject of frequent imperial constitutions, which sometimes extended, sometimes confirmed their privileges. Here are the principal of these :

1 *Constantinus*[1] *Augustus to Volusianus* (in 321).—" We order that physicians, grammarians, and the other learned professors be for the future, they and the property they possess in their respective cities, exempt from all municipal charges, but that, nevertheless, they may be capable of being invested with the *honores*.[2] We forbid them to be harassed by law, or that any wrong be done them. If any one annoys them, let him be prosecuted by the magistrates, to the end that they themselves may be spared that trouble, and let him pay one hundred thousand pieces to the exchequer; if a slave offend them let him be whipped by his master before him he has offended; and if the master has consented to the outrage, let him pay twenty thousand pieces to the exchequer, and let his slave remain in pledge till the whole sum be delivered. We order to be paid to the said professors their salaries; and as they must not be charged with onerous functions, we allow them to have the *honores* conferred upon them when they desire, but we do not oblige them to it."[3]

2. *Constantinus Augustus to the people* (in 133).—" Confirming the good deeds of our divine predecessors, we order that physicians and professors of letters, as well as their wives and children, be exempt from all public functions and charges; that they be not included in the service of the militia, nor obliged to receive guests, or to acquit themselves of any charge, to the end that they may have more facility to instruct many people in the liberal studies and the above-mentioned professions."[4]

3. *Gratianus Augustus to Antonius, pretorian prefect of the Gauls* (in 376).—" In the heart of the great cities which, in all the diocese confided to your Magnificence, flourish with illustrious masters, let the best preside over the education of youth (we mean the rhetoricians and grammarians in the Attic and Roman tongues), let the orators receive from

---

[1] Probably prætorian prefect.

[2] There was a distinction made in the Roman cities and municipalities between the *munera*, municipal functions of an inferior class, which conferred no privileges; and the *honores*, superior functions, regular magistracies, to which certain privileges were attached.

[3] Cod. Theod., l. III tit. 3., l. i.   [4] Ibid. l. 3.

the exchequer twenty-four rations;[1] let the less considerable number of twelve rations be, according to usage, accorded to Greek and Latin grammarians. And to the end that the cities which enjoy metropolitan rights may select famous professors, and as we do not think that each city should be left free to pay its rhetoricians and masters according to its inclination, for the illustrious city of Trèves we wish to do something more; accordingly, let thirty rations be there granted to the rhetoricians, twenty to the Latin grammarian, and twelve to the Greek grammarian, if a capable one can be found."[2]

Valentinian, Honorius, Theodosius II. issued many similar decrees. After the Empire was divided among many masters, each of them concerned himself rather more about the prosperity of his states and the public establishments which were in them. Thence arose a momentary amelioration, of which the schools felt the effects, particularly those of Gaul, under the administration of Constantius Clorus, of Julian, and of Gratian.

By the side of the schools were, in general, placed other analogous establishments. Thus, at Trèves there was a grand library of the imperial palace, concerning which no special information has reached us, but of which we may judge by the details which have reached us concerning that of Constantinople. This last had a librarian and seven scribes constantly occupied—four for Greek, and three for Latin. They copied both ancient works and new works. It is probable that the same institution existed at Trèves, and in the great towns of Gaul.

Civil society, then, was provided with means of instruction and intellectual development. It was not the same with religious society. It had at this epoch no institution especially devoted to teaching; it did not receive from the state any aid to this particular aim. Christians, as well as others, could frequent the public schools; but most of the professors were still pagans, or indifferent in religious matters, and in their indifference, had sufficient ill-will towards the new

---

[1] *Annona,* a certain measure of wheat, oil, and other provisions, probably what was necessary for the daily consumption of a single person, ἡμερήσιον.

[2] Cod. Theod., XIII., tit. 3., b. 11

religion.   They therefore attracted very few Christians.
The sciences which they taught, grammar and rhetoric, pagan
by origin, dominated by the ancient pagan mind, had besides
but little interest for Christianity.   Lastly, it was for a long
time in the inferior classes, among the people, that Christianity
was propagated, especially in the Gauls, and it was the superior
classes which followed the great schools.   Moreover, it was
hardly until the commencement of the fourth century that the
Christians appeared there, and then but few in number.

No other source of study was open to them.   The establishments which, a little afterwards, became, in the Christian
church, the refuge and sanctuary of instruction, the monasteries,
were hardly commenced in the Gauls. It was only after the year
360 that the two first were founded by Saint Martin—one at
Ligugé, near Poitiers, the other at Marmoutiers, near Tours;
and they were devoted rather to religious contemplation than
to teaching.

Any great school, any special institution devoted to the
service and to the progress of intellect, was at that time, therefore, wanting to the Christians; they had only their own ideas,
the internal and personal movement of their thought.   It was
necessary that they should draw everything from themselves;
their doctrines, and the empire of their doctrines over the
will—the desire which they had to propagate themselves, to
take possession of the world—that was their whole power.

Still the activity and intellectual strength of the two societies
were prodigiously unequal. With its institutions, its professors,
its privileges, the one was nothing and did nothing—with its
single ideas, the other incessantly laboured and seized everything.

All things in the fifth century attest the decay of the civil
schools.   The contemporaneous writers, Sidonius Apollinaris
and Mamertius Claudianus, for example, deplore it in every page,
saying that the young men no longer studied, that professors
were without pupils, that science languished and was being
lost. They attempted, by a multitude of petty expedients, to
escape the necessity of long and vigorous studies.   This was
a time of abbreviators of history, philosophy, grammar, and
rhetoric; and they evidently proposed to themselves not to
propagate instruction in the classes who would not study, but
to spare the labour of science to those who could but would

not devote themselves to it.   It was especially the young men of the superior classes who frequented the schools; but these classes, as has been seen, were in rapid dissolution. The schools fell with them; the institutions still existed, but they were void.—the soul had quitted the body.

The intellectual aspect of Christian society was very different.   Gaul, in the fifth century, was under the influence of three spiritual chiefs, of whom none lived there: Saint Jerome[1] residing at Bethlehem, Saint Augustin[2] at Hippo, Saint Paulin[3] at Nola: the latter only was a Gaul by birth. They truly governed Gaulish Christianity; it was to them that it addressed itself on all occasions, to receive ideas, solutions, councils.   Examples abound.   A priest, born at the foot of the Pyrenees, and who was called Vigilantius, travelled to Palestine.   He there saw Saint Jerome, and engaged with him in controversy concerning some questions of ecclesiastical doctrine or discipline.   Upon his return to the Gauls, he wrote concerning what he regarded as abuses.   He attacked the worship of martyrs, their relics, the miracles worked at their tombs, frequent fasts, austerities, even celibacy.   Scarcely was his work published, than a priest, named Reparius, who lived in his neighbourhood, probably in Dauphiny or Savoy, acquainted Saint Jerome with it, giving him an account at large of the contents of the book, and of its danger, as he said. Saint Jerome immediately answered Reparius, and his answer is a first refutation, which promises a second more in detail. Reparius and another neighbouring priest, Didier, immediately sent to Bethlehem by a third priest, Sisinnius, the writings of Vigilantius; and in less than two years after the commencement of the contest, Saint Jerome sent into the Gauls a complete refutation, which rapidly spread there. The same fact took place almost at the same moment between Gaul and Saint Augustin, upon the subject of the heresy of Pelagius concerning free-will and grace; there was the same care on the part of the Gaulish priests to inform the grand bishop of everything; the same activity on his part to answer their questions, to remove their doubts, to sustain, to direct their faith.   Every heresy which

[1] Born in 331, died in 420.   [2] Born in 354, died in 430.
[3] Born in 354, died in 431.

A A

threatened, every question which arose, became, between
the Gauls on one side, and Hippo, Bethlehem, and Nola on
the other, the occasion of a long and rapid succession of
letters, messages, journeys, pamphlets. It was not even
necessary that a great question should arise, that general
and pressing religious interest should be involved. Simple
Christians, and women, were pre-occupied with certain ideas,
certain scruples; light was wanting to them; they had recourse
to the same doctors, the same remedies. A woman of Bayeux,
Hédibie, and at the same time a woman of Cahors, Algasie,
drew up, in order to address them to Saint Jerome, the one
twelve, the other eleven questions concerning philosophical,
religious, historical matters: they asked him the explanation
of certain passages of the Holy Scriptures; they wished to
know from him what were the conditions of moral perfection, or what conduct should be pursued in certain circumstances of life. In a word, they consulted him as a family
spiritual director; and a priest named Apodemus set out from
the heart of Brittany, charged to carry these letters into
the heart of Palestine, and to bring back the answers. The
same activity, the same rapidity of circulation reigned in the
interior of Gaulish Christianity. Saint Sulpicius Severus, the
companion and friend of Saint Martin of Tours, wrote a *Life*
of that saint while still living. It spread everywhere, in
Gaul, in Spain, and in Italy; copies of it were sold in all the
great towns; bishops sent for it with eagerness. Whenever
a religious desire, doubt, or difficulty was manifested, doctors
laboured, priests travelled, writings circulated. And this
was no easy thing, this quick and vast correspondence.
Physical means were wanting; the roads were few and perilous; questions had far to be carried, and long to wait for an
answer; active zeal—immovable, inexhaustible patience—was
necessary; lastly, that perseverance in moral wants was necessary which at all times is a rare virtue, and which can alone
supply the imperfection of institutions.

Nevertheless, institutions began to rise, and to be regulated
among the Christians of Gaul. The foundation of the greater
portion of the large monasteries of the southern provinces
belongs to the first half of the fifth century. That of Saint
Faustin at Nimes, and another in his diocese, has been
attributed to Saint Castor, bishop of Apt about 422. About

the same time, Cassienus founded at Marseilles that of Saint Victor; Saint Honoratus and Saint Caprais that of Lerins, the most celebrated of the age, in one of the isles of Hyères; rather later arose that of Condat or Saint Claude in Franche-Comté, that of Grigny in the diocese of Vienne, and many others of less importance. The primitive character of the Gaulish monasteries was entirely different from that of the eastern monasteries. In the east, the monasteries were chiefly for the purposes of solitude and contemplation; the men who retired into the Thebaid desired to escape pleasures, temptations, and the corruption of civil society; they wished to abandon themselves, far from social intercourse, to the transports of their imagination, and to the rigours of their conscience. It was not until a later period that they drew near each other in places where at first they had been dispersed, and anchorites or solitaries became cenobites, κοινοβιοὶ, living in common. In the west, despite the imitation of the east, monasteries had a different origin; they began with life, in common with the desire, not of isolation, but of union. Civil society was a prey to all kinds of disorders; national, provincial, or municipal, it was dissolving on all sides; a centre and an asylum was entirely wanting to men who wished to discuss, exercise themselves, live together; they found one in the monasteries; thus monastic life, in its rise, had neither the contemplative nor solitary character; on the contrary, it was highly social and active; it kindled a focus of intellectual development; it served as the instrument of fermentation and propagation of ideas. The monasteries of the south of Gaul were philosophical schools of Christianity; it was there that intellectual men meditated, discussed, taught; it was from thence that new ideas, daring thoughts, heresies, were sent forth. It was in the abbeys of Saint Victor and of Lerins that all the great questions of free will, predestination, grace, original sin, were the most warmly agitated, and where the Pelagian opinions, for fifty years, found the greatest nourishment and support.

It will be seen that the intellectual state of religious society, and that of civil society, cannot be compared; on one side all is decay, languor, inertia; on the other, all is movement, eagerness, ambition, progress. What are the causes of such a contrast? It is necessary to know from whence so striking a difference arose, how it continued, why each day it was

▲ ▲ 2

aggravated: by this only shall we arrive at a full knowledge and comprehension of their moral state.

There were, I believe, two great causes for the fact which I have just described: 1st. the very nature of the subjects, questions, intellectual labours with which the two societies occupied themselves: 2nd. the very unequal freedom of minds in one and the other.

Civil literature, if I may use the expression, presents at this epoch in Gaul only four kinds of men and of works: grammarians, rhetoricians, chroniclers, and poets; poets not on a large scale, but on a small one, makers of epithalamiums, inscriptions, descriptions, idyls, eclogues. These are the subjects upon which what remained of the Roman mind exercised itself.

Christian literature was entirely different. It abounded in philosophers, politicians, and orators; it agitated the most important questions, the most pressing interests. I shall now place before you, always taking heed to confine myself to Gaul, some proper names and some titles, a comparative view ot the principal writers and works of the two literatures. You yourselves will deduce the consequences.

I do not here pretend to give a biographical or literary enumeration, however far from complete. I only point out the most eminent names and facts.

Among the grammarians with whom civil literature was crowded, I shall name, 1st, Agroetius or Agritius, professor at Bordeaux about the middle of the fourth century, by whom we have remaining a treatise, or fragment of a treatise on the property and varieties of the Latin tongue; Latin synonymes, for example, *temperantia*, *temperatio* and *temperies*, *percussus* and *perculsus*; the author rests upon examples drawn from the best authors—Cicero, Horace, Terence, Livy, &c.— for the distinctions which he establishes. 2nd, Urbicus, also professor at Bordeaux, celebrated chiefly for his profound knowledge of the Greek language and literature. 3rd, Ursulus and Harmonius, professors at Trèves. Harmonius collected the poems of Homer, adding thereto notes on false readings, interpretations, &c.

By the side of the grammarians are the rhetoricians, whose business was not only with teaching eloquence, but with writing discourses, panegyrics on all the chief circumstances of life, upon the occasion of fêtes, civil solemnities. the death or accession of an emperor, &c. Twelve of these bravuras of vain eloquence have been specially preserved and collected. The four principal panegyrists are—first, Claudius Mamertinus, author of an eulogy on the emperor Maximian, delivered at Trèves, the 20th of April, 292, the day on which the foundation of Rome was celebrated; secondly, Eumenius, professor of eloquence at Autun, author of four discourses delivered from 297 to 311, in the presence and in honour of Constantius Chlorus, and of Constantine; thirdly, Nazarius, professor at Bordeaux, author of a panegyric on Constantine, fourthly, Claudius Mamertinus, perhaps the son of the first, author of a discourse delivered in 362 before Julian.

Among the Gaulish and pagan chroniclers of this epoch, the most distinguished is Eutropius, who wrote his abridgment of Roman history about the year 370.

I might extend the list of poets at pleasure, but it will not be complained of that I only name three of them. The most fertile, the most celebrated, and incontestably the most spiritual and elegant, is Ausonius, who was born at Bordeaux about 309, and died upon one of his estates in 394, after having filled the highest public offices, and composed—first, one hundred-and-forty epigrams; secondly, thirty-eight epitaphs; thirdly, twenty idyls ; fourthly, twenty-four epistles; fifthly, seventeen descriptions of towns, and a multitude of small poems upon such subjects as the professors of Bordeaux, the persons and incidents of his family, the twelve Cæsars, the seven wise men of Greece, &c. &c.

An uncle of Ausonius, named Arborius, of Toulouse, has left a small poem, addressed to a young girl too finely dressed, *Ad virginem nimis cultam.*

A poet of Poitiers, Rutilius Numatianus, who lived for some time at Rome, and who returned to his country about the year 416, upon his return wrote a poem entitled *Itinerarium;* or *de Reditu ;* a curious work enough for details or places, manners, and for the anger of the poet, against the invasion of society by the Jews and the monks. He was evidently a pagan.

I pass to the Gaulish Christian society at the same epoch.

The first name that I meet with is that of Saint Ambrose; although he passed his life in Italy, I reckon him as a Gaul, for he was born at Trèves, about the year 340. His works have been collected in two volumes folio. They contain thirty-six different works—religious treatises, commentaries upon the Bible, discourses, letters, hymns, &c. The most extensive, and also the most curious, is entitled De Officiis Ministrorum, (concerning the duties of ministers of the church.)

At a future period I shall, perhaps, return to this work in detail; at present I only wish to explain its character. You would be tempted to believe, from the title, that it was a treatise upon the particular duties of priests, and on the manner in which they should acquit themselves of their duties. You would be deceived; it is a complete moral treatise, in which the author, while on the subject of priests, passes in review all human duties; he there sets down and resolves a multitude of questions of practical philosophy.

By the side of Saint Ambrose I shall place Saint Paulin, born, like him, in Gaul (at Bordeaux, about the year 353), and who died, like him, a bishop, in Italy (at Nola, in 431). Many of his works, among others his book against the pagans, are lost; all that remains of him are some letters and poems; but letters, at this period, had a very different importance from what they have in modern times. Literature, properly so called, held but little place in the Christian world; men wrote very little for the sake of writing; for the mere pleasure of manifesting their ideas; some event broke forth, a question arose, and a book was often produced under the form of a letter to a Christian, to a friend, to a church. Politics, religion, controversy, spiritual and temporal interests, general and special councils—all are met with in the letters of this time, and they are among the number of its most curious monuments.

I have already named Saint Sulpicius Severus, of Toulouse[1] (or of some other town of Aquitaine, for his origin is not known with certainty), and his *Life of Saint Martin*, of Tours. He moreover wrote a *Sacred History*, one of the first essays at ecclesiastical history attempted in the west; it reaches from the beginning of the world up to the year 400, and contains many important facts which are not found elsewhere.

[1] Born about 355, died about 420.

Nearly at the same time, or rather later, the monk Cas-sienus,[1] a provincial by birth, as it would appear, though he lived for a very long time in the east, published at Mar-seilles, at the request of Saint Castor bishop of Apt, his *Institutions* and his *Conferences*, works written for the pur-pose of making the western world acquainted with the origin, principles, practices, and ideas, of the eastern monks. It was at this period, as you have heard, that most of the earlier monasteries in southern Gaul were founded by the co-operation of Cassienus himself; so that these books of his were prepared to meet an actual and practical want.

It recurs to me that before Cassienus I should have men-tioned Saint Hilary, bishop of Poitiers, one of the most active, most upright, and most eminent chiefs of the Gaulish church,[2] who wrote a number of works, all of them of limited extent, but all highly important in their time. They are, in fact, for the most part, mere pamphlets upon the various questions which were then engaging attention. After Chris-tianity had grown beyond its infancy, the more eminent bishops had two parts to play at one and the same time—that of philosopher and that of statesman. They possessed the empire over ideas, or, at all events, the preponderating influence in the intellectual order; and they had also to administer the temporal affairs of the religious society. They were called upon concurrently to fulfil two missions—to mediate and to act, to convince and to govern. Hence the prodigious variety, and hence also the haste, which very often characterise their writings. These, in general, were works got up altogether for the occasion—pamphlets intended, now to solve a question of doctrine, now to discuss a matter of business, to enlighten a soul, or oppose a civil disorder, to answer a heresy, or to obtain a concession from the govern-ment. The works of Saint Hilary are more especially im-pressed with this character.

A monk, who was possibly acquainted with Saint Hilary, since he lived for some time with St. Martin of Tours, Evagrius, wrote two dialogues, entitled—the one, *Conference between Theophilus, a Christian, and Simon, a Jew*—the other, *Conference between Zacheus, a Christian, and Apollo-*

---

[1] Born about 360, died about 440.   [2] Died about 368.

nius, a philosopher—curious monuments of the manner in which a Christian monk of the end of the fourth century framed in his mind the question, on the one hand, between Judaism and Christianity; and on the other, between Christianity and philosophy.

A little later than this, a priest of Marseilles, Salvienus, a native of Trèves, wrote his treatise *On Avarice*, a treatise on religious morality, and his book, which I have already mentioned, *De Gubernatione Dei*, a work remarkable both as a picture of the social state and manners of the period, and as an attempt to acquit Providence from any share in the miseries of the world, the blame of which he entirely throws upon mankind themselves.

The Pelagian schism gave rise to a vast number of works, among which, however, I will only mention those of Saint Prosper of Aquitaine, and especially his poem, *Against Ingrates*, one of the happiest efforts of philosophical poetry that ever emanated from the bosom of Christianity. His Chronicle, which extends from the origin of the world to the year 455, is not without importance.

While the question of free will and of grace was agitating the whole church, and more especially that of Gaul, that of the immateriality of the soul was being more quietly discussed in the Narbonnese, between Faustus,[1] bishop of Riez, who maintained that the soul is material, and Mamertius Claudienus,[2] priest of Vienne, and brother of the bishop Saint Mamertius, who defended the contrary opinion. The letter in which Faustus sets forth his views, and the treatise of Mamertius Claudienus, entitled *On the Nature of the Soul*, are amongst the most curious monuments of the state of the human mind in the fifth century, and I therefore propose to make you acquainted with them in detail at a future period.

Of the Christian literature of this period, I will cite but one more name, that of Gennadius, priest at Marseilles, who in his work entitled, *Treatise on Illustrious Men, or Ecclesiastical Authors, from the middle of the fourth century to the end of the fifth*, has given us more information on the literary history of the period than we find anywhere else. When you compare these two lists, dry and incomplete as they are, of

[1] Died in 490.   [2] Died about 473

authors and of works, do not the names, the titles alone, explain the difference in the intellectual state of the two societies? The Christian writers address themselves at once to the highest interests of thought and of life; they are active and potent at once in the domain of intellect, and in that of reality; their activity is rational, and their philosophy popular; they treat of things which alike stir up the soul of the anchorite in his solitude, and of nations in their cities. The civil literature, on the contrary, has no reference to questions either of principle or of passing events, to either the moral wants or the household sentiments of the masses; it is entirely a literature of convention and luxury, of coteries and of schools, wholly and solely devoted, from the very nature of the subjects which engage its attention, to the passing entertainment of the nobles and the wits.

This is not all; we find another and a far different cause for the diversity of the moral condition of the two societies: liberty, that is to say, liberty of mind, was entirely wanting to the one, while in the other it was real and powerful.

Indeed, it was impossible but that liberty should be wholly wanting to the civil literature; that literature belonged to civil society, to the old Roman world; it was its image, its amusement; it bore all its characteristics,—decay, sterility, fertility, servility. The very nature, however, of the subjects upon which it exercised itself, rendered the presence of these characteristics very endurable. It kept entirely apart from all the great moral questions, from all the real interests of life, that is to say, from every career in which freedom of mind is indispensable. Grammar, rhetoric, minor poetry, very readily adapt themselves to servitude. To compile Latin synonymes like *Agræcius*—to criticise, like Arborius, a girl over dressed—or even to celebrate, like Ausonius, the beauties of the Moselle, required neither freedom nor, in truth, even movement of mind. This subordinate literature has more than once prospered extremely well under despotism, and in the decline of societies.

In the very heart of the schools, there was an entire absence of liberty; the whole of the professors were removable at any time. The emperor had full power, not only to transfer them from one town to another, but to cancel their appointment whenever he thought fit. Moreover, in a great many

of the Gaulish towns, the people themselves were against
them, for the people were Christians, at least in a great
majority, and as such had a distaste for schools which were
altogether pagan in origin and intention. The professors,
accordingly, were regarded with hostility, and often mal-
reated; they were, in fact, quite unsupported except by the
remnant of the higher classes, and by the imperial authority,
which still maintained order, and which having heretofore
often persecuted the Christians solely in compliance with the
clamorous demands of the people, now, in the fourth century,
protected the pagans against the people, either from an abstract
desire to preserve order, from deference to the wishes of distinguished citizens, themselves pagans or indifferent about
the matter, or out of that respect for old institutions, old
principles, which an old government ever retains. You may
thus readily perceive, in how dependent, powerless, precarious, painful a position the professors were placed. That
of the students was scarcely any better. They were the
object of a multitude of inquisitorial, vexatious, police regulations, against which they had no practical security. I will
read to you an edict of Valentinian, which will give you a
clear idea of their situation; the edict itself only refers to the
students of the school at Rome, but the other schools of the
empire were conducted upon analogous rules and principles:

" *Valentinian, Valerius, and Gratian, to Olybrius, Prefect
of Rome. (370.)*

" 1. All persons coming to study at Rome, must immediately upon their arrival lay before the master of the census[1]
letters from the provincial governors who have given them
permission to travel, setting forth their place of abode, their
age, their name, condition, and description. 2. They must declare, also, at the same time, what studies they intend more
especially to pursue. 3. They must let the census office know,
from time to time, their place of abode in Rome, so that the
officers of that department may see to their following out the
studies which they have indicated as the object of their pursuit. 4. The aforesaid officers are charged to take care that

---

[1] A magistrate, some of whose functions were analogous with those of
our prefect of police.

the students conduct themselves at the lectures in a becoming manner, avoiding all occasion of gaining an ill reputation, and taking no part in any of those private associations among themselves, which we regard as very little short of crimes; they are not to visit the theatre too frequently, nor to indulge in overfeasting and revelry. Any student who shall forget the dignified demeanour due from him who pursues the liberal arts, shall be publicly beaten with rods, put on board some vessel, and, ignominiously expelled the city, be sent back whence he came. They who apply themselves assiduously to their studies, may remain in Rome until their twentieth year; should they then omit to return home of their own accord, let the prefect have them removed, whether they will or no. And that these regulations may be properly attended to, your High Sincerity will forthwith direct the chief officers of the census department to have drawn up, every month, a report upon the said students, setting forth how many there are, who they are, whence they came, their general character, and who of them, their time in Rome being completed, have to be sent back to Africa, or other provinces. . . . . Let a copy of these reports be annually sent to us, that, thereby made acquainted with the merits and acquirements of the students, we may judge how far any of them are necessary cr desirable for our service."[1]

Some of these precautions may very possibly have been, in certain cases, necessary and proper; but it is at the same time quite clear that in the system of which they were a leading, a dominant feature, in the schools of whose discipline they formed the basis, there was no liberty.

In Christian literature, on the contrary, liberty manifests itself in full luxuriance: the activity of mind, the diversity of opinion publicly declared, are of themselves sufficient to prove the fact of this liberty. The human mind does not spread its wings so broadly, so energetically, when it is loaded with irons. Liberty, besides, was inherent in the intellectual situation of the church: she was labouring at the formation of her doctrines, which, as to a great number of points, she had not as yet promulgated or fixed. From time to time, some question was raised by an event, by a polemical writing; it was

[1] Cod. Theod. l. xiv. t. ix. l. i.

then examined and discussed by the chiefs of the religious society; and the decision formed, the belief adopted, the dogma was in due time proclaimed. It is evident that, in such a period as this, there must exist liberty, precarious, perhaps, and transitory, but still real, and. to a considerable extent, practical.

The state of the legislation against heresy was not as yet mortal to it; the principle of persecution, the idea that truth had a right to govern by force, occupied men's minds, but it did not yet dominate in facts. Civil power began to lend a strong hand to the church against the heretics, and to be severe against them; they were exiled, certain functions were interdicted them, they were despoiled of their property; some even, as the Priscillianists, in 385, were condemned to death: the laws of the emperors, especially those of Theodosius the Great, were full of menaces and provisions against heresy; the course of things, in short, evidently tended to tyranny: civil power, however, still hesitated to make itself the instrument of doctrines; the greatest bishops, Saint Hilary, Saint Ambrose, Saint Martin, still cried out against all capital condemnation of heretics, saying that the church had no right to employ other than spiritual arms. In a word, although the principle of persecution was in progress, and in very threatening progress, liberty was still stronger: a dangerous and tempestuous liberty, but active and general; a man was an heretic at his peril; but he might be one if he pleased; and men might sustain, they did sustain, their opinions, for a long period, with energy, with publicity. It will suffice to glance at the canons of the councils of this epoch in order to be convinced that liberty was still great: with the exception of two or three great general councils, these assemblies, particularly in Gaul, scarcely concerned themselves with anything more than discipline; questions of theory, of doctrine, appeared there rarely and only upon great occasions; it was more especially the government of the church, her situation, the rights and duties of priests, that they treated of and decided upon: a proof that, in numerous points, diversity of ideas was admitted and debate still open.

Thus, on one side, the very nature of the labours, and on the other the situation of minds, fully explain the intellectual superiority of the religious society over the civil society; the one state was earnest and free, the other servile and frivolous: what is there to add?

But one final observation, one, however, which is not without importance, and which, perhaps, fully explains why civil literature was on the point of death, while religious literature lived and prospered so energetically.

For the culture of mind, for the sciences, for literature, to prosper by themselves, independently of all near and direct interest, happy and peaceable times are requisite, times of contentment and good fortune for men. When the social state becomes difficult, rude, unhappy, when men suffer much and long, study runs a great risk of being neglected and of declining. The taste for pure truth, the appreciation of the beautiful, apart from all other desire, are plants as delicate as they are noble; they must have a pure sky, a brilliant sun, a soft atmosphere; amid storms they droop the head and fade. Intellectual development, the labour of mind to attain truth, will stop unless placed in the train, and under the shield, of some one of the actual, immediate, powerful interests of humanity. This is what happened at the fall of the Roman empire: study, literature, pure intellectual activity, were unable alone to resist disasters, sufferings, universal discouragement; it was necessary that they should be attached to popular sentiments and interests; that they should cease to appear a luxury, and should become a need. The Christian religion furnished them with the means; by uniting with it, philosophy and literature were saved the ruin which menaced them; their activity had then practical, direct results; they showed an application to direct men in their conduct, towards their welfare. It may be said without exaggeration that the human mind proscribed, beaten down with the storm, took refuge in the asylum of churches and monasteries; it supplicatingly embraced the altars, and entreated to live under their shelter and in their service, until better times permitted it to re-appear in the world and to breathe the free air

I shall not go any further into this comparison of the moral state of the two societies in the fifth century; we know enough of it, I think, to understand them both clearly. It is

now necessary to enter deeper into the examination of the
religious society, alone living and fertile; it is necessary to
seek to discover what questions occupied it, what solutions
were proposed to it, what controversies were powerful and
popular, what was their influence upon the life and actions
of mankind.   This will be the subject of o'   next lectures.

FIFTH LECTURE.

Of the principal questions debated in Gaul in the fifth century—Of Pelagianism—Of the method to follow in its history—Of the moral facts
which gave place to this controversy: 1st, of human liberty; 2nd, of the
impotency of liberty, and the necessity for an external succour; 3rd, of
the influence of external circumstances upon liberty; 4th, of the moral
changes which happen in the soul without man attributing them to his
will—Of the questions which naturally arose from these facts—Of the
special point of view under which we should consider them in the
Christian church in the fifth century—History of Pelagianism at Rome,
in Africa, in the East, and in Gaul—Pelagius—Celestius—Saint Augustin—History of semi-Pelagianism—Cassienus—Faustus—Saint
Prosper of Aquitaine—Of predestination—Influence and general results
of this controversy.

In the last lecture, I attempted to picture, but only under its
general features, the comparative moral state of civil society
and of religious society in Gaul at the fifth century. Let us
enter deeper into the examination of religious society, the
only one which furnishes ample matter for study and reflection.

The principal questions which occupied the Gaulish
Christian society in the fifth century were—1st, Pelagianism,
or the heresy of Pelagius, the principal opponents of which
were Saint Augustin; 2nd, the nature of the soul, debated
in the south of Gaul between bishop Faustus and the priest
Mamertius Claudienus; 3rd, various points of worship and of
discipline, rather than of doctrine, such as the worship of
the martyrs, the value to be attached to fastings, austerities,
celibacy, &c.; these, as you have seen, were the objects to
which Vigilantius applied his writings; 4th, the prolongation
of the struggle of Christianity against Paganism and Judaism, the theses of the two dialogues of the monk Evagrius,

between the Jew Simon and the Christian Theophilus, and the Christian Zacheus and the philosopher Apollonius.

Of all these questions, Pelagianism was by far the most important: it was the great intellectual controversy of the church in the fifth century, as Arianism had been in the fourth. It is with its history that we are now about to occupy ourselves.

Every one is aware that this controversy turned upon the question of free-will and of grace, that is to say, of the relations between the liberty of man, and the Divine power, of the influence of God upon the moral activity of men.

Before proceeding with the history of this affair, I will indicate the method upon which I propose to proceed.

The mere statement of the question will show you that it was one not peculiar either to the fifth century or to Christianity, but that it is a universal problem common to all times and all places, and which all religions, all systems of philosophy, have propounded to themselves, and have endeavoured to solve.

It has, therefore, manifest reference to primitive, universal, moral facts, facts inherent in human nature, and which observation may discover there. I will, in the first place, seek out these facts; I will endeavour to distinguish in man in general, independently of all considerations of time, place, cr particular creed, the natural elements, the first matter, so to speak, of the Pelagian controversy. I shall bring these facts to light, without adding anything thereto, without retrenching anything therefrom, without discussing them, solely applied to prove and describe them.

I shall then show what questions naturally flowed from natural facts, what difficulties, what controversies, arose out of them, independently of all particular circumstances of time, place, or social state.

This done, and, if I may so express myself, the general theoretical side of the question once thoroughly established, I shall determine under what special point these moral facts should be considered at the fifth century, by the defenders of the various opinions in debate.

Finally, after having thus explained from what sources and under what auspices Pelagianism was born, I shall recount its history; I shall attempt to follow, in their relations and their progress, the principal ideas which it suscitated, in order properly to understand what was the state of mind at the moment when this great controversy arose, what it did therein, and at what point it left it.

I must request your most scrupulous attention, especially in the examination of the moral facts to which the question attaches itself: they are difficult properly to understand, to express with precision; I should wish nothing should be wanting to them in clearness and certainty, and I have hardly time to indicate them in a cursory manner.

The first, that which forms the foundation of the whole quarrel, is liberty, free will, the human will. In order to understand this fact exactly, it must be disengaged from all foreign element, and strictly reduced to itself. It is, I believe, for want of this care that it has been so often but ill comprehended; men have not placed themselves in front of the fact of liberty, and of that alone; they have seen and described it, so to speak, mixed up with other facts which occupy a very close position to it in moral life, but do not the less essentially differ from it. For example, they have made human liberty to consist in the power to deliberate and choose between motives of action; the deliberation and judgment which proceed therefrom have been considered as the essence of free will. It is nothing of the kind. These are acts of intellect, and not of liberty; it is before the intellect that the different motives of action, interests, passions, opinions, &c., appear: the intellect considers, compares, estimates, weighs, and finally judges them. This is a preparatory work, which precedes the act of will, but does not in any way constitute it. When the deliberation has taken place, when man has taken full cognizance of the motives which presented themselves to him, and of their value, then comes an entirely new fact, entirely different, the fact of liberty; man takes a resolution, that is to say, commences a series of facts which have their source in himself, of which he looks upon himself as the author, which arise because he wishes it, and which would not arise unless he wished it, which would be different if he desired to produce them differently. Remove all recollection of intellectual deliberation, of motives known and appreciated; concentre your thought and that of the man who takes a resolution at the very moment that it occurs to him, when he says: "I will,

B B

I will do so," and ask yourself, ask him, if he could not will and do otherwise. Of a surety, you will answer—he will answer, " Yes." Here the fact of liberty is shown : it resides complete in the resolution which man takes after deliberation: it is the resolution which is the proper act of man, which subsists by him, and by him alone; a simple act, independent of all the facts which precede it, or surround it; identical in the most diverse circumstances; always the same, whatever may be its motives and its results.

Man sees this act just as he produces it; he knows himself to be free, he is conscious of his liberty. The conscience is that faculty which man possesses of contemplating what passes within him, of being present at his own existence, of being as it were a spectator of himself. Whatever may be the facts which are accomplished within man, it is by the fact of con- science that they are shown to him; the conscience attests liberty, the same as sensation, as thought; man sees, knows himself free, as he sees, as he knows himself thinking, reflect- ing, judging. People have often attempted, even now they attempt to establish, between these various facts, some sort of inequality of clearness, of certainty: they rise against what they call the assumption of introducing the facts of conscience, unknown and obscure facts, into science; sensation, percep- tion, say they, these are clear, proved; but the facts of con- science, where are they? what are they? I do not think there is any need to insist long on this point: sensation, perception, are facts of conscience as well as liberty; man sees them in the same manner, with the same degree of light, and of certainty. He may lend his attention to certain facts of conscience, rather than others, and forget or misunderstand those which he regards not: the opinion to which I have this moment made allusion is proof of this: but when he observes himself in a complete manner, when he is present without losing any part of it, at the spectacle of his internal life, he has little trouble in being convinced that all the scenes pass upon the same stage, and are known to him on the same principle and in the same manner.

I desire that the fact of human liberty, thus reduced to its proper and distinctive nature, should remain fully present to your thought; for its confusion with other facts, bordering upon, but different from it, was one of the chief causes of trouble and debate in the great controversy with which we have to occupy ourselves.

A second fact, equally natural, equally universal, played a considerable part in this controversy.

At the same time that man felt himself free, that he saw in himself the faculty of commencing, by his will alone, a series of facts, he also acknowledged that his will was placed under the empire of a certain law which, according to the occasions to which it applied itself, took different names, moral law, reason, good sense, &c. He is free; but, in his own thought, his freedom is not arbitrary; he may use it in a senseless, unjust, guilty manner; and each time that he uses it, a certain rule must preside at it. The observation of this rule is his duty, the task of his liberty.

He will soon see that he never fully acquits himself of this task, nor acts perfectly according to reason, moral law; that, always free, that is to say, morally capable of conforming himself to this rule, he, in fact, does not accomplish all that he ought, or even all that he can. Upon every occasion, when he scrupulously interrogates himself, and sincerely answers himself, he is forced to say: "I might have done so and so, if I had chosen;" but his will was enervated, backward; it went neither to the end of its duty, nor of its power.

This fact is evident, one of which all may give witness: there is even this singularity, that the feeling of this weakness of the will becomes often so much the more clear, so much the more pressing, as the moral man is developed and perfected: the best men, that is, those who have best conformed their will to reason, to morality, have often been the most struck with their insufficiency, the most convinced of the profound inequality between the conduct of man and his task, between liberty and its law.

Hence arises a sentiment which is found under various forms, in all men; the feeling of the necessity of an external support, of a fulcrum for the human will, a power which may be added to its present power, and sustain it at need. Man seeks on all sides to discover this fulcrum, this aiding power; he demands it in the encouragements of friendship, in the councils of the wise, in the example, the approbation of those like himself; in the fear of blame; there is no one but has every day, in his own conduct, a thousand proofs to cite

B B 2

of this movement of the soul, eager to find beyond itself an
aid to its liberty, which it feels at once to be real and insufficient. And as the visible world, the human society, do not
always answer to his desire, as they are afflicted with the same
unsufficingness which is seen in his own case, the soul goes
beyond the visible world, above human relations, to seek this
fulcrum of which it has need: the religious sentiment develops itself; man addresses himself to God, and invokes his
aid. Prayer is the most elevated, but not the only form,
under which the universal sentiment of the weakness of human
will, this recourse to an external and allied power, is manifested.

And such is the nature of man, that when he sincerely
asks this support, he obtains it, that his merely seeking it is
almost sufficient to secure it. Whosoever, feeling his will
weak, sincerely invokes the encouragement of a friend, the
influence of wise councils, the support of public opinion, or
addresses himself to God by prayer, soon feels his will
fortified, sustained, in a certain measure, and for a certain
time. This is a fact of daily experience, and which is easy of
verification.

Here is a third whose importance should not be forgotten;
I mean the influence of circumstances independent of man
upon the human will, the empire of the external world upon
liberty. No one denies the fact, but it is necessary to
estimate it with exactness, for, if I do not deceive myself, it
is generally ill comprehended.

I just now distinguished liberty from the deliberation which
precedes it, and which is accomplished by the intellect. Now
the circumstances independent of man, whatsoever they be,
the place, the time when the man was born, habits, manners,
education, events, influence in no way the act of liberty,
such as I have endeavoured to describe it; it is not reached
nor modified by them; it always remains identical and complete, whatever the motives which call it forth. It is upon
these motives, in the sphere where intellect displays itself,
that external circumstances exercise and exhaust their power.
The age, the country, the world, in the heart of which life
passes away, infinitely vary the elements of the deliberation
which precedes the will: in consequence of this variation,
certain facts, certain ideas certain sentiments, in this intellec-

tual labour, are present or absent, near or at a distance, powerful or weak; and the result of this deliberation, that is to say the judgment formed upon the motives, is greatly affected by it. But the act of the will which follows it remains essentially the same: it is only indirectly, and by reason of the diversity of the elements introduced into the deliberation, that the conduct of men undergoes this influence of the external world. One illustration, I hope, will make me fully understood. In accordance with the customs of his tribe, to fulfil what he regards as a duty, a savage reluctantly kills his aged and infirm father: a European, on the contrary, supports his parent, tends him, devotes himself to the alleviation of his old age and infirmities; nothing assuredly can be more different than the ideas which, in the two cases, constitute the groundwork of the deliberation which precedes the action, and the results which accompany it: nothing more unequal than the legitimacy, the moral worth of the two actions in themselves, but as to the resolution, the free and personal act of the European, and of the savage, are they not alike, if accomplished with the same intention, and with the same degree of effort?

Thus the influence of circumstances independent of the will, upon the motives and the consequences of free action, is immense, but that is the only field in which it exercises itself: the lower fact placed between deliberation and exterior action, the fact of liberty, remains the same, and accomplishes itself in like manner amidst the most varying elements.

I now come to the fourth and last of the great moral facts, a knowledge of which is indispensable, before we can comprehend the history of Pelagianism. There are many others which I might enumerate; but these are of minor importance, obvious results of those which I here describe, and I have no time to enter into an account of them.

There are certain changes, certain moral events, which accomplish and manifest themselves in man without his being able to refer their origin to an act of his will, or being able to recognise their author.

This assertion may at first glance surprise some of you; I will endeavour to illustrate it by analogous facts, which occur more frequently within the domain of intelligence, and are more readily apprehended

There is no one who at some time or other of his life after laboriously seeking some idea, some reminiscence, has not fallen asleep in the midst of the search without having succeeded in it, and next morning, on awaking, found the desired object fully present to his mind. There is no scholar to whom it has not occurred to have retired to rest without having acquired the lesson he has been studying, and to have arisen next morning and learned it without the least difficulty. I might show many other illustrations of the same description: I select these as the simplest and most incontestable.

I deduce from them this consequence: independently of the voluntary and deliberate activity of the will, a certain interior and spontaneous labour accomplishes itself in the understand-ing of man, a labour which we do not direct or control, of which we have no opportunity of observing the progress, and yet a real and productive labour.

There is, after all, nothing strange in this: every one of us brings with him into the world an intellectual nature of his own. Man, by the operation of his will, directs and modifies, exalts or debases his moral being, but he does not create it; he has received it, and received it endowed with certain indi-vidual dispositions, with a spontaneous force. The inborn diversity of men in the moral point of view, as in the physical, is beyond dispute. Now, in the same way that the physical nature of each man develops itself spontaneously and by its own virtue, so, in the same way, though in a very unequal degree, there is operated in his intellectual nature, set in motion by his relations with the external world, or by his will itself, a certain involuntary, imperceptible development, and, to use an expression, which I only avail myself of because it figuratively expresses the idea I wish to convey, a sort of vegetation, bearing naturally, and in due course, its fruits.

That which takes place in the intellectual order, happens in like manner in the moral order. Certain facts occur in the interior of the human soul which it does not refer to itself; which it does not recognise as the work of its own will; there are certain days, certain moments, in which it finds itself in a different moral state from that which it was last conscious of under the operation of its own will. It cannot trace back the progress of the change to its source; it had nothing to do with it, it took place without its concurrence. In other words, the moral man does not wholly create himself, he is conscious that causes, that powers external to himself, act upon him and modify him imperceptibly; in his moral life, as in his future destiny, there are points utterly inexplicable to him, of which he knows nothing.

Nor is it necessary, to convince himself of this fact, that he should turn to those great moral revolutions, those sudden, marked changes, which the human soul, undoubtedly, may at times experience, but which ever receive a high colouring from the imagination of the narrators, and of which it is difficult to form an adequate appreciation. It is only necessary to look into oneself, to discover there more than one example of these involuntary modifications. There is no one, who, on observation of his internal life, will not easily recognise that the vicissitudes, the development of his moral being, are not all the result, either of the action of his will, or of the external circumstances that are known to him.

Such are the principal moral facts connected with the Pelagian controversy, such as human nature, simple, universal nature, communicates them to us, apart from the historical details, the particular circumstance of Pelagianism itself. You at once see, that from these facts alone, still apart from all special and accidental elements, there results a multitude of questions, the groundwork of many a grave discussion. And, in the first place, we may question the reality of the facts themselves: all of them, indeed, are not equally exposed to this danger; the fact of human liberty, for instance, is more evident, more irresistible, than any of the rest; yet even this has been denied, as all things may be denied, seeing that there are no bounds to the vast field of error.

Admit the facts, acknowledge them fully: then comes the question, whether we may not be mistaken as to the place which each occupies, or to the part which each plays in the moral life; we may have measured inexactly their extent, their importance; we may have given too large or too small a part to liberty, to external circumstances, to the weakness of the will, to unknown influences, &c.

Again, altogether different explanations of the facts themselves may be suggested. In reference, for example, to the involuntary, imperceptible changes which occur in the moral state of man; it may be said that these are assignable to some

want of due attention on the part of the soul, to its not re
membering all that passes within itself, to its having forgotten
some act of the will, some resolution, some impression, which
has produced consequences, the thread of which it has not
followed, the development of which it has not observed. Or,
to explain these obscure, doubtful facts of the moral life, recourse may at once be had to a direct, special action, of God
upon man, to a permanent relation between the action of God
and the activity of man. Or, finally, attempts may be made
to reconcile these facts together in various ways; to reduce
them into a system upon such or such a principle, to refer
them to such or such a general doctrine upon the nature and
destiny of man and of the world. Thus, in a variety of ways,
an infinity of questions may arise; from the nature alone of
the facts under consideration, taken in themselves and in their
generality, they are a fruitful subject of discussion.

And how much wider still the field of controversy, when
particular, local, temporary causes vary still more the point of
view under which we regard these questions, modify the cognizance which the human mind takes of them, diverting its
inquiries into one direction rather than into another, giving
greater or less prominence, greater or less effect to this or to
that fact. This, which always happens, happened of course
in the fifth century. I have endeavoured to reascend with
you to the natural and purely moral sources of the Pelagian controversy: it is now necessary that we should consider
its historical origins; they are no less necessary to the proper
comprehension of it.

In the bosom of the Christian church, the moral facts which
I have described were, as a matter of inevitable course, considered in various points of view.

Christianity was an essentially practical revolution, not a
mere scientific, speculative reform. Its prominent aim was
to change the moral state, to govern the life of men; and not
only that of particular men, but of whole nations, of the entire
human race.

This was a prodigious innovation. The Greek philosophy,
at least since the period when its history becomes clear and
certain, was essentially scientific, was applied far more to the
research of truth than to the reformation and direction of
manners. There were only two of its schools which took a

somewhat different direction. It entered into the formal plan of the stoics, and of the new Platonists, to exercise a moral influence, to regulate the conduct, as well as to enlighten the understanding; but their ambition in this respect was limited to a small number of disciples—to a sort of intellectual aristocracy.

It was, on the contrary, the special and characteristic design of Christianity to effect a moral reformation, a universal reformation—to govern throughout the world, in the name of its doctrines, the will and the life of men.

As an almost inevitable consequence, among the moral facts which constitute our nature, the chiefs of the Christian society would apply themselves especially to give prominence to those which are more peculiarly calculated to exercise a reforming influence, to bring about with greater promptitude practical effects. Towards these would the attention of the great bishops, of the fathers of the church, be drawn; for from them they derived the means of impelling Christianity onward in its career, and of accomplishing their own mission.

Again, the fulcrum of the moral Christian reformation was religion; it was religious ideas, the relations of man with the Divinity, of the present with the future life, that constituted her force. Her chiefs accordingly would, among moral facts, prefer and favour those whose tendency is religious, which belong to the religious part of our nature, and are, so to speak, placed on the limits of present duties, and of future hopes, of morality and of religion.

The wants of Christianity, and its means of action for effecting moral reform, and governing men, varied necessarily with time and place: it had to address itself in the human soul now to one fact, now to another; to-day, to one condition of things—to-morrow, to another. It is evident, for instance, that at various times, from the first to the fifth century, the task of the chiefs of the religious society was not uniformly the same, and could not be accomplished by the same means. The predominant fact of the first century was the struggle against paganism—the necessary efforts to overthrow an order of things odious to the state of men's souls—the work, in a word, of revolution, of war. There was incessant necessity for appealing to the spirit of liberty, of examination, to the energetic display of the will; this was the moral fact which Christian society of this period invoked and displayed constantly, on all occasions.

In the fifth century, things were in a different situation. The war was at an end, or nearly so—the victory achieved. The Christian leaders had now to regulate the religious society, to promulgate its articles of faith, to order its discipline, to constitute it, in a word, on the ruins of that pagan world over which it had triumphed. These vicissitudes are to be met with in all great moral revolutions. I need not give you further instances of it. You perceive that at this period it was no longer the spirit of liberty which it was necessary constantly to invoke. That which was now to be cultivated in its turn, was a disposition in the people favourable to the establishment of rule, of order; to the exercise of power.

Apply these considerations to the natural and moral facts which I have pointed out as the sources of the Pelagian controversy, and you will easily distinguish those whose development the chiefs of the church were more especially called upon to promote in the fifth century.

There was another cause which modified the point of view under which they considered our moral nature. The facts which relate to human liberty, and the problems which arise out of those facts, are not isolated facts or isolated problems; they are closely connected with other facts, with other problems still more general and complex; for instance, with the question of the origin of good and evil, with the question of the general destiny of man, and its essential relations with the designs of God as to the world. Now, upon these higher questions, there already existed in the church determinate doctrines, fixed propositions, accepted solutions; so that when new questions arose, the chiefs of the religious society had to adapt their ideas to the general ideas, to the established opinions. Hence for them this complicated situation: certain facts, certain moral problems attracted their attention; they might have examined and judged them as philosophers, with all the freedom of their minds, apart from all external considerations, from all but the scientific point of view; but then they were invested with an official power; they were called upon to govern their people, to regulate their actions, and to direct their will. Hence a practical political necessity, which weighed down upon the philosophic operation and turned it aside. Nor was this all; philosophers and politicians, they were at the same time compelled to the functions of pure logicians, to conform implicitly on all occasions to the consequences of certain principles, of certain immutable doctrines. They thus, as it were, played three parts at once, underwent at once three yokes; they had to consult at one and the same time the nature of things, practical necessity, and hope. Whenever a new question arose, whenever they were called upon to take cognizance of moral facts to which they had not as yet applied particular attention, they had to think and to act in this triple character, to fulfil this triple mission.

This, however, was not, in the religious society, the position of all its members; there were many Christians who did not regard themselves as called upon, on the one hand, to direct the moral government of the church, nor as bound, on the other, to follow out, through all its consequences, its system of doctrines. Among the numbers so situated, there could not fail to arise men who assumed the right of observing and of acquiring for themselves such or such moral facts, without taking much heed to their practical influences, or to their place in, and connexion with, a general system; men with minds less capacious, less powerful than those of the great chiefs of the church, but who, having fuller career in a less crowded field, imposing upon themselves a simpler and more easy task, might very well arrive at more precise and definite knowledge upon particular points. Thus arose the heresiarchs.

Thus arose Pelagianism. You are by this time, I hope, acquainted with the great preliminary, and, as it were, external circumstances which influenced its destiny; you have before you: 1, the principal natural facts upon which the dispute turned; 2, the questions which naturally arose out of those facts; 3, the special point of view under which these facts and these questions were considered in the fifth century by the leaders of the religious society, and by the active and investigating minds which spring up in its bosom. Thus possessed of the guiding thread, the illuminating torch, we may now advantageously proceed to the history of the Pelagian controversy itself.

The controversy arose early in the fifth century. The question of free will, and of the action of God upon the human soul, had, indeed, already occupied the attention of the Christians, as is attested by the letters of St. Paul, and by many other monuments; but the facts brought forward had been either accepted or rejected, as the case might be, almost without discussion. Towards the close of the fourth century, men began to examine them more closely; and some of the chiefs of the church already began to entertain some uneasiness on the subject. "We must not," says St. Augustin himself, " we must not discourse much of grace to men who are not yet Christians, or thoroughly confirmed Christians; for it is a knotty question, and one which may give the faith much trouble."

About the year 405, a British monk, Pelagius (this is the name given him by the Greek and Latin writers; his real name, it appears, was Morgan), was residing at Rome. There has been infinite discussion as to his origin, his moral character, his capacity, his learning; and, under these various heads, much abuse has been lavished upon him; but this abuse would appear to be unfounded, for, judging from the most authoritative testimony, from that of St. Augustin himself, Pelagius was a man of good birth, of excellent education, of pure life. A resident, as I have said, at Rome, and now a man of mature age, without laying down any distinct doctrines, without having written any book on the subject, Pelagius began, about the year I have mentioned, 405, to talk much about free will, to insist urgently upon this moral fact, to expound it. There is no indication that he attacked any person about the matter, or that he sought controversy; he appears to have acted simply upon the belief that human liberty was not held in sufficient account, had not its due share in the religious doctrines of the period.

These ideas excited no trouble in Rome, scarcely any debate. Pelagius spoke freely; they listened to him quietly. His principal disciple was Celestius, like him a monk, or so it is thought at least, but younger, more confident, of a more daring spirit, and more determined to prosecute the consequences of his opinions to the end.

In 411, Pelagius and Celestius are no longer at Rome; we find them in Africa, at Hippo and at Carthage. In the latter town, Celestius put forth his ideas: a controversy was immediately begun between him and the deacon Paulinus, who accused him of heresy before the bishop. In 412 a council was assembled; Celestius appeared there, and vigorously defended himself; he was excommunicated, and, after having in vain essayed an appeal to the bishop of Rome, passed into Asia, whither Pelagius, it seems, had preceded him.

Their doctrines spread; they found in the islands of the Mediterranean, among others in Sicily and at Rhodes, a favourable reception; they sent to Saint Augustin a small work of Celestius, entitled *Definitiones,* which many people were eager to read. Hilary, a Gaul, wrote to him about it with great uneasiness. The bishop of Hippo began to be alarmed; he saw in these new ideas error and peril.

At first, among the facts relative to the moral activity of man, that of free will was almost the only one with which Pelagius and Celestius seemed to be occupied. Saint Augustin was of the same belief as they, and had more than once proclaimed it; but other facts, in his opinion, ought to occupy a place by the side of this one; for example, the insufficiency of the human will, the necessity for exterior aid, and the moral changes which happen in the soul, without her being able to claim them. Pelagius and Celestius seemed to count these nothing: this was the first cause of the contest between them and the bishop of Hippo, whose greater mind considered moral nature under a greater number of aspects.

Besides, Pelagius, by the almost exclusive importance which he gave to free-will, weakened the religious side of the Christian doctrine, and strengthened, if I may use the expression, the human side. Liberty is the fact of man; he appears there alone. In the insufficiency of the human will, on the contrary, and in the moral changes which it does not claim, there is a place for Divine intervention. Now, the reforming power of the church was essentially religious; it could not but lose, under the practical point of view, from a theory which placed in the first rank a fact with which religion had nothing to do, and left in the shade those in which its influence found occasion for exercise.

Saint Augustin was the chief of the doctors of the church, called upon more than any other to maintain the general system of her doctrines. Now, the ideas of Pelagius and of Celestius seemed to him in contradiction with some of the fundamental points of the Christian faith, especially with the doctrine of original sin and of redemption. He attacked them, therefore, in a triple relation: as a philosopher, because their knowledge of human nature was, in his eyes, narrow and incomplete; as a practical reformer, and charged with the government of the church, because, according to him, they weakened his most efficacious means of reformation and government; as a logician, because their ideas did not exactly agree with the consequences deduced from the essential principles of the faith.

You see, from that time, what a serious aspect the quarrel took: everything was engaged in it, philosophy, politics, and religion, the opinions of Saint Augustin and his business, his self-love and his duty. He entirely abandoned himself to it, publishing treatises, writing letters, collecting information, which came to him from all parts, prodigal of refutations, and of counsels, and carrying into all his writings, all his proceedings, that mixture of passion and mildness, of authority and of sympathy, extent of mind and logical rigour, which gave him so rare a power.

Pelagius and Celestius, on their side, did not remain inactive; they had found powerful friends in the east. If Saint Jerome fulminated against them at Bethlehem, John, bishop of Jerusalem, zealously protected them: he convoked, on their account, an assembly of the priests of his church. Orosius, the Spaniard, a disciple of Saint Augustin, and who happened to be in Palestine, repaired thither, and stated all that had passed in Africa upon the subject of Pelagius, as well as the errors of which he was accused. On the recommendation of bishop John, Pelagius was called; they asked him if he really taught what Augustin had refuted. "What is Augustin to me?" answered he. Many present were shocked. Augustin was then the most celebrated and most respected doctor of the church. They desired to expel Pelagius, and even to excommunicate him; but John turned aside the blow, caused Pelagius to be seated, and interrogated him, saying, "It is I who am Augustin here; it is me that thou shalt answer." Pelagius spoke Greek, his accuser Orosius spoke only Latin; the members of the assembly did not understand him; they separated without deciding anything.

A short time afterwards, in the month of December, 415, a council was held in Palestine, at Diospolis, the ancient Lydda, composed of fourteen bishops, and under the presidency of Eulogius, bishop of Cæsaria. Two Gaulish bishops, exiles from their sees, Heros, bishop of Arles, and Lazarus, bishop of Aix, had addressed to him a new accusation against Pelagius. They were not present at the council, alleging illness, and probably informed that he was little favourable to them. Pelagius appeared there, still protected by the bishop of Jerusalem: they interrogated him concerning his opinions; he explained them, modified them, adopted all that the council presented to him as the true doctrine of the church, recounted what he had already suffered, spoke of his relations with many holy bishops, with Augustin himself, who, two years previously, had written him a letter intended to contest some of his ideas, but full of benevolence and mildness. The accusation of Heros and of Lazarus was read, but only in Latin, and by the interposition of an interpreter. The council declared itself satisfied; Pelagius was acquitted and declared orthodox.

The report of this decision soon arrived in Africa, from Africa into Europe, from city to city. As soon as Saint Augustin was informed of the results of the council of Diospolis, although he had not yet received its acts, he put everything in motion to resist their effects.

About the same time an incident occurred in Palestine which threw a gloomy hue over the cause of Pelagius. He remained at Jerusalem, and there had professed his ideas with a greater degree of assurance. A violent commotion broke out at Bethlehem against Saint Jerome and the monasteries which were formed near him: serious excesses were committed, houses were pillaged, burnt, a deacon killed; and Jerome was obliged to seek safety in a tower. The Pelagians, it is said, were the authors of these disorders: nothing proves this, and I am rather inclined to doubt it; still there was room for suspicion; it was generally believed, and a great clamour arose; Saint Jerome wrote to the bishop of Rome, Innocent I., about it and Pelagianism was seriously compromised.

Two solemn councils sat this year (416) in Africa, at Carthage and at Milevum; sixty-eight bishops were present at the one, sixty-one at the other. Pelagius and his doctrines were there formally condemned; the two assemblies informed the pope of their decision, and St. Augustin wrote to him privately, with four other bishops, giving him a more detailed account of the whole affair, and induced him to examine Pelagius in order to proclaim truth and anathematise error.

On the 27th January, 417, Innocent answered the two councils, to the five bishops, and condemned the doctrines of Pelagius.

He did not deem himself beaten; two months afterwards, Innocent died; Zosimus succeeded him; Celestius returned to Rome; he obtained from the new pope a new examination, at which he probably explained his opinion, as Pelagius had at Diospolis; and on the 21st September, 417, Zosimus informed the bishops of Africa, by three letters, that he had scrupulously employed himself in this affair; that he had heard Celestius himself, at a meeting of priests held in the church of Saint Clement; that Pelagius had written to him to justify himself; that he was satisfied with their explanations, and had reinstated them in the communion of the church.

Hardly had these letters arrived in Africa, when a new council met at Carthage (in May, 418); two hundred and three bishops[1] were present at it; in eight express canons it condemned the doctrines of Pelagius, and addressed itself to the emperor Honorius in order to obtain from him, against the heretics, measures which might place the church under shelter from peril.

From 418 to 421, appeared many edicts and letters of the emperors Honorius, Theodosius II., and Constantius, which banished Pelagius, Celestius, and their partisans, from Rome, and all towns where they should attempt to propagate their fatal errors.

Pope Zosimus did not long resist the authority of the councils and of the emperors; he convoked a new assembly, in order to hear Celestius again; but Celestius had quitted Rome, and Zosimus wrote to the bishops of Africa that he had condemned the Pelagians.

---

[1] According to others, two hundred and fourteen.

'The quarrel continued yet some time; eighteen bishops of Italy refused to subscribe to the condemnation of Pelagius; they were deprived of their sees, and banished into the east. The triple decision of the council, the pope, and the emperor, gave a death-blow to this cause. After the year 418, we discover, in history, no trace of Pelagius. The name of Celestius is sometimes met with until the year 427; it then disappears. These two men once off the scene, their school rapidly declined. The opinion of Saint Augustin, adopted by the councils, by the popes, by the civil authority, became the general doctrine of the church. But the victory had yet to cost her some struggles; Pelagianism dying, left an heir; the semi-Pelagians engaged in the struggle which the Pelagians could not maintain.

In the south of Gaul, in the heart of the monasteries of Saint Lerins and of Saint Victor, where boldness of thought then took refuge, it appeared to some men, among others to Cassienus, the monk of whom I have already spoken, that the fault of Pelagius was in being too exclusive, and not holding sufficient account of all the facts relative to human liberty, and to its relation with the Divine power. The insufficiency of the human will, for example, the necessity for exterior relief, the moral revolutions which operate in the soul, and are not its work, were, he felt, real, important facts, that should neither be disputed nor even neglected. Cassienus admitted them fully, loudly, thus giving to the doctrine of free-will something of the religious character which Pelagius and Celestius had so much weakened. But, at the same time, he disputed, more or less openly, many of the ideas of Saint Augustin; among others, his explanation of the moral reformation and progressive sanctification of man. Saint Augustin attributed them to the direct, immediate, special action of God upon the soul, to grace, properly so called, a grace to which man had not title of himself, and which proceeded from absolutely gratuitous gift, from the free choice of the Divinity.

Cassienus allowed more efficacy to the merits of man himself, and maintained that his moral amelioration was partly the work of his own will, which drew upon him divine support, and produced, by a natural concatenation, although often unseen, the internal changes by which the progress of sanctification made itself known.

c c

Such, between the semi-Pelagians and their redoubtable
adversary, was the principal subject of controversy: it commenced about the year 428, upon letters from Prosper of
Aquitaine and from Hilary, who had hastened to inform Saint
Augustin that Pelagianism was again rising under a new
form.   The bishop of Hippo immediately wrote a treatise
entitled: *De Prædestinatione Sanctorum et de dono perseve-
rantiæ.*   Prosper published his poem *Against Ingrates;* and
the war of pamphlets and letters regained all its activity.

Saint Augustin died in 430; Saint Prosper and Hilary
alone remained charged with prosecuting his work.   They
went to Rome, and had the semi-Pelagians condemned by
pope Celestin.   However modified this doctrine was, it was
but little favourable in the church; it reproduced a heresy
already vanquished; it weakened, although to a less degree,
the religious influence of morality and of government; it was
in discord with the general course of ideas, which tended to
give the greater share to the Divine intervention on every
occasion; it would have fallen almost without resistance, if a
directly contrary doctrine, that of the predestinarians, had not
appeared and lent it a few moments' power and credit.

From the writings of Saint Augustin upon the impotence
of human will, the nullity of its merits, and the perfectly
free and gratuitous nature of Divine grace, some refractory
logicians deduced the predestination of all men, and the irre-
vocability of the decrees of God as to the eternal lot of everyone.
The first manifestations of this doctrine in the fifth century are
obscure and doubtful; but from the time that it appeared, it
shocked the good sense and moral equity of most Christians.
Accordingly, the semi-Pelagians took up the combat, and
presented their ideas as the natural counterpoise of such
an error.   Such was especially the characteristic which was
laboured to be impressed upon semi-Pelagianism, about the
year 445, by Faustus, bishop of Riez, whom I have already
named, and of whom, at a later period, I shall speak more
particularly; he presented himself as a kind of mediator
between the Pelagians and the predestinarians.   "It is necessary," said he, "in the question of the grace of God and the
obedience of man, to keep to the middle path, and incline
neither to the right nor to the left."   According to him,
Pelagius and Saint Augustin were both of them too exclusive:

one allowed too much to human liberty and not enough to the action of God; the other was too forgetful of human liberty. This species of compromise at first obtained much favour in the Gaulish church; two councils met, one at Arles, in 472, the other at Lyons, in 473, formally condemned the predestina rians, and charged Faustus to publish a treatise which he had written against them, entitled, *Of Grace and of the Liberty of the Human Will*, even ordering him to add some further developments. This, however, was but a day's respite for semi-Pelagianism, a glimmer of fortune; it was not long in again falling into discredit.

While still living, Saint Augustin had been accused of advocating the doctrine of predestination, the total abolition of free-will, and he had energetically defended himself from it. He deceived himself, I think, as a logician, in denying a consequence which inevitably resulted from his ideas, on the one hand, concerning the impotence and corruption of the human will—on the other, concerning the nature of the Divine intervention and fore-knowledge.

But the superiority of Saint Augustin's mind saved him, on this occasion, from the errors into which logic had nearly brought it, and he was inconsistent precisely because of his lofty reason. Allow me to dwell a moment on this moral fact, which alone explains the contradictions of so many fine geniuses: I shall take an example near to us all, and one of the most striking. Most of you, of course, have read the *Contrat Social* of Rousseau; the sovereignty of number, of the numerical majority is, as you know, the fundamental principle of the work, and Rousseau, for a long time, follows out the consequences of it with inflexible rigour; a time arrives, however, when he abandons them, and abandons them with great effect; he wishes to give his fundamental laws, his constitution, to the rising society; his high intellect warned him that such a work could not proceed from universal suffrage, from the numerical majority, from the multitude: " A God," said he, " must give laws to men." .... It is not magistracy, it is not sovereignty .... It is a particular and superior function, which has nothing in common with the human empire.[1] And hereupon he sets up a sole legislator, a sage; thus violating his

---

[1] *Contrat Social*, b. ii. ch. vii.

principle of the sovereignty of number, in order to turn to an
entirely different principle, to the sovereignty of intellect, to
the right of superior reason.

The *Contrat Social*, and almost all the works of Rousseau,
abound in similar contradictions, and they are, perhaps, the
clearest proof of the great mind of the author.

It was by an inconsistency of the same kind that Saint
Augustin resolutely repelled the predestination which had been
imputed to him. Others, afterwards, acute dialecticians,
unhesitatingly went on to this doctrine and settled to it:
for him, when he perceived it, enlightened by his genius,
he turned aside, and without entirely retracing his steps,
took flight in another direction, in absolutely refusing to
abolish liberty. The church acted like Saint Augustin; it
had adopted his doctrines concerning grace, and on this score
condemned the Pelagians and semi-Pelagians; she likewise
condemned the predestinarians, thus taking from Cassienus and
Faustus, and from their disciples, the pretext by favour of
which they had somewhat regained the ascendant. Semi-
Pelagianism from that time did nothing but decline; Saint
Cesarius, bishop of Arles, at the commencement of the sixth
century, again declared war against it, as Saint Augustin and
Saint Prosper had done: in 529, the councils of Orange and
Valencia condemned it; in 330, pope Boniface II., in his turn,
struck it with a sentence of anathema, and it soon ceased, for
a long time, at least, to agitate minds. Predestination experienced the same fate.

None of these doctrines gave rise to a sect, properly so called:
they were not separated from the church, nor did they constitute a distinct religious society; they had no organization, no
worship: they were mere opinions debated between men of mind;
more or less accredited, more or less contrary to the official doctrine of the church, but which never threatened her with a
schism. Accordingly, of their appearance, and of the debates
which they excited, there only remained certain tendencies,
certain intellectual dispositions, not sects nor veritable schools.
We meet at all epochs in the course of European civilization,
1st, With minds preoccupied especially with what there is of
humanity in our moral activity, with the fact of liberty, and
which thus attach themselves to the Pelagians. 2nd, With minds
more especially struck with the power of God over man, with

Divine intervention in human activity, and inclined to make human liberty vanish under the hand of God; these hold with the predestinarians. 3rd, Between those two tendencies was placed the general doctrine of the church, which strove to take into account all natural facts, human liberty and Divine intervention; denies that God effects all in man, that man can do all without the assistance of God, and thus establishes itself, perhaps with more of reason than of scientific consistency, in the regions of good sense, the true country of the human mind, which always returns there, after having strayed in all directions. (*Post longos errores.*)

SIXTH LECTURE.

Object of the lecture—General character of the literature of the middle ages—Of the transition from pagan philosophy to Christian theology—Of the question of the nature of the soul in the Christian church—The ancient priests for the most part pronounced in favour of the system of materialism—Efforts to escape from it—Analogous march of ideas in pagan philosophy—Commencement of the system of spirituality—Saint Augustin, Nemesius, Mamertius Claudienus—Faustus, bishop of Riez—His arguments for the materiality of the soul—Mamertius Claudienus answers him—Importance of Mamertius Claudienus in Gaul—Analysis of, and quotations from his treatise on the nature of the soul—The dialogue of Evagrius between Zacheus the Christian and Apollonius the philosopher—Of the effects of the invasion of the barbarians upon the moral state of Gaul.

BETWEEN the question which occupied us in the last lecture, and that with which we shall now occupy ourselves, the difference is very great. Pelagianism was not only a question, but also an event; it gave rise to parties, interests, passions; it put in movement councils, emperors; it influenced the fate of many men. The question of the nature of the soul produced nothing of the kind; it was carried on between a few able men in a corner of the empire. In the last lecture, I had many facts to recount; at present I have to speak of books and of arguments.

I pray you to mark the course of our studies. We commenced by examining the social state, the external and public facts; we then passed to the moral state of Gaul; we sought it first in general facts, in the entirety of society; then in a great religious debate, in a doctrine, an active powerful doctrine, which became an event; we will now study it in a simple philosophical discussion. We shall thus penetrate more and more into the interior of men's minds; we first con

sidered facts, then ideas mingled with facts, and subject to
their influences; we will now consider ideas by themselves.

Before entering upon the question, permit me to say a few
words upon the general character of the literary writers of
this period and of the middle ages in general.

If you compare, on the one hand, ancient literature, Greek
and Roman literature, and on the other hand, modern literature, especially so called, with that of the middle ages, the
principal points. which, as I think, will strike you, will be the
following:

In ancient literature, the form of the works, the art of their
composition, and the language, are admirable; even when its
materials are poor, the ideas false or confused, the workmanship is so skilful, that it cannot fail to please; manifesting in
the author, a mind at once natural and refined, whose inward
development far surpasses its acquired knowledge, which has
an exquisite appreciation of the beautiful, and a peculiar aptitude for reproducing it.

In modern literature, since the sixteenth century for instance, the form is very often imperfect; there is frequently a
deficiency at once of nature and of art, but the groundwork is
in general sound; we meet with less and less of gross ignorance, of wanderings from the question, of confusion; method,
common sense, in a word, artistic merit, is the prominent
feature; if the mind is not always satisfied, it is at least very
seldom shocked; the spectacle is not invariably a fine one, but
chaos has disappeared.

The intellectual labours of the middle ages present a different aspect; as a general proposition, they are entirely deficient in artistic merit; the form is rude, fantastic; they are
full of divergences, of incoherent ideas; they manifest a state
of mind, crude, uncultivated, alike without interior development or acquired knowledge, and accordingly neither our
reason nor our taste is satisfied. This is the reason why they
have been forgotten, why Greek and Roman literature have
survived, and will eternally survive the people among whom
it respectively arose. Yet under this so imperfect form,
amidst this so strange medley of ideas and of facts, ill understood and ill combined, the books of the middle ages are very
remarkable monuments of the activity and wealth of the
human mind, we meet in them with many vigorous and

original conceptions; important questions are often sounded to their lowest depths, flashes of philosophical truth, of literary beauty, glance at every moment from the darkness; the mineral in this mine is altogether in a rough state, but the metal is plentiful, and well merits our research.

The writings of the fifth and sixth centuries, moreover have a character and an interest peculiar to themselves. It was the period at which ancient philosophy was giving way before modern theology, in which the one was becoming transformed into the other; in which certain systems became dogmas, certain schools sects. These periods of transition are of great importance, are, perhaps, in the historical point of view, the most instructive of all. It is at these periods only that we are able to view simultaneously and face to face certain facts, certain states of man and of the world, which are generally only to be seen by themselves, and separated by whole centuries; they are the only periods, therefore, in which it is easy for us to compare these facts and these states, to explain them, connect them together. The human mind is but too prone to walk in but one single path, to see things but under one partial, narrow, exclusive aspect, to place itself in prison; it is, therefore a very fortunate circumstance for it, when it is compelled, by the very nature of the spectacle placed before its eyes, to look around it in all directions, to embrace a vast horizon, to contemplate a great number of different objects, to study the great problems of the world under all their aspects, and in all their various solutions. It is more especially in the south of Gaul that this character of the fifth century manifests itself. You have seen the activity which prevailed in the religious society, and, among others, in the monasteries of Lerins and Saint-Victor, the focus of so many daring opinions. The whole of this movement of mind did not emanate from Christianity; it was in the same districts, in the Lyonnese, the Viennese, the Narbonnese, Aquitaine, that ancient civilization in its decline concentrated itself. It was here that it still exhibited most life. Spain, Italy herself, were at this period far less active than Gaul, far less rich in literature and in literary men. We must, perhaps, attribute this result to the development which had been assumed in these provinces by Greek civilization, and to the prolonged influence there of its philosophy. In all the great towns of southern Gaul, at Marseilles, at Arles, at Aix, at Vienne, at Lyons itself, the Greek language was understood and spoken. There were regular Greek exercises under Caligula, in the Athanacum, an establishment at Lyons, especially devoted to that purpose; and in the beginning of the sixth century, when Cesarius, bishop of Arles, required the faithful to sing with the clergy previous to the sermon, many of the people sang in Greek. We find among the distinguished Gauls of this period philosophers of all the Greek schools; some are mentionned as Pythagoreans, others as Platonists, others as Epicureans, others as Stoics.

The Gaulish writings of the fourth and fifth century, among others that which I am about to introduce to you, the treatise of Mamertius Claudienus, *On the Nature of the Soul,* quote passages from philosophers whose names even we do not meet with elsewhere. In short, there is every evidence that, in the philosophical as in the religious point of view, Greek and Roman as well as Christian Gaul was at this period the most animated, the most living portion of the Empire; of the western empire at all events. It is here, accordingly, that the transition from pagan philosophy to Christian theology, from the ancient world to the modern, is most strongly marked, most clearly observable.

In this movement of mind, it was not likely that the question of the nature of the soul should remain long untouched. From the first century upwards, we find it the subject of discussion amongst the doctors of the church, the majority of whom adopted the material hypothesis; passages to this effect are abundant. I will select two or three, which leave no doubt as to the prevalent opinion on the subject. Tertullian says expressly:

" The corporeality of the soul is perfectly manifest to all who read the gospel. The soul of a man is there represented suffering its punishment in hell; it is placed in the midst of the flame; it feels a tormenting agony in the tongue, and it implores, from the hand of a soul in bliss, a drop of water to cool it. . . There can be nothing of all this without the presence of the body. The incorporeal being is free from every description of restraint, from all pain or from all pleasure, for it is in the body alone that man is punished or rewarded.[1]

---

[1] *De Animá,* 5, 7.

"Who does not see," asks Arnobius, "that that which is ethereal, immortal, cannot feel pain."[1]

"We conceive," says St. John of Damascus, "we conceive of incorporeal and invisible beings, in two ways: by essence and by grace; the former incorporeal by nature, the latter only relatively, and in comparison with the grossness of matter. Thus, God is incorporeal by nature ; as to angels, devils, and men's souls, we only call them incorporeal by grace, and comparatively with the grossness of matter."[2]

I might multiply *ad infinitum* similar quotations, all proving that in the first ages of our era, the materiality of the soul was not only the admitted, but that it was the dominant opinion.

After a while, the church manifested a tendency to quit this opinion. We find the fathers placing before themselves every argument in favour of immateriality. The sentence I have just quoted from St. John of Damascus itself gives a proof of this; you find him laying down a certain distinction between material beings. The philosophical fathers entered upon the same path, and advanced in it with more rapid strides. Origen, for instance, is so astonished at the idea of a material soul having a conception of immaterial things, and arriving at a true knowledge, that he concludes it to possess a certain relative immortality, that is to say, that material in relation with God, the only being truly spiritual; it is not so in relation with earthly things, with visible and sensual bodies.[3]

Such was the course of ideas in the heart of pagan philosophy ; in its first essays dominated both the belief in the immateriality of the soul, and at the same time a certain progressive effort to conceive the soul under a more elevated, a more pure aspect. Some made of it a vapour, a breath; others declared it a fire; all wished to purify, to refine, to spiritualize matter, in the hope of arriving at the end to which they aspired. The same desire, the same tendency existed in the Christian church; still the idea of the materiality of the soul was more general among the Christian doctors from the first to the fifth century, than among the

<hr/>

[1] *Adversus Gentes*, ii.   [2] *De Orthodoxa fide*, ii. 3, 12.
[3] Origen, *de Principiis*, l. i. c. 1. l. 2. c. 2.

pagan philosophers of the same period. It was against the pagan philosophers, and in the name of the religious interest, that certain fathers maintained this doctrine; they wished that the soul should be material in order that it might be recompensed or punished, in order that in passing to another life it might find itself in a state analogous to that in which it had been upon earth; in fine, in order that it should not forget how inferior it is to God, and never be tempted to compare itself with Him.

At the end of the fourth century, a kind of revolution concerning this point was wrought in the breast of the church; the doctrine of the immateriality of the soul, of the original and essential difference of the two substances, appeared there, if not for the first time, at least far more positively, with far more precision than hitherto. It was professed and maintained—first, in Africa, by Saint Augustin in his treatise *de quantitate Animæ;* secondly, in Asia, by Nemesius, bishop of Emessa, who wrote a very remarkable work *upon the nature of man* (περιφύσεος άνθρώπου); thirdly, in Gaul, by Mamertius Claudienus, *de naturâ Animæ.* Confined to the history of Gaulish civilization, this last is the only one with which we have to occupy ourselves.

This is the occasion upon which it was written. A man whom you already know, Faustus, bishop of Riez, exercised a great influence in the Gaulish church; born a Breton, like Pelagius, he came—it is not known why—into the south of Gaul. He became a monk in the abbey of Lerins, and in 433 was made abbot of it. He instituted a great school, where he received the children of rich parents, and brought them up, teaching them all the learning of the age. He often conversed with his monks upon philosophical questions, and, it appears, was remarkable for his talent of improvisation. About 462 he became bishop of Riez. I have spoken of the part taken by him in the semi-Pelagian heresy, and of his book against the predestinarians. He was of an active, independent spirit, rather intermeddling, and always eager to mix in all the quarrels which arose. It is not known what called his attention to the nature of the soul: he treated of it at length in a long philosophical letter addressed to a bishop, and in which many other questions are debated; he declares himself for materiality, and thus sums up his principal arguments:

1　Invisible things are of one kind, incorporeal things of another.

2. Everything created is matter, tangible by the Creator; is corporeal.

3. The soul occupies a place. 1. It is enclosed in a body. 2. It is not to be found wherever its thought is. 3. At all events, it is to be found only where its thought is. 4. It is distinct from its thoughts, which vary, which pass on, while it is permanent and always the same; 5. It quits the body at death, and re-enters it by the resurrection; witness Lazarus; 6. The distinction of hell and heaven, of eternal punishments and rewards, proves that even after death souls occupy a place, and are corporeal.

4. God alone is incorporeal, because he alone is intangible and omnipresent.[1]

These propositions, laid down in so unhesitating and distinct a manner, are not elaborated to any extent; and such details as the author does enter into are taken in general from the theology, narratives, and authority of the holy scriptures.

The letter of Faustus, which, circulated anonymously, occasioned considerable excitement; Mamertius Claudienus, brother of St. Mamertius, bishop of Vienne, and himself a priest in that diocese, answered it in his treatise *On the Nature of the Soul*, a work of far higher importance than the one which it refuted. Mamertius Claudienus was in his day the most learned, the most eminent philosopher of southern Gaul; to give you an idea of his reputation, I will read a letter written shortly after the philosopher's death, to his nephew Petreius, by Sidonius Apollinarius, a letter, I may observe, stamped with all the ordinary characteristics of this writer, exhibiting all the puerile elaboration of the professed *bel esprit*, with here and there just perceptions, and curious facts.

" SIDONIUS TO HIS DEAR PETREIUS.[2]　HEALTH.[3]

" I am overwhelmed with affliction at the loss which our age has sustained in the recent loss of your uncle Claudienus:

---

[1] I have adopted the text of Faustus, inserted in the edition of the treatise on the Nature of the Soul, by Claudienus, published, with notes, by Andrew Schoff and Gaspard Barth, at Zwickau, in 1665

[2] Son of the sister of Mamertius Claudienus.　　　[3] Lib. iv. ep ii

we shall never see his like again. He was full of wisdom and
judgment, learned, eloquent, ingenious; the most intellectual
man of his period, of his country. He remained a philosopher,
without giving offence to religion; and though he did not indulge in the fancy of letting his hair and his beard grow,
though he laughed at the long cloak and stick of the philosophers, though he sometimes even warmly reprehended these
fantastic appendages, it was only in such matters of externals
and in faith, that he separated from his friends the Platonists.
God of Heaven! what happiness was ours whenever we repaired to him for his counsel. How readily would he give
himself wholly to us, without an instant's hesitation, without
a word, a glance of anger or disdain, ever holding it his
highest pleasure to open the treasures of his learning to those
who came to him for the solution of some, by all others insoluble, question! Then, when all of us were seated around
him, he would direct all to be silent, but him to whom—and
it was ever a choice which we ourselves should have made—
he accorded the privilege of stating the proposition; the
question thus laid before him, he would display the wealth of
his learning deliberately, point by point, in perfect order,
without the least artifice of gesture, or the slightest flourish of
language. When he had concluded his address, we stated
our objections syllogistically; he never failed to refute at
once any propositions of ours which were not based upon
sound reason, and thus nothing was admitted without undergoing mature examination, without being thoroughly demonstrated. But that which inspired us with still higher respect,
was that he supported, without the least ill humour, the dull
obstinacy of some amongst us, imputing it to an excusable
motive, we all the while admiring his patience, though unable to imitate it. No one could fear to seek the counsel, in
difficult cases, of a man who rejected no discussion, and
refused to answer no question, even on the part of the most
foolish and ignorant persons. Thus much for his learning:
enough concerning his studies and his science; but who can
worthily and suitably praise the other virtues of that man,
who, always remembering the weaknesses of humanity,
assisted the priests with his work, the people with his discourses, the afflicted with his exhortations, the forsaken with
his consolations, prisoners with his gold; the hungry received

food fr<m him, the naked were clothed by him. It would, I think, be equally superfluous to say any more upon this subject. . . .

" Here is what we wished to have said at first: in honour of the ungrateful ashes, as Virgil says, that is to say, which cannot give us thanks for what we say, we have composed a sad and piteous lamentation, not without much trouble, for having dictated nothing for so long, we found unusual difficulty therein ; nevertheless, our mind, naturally indolent, was reanimated by a sorrow which desired to break into tears. This, then, is the purport of the verses:

" ' Under this turf reposes Claudienus, the pride and sorrow of his brother Mamertius, honoured like a precious stone by all the bishops. In this master flourished a triple science, that of Rome, that of Athens, and that of Christ: and in the vigour of his age, a simple monk, he achieved it completely and in secret. Orator, dialectician, poet, a doctor learned in the sacred books, geometrician, musician, he excelled in unravelling the most difficult questions, he struck with the sword of words the sects which attacked the Catholic faith. Skilful at setting the psalms and singing, in front of the altars, and to the great gratitude of his brother, he taught men to sound instruments of music. He regulated, for the solemn feasts of the year, what in each case should bo read. He was a priest of the second order, and relieved his brother from the weight of the episcopacy; for his brother bore the ensigns, and he all the duty. You, therefore, reader, who afflict yourself as if nothing remained of such a man, whoever you be, cease to sprinkle your cheeks and this marble with tears; the soul and the glory cannot be buried in the tomb.'

" These are the lines I have engraved over the remains of him who was a brother to all . . . ."

It was to Sidonius that Mamertius Claudienus had dedicated his work.

It is divided into three books. The first is the only truly philosophical one; the question is there examined in itself, independently of every special fact, of all authority, and under a purely rational point of view. In the second the author invokes authorities to his aid; first that of the Greek philosophers—then, that of the Roman philosophers—lastly, the sacred writings, Saint Paul, the Evangelists, and the fathers of the church. The special object of the third book is to explain, in the system of the spirituality of the soul, certain events, certain traditions of the Christian religion; for example, the resurrection of Lazarus, the existence of the angels, the apparition of the angel Gabriel to the Virgin Mary; and to show that, so far from contradicting them, or being embarrassed by them, this system admits them and makes at least as much of them as any other.

The classification is not as rigorous as I have made it out: the ideas and arguments are often mixed; philosophical discussions appear here and there in the books which are not devoted to them; still, upon the whole, the work is not wanting in either method or precision.

I shall now place before you the summary of it, as prepared by Mamertius Claudienus himself, in ten theses or fundamental propositions, in the last chapter but one of the third book. I shall then literally translate some passages, which will enable you to understand, on one hand, with what profundity and with what force of mind the author has penetrated into the question; on the other, what absurd and fantastical conceptions could, at this epoch, be combined with the most elevated and the most just ideas:

"Since many of the things which I have asserted in this discussion," says Mamertius Claudienus, "are scattered, and might not easily be retained, I wish to bring them together, compress them, place them, so to speak, in a single point, under the mind's eyes.

"1st. God is incorporeal; the human soul is the image of God, for man was made in the image and likeness of God. Now a body cannot be the image of an incorporeal being; therefore the human soul, which is the image of God, is incorporeal.

"2nd. Everything which does not occupy a determined place is incorporeal. Now the soul is the life of the body; and, living in the body, each part lives as truly as the whole body. There is, therefore, in each part of the body, as much life as in the whole body; and the soul is that life. Thus, that which is as great in the part as in the whole, in a small space as in a large, occupies no space; therefore the soul occupies no place. That which occupies no place is not corporeal; therefore the soul is not corporeal.

"3rd. The soul reasons, and the faculty of reasoning is inherent in the substance of the soul. Now, the reason is incorporeal, occupies no position in space; therefore the soul is incorporeal.

"4th. The will of the soul is its very substance, and when the soul chooses it is all will. Now will is not a body; therefore the soul is not a body.

"5th. Even so the memory is a capacity which has nothing local; it is not widened in order to remember more of things; it is not contracted when it remembers less of things; it immaterially remembers material things. And when the soul remembers, it remembers entire; it is all recollection. Now, the recollection is not a body; therefore, the soul is not a body.

"6th. The body feels the impression of touch in the part touched; the whole soul feels the impression, not by the entire body, but in a part of the body. A sensation of this kind has nothing local; now what has nothing local is incorporeal; therefore the soul is incorporeal.

"7th. The body can neither approach nor absent itself from God; the soul does approach and does absent itself from them without changing its place; therefore the soul is not a body.

"8th. The body moves through a place, from one place to another; the soul has no similar movement; therefore the soul is not a body.

"9th. The body has length, breadth, and depth; and that which has neither length, breadth, nor depth, is not a body. The soul has nothing of the kind; therefore the soul is not a body.

"10th. There is in all bodies the right hand and the left— the upper part and the lower part, the front and the back; in the soul there is nothing of the kind; therefore the soul is incorporeal."[1]

Here are some of the principal developments in support of these propositions:

I. You say that the soul is one thing, the thought of the soul another: you ought rather to say, that the things upon which the soul thinks . . . are not the soul; but thought is nothing but the soul itself.

Book iii. chap. 14, pp. 201, 202.

" The soul, you say, is in such profound repose, that it has no thought at all. This is not true; the soul can change its thought, but not be without thought altogether.

" What do our dreams signify if not that, even when the body is fatigued and immersed in sleep, the soul ceases not to think?

" What greatly deceives you concerning the nature of the soul, is that you believe that the soul is one thing, and its faculties another. What the soul thinks is an accident, but that which thinks is the substance of the soul itself.[1]

" II. The soul sees that which is corporeal through the medium of the body; what is incorporeal it sees by itself. Without the intervention of the body, it could see nothing corporeal, coloured, or extensive; but it sees truth, and sees it with an immaterial view. If, as you pretend, the soul, corporeal itself, and confined within an external body, can see of itself a corporeal object, surely nothing can be more easy to it than to see the interior of that body in which it is confined. Well, then, do this—apply yourself to this work; direct inward this corporeal view of the soul, as you call it; tell us how the brain is disposed, where the mass of the liver is situated; where and what is the spleen . . . . what are the windings and texture of the veins, the origins of the nerves. . . . . How! you deny that you are called upon to answer concerning such things: and wherefore do you deny it? Because the soul cannot see directly and of itself corporeal things. Why can it not, then, that which is never without thinking—that is to say, without seeing? Because it cannot see corporeal objects without the medium of the corporeal view. Now, the soul which sees certain things of itself, but not corporeal things, sees, therefore, with an incorporeal view; now an incorporeal being can alone see with an incorporeal view; therefore the soul is incorporeal.[2]

" III. If the soul is a body, what then is that which the soul calls its body, if not itself. Either the soul is a body, and in that case it is wrong to say *my body*, it ought rather to say *me*, since it is itself; or if the soul is right in saying *my body*, as we suppose, it is not a body.[3]

" IV. It is not without reason that it is said that memory is

---

[1] Book i. chap. 24, p. 83.   [2] Book iii. chap. 9, pp. 187, 188.
[3] Book i. chap. 16, p. 53.

common to men and to animals; storks and swallows return to
their nest, horses to their stable; dogs recognise their master. But as the soul of animals, although they retain the
image of places, has no knowledge of its own being, they
remain confined to the recollection of corporeal objects which
they have seen by the bodily senses; and, deprived of the
mind's eye, they are incapable of seeing, not only what is
above them, but themselves.[1]

  " V. A formidable syllogism, which is thought insolvable,
is addressed to us; the soul, it is said, is where it is, and is
not where it is not. The anticipation is, that we shall be
driven to say, either that it is everywhere, or that it is nowhere : and then it will be rejoined, if it is everywhere, it is
God; if it is nowhere, it is non-existent. The soul is not
wholly in the whole world, but in the same way that God is
wholly in the whole universe, so the soul is wholly in the
whole body. God does not fill with the smallest part of himself the smallest part of the world, and with the largest the
largest; he is wholly in every part and wholly in the whole;
so the soul does not reside in parts in the various parts of the
body. It is not one part of the soul which looks forth
through the eye and another which animates the finger; the
whole soul lives in the eye and sees by the eye, the whole
soul animates the finger and feels by the finger.[2]

  " VI. The soul which feels in the body, though it feels by
visible organs, feels invisibly. The eye is one thing, seeing
another: the ears are one thing, hearing another; the nostrils
are one thing, smelling another; the mouth one thing, eating
another; the hand one thing, touching another. We distinguish by the touch what is hot and what cold, but we do
not touch the sensation of the touch, which in itself is neither
hot nor cold; the organ by which we feel is a perfectly different thing from the sensation of which we are sensible." [3]

  You will readily admit that these ideas are deficient neither
in elevation nor profundity; they would do honour to the
philosophers of any period; seldom have the nature of the
soul and its unity been investigated more closely or described
with greater precision. I might quote many other passages

---

[1] Book i. chap. 21, p. 65.   [2] Book iii. chap. 2 , p.164.
                [3] Book i. chap. 6, p. 31.

remarkable for the subtlety of perception, or energy of debate, and, at times, for a profound moral emotion, and a genuine eloquence.

I will read to you two extracts from the same book of the same man; Mamertius Claudienus is replying to the argument of Faustus, who maintains that the soul is formed of air, reasoning upon the ancient theory which regarded air, fire, earth, and water as the four essential elements of nature: " Fire," says he, " is evidently a superior element to air, as well by the place which it occupies as by its intrinsic power This is proved by the movement of the terrestrial fire, which, with an almost incomprehensible rapidity, and by its own natural impulse, reascends towards heaven as towards its own country. If this proof be not sufficient, here is another: the air is illumined by the presence of the sun, that is to say fire, and falls into darkness in its absence. And a still more powerful reason is, that air undergoes the action of fire and becomes heated, while fire does not undergo the action of air, and is never made cold by it. Air may be inclosed and retained in vases; fire never. The preeminence of fire, then, is clearly incontestable. Now, it is from fire (that is to say, from its light) that we derive the faculty of sight, a faculty common to men and to animals, and in which, indeed, certain irrational animals far surpass man in point of both strength and of delicacy. If, then, which is undeniable, sight proceeds from fire, and if the soul, as you think, is formed of air, it follows that the eye of animals is, as to its substance, superior in dignity to the soul of man."[1]

This learned confusion of material facts and of intellectual facts, this attempt to establish a sort of hierarchy of merit and of rank among the elements, in order to deduce from them philosophical consequences, are curious evidences of the infancy of science and of thought.

I will now quote, in favour of the immateriality of the soul, an argument of as little value in itself, but less fantastic in its outward appearance. " Every incorporeal being is superior, in natural dignity, to a corporeal being; every being not confined within a certain space, to a localized being; every indivisible being to a divisible being. Now, if the Creator

---

[1] Book i. chap. 9, p. 38

D D 2

sovereignly powerful and sovereignly good, has not created, as he ought to have done, a substance superior to the body, and similar to himself, it is either that he could not or would not; if he would, and could not, almightiness was wanting to him; if he could, and would not (the mere thought is a crime), it could only have been through jealousy. Now, it is impossible that the sovereign power cannot do what it wills, that sovereign goodness can be jealous. It results that he both could and would create the incorporeal being; final result, he did create it."[1]

Was I wrong in speaking just now of the strange combinations, the mixture of high truths and gross errors, of admirable views and ridiculous conceptions, which characterize the writings of this period—those of Mamertius Claudienus, I may add, present fewer of these contrasts than do those of most of his contemporaries.

You are sufficiently acquainted with this writer to appreciate his character; taken as a whole, his work is rather philosophical than theological, and yet the religious principle is manifestly predominant throughout, for the idea of God is the starting point of every discussion in it. The author does not commence by observing and describing human, special, actual facts, proceeding through them up to the Divinity: God is with him the primitive, universal, evident fact; the fundamental datum to which all things relate, and with which all things must agree; he invariably descends from God to man, deducing our own from the Divine nature. It is evidently from religion, and not from science, that he borrows this method. But this cardinal point once established, this logical plan once laid down, it is from philosophy that he draws, in general, both his ideas and his manner of expressing them; his language is of the school, not of the church; he appeals to reason, not to faith; we perceive in him, sometimes the academician, sometimes the stoic, more frequently the platonist, but always the philosopher, never the priest, though the Christian is apparent, is manifest in every page.

I have thus exhibited the fact which I indicated in the outset, the fusion of pagan philosophy with Christian theology, the metamorphosis of the one into the other. And it is

---

[1] Book i. chap. v. p. 26.

remarkable, that the reasoning applied to the establishment of the spirituality of the soul is evidently derived from the ancient philosophy rather than from Christianity, and that the author seems more especially to aim at convincing the theologians, by proving to them that the Christian faith has nothing in all this which is not perfectly reconcilable with the results derived from pure reason.

It might be thought that this transition from ancient philosophy to modern theology would be more manifest, more strongly marked in the dialogue of the Christian Zacheus and the philosopher Apollonius, by the monk Evagrius, where the two doctrines, the two societies, are directly confronted and called upon to discuss their respective merits; but the discussion is only in appearance, exists, in fact, only on the title-page. I am not acquainted with any work, with any monument, which proves more clearly the utter indifference with which the popular mind regarded paganism. The philosopher Apollonius opens the dialogue in an arrogant tone, as if about utterly to overwhelm the Christian, and to deliver over to general scorn any arguments which he may adduce.[1] " If you examine the matter with care," says he, " you will see that all other religions and all other sacred rites had rational origins; whereas, your creed is so utterly vain and irrational, that it seems to me none but a madman could entertain it."

But this arrogance is sterile: throughout the dialogue Apollonius does not advance one single argument, one solitary idea; he proves nothing, he confutes nothing; he does not open his lips except to suggest a topic to Zacheus, who, on his part, takes no notice whatever of paganism nor of the philosophy of his adversary, does not refute them, scarcely makes here and there an allusion to them, and only occupies himself relating history and describing the Christian faith so as to show forth its entirety and authority. Doubtless, the book is the work of a Christian, and the silence which he makes his philosophers preserve does not prove that philosophers were really silent. But such is by no means the character of the first debates of Christianity with the ancient philosophy,

---

[1] Dialogue of Zacheus and Apollonius, in the *Spicilegium* of D'Achery, vol. x p. 3.

when the latter was still living and powerful. Christianity
at that time condescended to notice the arguments of its adversaries; it spoke of them, it refuted them; the controversy
was a real and an animated one. In the work before us there
is no longer any controversy at all; the Christian indoctri-
nates and catechises the philosopher, and seems to consider
that this is all that can be required of him.

Nay, he even makes this a matter of concession, a favour:
discussions with pagans had by this time become a sort of
superfluity in the eyes of the Christians.

" Many persons," says Evagrius, in the preface to his book,
" think that we should despise, rather than refute, the objections advanced by the Gentiles, so vain are they, so devoid
of true wisdom; but, in my opinion, such scorn were worse
than useless. I see two advantages in instructing the Gentiles;
in the first place, we prove to all how holy and simple our
religion is; and secondly, the heathen thus instructed come
at last to believe that which, unknowing, they had despised
.... Besides, by approaching the candle to the eyes of the
blind, if they do not see its light, they at all events feel its
warmth."   This last phrase appears to me a fine one, full of
a sympathetic sentiment.

There is one thing only which appears to me remarkable
in this dialogue: it is that here the question is broadly laid
down between rationalism and the Christian revelation; not
that this subject is more really or more extensively developed
than any other: it is only in a few sentences that the idea
manifests itself, but from these it is evident that the question
was full in the minds of all controversialists, and formed, as it
were, the last intrenchment behind which philosophy defended itself. Apollonius, as you have seen, makes it an
especial charge against the Christian doctrine that it is irrational; to this Zacheus replies : " It is easy for every one to
understand and appreciate God, that is to say, if the Divine
Word is compatible with your notion of wisdom . . . for your
view is, that the sage believes nothing out of himself, that he
is never deceived, but that he of himself knows all things infallibly, not admitting that there is anything whatever either
hidden or unknown, or that anything is more possible to the
Creator than to the creature. And it is more especially against

the Christians that you make use of this mode of reasoning."[1] And elsewhere: " The understanding follows faith, and the human mind knows only through faith the higher things which come near God."[2]

It were a curious study to consider the state of rationalism at this period, the causes of its ruin, and its efforts, its various transformations in order to avert that ruin: but it is an inquiry which would carry us too far, and, besides, it was not in Gaul that the grand struggle between rationalism and Christianity took place.

The second dialogue of Evagrius, between the Christian Theophilus and the Jew Simon, is of no sort of importance; it is a mere commentary, a mere trifling controversy on a few scriptural texts.

I might mention to you, and make extracts from, a great number of other works of the same period and the same class. This, however, were unnecessary, as I have selected from among them the two most remarkable, the most characteristic, the most calculated to convey an accurate idea of the state of mind, and of its activity at this period. That activity was great, though exclusively confined within the limits of the religious society; whatever vigour and life had remained to the ancient philosophy, passed over to the service of the Christians; it was under the religious form, and in the very bosom of Christianity, that were reproduced the ideas, the schools, the whole science of the philosophers; but subject to this condition, they still occupied men's minds, and played an important part in the moral state of the new society.

It was this movement which was arrested by the invasion of the barbarians and the fall of the Roman empire: a hundred years later we do not find the slightest trace of what I have been describing to you; the discussions, the travels, the correspondence, the pamphlets, the whole intellectual activity of Gaul in the seventh century, all these had disappeared.

Was this loss of any consequence? was the movement thus put a stop to by the invasion of the barbarians an important and fruitful movement? I doubt it very much. You will perhaps remember my observations on the essentially practical character of Christianity; intellectual progress, science, especi-

[1] Page 3.   [2] Page 9.

ally so called, was not at all its aim; and although it had a connexion upon several points with the ancient philosophy—though it had been very willing to appropriate the ideas of that philosophy, and to make the most of it, it was by no means anxious for its preservation, nor to replace it by any other philosophy. To change the manners, to govern the life of men, was the predominant idea of its leaders.

Moreover, notwithstanding the freedom of mind which practically existed in the fifth century, in the religious society, the principle of liberty made no progress there. It was, on the contrary, the principle of authority, of the official domination over intellect by general and fixed rules, which sought the ascendancy. Though still powerful, intellectual liberty was on the decline; authority was rapidly taking its place; every page of the writings of this period proves the fact. It was, indeed, the almost inevitable result of the very nature of the Christian reformation; moral, rather than scientific, it proposed to itself as its leading aim to establish a law, to govern men's will; it was consequently authority that was above all things needful to it; authority in the existing state of manners was its surest, its most efficacious means of action.

Now, what the invasion of the barbarians, and the fall of the Roman empire more especially arrested, even destroyed, was intellectual movement; what remained of science, of philosophy, of the liberty of mind in the fifth century, disappeared under their blows. But the moral movement, the practical reformation of Christianity, and the official establishment of its authority over nations, were not in any way affected; perhaps even they gained instead of losing: this at least, I think, is what the history of our civilization, in proportion as we advance in its course, will allow us to conjecture.

The invasion of the barbarians, therefore, did not in any way kill what possessed life; at bottom, intellectual activity and liberty were in decay; everything leads us to believe that they would have stopped of themselves; the barbarians stopped them more rudely and sooner. That, I believe, is all that can be imputed to them.

We have now arrived at the limits to which we should confine ourselves, to the end of the picture of the Roman society in Gaul at the time when it fell: we are acquainted with it, if not completely, at least in its essential features. In order to prepare ourselves to understand the society which followed it, we have now to study the new element which mixed with it, the barbarians.   Their state before the invasion, before they came to overthrow the Roman society, and were changed under its influence, will form the subject of our next lecture.

SEVENTH LECTURE.

WE approach successively the various sources of our civilization.   We have already studied, on one side, what we call
the Roman element, the civil Roman society; on the other,
the Christian element, the religious society.   Let us now
consider the barbaric element, the German society.
   Opinions are very various concerning the importance of
this element, concerning the part and share of the Germans
in modern civilization; the prejudices of nation, of situation,
of class, have modified the idea which each has formed of it.
   The German historians, the feudal publicists, M. de Boulainvilliers, for example, have in general attributed too
extensive an influence to the barbarians; the burgher publicists, as the abbé Dubos, have, on the contrary, too much
reduced it, in order to give far too large a part to Roman
society; according to the ecclesiastics, it is to the church
·that modern civilization is the most indebted.   Sometimes
political doctrines have alone determined the opinion of the

writer; the abbé de Mably, all devoted as he was to the popular cause, and despite his antipathy for the feudal system, insists strongly upon the German origins, because he thought to find there more institutions and principles of liberty than anywhere else. I do not wish to treat at present of this question; we shall treat of it, it will be resolved as we advance in the history of French civilization. We shall see from epoch to epoch what part each of its primitive elements has there played, what each has brought and received in their combination. I shall confine myself to asserting beforehand the two results to which I believe this study will conduct us:—First, that the state of the barbaric element in modern civilization has, in general, been made a great deal too much of. Second, its true share has not been given it: too great an influence upon our society has been attributed to the Germans, to their institutions, to their manners; what they have truly exercised has not been attributed to them; we do not owe to them all that has been done in their name; we do owe to them what seems not to proceed from them.

Until this twofold result shall arise under our eyes, from the progressive development of facts, the first condition, in order to appreciate with accuracy the share of the Germanic element in our civilization, is to correctly understand what the Germans really were at the time when it commenced, when they themselves concurred in its formation; that is to say, before their invasion and their establishment on the Roman territory; when they still inhabited Germany in the third and fourth centuries. By this alone shall we be enabled to form an exact· idea of what they brought to the common work, to distinguish what facts are truly of German origin.

This study is difficult. The monuments where we may study the barbarians before the invasion are of three kinds; first, the Greek or Roman writers, who knew and described them from their first appearance in history up to this epoch; that is to say, from Polybius, about one hundred and fifty years before Christ, down to Ammianus Marcellinus, whose work stops at the year of our Lord 378. Between these two eras a crowd of historians, Livy, Cæsar, Strabo, Pomponius Mela, Pliny, Tacitus, Ptolemy, Plutarch, Florus. Pausanias,

&c., have left us information, more or less detailed, concerning the German nations; secondly, writings and documents posterior to the German invasion, but which relate or reveal anterior facts; for example, many Chronicles, the Barbaric laws, Salic, Visigoth, Burgundian, &c.; thirdly, the recollection and national traditions of the Germans themselves concerning their fate and their state in the ages anterior to the invasion, reascending up to the first origin and their most ancient history.

At the mere mention of these documents, it is evident that very various times and states are comprehended in them. The Roman and Greek writers, for example, embrace a space of five hundred years, during which Germany and her nations were presented to them in the most different points of view. Then came the first expeditions of the wandering Germans, especially that of the Teutones and the Cimbrians. Rather later, dating from Cæsar and Augustus, the Romans, in their turn, penetrated into Germany; their armies passed the Rhine and the Danube, and saw the Germans under a new aspect and in a new state. Lastly, from the third century, the Germans fell upon the Roman empire, which repelling and admitting them alternately, came to know them far more intimately, and in an entirely different situation from what they had done hitherto. Who does not perceive that, during this interval, through so many centuries and events, the barbarians and the writers who described them, the object and the picture, must have prodigiously varied?

The documents of the second class are in the same case: the barbaric laws were drawn up some time after the invasion; the most ancient portion of the law of the Visigoths belonged to the last half of the fifth century; the Salic law may have been written first under Clovis, but the digest which we have of it is of a far posterior epoch; the law of the Burgundians dates from the year 517.

They are all, therefore, in their actual form, much more modern than the barbaric society which we wish to study. There can be no doubt but that they contain many facts, that they often describe a social state anterior to the invasion; there can be no doubt but that the Germans, transported into Gaul, retained much of their ancient customs, their ancient relations. But there can also be no doubt here that, after the invasion, Germanic society was profoundly modified, and that these modifications had passed into laws; the law of the Visigoths and that of the Burgundians are much more Roman than barbarian; three fourths of the provisions concern facts which could not have arisen until after these nations were established upon Roman soil. The Salic law is more primitive, more barbaric; but still, I believe it may be proved that, in many parts—among others, in that concerning property—it is of more recent origin. Like the Roman historians, the German laws evidence very various times and states of society.

According to the documents of the third class, the national traditions of the Germans, the evidence is still more striking: the subjects of these traditions are almost all facts, so far anterior as probably to have become almost foreign to the state of these nations at the third and fourth centuries; facts which had concurred to produce this state and which may serve to explain it, but which no longer constituted it. Suppose, that, in order to study the state of the highlanders of Scotland fifty years ago, one had collected their still living and popular traditions, and had taken the facts which they express as the real elements of Scotch society in the eighteenth century: assuredly the illusion would be great and fruitful of error. It would be the same and with much greater reason, with regard to the ancient German traditions; they coincide with the primitive history of the Germans, with their origin, their religious filiation, their relations with a multitude of nations in Asia, on the borders of the Black sea, of the Baltic sea; with events, in a word, which, doubtless, had powerfully tended to bring about the social state of the German tribes in the third century, and which we must closely observe, but which were then no longer facts but only causes.

You see that all the monuments that remain to us of the state of the barbarians before the invasion, whatever may be their origin and their nature, Roman or German, traditions, chronicles, or laws, refer to times and facts very far removed from one another, and among which it is very difficult to separate what truly belongs to the third and fourth centuries. The fundamental error, in my opinion, of a great number of German writers, and sometimes of the most distinguished, is not having sufficiently attended to this circumstance: in order to picture German society and man

ners at this epoch, they have drawn their materials pell-mell
from the three sources of documents I have indicated, from
the Roman writers, from the barbaric laws, from the national
traditions, without troubling themselves with the difference
of times and situations, without observing any moral
chronology. Hence arises the incoherence of some of these
pictures, a singular mixture of mythology, of barbarism,
and of rising civilization, of fabulous, heroic, and semi-
political ages, without exactitude and without order in the
eyes of the more severe critic, without truth for the imagination.

I shall endeavour to avoid this error; it is with the state
of the Germans, a little before the invasion, that I desire to
occupy you; that is what it imports us to know, for it was that
which was real and powerful at the time of the amalgamation of the nations, that which exercised a true influence
upon modern civilization. I shall in no way enter into
the examination of the German origins and antiquities; I
shall in no way seek to discover what were the relations
between the Germans and the nations and religions of
Asia; whether their barbarism was the wreck of an ancient
civilization, nor what might be, under barbaric forms, the
concealed features of this original society. The question
is an important one; but it is not ours, and I shall not stop
at it. I would wish, too, never to transfer into the state of
the Germans, beyond the Rhine and the Danube, facts which
belong to the Germans established upon Gaulish soil. The
difficulty is extreme. Before having passed the Danube or
the Rhine, the barbarians were in relation with Rome; their
condition, their manners, their ideas, their laws, had perhaps
already submitted to its influence. How separate, amidst
notices so incomplete, so confused, these first results of foreign
importation? How decide with precision what was truly
Germanic, and what already bore a Roman stamp? I shall
attempt this task; the truth of history absolutely requires it.

The most important document we possess concerning the state
of the Germans, between the time when they began to be known
in the Roman world, and that in which they conquered it, is
incontestably the work of Tacitus. Two things must be here
carefully distinguished: on one side, the facts which Tacitus

has collected and described; on the other, the reflections which he mixes with them, the colour under which he presents them, the judgment which he gives of them. The facts are correct: there are many reasons for believing that the father of Tacitus, and perhaps himself, had been procurator of Belgium; he could thus collect detailed information concerning Germany; he occupied himself carefully in doing so; posterior documents almost all prove the material accuracy of his descriptions. With regard to their moral hue, Tacitus has painted the Germans, as Montaigne and Rousseau the savages, in a fit of ill humour against his country: his book is a satire on Roman manners, the eloquent sally of a philosophical patriot, who is determined to see virtue, wherever he does not happen to find the disgraceful effeminacy and the learned depravation of an old society. Do not suppose, however, that everything is false, morally speaking, in this work of anger—the imagination of Tacitus is essentially vigorous and true; when he wishes simply to describe German manners, without allusion to the Roman world, without comparison, without deducing any general consequence therefrom, he is admirable, and one may give entire faith, not only to the design, but to the colouring of the picture. Never has the barbaric life been painted with more vigour, more poetical truth. It is only when thoughts of Rome occur to Tacitus, when he speaks of the barbarians with a view to shame his fellow-citizens; it is then only that his imagination loses its independence, its natural sincerity, and that a false colour is spread over his pictures.

Doubtless, a great change was brought about in the state of the Germans, between the end of the first century, the epoch in which Tacitus wrote, and the times bordering on the invasion; the frequent communications with Rome could not fail of exercising a great influence upon them, attention to which circumstance has too often been neglected. Still the ground-work of the book of Tacitus was true at the end of the fourth as in the first century. Nothing can be a more decisive proof of it than the accounts of Ammianus Marcellinus, a mere soldier, without imagination, without instruction, who made war against the Germans, and whose brief and simple descriptions coincide almost everywhere with the lively and learned colours of Tacitus. We may, therefore, for the epoch which occupies us, give almost entire confidence to the picture *of the manners of the Germans.*

If we compare this picture with the description of the ancient social state of the Germans, lately given by able German writers, we shall be surprised by the resemblance. Assuredly the sentiment which animates them is different; it is with indignation and sorrow that Tacitus, at corrupted Rome, describes the simple and vigorous manners of the barbarians; it is with pride and complaisance that the modern Germans contemplate it; but from these diverse causes rises a single and identical fact; like Tacitus, nay, far more than Tacitus, the greater part of the Germans paint ancient Germany, her institutions, her manners, in the most vivid colours; if they do not go so far as to represent them as the ideal or society, they at least defend them from all imputation of barbarism. According to them: 1st, the agricultural or sedentary life prevailed there, even before the invasion, over the wandering life; the institutions and ideas which create landed property were already very far advanced; 2nd, the guarantees of individual liberty, and even security, were efficacious, 3rd, manners were indeed violent and coarse, but at bottom the natural morality of man was developed with simplicity and grandeur; family affections were strong, characters lofty, emotions profound, religious doctrines high and powerful; there was more energy and moral purity than is found under more elegant forms, in the heart of a far more extended intellectual development.

When this cause is maintained by ordinary minds, it abounds in strange assumptions and ridiculous assertions. Heinrich, the author of an esteemed *History of Germany,* will not have it that the ancient Germans were addicted to intoxication;[1] Meiners, in his *History of the Female Sex,* maintains that women have never been so happy nor so virtuous as in Germany, and that before the arrival of the Franks, the Gauls knew not how either to respect or to love them.[2]

I shall not dwell upon these puerilities of learned patriotism; I should not even have touched upon them, if they were not the consequence, and as it were, the excrescence

[1] *Reichsgeschichte,* vol. i. p. 69.
[2] *Geschichte des Weiblichen Geschlechts,* vol. i. p. 198

of a system, maintained by very distinguished men, and which, in my opinion, destroys the historical and poetical idea which is formed of the ancient Germans. Considering things at large, and according to mere appearances, the error seems to me evident.

How can it be maintained, for example, that German society was well nigh fixed, and that the agricultural life dominated there, in the presence of the very fact of migrations, of invasions, of that incessant movement which drew the Germanic nations beyond their territory? How can we give credit to the empire of manorial property, and of the ideas and institutions which are connected with it, over men who continually abandoned the soil in order to seek fortune elsewhere? And mark, that it was not only on the frontiers that this movement was accomplished; the same fluctuation reigned in the interior of Germany; tribes incessantly expelled, displaced, succeeded one another: some paragraphs from Tacitus will abundantly prove this:

" The Batavians," says he, " were formerly a tribe of the Catti; intestine divisions forced them to retire into the islands of the Rhine, where they formed an alliance with the Romans." (Tacitus, *de Morib. Germanorum*, xxix.)

" In the neighbourhood of the Tencteres were formerly the Bructeres; it is said, however, that now the Chamaves and the Angrivarians possess the district, having, in concert with the adjoining tribes, expelled and entirely extirpated the ancient inhabitants." (*ib.* xxxii.)

" The Marcomannians are the most eminent for their strength and military glory; the very territory they occupy is the reward of their valour, they having dispossessed its former owners, the Boians." (*ib.* xlii.)

" Even in time of peace the Cattians retain the same ferocious aspect, never softened with an air of humanity. They have no house to dwell in, no land to cultivate, no domestic cares to employ them. Wherever they chance to be, they live upon the produce they find, and are lavish of their neighbours' substance, till old age incapacitates them for these continuous struggles." (*ib.* xxxi.)

" The tribes deem it an honourable distinction to have their frontiers devastated, to be surrounded with immense deserts. They regard it as the highest proof of valour for their

E E

neighbours to abandon their territories out of fear of them, moreover, they have thus an additional security against sudden attacks." (Cæsar, de *Bell. Gall.* vi. 23.)

Doubtless, since the time of Tacitus, the German tribes, more or less, had made some progress; still, assuredly, the fluctuation, the continual displacement had not ceased, since the invasion became daily more general and more pressing.

Hence, if I mistake not, partly proceeds the difference which exists between the point of view of the Germans and our own. There was, in fact, at the fourth century, among many German tribes or confederations, among others with the Franks and Saxons, a commencement of the sedentary, agricultural life; the whole nation was not addicted to the wandering life. Its composition was not simple; it was not an unique race, a single social condition. We may there recognise three classes of men: 1st, freemen, men of honour or nobles, proprietors; 2ndly, the *lidi, liti, lasi,* &c., or labourers, men attached to the soil, who cultivated it for masters; 3rdly, slaves properly so called. The existence of the first two classes evidently indicate a conquest; the class of freemen was the nation of conquerors, who had obliged the ancient population to cultivate the soil for them. This was an analogous fact to that which, at a later period, in the Roman empire, gave rise to the feudal system. This fact was accomplished at various epochs, and upon various points, in the interior of Germany. Sometimes the proprietors and the labourers—the conquerors and the conquered —were of different races; sometimes it was in the bosom of the same race, between different tribes, that the territorial subjection took place; we see Gaulish or Belgian colonies submit to German colonies, Germans to Slavonians, Slavonians to Germans, Germans to Germans. Conquest was generally effected upon a small scale, and remained exposed to many vicissitudes; but the fact itself cannot be disputed; many passages in Tacitus positively express it:

" The slaves, in general, are not arranged in their several employments in household affairs, as is the practice at Rome. Each has his separate habitation or home. The master considers him as an agrarian dependent, who is obliged to furnish, by way of rent, a certain quantity of grain, of cattle, or of wearing apparel. The slave does this, and there his servitude ends. All domestic matters are managed by the master's own wife and children. To punish a slave with stripes, to load him with chains, or condemn him to hard labour, is unusual." (*Ib.* xxv.)

Who does not recognise in this description, ancient inhabitants of the territory, fallen under the yoke of conquerors.

The conquerors in the earliest ages, at least, did not cultivate. They enjoyed the conquest—sometimes abandoned to a profound idleness, sometimes excited with a profound passion for war, hunting, and adventures. Some distant expedition tempted them; all were not of the same inclination—they did not all go; a party set off under the conduct of some famous chief; others remained, preferring to guard their first conquests, and continued to live upon the labour of the ancient inhabitants. The adventurous party sometimes returned laden with booty, sometimes pursued its course, and went to a distance to conquer some province of the empire, perhaps found some kingdom. It was thus that the Vandals, the Suevi, the Franks, the Saxons, were dispersed; thus we find these nations over-running Gaul, Spain, Africa, Britain, establishing themselves there, beginning states, while the same names are always met with in Germany—where, in fact, the same people still live and act. They were parcelled out: one part abandoned themselves to the wandering life; another was attached to the sedentary life, perhaps only waiting the occasion or temptation to set out in its turn.

Hence arises the difference between the point of view of the German writers, and that of our own; they more especially were acquainted with that portion of the German tribes which remained upon the soil, and was more and more addicted to the agricultural and sedentary life; we, on the contrary, have been naturally led to consider chiefly the portion which followed the wandering life, and which invaded western Europe. Like he learned Germans, we speak of the Franks, the Saxons, the Suevi, but not of the same Suevi, the same Saxons, the same Franks; our researches, our words, almost always refer to those who passed the Rhine, and it is in the state of wandering bands that we have seen them appear in Gaul, in Spain, in Britain, &c. The assertions of the Germans chiefly allude to the Saxons, the Suevi, the Franks who

E E 2

remained in Germany; and it is in the state of conquering nations, it is true, but fixed, or almost fixed in certain parts of the land, and beginning to lead the life of proprietors, that they are exhibited by almost all the ancient monuments of local history. The error of these scholars, if I mistake not, is in carrying the authority of these monuments too far back—too anterior to the fourth century,—of attributing too remote a date to the sedentary life, and to the fixedness of the social state in Germany; but the error is much more natural and less important than it would be on our part.

With regard to ancient German institutions, I shall speak of them in detail when we treat especially of the barbarian laws, and more especially of the Salic law. I shall confine myself at present to the characterizing, in a few words, their state at the epoch which occupies us.

At that time, we find among the Germans the seeds of the three great systems of institutions which, after the fall of the Roman empire, contested for Europe. We find there: 1st, assemblies of freemen, where they debate upon the common interests, public enterprises, all the important affairs of the nation; 2ndly, kings, some by hereditary title, and sometimes invested with a religious character, others by title of election, and especially bearing a warlike character; 3rdly, the aristocratical patronage, whether of the warlike chief over his companions, or of the proprietor over his family and labourers. These three systems, these three modes of social organization and of government may be seen in almost all the German tribes before the invasion; but none of them are real, efficacious. Properly speaking, there are no free institutions, monarchies, or aristocracies, but merely the principle to which they relate, the germ from whence they may arise. Everything is abandoned to the caprice of individual wills. Whenever the assembly of the nation, or the king, or the lord, wished to be obeyed, the individual must either consent, or disorderly brute force obliged him. This is the free development and the contest between individual existences and liberties; there was no public power, no government, no state.

With regard to the moral condition of the Germans at this epoch, it is very difficult to estimate it. It has been made

the text of infinite declamation in honour of or against civilization of savage life, of primitive independence or of developed
society, of natural simplicity or of scientific enlightenment; but we are without documents enabling us to estimate the true nature of these generalities. There exists,
however, one great collection of facts, posterior, it is true, to
the epoch of which we are speaking, but which yet presents
a sufficiently faithful image of it; this is the *Histoire des
Francs*, by Gregory of Tours, unquestionably, of all others,
the work which furnishes us with the most information, which
throws the clearest light upon the moral state of the barbarians; not that the chronicler made it any part of his plan,
but, in the ordinary course of his narrative, he relates an
infinite number of private anecdotes, of incidents of domestic
life, in which the manners, the social arrangements, the moral
state, in a word, the man of his period, are exhibited to us
more clearly than in any other work we possess.

It is here that we may contemplate and understand this
singular mixture of violence and deceit, of improvidence and
calculation, of patience and bursts of passion; this egoism of
interest and of passion, mixed with the indestructible empire
of certain ideas of duty, of certain disinterested sentiments:
in a word, that chaos of our moral nature which constitutes
barbarism; a state of things very difficult to describe with precision, for it has no general and fixed feature, no one decided
principle; there is no proposition we can make it, which we
are not compelled the next instant to modify, or altogether to
throw aside. It is humanity, strong and active, but abandoned to the impulse of its reckless propensities, to the incessant mobility of its wayward fancies, to the gross imperfection of its knowledge, to the incoherence of its ideas, to the
infinite variety of the situations and accidents of its life.

It were impossible to penetrate far enough into such a
state, and reproduce its image, by the mere aid of a few dry
and mutilated chronicles, of a few fragments of old poems, of
a few unconnected paragraphs of old laws.

I know but of one way of attaining anything like a correct
idea of the social and moral state of the German tribes—it is
to compare them with the tribes who, in modern times, in
various parts of the globe, in North America, in the interior
of Africa, in the North of Asia, are still almost in the same

degree of civilization, and ... ~ry nearly the same life.
The latter have been observe... ~ nearly, and described
in greater detail; fresh accounts or t.. n reach us every day
We have a thousand facilities for regulating and completing
our ideas with respect to them; our imagination is constantly
excited, and at the same time rectified, by the narratives of
travellers. By closely and critically observing these narratives, by comparing and analyzing the various circumstances,
they become for us as it were a mirror, in which we raise up
and reproduce the image of the ancient Germans. I have
gone through this task; I have followed, step by step, the
work of Tacitus, seeking throughout my progress, in voyages
and travels, in histories, in national poetry, in all the documents which we possess concerning the barbarous tribes in
the various parts of the world, facts analogous to those
described by the Roman writer. I will lay before you the
principal features of this comparison, and you will be
astonished at the resemblance between the manners of the
Germans and those of the more modern barbarians—a resemblance which sometimes extends into details where one
would have had not the slightest idea of finding it.

1.

" To retreat, if you afterwards return to the charge, is considered prudent skill, not cowardice."—De Moribus Germanorum. vi.

1.

" Our warriors do not pique them-selves upon attacking the enemy in front, and while he is on his guard; for this they must be ten to one." Choix de Litt. edif. Missions d'Ame-rique, vii. 49.

" Savages do not pride themselves upon attacking the enemy in front and by open force. If, despite all their precautions and their address, their movements are discovered, they think the wisest plan is to retire."— Robertson's Hist. of America, ii.

The heroes of Homer fly when-ever, finding themselves the weaker party, they have the opportunity.

2

" Their wives and mothers ac-company them to the field of battle; and when their relatives are wounded, count each honourable gash, and suck the blood. They are even daring enough to mix with the com-

2.

" The Tungusian women in Si-beria go to war as well as their hus-bands; and they have as rough treat-ment."—Meiners' Hist. of the Fe-male Sex, i. 18, 19.

" At the battle of Yermuk, in

lutants, taking refreshments to them and reanimating their courage."—Ib. vii.

"They have accounts of armies put to the rout, who have been brought to the charge by the women and old men preventing their flight." —Ib. viii

3.

"There is in their opinion something sacred in the female sex, and even the power of foreseeing future events; the advice of the women, therefore, is frequently sought, and their counsels respected."—Ib.

4.

"Their attention to auguries, and the practice of divination, is conducted with a degree of superstition not exceeded by any other nation. .... The branch of a fruit tree is cut into small pieces, which being all distinctly marked, are thrown at random on a white cloth. If a question of public interest be depending, the high priest performs the ceremony; if it be only a private matter, the master of the family officiates. Having invoked the gods, with his eyes devoutly raised to heaven, he holds up three times each segment of the twig, and, as the marks rise in succession, interprets the decrees of fate.

"The practice of consulting the notes and flight of birds is also in use among them."—Ib. x.

Syria, in 630, the last line was occupied by the sister of Dezar, with the Arabian women, who were accustomed to wield the bow and the lance. Thrice did the Arabs retreat in disorder, and thrice were they driven back to the charge by the reproaches and blows of the women."— Gibbon's Hist. of the Dec. and Fall of the Roman Empire.

3.

"When a national war breaks out, the priests and diviners are consulted; sometimes, even, they take the advice of the women."—Rob. Hist. of America, ii.

"The Hurons, in particular, pay particular respect to women." — Charlevoix, Hist. of Canada.

"The Gauls consulted the women in important affairs; they agreed with Hannibal that if the Carthaginians had to complain of the Gauls, they should carry their complaint before the Gaulish women, who should be the judges of them."—Mem. de l'Académ. des Inscrip. xxiv. 374, Memoire de l'Abbé Fenel.

4.

"This mode of divination, by rod, has some relation with divination by arrow, which was in usage throughout the East. When Turkmans were established in Persia, after the defeat of the Ghaznevides, (A.D. 1038,) they chose a king by writing upon arrows the names of the different tribes, of the different families of the tribes, taken by lot, and of the different members of the family."—Gibbon, Hist. of the Decl. and Fall of the Roman Empire, xi. 224.

"Presages drawn from the song and flight of birds were known among the Romans, among the Greeks, among the greater part of the savages of America, Natchez, Moxes Chequites, &c."—Lett. edif. vii. 255, viii. 141, 264.

5.

"The kings in Germany owe their election to the nobility of their births; the generals are chosen for their valour. The power of the former is not arbitrary or unlimited; the latter command more by warlike example than by their mere orders; to be of a prompt and daring spirit in battle, to appear in the front of the lines, insures the obedience of the soldiers, admirers of valour. The whole nation takes cognizance of important affairs. The princes and chiefs gain attention rather by the force of their arguments than by any authority. If their opinion is unsatisfactory to the warriors, the assembly reject it by a general murmur. If the proposition pleases, they brandish their javelins."—Ib. vii 11.

6.

"In that consists his dignity; to be surrounded by a band of young men is the source of his power; in peace, his highest ornament, in war, his strongest bulwark. Nor is his fame confined to his own country; it extends to foreign nations, and he is then of the first importance, if he surpasses his rivals in the number and courage of his followers. If, in the course of a long peace, a tribe languishes under indolence, the young men often seek in a body a more active life with another tribe that is engaged in war. The new chief must show his liberality; he must give to one a horse, to another a shield, to another a blood-stained and victorious spear; to all plentiful food and potations. These are their only pay."—Ib. xiii.

7.

"When the State has no war on its hands, the men pass their time partly in the chase, partly in sloth and gluttony. The intrepid warrior, who in the field braved every danger, becomes in time of

5.

"Savages know among themselves neither princes nor kings. They say in Europe that they have republics; but these republics have no approach to stable laws. Each family looks upon itself as absolutely free; each Indian believes himself independent. Still they have learned the necessity of forming among them a kind of society, and of choosing a chief whom they call *cacique*, that is to say, commander. In order to be raised to this dignity, it is necessary to have given striking proofs of valour."—Lett. edif. viii. 133.

6

"The most powerful order among the Iroquois is that of warlike chiefs. It is first necessary that they should be successful, and that they should by no means lose sight of those who follow them; that they should deprive themselves of whatever is dear to themselves in favour of their soldiers."—Mém. sur les Iroquois, *in the* Variétés Littéraires i. 543.

"The influence of the warlike chiefs over the young men is more or less great, according as they give more or less, as they more or less keep open table."—Journal des Campagnes de M. de Bougainville in Canada, *in the* Variétés Littéraires, i. 488.

7.

"With the exception of some trifling huntings, the Illinois lead a perfectly indolent life. They pass their time in smoking and talking, and that is all. They remain tranquil upon their mats, and pass their peace a listless sluggard. The management of his house and lands he leaves to the women, to the old men, and to the other weaker portions of his family."—Ib. xv.

8.

" The Germans, it is well known, have no regular cities, nor do they even like their houses to be near each other. They dwell in separate habitations, dispersed up and down, as a grove, a spring, or a meadow, happens to invite. They have villages, but not in our fashion, with connected buildings. Every tenement stands detached."—Ib. xvi.

9.

" They are almost the only barbarians who content themselves with one wife. There are, indeed, some cases of polygamy among them, not, however, the effect of licentiousness, but by reason of the rank of the parties."—Ib. xviii

10.

" It is not the wife who brings a dowry to her husband, but the husband who gives one to his bride; not presents adapted for female vanity, but oxen, a caparisoned horse, a shield and spear and sword."—Ib.[1]

time in sleeping or making bows. As to the women, they labour from morning till night like slaves."—Lett. edif. vii 32, 867. See also Robertson's History of America, ii.

8.

" The villages of the American savages and of the mountaineers of Corsica, are built in the same way; they are formed of houses scattered and distant from one another, so that a village of fifty houses sometimes occupies a quarter of a league square."—Volney, Tableau des Etats Unis d'Amerique, 484—486.

9.

" Among the savages of North America, in districts where the means of subsistence were rare, and the difficulties of raising a family very great, the man confined himself to a single wife."—Robertson's Hist. of America.

" Although the Moxes (in Peru) allow polygamy, it is rare for them to have more than one wife; their poverty will not allow of their having more."—Lett. edif., viii. 71.

" Among the Guaranis (in Paraguay) polygamy is not permitted to the people; but the caciques may have two or three wives."—Ib. 261.

10.

This takes place wherever the husband buys his wife, and where the wife becomes the property, the slave of her husband. " Among the Indians of Guiana the women have no dowry on marrying. An Indian, who wishes to marry an

---

[1] There is no doubt that the Germans bought their wives: a law of the Burgundians declares — " If any one dismiss his wife without a good reason, he must give her a sum equal to what he paid for her."—Tit. xxxiv Theodoric, king of the Ostrogoths, in giving his niece in marriage to Hermanfried, king of the Thuringians, writes to him, by the hand of Cassiodorus: " We inform you that on the arrival of your envoys, they punctually delivered to us the horses harnessed with the silver trappings, be-

Indian woman, must make considerable presents to the father;—a canoe, bows and arrows, are not sufficient; he must labour a year for his future father-in-law, cook for him, hunt for him, fish for him, &c. Women among the Guanis are true property."—MS. Journal of a Residence in Guiana, by M. de M.

"It is the same among the Natchez, in many Tartar tribes in Mingrélia, in Pegu, among many Negro tribes in Africa."—Lett. édif. vii. 221; Lord Kaime's Sketches of the History of Man, i. 184—186.

11.

Populous as the country is, adultery is rarely heard of; when detected the punishment is immediate, and inflicted by the husband. He cuts off the hair of his guilty wife, and having assembled her relations, expels her naked from his house, pursuing her with stripes through the village.—Ib. xix.

11.

It is pretended that adultery was unknown among the Caribbees of the islands, before the establishment of the Europeans.—Lord Kaime, i. 207.

"Adultery among the savages of North America is generally punished without form or process, by the husband, who sometimes severely beats his wife, sometimes bites off her nose."—Lang's Travels among the different savage nations of North America, 177. See also the History of the American Indians by James Adair, (1775) 144; Variétés Littéraires, i. 458.

12.

It is generally late before their young men enjoy the pleasures of love, and consequently they are not exhausted in their youth. Nor are the virgins married too soon.—Ib. xv.

12.

The coldness of wandering savages, in matters of love, has often been remarked: Bruce was struck with it among the Gallas and Shangallas, on the frontiers of Abysinia: Levaillant, among the Hottentots. "The Iroquois know and say that the use of women enervates their courage and their strength, and that, wishing to be warlike, they should abstain

---

fitting royal marriage horses, the price you, after the custom of the Gentiles, gave us for our niece."—Cassiodorus, Varior., iv. 1.

Down to a very recent period, the betrothing in Lower Saxony was called *bruakop*, that is to say, *brautkauf* [vide purchase].—Adelung, History of the Ancient Germans, 301.

from using them, or use them with moderation."—Mem. sur les Iroquois, in the Varietes Litteraires i. 455; see also Volney, Tabl. des Etats—Unis, 448; Malthus's Essays upon the principle of Population, i. 50; Robertson's Hist. of America, ii. 237.

Among the Greenlanders, the girls marry at twenty; it is the same among most of the northern savages.—Meiner's Hist of the Female Sex, i. 20.

13.

The uncle on the mother's side regards his nephews with an affection nothing inferior to that of their father. With some, this relationship is held to be the strongest tie of consanguinity, insomuch that in demanding hostages, maternal nephews are preferred, as the most endearing objects, and the safest pledges.—Ib.

13.

Among the Natchez, "it is not the son of the reigning chief who succeeds to his father; it is the son of his sister. . . . This policy is founded on the knowledge of the licentiousness of their wives; they are sure, say they, that the son of the sister of the great chief, is of the blood royal, at least on his mother's side."—Lett. édif. vii. 217.

Among the Iroquois and the Hurons, the dignity of a chief always passes to the children of his aunts, of his sisters, or of his nieces on the maternal side.—Mœurs des Sauvages, by father Lafitau, i. 73, 471.

14.

"To adopt the quarrels as well as the friendships of their parents and relations, is held to be an indispensable duty."—Ib. xxi.

14.

"Every one knows that this feature is found among all nations in the infancy of civilization, where as yet there was no public power to protect or punish. I shall cite but one example of this obstinacy of savages in taking vengeance; it appears to me striking and very analogous to what is recounted of the Germans by Gregory of Tours and other characters.

"An Indian, of a tribe established on the Maroni, a violent and bloodthirsty man, had assassinated one of his neighbours of the same village; to escape the resentment of the family of his enemy, he fled, and established himself at Simapo, at a distance of four leagues from our desert; a brother of the deceased did not delay following the murderer.

On his arrival at Simapo, the captain
asked him what he came there to do.
'I came,' said he, 'to kill Averani,
who has killed my brother.' 'I
cannot prevent you,' said the captain to him. But Averani was warned
during the night, and fled with his
children. His enemy, informed of his
departure, and that he had repaired
by the interior towards the river
Aprouague, resolved to follow him.
'I will kill him,' said he, 'though he
flee to the Portuguese.' He immediately set out. We know not whether
he attained his end."—Journal Manuscript d'un séjour à la Guyanne par
M. de M.

15.

"Hospitality is nowhere more
liberally observed. To turn any
man from their door was regarded as
a crime."—Ib.

15.

"The hospitality of all savage
nations is proverbial."—See in the
Histoire de l'Académie des Inscriptions, iii. 41, the extract from a
memoir of M. Simon, and a number
of accounts of travellers.

16.

"A German delights in the gifts
which he receives; yet in bestowing,
he imputes nothing to you as a
favour, and for what he receives, he
acknowledges no obligation."—Ib.

16.

"It is the same with the American
savages; they give and receive with
great pleasure, but they do not think
of, nor will they accept any acknow-
ledgment. 'If you have given me
this,' say the Galibis, 'it is because
you have no need of it.'"—Aublet,
Histoire des Plantes de la Guyane
Francaise, ii. 110.

17.

"To devote both day and night to
deep drinking, is a disgrace to no
man."—Ib. xxii.

17.

"The inclination of savage nations
for wine and strong liquors is universally known; the Indians of
Guiana take long journeys to procure it; one of them, of the colony
of Simapo, replied to M. de M——
who asked him where they were
going: *to drink*, as our peasantry
say: *to the harvest, to the fair*."—
Manuscript Diary of a Residence in
Guiana, by M. de M——.

18.

"They have but one sort of
public spectacle; the young men
dance naked amidst swords and
javelins pointed at their breasts."—
Ib. xxiv.

18.

"Love does not enter the least
into the dances of the North American
savages; they are only warlike
dances."—Robertson's History of
America, ii. 450—461

19.

"They yield to gambling with such ardour, that when they have lost everything else, they place their own liberty on the hazard of the die."—Ib.

20.

It was not in order to succeed in love, or to please, that they decked themselves, but in order to give themselves a gigantic and terrible appearance, as they might have decked themselves to go before their enemies."—Ib. c. 38.

21.

From the age of early manhood they allow their hair and beard to grow, until they have killed an enemy."—Ib. c. 31.

19.

"The Americans play for their furs, their domestic utensils, their clothes, their arms, and when all is lost, we often see them risk, at a single blow, their liberty.

20.

"When the Iroquois choose to paint their faces it is to give themselves a terrible air, with which they hope to intimidate their enemies; it is also for this reason that they paint themselves black when they go to war."—Variétés Litteraires, i. 472.

22.

After the Indians are twenty years old they allow their hair to grow.—Lett. édif., viii. 261.

The custom of scalping, or taking off the hair of their enemies, so common among the Americans, was also practised among the Germans: this is the *decalvare* mentioned in the laws of the Visigoths; the *capillos et cutem detrahere*, still in use among the Franks towards the year 879, according to the annals of Fulda; the *hettinan* of the Anglo-Saxons, &c.—Adelung, Ancient History of the Germans, 303.

Here are numerous citations; I might extend them much more, and might almost always place, side by side with the most trifling assertion of Tacitus concerning the Germans, an analogous assertion of some modern traveller or historian, concerning some one of the barbarous tribes at present dispersed over the face of the globe.

You see what is the social condition which corresponds to that of ancient Germany: what, then, must we think of those magnificent descriptions which have so often been drawn? Precisely that which we should think of Cooper's romances, as pictures of the condition and manners of the savages of North America. There is, without doubt, in these romances and in some of the works in which the Germans have attempted to depict their wild ancestors, a sufficiently vivid and true perception of certain parts and certain periods of barbarous society and life — of its independence, for instance; of the activity and indolence which it combines; of the skilful energy which man therein displays against the obstacles and perils wherewith material nature besieges him; of the monotonous violence of his passions, &c. &c. But the picture is very incomplete—so incomplete that the truth of even what it represents is often much changed by it. That Cooper, in writing of the Mohicans or the Delawares, and that the German writers, in describing the ancient Germans, should allow themselves to represent all things under their poetic aspect—that, in their descriptions, the sentiments and circumstances of barbarous life should become exalted to their ideal form—is very natural, and, I willingly admit, is very legitimate: the ideal is the essence of poetry —history itself is partial to it; and perhaps it is the only form under which times gone by can be duly represented. But the ideal must also be true, complete, and harmonious; it does not consist in the arbitrary and fanciful suppression of a large portion of the reality to which it corresponds. Assuredly, the songs which bear the name of Homer, form an ideal picture of Greek society; nevertheless, that society is therein reproduced in a complete state, with the rusticity and ferocity of its manners, the coarse simplicity of its sentiments, and its good and bad passions, without any design of particularly drawing forth or celebrating such or such of its merits and its advantages, or of leaving in the shade its vices and its evils.

This mixture of good and evil, of strong and weak— this co-existence of ideas and sentiments apparently contra- dictory—this variety, this incoherence, this unequal develop- ment of human nature and human destiny—is precisely the condition which is the most rife with poetry, for through it we see to the bottom of things, it is the truth concerning man and the world; and in the ideal pictures which poetry, romance, and even history, make of it, this so various and yet harmonious whole ought to be found, for without it the true ideal will be wanting, no less than the reality. Now it is into this fault that the writers of whom I speak have always fallen; their pictures of savage man and of savage life are essentially incomplete, formal, factitious, and wanting in simplicity and harmony. One fancies that one sees melo- dramatic barbarians and savages, who present themselves to display their independence, their energy, their skill, or such and such a portion of their character and destiny, before the eyes of spectators who, at once greedy of, but worn out with excitement, still take pleasure in qualities and adventures foreign to the life they themselves lead, and to the society by which they are surrounded. I know not whether you are struck, as I am, with the defects of the imagination in our times. Upon the whole, it seems to me that it lacks nature, facility, and extension; it does not take a large and simple view of things in their primitive and real elements; it arranges them theatrically, and mutilates them under the pretence of idealizing them. It is true that I find, in the modern descriptions of ancient German manners, some scattered characteristics of barbarism, but I can discover nothing therefrom of what barbarous society was as a whole.

If I were obliged to sum up that which I have now said upon the state of the Germans before the invasion, I confess I should be somewhat embarrassed. We find therein no precise and well defined traits which may be detached and distinctly exhibited; no fact, no idea, no sentiment had as yet attained to its development, or as yet presented itself under a determinate form; it was the infancy of all things, of the social and moral states, of institutions, of relations, of man himself; everything was rough and confused. There are, however, two points to which I think I ought to direct your attention:

1st. At the opening of modern civilization, the Germans influenced it far less by the institutions which they brought with them from Germany, than by their situation itself, amidst the Roman world. They had conquered it: they were, at least upon the spot where they had established themselves, masters of the population and of the territory. The society which formed itself after this conquest, arose rather from this situation, from the new life led by the conquerors in their relations with the conquered, than from the ancient German manners.

2nd. That which the Germans especially brought into the Roman world was the spirit of individual liberty, the need, the passion for independence and individuality. To speak properly, no public power, no religious power, existed in ancient Germany; the only real power in this society, the only power that was strong and active in it, was the will of man; each one did what he chose, at his own risk and peril.

The system of force, that is to say, of personal liberty, was at the bottom of the social state of the Germans. Through this it was that their influence became so powerful upon the modern world. Very general expressions border always so nearly upon inaccuracy, that I do not like to risk them. Nevertheless, were it absolutely necessary to express in few words the predominating characters of the various elements of our civilization, I should say, that the spirit of legality, of regular association, came to us from the Roman world, from the Roman municipalities and laws. It is to Christianity, to the religious society that we owe the spirit of morality, the sentiment and empire of rule, of a moral law, of the mutual duties of men. The Germans conferred upon us the spirit of liberty, of liberty such as we conceive of, and are acquainted with it, in the present day, as the right and property of each individual, master of himself, of his actions, and of his fate, so long as he injures no other individual. This is a fact of universal importance, for it was unknown to all preceding civilizations: in the ancient republics, the public power disposed all things; the individual was sacrificed to the citizen. In the societies where the religious principle predominated, the believer belonged to his God, not to himself. Thus, man hitherto had always been absorbed in the church or in the state. In modern Europe, alone, has he existed and developed himself on his own account and in his own way, charged, no doubt, charged continually, more and more heavily with toils and duties, but finding in himself his aim and his right. It is to German manners that we must trace this distinguishing characteristic of our civilization. The fundamental idea of liberty, in modern Europe, came to it from its conquerors.

EIGHTH LECTURE

Object of the lecture—True character of the German invasions—Cause of errors on this subject—Description of the state of Gaul in the last half of the sixth century—Dissolution of Roman society: 1. In rural districts; 2. In towns, though in a lesser degree—Dissolution of German society: 1. Of the colony or tribe; 2. Of the warfaring band—Elements of the new social state: 1. Of commencing royalty; 2. Of commencing feudalism; 3. Of the church, after the invasion—Summary.

WE are now in possession of the two primitive and fundamental elements of French civilization; we have studied, on the one hand, Roman civilization, on the other, German society, each in itself, and prior to their apposition. Let us endeavour to ascertain what happened in the moment at which they touched together, and became confounded with one another; that is to say, to describe the condition of Gaul after the great invasion and settlement of the Germans.

I should wish to assign to this description a somewhat precise date, and to inform you, beforehand, to what age and to what territory it especially belongs. The difficulty of doing this is great. Such, at this epoch, was the confusion of things and minds, that the greater part of the facts have been transmitted to us without order and without date, particularly general facts, those connected with institutions, with the relations of the different classes, in a word, with the social condition; facts which, by nature, are the least apparent and the least precise. They are omitted or strangely confused in contemporary monuments; we must, at every step, guess at and restore their chronology. Happily, the accuracy of this chronology is of less importance at this epoch than at any other. No doubt, between the sixth and eighth centuries, the state of Gaul must have changed; rela-

F F

tions of men, institutions and manners must have been modi
fied; less, however, than we might be tempted to believe,
The chaos was extreme, and chaos is essentially stationary.
When all things are disordered and confounded to this degree, they require much time for unravelling and re-arranging
themselves; much time is needed for each of the elements to
return to its place, to re-enter its right path, to place itself
again in some measure under the direction and motive force
of the special principle which should govern its development.
After the settlement of the barbarians upon the Roman
soil, events and men revolved for a long time in the same
circle, a prey to a movement more violent than progressive.
Thus, from the sixth to the eighth century, the state of
Gaul changed less, and the strict chronology of general facts
is of less importance than we might naturally presume from
the length of the interval. Let us, nevertheless, endeavour
to determine, within certain limits, the epoch of which we are
now to trace the picture.

The true Germanic people who occupied Gaul were the
Burgundians, the Visigoths, and the Franks. Many other
people, many other single bands, of Vandals, Alani, Suevi,
Saxons, &c., wandered over its territory; but of these,
some only passed over it, and the others were rapidly
absorbed by it; these are partial incursions which are
without any historical importance. The Burgundians, the
Visigoths, and the Franks, alone deserve to be counted
among our ancestors. The Burgundians definitively established themselves in Gaul between the years 406 and
413; they occupied the country between the Jura, the
Saône, and the Durance; Lyons was the centre of their
dominion. The Visigoths, between the years 412 and 450,
spread themselves over the provinces bounded by the Rhone,
and even over the left bank of the Rhone to the south of the
Durance, the Loire, and the Pyrenees: their king resided at
Toulouse. The Franks, between the years 481 and 500,
advanced in the north of Gaul, and established themselves
between the Rhine, the Scheldt, and the Loire, without including Brittany and the western portions of Normandy;
Clovis had Soissons and Paris for his capitals. Thus, at the
end of the fifth century, was accomplished the definitive occupation of the territory of Gaul by the three great German
tribes.

The condition of Gaul was not exactly the same in its various parts, and under the dominion of these three nations. There were remarkable differences between them. The Franks were far more foreign, German, and barbarous, than the Burgundians and the Goths   Before their entrance into Gaul, these last had had ancient relations with the Romans; they had lived in the eastern empire, in Italy; they were familiar with the Roman manners and population. We may say almost as much for the Burgundians. Moreover, the two nations had long been Christians. The Franks, on the contrary, arrived from Germany in the condition of pagans and enemies. Those portions of Gaul which they occupied became deeply sensible of this difference, which is described with truth and vivacity in the seventh of the " Lectures upon the History of France," of M. Augustin Thierry. I am inclined, however, to believe that it was less important than has been commonly supposed. If I do not err, the Roman provinces differed more among themselves than did the nations which had conquered them. You have already seen how much more civilized was southern than northern Gaul, how much more thickly covered with population, towns, monuments, and roads. Had the Visigoths arrived in as barbarous a condition as that of the Franks, their barbarism would yet have been far less visible and less powerful in Gallia Narbonensis and in Aquitania; Roman civilization would much sooner have absorbed and altered them. This, I believe, is what happened; and the different effects which accompanied the three conquests resulted rather from the differences of the conquered than from that of the conquerors.

Besides, this difference, sensible so long as we confine ourselves to a very general view of things, becomes effaced, or at least very difficult to be perceived, when we go farther on with the study of the society. It may be said that the Franks were more barbarous than the Visigoths; but, that being said, we must stop. In what consisted the positive differences between the two peoples, in institutions, ideas, and relations of classes? No precise record contains an answer to this question. Finally, the difference of condition in the provinces of Gaul, that difference, at least, which was referable to their masters soon disappeared or became greatly

F F 2

lessened. About the year 534, the country of the Bur
gundians fell under the yoke of the Franks; between the
years 507 and 542, that of the Visigoths became subject to
nearly the same fate. In the middle of the sixth century,
the Frank race had spread itself and obtained dominion
throughout Gaul. The Visigoths still possessed a part of
Languedoc, and still disputed the possession of some towns
at the foot of the Pyrenees; but, properly speaking, Brittany excepted, the whole of Gaul was, if not governed, at
least overrun by the Franks.

It is with the Gaul of this epoch that I desire to make you
acquainted; it is the state of Gaul about the last half of
the sixth century, and, above all, of Frankish Gaul, that I
shall now endeavour to describe. Any attempt to assign
a more precise date to this description would be vain and
fertile in errors. No doubt there was still, at this epoch,
much variety in the condition of the Gaulish provinces;
but I shall attempt to estimate it no farther, remaining
satisfied with having warned you of its existence.

It seems to me that people commonly form to themselves
a very false idea of the invasion of the barbarians, and
of the extent and rapidity of its effects. You have, in your
reading upon this subject, often met with the words *inun-
dation, earthquake, conflagration*. These are the terms
which have been employed to characterize this revolution.
I think that they are deceptive, that they in no way
represent the manner in which this invasion occurred, nor
its immediate results. Exaggeration is natural to human
language; words express the impressions which man receives
from facts, rather than the facts themselves; it is after
having passed through the mind of man, and according to
the impressions which they have produced thereupon, that
facts are described and named. But the impression is
never the complete and faithful image of the fact. In the
first place, it is individual, which the fact is not; great
events, the invasion of a foreign people, for instance, are
related by those who have been personally affected, as
victims, actors, or spectators: they relate the event as
they have seen it; they characterize it according to what they
have known or undergone. He who has seen his house or
his village burnt, will, perhaps, call the invasion a confla-

gration; to the thought of another, it will be found arrayed in the form of a deluge or an earthquake. These images are true, but are of a truth which, if I may so express myself, is full of prejudice and egoism; they re-produce the impressions of some few men; they are not expressions of the fact in its entire extent, nor of the manner in which it impressed the whole of the country.

Such, moreover, is the instinctive poetry of the human mind, that it receives from facts an impression which is livelier and greater than are the facts themselves; it is its tendency to extend and ennoble them; they are for it but matter which it fashions and forms, a theme upon which it exercises itself, and from which it draws, or rather over which it spreads beauties and effects which were not really there. Thus, a double and contrary cause fills language with illusion; under a material point of view, facts are greater than man, and he perceives and describes em only that which strikes him personally; under the moral point of view, man is greater than facts; and, in describing them, he lends them something of his own greatness.

This is what we must never forget in studying history, particularly in reading contemporary documents; they are at once incomplete and exaggerated; they omit and amplify: we must always distrust the impression conveyed by them, both as too narrow and as too poetical; we must both add to and take from it. Nowhere does this double error appear more strongly than in the narratives of the Germanic invasion; the words by which it has been described in no way represent it.

The invasion, or rather, the invasions, were events which were essentially partial, local, and momentary. A band arrived, usually far from numerous; the most powerful, those who founded kingdoms, as the band of Clovis, scarcely numbered from 5,000 to 6,000 men; the entire nation of the Burgundians did not exceed 60,000 men. It rapidly over-ran a limited territory; ravaged a district; attacked a city, and sometimes retreated, carrying away its booty, and sometimes settled somewhere, always careful not to disperse itself too much. We know with what facility and promptitude such events accomplish themselves and disappear. Houses are burnt, fields are devastated, crops carried off, men killed or led away prisoners: all this evil over, at the end of a few days the waves close, the ripple subsides, individual sufferings are forgotten, society returns, at least in appearance, to its former state.   This was the condition of things in Gaul during the fourth century.

But we also know that the human society, that society which we call a people, is not a simple juxta-position of isolated and fugitive existence: were it nothing more, the invasions of the barbarians would not have produced the impression which the documents of the epoch depict; for a long while the number of places and men that suffered there-from was far inferior to the number of those who escaped. But the social life of each man is not concentrated in the mate-rial space which is its theatre, nor in the passing moment; it extends itself to all the relations which he has contracted upon different points of the land; and not only to those relations which he has contracted, but also to those which he might contract, or can even conceive the possibility of contracting; it embraces not only the present, but the future; man lives in a thousand spots which he does not inhabit, in a thousand moments which, as yet, are not; and if this development of his life is cut off from him, if he is forced to confine himself to the narrow limits of his material and actual existence, to isolate himself in space and time, social life is mutilated, and society is no more.

And this was the effect of the invasions, of those appa-ritions of barbarous hordes, short, it is true, and limited, but reviving without cessation, everywhere possible, and always imminent: they destroyed, 1st, all regular, habitual, and easy correspondence between the various parts of the territory; 2nd, all security, all sure prospect of the future; they broke the ties which bound together the inhabitants of the same country, the moments of the same life, they isolated men, and the days of each man.   In many places, and for many years, the aspect of the country might remain the same; but the social organization was attacked, the members no longer held together, the muscles no longer played, the blood no longer circulated freely or surely in the veins: the disease appeared sometimes at one point, sometimes at another: a town was pillaged, a road rendered impassable, a bridge destroyed; such or such a communication ceased: the culture of the land became impossible in such or such a district: in a word, the organic harmony, the general activity of the social body, were each day fettered and disturbed; each day dissolution and paralysis made some new advance.

Thus was Roman society destroyed in Gaul; not as a valley is ravaged by a torrent, but as the most solid body is disorganised by the continual infiltration of a foreign substance. Between all the members of the state, between all the moments of the life of each man, the barbarians continually intruded themselves. I lately endeavoured to paint to you the dismemberment of the Roman empire, the impossibility under which its masters found themselves of holding together the different parts, and how the imperial administration was obliged to retire spontaneously from Britain, from Gaul, incapable of resisting the dissolution of that vast body. What occurred in the Empire occurred equally in each province; as the Empire had suffered disorganization, so did each province; the cantons, the towns detached themselves, and returned to a local and isolated existence. The invasion operated everywhere in the same manner, and everywhere produced the same effects. All the ties by which Rome had been enabled, after so many efforts, to combine together the different parts of the world; that great system of administration, of imposts, of recruiting, of public works, of roads, had not been able to support itself. There remained of it nothing but what could subsist in an isolated and local condition, that is to say, nothing but the wrecks of the municipal system. The inhabitants shut themselves up in the towns, where they continued to govern themselves nearly as they had done of old, with the same rights, by the same institutions. A thousand circumstances prove this concentration of society in towns; here is one which has been little noticed. Under the Roman administration, it is the governors of provinces, the consuls, the correctors, the presidents who fill the scene, and reappear continually in the laws and history; in the sixth century, their names become much more rare; we, indeed, still meet with dukes and counts, to whom the government of the provinces was confided; the barbarian kings strove to inherit the Roman administration, to preserve the same officers, and to induce their power to flow in the same channels; but they succeeded only very incompletely, and with great dis-

order; their dukes were rather military chiefs than administrators; it is manifest that the governors of provinces had no
longer the same importance, and no longer played the same
part; the governors of towns now filled history; the majority
of these counts of Chilperic, of Gontran, of Theodebert,
whose exactions are related by Gregory of Tours, are counts
of towns established within their walls, and by the side of
their bishop. I should exaggerate were I to say that the
province disappeared, but it became disorganized, and lost all
consistency, and almost all reality. The towns, the primitive
elements of the Roman world, survived almost alone amidst
its ruin. The rural districts became the prey of the barbarians; it was there that they established themselves with their
men; it was there that they were about to introduce by
degrees totally new institutions, and a new organization,
but till then the rural districts will occupy scarcely any place
in society, they will be but the theatre of excursions, pillages,
and misery.

Even within the towns the ancient society was far from
maintaining itself strong and entire. Amidst the movement
of the invasions, the towns were regarded above all as fortresses; the population shut themselves therein to escape
from the hordes which ravaged the country. When the barbarous immigration was somewhat diminished, when the new
people had planted themselves upon the territory, the towns
still remained fortresses: in place of having to defend themselves against the wandering hordes, they had to defend themselves against their neighbours, against the greedy and tur-
bulent possessors of the surrounding country. There was
therefore little security behind those weak ramparts. Towns
are unquestionably centres of population and of labour,
but under certain conditions; under the condition, on the
one hand, that the country population cultivate for them; on
the other, that an extended and active commerce consume the
products of the citizen's labour. If agriculture and commerce
decay, towns must decay; their prosperity and their power
cannot be isolated. Now you have just seen into what
a condition the rural districts of Gaul had fallen in the sixth
century; the towns were able to escape for some time, but
from day to day the evil threatened to conquer them. Finally,
it did conquer them, and very soon this last wreck of the

Empire seemed stricken with the same weakness, and a prey to the same dissolution.

Such, in the sixth century, were the general effects of the invasion and establishment of the barbarians upon Roman society; that was the condition in which they had placed it. Let us now inquire, what was the consequence of these facts, with regard to the second clement of modern civilization, the German society itself?

A great mistake lies at the bottom of most of the researches which have been made upon this subject. The institutions of the Germans have been studied in Germany, and then transported just as they were into Gaul, in the train of the Germans. It has been assumed that the German society was in much the same condition after as before the conquest; and persons have reasoned from this postulate in determining the influence of the conquest, and in assigning to it its part in the development of modern civilization. Nothing can be more false and more deceptive. The German society was modified, defaced, dissolved, by the invasion, no less than the Roman society. In this great commotion a wreck was all that remained to each; the social organization of the conquerors perished like that of the conquered.

Two societies—at bottom perhaps more like each other than has been supposed, distinct, nevertheless—subsisted in Germany: first, the society of the colony or tribe, tending to a sedentary condition, and existing upon a limited territory, which it cultivated by means of labourers and slaves; second, the society of the warfaring horde, accidentally grouped around some famous chief, and leading a wandering life. This manifestly results from the facts which I have already described to you

To the first of these two societies, to the tribes, are, in a certain measure, applicable those descriptions of the condition of the ancient Germans by modern Germans, concerning which I have already spoken. When, in fact, a tribe, small in number as were all the tribes, occupied a limited territory; when each head of a family was established upon his domain, in the midst of his people, the social organization which has been described by these writers might well exist, if not completely and effectively, at least in the rough sketch; the assembly of proprietors, of heads of families, decided upon all matters; each

horde had its own assembly; justice was dispensed to them by
the freemen themselves, under the direction of the aged;
a kind of public polity might arise between the confederate
hordes; free institutions were then under the form in which
we meet them in the infancy of nations.

The organization of the warfaring band was different;
another principle presided in it, the principle of the patronage
of the chief, of aristocratic clientship, and military subordination.   It is with regret that I make use of these last words;
they are ill suited to barbarian hordes; yet, however
barbarian men may be, a kind of discipline necessarily in-
troduces itself between the chief and his warriors; and in
this case there must assuredly exist more arbitrary authority,
more forced obedience, than in associations which have not
war for their object.   The German warfaring band therefore
contained a political element that was not possessed by the
tribe. At the same time, however, its freedom was great: no
man engaged therein against his will; the German was born
within his tribe, and thus belonged to a situation which was
not one of his choice; the warrior chose his chief and his
companions, and undertook nothing but with the consent of
his own free will.   Besides, in the bosom of the warfaring
band, the inequality was not great between the chiefs and
their men; there was nothing more than the natural inequality
of strength, skill, or courage; an inequality which afterwards
becomes fruitful, and which produces sooner or later immense
results, but which, at the outset of society, displays itself
only in very narrow limits.   Although the chief had the
largest share of the booty, although he possessed more horses
and more arms, he was not so superior in riches to his companions as to be able to dispose of them without their consent; each warrior entered the association with his strength
and his courage, differing very little from the others, and
at liberty to leave it whenever he pleased.

Such were the two primitive German societies: what did
they become by the fact of the invasion? what change
did it necessarily work upon them? By ascertaining this
alone it is that we can learn what German society truly was
after its transplantation to the Roman soil.

The characteristic fact, the grand result of the invasion, as
regards the Germans, was their change to the condition of

proprietors, the cessation of the wandering life, and the definitive establishment of the agricultural life.

This fact accomplished itself gradually, slowly, and unequally; the wandering life continued for a long time in Gaul, at least it so continued for a great number of the Germans. Nevertheless, when we have estimated all these delays and disorders, we see that, in the end, the conquerors became proprietors, that they attached themselves to the soil, that landed property was the essential element of the new social state.

What were the consequences of this single fact, as regards the regulation of the warfaring band and of the tribe?

As to the tribe, remember what I have told you of the manner of its territorial establishment in Germany, of the manner in which the villages were constructed and disposed. The population was not condensed therein; each family, each habitation was isolated and surrounded with a plot of cultivated ground. It is thus that nations, who have only arrived at this degree of civilization, arrange themselves, even when they lead a sedentary life.

When the tribe was transplanted to the soil of Gaul, the habitations became yet further dispersed; the chiefs of families established themselves at a much greater distance from one another; they occupied vast domains; their houses afterwards became castles. The villages which formed themselves around them were no longer peopled with men who were free, who were their equals, but with labourers who were attached to their lands. Thus, in its material relations, the tribe became dissolved by the single fact of its new establishment.

You may easily guess what effect this single change was calculated to exert upon its institutions. The assembly of freemen, wherein all things were debated, was now got together with much greater difficulty. So long as they had lived near to one another, there was no need of any great art, or wise combinations, in order that they might treat in common of their affairs; but when a population is scattered, in order that the principles and forms of free institutions may remain applicable to it, great social development is necessary, riches, intelligence, in short, a thousand things are necessary, which were wanting to the German horde, transported suddenly to a territory far more extensive than that which it had hitherto occupied. The system which regulated its

existence in Germany now perished.   In looking over the
most ancient German laws—those of the Allemanni, Boii,
and Franks—we see that, originally, the assembly of freemen
in each district was held very frequently, at first, every week,
and afterwards, every month.   All questions were carried
before it; judgments were given there, and not only criminal,
but also civil judgments: almost all acts of civil life were
done in its presence, as sales, donations, &c.   When once the
tribe was established in Gaul, the assemblies became rare and,
difficult; so difficult, that it was necessary to employ force
to make the freemen attend: this is the object of many
legal decrees.   And if you pass suddenly from the fourth
to the middle of the eighth century, you find that at this last
epoch there were in each county but three assemblies of freemen in the year: and these not regularly kept, as is proved
by some of Charlemagne's laws.

   If other proofs were necessary, here is one which deserves
to be noticed.   When the assemblies were frequent, freemen,
under the name of *rachimburgi, arhimanni, boni homines*,
and in various forms, decided upon affairs.   When they no
longer attended, it became necessary, upon urgent occasions,
to supply their places; and thus we see, at the end of the
eighth century, the freemen replaced in judicial functions by
permanent judges.   The *scabini*, or sheriffs of Charlemagne,
were regular judges.   In each county, five, seven, or nine freemen were appointed by the count, or other local magistrate,
and charged to present themselves at the assembly of the
country to decide upon cases.   The primitive institutions
were become impracticable, and the judicial power passed
from the people to the magistrates.

   Such was the state into which the first element of German
society, the colony or tribe, fell after the invasion and under
its influence.   Politically speaking, it was disorganised, as
Roman society had been.   As to the warfaring band, facts
accomplished themselves in another way, and under a different
form, but with the same results.

   When a band arrived anywhere, and took possession of the
land, or of a portion of it, we must not believe that this occupation took place systematically, or that the territory was
divided by lots, and that each warrior received one,
proportionate to his importance or his rank.   The chiefs

of the band, or the different chiefs who were united in it, appropriated to themselves vast domains. The greater part of the warriors who had followed them continued to live around them, with them, and at their table, without possessing any property which belonged especially to them. The band did not dissolve into individuals of whom each became a proprietor; the most considerable warriors entered almost alone into this situation. Had they dispersed themselves, in order that each one might establish himself upon a spot of the territory, their safety amidst the original population would have been compromised; it was necessary that they should remain united in groups. Moreover, it was by the life in common that the pleasures of the barbarians, gaming, the chase, and banquets, could alone subsist. How could they have resigned themselves to isolation? Isolation is only supportable in a laborious condition; man cannot remain idle and alone. Now, the barbarians were essentially idle; they therefore required to live together, and many companions remained about their chief, leading upon his domains pretty nearly the same life which they had led before in his train. But from these circumstances it arose that their relative situation was completely altered. Very soon a prodigious inequality sprang up between them: their inequality no longer consisted in some personal difference of strength or of courage, or in a more or less considerable share of cattle, slaves, or valuable goods. The chief, become a great proprietor, disposed of many of the means of power; the others were always simple warriors; and the more the ideas of property established and extended themselves in men's minds, the more was inequality, with its effects, developed. At this period we find a great number of freemen falling by degrees into a very inferior position. The laws speak constantly of freemen, of Franks living upon the lands of another, and reduced almost to the situation of the labourers.[1] The band, regarded as a peculiar society, reposed upon two facts—the voluntary association of the warriors in order to lead in common a wandering life, and their equality. These two facts perished in the results of the invasion. On one hand, the wandering life ended—on the other, inequality introduced itself, and increased from day to day, among the sedentary warriors.

[1] Essais sur l'Histoire de France, pp. 109—111.

The progressive parcelling out of lands, during the three centuries after the invasion, did not change this result. There are none of you who have not heard of the fees that the king, or the great chiefs who occupied a vast territory, distributed to their men, to attach them to their service, or to recompense them for services done. This practice, in proportion as it extended, produced, upon what remained of the warfaring band, effects analogous to those which I have pointed out to you. On one hand, the warrior upon whom the chief had conferred the fee, departed to inhabit it,—a new source of isolation and individuality; on the other, this warrior had usually a certain number of men attached to him; or he sought and found men who would come to live with him upon his domain;—a new source of inequality. Such were the general effects of the invasion upon the two ancient Germanic societies, the tribe and the wandering band. They became equally disorganized, and entered upon totally different situations, upon totally new relations. In order to bind them among themselves anew, in order to form society anew, and to deduce from that society a government, it became necessary to have recourse to other principles, to other institutions. Dissolved, like Roman society, German society, in like manner, furnished to the society which followed it nothing but wrecks.

I hope that these expressions, *society dissolved, society which perished,* do not mislead you, and that you understand them in their right sense. A society never dissolves itself, but because a new society is fermenting and forming in its bosom; the concealed work it is there going on which tends to separate its elements, in order to arrange them under new combinations. Such a disorganization shows that facts are changed, that the relations and dispositions of men are no longer the same; that other principles and other forms are ready to assume the predominance. Thus, in affirming that, in the sixth century, ancient society, Roman as well as German, was dissolved in Gaul by the results of the invasion, we say that, by the same causes, at the same epoch, and upon the same ground, modern society began.

We have no means of explaining or clearly contemplating this first labour; the original sources, the original creation, is profoundly concealed, and does not manifest itself outwardly until later, when it has already made considerable progress. Nevertheless, it is possible to foresee it; and it is important that you should know, at once, what was fermenting and being formed beneath this general dissolution of the two elements of modern society; I will endeavour to give you an idea of this in few words.

The first fact of which we catch a glimpse at this period, is a certain tendency to the development of royalty. Persons have often praised barbarian at the expense of modern royalty, wrongfully, as I think: in the fourth and in the seven teenth centuries this word expresses two institutions, two powers which are profoundly different from each other. There were, indeed, among the barbarians, some germs of hereditary royalty, some traces of a religious character inherent in certain families descended from the first chiefs of the nations, from heroes become gods. There can, however, be no doubt but that choice, election, was the principal source of royalty, and that the character of warlike chiefs predominates in the barbarous kings.

When they were transplanted to the Roman territory, their situation changed. They found there a place which was empty, namely, that of the emperors. Power, titles, and a machine of government with which the barbarians were acquainted, and of which they admired the splendour and soon appreciated the efficacy, were there; they were, of course, strongly tempted to appropriate these advantages. Such, indeed, was the aim of all their efforts. This fact appears everywhere: Clovis, Childebert, Gontran, Chilperic, Clotaire, laboured incessantly to assume the names and to exercise the rights of the Empire; they wished to distribute their dukes and their counts as the emperors had distributed their consuls, their correctors, and their presidents; they tried to reestablish all that system of taxes, enlistment, and administration which had fallen into ruin. In a word, barbaric royalty, narrow and crude as it was, endeavoured to develop itself, and fill, in some measure, the enormous frame of imperial royalty.

For a long while the course of things was not favourable to it, and its first attempts were attended with little success; nevertheless, we may see, from the beginning, that something of the imperial royalty will remain to it; that the new royalty will by and bye gather a portion of that imperial inheritance, the whole of which it desired to appropriate at the first; immediately after the invasion, it became less war- like, more religious, and more politic than it had hitherto been, that is to say, it assumed more of the character of the imperial royalty. Here, if I mistake not, is the first great fact of that labour which was about to give birth to the new society; that fact is not clearly manifest as yet, but glimpses of it are easily to be caught.

The second great fact is the birth of the territorial aris- tocracy. Property, for a long time after the settlement of the barbarians, seemed uncertain, fluctuating and confused, passing from one hand to another with surprising rapidity. Nevertheless, it is clear that it prepared to become fixed in the same hands, and to regulate itself. The tendency of fees is to become hereditary; and, in spite of the ob- stacles which oppose it, the principle of inheritance pre- vails therein more and more. At the same time there arose between the possessors of the fees that hierarchical organization which afterwards became the feudal system. We must not transport into the sixth and seventh centuries the feudalism of the thirteenth; nothing like it then ex- isted; the disorder of property and personal relations was infinitely greater than under the feudal system; never- theless all things concurred, on the one hand, to render pro- perty fixed; on the other, to constitute the society of the proprietors according to a certain hierarchy. As we have seen royalty dawning from the end of the sixth century, so, likewise, we may discover, from that period, the dawn of feudalism.

Finally, a third fact also developed itself at this epoch. I have engaged your attention with the state of the church; you have seen what power it had, and how it was, so to speak, the sole living remnant of Roman society. When the barbarians were established, let us see in what situation the church found itself, or, at least, what that situation soon be- came. The bishops were, as you know, the natural chiefs of the towns; they governed the people in the interior of each city, they represented them in the presence of the barbarians, they were their magistrates within, and their protectors without. The clergy were therefore deeply rooted in the municipal system, that is to say, in all that remained of Roman society. And they very soon struck root in other directions; the bishops became the counsellors of the barbarous. kings; they counselled them upon the conduct which they ought to observe towards the vanquished people, upon the. course they ought to take in order to become the heirs of the Roman emperors. They had far more experience and. political intelligence than the barbarians, who came fresh. from Germany; they had the love of power, they had been accustomed to serve and to profit by it. They were thus the counsellors of the nascent royalty, while they remained the magistrates and patrons of the still surviving municipality.

Behold them connected on the one hand with the people, on. the other with thrones. But this was not all; a third position. now opened itself to them; they became great proprietors; they entered into that hierarchical crganization of manorial property which, as yet, scarcely existed but in tendency; they laboured to occupy, and soon succeeded in occupying, a considerable place therein. So that at this epoch, while yet the new society was in its first rudiments, the church was already connected with all its parts, was everywhere in good repute and powerful; a sure sign that it would be the first to attain. dominion; as happened.

Such were the three great facts—obscure as yet, but visible— by which the new social order announced itself, at the end of the sixth and the beginning of the seventh century. It is, I believe, impossible to mistake them; but, in recognising them, we must remember that neither of them had as yet taken the position and the form which it was to retain. All things were still mixed and confused to such a degree, that it must have been impossible for the shrewdest sight to have discerned any of the characteristics of the future. I have already had occasion to say, and in your studies you have had opportunities of becoming convinced, that there exists no modern system, no pretension to power, which has not discovered grounds for its legitimacy in these beginnings of our society. Royalty regards itself as the only heir of the Roman empire. The feudal aristocracy asserts that, at that, time, it possessed the entire country, men and lands; the towns affirm that they succeeded to all the rights of the Roman municipalities; the clergy, that they then shared.

G G

all power.   This singular epoch has lent itself to all the requirements of party spirit, to all the hypotheses of science; it
has furnished arguments and arms to nations, to kings, to
grandees, to priests, to liberty as well as to aristocracy, to
aristocracy as well as to royalty.

The fact is, it carried all things in its bosom, theocracy,
monarchy, oligarchy, republics, mixed constitutions; and all
things in a state of confusion which has allowed each to see
all that it chose to see therein.   The obscure and irregular
fermentation of the wrecks of former society, German as well
as Roman, and the first labours of their transformation into
elements of the new society, constituted the true condition of
Gaul during the sixth and seventh centuries, and this is the
only character we can assign to it.

NINTH LECTURE.

Object of the lecture—False idea of the Salic law—History of the formation of this law—Two hypotheses upon this matter—Eighteen manuscripts — Two texts of the Salic law — M. Wiarda's work upon the history and exposition of the Salic law—Prefaces attached to the manuscripts—Value of national traditions concerning the origin and compilation of the Salic law—Concerning its tendencies—It is essentially a penal code—1st. Of the enumeration and definition of offences in the Salic law; 2nd. Of penalties; 3rd. Of criminal procedure—Transitory character of this legislation.

WE are to occupy ourselves now with the barbarian laws, and especially with the Salic law, upon which I must give certain minute details, indispensable to a knowledge of the true character of this law, and of the social state which is indicated thereby. People have been deeply, and for a long while, deceived upon this point. A greatly exaggerated importance has been attributed to the Salic law. You are acquainted with the reason of this error; you know that at the accession of Philippe-le-Long, and during the struggle of Philippe-de-Valois and Edward III. for the crown of France, the Salic law was invoked in order to prevent the succession of women, and that, from that time, it has been celebrated by a crowd of writers, as the first source of our public law, as a law always in vigour, as the fundamental law of monarchy. Those who have been the most free from this illusion, as, for example, Montesquieu, have yet experienced, to some degree, its influence, and have spoken of the Salic law with a respect which it is assuredly difficult to feel towards it when we attri-

a a 2

bute to it only the place that it really holds in our history.
We might be tempted to believe that the majority of the
writers who have spoken of this law had studied neither its
history nor its scope; that they were equally ignorant of its
source and of its character. These are the two questions which
we have now to solve: we must learn, on the one hand, in
what manner the Salic law was compiled, when, where, by
whom, and for whom; on the other, what the object and plan
of its dispositions were.

As regards its history, I pray you to recal that which I
have already told you touching the double origin and the incoherence of the barbarous laws; they were, at once, anterior
and posterior to the invasion; at once, German, and Germano-
Roman: they belonged to two different conditions of society.
This character has influenced all the controversies of which
the Salic law has been the object; it has given rise to two
hypotheses: according to one, this law was compiled in Germany, upon the right bank of the Rhine, long before the
conquest, and in the language of the Franks; everything in its
provisions which is not suitable to that period, and to ancient
German society, according to this hypothesis, was introduced
afterwards, in the successive revisions which occurred after
the invasion. According to the other hypothesis, the Salic
law was, on the contrary, compiled after the conquest, upon
the left bank of the Rhine, in Belgium or in Gaul, perhaps in
the seventh century, and in Latin.

Nothing is more natural than the conflict of these hypotheses; they necessarily arose from the Salic law itself. A
peculiar circumstance tended to provoke them.

In the manuscripts which remain to us, there are two texts
of this law: the one unmixedly Latin; the other Latin also,
but mixed with a great number of German words, of glosses,
and of expositions, in the ancient Frankish tongue, interca-
lated in the course of the articles. It contains two hundred
and fifty-three intercalations of this kind. The second text
was published at Basil, in 1557, by the juris-consult, John
Herold, from a manuscript in the Abbey of Fulda. The
purely Latin text was published, for the first time, in Paris,
without date, or the name of the editor; and, for the second
time, by John Dutillet, also in Paris, in 1573. Both texts
have since gone through many editions.

Of these two texts there exist eighteen manuscripts[1]—
namely, fifteen of the unmixedly Latin text, and three of
that in which Germanic words appear.   Of these manuscripts,
fifteen have been found upon the left bank of the Rhine, in
France, and only three in Germany.   You might be inclined
to suppose that the three manuscripts found in Germany, are
those which contain the German glosses: but such is not the
case; of the three manuscripts with the comments, two only
come from Germany, the third was found in Paris; of the fifteen
others, fourteen were found in France, and one in Germany.

The fifteen manuscripts of the unmixedly Latin texts are
pretty nearly alike.   There are, indeed, some various readings
in the prefaces, the epilogues, and in the arrangement or the
compilation of the articles, but these are of little importance.
The three manuscripts containing the German comments differ
much more widely; they differ in the number of titles and
articles, in their arrangement, even in their contents, and still
more in their style.   Of these manuscripts, two are written
in the most barbarous Latin.

Here, then, are two texts of the Salic law which support
the two solutions of the problem; the one appears rather of a
Roman origin, the other more entirely Germanic.   Thus the
question assumes this form: of the two texts, which is the
most ancient ?—to which of them should priority be attributed ?

The common opinion, especially in Germany, attributes
the highest antiquity to the text which bears the German
gloss.   There are, indeed, some arguments which seem, at
first sight, to support this view.   The three manuscripts of
this text bear the words, *Lex Salica antiqua, antiquissima,
vetustior;* whilst, in those of the unmixedly Latin text, we
commonly read: *Lex Salica recentior, emendata, reformata.*
If we referred the question to these epigraphs, it would be
resolved.

Another circumstance seems to lead us to the same solution.
Several manuscripts contain a kind of preface, in which the
history of the Salic law is related.   The following is the
most comprehensive.   You will immediately see what come

If I do not err, M. Pertz has recently discovered two others; but nothing
has as yet been published concerning them.

quences are to be deduced from it concerning the antiquity of the law:

" The nation of the Franks, illustrious, founded by God, mighty in arms, firm in treaties of peace, profound in council, noble and healthy in body, of a singular fairness and beauty, bold, active, and fierce in fight; lately converted to the catholic faith, free from heresy; while it was yet under a barbarous belief seeking the key of knowledge by the inspiration of God, desiring justice, and observing piety according to the nature of its qualities: the Salic law was dictated by the chiefs of their nation, who, at that time, commanded therein.

" Four men were chosen of many—namely, Wisogast, Bodogast, Salogast, and Windogast,[1] in the places called Salagheve, Bodogheve, Windogheve. These men met in three *mâls*,[2] discussed with care all judicial processes, treated of each in particular, and decreed their judgment in the following manner. Afterwards, when, with the help of God, Choldwig the long-haired, the beautiful, the illustrious king of the Franks, had received the first catholic baptism, everything in this covenant that was considered unfitting was amended with perspicuity by the illustrious kings, Choldwig, Childeberg, and Chlotaire; and in this manner was the following decree produced:

" ' Honour to Christ who loves the Franks! May he preserve their kingdom, and fill their chiefs with the light of his grace! May he protect their army; may he give them signs which shall bear witness to their faith, awarding unto them joys of peace and an entire felicity! May the Lord Jesus Christ direct in the ways of piety those who govern! For this is the nation which, small in number but valorous and powerful, shook from its head the hard yoke of the Romans, and which, after having recognised the sacredness of baptism, sumptuously adorned with gold and precious stones the bodies of the holy martyrs whom the Romans had burnt with fire, massacred, mutilated with the sword, or delivered to be torn to pieces by wild beasts.

---

[1] *Gast* means guest; *gheve* or *gau*, canton, district; *salogast* is the guest inhabiting the canton of Sale; *bodogast*, the guest of the canton of Bode, &c.

[2] *Mallum*, an assembly of free men.

"*Concerning the inventors of laws and their order.*—
"Moses was the first of all those who expounded, in sacred
letters, the divine laws to the Hebrew nation. King Pho-
roneus was the first to establish laws and judgments among
the Greeks ; Mercury Trismegistus gave the first laws to
the Egyptians; Solon gave the first laws to the Athenians;
Lycurgus established the first laws among the Lacedemonians,
by the authority of Apollo; Numa Pompilius, who succeeded
to Romulus, gave the first laws to the Romans. Afterwards,
because the factious people would not tolerate its magistrates, it created decemvirs to write laws, and these placed
upon twelve tables the laws of Solon, translated into Latin.
They were: Appius Claudius Sabinus, T. L. Genutius, P. Ses-
tius Vaticanus, T. Veturius Cicurinus, C. Julius Tullius,
A. Manilius, P. Sulpicius Camerinus, Sp. Postumius Albus,
P. Horatius Pulvillus, T. Romilius Vaticanus. These decemvirs were nominated to write the laws. The consul
Pompey was the first to desire that the laws should be
written in books; but he did not prosecute his desire from
the dread of calumniators. Cæsar afterwards began this
work, but he was killed before he completed it. Little
by little the ancient laws fell into disuse through age and
neglect; but although they were no longer used, it was nevertheless necessary that they should be known. The new
laws began to count from Constantine and his successors;
they were mixed and without order. Afterwards, the august
Theodosius II., in imitation of the Codes of Gregory and of
Hermogenes, caused the constitutions given out since Constantine to be collected and arranged under the name of each
emperor; and this is called, after himself, the Theodosian
Code. Afterwards, each nation selected, according to its
customs, the laws which were suited to it; for a long custom
passes for a law: law is a written constitution; custom is
usage founded upon antiquity, or unwritten law ; for the
word *law* is derived from the word *legere* (*lex a legendo*),
because it is written; custom is a long habit founded solely
upon manners; habit is a certain right which is established
by manners, and which is regarded as law; law is all that
which has already been established by reason, which is agreeable to good discipline and profitable to salvation; but we
call that habit which is in common use.

"Theodoric, king of the Franks, when he was at Chalons, selected the wise men of his kingdom, and those who were learned in ancient laws, and dictating to them himself, he commanded them to write the laws of the Franks, of the Allemanni, of the Boii, and of all the nations which were under his power, according to the customs of each. He added what was necessary thereto, and took away what was improper, and amended, according to the laws of the Christians, that which was according to the ancient pagan customs. And of that which king Theodoric was unable to change, on account of the great antiquity of the pagan customs, king Childebert began the correction, which was finished by king Chlotaire. The glorious king Dagobert renewed all these things by means of the illustrious men, Claudius, Chadoin, Domagne, and Agilof; he caused to be transcribed, with ameliorations, the ancient laws, and gave them written to each nation. Laws are made in order that human wickedness should be restrained by fear, that innocence should be shielded from all danger in the midst of the wicked, that the wicked should dread punishment, and that they should curb their lust for mischief.

"This has been decreed by the king, the chiefs, and all the Christian people who dwell in the country of the Merovingians.

*   *   *   *   *   *   *

"In the name of Christ:—

"Here commences the compact of the Salic law.

"'Those who have written the Salic law are Wisogast, Aregast, Salogast, Windogast, in Bodham, Saleham, and Widham....'"

From this preface, from the words *antiqua, vetustior*, inserted in a text, and from some other analogous indications, it has been concluded—1st. That the Salic law was written before the invasion, beyond the Rhine, and in the language of the Franks. 2nd. That the manuscript mixed with German words was the most ancient, and that it contained the remains of the primitive text.

The most learned work in which this controversy has been recapitulated is that of M. Wiarda, entitled, "*Histoire et explication de la loi Salique*," and published at Bremen in 1808. I will not carry you through the labyrinth of discus·

sions which he engages in upon the different questions which his work embraces; but merely point out his principal results. They are generally supported by sufficient proofs, and the criticism upon them is very careful.

According to M. Wiarda, the text mixed with German words—in the copies, at least, which we possess of it—is not more ancient than the other; one might be tempted, indeed, to believe it more modern. Two articles especially seem to indicate that this is the case:—1st. Title 61, entitled *De Chrenecruda*,[1] which treats of the cession of property, is found alike in both texts; but the purely Latin text gives it as a rule in vigour, while the text with the German gloss adds: " In present times this no longer applies." 2nd. Under title 58, § 1st, the text with the gloss runs thus: " According to the ancient law, whoever disinterred or stripped a dead and buried body, was banished," &c. This law, described here as ancient, exists in the unmixedly Latin text without any observation

It is impossible to deny that these two passages of the text with the gloss seem to indicate posterior date.

From this comparison of the texts, M. Wiarda passes to an examination of the preface, and easily discovers improbabilities and contradictions therein. Many manuscripts have no preface; in those which have, they vary much. Even that which I have just read to you is composed of incoherent parts; the second part, from the words, *the inventors of laws*, &c. &c., is copied textually in the treatise *Of Etymologies and Origins*, by Isidore of Seville, a writer of the seventh century; the third, from these words: *Theodoric, king of the Franks*, is also found at the head of a manuscript of the law of the Bavarians. The names of the first compilers of the law of the Salian Franks are not the same in the preface and in the body of the law itself. From these, and many other circumstances, M. Wiarda concludes that the prefaces are merely additions written at the head of the text, by the copyists, who collected, each in his own fashion, the popular reports, and that therefore no authority is to be attributed to them.

Moreover, none of the ancient documents, none of the first

---

[1] That is to say, *concerning green herbage*, from ancient German words which answer to the modern words *grün*, green, and *kraut*, herb or plant.

chroniclers who have minutely related the history of the
Franks, neither Gregory of Tours, nor Fredegaire, for instance, speak of any compilation of their laws. We must
come down to the eighth century in order to find a passage in
which such compilation is mentioned, and then it is in one of
the most confused and most fabulous chronicles of the time,
the *Gesta Francorum*, that we read:

"After a battle with the emperor Valentinian, in which
their chief, Priam, fell, the Franks left Sicambria, and came
to establish themselves in the regions of Germany, at the
extremity of the river Rhine .... There they elected king
Pharamond, son of Marcomir, and, elevating him upon their
shields, they proclaimed him the long-haired king; and then
they began to adopt a law which their ancient gentile
councillors, Wisogast, Windogast, Aregast, and Salogast,
wrote in the German villages of Bodecheim, Salecheim, and
Windecheim." (*Gesta Franc.* c. 3.)

It is upon this paragraph that all the prefaces, inscriptions,
or narratives, placed at the head of manuscripts, are founded;
they have no other warrant, and merit no more faith.

After having thus discarded the indirect documents advanced in support of the high antiquity and of the purely
German origin of this law, M. Wiarda comes directly to the
question, and conceives, 1st, That the Salic law was written
for the first time upon the left bank of the Rhine, in Belgium,
upon the territory situated between the forest of Ardennes,
the Meuse, the Lys, and the Scheldt; a country which, for a
long time, was occupied by the Salian Franks, whom especially this law governed, and from whom it received its name;
2nd, that, in none of the texts actually existing does this
law appear to go further back than the seventh century;
3rd, that it has never been written except in Latin. This
is acknowledged with regard to all other barbarous laws,
the Ripuarian, Bavarian, and Allemannic laws; and nothing
indicates that the Salic law was an exception. Moreover,
the Germanic dialects were not written before the reign of
Charlemagne ; and Otfried of Weissemburg, the translator
of the Gospel, calls the Frankish tongue, even in the ninth
century, *linguam indisciplinabilem.*

Such are the general results of the learned labour of M.
Wiarda; and, upon the whole, I believe that they are legiti-

mate. He even places too little importance upon a kind of proof, which is, in my opinion, more forcible than the greater portion of those which he has so ingeniously examined—I mean, the contents themselves of the Salic law, and the facts which are clearly deducible therefrom. It seems evident to me, from the dispositions, the ideas, and the tone of their law, that it belongs to a period at which the Franks had for a long time existed amidst a Roman population. It constantly makes mention of the Romans; and not as of inhabitants scattered thinly here and there over the territory, but as of a population numerous, industrious, agricultural, and already reduced, in great part at least, to the condition of labourers. We also perceive from this law, that Christianity was not of recent date among the Franks, but that it already held an important place in society and men's minds. Churches, bishops, deacons, clerks, are often treated of; and we may recognise, in more than one article, the influence of religion upon moral notions, and the change which it had already wrought upon barbarous manners. In short, the intrinsic proof, derivable from the law itself, appears to me conclusive in favour of the hypothesis maintained by M. Wiarda.

I believe, however, that the traditions which, through so many contradictions and fables, appear in the prefaces and epilogues annexed to the law, have more importance, and merit more consideration, than he gives them. They indicate that, from the eighth century, it was a general belief, a popular tradition, that the customs of the Salian Franks were anciently collected—they were Christians before, in a territory more German than that which they now occupied. However little their authenticity, and however defective the documents where these traditions are preserved may be, they at least prove that the traditions existed. We are not obliged to believe that the Salic law, such as we have it, is of a very remote date, nor that it was compiled as recounted, nor even that it was ever written in the German language; but that it was connected with customs collected and transmitted from generation to generation, when the Franks lived about the mouth of the Rhine, and modified, extended, explained, reduced into law, at various times, from that epoch down to the end of the eighth century—this, I think, is the reasonable result to which this discussion should lead.

Allow me, before quitting the work of M. Wiarda, to call your attention to two ideas which are developed there, and which contain, in my opinion, a large portion of truth. The Salic law, according to him, is, properly speaking, no law at all, no code; it was not compiled and published by a legal, official authority, whether that of a king, or of an assembly or the people or great men. He has been disposed to see in it a mere enumeration of customs and judicial decisions—a collection made by some learned man, some barbarian priest—a collection analogous to the *Mirror of the Saxons*, to the *Mirror of the Swabians*, and many other ancient monuments of the Germanic legislation, which have evidently only this character. M. Wiarda founds the conjecture upon the example of many other nations at the same degree of civilization, and upon a number of ingenious arguments. One has escaped him— perhaps, the most conclusive; this is a text of the Salic law itself. There we read:—

" If any one strips a dead person before he is placed in the earth, let him be condemned to pay 1800 deniers, which make 45 sous; and, according to another decision, (*in alia sententia*,) 2500 deniers, which make 62 sous and a-half."[1]

This is evidently not a legislative text, for it contains two different penalties for the same crime; and the words, *according to another decision*, are exactly those which would be found in the language of jurisprudence, in a collection of decrees.

M. Wiarda thinks, moreover, and this will confirm the preceding opinion, that the Salic law does not contain all the legislation, all the law of the Salian Franks. We find, in fact, in the monuments of the ninth, tenth, and eleventh centuries, a certain number of cases which are called rules *secundum legem salicam*, and of which the text of that law makes no mention. Certain forms of marriage, certain rules of affiancing, are expressly called *secundum legem salicam*, which do not figure there at all. From whence one might conclude that a large number of the customs of the Salian Franks had never been written, and form no part of the text which we possess.

Here are a great many details, and I have suppressed many more; I have given only the result of the controversies of

---

[1] *Pact. Leg. Sal.*, ed. Herold, tit. xvii. de Expoliationibus, § 1.

which the history of the Salic law alone has been the object. It is from not having given proper attention to it, from not having scrutinized with care the origins and vicissitudes of this law, that such strange mistakes have been fallen into as to its character. Let us now enter into the examination of the legislation itself, and endeavour to bring to bear upon it a rather close criticism, for here also people have strangely fallen into vagueness and declamation.

The two texts are of unequal extent : the text, mixed with Germanic words, contains 80 titles and 420 articles or paragraphs; the purely Latin text has but 70, 71, 72 titles, according to the different manuscripts, and 406, 407, or 408 articles. One manuscript, that of Wolfenbuttel, a very confused one in its arrangements, contains even a greater number.

At the first aspect it is impossible not to be struck with the apparent utter chaos of the law. It treats of all things—of political law, of civil law, of criminal law, of civil procedure, of criminal procedure, of rural jurisdiction, all mixed up together without any distinction or classification. If we were to write out, each on a separate piece of paper, the various articles of our various codes, and after having thrown them together into an urn, draw them out as each presented itself, the order, or rather disorder, in which chance would throw them, would differ very little from their arrangement in the Salic law.

When we examine this law more closely, we perceive that it is essentially a penal regulation, that in it the criminal law occupies the first, and, indeed, almost the whole place. The political law makes its appearance quite incidentally and indirectly, and in reference only to institutions, to facts which are regarded as established, and with the foundation or even declaration of which the law looks upon itself as having nothing to do; as to the civil law, it contains some enactments of a more precise and distinct nature, to the preparation of which much attention seems to have been paid. The same is the case with regard to civil procedure. As to criminal procedure, the Salic law appears to consider almost every point established and understood; all that it does under this head, is to supply a few obvious deficiencies, and to lay down in certain cases the duties of judges, of witnesses, &c. Pains and penalties are here entirely dominant; the great aim is to repress crime, and to inflict punishment. It is a penal code

It contains three hundred and forty-three penal articles, and
but sixty-five upon all other subjects.

Such, indeed, is the character of all legislations in their
infancy; it is by penal laws that nations make the first visible
steps—the first written steps, if I may use the expression—
out of barbarism.   They have no idea of writing the political
law; the powers which govern them, and the forms in which
those powers are exercised, are clear, certain, understood
facts: it is not in this period of their existence that nations
discuss constitutions.   The civil law exists in like manner as
a fact; the mutual relations between men, their covenants
and agreements, are left to the rules of natural equity, are
conducted according to certain fixed principles, certain generally admitted forms.   The legal settlement of this portion of
law does not take place until after a much fuller development
of the social state.   Whether under a religious form, or under
one purely secular, the penal law is the first that makes its
appearance in the legislative career of nations; their first
effort towards the perfecting of civil life consists in raising
barriers against, in proclaiming, beforehand, punishments for
excesses of individual liberty.   The Salic law belongs to this
period of the history of our society.

In order to acquire a true knowledge of this law, apart
from the vague assertions and discussions of which it has
been made the object, let us endeavour to consider it—first,
in the enumeration and definition of crimes; secondly, in its
application of punishments; thirdly, in its criminal procedure.
These are the three essential elements of all penal legislation.

I. The crimes taken cognisance of in the Salic law are
almost all of them classed under two heads : robbery, and
violence against the person.   Of three hundred and forty-
three articles in the penal law, one hundred and fifty have
reference to cases of robbery, and of these seventy-four
relate to and assign punishments for the stealing of animals—
twenty, namely, to pig stealing; sixteen to horse stealing;
thirteen to the stealing of bulls, cows, and oxen; seven to
sheep and goat stealing; four to dog stealing; seven to bird
stealing; and seven to bee stealing.   Under these heads the
laws enter into the most minute details; the crime and the
punishment vary according to the age and sex of the thief,
the number of animals stolen, the place and time of the robbery, &c.

Cases of violence against the person furnish matter for 113 articles, of which 30 relate to mutilation in every possible variety, 24 to violence against women, &c.

I need proceed no further in this enumeration of crimes. They exhibit to us in a clear light two marked characteristics of the law: 1st, it belongs to a society in a very low and inartificial state. Open the criminal codes of another period, you find a far greater variety in the classes of crimes, while in each class the specification of cases is infinitely less detailed; we recognise at once more various facts and more general ideas. The crimes set forth here are, for the most part, such only as may be anticipated in a condition of things under which mankind becomes more united, however simple their relations may be, however monotonous their life. 2nd. It is also evidently a very coarse and brutal society, in which the confusion of individual wills and forces is carried to an extremity, where there is no kind of public power to prevent their excesses, where the safety of persons and properties is every instant in peril. This absence of all generalization, of all attempt to give a simple and common character to crimes, attests at once the want of intellectual development, and the precipitation of the legislator. It combines nothing; it is under the influence of a pressing necessity; it takes, so to speak, every action, every case of robbery, of violence in the very fact, in order to immediately inflict a penalty upon them. Rude itself, it had to do with rude men, and had no idea but of adding a new article of law whenever a new crime was committed, however trifling its difference from those it had already contemplated.

II. From the crimes let us pass to the punishments, and let us see what was the character of the Salic law in this respect.

At the first glance, we shall be st uck with its mildness. This legislation, which as to crimes reveals such violent and brutal manners, contains no cruel punishments, and not only is it not cruel, but it seems to bear a singular respect towards the person and liberty of men: of free men, that is to say; for whenever slaves or even labourers are in question, cruelty reappears—the law abounds in tortures and in corporeal punishments for them; but for free men, Franks and even Romans, it is extremely moderate. There are but

few cases of the punishment of death, and from this criminals
could always redeem themselves; no corporeal punishments,
no imprisonments. The only punishment put forth in
writing in the Salic law, is composition, *wehrgeld*, *wid-
rigeld*[1]—that is, a certain sum which the guilty person was
obliged to pay to the offended person, or to his family. To
the *wehrgeld* is added, in a great number of cases, what the
German laws call the *fred*,[2] a sum paid to the king or to the
magistrate, in reparation for the violation of public peace.
The penal system of the law reduces itself to this.

Composition is the first step of criminal legislation out of
the system of personal vengeance. The right concealed under
this penalty, the right which exists at the foundation of the
Salic law, and all barbaric laws, is the right of each man to
do justice to himself, to revenge himself by force ; war
between the offender and the offended. Composition is
an attempt to substitute a legal system for this war; it is the
right of the offender, by paying a certain sum, to protect
himself from the vengeance of the offended; it obliges the
offended party to renounce the employment of force.

Be careful, however, not to suppose that it had this effect
from its origin; the offended party for a long time preserved
the privilege of choosing between composition and war, of
refusing the *wehrgeld*, and having recourse to vengeance.
The chronicles and documents of all kinds leave no doubt on
the subject. I am inclined to think that at the eighth century
composition was obligatory, and the refusal to be contented
therewith was regarded as a violence, not as a right; but
assuredly, it had not always been so, and composition was at
first only a rather inefficacious attempt to put an end to the
disorderly contest of individual force—a kind of legal offer
from the offender to the offended.

In Germany, and especially in later times, a far higher
idea has been attached to it. Men of learning and of rare
minds have been struck, not only with the respect for the
power and liberty of man which appears in this kind of
penalty, but with many other characteristics which they think

---

[1] Probibition money, (from *wheren*, *wharen*, *bewahren*,) guarantee. See
my *Essais sur l'Histoire de France*, p. 197.
[2] From *frieden*, peace.

are to be recognised in it. I shall arrest your attention but upon one: what, from the time that we consider things under an elevated and moral point of view, what is the radical vice of modern penal legislations? They strike, they punish, without troubling themselves to know whether the guilty party accepts the penalty or not, whether he acknowledges his wrong, whether his will does or does not concur with the will of the law; they act only by constraint, justice cares not to appear to him she condemns, under other features than those of force.

Composition has, so to speak, an entirely different penal physiognomy; it supposes, it involves the avowal of wrong by the offender; it is, in its way, an act of liberty; he may refuse it, and run the risk of the vengeance of the offended; when he submits to it, he acknowledges himself guilty, and offers reparation for the crime. The offended party, on his side, in accepting the composition, reconciles himself with the offender; he solemnly promises to forget, to abandon vengeance: so that composition as a penalty has characteristics much more moral than the punishments of more learned legislations; it gives evidence of a profound feeling of morality and liberty.

I here resume, in bringing them to more precise terms, the ideas of some modern German writers; among others, of a young man lately dead, to the great sorrow of science, M. Rogge, who has set them forth in an *Essay upon the Judicial System of the Germans*, published at Halle, in 1820. Among many ingenious views, and some probable explanations of the ancient social German state, there is, I think, in this system a universal mistake, a great want of understanding man and barbaric society.

The source of the error, if I mistake not, is the very false idea which is frequently formed of the liberty which seemed to exist in the earliest age of nations. There can be no doubt but that, at this epoch, the liberty of individuals was, in fact, very great. On the one hand, there existed between men inequalities but little varied, and little powerful; those which arose from wealth, from antiquity of race, and from a multitude of complex causes, could not yet have been developed or have produced anything more than very transitory effects. On the other hand, there was no longer any, or scarcely any, public power capable of holding in check or restraining

H H

individual wills. Men were firmly governed neither by other men nor by society: their liberty was real; each did almost what he wished according to his power, at his own risk and perils. I say according to his power; this co-existence of individual liberties was, in fact, at this epoch a mere contest of powers; that is, warfare between individuals and families, war incessant, capricious, violent, and barbarous as the men who carried it on.

This was not society; and it was not long before they found this out; efforts were made on all sides to escape from such a state, in order to enter upon social order. The evil everywhere sought its remedy. Thus it was ordered by this mysterious life, this secret power which presides over the destinies of the human race.

Two remedies appeared: 1st, inequality between men declared itself; some became rich, others poor; some noble, some obscure; some were patrons, others clients; some masters, others slaves. 2ndly. Public power developed itself; a collec- tive force arose, which, in the name and interest of society, proclaimed and executed certain laws. Thus originated, on the one side, aristocracy, and on the other, government—that is to say, two methods of restraining individual will, two means of subduing many men to a will different from their own.

In their turn the remedies became evils; the aristocracy tyrannized, and the public power tyrannized; this oppression led to a disorder, different from the first, but profound and intolerable. Still, in the heart of social life, by the sole effect of its continuance, and by the concurrence of numerous influ- ences, individuals, the sole real beings, developed, enlightened, and perfected themselves; their reason was less contracted, their will less irregular; they began to perceive that they might live very well in peace without so great an amount of inequality or public power—that is to say, that society could subsist very well without so dear a sacrifice to liberty. At this time, just as there had been an effort for the creation of public power, and for inequality between men, so now there commenced an effort which tended to the attainment of a contrary end, towards the reduction of the aristocracy and the government; that is to say, society tended towards a state which, externally, at least, and judging only from that point of view, resembled what it had been in its earliest age, at the free development of individual wills, in that situation in which each man did what he pleased, and at his own risk and peril.

If I have explained myself clearly, you now know where the great mistake lies of the admirers of the barbarous state: Struck, on the one hand, by the slight development, whether of public power, or of inequality, and on the other, by the extent of individual liberty which they met with, they thence concluded that society, despite the rudeness of its forms, was at bottom, in its normal state, under the empire of its legitimate principles, such, in fact, as, after its noblest progressions, it evidently tends again to become. They forgot but one thing; they did not trouble themselves to compare men themselves, in these two terms of social life; they forgot that in the first, coarse, ignorant and violent, governed by passion, and always ready to have recourse to force, they were incapable of living in peace according to reason and justice—that is to say, of living in society, without an external force compelling them. The progress of society consists, above all, in a change in man himself, in his being rendered capable of liberty—that is to say, of governing himself according to reason. If liberty perished at the beginning of the social career, it was because man was incapable, while keeping it, of advancing in it; his recovering and exercising it more and more, is the end and perfection of society, but it was by no means the primitive state, the condition of barbarous life. In the barbarous life, liberty was nothing but the empire of force—that is to say, the ruin, or rather the absence, of society. It is thence that so many men of talent have deceived themselves concerning the barbaric legislations, and particularly concerning that which now occupies us. They have there seen the principal external conditions of liberty, and in the midst of these conditions they have placed the sentiments, ideas, and men of another age. The theory of composition, I have just stated, has no other source: its incoherence is evident; and instead of attributing so much moral worth to this kind of penalty, it should be regarded only as a first step out of a state of warfare and the barbarous struggle of forces.

III. With regard to criminal procedure, the manner of the

H H 2

prosecution and judgment of offences, the Salic law is very imperfect, and almost silent; it takes the judicial institutions as a fact, and speaks neither of tribunals, judges, nor forms. One meets here and there, as to summoning, the appear-·ance in court, the obligations of witnesses and judges, the proof by hot water, &c., a few special dispositions; but in order to complete them, to reconstruct the system of institutions and manners to which they attach themselves, it is necessary to carry our investigations far beyond the text, and even the object of the law. Among the features of information which they contain concerning criminal procedure, I shall arrest your attention upon two points only, the distinction of fact and law, and the compurgators or *conjuratores*.

When the offender, upon the citation of the offended party, appeared in the *mâl*, or assembly of free men, before the judges, no matter whom, called upon to decide, counts, rachim-burgs, ahrimans, &c., the question submitted to them was, what the law commanded as to the alleged fact: people did not come before them to discuss the truth or falsehood of the fact; they fulfilled before them the conditions by which this first point should be decided; then, according to the law under which the parties lived, they were required to determine the rate of composition and all the circumstances of the penalty.

As to the reality of the fact itself, it was established before the judges, in various ways, by recourse to the judgment of God, the test of boiling water, single combat, &c., sometimes by the depositions of witnesses, and most fre-quently by the oath of the *conjuratores*. The accused came attended by a certain number of men, his relations, neighbours, or friends—six, eight, nine, twelve, fifty, seventy-two, in certain cases even a hundred—who came to make oath that he had not done what was imputed to him. In certain cases, the offended party also had his *conjuratores*. There was there neither interrogation, nor discussion of evidence, nor, properly speaking, examination of the fact; the *conjuratores* simply attested, under oath, the truth of the assertion of the offended party, or the denial of the offender. This, as regards the discovery of facts, was the great means and general system of the barbarous laws: the *conjuratores* are mentioned less frequently in the law of the Salian Franks, than in the other barbarous laws—in that of the Ripuarian Franks, for instance; yet there is no doubt that they were everywhere equally in use, and the foundation of criminal procedure.

This system, like that of composition, has been an object of great admiration to many learned men; they have seen in it two rare merits; the power of the ties of family, friendship, or neighbourhood, and the confidence placed by the law in the veracity of man: " The Germans," says Rogge, " have never felt the necessity for a regular system of proofs. What may appear strange in this assertion vanishes, if one is thoroughly impressed, as I am, with a full faith in the nobility of character, and, above all, the unbounded veracity of our ancestors."[1]

It would be amusing to pass from this sentence to Gregory of Tours, the poem of the Niebelungen, and all the poetical or historical monuments of the ancient German manners: to the artifice, deceit, and want of faith, shown there at every step, sometimes with the most dexterous refinement, and sometimes with the coarsest audacity. Can you believe that the Germans were any different when before their tribunals than in common life, and that the registers of their law-suits, if such things as registers then existed, should give the lie to their history?

I do not attach any special reproach to them for these vices; they are the vices of all barbarous nations, in all epochs, and under every zone; American traditions bear witness to it, as well as those of Europe, and the Iliad as well as the Niebelungen. I am far, too, from denying that natural morality in man, which abandons him in no age or condition of society, and mixes itself with the most brutal empire of ignorance or passion. But you will readily comprehend, what, in the midst of such manners, the oaths of the *conjuratores* must very frequently have been.

With regard to the spirit of tribe or family, it is true, it was powerful among the Germans; of this, among many other proofs, the *conjuratores* give one; but it had not all the causes, nor did it produce all the moral consequences which are attributed to it: a man accused was a man attacked; his neighbours followed and surrounded him before the tribunal

---

[1] Ueber das gerichtwesen der Germanen, Preface, p. 0

as at a combat. It was between families that the state of warfare subsisted in the heart of barbarism: can we be surprised that they should group and put themselves in movement when, under such a form, war menaced them?

The true origin of the *conjuratores* was, that all other means of establishing facts were almost impracticable. Think what such an inquiry exacts, what a degree of intellectual development and public power are necessary in order to confront the various kinds of proofs, to collect and contest the evidence, to bring the witnesses before the judges, and to obtain truth from them in the presence of the accusers and the accused. Nothing of this was possible in the society governed by the Salic law; and it was neither from choice nor moral combination that they then had recourse to the judgment of God and the oath of relations, but because they could neither do, nor apprehend anything better.

Such are the principal points of this law which seemed to me to merit your attention. I say nothing of the fragments of political law, civil law, or civil procedure, which are found dispersed through it, nor even of that famous article which orders that " Salic land shall not fall to women; and that the inheritance shall devolve exclusively on the males." No person is now ignorant of its true meaning. Some dis positions, relative to the forms by which a man may separate himself from his family,[1] the getting free of all obligation of relationship, and entering upon an entire independence, are very curious, and give a great insight into social life; but they hold an unimportant place in the law, and do not determine its end. I repeat, that it is essentially a penal code, and you now comprehend it under this view. Considering it in its whole, it is impossible not to recognise in it a complex, uncertain, and transitory legislation. One feels at every moment the passage from one country into another, from one social state into another social state, from one religion into another religion, and from one language into another language; almost every metamorphosis which can take place in the life of a nation is stamped upon it. Its existence also was precarious and brief; from the tenth century, perhaps, it was replaced by a multitude of local customs, to which, of a

---

[1] Tit. liii. § 1—8

surety, it had contributed a great deal, but which were likewise drawn from other sources, in the Roman law, the canon law, and the necessities of circumstances; and when, in the fourteenth century, they invoked the Salic law, in order to regulate the succession to the crown, it had certainly been a long time since it had been spoken of, except in remembrance, and upon some great occasion.

Three other barbarian laws ruled over the nations established in Gaul, those of the Ripuarians, the Burgundians, and the Visigoths; these will form the subject of our next lecture.

TENTH LECTURE.

Object of the lecture—Is the transitory character of the Salic law found in the laws of the Ripuarians, the Burgundians, and the Visigoths?—1st, The law of the Ripuarians—The Ripuarian Franks—History of the compilation of their law—Its contents—Difference between it and the Salic law—2nd, The law of the Burgundians—History of its compilation—Its contents—Its distinctive character—3rd, The law of the Visigoths—It concerns the history of Spain more than that of France—Its general character—Effect of Roman civilization upon the barbarians.

In our last lecture, the character which, on summing up, appeared to us dominant and fundamental in the Salic law, was that of being a transitory legislation, doubtless essentially German, yet distinguished by a Roman stamp; which would have no future; and which showed, on the one hand, the passage from the German into the Roman social state, and on the other, the decay and fusion of the two elements for the good of a new society, to which they both concurred, and which began to appear amidst their wreck.

This result of the examination of the Salic law will be singularly confirmed, if the examination of the other barbarous laws likewise lead us to it; still more, if we find in these various laws, different epochs of transition, different phases of transformation, which may be imperfectly discovered in the other; if we recognise, for example, that the law of the Ripuarians, the law of the Burgundians, and the law of the Visigoths, are in some measure placed in the same career as the Salic law, at unequal distances, and leave us, if the term be permitted, products more or less advanced in the combination of the German and Roman society, and in the formation of the new state which was to be the result.

It is to this, I believe, that the examination of the three
laws will, in fact, conduct us, that is to say, of all those which,
within the limits of Gaul, exercised any true influence.
The distinction between the Ripuarian Franks and the
Salian Franks is known to you; these were the two principal
tribes, or rather the two principal collections of tribes of the
great confederation of the Franks. The Salian Franks probably took their name from the river Yssel, (Ysala,) upon the
banks of which they were established, after the movement of
nations which had driven them into Batavia; their name was
therefore of German origin, and we may suppose that it was
given them by themselves. The Ripuarian Franks, on the
contrary, evidently received theirs from the Romans. They
inhabited the banks of the Rhine. As the Salian Franks
advanced towards the south-west, into Belgium and Gaul,
the Ripuarian Franks spread also towards the west, and
occupied the territory between the Rhine and the Meuse, to
the forest of Ardennes. The first became, or well nigh,
the Franks of Neustria; the last, the Franks of Austrasia.
These two names, without exactly corresponding to the primitive distinction, reproduce it faithfully enough.

At the beginning of our history, the two tribes appear for
a time re-united in a single nation and under a single empire.
I will read to you, upon this subject, the account of Gregory
of Tours; always, without his knowing it, the truest painter
of the manners and events of this epoch. You will there
see what, at that time, was understood by the words union of
nations and conquest.

" When Clovis came to battle against Alaric, king of the
Goths, he had for an ally the son of Sigebert-Claude, (king
of the Ripuarian Franks, and who resided at Cologne,)
named Chloderic. This Sigebert limped, from a blow on the
knee which he had received at the battle of Tolbiac, against
the Germans. .... King Clovis, during his sojourn at Paris,
sent secretly to the son of Sigebert, saying to him: ' Your
father is aged, and he limps with his bad leg: if he should
die, his kingdom belongs to you of right, as well as our friendship. Seduced by this ambition, Chloderic formed the project of killing his father.

" Sigebert had gone out of the town of Cologne, and,
having passed the Rhine, was walking in the forest of Bu-

conia; he slept at noon in his tent; his son sent assassins
against him and procured his death, in the hope that he
should possess his kingdom.   But, by the judgment of God,
he fell into the very grave which he had maliciously dug for
his father.   He sent to king Clovis messengers announcing
the death of his father, and said to him: ' My father is dead,
and I have in my power his treasures and his kingdom.   Send
to me and I will willingly give you what treasures you please.'
Clovis returned for answer: ' I return thee thanks for thy
good will, and pray thee show thy treasures to my deputies,
after which thou shalt possess them all.'   Chloderic then
showed his father's treasures to the deputies.   Whilst they
examined them, the prince said: ' This is the coffer in which
my father was accustomed to amass his gold coin.'   They
said to him, ' Plunge your hand to the bottom, in order to
find all.'   Having done this, and while he stooped low, one
of the deputies raised his axe and broke his skull.   Thus did
this unworthy son suffer the same death which he had inflicted
on his father.   Clovis learning that Sigebert and his son were
dead, came to this same town, and having convoked all the
people, he said to them: ' Listen to what has happened.
While I was sailing upon the river Scheld, Chloderic, my
cousin's son, alarmed his father by telling him that I wished
to kill him.   As Sigebert fled through the forest of Buconia,
Chloderic sent murderers after him, who put him to death;
he himself was assassinated, I know not by whom, at the
moment of his opening his father's treasures.   I am no
accomplice in these things.   I could not shed the blood of my
friends, because it is forbidden; but since these things have
happened, I have some advice to give you.   If it is agreeable
to you, follow it.   Have recourse to me; put yourselves
under my protection.'   The people answered these words
by plaudits of hand and mouth; and having raised him upon
a shield, they created him their king.   Clovis then received
the kingdom and treasures of Sigebert.   Every day God
caused his enemies to fall into his hands, and augmented his
kingdom, because he walked with an upright heart before the
Lord, and did the things that were pleasing in his sight."[1]

[1] Gregory of Tours, in my *Collection des Memoires de l'Histoire de
France*, i. pp. 104—107.

This union of the two nations, if such a fact may bear the name, was not of long duration. On the death of Clovis, his son, Theodoric, was king of the eastern Franks; that is to say, of the Ripuarian Franks; he resided at Metz. To him is generally attributed the compilation of their law. This, in fact, is indicated by the preface of the Salic law, which I have already read, and which is likewise found at the beginning of the Bavarian law. According to this tradition, then, the law of the Ripuarians should be placed between the years 511 and 534. It could not have, like the Salic, the pretension of ascending to the right-hand bank of the Rhine, and to ancient Germany. Still its antiquity must be great. I am inclined to abridge it, in its actual form at least, of nearly a century of existence. The preface, which describes it as digested under Theodoric, attributes to this chief also the law of the Germans; now it is almost certain that this was not digested until the reign of Clotaire II., between the years 613 and 628; this is what the best manuscripts give us reason to suppose. The authority of this preface, therefore, becomes very doubtful with regard to the law of the Ripuarians; and, after an attentive comparison of the evidence, I am inclined to believe that it was only under Dagobert I., between the years 628 and 638, that it took the definite form under which it has reached us.

Let us now pass to the history of its contents. I have submitted it to the same analysis as the Salic law. It contains 89 or 91 titles, and (according to various distributions) 224 or 227 articles; namely, 164 of penal law, and 113 of political or civil law, and civil or criminal procedure. Of the 164 articles of penal law, we reckon 94 for violence against persons, 16 for cases of theft, and 64 for various offences.

At the first glance, according to this simple analysis, the Ripuarian law a good deal resembles the Salic law; it is also an essentially penal legislation, and gives evidence of nearly the same state of manners. Still, when regarded more closely, we discover important difference. I spoke to you at our last meeting of the *conjuratores*, or compurgators, who, without, properly speaking, bearing witness, came to attest by their oath the truth or falsehood of the facts alleged by the offended or the offender. The *conjuratores* held a specially important place in the law of the Ripuarians. There is mention made of them in fifty-eight articles of this law, and on every occasion it minutely regulates the number of the compurgators, the forms of their appearance, &c. The Salic law speaks much more rarely of them—so rarely, that some persons have doubted whether the system of the *conjuratores* was in force among the Salian Franks. This doubt does not seem well founded. If the Salic law has scarcely spoken of it, it is because it looked upon the system as an established and understood fact, of which there was no need to write. Besides, everything indicates that this fact was real and powerful. What were the reasons for its frequent insertion in the law of the Ripuarians? I will presently give the only explanation of this that I can catch a glimpse of.

Another custom is also much more frequently mentioned in the Ripuarian than in the Salic law; I mean judicial combat. There are many traces of it in the Salic law; but the Ripuarian law formally institutes it in six distinct articles. This institution, if such a fact merits the name of institution, played too important a part in the middle ages to allow of our not endeavouring to understand it at the moment that it appears for the first time in laws.

I have endeavoured to show how composition—properly speaking, the only punishment of the Salic law—was a first attempt to substitute a legal system in place of the right of war, in place of vengeance, and the contest of physical force. Judicial combat was an attempt of the same kind; its aim was to subdue war itself, individual vengeance, to certain forms and rules. Composition and judicial combat were intimately connected, and simultaneously developed themselves. A crime had been committed, a man offended; it was generally believed that he had a right to revenge himself, to pursue by force the reparation of the wrong to which he had been subjected. But a commencement of law, a shadow of public power interfered, and authorized the offender to offer a certain sum to repair his crime. But, originally, the offended party had the right to refuse the composition, and to say—"I will exercise my right of vengeance, I desire war." Then the legislator, or rather the customs, for we personify under the name legislator, mere customs which for a long period had no legal authority, the customs then interfered, saying —"If you wish to revenge yourself, and make war upon your enemy, you must do so according to certain terms, and in the presence of certain witnesses."

Thus was judicial combat introduced into the legislation as a regulation of the right of war, a limited arena opened to vengeance. Such was its first and true source; the recourse to the judgment of God, the truth proclaimed by God himself in the issue of the combat, are ideas whose association with it is of later date, when religious creeds and the Christian clergy played an important part in the thought and life of the barbarians. Originally, judicial combat was only a legal form of the right of the strongest—a form much more explicitly recognised in the law of the Ripuarians than in the Salic law.

Judging from the two differences, one would be, for the moment, inclined to suppose that the first of these two laws was the most ancient. In fact, there can be no doubt that the system of the *conjuratores* and judicial combat belonged to the primitive German society. The Ripuarian, therefore, would seem their most faithful image. It was nothing of the kind. And, first, these two differences, which seemed to give to this law a more barbarous physiognomy, themselves indicate an effort, a first step out of barbarism, for they give evidence of the design, if not to abolish it, at all events to regulate it.

Silence upon this subject leaves all things under the empire of custom—that is to say, of violence and chance: the Ripuarian law attempted in writing, by determining the custom, to convert it into law—that is to say, to render it fixed and general. A certain symptom of a more modern date, and of a society rather more advanced.

Besides, there were other differences between these two laws which incontestably prove this result.

1st, You have seen, by the simple enumeration of the articles, that civil law held a greater place in the Ripuarian than in the Salic law. There penal law always dominated. Still the law is less exclusively a penal code; the procedure, the rule of evidence, the state of persons, property and its various modes of transmission—in a word, all parts of legislation not penal, are, at least indicated in it, and often with a great deal of precision.

2nd, Moreover, and this is an important fact, royalty appeared more in the Ripuarian law than in the other. It appeared but little in a political relation: it was not a question of royal power, nor the manner of exercising it; but it was a question of the king, as of an individual more important in all respects, and with whom the law should specially occupy itself. It regarded him, above all, as a proprietor or patron, as having vast domains, and upon these domains serfs who cultivated them—men engaged in his service or placed under his protection; and by reason of this title they accorded to him, to himself or those belonging to him, numerous and very important privileges. I will give a few examples.

" I. If any one carry off by violence anything belonging to one of the king's men, or to any one attached to the church, he shall pay a composition treble what he would have had to pay had the crime been committed towards any other Ripuarian."—Tit. xi. § 4.

" II. If the crime be committed by a man attached to the church, or to one of the king's domains, he shall pay half the composition which another Frank would have paid. In case of denial, he must appear with thirty-six compurgators."—Tit. xviii. § 5.

" III. A man attached to the domains of the king, Roman or freedman, cannot be the object of a capital accusation."—Tit. lx. § 22.

" IV. If he be summoned to appear in justice, he shall make known his condition by a declaration which he shall affirm upon the altar; after which proceedings with regard to him shall be different from those with regard to the Ripuarians."—Ibid. § 23.

" V. Slaves belonging to the king or to a church do not plead by means of a defender; but they defend themselves, and are allowed to justify themselves by oath, without being obliged to answer the summonses which may be addressed to them."—Ibid. § 24.

" VI. If any one shall seek to overthrow a royal charter without being able to produce another repealing the first, he shall answer this attempt with his life."—Tit. lvii. § 7.

" VII. Whoever shall commit treason towards the king

shall forfeit his life, and all his goods shall be confiscated."—Tit. lxxi. § 1.

The Salic law says nothing of this kind; here royalty has evidently made an important progress.

3rd. The same difference exists between the two laws with regard to the church; the articles which I have just read completely prove it; the church is everywhere assimilated to royalty; the same privileges are accorded to her lands and her labourers.

4th. One discovers, also, in the Ripuarian law, a rather more marked influence of the Roman law; it does not confine itself to mentioning it merely in order to say that the Romans lived under its empire; it accepts some of its provisions. Thus, in regulating the formulæ of enfranchisement, it says :

" We desire that every Ripuarian Frank, or freed man, who, for the good of his soul, or for a sum, wishes to free his slave in the forms indicated by the Roman law, present himself at the church, before the priests, deacons, and all the clergy and people. . . ." (The formulæ of enfranchisement follow.)—Tit. lx. § 1.

This, although a slight, is a real indication of a more advanced society.

5th. Lastly, when we read the Ripuarian law attentively in its whole, we are struck with a character less barbarous than that of the Salic law. The provisions are more precise and extensive; we discover more purpose in them, and purpose more matured and political, and inspired by more universal views. They are not always mere customs which they digest; the legislators say at times, " We establish, we order."[1] In fact, everything indicates that this legislation, if not in its form, at least in the ideas and manners which are its foundation, belongs to a posterior epoch, to a state somewhat less barbarous, and shows a new step in the transition from the German to the Roman society, and from these two societies to a new society arising from their amalgamation.

From the law of the Ripuarians let us pass to that of the Burgundians, and let us see if we shall there find the same fact.

The compilation of the law of the Burgundians fluctuates

Tit. lxxvi. § 1. lit. xc.

between the year 467 or 468, the second of the reign of Gondebald, and the year 534, the time of the fall of this kingdom under the arms of the Franks. Three parts, probably of different dates, compose this law. The first, which comprehends the first forty-one titles, evidently belongs to king Gondebald, and appears to have been published before the year 501. From the forty-second title, the character of the legislation changes. The new laws are scarcely anything more than modifications of the old ones; they explain, reform, complete, and announce them definitely. From the consideration of many facts, into the details of which I shall not enter here, one is inclined to believe that this second part was digested and published towards the year 517, by Sigismond, the successor of Gondebald. Lastly, two supplements form a third part, added to the law, under the positive name of *Additamenta*, probably also by Sigismond, who died in 523.

The preface, placed in front of the text, confirms these conjectures; it is evidently composed of two prefaces of different epochs; one by King Gondebald, and the other by King Sigismond. Some manuscripts have attributed the latter also to Gondebald; but those which give it to Sigismond certainly merit the preference.

This preface throws light upon questions much more important than the date of the law, and at once clearly distinguishes it from the two laws which have just occupied our attention. It is necessary that I should read it to you throughout.

" The most glorious king of the Burgundians, after having, for the interest and repose of our people, deliberately reflected upon our institutions and those of our ancestors, and upon what, in every matter and every business, is expedient for honesty, regularity, reason, and justice, we have weighed all this in our great assemblies; and as much by our advice as theirs, we have ordered the following statutes to be written. to the end that the laws may remain eternal:—

" By the grace of God, in the second year of the most glorious Lord King Sigismund, the book of ordinances touching the eternal maintenance of the laws past and present, made at Lyons the 4th day of the calends of April.

" By love of justice, through which God becomes favourable

to us, and by which we acquire power upon earth, having first held counsel with our counts and nobles, we have applied ourselves to regulate all things in such a manner that integrity and justice in judgments may dispel all corruption. All those who are in power, counting from this day, must judge between the Burgundian and the Roman according to the tenour of our laws, composed and amended by common accord; in such manner that no person shall hope or dare, in a judgment or law-suit, to receive anything of one of the parties by way of gift or advantage; but that the party having justice on his side shall obtain it, and that to this end the integrity of the judge shall suffice. We think it our duty to impose this duty on ourselves, to the end that no one, in what case soever, shall tempt our integrity by solicitations or presents, thus, from love of justice, repelling far from ourselves, what, throughout our kingdoms, we interdict all judges from doing. Our treasury shall no longer pretend to exact more as penalty than is found established in the laws. Let the nobles, counts, counsellors, domestics, and mayors of our house, the chancellors and counts of cities and districts, both Burgundians and Romans, as well as all deputy judges, even in case of war, know then that they are to receive nothing for causes treated or judged before them; and that they shall ask nothing of the parties by way of promise or recompence. The parties shall not be forced to compound with the judge in such a manner that he shall receive anything. If any of the said judges allow themselves to be corrupted, and, despite our laws, be convicted of receiving a recompence in a law-suit or judgment, however justly tried, for the example of all, if the crime be proved, let him be punished with death, in such a manner, however, that he who is convicted of venality, having been punished himself, his possessions be not taken from his children or legitimate heirs. With regard to the secretaries of deputy judges, we think that, for their fee in cases, a third of a penny should be allowed them in causes above ten *solidi;* below that sum they must demand less. The crime of venality being interdicted under the same penalties, we order that Romans be judged according to Roman laws, as was done by our ancestors; and let these latter know that they shall receive in writing the form and tenour of the laws according

I I

to which they shall be judged; to the end that no person can excuse himself upon the score of ignorance. As regards what may have been ill judged formerly, the tenour of the ancient law must be preserved. We add this, that if a judge accused of corruption cannot in any way be convicted, the accuser shall be liable to the penalty which we have ordered to be inflicted upon a prevaricating judge.

"If some point be found unprovided for in our laws, we order that it be referred to our judgment, upon that point only. If any judge, whether barbarian or Roman, through simplicity or negligence, judge not a cause upon which our law has determined, and if he be exempt from corruption, let him know that he shall pay thirty Roman *solidi*, and that the parties being interrogated, the cause shall be judged anew. We add that if, after having been summoned three times, the judges decide not; and if he whose cause it is thinks it should be referred to us; and if he prove that he has summoned his judges three times, and has not been heard, the judge shall be condemned to a fine of twelve solidi. But if any person, in any case whatsoever, having neglected to summon the judges three times, as we have prescribed, dares to address himself to us, he shall pay the fine which we have established for a tardy judge. And in order that a cause may not be delayed by the absence of the deputy judges, let no Roman or Burgundian count presume to judge a cause in the absence of the judge before whom it should be tried, to the end that those who have recourse to the law may not be uncertain as to the jurisdiction. It has pleased us to confirm this series of our ordinances by the signature of the counts, to the end that the rule which has been written by our will, and the will of all, be preserved by posterity, and have the solidity of an eternal compact." (Here follow the signatures of thirty-two counts).

Without going further, from this preface only the difference of the three laws is evident; this latter is not a mere collection of customs, we know not by whom digested, nor at what epoch, nor with what view; it is a work of legislation, emanating from a regular power, with a view to public order, which offers some truly political characteristics, and gives evidences of a government, or, at least, the design of a government.

Let us now enter into the law itself; it does not belie the preface.

It contains 110 titles, and 354 articles, namely: 142 articles of civil law, 30 of civil or criminal procedure, and 182 of penal law. The penal law is divided into 72 articles for crimes against persons, 62 for crimes against property, and 44 for various crimes.

These are the principal results to which we are conducted by the examination of the provisions thus classified:

I. The condition of the Burgundian and the Roman is the same; all legal difference has vanished: in civil or criminal matters, whether as offended or offenders, they are placed upon a footing of equality. The texts abound in proofs of it. I select some of the most striking:—

1. "Let the Burgundian and the Roman be subjected to the same condition."—Tit. x. § 1.

2. "If a young Roman girl be united to a Burgundian without the consent or knowledge of her parents, let her know that she shall receive none of her parents' possessions." —Tit. xii. §. 5.

3. "If any free Burgundian enter into a house for any quarrel, let him pay six *solidi* to the master of the house, and twelve *solidi* as a fine. We wish in this that the same condition be imposed upon the Romans and the Burgundians." —Tit. xv. §. 1.

4. "If any man travelling on his private business, arrive at the house of a Burgundian and demand hospitality of him, and if the Burgundian show him the house of a Roman, and this can be proved, let the Burgundian pay three *solidi* to him whose house he pointed out, and three *solidi* by way of fine."—Tit. xxxviii. §. 6.

These regulations certainly exhibit care to maintain the two people on the same footing. We thus read in Gregory of Tours: "King Gondebald instituted, in the country now named Burgundy, the most mild laws, in order that the Romans might not be oppressed.[1]

II. The penal law of the Burgundians is not the same as that of the Franks. Composition had always existed

---

[1] Tom. i. p. 96, of my *Collection des Mémoires relatifs a l'Histoire de France.*

in it, but it was no longer the sole penalty; corporal penalties appeared; we find also certain moral penalties; the legislator attempted to make use of shame.[1] Already, even, it invented strange punishments, such as are so often found in the legislation of the middle ages. If, for example, a hunting sparrow-hawk was stolen, the robber was condemned to let the sparrow-hawk eat six ounces of flesh from his body, or to pay six *solidi*. This is but a piece of fantastical savageness; but it indicated attempts at punishment very different from the ancient German customs. The difference manifests itself also by other symptoms; crimes are much more various, fewer of them are against persons, and we see some arise which bespeak more regular and complicated social relations.

III. Civil right and procedure also occupy a much greater place in the law of the Burgundians than in the two preceding laws. They form the subject of nearly half the articles; in the law of the Ripuarians they only occupy two-fifths, and only the sixth of the Salic law. One need only open the laws of Gondebald and Sigismund in order to perceive there a multitude of provisions upon successions, testaments, bequests, marriages, contracts, &c.

IV. One even meets there with some positive marks of the Roman law. We could scarcely discover any traces of such a fact in the Ripuarian law; here it is plainly visible, particularly in what concerns civil law; nothing can be more simple; civil law was rare and weak in barbarous laws; from the time that the progress of civil relations furnished the matter, as it were, it was from the Roman legislation that they were obliged to borrow the form.

Here are two provisions where the imitation is certain:

1.

" If a Burgundian woman, after the death of her husband, enters, as happens, into a second or a third marriage, and if she has sons by each marriage, let her possess in usufruct, while she lives,[2] the nuptial

1.

" Let no person be ignorant that if women, the lawful time being passed, enter into a second marriage, having children by the former marriage, they shall preserve, during their life, the usufruct of what they

[1] See the first Supplement, tit. x.
[2] *Dum advivit usufructu possideat.*

donation; but after her death, each of her sons shall come into the possession of what his father gave to his mother; and thus the woman has no right to give, sell, or alienate anything that she received as a nuptial donation."—Tit. xxiv. § 1.

2.

" Bequests and testaments made among our people shall be valid when five or seven witnesses have set thereto, as best they can, their seal or signature."—Title, xliii. § 2.

received[1] at the time of their marriage, the property coming entire to their children, to whom the most sacred laws preserve the right of it after their parents' death." — Cod. Theod., liv. iii. tit. viii. l. 8; Ibid. l. 2.

2.

" In codicils that are not preceded by a testament, as in wills, the mediation of five or seven witnesses must never be wanting." — Cod. Theod. liv. iv., tit. iii. l. 1.

I might indicate other apparent analogies.

V. Lastly, the law of the Burgundians clearly shows that royalty had made great progress among that people. Not that it is more in question there than elsewhere; it was not in question at all in a political point of view; the Burgundian law is the least political of the barbarian laws, the one which most exclusively confines itself to penal and civil law, and contains the fewest allusions to general government; but by this law in its whole, by its preface, and by the tone and spirit of its compilation, one is reminded at every step that the king is no longer merely a warrior chief, or merely a great proprietor; and that royalty has left its barbarous condition, in order to become a public power.

You see all this gives evidence of a more developed and better regulated society; the Roman element prevails more and more over the barbarous element; we visibly advance in the transition from one to the other, or rather in the work of fusion which is to combine them together. What the Burgundians appear to have chiefly borrowed from the Roman empire, independently of some traits of civil law, is the idea of public order, of government properly so called; hardly can we catch a glimpse of any trace of the ancient German assemblies; the influence of the clergy does not appear dominant; it was royalty which prevailed, and strove to reproduce the imperial power.

The Burgundian kings seems to have the most completely followed the emperors and reigned after their model. Perhaps

---

[1] *Dum advixerit in usufructu possideat (Interpret.)*

the cause should be sought for in the date of their kingdom,
which was one of the earliest founded, while the organization
of the empire still existed, or nearly so; perhaps, also, their
establishment, enclosed within narrower limits than those of
the Visigoths or the Franks, may have promptly invested it
with a more regular form. However this may be, the fact
is certain, and characterizes the nation and its legislation.

It continued in vigour after the Burgundians had passed
under the yoke of the Franks; the formulas of Marculf and
the capitularies of Charlemagne prove it.[1] We find it even
formally mentioned in the ninth century by the bishops
Agobard and Hincmar; but few men, they observe, now live
under this law.

III. The destiny of the law of the Visigoths was more
important, and of greater duration. It formed a considerable
collection, entitled *Forum judicum*, and was successively
digested, from the year 466, the epoch of the accession of
king Euric, who resided at Toulouse, to the year 701, the
time of the death of Egica or Egiza, who resided at Toledo.
This statement alone announces that, in this interval, great
changes must have taken place in the situation of the people
for whom the law was made. The Visigoths were first
established in the south of Gaul: it was in 507 that Clovis
drove them hence, and took from them all Aquitaine; they
only preserved on the north of the Pyrenees a Septimani.
The legislation of the Visigoths, therefore, is of no importance
in the history of our civilization until this epoch; in later
times, Spain is almost solely interested in it.

While he reigned at Toulouse, Euric caused the customs
of the Goths to be written; his successor, Alaric, who was
killed by Clovis, collected and published the laws of his
Roman subjects under the name of *Breviarium*. The
Visigoths, then, at the commencement of the sixth century
were in the same situation as the Burgundians and the Franks;
the barbarous law and the Roman law were distinct; each
nation retained its own.

When the Visigoths were driven into Spain, this state
was altered; their king, Chindasuinthe (642-652) fused
the two laws into one, and formally abolished the Roman

[1] *Marculf*, b. 1. f. 8; capit. 2 s 813. Baluze, 1505.

law ; there was from that time but one code, and one nation. Thus was substituted among the Visigoths the system of real laws, or according to territory, in the place of personal laws, or according to origin or races. This last had prevailed and still prevailed among all barbarous nations, when Chindasuinthe abolished it from among the Visigoths. But it was in Spain that this revolution was completed; it was there that from Chindasuinthe to Egica, (642-701) the *Forum judicum* was developed, completed, and took the form under which we now see it. As long as the Visigoths occupied the south of Gaul, the compilation of their ancient customs and the *Breviarium* alone ruled the country. The *Forum judicum* has, therefore, for France, only an indirect interest; still it was for some time in vigour in a small portion of southern Gaul; it occupies a great place in the general history of barbarous laws, and figures there as a very remarkable phenomenon. Let me, therefore, make you acquainted with its character and its whole.

The law of the Visigoths is incomparably more extensive than any of those which have just occupied our attention. It is composed of a title which serves as a preface, and twelve books, divided into 54 titles, in which are comprehended 595 articles, or distinct laws of various origins and date. All the laws enacted or reformed by the Visigoth kings, from Euric to Egica, are contained in this collection.

All legislative matters are there met with; it is not a collection of ancient customs, nor a first attempt at civil reform; it is a universal code, a code of political, civil, and criminal law: a code systematically digested, with the view of providing for all the requisites of society. It is not only a code, a totality of legislative provisions, but it is also a system of philosophy, a doctrine. It is preceded by, and here and there mixed with dissertations upon the origin of society, the nature of power, civil organization, and the composition and publication of laws, and not only is it a system, but also a collection of moral exhortations, menaces, and advice. The *Forum judicum*, in a word, bears at once a legislative, philosophical, and religious character; it partakes of the several properties of a law, a science, and a sermon.

The course is simple enough; the law of the Visigoths was the work of the clergy; it emanated from the councils of

Toledo. The councils of Toledo were the national assemblies
of the Spanish monarchy. Spain has this singular characteristic, that, from the earliest period of its history, the clergy
played a much greater part in it than elsewhere; what the
field of Mars or May was to the Franks, what the Witten-
agemote to the Anglo-Saxons, and what the general assembly
of Pavia was to the Lombards, such were the councils of
Toledo to the Visigoths of Spain. It was there that the laws
were digested, and all the great national affairs debated.
Thus, the clergy was, so to speak, the centre around which
grouped royalty, the lay aristocracy, the people and the
whole of society. The Visigoth code is evidently the work
of the ecclesiastics; it has the vices and the merits of their
spirit ; it is incomparably more rational, just, mild, and
exact; it understands much better the rights of humanity, the
duties of government, and the interests of society; and it
strives to attain a much more elevated aim than any other of
the barbarous legislations. But, at the same time, it leaves
society much more devoid of guarantees; it abandons it on
one side to the clergy, and on the other to royalty. The
Frank, Saxon, Lombard, and even Burgundian laws, respect
the guarantees arising from ancient manners, of individual
independence, the rights of each proprietor in his domains,
the participation, more or less regular, and more or less extensive, of freemen in the affairs of the nation, in judgments,
and in the conduct of the acts of civil life. In the *Forum
iudicum*, almost all these traces of the primitive German
society have disappeared; a vast administration, semi-ecclesi-
astical and semi-imperial, extends over society. I surely need
not observe, for your thoughts will have outrun my words,
that this is a new and prodigious step in the route on which
we proceed. Since we have studied the barbarous laws, we
advance more and more towards the same result, the fusion of
the two societies becomes more and more general and profound;
and in this fusion, in proportion as it was brought about, the
Roman element, whether civil or religious, dominated more
and more. The Ripuarian law is less German than the Salic;
the law of the Burgundians less so than the Ripuarian law;
and the law of the Visigoths still less so than that of the Bur
gundians. It is evidently in this direction that the river
flows, towards this aim that the progress of events tends.

Singular spectacle! Just now we were in the last age of Roman civilization, and found it in full decline, without strength, fertility, or splendour, incapable, as it were, of subsisting; conquered and ruined by barbarians; now all of a sudden it reappears, powerful and fertile; it exercises a prodigious influence over the institutions and manners which associate themselves with it; it gradually impresses on them its character; it dominates over and transforms its conquerors.

Two causes, among many others, produced this result; the power of a civil legislation, strong and closely knit; and the natural ascendency of civilization over barbarism.

In fixing themselves and becoming proprietors, the barbarians contracted, among themselves, and with the Romans, relations much more varied and more durable, than any they had hitherto known; their civil existence became much more extensive and permanent. The Roman law alone could regulate it; that alone was prepared to provide for so many relations. The barbarians even in preserving their customs, even while remaining masters of the country, found themselves taken, so to speak, in the nets of this learned legislation, and found themselves obliged to submit, in a great measure, doubtless not in a political point of view, but in civil matters, to the new social order. Besides, the mere sight of Roman civilization exercised great influence on their imagination. What now moves ourselves, what we seek with eagerness in history, poems, travels, novels, is the representation of a society foreign to the regularity of our own; it is the savage life, its independence, novelty, and adventures. Very different were the impressions of the barbarians; it was civilization which struck them, which seemed to them great and marvellous; the remains of Roman activity, the cities, roads, aqueducts, and amphitheatres, all that society so regular, so provident, and so varied in its fixedness—these were the objects of their astonishment and admiration. Although conquerors, they felt themselves inferior to the conquered; the barbarian might despise the Roman individually; but the Roman empire in its whole appeared to him something superior; and all the great men of the age of conquests, the Alarics, the Ataulphs, the Theodorics, and many others, while destroying and throwing to the ground the Roman empire, exerted all their power to imitate it.

These are the principal facts which manifested themselves in the epoch which we have just reviewed, and, above all, in the compilation and successive transformation of the barbaric laws. We shall seek, in our next lecture, what remained of the Roman laws to govern the Romans themselves, while the Germans were applying themselves to writing their own

END OF VOL I.

LONDON: PRINTED BY WILLIAM CLOWES AND SONS, LIMITED, STAMFORD STREET
AND CHARING CROSS.

Lightning Source UK Ltd.
Milton Keynes UK
UKOW07f2141230315

248389UK00007B/66/P

For Marjorie

With very best wishes

Nigel Bex

The Lost
Pre-Raphaelite

The Secret Life & Loves of
Robert Bateman

THE LOST PRE-RAPHAELITE

The Secret Life & Loves of ROBERT BATEMAN

NIGEL DALY

WILMINGTON SQUARE BOOKS
an imprint of Bitter Lemon Press

WILMINGTON SQUARE BOOKS
An imprint of Bitter Lemon Press

First published in 2014 by
Wilmington Square Books
47 Wilmington Square
London WC1X 0ET

www.bitterlemonpress.com

A CIP record for this book is available from the British Library

ISBN 978-1-908524-386

Edited, designed and typeset by Jane Havell Associates
Printed in China

2 4 6 8 9 7 5 3 1

Endpapers: Robert Bateman, The Four Seasons,
watercolour on gold medium, private collection.
Frontispiece: Robert Bateman, Rose 1877 *(detail), 1906–8,*
oil on canvas, private collection.
Sculptures by Robert Bateman on pages 1, above and 323 at Biddulph Old Hall,
1874–5, on page 6 at St Bartholemew's Church, Benthall, 1893, and on page 336
at Rockfield House, Nunney (Nunney Delamere), after 1906.

CONTENTS

INTRODUCTION

Beyond the safe confines of popular fiction, being drawn into a mystery is one of the most disturbing and disorientating experiences that can befall anyone. One hopes that acquiring more information will dispel uncertainty, but if new facts simply aggravate disquiet by adding further contradictions and non-sequential data, it can trigger a dangerous addiction.

My partner Brian Vowles and I discovered this when the first flush of our innocuous dalliance with the double mystery of Biddulph Old Hall and Robert Bateman ought to have been fading away. The fact that the two narratives were woven together was an integral part of their compulsive allure. Cryptic evidence of the artist's story had literally been carved into the fabric of the ancient building, intensifying the sensation of decoding arcane symbols recording a lost civilisation.

The Old Hall's story, with the emergence of its single-cell structure and massive crude fire-openings, gradually undermined the previously accepted chronology of its age and construction. Of course, none of these archaelogical revelations, in themselves, compared with the academic information preserved within the fabric of the great contemporary treasure houses such as Haddon and Little Moreton halls, but Biddulph's uncossetted recent history enabled it to illuminate the past with its own unique candour. The grubby struggle of life sustained by its soot-grimed working hearth and the raw hatred that informed a civil war waged against neighbours and family within the sanctity of their own homes is here brutally laid bare. These blackened, cratered walls insisted we take the past seriously, both in its crudity and its slow abiding contentment that mocked our own hectic neuroses. In doing so it allowed us to feel the rythm – the pulse of the forgotten people who had inadvertently determined its present form.

Nowhere was this disconcerting ability more hypnotically deployed than in the silent emergence, from tiny clues left on its surface, of a forgotten man of genius – Robert Bateman, the lost Pre-Raephaelite.

Bateman's response to the ruined building was captured in his portrayal of it in several of his most personal and deeply felt paintings. Its melancholic atmosphere allowed him to express the isolation he experienced after his brutal separation from the love of his life, Caroline Howard. Under the influence of these fragmented remains he was able to sublimate his desolation at her marriage to an elderly clergyman into the spectral stillness of his masterpiece, *The Pool of Bethesda.* This was the work which rescued him from oblivion in the 1960s, when its originality, technical prowess and emotional intensity led to its being acquired and put on display at the Yale Center for British Art in New Haven, Connecticut. It was also the haunting vision that inspired our quest to discover every retrievable drawing, painting and sketch, every discarded fragment of evidence that would illuminate his life and personality.

We little knew, when we set ourselves that task, that it would take us from Biddulph into the glories of Castle Howard, the glamour of the Grosvenor Gallery, and to the heart of Queen Victoria's Imperial Court and Benjamin Disraeli's political machine. Nor did we expect to encounter the furtive despair, cruelty and abject poverty that accompanied social rejection from Victorian society. We could not have guessed that we would be taken into the sweltering heat of the Punjab, amid itinerant missionaries and religious rivalries, nor experience the frozen starvation of the pioneering settlers in Canada. We did not expect to meet real, unglamorised cowboys – and certainly not the great Buffalo Bill.

We set out to try to understand what had caused Bateman to leave London suddenly in the mid 1870s to live a reclusive life at Biddulph Old Hall for the next sixteen years. On our journey we found cruelty, rejection, fear and subterfuge but, perhaps more surprisingly, loyalty, integrity and pure, unselfish love. The purpose of our search for answers to the conundrums surrounding Robert Bateman's life has been to bring this consummately gifted artist and his wise, beautiful wife out of the obscurity that has enveloped them and their world, so that they may take their rightful place as inspirational romantic figures of the late Victorian age.

ACKNOWLEDGEMENTS

I have more reason than most writers to be grateful to the many people who have generously given their time, expertise and enthusiasm to the creation of this book. This is because it did not begin life as an investigation of a Pre-Raphaelite artist, nor an account of a compulsive love story, nor indeed as the proposal for a book of any kind.

It began as no more than a simple enquiry into the building history of a minor historic house, with the purpose of informing its restoration. In these circumstances, there was little incentive for anyone to become entangled in the confusion thrown up by our first faltering discoveries. Even after Robert Bateman had emerged to enrich the narrative, the project revolved only around a maltreated house, an obscure artist and an unknown, aspiring author – scarcely an enthralling prospect for a potential contributor to engage in.

Yet from the very beginning I have been overwhelmed by people's willingness to go to untold trouble and inconvenience in order to contribute to the research process. They appeared magically from every hidden place and condition of life. They ranged from local people, through historical societies, art critics, museum curators, crafts-men, writers and heritage bodies, to friends, family and descendants of characters in the story. It takes a special kind of good nature to provide support for an unknown, untried endeavour – especially if it holds out no prospect of direct return or recog-nition. None the less, that help is exactly what I received over and over again during the long gestation of this book, and I am profoundly grateful to all the patient people who gave so unstintingly to enable it to be brought to completion.

To begin at the beginning, with Biddulph Old Hall. All the members of the local Historical and Genealogical Society were dedicated to saving the building and had played a key role before our arrival in having it registered as a Building at Risk. Derek Wheelhouse and Roland Machin, in particular, brought us crucial pieces of evidence that opened the way to our discovery of Robert Bateman's association with the house and the Clough stream. Countless local people gave us valuable information about the history of the area, including Fred Hughes, Paul Baker, Michael Bond, the Bostock family, Margaret Smith, Bill Ridgway, Terry and Mavis Woods, and Stuart and Ann Thomas.

As the serious process of starting to halt the decay of the building's fabric got under way, we had invaluable support from our own wonderfully loyal team of Jeff Black, Ian Metcalf, Damion Moss, Barry Gold and Mark Thompson. Graham Holland gave wise counsel, as did John Yates, Stuart Ellis, John Tiernan and Ian George of English Heritage, Dr Martin Bridge of the Oxford Dendrochronology Lab and Dr Faith Cleverdon. The saving of the Tower drew heavily on the experience of Will Mellor and Rory Moore of Grosvenor Construction and the skills of Dennis Holgate. The renovation of the Great Hall relied on the finesse of Linda Walton and Dennis Eckersley from Design Lights, John Fosker, Ben Allport and his team, Richard Rhodes, Dave Broadbent, David Clayton, John Hetherington and Ben Newman. As the story led us into the world of Pre-Raphaelite art, we would have been lost without the guidance of Richard Dorment, Julian Hartnoll, Amanda Kavanagh, Colin Cruise, Fiona McCarthy, Dennis Lannigan, Janet Street Porter, Bob Maddocks and Robert Tichenor-Barrett. The Yale Center for British Art, particularly Gillian Forrester, Cassandra Albinson, Melissa Fournier, Abigail Armitstead and Scott Wilcox, set our search for Bateman in motion by sending us an image of their painting and explaining the strange story of its acquisition under a wrong attribution.

Equally vital was the help of Crestina Forcina at the Wellcome Foundation and Claire Hancock at Bridgeman Art. The staff at the Whitworth Art Gallery, Manchester, Lichfield Cathedral, Ironbridge Heritage Centre and the Staffordshire Archives provided important information at crucial moments in the research, as did Thomas Lloyd of the Lockinge Trust, Piers Monckton at Stretton Hall, Anna-Louise Mason at Castle Howard, Craig Sherwood at the Warrington Museum and Art Gallery, Dominic Farr from the William Salt Library and also Jean Milton and Sam Richardson from the Potteries Museum and Art Gallery. Special thanks also to all the long-suffering individuals and families who allowed us to invade their beautiful homes in pursuit of images or records, particularly Sir Richard and Lady Anne Baker-Wilbraham, The Earl and Countess of Oxford and Asquith, Edward Benthall, Lord Camoys, Anne Pommeroy, Viscount Harberton and Robin de Beaumont.

I am especially grateful for the cooperation and help of the descendants of the Bateman family, many of whom were startled to discover their relationship to Robert. These include John and Joyce Beauchamp, Jeremy and Prudence Burke, Jenifer Beauchamp and her children, Ruth Vilmi, and her brother Gordon Humphreys.

Thanks also to Heather Holden-Brown for being the first professional person to interface with the manuscript and her advice on how to proceed from there. A special thank you to naughty Roger Murray, not only for his lovely cartoon, but for his impeccably correct assessment of the manuscript as far too long! Almost as irrepressible was Paul Worpole, whose infectious enthusiasm was surpassed only by the brilliance of his photographs.

The other friend to whom I owe a real debt of gratitude is Pat Harvey who, at an unhappy time for her, dedicated endless hours to proofreading and annotating every single page of the huge original manuscript before we sent it out, and patiently nursing me through every twist and turn of the publishing process since then. Equally I cannot ignore the encouragement of my brother David, whose constant conviction that the book was sure to become a blockbuster movie was important at several dispiriting moments, and Iris Vowles for intervening to help us acquire the Clough, which would have been impossible without her.

But without doubt the defining moment in the book's fortunes arrived when John Nicoll opened the manuscript during his Christmas holidays and read it. He spent the next three days working out how best to publish it. He visited Biddulph, then put in place the editorial and design skills of Jane Havell to distil its potential and shape, and hone it for publication. The debt I owe to both these consummately gifted and professional people is immeasurable.

Of course, anyone who reads this book will understand that the whole of the adventure it records was a joint experience. Every single triumph and frustration was filtered through the prism of the relationship between Brian Vowles and myself. Together we perceived and reacted to each revelation and pondered its significance until its meaning became clear. Beyond that, all the labour of transcribing, correcting and ordering it was done by him alone. Only the will to capture the fleeting sensations in words before they were lost was mine. I could not and would not have created this piece of work without him. I think he knows that, so I don't need to attempt an impossible thank you.

NIGEL DALY
February 2014

Part 1

LOST AMONG THE RUINS

Fig. 1. 'We'll have to buy it, obviously' – our first glimpse of Biddulph Old Hall.

Chapter 1

INFATUATION

The moment Brian saw a magazine advertisement for the sale of Biddulph Old Hall, he was gripped by foreboding. He felt sure that if I were ever to catch sight of the photograph of the gaunt stone tower rising out of a cluster of mournful ruins, a calamitous chain of events would be set in motion. It was an uncannily wise and perceptive worry, which led him to hide the magazine and not mention it for two or three days. Then his own curiosity got the better of him and he slipped it, open, on to my desk (fig. 1).

I glanced at the picture and began to read. The text described the remnants of a great Elizabethan mansion on the edge of the Staffordshire moorlands which had been attacked in the English Civil War and brought to ruin. Alongside them, in fact built in to them, was a seventeenth-century inhabited stone farmhouse.

'What do you think?' Brian asked nonchalantly.

I slowly took off my glasses and rubbed my eyes.

'We'll have to buy it, obviously.'

Ten minutes later we had made an appointment to view it the following day. Worse still, an hour after that we had set off to find it.

Brian and I run a design business restoring period houses for clients, and for years had been searching for one special project to renovate ourselves. We had recently borrowed a lot of money to buy Bletchley Manor, a ruinous manor house in north Shropshire. It was desperately in need of major surgery if the disintegration of its timber frame was to be halted before it reached the point of collapse, and demolition. We had drawn up plans and got listed building consent for a radical restoration of the building from a sad collection of bedsits to the important historic house it really was. Work had begun with a drastic strip-out so that the deep-seated structural problems could be assessed, and a programme for tackling them put in hand. So what were we doing, meandering about the back lanes of Staffordshire on a rain-sodden January evening searching for yet another decrepit manor house?

We arrived at two low stone piers supporting a fractured iron gate, newly painted brilliant white over its pitted, corroded surface to try to disguise its decay. The gate was standing open and in the car headlights we could see a rutted drive disappearing steeply downhill between dripping, leafless beech trees. Without warning, a light flicked on – and a surreal apparition emerged from the impenetrable void. It was a building so incomprehensible in shape, mass and texture that we could not begin to decipher it. Facades from moorland farmhouses were juxtaposed with reticent ashlar elements which in turn collided with mighty, castle-like, sandstone blocks. Above all this, a cacophony of anarchic twisted roofs straddled their way upwards till they were crowned by an octagonal tower, the ogee dome of which provided a climax of ghoulish melodrama to the whole fantastic edifice. It utterly defied classification. Some parts were symmetrically arranged, but they made no attempt to conform to Italianate ideals of harmony. Equally, there was no hint of the contrived, spiky disorder of Victorian medievalism.

As suddenly as we had been admitted to this startling world, it vanished when the security light went off. We had been initiated into the mystical world of Biddulph Old Hall and we knew that, despite our better judgement, we would be back the next morning to view it. The following day the rain was replaced by pallid January sun. The clash of discordant fragments of masonry was no less peculiar than it had been the night before, but now the cumulative effect was more gently eccentric than monstrously assertive. The tower and the highest chimney stacks were revealed as being of a different stone, which at least made them understandable as distinct phases of construction.

The undisturbed quality of the hall and its setting seemed even more unusual in daylight than it had when the surrounding countryside was lost in darkness. The land fell away into a gentle valley beyond the building, made up of a series of hedged or stone-walled fields interspersed with copses and larger patches of woodland. There were glimpses of a river in the valley bottom, beyond which the land rose to a long ridge, sparsely dotted by sandstone farmsteads with long tracks snaking up to them. Even though it was January, there was only a single gap in the trees bordering the river far below, through which we could catch a glimpse of traffic. The whole pattern of the land was lyrically evocative of an age before intensive farming or ribbon housing development. The tower and its cluster of supporting structures lay in a context of enduring repose that was so improbable near Stoke-on-Trent that it was difficult to believe it had not been deliberately contrived for effect (fig. 2).

The car came to a halt in oozing mud and we sat in silence, absorbed by the still presence of the old house in its remote hiding place, apparently oblivious to the neurotic world around it. Far away across the Cheshire plain the weak sun shone through a slight haze on to the great white dish of the Jodrell Bank telescope.

Fig. 2 (right). Biddulph Old Hall from the entrance gate – a disconcerting collision of shapes and textures.

Fig. 3 (below). 'The mud comes free' – the back elevation of the Old Hall.

We had just remarked on the comparatively conventional character of the house's back elevation when the door opened and a slim woman emerged.

'The mud comes free, you'll be glad to hear!' she called as we got out of the car and squelched our way towards her. She stepped back into the house as we approached, revealing a step down from the threshold, over which two alarming little rivulets of water were flowing (fig. 3).

We shook her proffered hand. Mrs Smith was about sixty, with the manner of a slightly acerbic schoolmistress taking in hand two dawdling nine-year-olds. Brian and I gazed along a narrow passage with steep stairs rising along its left-hand wall. There were two poor-quality flush doors with plastic handles to left and right. The absolute predictability of the layout gave us the feeling of having walked into a conventional semi-detached house of the 1930s. The space felt mean, dark and dismayingly commonplace. How could this meagre corridor be the first experience of being enveloped by the hidden tower house we had driven up to? Every part of what we were looking at was a banal travesty, ruthlessly imposed upon the ancient fabric of the house.

Even then, in that first moment of engagement, we had a sense of outrage that something so inherently unique and precious, all the more valuable for being difficult to comprehend, had been deliberately suppressed and tamed. Before we had regained our equilibrium, Mrs Smith was chivvying us through the door on the right to her kitchen.

After the hall, it was at least animated by the cluttered chaos of everyday use. Indeed, such a density of necessities and bric-à-brac had been compressed into one low, dimly lit space that it had aquired the all-embracing claustrophobia of a caravan or canal barge. The confrontation of decorative idioms, working one against the other, and all, to varying degrees, in conflict with the underlying character of the building, was eclectic to the point of exhaustion. The walls at the far end of the room had been clad in varnished pine boards, and fitted with starkly simple white melamine units. However, the reticent intent of this ensemble had been completely submerged beneath a conglomeration of wine racks, sieves, painted plates, trivets, microwave cookers, abstract drawings, Greek peasant jars, cacti, ferns and scented candles. In the centre of the room this homely hotch-potch collided with the stern mass of a great corbelled chimney breast, obscured beneath an ill-fitting skin of woodchip wallpaper above a venerable cream Aga.

'So that's the kitchen – no doubt as designers you think it very passé!'

She led the way out into the hall.

'Not that I'm out of sympathy with that! If I'd not got bogged down here who knows what subversive innovations might not have sheltered me. After all, I'm a modernist at heart!'

As she spoke she reached the end of the hall and opened a door into another world. It was a disturbing place, with an atmosphere as distinct as it was possible to get from the banality of the hall and kitchen. It rode roughshod over the contrived ordinariness of those spaces.

Brian and I literally gasped as we stepped across the stone-flagged threshold of the room. Never in all our years of working with period houses, in every stage of dereliction or cosseted preservation, had we walked into a space that so vividly and brutally conveyed a sense of the remote past.

Fig. 4. 'She opened the door into another world' – The Great Hall as we first saw it.

It spoke of a harsh, workaday existence. There was no attempt to embellish or elaborate in order to impress – and yet the height of the room and its wide, stone-mullioned window were a world away from the cramped hovels that housed hill farmers, high on these icy moorlands, before the agricultural revolution. The window was set high in the wall. A short passageway led to an outside door, and three other doors indicated that it was intended to function as some sort of hall from which the other rooms radiated. It was not a particularly big room, perhaps twenty feet square, so it was a surprise when Margaret Smith announced it with a flourish as the 'Great Hall' (fig. 4).

However, she made clear that she concurred with the opinion of Sir Nikolaus Pevsner, who had described Biddulph Old Hall as 'the ruins of an Elizabethan mansion into which is built a late seventeenth-century house of no pretension'. Since Restoration farmhouses were not built with great halls, Mrs Smith had felt compelled to conclude that the name was derived not from historical evidence, but Victorian affectation. Her distaste for this and all things Victorian was evident in her next words:

'It is to banish the baleful ambience of that benighted age that I have made pure white the leitmotiv of my rejuvenation of this place.'

As she said this, it dawned on us that it was the contrast between the impossibly staring white walls and the blackened beams, floor slabs and furniture that accounted for the stark cheerlessness of the room. Not only was the uniform, brilliant whiteness of the paint an historical impossibility, but the flawless texture achieved by the latex in its composition blotted out every vestige of animating patina, built up by accidents and adaptations over the centuries. Had these been visible, the fractured, time-worn materials from which the hall was made would have softened and enhanced the enigmatic character of this precious survival from a lost world.

Certainly until we, or someone else, looked into it, we were not prepared to join Mrs Smith in her whitewashed certainty that the received name 'Great Hall' was no more than Victorian snobbery. We knew that it did not have all the defining characteristics of a medieval hall – there was no surviving cross-passage, or visible dais. However, we could see that it had been badly mutilated over the years, so it would be foolhardy to accept everything at face value. What had been hidden or lost? What had these changes concealed about the origins of this room? The more we gazed about us, the more curious we became about what we were actually looking at.

On the far wall there was an absurdly under-scaled fire-surround dating from the 1950s, which was almost endearing in its comic inadequacy for the task of heating the space. Above it a huge blackened timber, at least 14 feet long, was set into the wall. We could easily imagine how different the character of the Great Hall would be if the original fireplace had related to the width of that beam. The whole scale and dynamics of the room would be transformed into something inherently earlier and more communal in intent. Its archaic resonance, already so arresting, would be distilled and intensified. Also, crucially, a fireplace that size would be impossible to reconcile with the house being built after 1660, as Pevsner had suggested.

Mrs Smith led the way up another intriguingly individual feature of the room. It was a set of three steps, fixed within what looked like the stalls of a stable. They were incredibly simple and massive, being formed of heavy oak boards joined directly together and fronted by posts with crudely carved square finials. They led to the 'parlour', which proved to be a dark room with a pungent smell of sodden soot hanging in the musty air. It was ironic in the light of Mrs Smith's preferences, and the continuation of her brilliant white offensive, that the 'parlour' contrived to capture the very essence of that most doleful of British institutions, the unused front room.

However, Brian and I had already become dangerously impervious to even the most glaring defects of the house. We were too enthralled by the atmosphere of this bewitching place to do more than follow in Mrs Smith's wake, as she chivvied us from one outlandishly improbable space to the next. We found ourselves being herded back down the steps and through a wide door on the far side of the Great Hall, where even Mrs Smith faltered for a moment in mid-sentence. She was announcing yet another 'hall', the Staircase Hall, as she opened the door.

Fig. 5. The puzzling Staircase Hall.

It was night in the room beyond, apart from a single strip of brightness at floor level ahead of us. As our eyes adjusted, the handrail of a staircase appeared in ghostly silhouette, its skinny spindles spaced unnaturally wide apart. It seemed to be lit by a hidden source of daylight far away in the floor above. The next moment there was a click and a paper globe above our heads illuminated the blinding white dungeon or crypt surrounding us (fig. 5).

Ahead was a low archway set at a strangely unnatural height, barely five feet at the centre. Behind it was an unplastered niche of whitewashed rubble-stone. Our sense of disquiet was increased by the presence of a door in the back wall of the niche, which was logically out of kilter with the preceding arch and so defied the coherence of everyday common sense. The stone floor was black and glistened with beads of water.

The room contained the principal staircase of the house. As Mrs Smith pointed to it, the truly abysmal workmanship of this flight of stairs became clear to us. The mitres gaped, the tiny spindles were spaced so sparsely they were clearly illegal. The gaps and mismatches had been larded with filler and then heavily overpainted with brilliant white gloss, which hung in disfiguring runs over every element of the structure. It was utterly inconceivable that anything so feeble and inept had ever formed an integral part of the fabric of a building as massive and robust as Biddulph Old

Hall. The devastating effect upon the architectural integrity of the building was tragic and had the effect of devaluing the importance of what still remained. But far from discouraging us, the more the house displayed the contempt with which it had been treated the stronger our compulsion to bond with it became.

Mrs Smith crossed the hall to what she described as her pièce de resistance, the 'quintessence' of her contribution to the building – the Library. To our surprise the ubiquitous white walls gave way to duck-egg blue. There had been a real attempt to achieve a comfortable sitting room with a studious theme. There was a complete wall of bookshelves with upholstered chairs grouped around a brick fireplace of the inter-war era. A window looked out on to the ruins of the mansion, through which weak sunlight fell into the room. The chintz curtains and patterned fabrics ought to have created a relaxed intimate haven but, for some reason, carried no conviction. The room seemed ill at ease, forlorn and empty, rather than exuding the hush of a secluded sanctuary. There was a sense of the books being working documents or agents of self-improvement rather than beloved companions.

As we followed Mrs Smith up the dismal staircase we were careful to heed her warning not to put too much faith in the handrail. We crossed a landing and into the room above the library. Although the same dimensions as the room below, it had been painted an impenetrable black-green and seemed cavernous and sombre. Uniquely, it was lit by a huge north-facing sash window, indicating a later date than the rest of the building. The window, however, was in the last stages of dilapidation. The glazing bars were rotted through, and the discoloured glass panes were cracked or replaced by distorted hardboard. The floor had been repaired with varnished pine boards, but this petered out part-way across the room. Two bulbs hung from frayed plaited wires. The walls were completely misted over with condensation. The cold air was achingly invasive, its stagnant stillness infinitely more desolate than the healthy outdoor chill. It was a junk room, piled with cardboard boxes, broken vacuum cleaners, faded garden loungers and appalling abstract paintings from the 1970s (fig. 6).

Fig. 6. The Green Room or Studio – Mrs Smith's 'Waterloo'.

Mrs Smith described this room as her 'Waterloo', the place where she had finally drawn a limit to her commitment to rescuing the house. She recalled how, after they had been in the house three or four years, her husband John had proposed restoring this derelict room. Until then, she explained, they had dedicated their entire lives, and every penny they earned, to repairing and modernising the crumbling anachronism that fate had put in their path. She told us that she and her husband had convinced themselves there was something mysterious here – a hidden story that would reveal itself as they worked on the room.

Then, one day, the spell broke. They realised that they had become caught up in a dream world that was devouring them. They understood, in that moment, that there was no limit to the rapacious demands of this building. They could either decide to devote themselves entirely to relieving its progressive infirmity, or they could enjoy it broadly as it was and return to the vibrant world of jazz records and radical politics that they had abandoned a few years before. Disturbingly, I too sensed something intangible about this room, something hidden or forgotten, locked into it, despite its short history relative to the rest of the building. When I asked Mrs Smith what she had discovered about it she laughed.

'Ah! You're a sensitive, a believer! It's drawing you in already! There was wild talk of forbidden Popish chapels and studios for nameless romantic artists. Not one jot of evidence for any of it. '

We set off on a chase through the rest of the house. But the pace was too unrelenting, and the labyrinth of landings, chilly bathrooms, crooked flights of stairs, bedrooms, derelict attics and box rooms was too bewildering to take in. Besides, the emotional tipping point, when our romantic infatuation with the place could have been mitigated by anything we saw, no matter how macabre, was far behind us.

Eventually we paused at the foot of a flight of stairs with the underside of the stone slates of the roof visible above us. Mrs Smith seemed intent on ignoring our interest, so we were forced to ask what it led to. She told us there was a room she never went in to. When she arrived it had contained a statue of Buddha, left by the community of Buddhist monks she had bought the house from. As we climbed the stairs she warned us that there were sometimes 'dead things' in the room. We pushed open an ancient plank door that caught and scraped over debris. Immediately at our feet lay the maggot-eaten carcass of a dead jackdaw, its tattered wings outstretched and its broken neck twisted into an impossible position.

The window to our right was broken, with blackened dried blood on the edge of the shattered pane and dotted across the sill. The whole floor was littered with droppings, feathers and lichen-encrusted twigs. Diagonally across the room was a tall recess with a brick stanchion rising in it that disappeared through the ceiling. Behind the stanchion was another small glassless window, with a huge bird's nest built just inside it. The walls were Artexed in energetic swirls. Two were fitted with wooden wall lights, one broken and dangling from its wires, the other retaining a single mutilated shade, its dirty bobble fringe sagging from it.

Through the broken window was a distant, tranquil view over the far side of the valley. We watched transfixed as, far away, a single tiny vehicle slowly made its way up one of the unmade tracks to a farm. Framed by the jagged window pane, it had the intriguing intensity of the opening sequence of a film. As we gazed at it, Mrs Smith was called to her next viewing. We listened as her footsteps clattered away down the stairs.

The silence returned. Away to the left a crowd of jackdaws clucked and chattered as they wheeled around the blackened ogee dome of the tower. A kestrel flew into the middle of our view and hovered motionless.

'Strange atmosphere,' murmered Brian.

We were silent for a time.

'Actually, it's overpowering, isn't it?'

'In here?'

'Yes, but all through the place. Outside as well. There's something here. Incredibly strong. Not the usual old house spooks. A residue of something real. Too real to be laughed off. It could be sad, or even threatening, I can't quite tell. But it pervades everything – intense, almost urgent.'

'Steady,' said Brian, turning to go. 'We haven't done the ruins yet!'

It was the scale.

Nothing had prepared us for the declamatory proportions or fractured massiveness of what confronted us when we ducked under the tomb-like arch and pulled open the door to the ruins. We blinked and gazed, unable to adjust our vision sufficiently quickly to respond to the awesome dimensions of our new surroundings. Without warning, the crooked confusion of the maltreated building, oscillating uncertainly between crude farmhouse and historic manor, was subsumed into an assertive new entity, which imposed its dominating presence upon the surrounding landscape with effortless self-assurance. The castle-like resonance of the bare stone curtain-walls, pierced by mighty arched apertures and blind openings, changed the whole character of the site. There was a greatness, a magnificence, about the scale that we had never anticipated (fig. 7).

In our minds, the poetical potency of ruins was rooted in the picturesque idylls beloved of Jane Austen's heroines, or illustrated in the watercolour renderings of landscape parks by Humphrey Repton. Whether they were entirely contrived pieces of whimsy or genuine ruined buildings, their surroundings were invariably manipulated to evoke a sensation of refined melancholy. The abandoned fortress perched on its howling crag with foaming breakers hurling themselves against it was another popular variant. However, this relied on spartan solitude to convey its exhilarating

Fig. 7. The ruins – they insisted that one engage with their former sense of self-importance, and the brutality of the forces that had been ranged against them.

appeal – it could not possibly coexist with avocado bathroom suites, crocheted table centres and kitchen-implement racks on the outskirts of Stoke-on-Trent.

The Elizabethan remnants we were looking at refused to conform to any cultural conditioning associated with ruins, either poetic or barren. They did manage to coexist alongside a fully lived-in domestic building, and their setting, although miraculously peaceful, gave no sense of being deliberately designed to heighten their scenic effect. They had an almost brutal candour, which retained clear evidence of the tumultuous struggle that had created them. There had been no attempt to soften or disguise their gaunt outlines, or repair the gaping craters where cannon balls had splintered their ashlar walls.

We had been told that the ruins were listed separately from the Grade II* house, and were designated as a Scheduled Ancient Monument. This implied a separate identity. However, as we walked round the site, we were conscious of a palpable underlying unity that bonded the ruins, the tower, the inhabited house and the great level plateau (the so-called Tilt Yard) together into a dramatic, thematic whole, despite its fragmented forms and materials. These pieces were interdependent components of a historical narrative that stretched back darkly into the distant past.

The tragedy was that no one seemed to have taken the trouble to read the story written into the fabric of this wonderful place.

Despite our longing to embrace that adventure, Brian and I knew instinctively what had daunted so many before us. Interwoven with the tantalising mysteries was a thread of real danger. If we once dared to search beneath the surface of these archaic remains and expose their secrets, they would never allow us to return to the workaday world unscathed should we become overwhelmed and try to abandon them. They had the power to impoverish us materially and spiritually if we trifled with them. If we tried to cheat by investing ourselves with their charisma but simultaneously with-holding our commitment to their needs, as Mrs Smith admitted she had done, they would take us prisoner, as they had her.

Yet we could not deny that the place had spoken to us. We could not ignore its yearning to be released from its current humiliating ugliness. It was no less than our duty to respond to that hypnotic cry for help, by overcoming every obstacle to getting possession of it, so that the process of saving it could begin. We had to take action. We had to risk and hazard all, or live for the rest of our lives with the knowledge that we had come face to face with our moment of destiny and fumbled the encounter so that it slipped from our grasp.

We became obsessed. We went back day after day, until eventually Mrs Smith began to ignore us. Away from the house the pace was too hectic to permit a moment's reflection. Within days our cottage was valued and on the market. It was priced reasonably for a quick sale, and soon attracted several potential purchasers. We made an offer on Biddulph, and were immediately told it had been capped. We attempted a preemptive strike by offering the full asking price. However, the agents had arranged for the house to be advertised in *Country Life* the following week, and Mrs Smith would not commit until she had tested Biddulph's appeal at national level.

The article produced new viewings and new offers. Higher offers. A Dutch auction was developing, pushing the price to a level where we could not, honestly, take part. None the less, we offered again and, when we were capped, a third time. Suddenly, without warning, the agents called for sealed bids. The effect was stunning. The ensuing days were eerily still and ordinary. Confronted by the need to write down a figure, we went through a traumatically realistic assessment of what we could actually afford, and wrote it down.

In a desperate attempt to sidestep the implications of this collision with the real world, we went to Biddulph. We skulked past the house and crossed the Tilt Yard, where we found the start of a long, falling path lined each side by huge yew and sycamore trees. We guessed it must be the Yew Walk that Mrs Smith had mentioned on one of our visits. We decided to explore it, and in no time our tentative hold on financial sobriety was swept away on a new surge of enthusiasm.

As ever at Biddulph, the correlation between the expectation set up by key words, and the shock of what actually lay before us, was disconcertingly out of kilter. What we were looking at did not even function as a passable footpath. The Yew Walk was only discernible by the high banks that bordered it. These had become home to a thriving community of badgers, whose sets dotted its whole length. Their spoil formed great mounds of rubble, which had become intermingled with fallen branches from the bordering trees. The living branches had woven themselves into a continuous canopy overhead, which drooped down in places to touch the peaks of the disorderly hillocks below. Many were gnarled yews that produced a disquieting twilight where they met, and transformed the banks below into contorted skeletons of knotted roots, sitting proud of the pitted ground like old arthritic hands.

Brian and I began to scrabble our way over the debris. As we did so, squirrels leapt across branches just above our heads, and startled rooks flapped up through the twiggy canopy. The atmosphere was distinctly forbidding, but strangely at one with the outline of the ruins when we glanced back over our shoulders.

At the far end of the walk, the path turned and fell sharply between unruly banks of holly, until it passed under a beautifully simple bridge made of large sandstone blocks. We scrambled down to it and, on the far side, found ourselves in a steep wooded valley, with a fast-running stream, known locally as the Clough. The sense of privacy or seclusion was so strong that we felt as though we were being watched. It was the mournful ghost of a beautiful place – disfigured, but still faintly discernible (fig. 8).

Below us was a wide flat area of black mud, smelling of putrefying vegetation and defaced by discarded plastic sacks, rusty corrugated iron, old tractor tyres, half-

Fig. 8. The ghost of a beautiful place – the drained upper lake in the Clough.

submerged supermarket trolleys and fallen trees. The stream threaded its way across the quagmire between the pieces of rubbish, until it disappeared into a concrete pipe that had been used to breach what must once have been a dam. Despite our wariness, we followed the stream until it cascaded out of the other end of the pipe, splashing down over fallen rocks and broken paving slabs, transforming them into an exuberant waterfall. Gradually, the rubbish petered out and the valley was undisturbed, except for the occasional fallen tree lying across the stream.

The further we went, the stronger the sensation became of being drawn into an isolated, personal space, with a consciously heightened atmosphere. The stream was too good to be true. The water tumbled over weirs, rushed down little stepped rapids, and rippled over great flat plains of rock, before arriving at a second broken dam. Although this had been a substantial feat of engineering – tall and well constructed out of coursed sandstone blocks – it had been blown up to breach it and release the water held behind it. The great slabs of ivy-covered masonry, haphazardly strewn across the valley floor, bore silent witness to some ambitious human endeavour, whose purpose had been forgotten long ago.

By now an inexplicable conviction had taken hold of us. We could not rid ourselves of the sensation that the atmosphere of the Clough stream was so closely allied to the disturbing intensity of the Yew Walk and the ruins that they were bound together, not merely by their proximity to each other, but by the intervention of some manipulating historical force which we felt, but could not guess at. By the end of our walk through the wood, we had convinced ourselves that uniting the Clough valley with the hall was a vital element in understanding the true historical significance of the whole site.

We discovered that the Clough and its surroundings belonged to the brewery that owned the local pub, the Talbot. I rang them and was told that the brewery did indeed own the valley, and that they were looking to sell it. We became so transfixed by the possibilities that this presented that we lost sight of the date when the bids were to be opened for the house, the acquisition of which had somehow become a foregone conclusion in our minds.

Then, at 2 o'clock on a busy Thursday afternoon, my phone rang.

'Hello, Mr Daly, this is Strutt & Parker. This is just a courtesy call, really. Mrs Smith has asked me to inform you that your bid for Biddulph Old Hall has not been successful. You were outbid by two other parties...'

I stopped hearing her. I had passed into a state of shock – a sort of pins and needles of the soul. Somewhere, miles away, I heard myself asking how much more they had been offered, and being told it was in excess of £100,000. Perhaps, mercifully, this figure was hopelessly out of our reach. The game was up – except that we had ceased to perceive it as a game long, long ago. By the time I put the phone down, Brian had heard enough, and did not ask.

What had happened to us? It was a house, bricks and mortar or, in this case, a haphazard pile of stones – that was all. How could it be that the two of us, Brian and I, hard-bitten old professionals at the property game, who had worked on houses old, new, ugly and beautiful all over the country and beyond, had so comprehensively lost contact with our sanity that we had honestly come to believe in some sort of mystical destiny that bound us and Biddulph Old Hall together? It was unthinkable.

Very gradually, with the aid of a few drinks, we began the agonising process of applying a dishonest film of rational ointment over our raw disappointment. By the end of the first evening, we had made a valiant effort to become resigned, rather than speechless with resentment and self-pity. After the first week it began to occur to us that it might, possibly, be for the best in the long run. After all, we still had Bletchley Manor, and this gave us the opportunity to concentrate wholeheartedly on that and, of course, our work for our clients. By the end of two weeks we were congratulating ourselves on a narrow escape, and vowing to learn the lessons of our stupidity.

That was when the phone rang again.

'Mr Daly?' I knew that voice. 'I'm ringing on behalf of Margaret Smith. She has instructed me to accept your offer for Biddulph Old Hall – if the house is still of interest to you. Both the overbidders have withdrawn . . .'

I was trembling.

'We've got it!' I whispered. 'We've bloody well got it!'

'Of course, I think it was meant,' said Brian as he enveloped me in a footballer's hug. 'Never doubted it for a moment!'

Fig. 9 (see page 45). The Staircase Hall after restoration – a conundrum resolved.

Chapter 2

TRIAL BY TV

When the time actually came to move into Biddulph Old Hall, the compulsive hold it had established on our imaginations and the uncanny way it had come into our ownership were once again making us distinctly uneasy. We felt an urgent need to reestablish a stable plateau of objective rationality, so that our decisions could be driven by shrewd calculation rather than sentimental voodoo if we were to avoid another collision with mundane, everyday life. To this end we made a solemn vow not to indulge our fascination with the house's aura, or divert scarce resources from the restoration of Bletchley Manor, until that project was completed and sold. This would avert the potential catastrophe of owning two deconstructed, valueless, listed buildings at the same time.

We decided we would live in Biddulph exactly as it was, and await the proper moment to begin investigating its fabric and its story. The one concession we allowed ourselves was to agree a programme of investigative work with our local Conservation Officer. This would enable us to prepare a carefully drawn-up application to obtain Listed Building consent from the council and English Heritage.

Three months after we had set out upon this virtuous path we received a phone call from someone we did not know called Amy. She had been part of the production team on the Channel 4 television programme *Grand Designs*, and remembered seeing the plans of two restoration projects that we had done for clients, which had been considered for inclusion in the programme. She had moved on, having secured funding from BBC2 for a new prime-time series, specifically focused on the restoration of historic houses. She wondered if we had anything interesting in the pipeline.

She went into eulogies over the quality of our drawings and the 'truly amazing' nature of our projects. She also appealed to our vanity by inferring that she was specifically searching for serious contributors with longstanding professional experience in period buildings whose work would be endorsed and explained to 'the punters' by a panel of experts from the heritage industry.

As she spoke the possibility occurred to me that public exposure might attract interest, or even funding, for one of the two huge projects we had so impulsively become entangled in. Surely, if nothing else, television had the power to sell Bletchley Manor quickly when it was finished, so that we could regroup and pursue our obsession with Biddulph. Sadly, despite my shameless hard sell, Amy could not be persuaded to take any interest in Bletchley, since the restoration was already under way and the essential 'before' shots would be missing.

Undaunted, I found myself luridly describing another project that, 'as luck would have it,' was on the very point of starting work. I described it as a disintegrating ruin standing in a waterlogged moon crater, with a six-storey stone tower damaged in the English Civil War. She was agog. Before the phone call was over she had proposed sending two researchers to carry out a 'recce' and get some footage for her to look at. The researchers would be able to explain the exciting format of the series to us without, of course, putting any pressure on us to do anything we were not comfortable with.

Naturally, I agreed – completely failing to recognise the critical moment when all our carefully laid plans were abandoned and we linked our fate to the fortunes of a plausible stranger and her untried television series. Within a month we had given a firm commitment to Amy and initiated a crash programme of work at Bletchley to establish sufficient protection and security to allow us to divert the team of men working there to Biddulph. It was arranged that the production team would film the work intermittently over the next year, focusing on the restoration of the Great Hall, the Staircase Hall and the creation of a small parterre garden by the front door.

At a stroke we were liberated from the stern discipline of our pledge not to investigate either the historic fabric or the documentary evidence of Biddulph's past until Bletchley Manor was sold. In fact, we convinced ourselves that it was our duty to put in hand a meticulous drive to discover the lost story of the building at once, to enable us to carry out an informed restoration.

All we knew at the outset was that a family by the name of Biddulph was recorded as being the feudal lords of the surrounding area back into the mists of history. From a privately published booklet on the Civil War skirmish in which the house had been attacked, we knew that they had been Royalists and that after the Restoration Charles II had described their defence of their home as a 'great service' to the monarchy.

The owner of Biddulph Hall at that time was a young man of twenty-two called Francis Biddulph, who was captured and imprisoned in Stafford. His mother, young wife and one-year-old baby were forced to flee the building when the local population completed the work of the fearsome cannon, Roaring Meg, by looting and setting fire to the Hall. Reduced almost to starvation, the women were recorded as petitioning the Parliamentary Committee at Stafford for permission to return to the charred remnants of their former home. The Committee acceded to their request only under a series of stringent conditions, which condemned them to continued poverty. They were described as dangerous, and 'a nest of Papists'. As our research progressed, we came to realise that this phrase held a vital clue to understanding the whole story of the house and its inhabitants.

We managed to reclaim a file of papers relating to Biddulph from a firm of solicitors where they had been languishing unseen for decades. These recorded that, despite the continuous occupation of the house from the earliest era of archaic documentation, there was no evidence of its ever having been sold until 1861. In that year it was sold by a Lord Camoys to James Bateman, Esq. We knew that James Bateman was a wealthy Victorian who had created a famous garden round his property Biddulph Grange, which adjoined Biddulph Old Hall and was now restored and maintained by the National Trust. But who was Lord Camoys? How had he come to own the house? What link, if any, was there between him, Francis Biddulph and the destitute women of the Cromwellian era?

It transpired that there was a living Lord Camoys, whose surname was Stonor. He lived in some style at Stonor Park, a country house near Henley-on-Thames. Once we began to investigate these disparate people from different ages, the connection between them began to emerge. At the core of that link lay the Roman Catholic faith. Francis Biddulph had been a prominent Catholic. His Roman Catholicism had caused his house to become a natural target for the predominantly Puritan Parliamentary forces in the Civil War. When Henry VIII split from Rome, the Biddulphs became Recusants – they refused to recognise Henry, or any subsequent sovereign, as the Supreme Head of the Church in England. Despite their equally fervent Royalism, this led them to be held in deep distrust by succeeding monarchs and made them liable to punitive taxes and restrictions. The Stonors were equally overt Recusants who maintained a private Roman Catholic chapel by their mansion.

When we traced Francis Biddulph's descendants it became clear why Biddulph Old Hall had never been rebuilt or demolished. Despite the Restoration of Charles II in 1660, it was not long before the Biddulph family were again the focus of deep suspicion by the Court and political establishment. Several members of the family were implicated in King James II's attempt to reinstate the old faith, and fled into exile with him when he was deposed in favour of William III. The punitive taxes they were subjected to, especially at the time of the 1715 and 1745 rebellions, meant that they remained impoverished until Francis Biddulph's son, Richard Biddulph, made a highly advantageous marriage to the sole heiress of another Recusant family, the Gorings of Burton Park in Sussex. Not only did Richard Biddulph acquire a magnificent new estate and mansion in the south of England, but the marriage made him eligible for another advantage, retained by the family of his new wife.

The Gorings were holders of the Camoys title, which had the extremely rare distinction in English law of being able to pass through the senior female line of the family if the male descent became extinct. Thus, as an only daughter and the sole heir, Anne Goring was able to pass the title to her husband Richard Biddulph and on down to their children. However, the laws against Recusancy debarred Richard or his children from using this title or being legally recognised as peers. This situation persisted until 1820, when the male line of the Biddulph family died out with the death of Charles Biddulph, a bachelor nearly a hundred years old. His estates were divided between his two sisters and their families. Burton Park went to the younger sister and the Biddulph estate to the elder, Mary, who was married to Thomas Stonor.

Shortly after this, in 1829, the Catholic Emancipation Act was passed, removing penalties and restrictions on Roman Catholics. Among the Biddulph papers we found an elaborate family tree drawn up in 1839 to demonstrate the descent of the Stonor children from Mary Biddulph. This enabled them to place a successful claim before the House of Lords for the Camoys title to be brought out of abeyance.

Brian and I visited Stonor Park, a deceptively symmetrical Carolean house which encases a much earlier medieval structure. Our formidable guide majored on the evolved architectural history of the house, deviating only occasionally to point out pictures or objects that emphasised the historic pre-eminence of the Stonors, particularly in relation to the royal family. After Catholic Emancipation the newly enobled Lord Camoys had been appointed Lord-in-Waiting to Queen Victoria, and begun a family tradition of discreet but devoted service to the British monarchy that has continued ever since. Judging by the plethora of silver-framed photographs, the present Lord Camoys and his forebears had been intimate with most of the people who occupied key public positions across the globe during the previous 150 years. The pictures ranged from Queen Mary, through the Queen Mother, to the Queen, Prince Philip and innumerable lesser luminaries of the House of Windsor. They were supplemented by an assortment of French and American presidents, leaders of the UN, popes, dalai lamas, Japanese emperors and boiler-suited Chinese Party chairmen.

In view of the imperial grandeur and global reach of this network of connections, it seemed faintly implausible when our guide paused in the dining room beside a portrait of a frail, homely lady in a lace cap and announced that she was 'Mary Biddulph, the wife of Thomas Stonor and mother of fourteen children, who brought the title Lord Camoys into the family'.

Brian and I stared transfixed at the quaint little figure gazing out at us. It was the first face from the story of Biddulph that we had ever seen. Could she really have come from our strange, fragmented, hobgoblin of a house on the gale-swept Staffordshire moorlands to this noble pile? Could she have relentlessly given birth to fourteen children and bestowed nobility on them in perpetuity, once conditions allowed it? Although the ancient prominence of the Stonor family was evident all around us, we wondered what part her unique bequest of elevation to the peerage had played in their ability to project themselves into the heart of the British establishment.

We sought out Lord Camoys and told him our story. He and his wife were intrigued, as they did not know that any remnant of a house had survived at Biddulph. They freely acknowledged that it was to emphasise their descent from Mary Biddulph and reinforce their claim to the Camoys title that the Stonors had held on to the estate. In the early nineteenth century the family had intended to rebuild the house for a younger son, but he had died young. After that, with no use for it and with the Camoys title secured, the Stonors gradually lost interest in their remote acreage in Staffordshire and sold it, for the first time in its long history, to James Bateman in 1861.

Gradually, we were beginning to discern the succession of human tragedies and cruel twists of fate that had created the fragmented ruins that we now lived in. Local folk-lore had always insisted that our house was not the original historic seat of the Biddulph family. This was supposed to be on a steeply rising hillock, two miles away, round which a river, the Biddulph Brook, formed a natural moat. Although it seemed plausible, we had never been able to find any confirmation of this, so it was exciting to discover the report of an archaeological dig that had been carried out on the mound in the 1960s. The results had confirmed the site as a medieval settlement containing artefacts from the twelfth to the end of the fourteenth centuries. The last finds were a cluster of objects, all associated with demolition, dating from around 1400. This suggested a family long settled in the area, on a defensible site, who had progressively abandoned it and built a new house nearby, completing the removal by demolishing the old building completely at about this date.

The date stone of 1580 on the porch of our surviving ruins suggested that in the sixteenth century they began to replace the disorderly medieval buildings, many moved from their original site, by an ambitious, symmetrical, stone mansion. This process had been critically delayed from the 1530s by the penalties for the family's Recusancy, so it was incomplete at the time of the Civil War attack that brought it to ruin. Accounts of the attack describe the critical moment of surrender occurring when a cannonball struck the bressummer of a timber-framed section of the building, causing a partial collapse. This indicated that not all the house had been rebuilt in stone by that time.

After the attack the Biddulphs had squatted in fearful poverty among the ruins of their former mansion. They regained their land after the Restoration but, as generations succeeded one another, never wavered in their commitment to the Roman Catholic faith. Thus they remained impoverished and unable to rebuild the house until they acquired another estate by marriage. Because the name of Biddulph was the basis of their claim to the Camoys title, their descendents were never prepared to sever their connection with the Old Hall despite being settled elsewhere.

While we were immersed in these investigations, the television crew had come up for a day to get some establishing shots of the house. The first full day's filming was fast approaching. Before they arrived we needed to look into the other character we had found in the sale documents. Unless we could gain some understanding of what had motivated James Bateman to buy the Old Hall in 1861, we might misread the traces his ownership had left on the fabric of the building and its surroundings.

A visit to his house, Biddulph Grange, seemed the obvious place to start. We had been there before, but now, with our sharper focus of interest, the domineering scale of his huge Victorian mansion and the complexity of its restored garden impressed themselves upon us. The National Trust curator explained that James's purchase of Biddulph Old Hall had marked the last phase of the continuous elaboration of his garden, after the rock works, stumperies, arboretums, and Chinese and Egyptian gardens were already complete and mature. He had regarded the nearby ruined hall as the ultimate picturesque garden folly. He had bought it to add a last twist of macabre excitement to his landscape creation – the spectral tower abandoned amid the forlorn ruins of its former grandeur. The visual potency of the ruin was heightened by the fact that it was partly habitable – meals were prepared and served within it to Bateman's wealthy friends.

Intriguingly, James was said to have built a connecting walk from Biddulph Grange to the Old Hall that passed through tunnels and over bridges before rising up the valley beside the Clough stream. However, since he bought the Hall in 1861 and moved permanently to London in 1868, there were almost no surviving records or documents relating to it. Another local tradition had it that James's third son, an artist called Robert, had lived in the Hall before the family moved to London. In a book on the Grange gardens by Peter Hayden, we discovered a photograph of Robert Bateman in what was claimed to be part of the walk through the Clough (fig. 10). He was a bearded, distinctly artistic-looking character in a soft hat and neckerchief, accompanied by a woman and a bowler-hatted man on a rustic bridge in front of a complex waterfall. This photograph instantly reignited our interest in the Clough stream, as it appeared to confirm our intuition that at some point in the past the valley had been manipulated to intensify its atmosphere.

Feeling that Robert Bateman might form an important component in the story of the house and its surroundings, we spent many fruitless hours over the next weeks searching for this elusive character. There seemed to be little evidence anywhere to support either the tradition of his being an artist or of his sojourn in Biddulph Old Hall. Then, by chance, a man called Bill Ridgway contacted us to discuss his forthcoming book 'James Bateman and his World'. He knew almost nothing about Robert Bateman but had come across a single letter from him. This indicated that Robert had been some sort of governor of a school at Biddulph Moor when a quarrel had broken out between the rector and the resident schoolmaster. A letter from a school governor did not seem likely to confirm Robert's life as an artist living in a ruined mansion, but we asked Bill if he would send us a copy so that at least we could put the myth to rest.

Fig. 10. Robert Bateman (right) – a distinctly artistic-looking character.

To our amazement, the letter appeared to support one aspect of the story while creating a mystery around the accepted chronology of another. It was addressed from Biddulph Hall and dated 2 March 1874. This appeared to suggest that Robert was living at Biddulph Hall and acting as a school governor six years after the family were documented as having moved to London.

The letter is about an acrimonious dispute and Robert's position is a difficult, semi-official one. It is written privately to the schoolmaster, to express sympathy and to try to persuade him to follow a path that will avoid personal humiliation and unhappiness at the hands of the rector. Bateman's human concern is clearly sincere and beyond the scope of his official duties. It opens:

My Dear Sir,

Enclosed you will find an official letter from me as one of the school managers, the contents of which you will see, but I cannot send it off without this line to say how very sorry I am to find there exists a disagreement between yourself and the Rector. I have tried to find out the truth and justice of the case without taking either side and it seems to me that however blameless you may have been it is strongly in your own interests to abide by the notice which it seems Mr Gordon [the Rector] has given you and go on May 12th quietly.

My reasons for so advising you are simply and solely that supposing you did stop your two years at Biddulph Moor

1st You would be in direct opposition to Mr Gordon – that would have a bad effect in every way on yourself, him, the school and the neighbourhood.

2nd You would only have a miserable pittance from the school, pence which could be *legally* halved if the management chose.

The third point shows a real will to see beyond the dispute to the longterm wellbeing of the man himself:

3rd You would scarcely be happy up there – and what is life without happiness.

He concludes by emphasising the personal nature of the letter:

Mr Gordon knows nothing of my writing to you, which I hope you will take in good part as it is meant.

The suggestion that Robert Bateman really had lived in our house and the humanity of his concern for the schoolmaster made us eager to know more about him, but the lack of available information and the arrival of the television crew at Biddulph Old Hall swept our curiosity aside.

The crew decided to film us removing the 1950s fireplace in the Great Hall and then knocking out two or three square blocks so that we could establish whether there was a deep void behind it. When eventually the blocks splintered we were almost overwhelmed by the acrid smell of sodden soot. On an impulse I fed a broom handle into the opening and was amazed when it disappeared to the brush head. With mounting excitement we set to work on the surrounding blocks.

By the end of the first day's filming, one half of the chimney was open, and the true dimensions of the whole structure were beginning to become clear. It was evident that the opening did span virtually the full width of the visible beam. The bottom metre of the fireplace was filled with a black slurry of slimy soot, so wet and heavy that it flowed out the moment the stone wall was removed. We had established beyond question that the scale of the fireplace was too massive and the construction too naive to have been built after 1660. By this date the understanding of flue construction had advanced way beyond this crude cavern, even in the remotest areas

Fig. 11. The Great Hall before the removal of the 1950s hearth that had been substituted for the original 14-foot opening defined by the beam above it.

of England. Suddenly, Pevsner's description of the inhabited part of the building as 'a late seventeenth-century house of no pretension' was unsustainable.

We began to explain the significance of this to the film crew, expecting them to perceive it as contributing a compelling new dimension to their programme. However, they were completely impervious to our fascination, and deferred all discussion to the next filming visit when 'the experts' would be with them. What did excite them, on the other hand, was our intention to use the fire. They were openly sceptical about this but were equally anxious not to discourage us as they were convinced the huge opening would fill the room with smoke, creating a wonderful moment of television. By the middle of the afternoon they had wished us good luck and set off back to the sanity of contemporary London.

Much of the next day was spent in back-breaking labour, shovelling the sinister, black mucus into wheelbarrows and dumping it in a skip. But despite our exhaustion, the following evening found us standing inside the massive hearth, staring up at its awesome construction. Hand-hewn, blackened boulders were heaped one upon another, and climbed towards the distant sky in coarsely tapered, irregular steps. The right-hand portion had been manipulated into a sophisticated system of brick ovens, with complex barrel-headed compartments. These had only partly survived, leaving gap-toothed apertures and scatterings of fractured, fallen bricks. We knew that this massively constructed vault was important both as a historical survival and for its ability to convey the actuality of an ancient working fire (fig. 11). Over the next years, when we did begin to use it, there was no mistaking the mesmeric attraction it exerted upon visitors. There was something almost primeval about the comfort derived from its robust, living presence, as if it awoke some half-remembered instinct, almost a folk memory of communal security and wellbeing. Our intuition that a fire opening related to the visible beam would totally transform the character of this strange room was amply confirmed. The rough-hewn generosity of this giant focus of warmth destroyed any vestige of the gaunt, puritan cell into which the Great Hall had been transformed by deliberate concealment and assertive modern whitening.

After I had shovelled the last pieces of rubble from the hearth into the wheelbarrow, I slumped back heavily against the wall near the steps up to the parlour. To my shock, the wall seemed to give way behind me, and the next moment a patch of modern gypsum plaster slithered to the floor, revealing a beautifully carpentered section of timber framing, complete with a clearly legible joiner's numbering mark. The studs were in-filled by rectangles of old lime-washed lime plaster, broken away in places so that the underlying wattle twigs and straw-filled daub were visible. All along the edge of the opening, the brittle pink finish of new plaster had detached itself from the surface of the underlying frame and was hanging loose. I could not resist the temptation of banging it. Another big circle of plaster fell. The new section of visible frame was pockmarked with little charred gauges where tapers or crude candles had scorched the exposed surface of the timbers long ago.

Without a word we put our shovels into the loose edges of the plaster covering, and within ten minutes it was all lying in a disorderly pile at our feet. The more we revealed, the more obvious it became that the timber-framed wall was a later insertion. We realised that the parlour and the Great Hall had originally formed a single unit, heated by the huge hearth which we had just found. This was a pattern of building abandoned by the early sixteenth century, rather than one employed for new houses a century and a half later.

The true age of the Great Hall meant that the relationship between the lived-in house and the ruined mansion must have been much closer than anyone had previously understood. The two buildings must have coexisted over many years. If this was the case, each would be able to shed vital light on the role of the other, and on the forgotten meaning of the complex whole. The house was responding to our interest in it by dropping cryptic hints of a longer, more convoluted tale of mutation and survival than anything suggested to us when we bought it.

Our frustration at the filmmakers' lack of interest in our first round of discoveries was exacerbated on the second filming day by their introduction of a huge superstructure of television 'format'. This took the shape of a band of three building conservation specialists known collectively as 'the experts', and a likeable, but lightweight, presenter. As individuals they were an interestingly diverse group of people, with a wide experience of conserving important listed buildings. Brian and I had been looking forward to this element of the programme, as a chance to enter into a constructive dialogue about approaches and techniques with a group of knowledgeable, sympathetic enthusiasts.

When they actually appeared, they were fussed over by make-up girls, lighting specialists and sound technicians. Every move they made was subject to elaborate preparation and set-dressing, all designed to project a forbidding group persona of patronising hauteur. The relationship between 'the experts' and 'the contributors' (us) had been preconceived as an adversarial one. The idea clearly was that the stuffy world of historic house restoration could not be expected to hold viewers' attention for fifty minutes, so had to be enlivened by being adjudicated, with devastating frankness, in the time-honoured tradition of TV talent contests. To be fair, even they found the continual pressure to be abrasive a trifle ridiculous and would often say, 'I can't say that – it isn't true,' when surreptitiously handed a note in the middle of an interview instructing them to draw blood for the entertainment of the masses.

Not that the filming wasn't fun, nor that the film crew treated it with anything but total commitment. The difficulty was that with so elaborate a presentational structure to maintain, involving a presenter and three commentators, all of whom were required to react to every development, the filming days became dominated by them recording pieces to camera. They had no time to explore the detailed discoveries that were revealing the story of the building and informing the restoration work. Naturally they acted as a group, with shared opinions snatched superficially in the first moments of arriving at a new site to enable them to film their contributions shortly afterwards. In these circumstances, 'the experts' could not help becoming immersed in the imperative of the programme makers, and progressively losing touch with the subtleties of the archaeological investigation itself.

Gradually, this approach led Brian and me to develop two parallel perceptions of the progress at Biddulph. These were born out of the marked contrast between filming days and the rest of the time when the real work moved steadily forward. The television visits were characterised by the enjoyable, but slightly frenetic, gladiatorial combat with 'the experts' over the surface texture of the changes , such as the inclusion of modern features, particularly downlighters. The other times were dominated by an utterly different excitement. This was generated by the experience of interpreting a series of tiny textural and structural discoveries, dating from different periods of the house's history, which slowly enriched the knowledge gained from our recent research.

This quiet, infinitely private adventure bore no relation to the agitated craving for confrontation that the television crew imposed upon us for a couple of days each month. The quiet progress went unnoticed and unrecorded, except by us, while the tawdry parade of the programme marched on down its predestined route. We followed the band, and enjoyed the fun while it was there, but our hearts were rooted in the other Biddulph, the one that silently re-emerged to enfold us when the last van had tooted and rattled off up the drive – the mystical place in which we had perceived some half-hidden force or presence that we felt compelled to engage with and understand.

After the cameras departed, our men returned to their long days of patient toil, in which they dedicated all their skills to the pursuit of uncompromising perfection in every detail of the regeneration of the Great Hall. Something wonderful was happening, something that we could not allow to pass without a gesture of recognition. We had to find some way of acknowledging not only the peerless achievement of the actual craftsmanship, but the joyful commitment with which it was offered and carried out. Several of the guys had joked about their wives or girlfriends complaining about their obsession with Biddulph, so we hit upon the idea of a Christmas party in the Great Hall, to which everyone could bring their families to admire their work.

When the day of the party arrived, none of us had anticipated the strange alchemy that using the room would work upon its atmosphere. Suddenly, it was more than the sum of its lovingly repaired stones. More than the crackling and flaring of the apple logs in its monumental working hearth. More than the tranquillity of its recessive colour harmonies, or the honeyed glow of its beeswaxed tables and chairs. Nor was it simply the beguiling counterpoint between these caressing comforts and the broken floor of discordant flags and the rude, hacked flanks of the fireplace. These things tingled across the senses, mischievously playing games with scale and texture, but they alone did not fully account for the room's compulsive resonance.

There was a new radiance, emanating from within the room itself, that existed separately, beyond, and distinct from, the sum of its disparate components. The alteration was hard to define, being assimilated through the consciousness of atmosphere rather than the direct physical senses, but it was none the less real, and too intense to ignore. That evening, scarcely one of the craftsmen or their partners entered the room without remarking on its 'special feel', or 'its wonderful atmosphere'. Several of the men said that something new had happened that they found hard to explain, which carried it beyond the restored room they had been working on (fig. 12).

In the new year we began on the Staircase Hall. This was the one place that had completely baffled us when we first walked into it with Mrs Smith. The whole space had been dark, dank and incomprehensible. The endless piecemeal adaption which had been inflicted on it over the centuries had left it devoid of meaning. Since the jumble of component parts was so incoherent, we felt that the best way of tackling the problem was initially to concentrate our attention on a single element – the low arch with the door behind it – and hope that this would suggest some clues to the rest of the room.

The moment we scraped away the top layer of brilliant white lining paper we discovered several layers of limewash coloured with 'dolly blue'. This was interesting, as dolly blue was traditionally used in the kitchens of old houses to deter flies and insects. The layers of limewash were very flaky, and fell away to reveal large, regular, sandstone blocks identical in size and colour to the exterior building blocks of the ruined mansion.

Fig. 12. The Great Hall, reborn with a new radiance, too intense to ignore.

So the Staircase Hall had been built directly against the outer wall of the Eliza-bethan mansion, presumably to form some kind of link between the Great Hall and the newer building. As soon as we began to uncover the stones of the low arch we realised that it defined the front opening of yet another massive fireplace. The confusing doorway had simply been knocked through its brick fireback to allow access to the ruins, after its flue had been blocked off and it was no longer used. On the front face of the arch we found a triangular pattern of wooden dowels and a 400mm groove cut into the face of the stonework. These were clearly the fixings for a spit mechanism. So the Staircase Hall had contained a huge cooking fire, suggesting that at some point it had functioned as a kitchen (fig. 13).

It was almost impossible, however, to reconcile the dimensions of the fireplace with the cramped ceiling height of the room. With only a tiny window in an alcove, it would have been virtually impossible to bear the heat of the fire, let alone cook on it. Something was wrong. The pieces of the jigsaw did not quite lock together to give a cogent picture of the room in use.

As we had experienced before at Biddulph, the clues came when we least expected them. While we were completing the stripping of the wall above the fireplace arch we made another surprising discovery. In the corner of the room, another stone arch sprung along the side wall. The intriguing thing about this high arch, as we stripped

Fig. 13. A treasure trove of concealed clues – the Staircase Hall starts to tell its story.

it back to the stonework, was that the top of it disappeared above the line of the ceiling, suggesting that at some point the room might have been much higher.

With this in mind, we carefully inspected the heavy old beam in the middle of the ceiling. To our amazement we found that, despite its obvious weight and age, it rested barely an inch into the wall at one end, and at the other was supported by an early 1930s steel girder, disguised as a whitewashed beam. It had been inserted as a decorative fake. We suddenly realised that if the ceiling was removed, the proportions of the great cooking arch would be completely natural within the stone wall above it, and the heat of the fire would be manageable as the window on the floor above would have lit and ventilated the whole space.

The Staircase Hall proved to be a treasure trove of concealed information, all of which combined to reinforce our thesis that the Great Hall had been an ancient, freestanding block that had subsequently been joined to the new mansion by means of this tall link. The suggestion that it had served as some sort of kitchen for the re-inhabited Great Hall after the Civil War was confirmed by the discovery of an extremely unusual early hatch in the lower part of it. The primitive weight and simplicity of the hatch related it directly to the great stone fire opening and side arches.

In response to the scale of these elements, I designed a sturdy new staircase in English oak, with closed, panelled sides to retain a relationship with the mass of the stonework. On the other side of the space, I allowed the height of the stone arches on the side wall to define the dimensions of the two oak doors I drew to fill them. With the ceiling removed, and the fireback rebuilt to block up the doorway to the ruins, the incomprehensible disposition of the massive structure was suddenly resolved: the elements were brought into cogent relationship with each other and with the soaring dimensions of the overall space (fig. 9, page 30).

Brian and I had become sufficiently seasoned campaigners to enjoy the terror the emergence of this intensely unconventional space generated in the breasts of the presenters and film crew of the television series, by now entitled *Restored to Glory*. Our contention that it was impossible to begin to interact with Biddulph Old Hall unless one was prepared to empathise to some extent with the deeply held convictions of the people who had created it and made up its story gave everyone around us palpitations.

The over-scaled arches and stone doorways were the residue of the actual story of violent conflict, religious conviction and brutal intolerance that had been played out in and around this place. It had led to the collapse of a proud family into squalid poverty and forced them to eke out an existence among the truncated remnants of their once-great home. The true value of Biddulph as a window into the past was not as a quantified accumulation of moulded timbers, shaped mullions, flue constructions or lead glazing patterns. The elusive ability of the Old Hall to communicate the vibrant aura of long-lost ways of life, and retain the essence of the forgotten people it had sheltered, could not be tabulated and codified in this way. It was part of an intuitive, emotional response to the past embraced by the Victorians, but held in derision by educated people ever since.

Brian and I watched *Restored to Glory* alone together at Biddulph. We enjoyed watching it, as we might any programme on a subject that interested us, but we had been too immersed in the project itself, and the filming, to be able to assess the impact it would have on the general public. As a result, we were taken completely off guard by the avalanche of highly personal reactions that engulfed us over the next weeks.

It was the strength of feeling that took us aback. The adversarial format produced a passionately partisan reaction in large swathes of the audience, who perceived Brian and me as being bullied by 'the experts' while we valiantly dedicated ourselves to preserving a precious piece of the nation's heritage. Their anxiety seemed to be that we would be discouraged by the nonsense of downlighters and distemper (see fig. 14) from continuing our mission to discover and liberate the essence of Biddulph Old Hall, in which they sensed a magical story. It was strangely moving that people shared our intuition of fabulous, forgotten things, still present in the fabric of the place. It refocused our determination to continue our journey into the history of the house.

Suddenly, the pressure, the deadlines, the tantrums and the momentary fame of the television programme were over. Brian and I found ourselves blinking in the stark light of another cold dawn. The brooding spectre of Bletchley Manor, abandoned and forlorn, reappeared out of the chill oblivion to which we had consigned it by our preoccupation with Biddulph Old Hall and the British Broadcasting Corporation. With the money for it gone, and its condition deteriorated even from the deplorable state in which we had left it, the gentle presence of the Manor acquired a forbidding air of menace.

We furtively consulted an estate agent, but were told it was unmarketable as it stood. We eventually summoned up the courage to return to Bletchley and actually go inside for the first time in over a year. The moment we did so, we knew we could not simply walk away and become the agents of its final destruction. We could not be the people who had fecklessly signed its death warrant by stripping it out then walking away, condemning it to almost certain demolition. Although we knew that it meant setting aside our longing to maintain the momentum at Biddulph, for the first time our instincts told us to save Bletchley Manor no matter what the cost. We had become so concentrated on our new project that at first we scarcely registered the onset of an insidious new process of discovery that was destined to grow in scope and intensity, until it dominated and transformed our lives.

Fig. 14. The adversarial format had produced a passionately partisan reaction in large swathes of the audience.

Fig. 15. On location at home: Nigel with camera in the emerging parterre.

Part 2

THE LOST PRE-RAPHAELITE

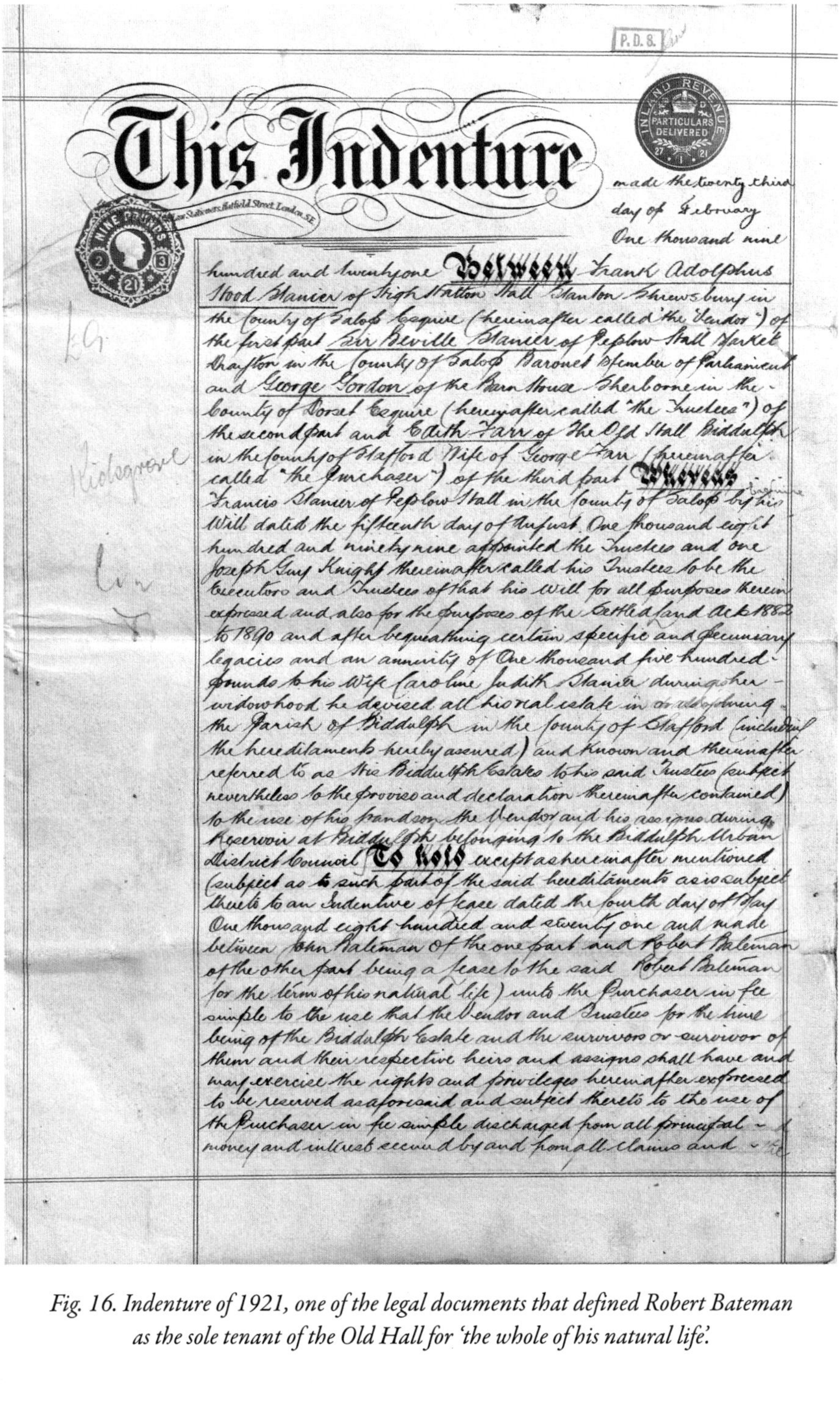

P. D. 8.

INLAND REVENUE PARTICULARS DELIVERED 27 1 21

NINE PENCE

This Indenture made the twenty third day of February One thousand nine hundred and twenty one **Between** Frank Adolphus Hood Stanier of High Hatton Hall Stanton Shrewsbury in the County of Salop Esquire (hereinafter called "the Vendor") of the first part Sir Beville Stanier of Peplow Hall Market Drayton in the County of Salop Baronet Member of Parliament and George Gordon of the Barn House Sherborne in the County of Dorset Esquire (hereinafter called "the Trustees") of the second part and Edith Farr of The Old Hall Biddulph in the County of Stafford Wife of George Farr (hereinafter called "the Purchaser") of the third part **Whereas** Francis Stanier of Peplow Hall in the County of Salop Esquire by his Will dated the fifteenth day of August One thousand eight hundred and ninety nine appointed the Trustees and one Joseph Guy Knight (hereinafter called his Trustees) to be the Executors and Trustees of that his Will for all purposes therein expressed and also for the purposes of the Settled Land Acts 1882 to 1890 and after bequeathing certain specific and pecuniary legacies and an annuity of One thousand five hundred pounds to his Wife Caroline Judith Stanier during her widowhood he devised all his real estate in or adjoining the Parish of Biddulph in the County of Stafford (including the hereditaments hereby assured) and known and thereinafter referred to as the Biddulph Estate to his said Trustees (subject nevertheless to the provisos and declaration thereinafter contained) to the use of his grandson the Vendor and his assigns during Reservoir at Biddulph belonging to the Biddulph Urban District Council **To Hold** except as hereinafter mentioned (subject as to such part of the said hereditaments as is subject thereto to an Indenture of Lease dated the fourth day of May One thousand eight hundred and seventy one and made between John Bateman of the one part and Robert Bateman of the other part being a Lease to the said Robert Bateman for the term of his natural life) unto the Purchaser in fee simple to the use that the Vendor and Trustees for the time being of the Biddulph Estate and the survivors or survivor of them and their respective heirs and assigns shall have and may exercise the rights and privileges hereinafter expressed to be reserved as aforesaid and subject thereto to the use of the Purchaser in fee simple discharged from all principal money and interest secured by and from all claims and

Fig. 16. Indenture of 1921, one of the legal documents that defined Robert Bateman as the sole tenant of the Old Hall for 'the whole of his natural life'.

Chapter 3

A FORGOTTEN FIGURE

Derek Wheelhouse had spent many years tracing and collecting documents and old photographs of the Biddulph area and publishing them in the form of illustrated histories of the town. He had made a habit of bringing us anything he came across relating to the Old Hall, so we were not surprised when he arrived one Sunday evening with an illustrated estate agent's sales booklet dating from the mid-1930s. One caption to a photograph of a rather conventional drawing room caught our attention. It read: 'A modern sitting room converted from the former studio of the artist Robert Bateman.'

From the letter that we had been given by Bill Ridgway, we knew that Robert had lived at the Old Hall for a time in the 1870s; however, this was the first written reference to him as an artist we had come across. We had suspected that, as the son of wealthy parents with private means, he might have been something of a dilettante operating on the periphery of the art world, rather than a serious working painter. The ancient house, surrounded by ruins, would have provided the perfect setting for him to project an image of romantic seclusion among his fashionable comtemporaries. In these circumstances, however, it would have been extraordinary for him and his studio to be remembered and thought worthy of mention in a commercial document some sixty years later. Suddenly we recollected a document in the papers of the house that we had never understood. Together with the fascinating sealed vellums and indentures had been a prosaic typewritten envelope containing the death certificate of Robert Bateman, Esq., dated August 1922.

When we re-read the death certificate another piece of chronological symmetry became clear to us. When the Biddulph Grange estate was sold to local industrialist Robert Heath in 1872 he had not kept the Old Hall but sold it on immediately to the Stanier family. They continued to own the Old Hall and its remnant of land until 1922, even though in 1921 they had sold all their other land in Biddulph. The presence of Robert Bateman's death certificate among the legal documents of the house suggested that, even though the Bateman family moved to London in 1868, Robert might have been left with some sort of legally binding life tenancy of the Old Hall, which was still in place when the Staniers wished to sell up in 1921. This would make the fact that Robert and his studio were still remembered when the house was sold in the mid-1930s much more understandable. If this was the case, we needed to find the proof, so we settled down to make a detailed study of the beautiful copperplate documents delineating the sale of Biddulph Grange and all its associated land holdings to Robert Heath.

Our first surprise was that James Bateman had not sold the property directly to Heath. When he moved to London in 1868, he passed the whole of the Biddulph Grange estate to his eldest son John. So it was John who sold it in 1872 to Robert Heath. The estate was large and complex, comprising many farms, cottages, almshouses, woods and paddocks, in addition to the main mansion and its exotic garden, so the documents were long, detailed and, in places, expressed in ponderous nineteenth-century legalese. Despite this we became intrigued by the lost world they illuminated, and we immersed ourselves in them. Eventually, hidden among the complexities of copses, bridleways and three-acre meadows, we found exactly what we were looking for – a description of the property known as Biddulph Castle or Biddulph Old Hall, along with its adjacent ruins of a former mansion house, the nearby lane, tilt yard or hemp drying ground and yew walk, believed to have been a former bowling alley. While these were clearly to be included in the sale, they were subject to an attached tenancy agreement between the vendor, John Bateman, and his brother Robert Bateman that was to last for the latter's natural life (fig. 16).

So, suddenly, there it was – proof that Robert Bateman had had a lifelong interest in the house, well into the twentieth century. Throughout that time, he had apparently maintained some kind of studio within the building which was not altered until the 1930s. Although none of this lifted the dense fog of obscurity that surrounded him, it motivated us to renew our investigations into the story of this shadowy figure who had had such a long and close relationship with our house.

For the next few weeks we perplexed the curators of every gallery and artistic institution across the north of England, no matter how obscure or parochial, with a remorseless barrage of enquiries about Robert Bateman. At the same time we immersed ourselves in countless expeditions to the outer reaches of the internet, usually involving irrelevant references to a living Canadian artist of the same name. It was while we were ensnared in one of these dispiriting adventures that the words 'Yale Center for British Art (Paul Mellon Collection)' appeared on the screen with below them in bold letters: 'Robert Bateman (1842–1922), *Pool of Bethesda*, oil on canvas, signed and dated 1877.'

Brian and I stared at the screen in silence.

We had long ago accepted that Bateman could only have been a very minor, provincial figure with, at best, a small local reputation during his lifetime. We had no actual proof, even of that. So it seemed almost cruel to find our first reference to him associated with the Yale Center for British Art. How could our forgotten figure possibly be part of a public collection that encompassed Turner, Gainsborough, Stubbs and Constable, the towering geniuses of British art, admired and collected the world over? The implication that Robert Bateman might be a figure of national or indeed international significance was impossible to adjust to at that moment.

We did not know how to treat it. We tried the Yale Center website but were too agitated at that moment to find a match with either 'Bateman' or 'Pool of Bethesda'. We decided to sleep on it and ring Yale when we had calmed down. The next day, after several nervous prevarications, I rang. The woman who answered spoke sparingly in a tone of modulated professionalism. I explained that I was engaged in research into a supposed artist by the name of Robert Bateman and that, by chance, I had seen on the internet that they appeared to have a painting entitled *Pool of Bethesda* by him in their collection.

'*The Pool of Bethesda*, yes, that's correct.'

Scarcely believing what she was saying, I filled the silence with more questions.

'I know it's absurd, but I just wondered if there was any possibility that the Robert Bateman who painted the picture might perhaps be the son of James Bateman, the creator of a celebrated Victorian garden in Staffordshire in England?'

She put me on hold. To my amazement, a moment later I found myself talking to someone who described himself as the Chief Curator of Art Collections. He told me that the painting was an oil on canvas dated 1877 and signed 'RB', with what was now known to be the characteristic elongated R of Robert Bateman. He described him as a leading figure in the so-called Dudley Group of second-generation Pre-Raphaelite artists mainly active in England during the 1860s, '70s and '80s. The signed initials, the date, a wealth of research into contemporary documentation and, perhaps more than anything, the intensely individual idiosyncratic style of the piece, both in overall design and technical execution, left no doubt as to its creator's identity.

I was stunned.

I knew, of course, that all museums had store rooms filled with paintings which were acquired, or bequeathed to them, when they were fashionable, but which never see the light of day because time and critical perspective have undermined their importance. Once I had explained my research into Bateman and his relationship to Biddulph Old Hall, I went to the heart of my worries by asking him about Yale's opinion of the painting.

He told me that it had been acquired personally by Paul Mellon, who formed the collection at the heart of the Yale Center, because he admired its quality. It had been attributed to another artist with the same initials, Richard Bevis, but Paul Mellon instigated research that led to an article by Basil Taylor in *Apollo* magazine in August 1966 that overturned this attribution and established beyond doubt that Bateman was the creator of this highly original and important work of art. Apparently Mellon then set in motion a search for other works by Bateman, in order to rescue him from almost complete obscurity and establish his reputation as a major figure in nineteenth-century British art. He also insisted that *The Pool of Bethesda* was one of the most popular pictures in the collection and was on permanent display, except for one or two occasions when it had been lent for special exhibitions elsewhere, most notably the Barbican Gallery in London.

I asked if I could get a copy of the magazine article he had mentioned and he promised to send it together with a good colour reproduction of the painting. At this point he suggested that if I wanted to know more about Bateman I should get a copy of the September 1989 issue of *Apollo* which contained a longer article on him by Amanda Kavanagh.

Now that we had found Robert, I wanted to like or at least admire his painting. I knew the Bible story of the Pool of Bethesda, where sick and disabled people waited for an angel to trouble the waters so that one person, the first to become immersed, could be cured. Christ performed a miracle there by curing a crippled man, and presumably that was the subject of Robert's canvas. But that was what worried me. How would a middle-class Victorian artist have envisaged that event? I dreaded the haloed Lord gazing languidly at the awe-struck invalid with his heart-breaking crutches and grubby cap with two meagre coins in it beside him. I could not control an urgent longing to see an image to which I could honestly relate – something that demanded and elicited a response, by its originality, its beauty, or the insight it gave into the mind of its creator. It was good to have the specific task of tracking down the back copy of *Apollo* magazine. We found it and arranged for it to be sent.

That evening we went outside and looked at the date stone on the later wing at Biddulph. It read 'RB 1874', with the elongated R just as Yale had described the signature on its 'important work of art'. We now realised it had been put there by Robert when he adapted the wing to form his studio. The rich, foppish, artistic poseur of our imagination had disappeared, and been replaced by an infinitely more formidable figure – the real Robert Bateman (fig. 17).

*Fig. 17. The date stone initialled RB by Robert to mark the conversion
of the former Roman Catholic chapel into his studio in 1874.*

Chapter 4

THE POOL OF BETHESDA

All our apprehension about Victorian sentimentality was banished with our first glance at *The Pool of Bethesda*. We did not, at that moment, have sufficient knowledge to understand the historical references in the grouping and configuration of the painting; however, the discipline of its spare design, the precise rendering of the contorted human forms, the sensitive textural treatment of stone, water and wood conveyed through an almost monochrome palette of colours, produced an effect of disquieting, still foreboding. The originality and power of the image communicated themselves without the need for explanation. This was not a conventional illustration of the Bible story. It is not the day of the miracle. Christ is not there to comfort the agonised and exhausted sufferers. They are forced to fight each other for the one moment of hope that the angel brings. Yet despite all this powerfully conveyed struggle, the whole image exuded a sense of unearthly, despairing silence (fig. 18).

The idea that the person who had generated this vision in his imagination and conveyed it, so exquisitely, to the canvas was forgotten by all but a handful of art experts seemed incomprehensible. The possibility that this process of inspiration and creation might have taken place within the walls of the place we now prosaically called 'home' seemed even more implausible. None the less, as Brian and I stood there taking in that extraordinary image, we made a pact to dedicate all our energy to the task of searching out every findable fact about the life of Robert Bateman, so that he could be rescued from obscurity and given the recognition his gifts deserved.

That undertaking was kicked into life the very next day with the arrival of the first article from *Apollo* magazine, dated August 1966. It was entitled 'A Forgotten Pre-Raphaelite: Robert Bateman's Pool of Bethesda' and was illustrated with a general view and two detailed enlargements of the picture, which was being published for the first time. The author, Basil Taylor, described the painting as a most knowledgeable and sensitive evocation of a historical style and went on to add:

Fig. 18. Robert Bateman, The Pool of Bethesda, *1877, oil on canvas, 50.8 × 73.6 cm, Yale Center for British Art, New Haven, Connecticut.*

it also has intrinsic qualities of drawing, colour, design, and visual observation that make it abundantly worth preserving. If only a few of Bateman's other pictures matched it he should be taken seriously into account, and another reason for bringing this work forward now is the hope of eliciting more information about a most obscure figure.

It was clear that Taylor knew almost nothing about Bateman's actual life. The only piece of biography he recorded was Bateman's entry into the Royal Academy schools in April 1865 at the age of 23 and his address at 21 Wigmore Street, London. He listed four other paintings that were exhibited at the Royal Academy – *As it fell upon a day*, 1878; *The Raising of Samuel*, 1879; *Roses*, 1889 and *Love in the Cloister*, 1889 – but made no comment on them, suggesting that he had not seen any of them even in reproduction. He noted that 1889 'seems to be the last year in which he showed work'.

He drew attention to the posture and faces of the suffering figures that 'bring a withdrawn emotionalism' to the picture 'which contributes to its disturbing individuality'. Interestingly, he suggested this power and originality might derive from Bateman's own experience: 'If, as seems likely, Bateman died prematurely or abandoned painting early, the choice of this not so common subject and the spirit in which it is treated may have had personal origin.' So in 1966 not even the date of his death was known. Taylor underlined the fact that the painting is atypical of its period and compared it with the work of Albert Moore and Whistler for its 'subtle tonality and clear pattern'. He concluded by again underlining the obscurity of Bateman even in his own lifetime:

> there is, however, strong indication that Bateman was missed by the critics. If the present picture was the one shown in 1876 at the RA, then it hung at Burlington House in what is still Gallery 1. But at that moment it was painters such as Leighton, Fildes, Waterhouse, Leader, Marcus Stone and John Gilbert who took the eye.

The article marked an important milestone for us. It was the first time we had ever seen any assessment of Robert Bateman as an artist, so it was exciting to see his ability and individuality endorsed in print. Secondly, it underlined what we already knew to our cost – that, despite his gifts, he had remained an almost completely obscure figure until 1966, and was overlooked even in his own lifetime. Most importantly, it had provided written confirmation of all that Yale had said, and launched us on a new phase of our research. Now we knew who we were searching for: a significant Pre-Raphaelite artist, with a recorded body of work at the Royal Academy and other galleries. Basil Taylor mentioned in passing that Bateman had fourteen pictures displayed at the Grosvenor Gallery and ten elsewhere. These were presumably all lost, since he gave no further detail of them. However, it provided a starting point for an intense programme of focused enquiry which was potentially far more fruitful than our previous blind meanderings.

The article also demonstrated the lack of any biographical information about Robert's life at the time it was written. We knew precious little ourselves, but it appeared to be more than Basil Taylor had known. We knew, from the Biddulph papers and local historical sources, that he had set up a studio in our house and marked it with a date stone. We also knew the date of his death in 1922. From Peter Hayden's book we knew that he got married, comparatively late in life, to Caroline Wilbraham, the widow of Charles Philip Wilbraham, a Church of England rector who came from Rode Hall, a Georgian country house about three miles from Biddulph. We had not, so far, taken much interest in either her or the marriage. We had been searching for an artist, and Caroline Wilbraham, a middle-aged clergyman's widow from a family of worthy Victorian churchmen, sounded decidedly conventional and dull. But now we felt we needed to know more about her, since she was one of the only solid pieces of information we had about Robert's life. A photograph or portrait of her would be a good place to start, so we rang up Rode Hall, in the hope that they might have a picture of her.

I explained to Sir Richard Baker-Wilbraham that we were researching the people who had lived at Biddulph Old Hall, one of whom was Robert Bateman. He had married the widow of a member of Sir Richard's family, Rev. Charles Philip Wilbraham, and her name was Caroline Octavia.

'We just wondered if you had a portrait of her in the house?'

'No, unfortunately not, sorry about that.'

I was ending the call and apologising for bothering him when he said, 'Of course, I know there is one. It's a huge thing, 7 or 8 feet high at least – you'll need a hell of a wall! There's a chap in London who's been trying to sell it to me for years because of the family connection. I don't want it – got enough portraits, particularly Victorian ones.'

For a moment I was speechless.

'I'm sorry, Sir Richard, are you saying that there is a full-length portrait of Caroline Octavia and the owner wants to sell it?'

'Yes, I've got the dealer's number here somewhere . . .'

Devastatingly, when we contacted the dealer, Julian Hartnoll, he told us he had sold the portrait two years earlier. Nevertheless, I wanted to hear more about the picture and Caroline. He emphasised the scale of the painting, describing it as a 'real whopper', perhaps 8 or 9 feet high. When I asked if she was beautiful he paused, then seemed to choose his words carefully.

'Not exactly, not conventionally. Certainly not what you would call pretty but a formidably attractive presence – strong, with a hint of sadness, composed, almost regal in bearing.'

I asked if he thought there was any possibility that the owner might sell it. He seemed very dubious but promised to contact him and ask. As I was about to say goodbye something made me ask who the portrait was by.

'Bateman, of course. It's by Bateman, I thought you knew that.'

The revelation that the life-size portrait of Caroline was by Bateman and that this man had owned it for fifteen long years, trying to find someone to buy it and had finally succeeded, almost broke our hearts. However, when Julian Hartnoll rang back to say that the owner was happy for us to visit him to see the picture provided we did not attempt to buy it, we shamefacedly agreed. At least we could meet Robert's wife face to face.

'He's a very interesting man, an acknowledged expert on this group of artists. His name is Richard Dorment and he is an art critic for the *Daily Telegraph*. You'll probably find him very helpful. He might be interested in what you have to say about your house.'

When we rang Richard Dorment, he was charming and listened with interest to our account of what we were doing at Biddulph, and our discovery of its links with Robert Bateman. He said he knew nothing of the house, or Bateman's connection to it. He asked us to bring a copy of the tenancy agreement between Robert and John and any photographs we had of the Hall, particularly the date stone with Robert's initials on it. We arranged to visit him the following month after he returned from America. In the meantime he suggested we go and see another of Robert's paintings, *Plucking Mandrakes*, which was in the Wellcome Foundation in London.

Chapter 5

A TWILIGHT WORLD

In the weeks leading up to our meeting with Richard Dorment, two events contributed to the gathering momentum. The first was that, out of the blue, we got a chance to buy the Clough, the steep valley with a swift little stream that ran past the end of our Yew Walk. We had been fascinated by it even before we bought the house.

After James Bateman had bought Biddulph Old Hall in 1861, he had constructed a walk which connected it with his own land at Biddulph Grange, about a mile away. This walk was an ambitious project, designed to heighten the picturesque effect of the Old Hall by approaching it on a gently rising path above a sheet of water created by damming the stream. The path passed under a small stone tunnel and up steps overhung with trees, to the bottom of an avenue of ancient yews, at the end of which the dramatic silhouette of the ruins could be seen. Further down the Clough, James had created another small lake behind a stone dam. Proof that both dams were the work of the Batemans was contained in the sale documents of the Old Hall. The maps of the estate drawn up for the sale by Lord Camoys to James Bateman in 1861 showed a continuous natural stream. The corresponding one for the sale by the Batemans to Robert Heath in 1871 showed the two dams and corresponding lakes. The document of 1871 described the route to the Old Hall as a picturesque walk passing through a tunnel, then down 'steps cut into the cliff face', over a lake and up past rapids and falling water to the ruined castle. This made it clear that the Batemans had manipulated the stream by damming it and blasting rock in order to create a dramatic water garden rising up the valley (figs. 19, 20).

From local enquiries we learned that the bare bones of this arrangement had survived well into the 1970s, when both dams were breached and the lakes drained for different reasons. The higher dam was breached by a concrete pipe to allow cattle to cross over, and the lower one was blown up for safety reasons after a dye works at the bottom of the Clough closed. Old photographs in Derek Wheelhouse's collec-

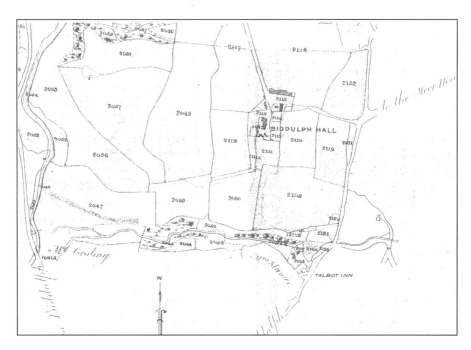

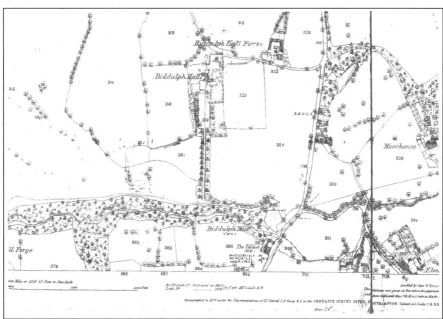

*Fig. 19 (top). The site map of Biddulph Old Hall drawn up for
the sale by Lord Camoys to James Bateman in 1861.*

*Fig. 20 (above). The OS map of 1877 which shows two new dams
and a formalised walk by the stream up to the Old Hall.*

tion showed flights of stone steps within the wood beside the stream as late as the 1930s, but all trace of these had been lost. We had made an offer to buy the Clough, but in the hurly-burly of moving we had not followed it up. We found out later it had been sold to someone local, who only wanted the flat fields adjoining it. The valley itself was still for sale.

The manager of our branch of the Royal Bank of Scotland had been enthusiastic about our creativity and specialist skills at the outset of our Bletchley project. But he was a changed character when we asked for a new loan to buy the Clough. He warned us that his colleagues at the bank were seriously concerned by the expense and length of time we were taking to complete Bletchley, so no further funding could be considered. He steadfastly ignored our special pleading and launched into a chilling analysis of the deterioration of the housing market nationally and locally. It was clear we could not make an offer.

The second event was that we managed to acquire the catalogue of the exhibition staged in 1989 at the Barbican Gallery entitled *The Last Romantics: The Romantic Tradition in British Art – Burne Jones to Stanley Spencer*. *The Pool of Bethesda* had been exhibited alongside another work by Bateman. The editorial notes on the exhibits dispelled any lingering doubts we had about Robert as a serious and gifted artist. Equally importantly, the biographical information the catalogue contained began dimly to illuminate the milieu in which he lived and worked. The more we became absorbed into that distant world, the more natural his association with our ruined hall seemed to be.

Robert was part of an identified circle of Romantic artists associated with and influenced by Burne-Jones. Walter Crane was quoted from his memoirs, *An Artist's Reminiscences*:

> Robert Bateman . . . had the leadership of a particular group or clique as it would be now called, I presume. The group consisted of H. Ellis Wooldridge, Edward Clifford, known as a water colour painter and for his graceful portraits of various members of our aristocracy. With these three painters was a poet, Boyd Montgomerie Maurice Ranking, author of *Fulgencius and other poems, streams from hidden sources*. I became more or less associated with this group from sympathy with their artistic aims . . . The group of young painters I have mentioned, of whom my friend Robert Bateman was a leading member, continued to show their work at the Dudley Gallery and were rather chaffed by the critics, if not occasionally abused. One of them, by a creative effort, even invented a phrase and characterised us as the 'Poetry without Grammar School', whatever that might mean.

This recognition of Robert's prominence by a contemporary seemed somewhat startling given that the article began with the familiar emphasis on his obscurity: 'Bateman is still a comparatively mysterious figure; though clearly an artist of great talent, he is known today by only a handful of works.' The catalogue named three other artists as members of the group: Theodore Blake Wirgman, Alfred Sacheverell Coke and E. H. Fahey.

The exhibition included two paintings by Bateman, *The Pool of Bethesda* and *The Dead Knight*. The catalogue described the first as 'probably the most important work by Bateman known today', describing its rediscovery and incorrect attribution to Richard Bevis and quoting the 1966 Basil Taylor article extensively.

At first glance, *The Dead Knight* appeared to be an almost monochrome green landscape of trees and long grass, speckled here and there with amorphous cream flower heads suggesting yarrow or cow parsley. The light was low and the dark trees almost impressionistically rendered. Through and above the branches, an uncanny white sky imparted a feeling of brooding melancholy to the whole piece. Careful examination revealed a small, featureless, light patch and a long, dark shadow among the grass of the foreground. This represented the knight of the title and his faithful dog, but they were so subservient to the landscape elements of the whole that one was left in little doubt that the true intention was to convey a sense of foreboding through an almost abstract interplay of low-toned shapes (fig. 21). The contrast between the taut architectural design and precise delineation of *The Pool of Bethesda* and the near-formless assemblage of green shapes of this picture could scarcely be more complete. Yet, strangely, despite that, both images vividly convey a similar sense of disturbing melancholy. The caption to *The Dead Knight* again quoted Walter Crane, who acknowledged the inspiration of Burne-Jones and outlined the aims of their group as being to depict

> a magic world of romance and pictured poetry, peopled with ghosts of ladies and lovely knights – a twilight world of dark mysterious woodlands, haunted streams, meads of deep green starred with burning flowers, veiled in a dim and mystic light.

I was reading these words out to Brian and before I had finished we both had the same idea. Crane was almost describing the mysterious little valley of arching trees that ran past the end of the Yew Walk, its stream falling from dark lakes down rocky waterfalls, past meads of deep green, veiled in the dim and mystic light that filtered here and there through the dense canopy of leaves (fig. 22).

We looked back at the picture in the Barbican catalogue. The similarity to the Clough was uncanny. Of course, you could not specifically identify the site. The picture was too amorphous and indistinct for that and, besides, it was painted in 1870. But the mood, the feel, the disposition of the trees, the long grass, the light – all these were hauntingly familiar. Besides, the logic of it was irresistible once one knew that Robert had effectively owned the Old Hall all of his life.

Robert was twenty when his father bought the house and ruins in 1861. We knew from Peter Hayden's book that James Bateman had consulted the artist E. W. Cooke (who had already done extensive design work on the gardens) on the connecting

Fig. 21. Robert Bateman, The Dead Knight, *1870, watercolour, 27.9 × 37.8 cm, private collection – a quintessential Dudley painting.*

Fig. 22. An unspoilt section of the Clough Valley today.

walk between the two properties. From the transcripts of Cooke's diaries held by the National Trust, we discovered that he made several visits to the Old Hall at this time: at one point he 'went up to the ruins with 40 men and began digging in all parts'. It became clear that Cooke, an extremely accomplished and prolific marine artist, acted as something of a mentor to Robert Bateman. Edited extracts from his diaries confirmed the close relationship between the two men. For example, in May 1862 Cooke recorded:

> Dear Mother's 80th birthday. James Bateman called in for tea before giving a lecture at the Royal Horticultural Society. In the evening Robert Bateman came to dinner. A lovely day.

Clearly Robert was a close friend of the Cooke family. The diaries also confirmed the fact that Robert had accompanied Cooke on painting trips to Spain and Algeria. After this, however, there was only one more reference to Robert, when Cooke recorded meeting him and a friend, Mr Wirgman, on a visit to the Grange in 1865. After that, although Cooke continues to keep his diaries until just before his death in 1880, there is not a single reference to Robert. Before we had seen Robert's paintings, we had reluctantly concluded that the likeliest explanation was that Robert had either failed to make a career out of his art or simply lost interest in it and the two men had drifted apart. Now it seemed more likely that Robert had taken an unconventional direction in his work, of which Cooke, from an older generation, thoroughly disapproved. We realised that the friend named by Cooke was Theodore Blake Wirgman, a member of the close circle of avant-garde artists around Robert.

It seems likely that in the early 1860s, when Cooke and Robert were close, the two artists had worked together in planning the romantic walk through the wooded valley. With Cooke's expertise in blasting and manipulating rock and Robert's intense romantic vision, they had created a thrilling, dynamic work of art. Later, when Robert had a studio at the Old Hall, surely he could not have resisted continuing to adapt the valley until he had effectively created around himself the very 'twilight world' that Crane depicts as the idealised world that their group was enthralled by. If the Clough had provided the strange hypnotic landscape of *The Dead Knight*, it would explain the highly charged, personal feel of the picture.

Suddenly, the intuitive fascination that we had always felt for the Clough seemed to have an explanation. Something of that magic world had survived and communicated itself to us, despite the dumped supermarket trolleys and rusted car bonnets that now resided there. How cruel that this insight into the Clough had presented itself just as an opportunity to gain control of the valley had appeared, and slipped away again.

While we were still looking at the catalogue the phone rang. It was Brian's mother, Iris. He began telling her about the portrait that Richard Dorment owned. Iris interrupted to say she was a devotee of Dorment and made a point of reading his articles.

Brian then told her about the Barbican catalogue and quoted Walter Crane's description of the twilight world that Bateman and his group aimed to evoke. He went on to describe the landscape of *The Dead Knight* and how, on seeing it and reading Crane's description, we suspected that the walk through the Clough had been organised to realise this idealised world. He told her about the amazing coincidence of the Clough being for sale, and our attempt to buy it being foiled by the bank.

Iris startled him by asking the price. Then she said, 'You must buy it now, today. Go round tonight. I'll organise the money and get it to you by next week.'

Iris is a capable and fiercely independent widow in her late seventies. She studied at Liverpool University and became a geography teacher before bringing up a family of strapping boys. She was raised a Methodist, on Sunday School, common sense and tapioca pudding, in the war-torn grime of industrial Widnes – not perhaps a location often associated with 'magic worlds of romance and pictured poetry'. None the less, something in the tale of lost artists and forgotten water gardens struck a chord with her and she was determined.

A week later the Clough was ours.

It felt as if some strange force emanating from the house itself was removing every obstacle to our being drawn ever deeper into the mystery of its past, so that we could breathe new life back into the building, and the forgotten figures hidden there.

We tried to be very responsible, and not allow the fact that the Clough now belonged to us to divert our attention from finishing Bletchley. But the act of actually signing the papers and handing over the money proved too much for our resolution. Within days we set out in our macs and wellies to walk the length of our new acquisition in a rainstorm. The rain penetrated through our wax coats and trickled from our woolly hats, inside our collars and down our backs. We stood on the upper dam and tried to imagine how it had looked as a lake, rather than a rank swamp colonised by elder and stinging nettles, embellished here and there by trailer loads of rubbish tipped from the fields above. We began to wonder if we had simply projected our own excitement at the discovery of Robert's story on to this grubby little stream.

Suddenly, we noticed a piece of plywood discarded in the mud near where the stream entered the concrete pipe. Some kids had clearly been playing about trying to block the pipe, but had got bored and thrown it away. The next moment we were wading into the mud to get it and, after a struggle, we managed to position it against the mouth of the pipe. Some water was still getting round the sides of the board, but almost at once a pool of water began to form in front of it. We had no idea what would happen, but we went back to the house laughing like two naughty schoolboys, and forgot about it.

The next morning the rain had stopped and we awoke to the most glorious English summer morning – green, silent and motionless, with just a hint of mist hanging over the valley. We remembered the blocked pipe with a start. We did not know what we were worried about, but felt vaguely that the dam might have been damaged or even destroyed. We hurried down the Yew Walk and under the stone bridge at the bottom, and stopped dead.

There before us was a motionless mirror of dark water, still, silent, with scarcely a quiver across its surface. The tall trees reflected deeply into it. The dim light was pierced here and there by bright spears of sunlight that sparked in the water, as leaves moved in the canopy above. The sense of it being secret, hidden in its woodland setting, communicated the same atmosphere of sad isolation that so strikingly characterised Robert's paintings (fig. 23).

It was as if we had been given a glimpse into the distant past and the future at the same moment. We knew we would have to let the water go again and begin the real work of clearing the rubbish, building a sluice and remaking the waterfall which had been filled up with hardcore and builder's debris. We knew all that – but in that moment, as Brian and I gazed at the hushed, concealed world before us, we instinctively knew that it was the lost, twilight world of Robert Bateman, the forgotten Pre-Raphaelite artist, who had emerged so mysteriously from obscurity to dominate our lives. No one else anywhere knew of this place or Robert's association with it – no academics, museum curators or art critics. By an extraordinary twist of fate we alone had been allotted the task of retrieving it from beyond the grave and, at the very moment of taking up that challenge, we had been given a fantastic vision of what it had been and could be again.

Under the influence of what we had seen in the Clough, we returned to our research with renewed enthusiasm. The drive to complete Bletchley continued but, as it came to its final phase, we felt it was important to keep increasing our understanding of Bateman and his world so that when Bletchley was sold we would be ready to move forward at Biddulph.

Fig. 23. Veiled in a dim and mystic light? The upper lake re-flooded.

Fig. 24. Robert Bateman, The Artist's Wife, *1886, oil on canvas,
82.8 × 91.4 cm, private collection.*

Chapter 6

A TRUE VICTORIAN?

We needed to trace the article in *Apollo* magazine by Amanda Kavanagh that the curator at Yale had advised us to read. When eventually we found it – 'Robert Bateman: A True Victorian' – it proved to be a watershed in our search for both the artist and the man. The author had clearly undertaken wide-ranging research in a serious attempt to pick up the challenge posed by Basil Taylor twenty-two years earlier. Since the article was published in September 1989, at the same time as *The Last Romantics* exhibition at the Barbican that featured *The Pool of Bethesda* and *The Dead Knight*, we supposed it was a response to the interest in Bateman created by that exposure. She had succeeded in bringing together a larger body of paintings on which to make a critical assessment of his work. In fact, we were soon to discover that almost all later references to Bateman, artistic and biographical, were sourced from this one article which was repeatedly quoted in subsequent years.

Of the pictures illustrated, the portrait of Caroline Bateman was the most instantly intriguing, as we had already learned so much about it and were shortly to see the original (fig. 24). Of course, by now we were as interested in the woman Robert had married as in the painting itself. The initial impression was one of dignified formality, both in the subject and the pictorial organisation of the image. Despite the large classical urn and the distant falling landscape, Caroline's figure and personality effortlessly dominated the canvas. She was an impressive and formidably attractive woman, of whom the artist was perhaps a little in awe. Kavanagh's text gave a possible reason for this: 'In 1883 Robert married Caroline Octavia Howard, daughter of the Very Rev. the Hon. Henry Edward Howard, Dean of Lichfield, son of the fifth Earl of Carlisle'.

By any standards, this was a daunting social connection in Victorian England. Caroline's grandparents were not only earls and countesses, but the owners of one of the greatest country house estates in Britain: Castle Howard. This might explain her intensely composed, aristocratic demeanour in the portrait. But the other factual information threw little light on either her or Robert:

> She had been married previously to the Reverend Charles Wilbraham, but he had died in 1879. The Wilbrahams of Rode Hall were near neighbours and close friends of the Batemans. Robert's elder brother John had married Rev. Charles Wilbraham's sister, the Hon. Jesse Caroline Bootle Wilbraham, in 1865.

The implication was that the marriage was the predictable, late union of a rector's widow and a bachelor of forty-one from the same provincial milieu, presumably to provide familiar, comfortable companionship to each other as they advanced into middle age. It also appeared that from the time of his marriage in 1883, Robert did not actually live at Biddulph Old Hall.

> Robert and Caroline spent the first years of their marriage at Benthall Hall, a beautiful sixteenth-century house in Shropshire, where he painted the imposing portrait of his wife which he exhibited at the Grosvenor Gallery in 1886, set within a gentle vista, probably inspired by the view of the Severn from Benthall Edge. Caroline Octavia Bateman stands against a classical stone urn, her formidable presence matched only by the austere elegance of her attire, in a manner reminiscent of Reynolds's most grandiose portraits.

Around 1910 the Batemans moved to Nunney, near Frome, Somerset. According to the *Somerset Standard*, Robert indulged his enthusiasm for bowling:

> His first work at Nunney was to make a bowling green in his own garden which necessitated a considerable amount of blasting and an extensive alteration to the garden. This he did in order that all the young men at Nunney, who so wished, might play bowls there every Saturday afternoon and this amateur bowling club continued until the war made it impossible.

A photograph of Robert holding a silver trophy, flanked by waistcoated bowling enthusiasts (fig. 79), reinforced the impression of comfortable, middle-class respectability which seemed slightly at odds with Caroline's commanding portrait. Kavanagh strengthened the impression of complacent domesticity by her assessment of Robert:

> Despite the undeniable quality of Bateman's artistic talent, his attitude was that of a dilettante who dabbled similarly in architecture, horticulture and sculpture with considerable degrees of success.

This implied his circumstances might have been too comfortable to enforce the necessary discipline to realise his full potential. However, having established Robert as the relaxed artistic dabbler, it came as a surprise that she chose to end the article by describing Robert's love for Caroline as the defining inspiration of his life:

Throughout his life Robert Bateman was inspired by the love of his wife; they both bravely bore grave illness, but after the death of Caroline on 30 July 1922, Robert relinquished his struggle to survive and succumbed to the anguish of his irreparably broken heart a few days later on 4 August 1922.

Nothing in the piece had prepared us for the emotional intensity of this conclusion, except that the person it portrayed seemed infinitely more plausible as the creator of the disquieting images that illustrated the article than the bowls-mad country squire and the middle-aged vicar's widow. Clearly, if we were to understand Robert and his work, we needed to know far more about his relationship with the fabulous figure in the portrait, whose death he was unable to survive by more than a few days.

Before our meeting with Richard Dorment, the owner of Caroline's portrait, we needed to get some understanding of the wider context of Robert's life as a late Pre-Raphaelite painter, and his place in the ferment of conflicting ideas that made up the mid-Victorian art world. Kavanagh's article described his association with a recognised group of young artists, who exhibited their work at the Dudley Gallery, which came to be associated with an avant-garde style of painting and choice of subject. She identified *The Dead Knight* as a quintessential example of the Dudley Gallery style, quoting a contemporary source, *The Art Journal*, of 1869:

> The Dudley style of landscape is, like the figure painting, a little peculiar ... for the most part, indeed, there is in these Dudley landscapes dreaminess instead of definite-ness and smudginess in place of sentiment ... landscapes of a peculiar impressiveness, either from a woolly touch or a thin dusky wash, which may be supposed symbolic of poetry ...

So 'Dudley' had come to define both a style of painting and the technical means by which it was executed. The influence of Burne-Jones upon the Dudley group and the distaste for both that was felt by the art establishment was made clear in *The Art Journal* of 1870:

> Mr Burne-Jones in the Old Water Colour Society stands alone: he has in this room no followers; in order to judge how degenerate this style may become in the hands of disciples, it is needful to take a walk to the Dudley Gallery.

However, *The Dead Knight* seems to be stylistically isolated from the others illus-trated in the article, both by its near-abstract subject and its relaxed, impressionistic execution. If this is a 'quintessential' Dudley Gallery style painting, the others seem far removed from it. For example, the black-and-white illustration of another oil painting dated 1879 entitled *Heloise and Abelard* was much more closely related to the disciplined precision of *The Pool of Bethesda* and to Caroline's portrait.

Plucking Mandrakes, which Richard Dorment had mentioned to us, was almost a hybrid work between the two contrasting styles: the overall design is much less

Fig. 25. Robert Bateman, Women Plucking Mandrakes, *1870, body colour on paper laid on canvas, 31.2 × 45.8 cm, Wellcome Foundation, London.*

formalised, and the wooded background and pale sky recall *The Dead Knight*. However, the figures, engaged in their strange ritualistic activity, dominate the canvas and are wonderfully rendered as solid, three-dimensional forms overlaid with animated swirling fabric that adds a slightly stylised, almost art-nouveau panache (fig. 25). We were intrigued by this versatility of technique which Robert seemed able to adapt at will to convey the essence of the highly eclectic range of subjects that he wanted to portray.

The critique of this work from *The Art Journal* of 1870 indicated that contemporaries perceived the Dudley exhibitors as a disturbing and loosely coherent entity, with Bateman a leading figure among them:

> These Dudley people are proverbially peculiar. Thus it would be hard to find anywhere talent associated with greater eccentricity than in the clever yet abnormal creations of Walter Crane, Robert Bateman and Simeon Solomon . . . 'Plucking Mandrakes' recalls a description in the works of Sir Thomas Browne, which recount how the mandrake shrieks when drawn from its roots. There is evidently much mystery in this process as depicted by Bateman, and this picture, in its form, action, colour removed as they are from common life and ordinary experience, is significant of something beyond the usual colours of nature. Though not wholly satisfactory, we hail with gladness the advent of an art which reverts to historic associations and carries the mind back to older times when painting was the twin sister of poetry.

The Kavanagh article illustrated three other works. One was an oil exhibited in 1900 which has an altogether less challenging feel. Entitled *At Romsey Abbey*, it portrays a small boy asleep beneath a portion of the ancient abbey walls with a relief sculpture of a crucifix set into it (fig. 26). For the first time in Bateman's work, this picture came perilously near to the sentimentality I had been frightened of at the outset. But every example of his work was valuable if we were to understand his story. We wondered if the late date might provide a clue to the change of intensity in this picture – by 1900 Robert was approaching sixty.

The other two pictures were each fascinating in a different way. Two anthropo-morphic studies of ravens strike a disconcerting, almost sinister note (figs. 27, 28). There is no attempt to mitigate the slightly forbidding associations attached to these uncompromisingly black birds. They are presented on a floor of stone slabs, only relieved by Robert's initials carved into their surface. Although these works bear the comparatively late date of 1889, there is no relieving prettiness or sentimentality here: it is clearly the meticulously delineated birds that interest the artist. The only hint of a narrative is that one of the birds is in prime condition, its wings and body feathers sleek and groomed, its head raised, eating a nut with its tiny beady eye bright and animated; the other is dishevelled, all its feathers ragged with an area of its head and neck apparently almost bald. It has one damaged wing hanging limply to the ground and its dull unfocused eye is starkly contrasted to the gimlet brightness of

Fig. 26. Robert Bateman, At Romsey Abbey, *1899, oil on panel, 40.6 × 30.5 cm, private collection.*

its companion, expressing the weariness of pain or great age. The choice of subject may be peculiar, but the austere clarity of the images and their meticulous precision relate these pictures stylistically to *The Pool of Bethesda* and the portrait of Caroline.

The underlying characteristic of all these pictures, regardless of the range of subject and varied technique, is that they all produce a strange sense of unease in the viewer. Whether this was consciously intended by Robert when he set about the paintings or was an innate part of his personality, expressing itself involuntarily in his work, is impossible to know. His figures, be they lovers or angels, ravens or women performing rituals, dogs with dead knights or even his beloved Caroline, seem pre occupied, detached from their outward surroundings, distracted and inhabiting an inner world dominated by their own thoughts, prayers or memories. Their surroundings, be they architectural or beautifully rendered landscapes, serve only to enhance this haunting sense of isolation.

The last picture in the Kavanagh article was a flower painting, *Wild Geranium and Great Master Wort* (fig. 29). This did not have quite the same imaginative intensity as his other paintings. Kavanagh quoted Crane's opinion that 'Bateman was the most remarkable draughtsman of flowers, among moderns, I have ever seen, after the best Japanese work'. Judging by the black-and-white photograph, it is certainly a wonderfully skilful piece of work. As Kavanagh put it:

> In this work of exquisite simplicity, he captures the pure beauty of the wild and wispy bloom, while his depiction of the exhibition label and tube of pigment contribute a capricious touch and allude to his profession as a painter.

Figs. 27, 28 (opposite). Robert Bateman, Two Ravens, *1889, oil on canvas, 40.6 × 20.3 cm, private collection.*

Fig. 29 (right). Robert Bateman, Wild Geranium and Great Master Wort, *1883, oil on canvas, 40.6 × 30.4 cm, private collection.*

This endearing component of the painting reveals an entirely new and unsuspected aspect of Robert's character. Without disturbing the spare clarity of the overall design, he incorporated a label attached by string to the neck of the vase which proves to be an advertisement for the fact that the painting is on sale at the Grosvenor Gallery. Nearby, but again so subtly handled that one could look at the painting without really taking it in, is a half-used tube of oil paint. At first one's attention is drawn to the exquisitely painted flowers and vase, and only later does one register the label and the paint. By referencing the grubby world of money, and the messy process of painting, they gently poke fun at the rarefied sensibilities of the arbiters of the fine art world, among whom this refined image so clearly belongs.

This is a new Bateman, at odds with the purveyor of poetic pathos and implied internalised conflict. Here, suddenly, the flawless technique is the partner of an impish sense of humour, not afraid to make fun of its own preciousness – a most unusual trait, especially for gifted artists in mid-Victorian England. Could it be that this mellowness was related to the date prominently incised on the stone wall in the background of the picture, 1883, the year of his marriage to Caroline?

One other painting, apparently lost, came in for special mention in the article. This was titled variously *The Witch of Endor* or *The Raising of Samuel.* Apparently never sold, it was in the artist's house at Nunney Delamere at his death in 1922. His obituary in the *Somerset Standard* described it as 'his most famous picture . . . Its technique is superb and it well deserves the notoriety given to it.' This judgement was endorsed by Walter Crane who identified its importance when he remarked:

His best-known picture is perhaps 'The Witch of Endor' which was in the Royal Acadamy Exhibition. It is a very weird and powerful scene of the Raising of Samuel and is worked out with extraordinary invention and detail.

If this was his masterpiece – and the fact that he elected to keep it with him all his life suggested he might have considered it to be so – it must have been a remarkable piece of work. Had it rivalled or surpassed *The Pool of Bethesda*? If so, it seems surprising that it has not survived, even in the dangerous years between the wars when the Pre-Raphaelites were ridiculed or ignored.

The remainder of Amanda Kavanagh's article was largely taken up with Robert's other interests of gardening, architecture and sculpture, in support of her underlying thesis that he was able to pursue these enthusiasms at will, as he was supported by private means. She produced no real evidence for the architecture, but claimed that he had made a new garden at Benthall. In the case of the sculpture, we were intrigued and uncertain. In support of his prowess, she described and illustrated a large stone frog, supposedly made in his youth and still in the gardens at Biddulph Grange. We had heard this story before, so had put it to the curator there – he told us that they had proof that the frog was not created by Robert, but by Waterhouse Hawkins.

We had been disappointed by this, as we had four pieces of carving at the Old Hall which we thought might be by him. Two were coats of arms, not particularly skilfully executed. One represented the Bateman family and the other the Staniers. Since the Staniers had never lived in the house, it seems unlikely that they put their crest on the building. However, we now knew that during their entire period of ownership the Staniers had only had one tenant, Robert Bateman. It therefore seems highly probable that Robert executed both coats of arms as well as two other, more interesting, pieces of sculpture on the building. The first of these takes the form of a small grotesque face with a gaping mouth that gives access to a recess in the stone behind it (fig. 30). The other is a well-rendered lizard or salamander, clinging to the stonework of the wall and peering into a square recess from which a baby lizard looks warily out (fig. 31).

Kavanagh had of course known nothing of Robert's association with the Old Hall. The fact that she discussed only the (wrongly attributed) frog made us wonder if there were any other known sculptures by him. If not, it was just possible that we

Figs. 30, 31. A typical Bateman grotesque head (far left) and sinister salamanders (left), both by Robert Bateman at Biddulph Old Hall.

owned the only four pieces of his sculpture to have survived. With what we were discovering about the working of Robert's imagination, it did seem plausible that these faintly sinister little pieces were his.

Since Kavanagh's article of 1989, there had been no further published material specifically on Bateman. The two *Apollo* articles appeared to represent the only serious attempt to rehabilitate him. Kavanagh's aim of re-evaluating his reputation was only partly successful, perhaps because the biographical material she uncovered was so slight and conventional in nineteenth-century terms that he remained an opaque and insubstantial figure with little personal or artistic context. This had led her to headline her article 'Robert Bateman: a True Victorian', indicating that she had come to see him as a highly gifted individual, socially and financially secure, who had applied his abilities and enquiring mind across a wide field of activities, while remaining fundamentally within the conventional middle-class religious and social structures of Victorian England. She acknowledged that he was elusive and difficult to categorise when she concluded:

> While it is possible to describe Robert Bateman as a 'Forgotten Pre-Raphaelite' and one of the 'Last Romantics' of the late Victorian and early Edwardian era, his works are characterised by a cryptic choice of subject matter, a peculiarity of imagination, and an acuity of observation which defy simple categorisation.

Something in this conclusion made us uneasy. The 'True Victorian' seemed hard to reconcile with the disquieting quality of his images, just as the bald facts of his marriage to Caroline gave no sense of the intensity of their relationship. Certainly he was interested in architecture, sculpture, gardening, bowls and a dozen other things, but this did not explain what inspired him to conceive and execute highly original images of haunting beauty and emotional intensity in paint.

Why, as a man described in his obituary as 'six feet four inches in height and with a profile that would have become a Grecian statue', did he not marry and settle down as a comfortable paterfamilias in his country house until he was over forty, and then chose a woman three years older than himself and therefore unable to bear him children, if he was a 'true Victorian'?

Where had he been before that?

It mattered because most of the pictures we had seen were from the 1870s, well before his marriage in 1883. If we were to find the answers to these questions we needed to move beyond the *Apollo* articles and see what we could find.

Fig. 32. Robert Bateman, Reading of Love, HE Being By, *1874, pencil and watercolour with gum arabic, heightened with touches of body colour and scratching out, 25.4 × 34.3 cm, private collection.*

Chapter 7

READING OF LOVE

Our visit to Richard Dorment to see Caroline's portrait was fast approaching. To get the most out of the meeting we wanted to gain an understanding of the Dudley Group. This was not initially as easy as we imagined. We were looking for detailed factual knowledge, rather than generalised references in books devoted to Pre-Raphaelitism. Eventually, however, we tracked down an essay by Dennis Lanigan published in 2000, 'The Dudley Gallery: Water Colour Drawings, Exhibitions 1865–1882'. This clarified the role of the gallery and the context that had led to its opening in 1865.

Since the beginning of the nineteenth century, there had been a growing demand among artists to break the monopoly of the Royal Academy Exhibitions over the display of their work, if it was to be seriously considered by the critics and the art-buying public. Not only was the RA's selection process in the hands of established artists of an older generation, whose tastes were, by definition, extremely conservative and opposed to experimentation or innovation, the exhibitions relied almost exclusively on oil paintings so drawings or water colours were excluded.

This had led to the founding of, first, the Old Water Colour Society in 1815, and later the New Water Colour Society in 1832. Both of these ran annual exhibitions but restricted the works shown to members of their societies, entry to which again tended to be controlled by committees of establishment figures in their field. The revolutionary changes brought about by the emergence of the Pre-Raphaelites and their followers in the late 1840s and '50s finally led to the opening of the Dudley Gallery in April 1865. It had a liberal exhibition policy and no membership requirement, so could display work by many artists, particularly young ones, who would otherwise not have been able to establish themselves.

The gallery was an instant success, and it continued in this format until 1883 when it came under new management and became The Dudley Gallery Art Society.

From the outset the gallery acquired a distinct character and notoriety:

The Dudley Gallery quickly became the main forum for the younger generation of artists associated with the early Aesthetic Movement, and it would remain so until the opening of the Grosvenor Gallery in 1877. Works in the characteristic 'L'art pour l'art' Dudley style rejected sentiment and morality as subjects and did not attempt to tell a story. These artists were more interested in the love of beauty. Even when some narrative content was retained the emphasis was primarily on achieving a harmonious arrangement of forms, colours and tones with the decorative effect of the work being predominant. Critics dubbed the more characteristic exhibitors in the Dudley style the 'Poetry-Without-Grammar School'. This term – commenting on the beauty of the works, whilst lamenting their obvious technical shortcomings – was first used by a reviewer for the *Westminster Review* in 1869 . . .

The 'Poetry-Without-Grammar School' is generally thought of today to have consisted of a group of young artists centred on Robert Bateman and Walter Crane, which also included Edward Clifford, Henry Ellis Wooldridge, Alfred Sacheverell Coke, Edward Henry Fahey and Theodore Blake Wirgman. In reality, however, the group of artists that could be included under this term, based on work they submitted, was much wider. The reviewer for the Westminster Review acknowledged this when he also discussed such artists as Lucy Madox Brown, A. B. Donaldson, Marie Spartali, Simeon Solomon and Alice and Helen Thorneycroft . . .

The art of the young Burne-Jones was particularly influential for the 'Poetry-Without-Grammar School'. His early work was also criticised for its technical faults and his guidance was recognised early on.

. . . Conservative critics from such periodicals as *The Art Journal*, the *Saturday Review* and the *Illustrated London News* were to continue in their denunciations of the early Aesthetic Movement until it became more respectable following the success of the Grosvenor Gallery.

More than a century later the artists of the 'Dudley School' have featured prominently in such exhibitions as *The Last Romantics* shown at the Barbican Gallery in 1989 and *The Age of Rossetti, Burne-Jones & Watts: Symbolism in Britain 1860–1910* shown at Tate Britain in 1997.

We felt a frisson of excitement at seeing Robert Bateman identified as a leading member of a group of young artists who clearly set out to revolutionise the artistic world of their day.

Attached to Dennis Lanigan's essay was a list of exhibitors and their works. These he defined as artists who epitomised the 'Dudley' style and therefore were similarly associated with Bateman and his group. Among these was E. R. Hughes who, although younger, came to be closely associated with both Simeon Solomon and Robert, who is documented as a witness at Hughes's wedding in 1883.

In 1866, Robert exhibited at the Dudley for the first time. His painting *Past and Present* was accompanied by an intriguing verse concerned with the emotional appeal of ruinous old buildings, in contrast to the soullessness of new ones:

> As the love-sculpted towers of ancient days,
> Though crumbling and defaced, the heart will thrill,
> While all unmoved on modern pile we gaze,
> The soulless offspring of a heartless skill.
>
> So these, though dying, live in all our hearts,
> This lives but in the eye, although it live,
> From these in death the sweetness scarce departs,
> Even strong life to this no charm can give.

Despite the laboured quality of the wording, one could scarcely select a clearer expression of the romantic appeal of ruinous buildings. We could not help wondering what the painting *Past and Present* would have shown. The possibility that it might have shown Biddulph with its 'love-sculpted tower of ancient days' and crumbling cannon-defaced walls was tantalising – but even without the painting, the poem gave an unmistakable pointer to how appealing Robert and his group would have found the Old Hall.

Of the other artists mentioned as being part of Robert's immediate circle, only his friends Walter Crane and Edward Clifford had paintings in the Dudley that year, but of the wider Dudley group A. B. Donaldson and Simeon Solomon were represented. What a glamorous figure Robert must have struck, especially to people of his own age – an exhibited artist, just twenty-four, with his tall, spare figure and Grecian good looks, part of a fast-forming group of talented artistic rebels, endorsed by the fashionable new London gallery at the heart of artistic controversy.

From 1866, Robert exhibited every year except one until 1874. Then, to our surprise, he stopped dead and never showed at the Dudley again. This was baffling as, at thirty-two, he was a young man, very probably at the height of his powers. We wondered what effect his departure would have had on the others in his group. Strangely, Simeon Solomon, who had been specifically linked with Robert in the 1870 *Art Journal* review of *Plucking Mandrakes*, also exhibited every year, often three or more pictures, until 1872 when he abruptly ceased and never showed again. Their friend E. R. Hughes also stopped exhibiting after 1874 and did not resume until 1880.

Robert's friend Walter Crane continued exactly as one would expect, exhibiting two or more paintings regularly every year until 1881, shortly before the Dudley closed. Apart from Crane, however, most of the other members of the group ceased to exhibit regularly at the Dudley after 1874. The only other exception appeared to be Edward Clifford, who exhibited every year from 1866 onwards, but there did seem to be a strange anomaly. Up to 1874 the titles of his pictures suggest they are in the romantic 'Dudley' style: *Head of an Angel, Some Have Entertained Angels Unawares, Meadows of Asphodel* and the like. Suddenly, in 1875, he exhibited a straightforward portrait, *The Earl of Tankerville*, and from then on he painted only portraits, usually of aristocrats.

While we were trying to see if there was any discernible pattern in all this, something struck us about the date 1874, which marked the end of Robert's association with the Dudley. This was the date on the carved stone built into the wing of the Old Hall, which Robert was said to have used as a studio. It seemed that Robert had undertaken sufficiently radical alterations at Biddulph to merit marking them with a signed and dated stone at the exact moment he ended his association with the Dudley after eight years of regular exhibiting. It suggested a sudden change in his circumstances, resulting in a closer relationship with the Old Hall which necessitated adapting it for his unique requirements.

As we now realised, these adaptations were very likely to have been the creation of a good-sized studio. The dates on several of his known paintings, including *The Pool of Bethesda* and *Heloise and Abelard*, confirm that he continued to produce important work after 1874. This raised the intriguing possibility that some of his best work might have been produced in his new studio at Biddulph.

We returned to our study of the lists of exhibits attached to Dennis Lanigan's article with a new zest, hoping to find some hint of the events that had caused Robert to abandon the Dudley. However, they confined themselves to dates, titles, exhibition numbers and prices at the annual exhibitions. Depressingly, of the sixteen paintings exhibited by Robert between 1866 and 1874, only one, *Plucking Mandrakes* of 1870, was known to have survived. This stylish work gives a tantalising hint of the possible quality of the missing fifteen. We realised we were basing the assumption they were lost on the fact that they were not mentioned or illustrated in either of the *Apollo* articles. But it was over twenty years since Kavanagh's piece – had others been discovered since then?

We tried searching by title on the internet but got no response – it seemed that they were completely forgotten. With some trepidation we rang Julian Hartnoll and asked him if he knew of any other Bateman paintings. He mentioned only one: *Reading of Love, HE Being By*. It had turned up in 2000 and was sold by Christie's for about £16,000 or £17,000. Brian and I were intrigued that this particular painting had been found as it was the very last one on the list before Bateman disappeared from the Dudley in 1874. Would the image itself, when we saw it, contain some coded message or clue to the sudden change in the pattern of Robert's life?

When we rang Christie's, we became embroiled in what we had come to think of as a classic 'Bateman' conversation. A confident young lady insisted that there was no record of a painting of that title being sold by Christie's around 2000, or at any other time. She said that if it was a water colour it was just possible it had been sold at South Kensington. We humbly asked if she could check South Kensington for us. After a pause in which she repeated the name continually under her breath as if frightened of forgetting it, she suddenly cried,

'Good Heavens, yes. It is here. Sold at Kensington on 28 November 2000. Lot No. 43, *Reading of Love, HE Being By*. Robert Bateman. Pencil and water colour heightened with body colour, 10 × 13.5 inches . . . It's just come up. Jeepers! That's a funny one! What do you want me to do with it?'

We asked her to email an image of it to us and send a hard copy in the post, which she agreed to do. As we waited by the computer screen we could not help feeling a little perplexed and uncertain about what we were about to see. The title was so peculiar. We could not quite imagine how these words would be transported into a visual image. To be truthful, the personification of spiritual attributes, such as mercy, valour or love, into suitably clad, symbolic winged figures was one of the staple ingredients of high Victorian art that we found particularly difficult to digest.

When suddenly the image began to work its way up the computer screen our fears were a little assuaged (fig. 32). The foreground showed three statuesque ladies in relaxed flowing garments of medieval character, one reading, the other two apparently transported into a state of almost trance-like rapture by what they were hearing. They were grouped by a small formal pond or well, on the far side of which sat Cupid in the form of an adolescent boy sporting a cream loincloth and wings. He is sitting, hands clasped round his knees, his quiver of arrows lying beside him, absorbed by the reading of his female companion. Immediately behind the figures are simple white rose bushes and wonderfully gnarled and shaped trees, all contained within an enclosure of architectural stone walls suggesting a secluded medieval garden. In the centre background are a man and a woman, looking through an unglazed window.

As the details of the background gradually became clear, we were galvanised. There, framing the whole foreground subject of the painting, was an exact depiction of a portion of the ruins at Biddulph. The detail of the walls were so painstakingly rendered that we could identify not only the precise location, but every individual door opening, glassless window and circular aperture of the original (fig. 33).

At first, we thought Bateman had omitted one detail, a circular stone opening low down within the plinth, but when we looked closely it was indicated faintly, as if it was filled in. As it was now empty and much more visible, we thought it must simply have been opened up since 1873 when Robert painted the picture, but when we went out to look at it later that day, we found a beautifully masoned circular stone plug lying in the long grass immediately below the opening.

The discovery of this picture, with its indisputable depiction of Biddulph, marked a thrilling development in our search for Robert Bateman. The painting demonstrated

Fig. 33. Love among the ruins – the setting of Reading of Love *as it is today.*

the intensity of Robert's emotional response to the Old Hall. It is clear that, to him, the place spoke of another world of heightened complex perceptions, beyond the commonplace round of day-to-day experience. This was generated by the sheer age of the structure, which carried evidence of the past into the present. However, that general sense of history was amplified by the gaunt ruins, which bore silent witness to violent struggle and high emotion, now spent and still. All these elements are used in *Reading of Love* to intensify the impact of this hypnotic image. It is an attempt to allow the viewer to experience the sensation of a world transformed by the presence of love into an earthly paradise. The ruins, while heightening the sense of separation from the prosaic, loveless outside world, subtly reference the attendant fears and intimations of mortality that such profound emotions generate.

The accompanying notes from Christie's gave no indication that the painting's background had any particular relevance, except as 'an architectonic design element partially paralleled in *The Pool of Bethesda* by the same artist'. Surely this painting on the subject of love, set in his own surroundings, was a highly personal statement by Robert. Could anyone not experiencing the delirium of an obsessional love affair have conceived such a distracted fantasy?

The subject was the potency of reading accounts of love when one was experiencing it first hand. Was there a clue here, in the last picture he was ever to exhibit at the Dudley Gallery, to events in Robert's life that may have led him to make such a marked change? Was the painting set in Biddulph because the chain of events that led to his leaving the Dudley took place there – and was love, in one form or another, at the heart of it? As a talented, good-looking artist of thirty-two, he may well have been in love, but that alone would not have caused him to cease showing his work. *Reading of Love* contains no hint of heartbreak or thwarted love which might have led to a crisis. All the figures seem transported into a thoughtful but blissful reverie; there are no tears or anger or suffering.

We went back to Dennis Lanigan's list of pictures exhibited at the Dudley Gallery, and were struck by a pattern we had not noticed before. In Robert's last two years at the Dudley he exhibited three paintings. In 1874, his last year, he showed *On The Way* and *Reading of Love*, but in 1873 he showed only one, *Paolo and Francesca*. Accompanying the main title of this picture was a quotation from Dante:

> Reading one day we were, for pleasure's sake,
> The Tale of Lancelot – how him Love thralled.
> Alone we were, and no suspicion near.
> Oft times the book did make our eyes to meet –
> Our faces faded at the words we read,
> But was one point alone that overcame!

So two of Robert's last three paintings were not only on the theme of love, but depicted an almost identical incident: people reading accounts of love with which they identify so closely that they are overcome by the strength of their feelings. The verse from Dante raised the possibility that Robert was inspired by a personal identification with the incident depicted. The two protagonists are in a private, secluded place – they seem to have had to contrive this secretly, for if it were known it would be the subject of 'suspicion'. The sense of trembling intimacy, part fear, part suppressed desire, at the very moment of declaration is wonderfully caught.

The book they are reading provides the catalyst for the acknowledgement of their pent-up feelings, by describing, in perfect words, the tumultuous emotions they are themselves experiencing at that very moment. The tension builds as their eyes meet more and more frequently, and their faces 'fade at the words we read', until a point is reached when their ability to contain their pretence of reading 'for pleasure's sake' is overcome and their own feelings take over.

Paolo and Francesca is a blood-soaked tale of star-crossed lovers, in which Paolo woos Francesca on behalf of his brother Giovanni, who is in love with her but has not the looks nor charm to woo her himself. Giovanni marries Francesca, but she and Paolo have fallen in love. It is not a platonic relationship. They are discovered together consummating their love and Paolo is stabbed and killed. The subject was beloved of many artists, particularly romantic ones, but it is much more usual for the moments of high drama to be portrayed – the couple being burst in on, or the weeping Francesca mourning over the corpse of her murdered lover.

Bateman's selection of this particular segment of the story, and his return to the subject so soon afterwards in *Reading of Love*, suggest that it is specifically the process of mutual love being revealed through the act of reading of love with which he identifies. The two pictures coming so close together, at the moment he abandoned the Dudley Gallery and adapted Biddulph Old Hall, suggested that they may have had some highly personal meaning for Robert, possibly centred on a real incident.

Of Robert's two paintings shown in 1874, only one was priced. *On The Way* had a price of £25 shown in brackets, but *Reading of Love* was not priced, indicating that it was not for sale. In the previous year *Paolo and Francesca* was similarly listed without a selling price. We had not before seen much significance in the original prices of the paintings, other than as a way of trying to assess their relative importance at the time. Now we went carefully through the whole list of Robert's paintings starting from 1866 to see which had been priced and which had not. We found to our surprise that every single painting had been exhibited with a price, except *Reading of Love* and *Paolo and Francesca*. This reinforced the thematic link between them and the sense that they held some deep significance for Robert, something perhaps that made them too personal to sell.

So at the moment he ceased to exhibit at the Dudley, Robert was executing highly personal paintings on the theme of love. Surely this held the answer to the riddle of why he had stopped exhibiting and adapted Biddulph. Presumably his dream world was invaded by barbaric complications of some kind – for there is no sign, either in his life or in his paintings, of the sublime creature who had inspired these poetic visions. Did she spurn him? The Dante poem suggests not – these lovers are mutually infatuated. Or was she out of reach? Was there a public scandal in the best Victorian tradition, which forced him to disappear from view and hide at Biddulph? Apparently not, as for the next few years he exhibited at the eminently respectable Royal Academy, showing *The Pool of Bethesda* there in 1876. He also remained single, because he was free to marry nine years later.

On the other hand there can be no dispute about the radical change in the style, subject and execution of his paintings in the short period between *Reading of Love* and *Pool of Bethesda*. The soft focus of the water colour with its flowing, almost molten forms and delicate colour harmonies is replaced two years later by a rigidly disciplined, angular composition in oil which conveys its painful subject with unflinching clarity and minimal colour. The love poems and palpitations have been banished, to be replaced by a sterner, more substantial world that encompasses pain and struggle.

One thing was clear: Robert was remaining true to his reclusive reputation. The more we discovered about him the more perplexing were the puzzles he set us. And yet with every new glimpse into the hypnotic world of his imagination the more compulsively we became absorbed in his story.

Chapter 8

THE BIG PICTURE

Our long-awaited visit to Richard Dorment came at a good time. We had managed to gain just enough information about the Dudley Group and later Pre-Raphaelites to begin to comprehend how diverse and complex a subject late nineteenth-century British art truly was. We hoped that our small body of background knowledge would be sufficient to enable us to have a meaningful discussion with Richard about Robert Bateman and his association with Biddulph Old Hall.

Of course, it was of crucial importance to us, in our aim of restoring Robert's life and reputation, that a working art critic with a national reputation should have admired a Bateman painting enough not merely to endorse it but actually to buy it and hang it in his own home. The subject of the painting was a figure of growing fascination for us, and it was to be the first time we had ever seen an original Bateman, all of which combined to generate a wonderful sense of occasion.

Richard greeted us warmly and ushered us in. He was a spare, elegant figure with a generous manner and no hint of intellectual arrogance. He walked down the narrow hall and indicated the wall beside the staircase. Despite being warned about its size, we were still not quite prepared for the fabulous scale of the image nor the commanding impact of Caroline's presence as she gazed steadily out at us from the huge canvas. From the first-floor landing we got a better view of her face and the lovely colouring of the top section of the portrait. Indeed, the colouring was the first thing to strike us. The small illustration we had seen gave no sense of the beautifully modulated tones of ochre, russet and grey that surrounded the black-clad figure, with her pale skin and almost white hair, in an iridescent glow of warmth. It was very beautiful.

Richard said that it truly came into its own when the morning light fell on it from the long window on the stairs. He described her clothes as 'half-mourning', a late stage in the highly structured Victorian expression of bereavement. He had published a paper specifically on the symbolic significance of Caroline's clothes in the portrait, and promised us a copy. Brian asked Richard if he knew anything about the landscape behind her. I knew what was in his mind – at this scale, where the landscape could be clearly seen, it seemed incredibly familiar. One element was idealised – the river in the valley, which looked too wide and prominent – but the lie of the land, the contours of the hills, the scattered copses of trees and irregular little fields were almost exactly the ones we could see looking west from Biddulph towards Congleton Edge.

Richard seemed fascinated by this proposition and looked closely at that part of the painting.

'So you think he was actually working from this place you've got?'

'We're pretty sure. Part of the ruined mansion forms the background to *Reading of Love, HE Being By*,' I said.

'Oh, the water colour, really?'

'Yes, there the representation is absolutely exact, unmistakable. We've got some photographs so you can compare them.'

'Remarkable. Well, if you've seen enough here we'll go down to the garden, have a glass of wine and you can show me what you've brought.'

We showed him the legal document between John Bateman and his brother, Robert, giving him a life tenancy over the Old Hall. Then we showed him a picture of the initialled date stone of 1874, which he agreed was directly related to the way Robert signed his paintings. We showed him photographs of the ruins and compared them with *Reading of Love*, which he agreed was indisputably the setting of the painting. As the wine slipped down, we all got thoroughly engrossed and enthusiastic.

We asked him if he was aware of any significance surrounding the year 1874 on the date stone at Biddulph, which coincided so exactly with Robert's abrupt break with the Dudley Gallery after years of regular exhibiting. Richard felt that the break with the Dudley might have been connected with a number of scandals that engulfed their mentor Edward Burne-Jones and several other artists who were seen as his followers, particularly Simeon Solomon, at about that time.

Burne-Jones had been involved in an increasingly intense extra-marital love affair with Mary Zambaco, a volatile and gifted Anglo-Greek sculptress. The affair had begun in about 1866 but had gradually become so obsessive that it led to several public incidents, usually triggered by Burne-Jones's attempts to end the relationship. These culminated in an attempt by Mary Zambaco to commit suicide by throwing herself into the Regent's Canal.

These incidents were compounded by a considerable artistic scandal that broke in 1870. Burne-Jones exhibited a painting entitled *Phyllis and Demophoon* at the Old Water Colour Society, the gallery where Bateman, Crane and others had been so influenced by his work. It was very badly received by the critics, who regarded it as expressing moral degeneracy in the nude depiction of the male figure Demophoon.

The highly conservative president of the society, Frederick Taylor, asked Burne-Jones to amend the painting, but he refused. He insisted on removing it from the exhibition and proffered his resignation, which the society accepted (fig. 34).

The public and critics had been equally outraged by the minimally draped female figure of Phyllis, who clasped her naked companion about the chest in a clinging embrace and whose head was a clearly identifiable portrait of Mary Zambaco. This was an affront to mid-Victorian morality and crystallised the perception of Burne-Jones and his followers as unhealthy, decadent mavericks. According to the critic of the *Illustrated London News*, the painting was 'something which, like the amatory poetry of Swinburne, might be loathsome were it not for its fantastic unreality'.

Fig. 34. Edward Burne-Jones, Phyllis and Demophoön, *1870, body colour and watercolour on composite layers of paper on canvas, 93.8 × 47.5 cm, Birmingham Museums and Art Gallery.*

This debacle had a huge impact on Burne-Jones. For the first time he joined his disciples by exhibiting three paintings at the Dudley Gallery in 1872–3. After that he ceased to exhibit completely and entered what he himself described as 'the desolate years', in which he was completely ignored and almost forgotten. He continued to work obsessively in private, supported by one or two loyal patrons, and in these secluded years developed the highly individual vision and technique that burst into public recognition in 1876 at the new Grosvenor Gallery, a glamorous custom-built institution dedicated to the promotion of advanced art.

As Richard described the hostility that had engulfed the figure who had inspired the Dudley Group's revolutionary new art, it was not difficult to imagine the traumatic impact it must have had on his disciples. Mockery and vilification of their subject matter and execution was bad enough, but to be accused of moral degeneracy must have made life extremely uncomfortable. We wondered what Robert's parents would have thought of their son's associates. His father, James Bateman, was a highly respected botanist, who regularly addressed the Royal Horticultural Society and had published a seminal treatise on orchids; he was also well known as a lay reader, and had published a collection of sermons of a particularly low-church Puritanical character. Robert's devoted mother was also noted for her piety, which was clearly expressed in a letter written to her middle son, Rowland, when he decided to dedicate his life to church missionary work:

> Treasure of my heart! And apple of my eye! It will be a gratification to you to know that this time twenty-one years ago I was beseeching the Gracious Giver of all good things to accept to his special service my newborn babe . . .

Robert and the Dudley Group must have been under enormous pressure. The decision of Burne-Jones, their acknowledged leader, to choose this moment to go into a life of artistic hibernation may have had some bearing on Robert's near-simultaneous disappearance from the Dudley and retreat to Biddulph. We were discussing this when Richard said cryptically,

'And then, of course, at almost exactly that moment there was the disaster of poor Simeon Solomon.'

All we knew about Solomon was that he had been linked with Bateman and Crane in *The Art Journal* in 1870, in an article discussing *Plucking Mandrakes*:

> These Dudley people are proverbially peculiar. Thus it would be hard to find talent associated with greater eccentricity than in the clever but abnormal creations of Walter Crane, Robert Bateman and Simeon Solomon.

After continuously exhibiting some 26 paintings between 1865 and 1871 Solomon, like Bateman, suddenly disappeared from the list at the Dudley Gallery and was never mentioned again.

Richard continued intriguingly, 'I know he stopped exhibiting a year or two before. I think he was abroad – in Rome if I remember rightly – but I think his actual crisis was very near your date.'

'His crisis?'

'Yes, poor chap, he got into a fearful mess. Unfortunately it wasn't women, this time it was men – which in Victorian London was catastrophically beyond the pale.'

Brian and I stared at him, conscious of the wine beginning to numb the outer edges of our conciousness. We thought we knew what he was saying, but we weren't quite sure and were afraid of making an absurd faux pas. I tried a tentative foray:

'Was he – arrested or something?'

'Oh, absolutely. Twice, actually. It was an utter disaster. He was ruined – completely ruined. He ended up destitute, an alcoholic living in St Giles's Workhouse. Appalling waste of talent.'

'Did he stop painting altogether?'

'Actually, no, not completely. But his work changed. Nearly all his late work is drawing – very hallucinogenic, obsessed with night, dreams, sleep, death and such like, haunting heads mostly with closed eyes, troubled, trance-like intensity. You need to know about him. There is a very good book about him that's come out recently called *Love Revealed*. The title's taken from an extraordinary prose poem he published not long before his disgrace.'

We mentioned the *Art Journal* article of 1870 linking Solomon with Crane and Bateman, and asked Richard whether he agreed that they formed a group.

'That's interesting. Because in his *Reminiscences* Walter Crane identifies himself with Bateman both as a personal friend and as part of an identified artistic clique, the two are always thought of together. But if you take the actual evidence of their known work, Solomon and Bateman show a stronger artistic empathy with one another, through the disturbing intensity of their images, than they do with the comparatively pretty and ephemeral early creations of Walter Crane.'

We asked Richard if he thought that might explain the anomaly that Crane alone, of the prominent members of the 'Poetry-Without-Grammar School', continued to exhibit annually right through the critical 1873–4 hiatus that marked the end of Burne-Jones's, Solomon's and Bateman's relationship with the Dudley Gallery. By this time, we had all become engrossed in the strange coincidence of the desertion of the gallery, at almost the same moment, by several of the leading figures of this circle. Richard sounded a note of caution, warning that there need not have been a single underlying cause for all these disparate events. But he felt, intuitively, that the causes for the change, in the cases of Solomon and Burne-Jones, had almost certainly sprung from events in their personal lives. He had no idea what had caused Bateman to follow a similar pattern – to his knowledge, there was no scandal or hiatus associated with his name at this time, or indeed at any other.

He did, however, proffer a possible explanation for Crane's bucking the trend. He was abroad throughout the crucial period, having married in late 1871. He and his new bride set out on an extended honeymoon tour of Italy, from which they did not return until the late summer of 1873. It seemed plausible that he had therefore avoided being contaminated by the suspicion and moral odium that became attached to other prominent members of the Dudley Group. Certainly, after referring to both Solomon and Bateman as friends in the early part of his autobiography, Crane never mentions Solomon again after his return from Italy and makes only a passing allusion to Bateman as a founding member of the Society of Artists in Tempera in 1901, some thirty years later. He may have continued to exhibit at the Dudley, but he did not renew his friendship with the group of artists he had identified with before his marriage.

If the cause of this lay in the irregular personal lives of some of them, it seemed a little surprising that Robert should have chosen to disappear and remain single for a further ten years, when he could have followed Crane's example and demonstrated his good character by marrying and settling down. It seemed especially odd since romantic love appeared to be the very subject dominating his mind and imagination at precisely this point in his life.

Richard was wonderfully good-natured in the face of our obsessional interest in the minutiae of every hypothesis. From his fund of information on nineteenth-century art he contributed facts and illumination on practically every point we raised. He was the perfect tutor to our intellectual curiosity. He insisted on accuracy, rigour and rationality, while continually encouraging us to research every nuance of what we were discovering, to extract the truth about the obscure figures we were pursuing and to increase the understanding of their work.

As we shook hands in the hall, we took a last glance up at the overwhelming presence of Caroline Octavia on the staircase. We were struck again by her disconcerting, still composure mingled with an unmistakable aura of controlled sadness. We walked away into the relaxed euphoria of a radiant summer evening in Little Venice, full of excitement and curiosity about the morbidly intense concoction of blissful hallucination and personal despair that we had glimpsed in the back alleys of the Victorian art world that Richard Dorment had begun to reveal to us.

Chapter 9

MANDRAGORA

We had been intrigued by the coincidence Richard Dorment had pointed out of the scandals engulfing the private lives of Edward Burne-Jones and Simeon Solomon at the very time that Bateman abandoned the Dudley Gallery and, like them, never exhibited there again. As time went on, we were to become immersed in the wider life and work of both these artists, but for the moment we concentrated our attention on the period 1873–4.

Solomon's extraordinary life held us spellbound by the titanic intensity of its triumphs and tragedies. Born the youngest son of a Jewish family of artists, he was precociously talented, entering the Royal Academy Schools at fifteen in 1861. He was taken up by the early members of the Pre-Raphaelite Brotherhood, especially Rossetti. At first, most of his work was heavily influenced by his Jewish roots, with subjects inspired by texts of the Old Testament to which he brought an intense Hebraic conviction. His technical skill, particularly in the rendering of complex metal surfaces such as chased silver or lustrous fabrics, was superb, especially in conjunction with his daring experimental colour palettes. Burne-Jones was a great admirer of his work from the first, and at one point described him as 'the greatest genius of us all'.

As time went on, Solomon's subjects moved away from his Jewish culture to become more classical in inspiration. A strong strand in many of his paintings was the depiction of people experiencing intense, almost trance-like spiritual states, brought on by the performance of ritualistic religious ceremonies. Another, clearly identifiable, strand was an increasing number of naked or near-naked male subjects which are, to modern eyes, blatantly homoerotic. Since these were criticised at the time for their 'unmanly' or 'unhealthy' connotations, one can only assume that Solomon set out deliberately to confront the sexual taboos of his time (figs. 35, 36).

By the early 1870s, Solomon's work was usually simultaneously exquisite and scandalous by the standards of the society about him. In 1871, he brought several of

Figs. 35, 36. Simeon Solomon, Bacchus, *1867, watercolour on paper, private collection, and* Carrying the Scrolls of the Law, *1867, watercolour with body colour on paper, Whitworth Art Gallery, Manchester.*

his preoccupations together in a long prose poem entitled *A Vision of Love Revealed in Sleep*. In view of the fervent intensity of this evocation of spiritual love, there was an element of almost macabre black comedy in his arrest for gross indecency with another man in a public lavatory just off Oxford Street in early 1873. At the same time, there was something truly heroic in his refusal, over the next thirty years, ever to conform to the hypocritical moral conventions of Victorian society. As a result he descended, literally, into the gutter. Shoeless, ragged and an alcoholic, he became an inmate of St Giles's Workhouse in Seven Dials, London, where he died in 1905.

After his crisis, Solomon continued to work mainly on drawings, illustrating aspects of his 'Vision of Love' poem. One recurrent figure was the personification of 'Passion', who was described as a Medusa-like figure, sunken-cheeked and hollow-eyed with snakes writhing in her hair. These drawings, and the description in the poem, intrigued us. They held out the possibility of an explanation of a strange feature at Biddulph that we had never understood. Inside the porch, on the left-hand wall, were two strange bits of decoration. The first was a lead plaque with a fragment of poetry carved into it:

> Hence rebel heart! Nor deem a welcome due
> To walls once ruined by a rebel's hand
> Thrice welcome thou if thou indeed be true
> To God and to the lady of the land.

Fig. 37. 'Hence rebel heart!', Robert's plaque in the porch at Biddulph.

Fig. 38 (left). The mask in the porch at Biddulph – the ghost of Simeon Solomon?

Fig. 39 (right). Simeon Solomon, The Tormented Conscience, *1889,*
red chalk on paper, 40.6 × 30.5 cm, private collection.

The extended Rs throughout this piece made us attribute the execution, if not the composition, to Robert (fig. 37).

Beneath it, however, was a strange mask carved in red sandstone with hollow cheeks and blank eyes. Two snakes rose through the sketchily represented hair, their heads meeting above the forehead (fig. 38). Solomon had annotated one of his drawings of such a head *The Tormented Conscience* (fig. 39). Was our sculpture an identification, by Bateman, with Solomon's image? Or was there even a remote possibility that Solomon himself had been to the Old Hall and attempted a sculptural representation of one of his most haunting images? A possible clue to this might lie in Solomon's well documented close relationship with a mysterious figure identified only as 'Willie', who lived in Warrington, some fifteen miles from Biddulph.

Shortly before his arrest, Solomon and Willie took an extended trip to Italy with Oscar Browning, a sympathetic Eton schoolmaster, and Gerald Balfour. Soon after their arrival, Solomon and his friend deliberately disappeared and went to separate lodgings. Browning took offence, and Solomon wrote to arrange a meeting in order to try to placate him:

> I will be at the Braccio Nuovo tomorrow soon after ten with Willie – who has been inexpressibly sweet to me. We shall dine this evening at the Botticella.

On his return, Solomon wrote again to Browning from Warrington, where he was visiting Willie:

> The dear Roman, Willie, lives here, or rather, near here. I have had him photographed in divers manners. I think the result very successful but you shall judge for yourself.

Did Solomon continue to meet his friend after the debacle of his arrest in 1873, and if so, did he take advantage of the remote seclusion of Biddulph Old Hall to facilitate this after Robert's return there in 1874?

One other person, known to be a friend of both Solomon and Bateman, might have provided a motive for him to visit the Old Hall. Solomon had known Edward Hughes since 1869, when he wrote to Oscar Browning telling him that he had taken 'the beautiful Hughes' to a choral concert at St James's Hall:

> He was much impressed and looked, leaning on his hand, quite lovely.

Later, Solomon used Hughes and his equally striking seventeen-year-old friend, Johnston Forbes-Robertson, to model for his drawing *Then I Knew my Soul Stood by Me and He and I went forth together* (fig. 40), which he published as the frontispiece to his prose poem *A Vision of Love Revealed in Sleep* in 1871. Whatever the truth of their intimacy with Solomon, this very public identification with him appeared to create a serious hiatus in both boys' lives after his disgrace became public knowledge in late 1873.

In 1874, Forbes-Robertson abandoned his artistic career altogether and became an actor. He quickly joined Henry Irving's company and travelled to America. In the same year Edward Hughes also stopped exhibiting at the Dudley Gallery and did not show any more work in London until 1880. At the same moment he announced his engagement to Mary Josephine MacDonald, whom he claimed to have been in

Fig. 40. Simeon Solomon, Then I Knew my Soul Stood by Me and He and I went forth together, *Hollyer photograph of drawing, 1871.*

love with for eight years since she was thirteen years old. In a letter, Mary's mother said the long delay before their betrothal had been caused by Hughes's wish to establish himself as an artist, 'but suddenly it couldn't be held back'. Despite the apparent new urgency, Hughes failed to marry Mary before her death of consumption four years later in Italy.

During this time, he worked as a portrait painter in Liverpool, a place he found deeply alienating. He wrote of it:

> I should enjoy myself more if I had more sympathetic people to deal with here . . . I simply hate working away from home (London).

After 1880, although he continued to spend several months each year in Liverpool, Hughes slowly re-established himself in the London galleries. In 1883 he married Emily Eliza Davies in Pimlico, a lady ten years his senior, with Robert Bateman as his principal witness.

During the previous difficult decade, had Biddulph Old Hall provided a secret place where Simeon Solomon could renew his acquaintanceship with 'the beautiful Hughes' undetected, when the young man mitigated his lonely life in Liverpool by visiting his good friend Robert Bateman?

Another aspect of Solomon's story interested us. The persistent trance-like state of his subjects, frequently with poppies entwined in their hair, is strongly suggestive of drug-induced torpor. *A Vision of Love* was written in 1870 and published the following year. At the same moment, Bateman exhibited *Plucking Mandrakes* at the Dudley Gallery. While we had taken a close interest in the style, colouring and technique of this painting, especially in relation to the work of the other artists in the Dudley Group, we had never paid much attention to the actual subject.

The rituals surrounding the extraction of the mandrake root from the ground went back to pre-history and were driven by the highly toxic nature of the plant. This danger, in conjunction with the narcotic and hallucinogenic effects of extracts of the bark, had led to the plant's becoming associated with magic and witchcraft. The soporific and aphrodisiac properties of the extracts meant that the drowsy visions they engendered tended to be vivid and highly erotic. It was thus associated with fertility as far back as the Old Testament, in Genesis 30, verses 16 to 17:

> So when Jacob came in from the fields that evening, Leah went out to meet him. 'You must sleep with me,' she said. 'I have hired you with my son's mandrakes.' So he slept with her that night. God listened to Leah, and she became pregnant and bore Jacob a fifth son.

In Hebrew, the word for mandrake is *dudaim*, meaning 'love plant'.

This renewed interest in the subject of Bateman's painting had been sparked by a vague recollection of studying *Othello* in my schooldays and recalling the wonderful phrase, 'Mandragora, and all the drowsy syrups of the night.' This phrase seemed to capture the essence of so many of Solomon's images and of his *Vision of Love*. We could not help wondering whether it had some relevance to the dreamlike visions portrayed by Burne-Jones, Bateman and other members of their group.

Rossetti and the original Pre-Raphaelite Brotherhood, we knew, used laudanum and chloral, both hallucinogenic drugs if consumed in any quantity. Burne-Jones's lover Mary Zambaco, when she attempted suicide, was described in a letter from Rossetti as 'wailing like Cassandra, threatening to take laudanum.' Was there a link here between the visionary paintings, the hallucinogenic drugs, now known to be extremely dangerous and addictive, and the erotic crises that overcame both Solomon and Burne-Jones in the early 1870s? If so, was *Women Plucking Mandrakes* an indication that Bateman too was involved in this experimentation with narcotics, and did it lead to some form of crisis that forced him, like them, to withdraw from London society and the Dudley Gallery? It seemed plausible – but, unlike them, he was not involved in any publicly acknowledged sexual scandal.

Burne-Jones called the period between 1870 and 1877 his 'desolate years', but the truth was that, out of the public eye, he had used the time for intense study. Over these seven years, he refined both his unique vision and the techniques by which he transferred that dream world to canvas. Despite their intensity of feeling and originality, earlier canvases such as *Green Summer* (fig. 41) or *The Merciful Knight* had been criticised as technically flawed and poorly finished, in the same spirit as his younger followers had been ridiculed as the 'Poetry-Without-Grammar School'. He clearly took this criticism to heart. In 1871 he set out on an extended tour of Italy,

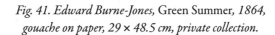

Fig. 41. Edward Burne-Jones, Green Summer, *1864,*
gouache on paper, 29 × 48.5 cm, private collection.

Fig. 42. Edward Burne-Jones, Wheel of Fortune, *1875–83, oil on canvas, 199 × 100 cm, Musée d'Orsay, Paris.*

in which he made a close study of the techniques of the Italian masters, not only of the early figures such as Mantegna, who had influenced him from the outset of his career, but others including Leonardo and Michelangelo. These studies had a dramatic effect upon his output, inspiring him to begin a large number of huge paintings, almost all in oil rather than the heightened water colour he had favoured previously. The new precision and accuracy he brought to these great canvases stunned the art world when they were exhibited for the first time at the opening of the new Grosvenor Gallery in 1877. Overnight Burne-Jones was transformed from a socially ignored, almost forgotten nonentity into the most successful artist of his generation. The roots of this transformation lay in those seven years of isolated concentration, when he had exhibited nothing but had worked obsessively, in private, adding a new discipline and clarity to his extraordinary images (fig. 42).

Here, surely, was a parallel with Bateman. We had already noted the completely changed style and execution of his work between his last pictures at the Dudley such as *Plucking Mandrakes* and *Reading of Love*, both heightened water colours, and the

Fig. 43. Detail of The Pool of Bethesda *(fig. 18) showing Bateman's changed technique.*

later oils such as *Pool of Bethesda, Heloise and Abelard* and the portrait of Caroline. Although he was never to achieve anything comparable to the impact of Burne-Jones's sensational exhibition at the Grosvenor, it seems that Robert used the isolated years at Biddulph to develop his techniques and produce his most important work (fig. 43).

In 1871 the people we had come to associate with Bateman – Solomon, Crane and Burne-Jones – were all in Italy. Since these visits had proved crucial in the development of all these men's careers, we wondered if Robert had been there with any of them. It was the year of the ten-year census and, intriguingly, Robert was nowhere to be found in Britain. But, try as we might, we could find no evidence anywhere to place him in Italy, either alone or with the others. It seemed the Bateman jinx was still with us.

While we were looking at the 1871 census, we casually tried the next one, for 1881. And, to our amazement, there he was: Robert Bateman, Artist, Biddulph Castle, alone except for a cook and her husband, a stonemason. Suddenly, we had absolute proof that Robert was operating as an artist at Biddulph – not a Victorian country gentleman, but a solitary figure with only a simple couple for company. This was two years before his marriage to Caroline Wilbraham, which apparently transformed his life.

Chapter 10

HEARTBREAKS AND MIRACLES

Before we were able to follow our instincts and immerse ourselves further in the lost world of Robert Bateman, we were confronted by the more mundane imperative of twenty-first-century financial reality. At the outset of our restoration of Bletchley Manor, we had made the controversial decision to allow the two distinct phases of its building – half-timbered Tudor gables and an early nineteenth-century stuccoed wing – to sit alongside each other undisguised, with no attempt to resolve the architectural disparity between them. It had been a radical approach and several times during the course of the work we had feared the result might be an uncoordinated hotchpotch rather than a stimulating juxtaposition of surviving historical fragments. So it was exciting as we reached the final phase to see the Manor emerge from its chrysalis of scaffolding and sheeting as both a usable family home and a striking historical building with a unique persona.

When the topiary garden was planted and a new approach from the busy main road was completed, Bletchley began to attract serious attention in the historic house world. It was recognised as a significant and hitherto unregistered element in the heritage of Shropshire. The architectural writer Marcus Binney asked to visit it and included it in a piece on timber-framed buildings in *The Times*. However, none of this had any influence over the catastrophic decline in the property market which had begun a year earlier and was gaining momentum. We wanted no more than to cover the cost of restoring the building, but in this climate the expense of the highly specialised technical and archaeological work involved in stabilising the timber frame was discounted by the market, leading to the perception that the house was over-priced.

Imperceptibly, as month followed month without any serious interest from buyers despite two price reductions, the impending trouble began to mutate from a financial loss on Bletchley Manor to an all-embracing disaster threatening Biddulph as well. Eventually, the bank sent us a letter almost doubling the interest rate on our loans

Fig. 44. Bletchley Manor, complete and ready to face the future.

and giving us just twenty-eight days before beginning the process of a compulsory sale of both properties.

As our problems grew more intractable we tried to believe that the hidden hand that had seemed to guide our fate since we first stepped over the threshold of Biddulph Old Hall would intervene again. We knew that if the house were to deploy a guardian angel to come to our rescue at the eleventh hour, it would be in a form we were least expecting. None the less, we were still dumbfounded when it arrived in the shape of Janet Street-Porter.

Months before, we had been contacted by television's Channel 4 informing us that they had heard about our restoration of Bletchley Manor and encouraging us to enter it for the restoration section of the *Grand Designs* awards. They had sent a form which we had filled in and returned without really engaging with the process. In the last week of our one-month grace period from the bank, they rang again. They told us that we had made it into the last three projects in the competition, and were to appear on live television where the viewers would see short films of each property and then vote for the overall winner. We would be supported by a celebrity advocate on the live programme who, in our case, was Janet Street-Porter.

Janet loved Bletchley and entered enthusiastically into the spirit of the competition by describing Brian and me as 'super-heroes of the restoration world'. When, to our astonishment, Kevin McCloud opened the envelope and announced Bletchley Manor the winner we were witnessed by the British nation kissing Janet Street-Porter on live television, sealing our claim to notoriety for all time. Winning the award worked as we prayed it might: now there was enormous interest in Bletchley Manor. It eventually went to a doctor, his wife and their three boys, and began a new life as a happy, living, family home. Our dream for it had been fulfilled, and we left it enriched by the privilege of being its custodians for a few short years in its long history. We had a sense of something achieved and brought to fruition (fig. 44).

Now we felt able to look forward again, and return to thinking about Biddulph, Robert Bateman, ruined towers, Pre-Raphaelite woodlands and waterfalls. One morning we decided to go for a walk along the Clough and into the woodland that surrounded the gardens at Biddulph Grange. The mist that hung between the trees seemed calculated to rekindle our sense of Robert Bateman's veiled, still world from which we had been exiled. No one seemed to be about, so we walked slowly in the pale haze until we chanced on a path we had never followed before. It led steeply up through the contorted outlines of ancient Himalayan rhododendrons which almost met over our heads.

After a sharp climb, there was a gap in the brooding undergrowth which gave a distant view down across the Cheshire plain. We stood and gazed at the misty land-scape, with the occasional spire or chimney providing a focus of interest. We talked quietly about the peculiarly contrasted atmosphere of the two houses, Bletchley and Biddulph. We continued up the path, which became steeper until the soil gave way to smooth rock under our feet. Suddenly, the sheer face of a huge outcrop of red sandstone loomed over us out of the mist. Our path skirted the front of it to a place where a set of steps had been cut into its surface (fig. 45). We climbed the steps and

Fig. 45. The steps in the Round Rock.

Fig. 46. The riddle on the rock: 'Remember this day', with extended Rs.

stood on the summit where we could see out across the surrounding countryside. I glanced down and there, in front of me, was a clearly incised message:

11ᵗʰ JUNE 04

REMEMBER THIS DAY

It had been properly cut and stood quite apart from the few other scratched names and initials nearby (fig. 46).

I called Brian over, and for a time the two of us stood staring down at the inscription without speaking. The lettering was not formalised, but the script was instantly recognisable from the plaque in the porch at Biddulph. The elongation of the Rs at each end of the word 'REMEMBER' were Robert Bateman's distinctive signature marks, used not only on the plaque, but on the 1874 date stone and almost all the pictures and prints that were known to be by him. Whoever had carved it was determined that the declared intention of the message should be fulfilled: the lettering had been deeply incised, and was easily legible after a century of exposure to the elements, even on the Staffordshire moorlands.

Of course, there was every reason to think it was Robert. He was known to have been an experienced sculptor, with the necessary chisels and equipment to carry out the job. Also, the rock stood within the grounds of his birthplace and childhood home, Biddulph Grange, and barely three-quarters of a mile from Biddulph Old Hall, the house in which he maintained a studio all his life.

But if Robert was the author of this enigmatic message, what riddle did it simultaneously conceal and perpetuate behind its few cryptic words? What event in his life had been commemorated on this day, and why was it invested with sufficient significance for him to mark it in this way, and seek to project the memory of it into the future, long after his own death? The message was specific to one particular day, but 11 June was not Robert's birthday or Caroline's, or their wedding day, so what significance did it have?

We were still discussing the inscription later that day when we went to the local pub for a beer. Two retired couples, whom we had chatted to several times, came in and sat at the table alongside us. Mavis, Terry, Stuart and Anne had all been brought up in the area and were interested in our renovation of the Old Hall. I asked them what they knew about the rock in the woods. Stuart, who was in his mid-seventies, immediately said,

'Do you mean the Round Rock?'

When we looked blankly at him, he went on,

'The huge, big one – with steps cut in it?'

'That's it.'

'My grandfather knew all about that. Apparently the steps were cut by an artist, a sculptor, so that his wife could climb it.'

We were stunned. It took a moment to realise that Stuart's grandfather could well have been a young man when the steps were cut, so his account stood a real chance of being accurate. When we asked him about the message, though, the Riddle of the Rock, he knew nothing. We were disappointed, but when we compared the photograph we had taken of the Riddle with the plaque in the porch at Biddulph the relationship of the lettering was too close to be coincidence.

Chapter 11

LOVE-SCULPTED TOWERS

Such is the power of television that winning the *Grand Designs* award had an extraordinary effect on the attitude of the local authority and of English Heritage. Their change of heart was most startling in the case of the incredibly dangerous six-storey tower at Biddulph (figs. 47, 48). They indicated that money might now be available to stabilise the structure, so we applied for a grant to restore it. We had conceived a scheme to install a tiny chapel or prayer room in the mid-point of the tower, where it had a semi-circle of mullioned windows. Our intention was to have the chapel consecrated by both Protestant and Catholic clergy, so the tower could become a symbol of reconciliation between the opposing religious convictions that had brought the mansion to ruin.

Fig. 47 (opposite). Love-sculpted tower? The tower at Biddulph after restoration.

Fig. 48 (right). A frightening prospect – the tower before!

The room at the top of the tower, with its complete circle of windows, we hoped to dedicate to the memory of Robert and Caroline. We aimed to return this double-height space to its historic format, by restoring the little stone fireplace and flue that it contained at the lower level, and the flight of oak stairs within the room that had led to the gallery under the ring of windows beneath the ogee-domed ceiling.

English Heritage agreed to send their own structural engineer to inspect the tower. His report, and the charisma of our momentary fame, combined to persuade them to offer a 50 per cent grant towards its restoration. This miraculous turn of events meant that the project to save the tower had mercifully returned to the realms of financial credibility. However, as the estimates for the work began to roll in we soon found our aspirations reduced from celestial chapels and astral viewing galleries to the thin gruel of reinforced concrete membranes and flanged steel pinions. Essential as these were, we could not help feeling that their contribution to the 'pictured poetry' reverie that had enveloped the tower in our imagination was perhaps a little uncouth.

The scheme agreed with English Heritage was to stabilise the fabric, insert three floors, unblock and glaze the windows, lead the dome, and insert four flights of English oak stairs to our own design. As we still hoped to create our tiny chapel at the mid-point, we had drawn a series of round panes in the leaded windows at this level into which we hoped to put some kind of figured or stained glass. We had heard of a skilled glass painter, who had copied some medieval roundels depicting the seasons as part of the renovation of a church. He had brought one over for us to look at and, while it had great naive charm, we felt that it was too generalised to become part of a chapel of reconciliation, inspired by the specific people and events that made up the Biddulph story. The whole issue was put on one side, and by the time the planning phase came to an end and work began on the tower, the question of the glass roundels was still unresolved.

As the manufacture of the leaded lights for the windows was being commissioned, we came under pressure to specify what the roundels were to be. Finally, unable to decide, we opted to insert clear glass instead. We were disappointed, since the chance of them ever being replaced was remote given the unlikelihood of finding anything affordable that would somehow reflect the Anglo-Catholic synthesis we were trying to express. For one thing, we could not think what it might be. Besides, if by chance we were to stumble upon anything, it was certain to be the wrong size and scale, so the roundels would be irrelevant anyway.

It was within days of this decision that we picked up a lead in our Bateman research from an avid book-collector friend. He had come across two extremely obscure titles, which appeared to be illustrated with woodcuts by Bateman. We knew that Bateman had done illustrations for books, as Amanda Kavanagh had noted two in her *Apollo* article. We asked him to buy them on our behalf and send them. The parcel arrived wrapped in brown paper and tied with knotted string in the old-fashioned way, which somehow heightened our impression that it contained a forgotten treasure from a lost culture, before padded envelopes and Sellotape, let alone the internet and electronic transmission.

Inside we found two small volumes, both compiled by the Rev. W. J. Loftie. The first was entitled *A Plea for Art in the House* and consisted of five chapters extolling the benefits of art as a part of the everyday environment, especially for children. It was clearly an earnest contribution to the growing Aesthetic Movement of the time when it was published in 1876. Robert had contributed four tail-piece woodcuts at the end of each section that represented the seasons. Two featured loving couples, walking hand in hand for spring and reclining by a lake, with the boy playing a lute, for summer. For autumn, the boy was sitting on the ground with his head bowed in a barren landscape while his love stood behind him in a cloak looking into the distance, apparently about to depart. The last illustration, for winter, was a skilful evocation of the bleakness of the season, with a figure struggling against an icy wind to open the door into a humble dwelling with sombre figures, perhaps children, gazing out from behind stone-mullioned windows. We were immediately interested in the fact that Robert was still drawn to the depiction of love subjects in 1875 or '76, and in the near certainty that the woodcuts were executed at Biddulph.

The second book was a sumptuous little volume bound in green leather with intricate tooling and heavily gilded page edges. The beautiful handmade paper was of a pale ivory colour. Beneath the title on the introductory page was written:

Compiled by Rev. W. J. Loftie, BA, FSA.

With illustrations by Robert Bateman

We turned the page and found a strange symbol of a divided circle surmounted by a double cross that stopped us dead (fig. 49). We had seen it before on Robert's date stone at Biddulph, but had never managed to discover its meaning since the stone was so weathered. This printed version was precise and clear, which allowed us to follow it up.

Fig. 49. A symbol we had seen before.

Fig. 50 (left). The surviving holy crown and orb with double cross which is preserved in the Hungarian Parliament Building.

Fig. 51 (right). St Stephen as portrayed in the Chronicum Pictum, *a fourteenth-century illustrated manuscript, showing the orb with double cross that became his heraldic badge.*

It transpired that the symbol represented the orb which formed part of the magnificent jewelled coronation regalia supplied by Pope Sylvester II to St Stephen, King of Hungary, the canonised founder of the Hungarian monarchy (fig. 50). The regalia, particularly the orb and 'holy crown' dedicated to the Virgin Mary, became intertwined with the legends of King Arthur by way of a surviving letter (c. 1025 AD) from St Stephen to his son Emeric, defining the virtues of Honour, Chastity, Humility and Patience to be pursued by a Christian king and his followers. The orb, or *globus cruciger*, surmounted by the double cross, became the heraldic badge of St Stephen, symbolising his dedication to establishing Christ as the *Salvator Mundi*, saviour of the whole world (fig. 51). King Arthur married Guinevere in St Stephen's Chapel at Camelot, and St Stephen's crown is included by Burne-Jones in his huge painting *The Sleep of Arthur in Avalon*.

Robert's inclusion of the symbolic orb and double crucifix in *The Latin Year* in 1873 and on his date stone at Biddulph in 1874 places him at the heart of the Arthurian cult dominated by Burne-Jones, who at that precise moment was completing *The Beguiling of Merlin*, perhaps his most celebrated canvas derived from the Morte D'Arthur legends. *The Latin Year* was a collection of poems, hymns and verses relating to the great festivals of the Christian year such as Christmas, Easter and the Ascension. They were all in Latin and, according to the index, were drawn from a variety of Christian sources dating from the sixth to the nineteenth centuries.

From the combination of its date and contents, I instantly understood what the purpose of this book was. I had been educated at Bloxham School, just outside

Banbury, founded in 1860 by a high church Anglican clergyman to further the aims of the Oxford Movement. This sought to invigorate the Church of England by studying and reintroducing much of the liturgy and symbolic ceremonial of the medieval Roman Catholic Church, so as to minimise, rather than emphasise, the differences between the two. Its founders were often known as Tractarians after the publication of *Tracts for the Times* in the 1840s. An important aspect of the *Tracts* was the exposition of the 'branch theory', which portrayed Greek Orthodoxy, Roman Catholicism and Anglicanism as branches of an essentially unified Christian Church.

The movement was heavily criticised and held in great suspicion by Methodists and indeed by many Anglicans for its Romanising influences on the church. It seemed incredible that Robert should have been part of such a publication – his father, James Bateman, was fanatically anti-Catholic and delivered sermons advocating traditional reformed practices as a lay preacher, and published stridently anti-Popish leaflets. Robert's small rectangular illustrations were extremely skilful, and for the most part very beautiful. The more of these exquisitely simple line drawings we saw, the more animated we became.

By luck we had stumbled across over twenty new images by Robert Bateman. We realised, at once, that these illustrations, whose whole purpose was to promote understanding between Protestants and Catholics, were the answer to our dilemma about what should fill the glass roundels. That they had been conceived and executed by Robert Bateman, of all people, was so uncanny that it really disturbed us. Despite spending so much of our time thinking about the creation of the chapel and the life of Robert Bateman, we had never even considered the possibility of a link between the two – the Civil War attack and the Victorian artist were two separate entities in our minds. What strange fate had brought Robert's own images to us now, at the very moment we needed them?

We knew that, to use them in the windows, we needed to enlarge the drawings and adapt them from rectangular to circular compositions. To achieve this we had to add small details to the edges. At first this felt like sacrilege. I wondered if Robert's disgruntled spirit would strike me down, but as I worked painstakingly on them I had a great feeling of enjoyment and fulfilment. No doubt it was all in my mind, but by the end I was sure he was there in those quiet hours of concentration, giving us his blessing (figs. 52–57).

Ubi crucifixerunt Eum.

Mors Illi ultra non dominabitur.

Magi ab Oriente.

*Figs. 52–54. Robert's woodcuts
for* The Latin Year: *Ubi
crucifixerunt Eum (top),
Mors Illi ultra non dominabitur
(centre) and Magi ab Oriente
(left).*

*Figs. 55–57 (opposite). Our
painted glass roundels derived
from them.*

Part 3

LOST IN THE VICARAGE

Fig. 58. The Deanery in the Cathedral Close at Lichfield, Caroline's childhood home.

Chapter 12

THE DEAN'S DAUGHTER

Robert's portrait of Caroline had already shattered our preconception of her as a middle-aged provincial rector's widow. Almost from the outset of our search, Caroline emerged as a cultured, elegant, glamorous and well-connected woman.

She was born in 1839, the eighth child of the Hon. Very Reverend Henry Edward Howard, Dean of Lichfield Cathedral, who was the sixth son of the 5th Earl of Carlisle, of Castle Howard in Yorkshire. By the time Caroline was born, the earldom had passed to the Dean's elder brother, her uncle George Howard, who was married to Georgiana Cavendish, daughter of the notorious Georgiana, Duchess of Devonshire. Two of Caroline's aunts were Baroness Cawdor of Castle Martin, and Elisabeth, Duchess of Rutland, the builder of Belvoir Castle and mistress of the Duke of York, second son of King George III. In the wider family, the Howards were not prolific begetters of children so only a single cousin, an only child, stood between the earldom passing to her elder brother and thus into her immediate family.

Her mother was Henrietta Elizabeth Wright, daughter of Ichabod Wright, a wealthy banker of Mapperley Hall, Northamptonshire.

The Dean's family was large, consisting of five boys and five girls. They lived in considerable splendour dividing their time between the Deanery, a fine Georgian edifice in the Cathedral Close at Lichfield (fig. 58), their country property Dean House at Brewood, and Donnington Rectory in Shropshire, which was held by the Dean as a secondary living. Contemporary records indicate that Caroline's mother used Donnington primarily as a place to go for her confinements, since most of her children were born there.

The Dean was a highly respected scholar who published English translations of biblical texts from the Greek and the poems of Claudian from the Latin. He was largely responsible for initiating the restoration of Lichfield Cathedral between 1842 and 1873. Censuses of the period show a full complement of domestic staff at the Deanery, including a butler, footman, cook, ladies' maids, parlour maids, coachmen,

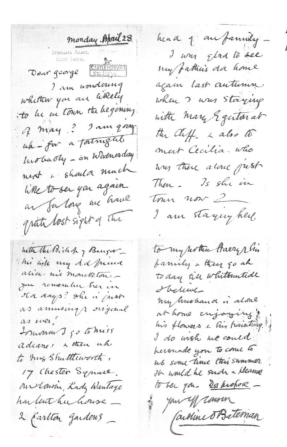

Fig. 59. 'Do propose': Caroline's letter inviting George Howard to Benthall Hall.

etc. Caroline was educated at home by a governess and grew up into a strikingly attractive, tall girl with fine blonde hair and a very good figure.

In the archives at Castle Howard we discovered a wonderful, animated letter from around the turn of the century written by Caroline Bateman to her cousin and contemporary, George Howard, 9th Earl of Carlisle, which gives a vivid sense of the verve and charm of its writer (fig. 59). She is writing to tell George that she is going to London, and to try to arrange to meet him there. She is staying with an old friend, Alice Monckton, whom he will remember from 'old days', but is going to London to join her younger brother Henry, a vicar, who has been lent a town house, 2 Carlton Gardens, by their cousin Lady Wantage. She mentions having recently been to York-shire and visited 'my father's old house', Castle Howard. She ends by begging George to visit her and her husband (who she describes as at home with his paintings and his flowers). Caroline's intimate, easy tone indicates that she and George have been close since childhood. Her friend, Alice Monckton, was brought up at Stretton Hall in Brewood, in the same village as Dean House. In the census of 1891 we found Caroline staying in Brewood Hall as the guest of Alice's two unmarried sisters, Mary and Leonora. Caroline obviously had a close, lifelong bond with the Moncktons.

Finding the letter to George Howard represented a decisive moment in our search for Caroline, both historically and personally. Nearly every reference opened up areas of research that revealed her world. When we checked the census returns to find Caroline and Robert it was interesting that in the next return for 1901 Caroline was a guest at Lockinge House, Berkshire, the country home of Lord and Lady Wantage. Lady Wantage proved to be another larger-than-life Edwardian personality. At her death in 1920 she was described as reputedly the richest woman in England. She was a towering figure in the art world who bequeathed a large part of her collection to the National Gallery. A copy of a painting done in 1889 by Henry Jamyn Brooks shows a large crowd attending a private view of the Old Masters Exhibition at the Royal Academy in 1888 (fig. 60). A key identifies the people present, which include all the artistic luminaries of the day: in a red coat in the foreground, being greeted by the President of the Academy, is Lady Wantage. Small wonder that the town house she was lending Caroline's brother was 2 Carlton Gardens, which fronted The Mall and the gardens of Marlborough House.

Before long another fascinating connection came to light. Lady Wantage's husband was the brother of Sir Coutts Lindsey, th e builder and founder of the Grosvenor Gallery which opened in 1877 to give a lavish new setting for the avant-garde painters who had previously exhibited at the Dudley. The Grosvenor caused a sensation when it opened and instantly turned Burne-Jones into a lionised celebrity; his wife Georgina said that, from the opening night, life was never the same for them again.

Fig. 60. Henry Jamyn Brooks, A Private View of the Old Masters Exhibition Royal Academy 1888, *1889, oil on canvas, 154.5 × 271.5 cm, National Portrait Gallery, London.*

It had begun to puzzle us why Robert had not been invited to exhibit at the Grosvenor until five years after the opening. He eventually showed his first picture there in 1881, two years before his marriage to Caroline.

In the excitement of discovering the evident closeness of Caroline to Lady Wantage, we had overlooked one vital phrase in her letter. She describes Lady Wantage as 'our cousin'. We thought this meant some kind of cousin to herself and George Howard, that is, on her father's side. We set out on a gruelling search for connections between the two families, which became ever more tenuous and convoluted until eventually we gave up. Then, as often happens, once we had stopped looking we suddenly saw the words in a different light: what if Caroline had meant her and her brother's cousin – that is, on her mother's side? Almost immediately everything became clear.

Lady Wantage was not a Howard – she was the only child of Harriet Wright, the sister of Henrietta Wright, Caroline's mother. The richest woman in England, the owner of 2 Carlton Gardens and Lockinge House, a fabulous estate in Berkshire of over 20,000 acres, and the owner of one of the most distinguished private art collections ever accumulated was Caroline's first cousin.

George Howard proved to be an equally unexpected and intriguing personality, particularly in the context of Caroline's later life. Born in 1843 to a grandson of the 5th Earl, he was a generation below Caroline but only three years her junior. The Dean's youngest children – Caroline, Elizabeth and Henry – were the only members of his wider family similar in age; he was an only child, so the relationship with his cousins was important to him as he grew up.

For someone destined from an early age to inherit prodigious wealth and power, he was a remarkable personality. Even as an Eton schoolboy he was gentle, unassertive and talkative. One of his tutor's reports read:

> It would be the greatest possible advantage to him to associate with manly, full-grown boys whom he would respect, so far as to be more reserved in their presence than he is with his present associates – and I particularly wish that he would be in the boats, which is nearly equivalent to being in the general society of the school.

George could not be persuaded to take any interest in 'manly' pursuits. From an early age he had a single, overriding interest and ambition: he loved drawing and aspired to be an artist. His tutor considered this most irregular for a boy with his prospects:

> If he spent his cash on boating and spent on the river some of the hours he gives to drawing he would become a regular Eton boy, none the worse for the special accomplishment.

George never lost his desire to become an artist. He was married at twenty to Rosalind Stanley, and produced a huge family of children. The couple mixed with all the artists of the day and became close personal friends of Burne-Jones and his wife Georgina. In 1868 they bought a building site at 1 Palace Green, Kensington. The house George built there became something of a cause célèbre: it was designed by Philip Webb and decorated throughout by William Morris, Burne-Jones and Robert's friend, Walter Crane. When it was finished, it became a mecca for the advanced art world in which George moved.

George showed little interest in the management of his great estates, or in politics. His continued determination to pursue art (he dedicated every possible moment to study under Alphonse Legros) became an important element in a real rift with his radical and ambitious wife. Rosalind was a fanatical Liberal who passionately espoused good causes from temperance to women's suffrage. As their biographer Virginia Surtees makes clear:

> Her own seedlings of ambition were developing with startling rapidity while George's were nonexistent; if he had any aspiration, it was solely to achieve greater proficiency in oil painting.

The longer this went on the more frustrated Rosalind became, as she confided in her diary:

> He has not any inventive genius and can one be a great painter without that? I think he is getting on but I don't know that he will ever be a really first-rate painter, and yet I see that daily he is becoming more engrossed by painting. He thinks and talks of nothing else now; he seems to care less about politics. All the friends he seeks out and cares to talk to, if they are not artists, are people who care to talk art.

Fig. 61. Milstead Manor, Kent, Henrietta Howard's home during her widowhood, from where Caroline was married.

George Howard failed to obtain entry to the Royal Academy Schools but in 1868 he had his first picture hung in a public exhibition at the Dudley Gallery. That year Robert Bateman had five paintings in the same exhibition. Following this the two men had paintings in the Dudley at the same time on three consecutive years in 1872, '73 and '74. This was the man that Caroline was writing to after he had come into his inheritance as the Earl of Carlisle and become the owner of Castle Howard and Naworth Castle.

Whilst George was creating a sensation in London building and decorating his new house, Caroline's father, Dean Howard, became gravely ill and died. He is commemorated by a tomb set in a gothic niche in Lichfield Cathedral upon which his full-size recumbent effigy rests. The next year Caroline and her mother moved south to Milstead Manor, a beautiful half-timbered house in Kent (fig. 61).

By then Caroline was an attractive woman of thirty with fabulous connections, particularly in the art world, from both sides of her illustrious family. It was high time for her to marry and take her place amid the glittering aristocratic connoisseurs who clustered around her family at Castle Howard, 1 Palace Green and 2 Carlton Gardens on The Mall.

Chapter 13

A COUNTRY PARSON

W hat appears to have happened, however, is that Caroline settled down to a life of spinsterhood – until suddenly, in 1876, at the age of thirty-seven, she married Charles Philip Wilbraham, a country parson almost thirty years her senior, who served a small mining and agricultural community in North Staffordshire. Such an age gap was not unknown in the mid-nineteenth century, but having seen Caroline's portrait and 'heard her voice', this development did not seem quite consistent with the woman we had got to know. So we set out to discover all we could about Reverend Wilbraham.

Charles and his brother Richard Wilbraham were born at Rode Hall in Cheshire. They both joined the army and were sent out to Canada by their regiment in 1838, when Charles was twenty-eight. They travelled extensively, crossing into the United States as far south as the Hudson River. Charles met a missionary whose toughness and dedication so impressed him that he decided to be ordained on his return to England and dedicate the rest of his life to the ministry. This he did, in 1844, and became rector of the parish of Audley, four miles from his family home where his older half-brother Randle was the squire. Since he was unmarried, his sister Fanny kept house for him.

Charles was clearly an energetic and devoted rector who had a dynamic effect on his parish. The village was dominated by coal pits which gave rise to regular injuries and fatal accidents. It was not a wealthy parish so he was not well paid, yet he and his sister started a school, which he subsidised from his own stipend. They also put in hand much-needed renovations and repairs to the church. He had been a tall, lean, fine-looking man, but this dedicated life took its toll. In a portrait of him in the early 1870s he looks a trifle sad. He has lost his hair and does not appear young for his age (fig. 62). He retained a lifelong love of travel. He regularly took trips of two to three months to exotic places such as India, Greenland and America, giving lectures on his return.

Fig. 62. Rev. Charles Philip Wilbraham, painted about the time of his marriage to Caroline Howard, oil on canvas, private collection.

In middle age he had suffered a thwarted love affair. The family archives contain an angry letter from Lord Egerton of Tatton, a wealthy and influential relative, to Randle Wilbraham:

> I have been excessively surprised and annoyed by being informed that Capt. Tarleton has been openly announcing in the Naval Club the intended marriage of your brother Charles to my daughter Beatrix. I think it therefore right to tell you that a day or two ago I again expressed to him in answer to a letter requesting me to allow him to pay his addresses to her, that I could never give my consent to it. As a parent I do not consider myself justified in allowing her, at her age, so young in every way, to marry a man near thirty years older than herself.

The letter is dated 1863, when Charles was fifty-three years old. Randle replied in Charles's defence that he was 'high principled, kind hearted and certainly very clever' and asked, not unreasonably, whether Egerton had even consulted his daughter. Lord Egerton replied that subsequent reflection had not induced him to alter his opinion that 'a girl of twenty-two is not a fit judge in such matters.'

Beatrix was eventually married, unhappily, to the Hon. Lionel Tollemache of Peckforton Castle in Cheshire, but there is some evidence that Charles's love for her might have been reciprocated. After her death in 1927 she left a generous legacy to the Wilbrahams in his memory, which allowed them to carry out much-needed repairs to their family home. In recognition of this they inscribed a handsome portico:

Ex Legato

Beatrix Tollemache

MCXXVII

Despite his devotion to his parish, Charles resigned as vicar of Audley in January 1874 and moved to Penkridge, a large parish about forty miles to the south. Given that he was the heir to Rode Hall as Randle had no children, this seems a radical departure for a man in his mid-sixties. He left the vicarage that had been his home for over thirty years and the family estate where he had been brought up and which remained the nucleus of family life for his closest relations. He abandoned the school and the restored church that he had rescued from virtual dereliction, and then two years later got married to a woman of thirty-seven.

To try to get a clearer understanding of the surprising events leading up to the marriage of Caroline and Charles Wilbraham, we arranged with Sir Richard Baker-Wilbraham to look at Charles's journal, which was kept in the library at Rode Hall. It was a large, leather-bound volume, which was on the whole factual and prosaic, majoring on texts for sermons and family occasions. It was about two-thirds filled, but in it we found no clue as to why Charles had left Audley. He simply announced his resignation from the living on 30 November 1873, recorded a first visit to

Penkridge on 7 December, the end of his ministry at Audley on 25 January 1874 and his induction at Penkridge on 1 February 1874. The journal entries continued meticulously in exactly the same format as for the previous thirty years, until 23 August of that year when, with no explanation, they ceased and were never resumed. Charles remained vicar of Penkridge until his death in 1879, but abandoned the ingrained habit of his working lifetime just eighteen months before his marriage to Caroline. He never mentions her name, or his betrothal to her, or their wedding day, or the marriage service itself. It seems extraordinary that an ordained priest, who had maintained so painstaking a record of his vocation, should fail to acknowledge his entry into the sacred state of matrimony, or offer a word of thanks for this almost miraculous turn of events so late in his life.

Charles Philip Wilbraham married Caroline Octavia Howard on 15 February 1876, at Milstead in Kent, after which they settled down as the vicar and vicar's wife at Penkridge in Staffordshire for the next three years. We were left with no explanation of the events leading up to the marriage of these two apparently incompatible personalities, thirty years apart in age, by then living at opposite ends of the country. Could Charles really have been in love with Caroline, if he omitted even to mention her name in the record of his life and work? And could the vivacious, self-confident Caroline, who was later to inspire forty years of unashamed devotion from a creative genius, really have chosen to commit her life to an elderly parson unable to declare his love in words, even to his private journal?

One aspect of the story especially intrigued us. Charles's life-changing decision to leave Audley was made in 1873–4, at the very moment that Robert Bateman returned from London to live in Biddulph, a mere five miles away. What role, if any, did Caroline Howard, who was destined to be wife to both men during the course of the next ten years, play in these puzzling decisions?

Chapter 14

A FURTIVE MARRIAGE AND
A GRAND FUNERAL

The strange fact about this unlikely marriage was that no one, from Charles Wilbraham's descendants to Amanda Kavanagh, in her research and subsequent article, appeared to have even the most rudimentary information as to why it came about. Caroline was thirty-seven years old, so her childbearing years were coming to an end. Perhaps marriage to a respectable clergyman, albeit much older, who was heir to a comfortable family estate, might have seemed preferable to the prospect of a long middle and old age as a patronised maiden aunt. What seems odd, however, is that this same person, shortly after Charles's death, married a strikingly handsome, unconventional artist, three years her junior, and embraced a dazzling life at the heart of social and artistic society. Similarly, why did a man who had committed the prime years of his life to the unselfish pastoral care of a poor mining community abandon it without explanation at the age of sixty-six, and marry a woman half his age?

Milstead Church in Kent, the site of Charles and Caroline's wedding, is a modest and pretty flint structure, whose stubby tower and tiny, single-cell nave convey a true sense of the simplicity of rural life. In the 1870s it sat at the heart of a little cluster of lanes that made up the village of just over 200 people, opposite the rambling half-timbered manor house to which Elisabeth Harriet Howard had retired, with her two unmarried daughters, after the death of the Dean in 1868.

The scale of the church makes it clear that the wedding must have been tiny by upper-class Victorian standards (fig. 63). The church would have struggled to accommodate Caroline's nine siblings and their families, let alone the hordes of titled aunts, cousins, nephews, nieces, godparents and clerical dignitaries that would normally attend such an occasion. Perhaps this helps to explain why only Caroline's mother and a second cousin, Beatrice Lascelles (who later that year married Frederick Temple, a future Archbishop of Canterbury), signed the marriage certificate as her

*Fig. 63. Milkmaid minimalism: the tiny village church in which
Caroline Howard and Charles Wilbraham were married.*

witnesses. Charles's only supporter was Henry Littleton, the third son of Lord
Hatherton, the patron of his new living at Penkridge. Henry Littleton could scarcely
have been more than an acquaintance: he was thirty-four years of age and only in
England for a few months' leave from his home in Australia.

Not a single member of the Wilbraham family was present – not Randle, the
squire of Rode Hall, nor Charles's younger brother Richard, nor even his beloved
sister Fanny, who supported him so devotedly in his ministry at Audley. Yet the
marriage would have been of great significance to the Wilbrahams – Randle and his
wife Sybella had no children and were nearing seventy. Richard had produced only
one child, a girl, before the death of his wife some twenty years earlier. Thus there
was no male heir to Rode Hall and the Wilbraham estates. Charles's marriage to an
eminently well-connected woman of thirty-seven held out the distinct possibility of
an heir to secure the estate's future.

If the marriage represented an escape from demeaning spinsterhood on one side,
and the acquisition of a beautiful younger bride on the other, why was it not a cause
for joyful celebration, in a setting commensurate with their exalted social position?
The richness of their clerical connections gave them a wide choice – St Michael's,
Penkridge, where they were to spend their married life; Audley, the site of Charles's

life's work; All Saints, Odd Rode, Randle Wilbraham's new church designed by Gilbert Scott where Charles was later to be buried, or even the sublime magnificence of Lichfield Cathedral, where the pale marble effigy of the Dean could be felt to have bestowed his benediction upon their union.

The marriage certificate held one further oddity. The ceremony was not conducted by Canon Henry Hilton, the inhabitant of the rectory, the only establishment in the village comparable in status to the manor house. It seems strange that on what must have been a momentous local occasion – the marriage in his parish church of an aristocratic neighbour – that Canon Hilton should have elected not to officiate, but to delegate the ceremony. The cumulative effect of all these discoveries was to suggest a sense of privacy or even secrecy around Caroline's marriage to Charles Wilbraham.

We wanted to try to understand why Charles's move to Penkridge had come about. If, in 1874, two years before his marriage, Charles had met and fallen in love with Caroline, might he have made the move to a better-paid living with a larger, more commodious vicarage? The vicarage at Penkridge was indeed a large Victorian pile built by Charles's predecessor, Rev. Fell, and described subsequently as Fell's Folly on account of its scale and pretentiousness (fig. 64).

Fig. 64. Penkridge Parish Church, where Charles went for a quiet life?

The living of Penkridge was controlled by Edward Richard Littleton, Lord Hatherton of nearby Teddesley Hall. Since a Littleton was witness to the wedding we assumed there must have been some connection between the two families. We were fortunate to find Bob Maddocks, who was researching the life of Lord Hatherton, and who was able to supply valuable information, letters and diary extracts.

On 5 November 1873 Lord Hatherton had visited the Sneyd family at their home, Keele Hall, for a grand dinner party attended by, among others, Mr and Mrs William Gladstone and the Rev. Charles Wilbraham. We already had a hint that Charles was on friendly terms with the great Liberal prime minister, so this was interesting corroboration of their intimacy. It gave an insight into Charles's broad education and intelligence. Apparently, after the dinner, Charles had, without invitation, proposed himself to Lord Hatherton for the living of Penkridge:

> Nov 17th 1873. Mr Wilbraham came here for a night from Audley (His Living) to see Penkridge church and parsonage. He had surprised me at Keele by leaving a note on his departure, saying that he would be willing to take the Living of Penkridge for 7 years, thus leaving it vacant for Cecil [Lord Hatherton's son] if his church views were then such that I could appoint him to it.

This appears to imply that Cecil was attracted to the High Church, Oxford Movement ritualists, then popular among young clerics, and that his father wanted to give him time to come to his senses before awarding the parish to him. No doubt the dilemma was discussed at the dinner, but Lord Hatherton was clearly surprised by Charles's unsolicited proposal to take the living after a lifetime in his own parish.

His next journal entry destroyed our conjecture on Charles's motivation for the move:

> Nov 18th. Drove Wilbraham to Penkridge to see the Church and Parsonage. He makes a great sacrifice of income by exchanging to Penkridge as he not only bought the advowson of Audley but has expended some £500.00 on the house; added to which the income from Audley is £600.00 a year while that for Penkridge is under £300.00.

This deepened rather than explained the mystery of Charles's motives. The advowson was the legal right to nominate a vicar or rector to a particular parish, making the holder the effective patron of the living. By buying it, Charles had protected his right to remain in the parish for the rest of his working life, and also acquired the right to nominate his successor. He had also expended a large sum of money on adapting the vicarage to suit his needs. Surely his intention must have been to provide a secure, comfortable future for himself at Audley, within the community he had served all his life. If his brother died before him, he could move the five miles to Rode Hall and install a successor of his own choice to continue his work in the parish. What had caused him to abandon these expensive and carefully organised arrangements in favour of a parish forty miles away, involving a drastic reduction in salary?

Whatever his motives, Charles carried out these radical changes at breakneck speed. From 5 November 1873, when he made the proposal to Lord Hatherton, it was barely a fortnight before he visited Penkridge on the 18th and only a further twelve days before he recorded in his own journal that he had announced his resig-nation from Audley. Lord Hatherton's journal even suggests that he may have risked jumping the gun, as it was not until 3 January 1874, a full month later, that he secured the new appointment:

> Rev'd C Wilbraham to Teddesley (Hall). I have appointed him to the living of Penkridge vice [in place of] Fell resigned on account of ill health.

The breathtaking pace continued, with Charles taking his first service at Penkridge the next day.

Charles and his four unmarried sisters – Sybylla, Fanny, Harriet and Emily – and Bishop Selwyn of Lichfield and Mrs Selwyn gathered at Teddesley Hall for Charles's induction on 1 February. We wondered, for a moment, if the haste might have been driven by some sort of scandal or ill-feeling between the vicar and his flock at Audley. But the celebrations in the village at Charles's marriage two years later, with flags, bellringing and dancing to Mr Coomer's Newcastle Quadrille Band, all faithfully recorded in the local newspaper, suggests a deep fund of affection and goodwill towards him, despite his absence.

Another possibility was that Charles had already met Caroline, perhaps at Stretton Hall, the home of her lifelong friends the Monktons, a mere four miles from Penkridge, and fallen in love. Had he been unable to resist the chance to be where he knew he could meet her, and grasped the opportunity that presented itself at the dinner at Keele Hall? Had he simply thrown away his old life for what he felt was his last chance of happiness, after the anguish of his frustrated love for Beatrix Egerton ten years before?

It seems surprising that, at sixty-four, he should be so much at the mercy of his emotions, but it was at least a credible explanation for the reckless series of events that began in November 1873, continued with his unexpected marriage in 1876 and culminated in his sudden death in 1879.

Charles seemed to have embraced the challenge of his new job with energy. By March 1874 Lord Hatherton comments, perhaps with some reservations:

> Church at Penkridge. W[ilbraham] making great alterations within. Old reading desk and pulpit removed and low pulpit replacing them. Cheadle, the clerk, to be placed I know not where. He looks sadly put out, though he is assured by his vicar that he ought to be much pleased by the changes.

Evidently the changes stirred up enough local controversy for Charles to issue a statement in the *Staffordshire Advertiser* that they 'involved no tendency to Ritualism, to which he had a decided aversion'. Presumably this met with the approval of Lord Hatherton, with his anxiety about his son Cecil's religious proclivities.

By May Charles was instigating special collections to finance his programme of changes. At a meeting in the Bishop's Palace in Lichfield in July he was effectively promoted by being appointed Rural Dean of Penkridge. He became a familiar figure covering the large parish on one of his two horses, Brobdignag ('to distinguish him from other nags!'), or Jacob ('to distinguish him from other cobs!'). One senses from the tone of Lord Hatherton's journal that his lordship may not have quite approved of Charles's levity with his parishioners. However, it is clear that he was generally on good terms with his patron and he was a frequent dinner guest at Teddesley Hall.

We were disappointed to find no reaction from Lord and Lady Hatherton to Charles's wedding in 1876; they were abroad in North Africa for over six months that year and made no comment on the marriage in letters or journals on their return. The first indication that the marriage had occurred was a dining list for 25 August 1876 which included 'Mr & Mrs Wilbraham'.

What was more perplexing was that despite the continual contact between Charles and the Hathertons at services, committees, civic ceremonies and private dinners there had never been the slightest hint or whisper in their letters and journals that their close friend had fallen in love with a beautiful younger woman and was about to marry. When they left, the marriage was only days away, in February. Marriage and matchmaking were part of the warp and weave of social speculation and gossip. With her large family of children, Lady Hatherton must have been alert to every nuance of behaviour that signalled the onset of a liaison. In the almost incestuous atmosphere of small-town genteel society, a romantic entanglement between the elderly vicar and an attractive younger woman would have been a topic of absorbing fascination to the Hathertons. Their curiosity to meet her would have been recorded by invitations to tea being issued, so that she could be vetted. That none of this occurred suggests that Charles must have kept every step of his courtship secret from them up to the very last moment. What his reasons were we could not guess, but at least it was consistent with the obscurity of the wedding ceremony itself.

After their return, the Hatherton letters and journals paint a vivid picture of Charles and Caroline, and their relationship to each other. Charles is clearly the more dominant and opinionated of the two. Fond of him as they undoubtedly are, there is an undertow of mockery about his continuous bombast about his travels and the repetitiveness of his stories. On 1 July 1877 Lord Hatherton describes them in a letter to his son Will:

> Parochial matters are going on much the same as usual, as do our vicar and his wife – living in the happy delusion that all they do is right and all approved of by their parishioners. He is still uxorious . . .

This description of them as being a little self-satisfied and out of touch is character-istic of many of the entries. However, the description of Charles as continuing to be 'uxorious', meaning adoring, besotted and protective towards his wife, is highly revealing. It gives a vivid picture of how Charles behaved towards Caroline, and how intense their relationship was perceived to be, fifteen months after their marriage. This is surprising as Charles is certainly not seen as young for his years. There are frequent references to his eccentricities and occasional cantankerousness, causing Lady Hatherton sometimes to strike a slightly exasperated note: 'Old Wilbraham has repeated all his American stories to Lady Fortescue – but one, I think, was new!'

His eccentricities mainly focus on his mania for using an outside plunge bath he had built at the vicarage, even in the depths of winter. This practice was universally blamed for his death. On 17 December 1879 Lord Hatherton wrote:

> Our poor friend and vicar W died today. I can have no doubt he brought on this illness which terminated in his death by bathing in the plunge bath, of which he was so proud, while he had a severe cold upon him. . . . on Wednesday 10th he broke the ice some 3 or 4 inches thick in his plunge bath of which he boasted in a letter to us in London. We used to laugh at his eccentricities. He was fond of alluding to his travels and never preached that he did not refer to some place or thing which 'I myself have seen', a phrase which usually called forth a smile from his congregation. He was fond of society and talking, chiefly of himself and his travels and told the same stories so frequently that those who knew him well could not help smiling at their repetition. But he was genial and kind-hearted and, according to his own views, did his duty in his parish, though frequently about on visits.

Lady Hatherton gave a clearer idea of the slight ridicule with which they regarded him and the truly obsessive nature of some of his behaviour:

> Poor Mr Wilbraham's death after a few days illness. He did insane things – as to cold bathing with a cold on him! Visiting Stallington, he could not do with ordinary means of ablution and actually went down to a pond to bathe – this in bitter weather – it must have been iced over. Humanly speaking he killed himself. Everyone is sorry and we feel much remorse recollecting mockeries of him.

Up until this pivotal tragedy, Caroline remained a slightly shadowy figure in Penkridge, her own personality subordinated to her kindly but garrulous and opin-ionated husband. She is never reported as questioning his proposals for change, either in the church or wider parish business, and was perceived as sharing his slightly complacent conviction that he was universally respected. On the few occasions when she is mentioned alone it is in relation to her gifts for playing the piano and singing. There is never the slightest intimation that she was exasperated by the tedious repe-tition of her husband's stories, although she must have been subjected to them more than anyone else. Her patience and loyalty, it seems, were repaid by his devotion.

Still, it is difficult to imagine how someone of her age would have come to terms with the more curmudgeonly and eccentric aspects of his behaviour. Did she regard his fetish for immersing himself in frozen pools in the dead of winter as exhilarating exercise or the deranged obsession of an old man beginning to lose his reason? She must have known that for a man of sixty-nine the practice posed a serious threat to his health, if not his life. When the final crisis struck on 10 December with the onset of seven days of 'inflammation of the lungs' (pneumonia on his death certificate), did Caroline share Lady Hatherton's view that 'humanly speaking' he had 'killed himself'?

Whereas the Wilbraham family had appeared to ignore Charles's wedding in 1876, in December 1879 they were very much present and taking control of events. His devoted sister Fanny appears as 'informant' on the death certificate, witnessing that she was 'present at the death'. Charles's younger brother Richard, by this time General Sir Richard, supervised all the arrangements to convey the body to the newly built Odd Rode church on the family estate.

The departure of the body from Penkridge was clearly a significant local occasion, as Lord Hatherton records in his journal:

Dec 22nd 1879.
Most of the principal inhabitants of Penkridge and the principal adjoining farmers with Foden and myself met the remains of our late vicar as they were taken from his house to the station and accompanied them there. Sir Richard Wilbraham took charge of the arrangements . . .

This ceremonial reclaiming of Charles's body by the Wilbrahams after six years of voluntary exile has a sense of deliberate symbolism. They clearly wanted him to be commemorated at the place where he had given a lifetime of service rather than to perpetuate the memory of his sudden decision to remove himself to Penkridge. The funeral service and interment at Rode allowed him to be mourned by those who had known and loved him all his life.

One wonders how daunting this process was for Caroline as she entered Randle Wilbraham's new church, crowded with Charles's tearful sisters, cousins and friends. Ostensibly she was the chief mourner, but how short her three-year marriage must have seemed to his lifelong companions.

With the funeral and Christmas over, Caroline wasted little time in organising a fairly comprehensive conclusion to this phase of her life. She sold almost all the contents of the vicarage on 25 February 1880. Lady Hatherton attributed this to her having been left short of money:

The sale of things at the vicarage took place today and I am told was a very good one, which I am glad of for poor Mrs W's sake. She is poorly, tho' not a pauper at all. I suppose he could make no settlement – he left her everything he had, however. The splendid bed inlaid with ivory and woods was sold for £70.

Caroline's persona now begins to emerge more clearly, as the poor but dignified widow driven to sell beautiful things by her husband's inability to provide an income for her from the residue of his meagre living. She is clearly sad, but there is an over-riding perception of her as bravely coming to terms with her future as a modest, retiring widow, who has decided to live out her days in 'a little house in London'. One must question whether she was being quite open with the Hathertons about the prodigious wealth of many of her relations. Perhaps she was afraid that unless they thought the sale of the contents of the vicarage was driven by financial necessity they might have been shocked by it.

After the sale she went to stay with her friends the Moncktons at Stretton Hall, in the nearby village of Brewood. During Caroline's farewell visit to Penkridge Lady Hatherton wrote to her son:

> Mrs W is being very nice … tendrie very often, otherwise wonderfully, as it seems to me, composed and fairly cheerful. She is looking for a small London house. She begged to be remembered to you.

Like 'poorly', 'tendrie' is clearly part of Lady Hatherton's personal patois, this time conveying a state of pensive, wistful sadness after her bereavement. It is a lovely little snapshot of Caroline that is easy to relate to the gentle, dignified figure in Robert's portrait of her.

We next encounter Caroline Octavia Wilbraham in the census of 1881. By then she was head of her own household at 14 Upper Berkeley Street, a fine Georgian house on five floors in the heart of Mayfair. She is being visited by her mother, replete with butlers, footmen and lady's maid. 'Tendrie' she may still have been, but 'poorly' – only relatively so!

Part 4

A LOST LOVE STORY

Fig. 65. Robert Bateman, Heloise and Abelard, *1879,*
oil on canvas, 50.8 × 62.2 cm, private collection.

Chapter 15

HELOISE AND ABELARD

One June evening Robert Bateman made another intervention in our lives that brought home to me just how disturbing his slumbering spirit might become. His name appeared on the list of a forthcoming sale at Christie's in London. The oil painting *Heloise and Abelard* (fig. 65), previously known only from a black-and-white photograph, had been discovered in the estate of Lincoln Kerstein, co-founder of the New York Ballet and a pivotal figure in post-war American cultural life.

Before we had even seen an image, Brian and I understood the challenge the painting presented to us. The reserve was £20,000–£30,000. Heloise and Abelard were about to force us to evaluate the true depth of our admiration for Bateman and our commitment to his being part of our lives. As a matter of fact we had not been over-enthusiastic about this painting when we saw it reproduced in Amanda Kavanagh's article. There was something staid and contrived about the scene of the two lovers reclining beside an idealised lake, surrounded by the fairly predictable detritus of romantic encounters such as lutes, baskets of fruit, fading roses and sheets of music. The characteristic Bateman stillness so haunting in *The Pool of Bethesda* here seemed a little mournful and inappropriate to adolescent lovers in their moment of bliss.

Since the precise depiction of the subject and the strong, clear design were reminiscent of *Bethesda*, we had imagined a similarly severe, controlled palette of subtly contrasted neutral colours. Our first glance at the coloured reproduction of *Heloise and Abelard* was a shock. The whole impact of this image was delivered through the gorgeous intensity of the interplay between the clarets, maroons and petrol blues of its foreground elements and the soft recessive landscape against which they are set.

We realised from the date, 1879, that it had almost certainly been painted at Biddulph Old Hall. It provided further evidence of Bateman's obsessive depiction of lovers, but as ever with him the loveliness of the surface texture, the beauty of the setting and the accumulated objects of delight could not dispel the preoccupied,

THE LOST PRE-RAPHAELITE *Part 4: A Lost Love Story*

internal sadness of the participants, trapped within their own unspoken thoughts. Even the beautifully expressive dog, the symbol of faithfulness, stared away out of the composition as if haunted by sad memories.

The true story of the medieval French lovers Heloise and Abelard was preserved by the intense letters they sent each other after their self-imposed separation, revealing a physical and spiritual longing that persisted unaltered through long years of loneliness. The scholar Abelard was Heloise's teacher, but her wit and questing intelligence put her intellectually on a par with him. They became lovers and had to flee Paris for Brittany after Heloise became pregnant. Her uncle, a canon of Notre Dame, had Abelard brutally attacked and castrated, as an appropriate retribution for his heinous crime. Heloise fled to a convent at Argenteuil where she gave birth to a son. However, she and Abelard could not reconcile their compulsive physical desire with their deeply held faith. They felt that they must offer their most valuable worldly possession, their relationship, as an act of repentance for falling short of their spiritual ideals. They separated and entered closed monastic communities. Heloise had to give up her adored child. She was utterly desolate and inconsolable, knowing she would never see him again.

They only met once more, years later, at a religious ceremony. They agreed it was their youthful experience of complete human love that had enabled them to grow spiritually and comprehend divine love in later life. They promised to remain true to the truth of their love and stay 'forever one'. They never met again, but the letters they exchanged have endured through the centuries as testament to the heroic invincibility of human love. Centuries later, Napoleon's Empress Josephine had their bodies exhumed and reburied at the Père Lachaise cemetery in Paris so that they could rest eternally together.

The Christie's catalogue pointed out some anomalies between the historical story and Robert's painting, initialled and dated 1879:

> On the face of it, the subject and its treatment hardly seem to fit. The famous star-crossed lovers . . . lived in late eleventh- and early twelfth-century France. Bateman's figures seem to belong to sixteenth-century Venice. The setting recalls some Italian Renaissance painting, if not indeed the work of Capability Brown, while Abelard, if that is who he is, has matinée idol good looks. It is hard to see this curiously modern figure as one of the greatest schoolmen of the Middle Ages.

One could not quarrel with this assessment: not only does Abelard seem strangely glamorous and contemporary, but the background does indeed have the uncannily familiar contours of an English landscape park.

The catalogue notes ascribed these apparent anomalies to 'the notoriously eccentric character of Bateman's work' which frequently made visual allusions to the Renaissance masters. However, the author considered that the quirks were outweighed by the symbolism of the objects depicted which confirmed the traditional identification of the subject by referencing the profound conflicts at the heart of the original story.

> The presence of the stone cupid underlies the amorous relationship between the two protagonists, while a host of other symbols points to themes that are central to the tragic story of Heloise and Abelard, notably redemption and the conflict between spiritual and carnal love. They include the Horacian injunction 'Carpe Diem' (Redeem the Day) inscribed on the sundial.

The biographical information on Bateman was clearly derived from Amanda Kavanagh's article and, although much of it was familiar, several things aroused our curiosity. First, Robert's selection of this subject in 1879 continued his earlier fascination with themes of love and lovers begun in 1873 with *Paolo and Francesca* and *Reading of Love*. While Heloise and Abelard might be considered fertile ground for romantic painters, the way Robert chose to portray the scene, with the two figures surrounded by highly symbolic objects (the wilting sunflower, the faithful dog, the butterfly, the apples, the rose bush, etc.) yet lost in thought, suggests that it is his awareness of their tragic future that preoccupies the artist rather than this blissful moment.

Secondly, the freedom he had taken with the historical interpretation of the story suggested that his intention was that we should empathise with the emotional and spiritual experience of the characters. He clearly had no interest in including fashionable medieval details which might detract from the immediacy of the couple's inner conflict. What had motivated and enabled him to portray the complex and contradictory emotions of these ill-fated lovers unless, to some extent, he identified with their situation and feelings himself?

Thirdly, what was the meaning of the roman numerals and the motto on the Cupid separate from the artist's initialling and dating of the picture? In a painting where every object had a symbolic meaning, they had to be important and yet, as the Christie's catalogue acknowledged, their significance remained a mystery.

At one level the quotation from the Roman poet Horace seemed a fairly predictable carved embellishment on a sundial. However, the numerals are placed immediately above the quotation and given equal prominence with it, strongly suggesting that the artist intended them to be read together as a single interrelated element. The catalogue translated 'Carpe Diem' as 'Redeem the Day', but this does not appear to be strictly accurate, and nor is 'Seize the Day', another popular variant in English. The verb *carpe* means to pluck or crop fruit as soon as it is ripe enough to eat. This implies a need to fulfil the potential of each day by seizing the opportunities it offers at once, and not assuming they will remain available afterwards.

The phrase was virtually unknown outside scholastic circles before Lord Byron included it in a letter published in 1830:

I never anticipate – carpe diem – the past at least is one's own, which is one reason for making sure of the present.

After this the phrase passed into common usage and was almost certainly the source of Robert's quotation. But his emphasis is subtly different. Here, the future is utterly unpredictable, so can be ignored, but the present must be consciously fulfilled as it passes into personal experience and becomes integral to one's personality. The essence of 'carpe diem' is that it can only operate at the moment of decision and initiative – the continuous present. It cannot be applied to a fixed date that has passed into history and can no longer be influenced by active intervention.

Disturbingly, it appears that Robert was attempting to link the phrase to an actual date – X.XII.III. Was this because he perceived the essence of the lovers' tragedy as a failure to 'make sure' of the opportunity presented by one crucial day while it was the present and before it vanished into the past and became impotently absorbed into their personalities as a memory? This would certainly be consistent with the intensely meditative, almost mournful quality of his treatment of the subject. In these circumstances 'Redeem the Day' might be a more accurate reflection of Robert's motives for including the phrase, the numerals and indeed the Cupid sundial itself in the composition.

The statement in the catalogue that the painting 'cannot be identified with any of Bateman's otherwise recorded works' meant that it was not exhibited at the Royal Academy, where meticulous records were kept and where all Robert's paintings were shown between his abandonment of the Dudley in 1874 and his first picture at the Grosvenor in 1882. There was simply no record of this highly finished oil having ever been exhibited at any point in Robert's life. Did this mean that, to an even greater extent than *Paolo and Francesca* and *Reading of Love, Heloise and Abelard* was too personal for Robert to put on public view, let alone sell? If so, his motive in painting it must have been primarily to give expression to deeply held emotions. Stripped of the extraneous considerations of painting for public display, this would represent a unique insight into his personality.

If Robert identified so profoundly with the subject of this picture that he could not be comfortable with the degree of self-revelation involved in exhibiting it, was it not possible that the long-legged youth with the 'matinée idol good looks' was a self-portrait and the pensive lady was the mysterious figure for whom we had been searching so diligently, who had caused him to return compulsively to the theme of love at the time of his disappearance in 1874?

Even the possibility of this redoubled our fascination with the painting and our longing to possess it. The difficulty was that the tower renovation at Biddulph was at its most critical phase and it was vital to keep moving forward and achieve at least a stable structure. How could we even contemplate diverting £30,000 to buy a small oil painting by an obscure Victorian artist who happened to have connections with the ruin we called home?

Just days after the catalogue arrived, our bank appointed a new Business Development Manager to our local branch. This turned out to be the very person who had arranged all the initial finance for Bletchley Manor, and had sportingly extended it as that endeavour sped past several cash limits and time deadlines. Even he, though, did initially find the £30,000 and the amorous oil painting a little tricky to reconcile. However, on the basis of our intimacy with Janet Street-Porter, he was soon devising tortuous procedures by which it could be achieved, under the guise of a business loan. We mercilessly emphasised the need for despatch, as the sale was less than a fortnight away. By the time we were boarding the London train, we were clutching a document underwritten by the bank entitling us to bid up to £40,000, to be repaid over ten years. We now knew that *Heloise and Abelard* was meant to be returned to the place where it was created!

Sensibly, we decided to reinforce the workings of fate by engaging the help of a seasoned veteran of the art auction circuit. A friend of my brother, Robert Titchenor-Barret, refused any fee for nannying us through the Machievellian world of art dealing. He would consult his contacts at Christie's to get a feel for the likely interest and bid for us, in return for a good lunch and a bottle of wine. So, over lobster and Chablis, he gave us his assessment of the painting then asked what had led us to want it, as he felt there were several other paintings in the auction that represented a better investment. We ran through the broad outlines of our journey since buying Biddulph and discovering its association with Bateman. When we had finished, Robert's glass was empty and I proffered the remains of the bottle.

'No, no. I need to be on my mettle. I thought this was just a bit of fun but now I realise it isn't. After that story I realise we've got to get the damn thing.'

The scene at the auction room was gratifyingly true to our preconceptions. Rows of chairs were filled with astute, immaculate women accompanied by self-satisfied men in broad chalk-stripe suits or custard-coloured corduroys. Seated among them were the art puritans, dressed for the most part in uncompromising navy linen. In magnificent counterpoint to them, in the front row, sat two African ladies of statuesque proportions, their voluptuous contours swathed in pillar-box red and lime green tribal prints of ferocious energy, with headdresses to match. The huge room, the lines of desks for internet and telephone bids, the handlers in white gloves and, indeed, the patrician master of ceremonies with half-moon glasses, were familiar to us from a hundred television news clips.

Although we were nervous as the auctioneer worked his way through the earlier lots, it was an exhilarating fear, like going too fast in your car at eighteen years old, or being on a gravity-crunching fairground ride as a child. We were not prepared for the horse-kick of real fear as *Heloise and Abelard* was carried in. The auctioneer described the picture as 'a gloriously coloured, glamorous portrayal of the famous lovers, the whereabouts of which had not been known for some thirty years'. Bateman was 'a truly fascinating and enigmatic artist, routinely described as "The Lost Pre-Raphaelite" . . . So, ladies and gentlemen, this is a genuinely rare opportunity to acquire an important piece by this gifted and mysterious figure, whose work is now beginning to take its rightful place within several of the great international collections.'

The bidding opened at £15,000 and rose rapidly to £23,000, where it faltered. By then two of the three bidders on the floor had pulled out. Then there was a telephone bid which was instantly capped from the floor. The auctioneer repeatedly put the £24,000 figure to the telephone bidder but got no response. Desperate as I was to put my trust in Robert and maintain a poker-player's inscrutability, the agonising possibility that the picture was about to be sold without a single bid on our behalf frayed my nerves. What was Robert up to? What if he had decided that the picture had already exceeded its value? What if he thought it was his role to protect us from our own ill-informed enthusiasm? We needed to act. We had the money. In a matter of seconds the gavel would come down, condemning us to a nightmare of regret and futile recriminations.

Involuntarily, I reached out and touched Robert on the shoulder just as he raised his programme. Both the auctioneer and the woman taking the telephone bid noticed my panicky gesture in the split second before Robert's nonchalant entry into the bidding. My loss of composure had probably given vital information to our opponents, but there was no time for self-reproach. Now we were in the bidding, things seemed to move at breathtaking speed. It was a two-way struggle between us and the other bidder from the floor. The pace was frenetic until, quite suddenly, at £27,000 our opponent dropped out. The auctioneer's laconic request for further interest seemed to proceed in the ghostly slow-motion of a car crash. Time became grotesquely distorted as the silences between his echoing exhortations grew longer and longer. 'So at 27 thousand, it's with the gentleman by the door . . . At 27 thousand . . . We're all done at 27 thousand . . . At 27 thousand then – it's against you, sir – At 27 thousand.'

Then, with no warning, the trembling silence was banished by a tiny gesture from the woman on the phone.

'28, I have 28 thousand.'

Instantly the haggling tumult of an oriental bazaar returned to smash the unearthly stillness. Now it was us and the woman on the phone. The process was faster and more belligerent than before.

'38 – 39 – 40 – 41 – 42 . . .'

We had smashed right through our ceiling. Mercifully, at £43,000, our opponent seemed to check the pace, which gave Robert a chance to whisper,

'I'll have to do it on gut feel, okay? If she comes back I'll have to go on without flinching until I know the game's up. You'll have to trust me.'

The truce ended.

'44 – 45 – 46 – 47 . . .'

Then all at once it was over. Robert shook his head, and *Abelard and Heloise* was knocked down to the woman on the phone for £48,000. There was a hubbub in the room. It was a record price for a Bateman. For a while Robert did not turn round, and when he did his eyes were glistening.

'Bugger. The way she went on from 44 meant her chap had come to terms with 50 plus.'

He threw an arm round each of our shoulders and for a minute we stood there, a stunned little scrum of misery. As we broke up he said,

'The strange thing is, when you told me your story I had no doubt we would get it. I thought it was meant!'

'So did we.'

Fig. 66. Biddulph Grange, built by James Bateman, Robert's childhood home.

Chapter 16

WORLDS APART

For a heady moment our foray into the cultured opulence of the fine art world gave us airs – but they did not long withstand the austere corrective of a new round of plodding, systematic research.

In the Bateman archive held at the Cheshire Record Office was a note relating to the family's unsuccessful attempt to auction the Biddulph Grange estate in 1871 (fig. 66). It read:

> The house did not reach its reserve and had to be withdrawn. It was sold the following year to the wealthy local industrialist Robert Heath. The accumulated mortgages outstanding on the property amounted to approximately £35,000.

This huge debt must have been a critical factor in the decision of Robert's father, James Bateman, to sell his house and move to London in 1868. Our previous perception of the move had been derived from Peter Hayden's book, *Biddulph Grange: A Victorian Garden Rediscovered*, which described the historical and botanical importance of the gardens and the process of their rediscovery and restoration in 1988. James and Maria Bateman, together with Edward Cooke, were the central characters as the creative forces in the formation of the garden, so Hayden was content to accept their own accounts of their motives for selling up and going to London, which effectively marked the end of his story.

According to Hayden, the move to London was driven by concern for Maria's health, and the opportunity presented by Cooke's decision to move out of London when he found the ideal site to build a house near Groombridge in Kent. Cooke's new house, Glen Andred, was completed by 1868 and Peter Hayden records that James Bateman was the very first guest invited to stay there in July 1868. During this visit the two friends discussed the possibility of the Batemans renting Cooke's old home, The Ferns in Hyde Park Gate South (fig. 67). A few days later James wrote

Fig. 67. The Ferns, 9 Hyde Park Gate South, the house James and Maria Bateman rented after the enforced sale of Biddulph Grange.

agreeing to take it. Peter Hayden portrays this as the acquisition of a town house in addition to the Grange:

> The Batemans intended to spend half of each year at The Ferns, hoping Maria's bronchitis would improve if she could avoid Biddulph in the winter.

However, events did not bear this out. What actually happened was that, almost immediately, James and Maria moved to London and never returned to live at Biddulph Grange again. They signed over ownership of both The Grange and the Knypersley estates to their son John in return for an annuity, and disappeared from local society.

Peter Hayden quotes from a letter of 1870 from James to his wife's brother Rowland Egerton-Warburton, in which he both distances himself from the need to sell by attributing the decision to John, and attempts some fairly tortuous justifications for the sale:

> ... partly because he thinks it too large ... and much more because he is constantly amazed by the perpetually advancing tide of population which renders game preserving almost hopeless and quietude out of the question.

The tone betrays a real anxiety that his wife's important local family might be sceptical about the reasons for the Batemans' unexplained abandonment of their estates, through which they had established a position among the gentry of Staffordshire and Cheshire. James continues by making light of a shaming social predicament by characterising his former home as 'a new – as distinguished from an old – family place' adding, with a plaintive burst of candour, 'I only wish now that I had not laid out so much money on it.'

Here, for the first time, we get a hint of the real disaster that had overtaken the Batemans. The Biddulph Grange estate, with its huge Italianate mansion and elaborate gardens replete with glasshouses laden with priceless orchid specimens, was at the heart of the perception of them among the worthy local squires as knowledgeable and discerning plutocrats. For it to become known that their dazzling possessions were no more than a deception, built upon incontinent borrowing, would have constituted a shocking scandal that proved they were 'not gentlemen' and would cause them to be ostracised from polite society.

Proof that something of this kind did affect the Batemans is supplied by Edward Cooke's diaries. After all the evidence of close friendship between himself and James Bateman over the period leading up to his move to Glen Andred, there are only three further references to him in the entire twelve years before Cooke's death in 1880. The final entry is a single phrase, 'Mr Bateman agreed to three feet.' This relates to the fact that at the time the lease for The Ferns was negotiated in 1868, Cooke withheld a substantial area of the garden as a site for a new house designed by Norman Shaw. Throughout the build, although James and Maria Bateman remained next door as his tenants, Cooke never once records speaking to them, visiting them or staying with them on his frequent visits to London. He regularly stayed or dined at the Athenaeum, and kept meticulous lists of the parties he joined there – but James Bateman is never among them. These two men, whose professional association and friendship went back twenty years and who were now thrown together as landlord and tenant, suddenly ceased to maintain even the most superficial social contact. There seems no option but to conclude that Cooke 'cut' the Batemans as no longer socially desirable.

To understand how this debacle would have affected the Bateman family, it is important to see it in the context of their comparatively recent rise to wealth and social prominence. Their fortunes followed a pattern familiar during the great upheaval of the ancient social order caused by the Industrial Revolution. James's grandfather, Old James, was born in 1749 into a family of remote, impoverished country squires in Westmorland, who made a modest living from their land. Although Old James was the eldest son, he had no interest in inheriting the estate and persuaded his father to buy out the stock of Wilson's of Kendal, an ironmonger, on the understanding that his inheritance would pass to his younger brother. Old James was clearly a natural entrepreneur and an astute businessman.

The sense of relentless driving energy, allied to the iron determination needed to prosper in the unregulated crucible of early nineteenth-century commerce, provides a daunting insight into Old James's personality. He formed a partnership with a gifted engineer, William Sherrat, and together they developed an extensive ironworks in Salford where they manufactured steam engines, and a factory in the Potteries where they made boilers and a wide range of other iron products. His interests were not confined to iron and coal: he built three large cotton mills in Manchester and a range of warehouses known as Bateman's Buildings. Towards the end of his career, he also went into banking.

His purchase in 1811 of the Knypersley estate (which included the building and land of the Grange) was a commercial venture to gain access to the abundant coal reserves that underlay parts of it, so as to set up furnaces to serve in conjunction with his ironworks in Manchester. He developed several small pits already working on the land into much more profitable enterprises, particularly the Childerplay Colliery, later known as the Victoria Pit.

Old James never lived in the house at Knypersley or at Biddulph Grange, but stayed in Manchester until he finally retired to his native Westmorland. It was his son John who moved into the pleasant house at Knypersley Hall with his homely wife Elizabeth, from Redivals near Bury, and their only son, James. When Old James died in 1824, John and Elizabeth Bateman inherited fabulous wealth, with factories, mines, warehouses and land scattered all over Manchester and the Potteries and an annual income from enterprises ranging from coal pits to blast furnaces, steel works and banks.

Little wonder that the ensuing generations began to turn their attention to acquiring the refinement and education that would make them acceptable in the exclusive club of ease and amusement that made up the enchanted circle of upper-class life. This transition was not easy to achieve as the rules governing entry were ruthlessly applied by those already in the club. The plain truth was that possession of money, preferably in prodigious quantity, constituted the strongest motivation for established families to integrate with you. However, they would not do so until you conformed to one of the cardinal rules of genteel society and ceased to be actively involved in the grubby process of wealth creation. Not being 'in trade' was a defining characteristic of a 'gentleman'. To achieve this, profits from commercial ventures had to be sanitised by being transferred into land holdings in the form of a landed manor or estate. These provided a substantial income from agricultural rents, with the most satisfactory resonances of ancient feudal lordship. If your acreage happened to contain coal or mineral deposits which could be sold at vast profit, this was mere good fortune and quite acceptable, provided you were not too closely involved in their extraction and marketing.

In the Batemans' case, the influence of these pressures is easy to discern. Old James provided the fortune, through relentless hard work, that financed the buying of the Knypersley estate for its coal and iron. His son, Old John, moved into Knypersley

Hall and, as well as continuing to oversee his father's business ventures, began to take an increasing interest in embellishing the comparatively modest house and grounds. He built extensively, including a new church and school at Knypersley, thereby increasingly assuming the role of squire and benefactor. He also used his wealth to obtain access to a better education for his only son, James, by sending him to Magdalen College, Oxford.

Under the influence of this new cultural environment, James lost all interest in the family business. He took wealth for granted and devoted his time to making his name as a leading amateur botanist and plant collector. He married into a Cheshire county family, the Egerton-Warburtons, and moved away from Knypersley to Biddulph Grange, to disassociate himself from the nearby industrial development instigated by his grandfather. He continued to extend and elaborate his ostentatious new house and grounds in order to impress the local gentry with whom he now associated.

During Old John's lifetime the vaunting ambition of James's plans for the Biddulph Grange estate were underpinned by his father's grasp of the family businesses, even though a relentless process of borrowing against their capital value had set in. This ensured that right up to Old John's death in 1857, the income from the principal sites, such as the Victoria colliery, continued to support households of some thirty permanent staff on the Biddulph and Knypersley estates. James Bateman's ignorance of and distaste for business meant that after his father's death he was forced to lease the sites, which, without astute supervision, ceased to deliver their former profits. This in turn undermined their value when he came to sell them to service his borrowings. It took only ten years from Old John's death in 1857 before the situation had become so intractable that James and Maria were forced to disappear to London so that the estate could be sold.

Those ten years saw the Batemans' surroundings and social cachet reach dizzy new heights, with the acquisition of Biddulph Old Hall and the construction of the initial phase of the tunnels, bridges, stone steps and dams that formed the linking walk from the Grange. This extravagant project was completed in time for the marriage in 1865 of Young John to Jessy Caroline Bootle-Wilbraham, sister of the 2nd Lord Skelmersdale – the family's first inter-relationship with titled aristocracy. In 1868, James and Maria's youngest child Katherine made a similarly satisfactory union with Ralph Ulick Burke, a clever young barrister and a younger son of a distinguished family of Irish baronets.

It was into this increasingly privileged lifestyle that the rude shock of the enforced sale of their entire estate fell. How can James Bateman have reacted to the abandonment of the house, estate and garden in which he had invested a lifetime of work and inspiration, as well as the great fortune he had inherited? He seems to have been genuinely profligate and bad at organising his financial affairs, as they continued to

Fig. 68. Spring Bank, the modest semi-detached villa on Victoria Road, Worthing, where James Bateman ended his days.

decline after his move to London. By 1884 he was again citing Maria's bronchitis as the justification for a further withdrawal from fashionable life when they moved from London to Worthing.

Although the need for better air is considerably more convincing than the earlier move from Biddulph into the choking smog of the capital, it none the less represented a marked loss of social status. Home House, Worthing, was a villa in a conventional residential road, surrounded by similar houses, all with comfortable but modest gardens. James and Maria continued to demonstrate their skill and creativity by laying out a charming garden, but their journey from wealth into relative poverty continued unchecked. When James died in 1897, he lived in a semi-detached villa, Springbank, in Victoria Road, a distinctly modest address (fig. 68).

Of course, it is important to keep a sense of proportion when recording the change in the Bateman family's fortunes. James's son John was still able to buy an estate of almost 1,500 acres at Brightlingsea in Essex after he successfully negotiated the sale of Biddulph Grange in 1872 and paid off his father's debts. However, the estate did not have a house of any scale or distinction at its centre, and the flat seabound acreage had no value except as agricultural land, quite unlike the land at Biddulph, underpinned by deep seams of coal and iron.

Indeed, the next owner of the Grange, Robert Heath, dedicated himself singlemindedly to the development of the commercial potential of the pits and ironworks of the estate, and ended his life as one of the wealthiest industrialists in England and MP for Stoke. He spent lavishly on the Grange – the year after he bought it in 1873, he employed Queen Victoria's interior designers, John Gregory Crace & Sons, to prepare schemes and redecorate the principal rooms – but he remained steadfastly committed to the personal supervision of his business enterprises, which came to number twenty-eight coal and ironstone mines and eight blast furnaces, among others. By 1885 his wealth and influence across the county were so great that he was created High Sheriff of Staffordshire, despite his refusal to conform to the feudal masquerade of the landed country gentleman of private means.

By a strange chance, John Bateman's actions after the sale of Biddulph Grange provides a fascinating insight into his motives for owning a country house estate. Immediately after the purchase of his new house, John Bateman set about the single piece of work for which he is remembered, the collation and publishing of an influential book listing the principal landowners of the country. Entitled *The Great Landowners of Great Britain and Ireland*, it is an alphabetical list of 'all owners of three thousand acres and upwards, worth £3,000 a year in England, Scotland, Ireland and Wales, their income from land, college, club and services.' This focus on landholding is clearly intended to imply a social distinction between this and wealth derived from other sources. The great aristocratic families were bound to appear by virtue of their historic estates, so the main beneficiaries of the book were the much more modest owners who just managed to qualify and who were aggrandised by association. For John to create such a work so soon after the sale of his own family estate betrays a real anxiety on the Batemans' part at the prospect of being perceived as having fallen out of the landed gentry.

John's own entry is intriguing. His acreage in Essex, 1,413, and one single acre retained at Knypersley, is a long way short of the 3,000 needed to qualify. He only managed to get in by including 2,997 acres in County Mayo, Ireland. Whatever the source of these acres, land in Ireland at that terrible stage in its history, with the population decimated by starvation and emigration, was almost valueless and pathetically easy to acquire as an absentee landlord. This suggests that John Bateman deliberately set out to define an elite club and manipulate the entry qualifications so that he himself could be included, in order to restore his family's social position after the calamity of the forced sale of their lavish estate at Biddulph.

Understanding the extent and consequences of his family's indebtedness was a crucial turning point in our search for the truth about the life and work of Robert Bateman, and his relationship with Caroline Howard. One of the most universally acknowledged facts about Robert's life, consistently restated in every attempt to give biographical information on him, no matter how brief, stated that he was the son of a wealthy, well-connected family which provided him with a secure social position and private means. It is easy to see why this had become so widely accepted. His parents have effectively been immortalised at the peak of their opulence by the restoration of their horticultural wonderland at Biddulph Grange by the National Trust. This has left them, in perpetuity, as the flamboyant begetters of beautiful places with their children as privileged cohabitants.

Amanda Kavanagh, in her article on Robert Bateman, follows exactly this line. She describes Robert as being born the year James and Maria moved into Biddulph Grange. He was brought up and educated there until he was sent to Brighton College in 1854. She then continues with a statement which not only informs the whole thrust of her article, depicting Robert as a wealthy amateur, but which has become the source of all subsequent accounts of his privileged circumstances:

> It is more than coincidence that George Howard, who became 9th Earl of Carlisle in 1889, was in many ways comparable to his contemporary Robert Bateman. Both were amateur though accomplished artists of similar social status under no financial pressure to pursue fully an artistic career. Their lives were as much associated with their land as with their art . . .

An assumed social equivalence between George Howard and Robert Bateman completely distorts and obscures our understanding of Robert's relationship to Caroline. The truth, as far as we are able to establish it from the known facts, is that the only way the two men were 'comparable' was in their aspiration to be considered accomplished artists. There is no evidence that Robert was an 'amateur artist'. Contemporary documents make no attempt to portray him as a man of private means, but rather describe him as a professional artist making a living from the sale of his paintings. In the census of 1881 he described his profession as 'Artist and Painter', and on his marriage certificate two years later he gave his profession as 'Artist'. He did not qualify these statements by adding the accepted term 'Gentleman' to denote private means. Nor could Robert conceivably be described as of 'similar social status' to a man who was heir to an historic earldom, a seat in the House of Lords and two of the grandest and most beautiful country houses in England. Howard connections ran like a band of geological strata across the whole ponderous rock-face of the Victorian elite. Robert Bateman was the third son of a Staffordshire family which had, for a blinding moment, burrowed their way out of the grime of commerce into the luminous uplands of gentility, only to lose their way and find the fog of exclusion closing around them again.

Amanda Kavanagh's contention that the lives of George Howard and Robert Bateman were 'associated as much with their land as with their art' also cannot be correct. Of course, George Howard could not avoid being associated with land – he owned some 9,000 acres at Castle Howard alone. There is no evidence that Robert Bateman owned a single acre of land anywhere. According to the census returns he lived at Biddulph Castle, the small habitable fragment of a ruined sixteenth-century house which he rented on a lifetime tenancy.

If one adds to these differences the contrast in their education and upbringing, with Bateman attending the minor public school Brighton College, and then the Royal Academy School, while Howard followed the prescribed upper-class regime of Eton and Trinity College, Cambridge, it becomes clear that Howard, far from being 'comparable' to his contemporary, was from an entirely different stratum of wealth, connections and social class. And what applied to George Howard must have applied equally to his cousin Caroline.

ANNUNCIATIO BEATÆ VIRGINIS.

Filius Altiſſimi vocabitur.

Fig. 69. The Annunciation, as depicted by Bateman in The Latin Year.

Chapter 17

PICTURES OF PASSION

Although our research had led us to be sceptical about some aspects of Amanda Kavanagh's account of Robert's life, the conclusion at the end of her article had the uncanny ring of truth about Robert as a personality:

> Throughout his life, Robert Bateman was inspired by the love of his wife; they both bravely bore grave illness but after the death of Caroline on 30 July 1922, Robert relinquished his struggle to survive and succumbed to the anguish of his irreparably broken heart a few days later on 4 August 1922.

The person depicted in these lines was instantly recognisable as the quiet man whose intense nature found expression in obsessive representations of love, mingling premonitions of despair with the ecstatic moment of fulfilment. We felt that Amanda Kavanagh had intuitively understood the pivotal importance of the relationship between Robert and Caroline as the source of inspiration for his work all his adult life – that is to say, long before their marriage in 1883. Our own journey into their story had brought us to the same place and the same conclusion.

We suspected that the key to the riddle of their story lay hidden, partly within the enigmatic events themselves but, much more importantly, within the intensely symbolic coded messages conveyed by Robert through his paintings. While Abelard and Heloise had immortalised their love through the letters they wrote, Robert used visual images to convey his deepest feelings and the anguish of his and Caroline's long struggle to be 'forever one'.

Once we had made the leap of seeing the story of Robert and Caroline's lives in this longer perspective, patterns began to emerge out of the implausible jumble of events and made sense of their decisions. First and foremost was Robert's addictive return to the subject of love, as witnessed in *Paolo and Francesca* and *Reading of Love*, the illustrations for *Art in the House* and, most tellingly, in the unexhibited *Heloise and Abelard*. If this last painting was indeed a portrait of Robert, and his companion was Caroline, it must have depicted a meeting many years before its execution in 1879. By then Caroline would have been forty and Robert thirty-seven.

If, in 1879, Robert had wanted to refer to his love for his future wife it would have been irrelevant to portray himself and her as they had been long before. If, on the other hand, it is a portrayal of the solemn moment of irrevocable commitment at the beginning of a compulsive love affair that was never fulfilled, then he, his love and the day would remain fixed in his memory unaltered, awaiting the miracle of redemption contained in the evocative riddle 'Carpe Diem'. The vividness of an obsessional memory might account for one of the most arresting characteristics of the image. The strongly defined foreground, crowded with minutely observed and opulently coloured objects, rich in spiritual and symbolic significance, is uncomfortably contrasted with the vacuous emptiness of its almost featureless monochrome background. Robert seems to be driven to convey the precise meaning and the intensity of his emotional response to the lovers' predicament, while unconsciously betraying his indifference to the forlorn world outside and beyond it.

For the lovers to be a symbolic representation of Caroline and Robert, the meeting would have to date from the mid 1860s. This was in fact the very period when they had by far the greatest opportunity to meet on anything approaching equal terms. The Batemans were at the height of their wealth and social prestige, with the Grange complete and the gardens at their most flamboyant and mature. Robert had attended the Royal Academy Schools and was making a name for himself, exhibiting at the Dudley Gallery and his work was being noticed by the leading art publications of the day. At home in Staffordshire, the Batemans had moved into ever more exalted circles through the marriage of Robert's elder brother John to the sister of the 2nd Lord Skelmersdale. Her family were cousins of the Wilbrahams of Rode Hall, who were friends of the Dean of Lichfield. The respectability of the Bateman family was further enhanced by the ordination of Robert's other brother, Rowland, in Durham Cathedral, and his decision to join the Christian Missionary Society, dedicating his life to spreading the Gospel among the Muslim population of Lahore and the surrounding area.

For a brief moment, the probability of Robert and Caroline encountering each other in the close-knit world of Staffordshire county society must have been very high. The glamour attaching itself to the good-looking artist, allied to the manifest wealth of his family and the good character of their connections, through the Wilbrahams and Rowland Bateman, would probably not have rung alarm bells at the Deanery. Should anything develop, Caroline would at least be well provided for as part of a respectable, pious family, even if they were a trifle vulgar and nouveau riche. However, this situation would have been irretrievably altered by the events of the next few years. First, the Dean became ill, and the Howards progressively withdrew from society until entering a protracted period of mourning after his death in 1868.

If Robert and Caroline had planned to marry, it would have been out of the question until the early 1870s.

Almost at this precise moment, the Batemans' debt crisis broke and they disappeared from Staffordshire society, never to return. In January 1869, Burne-Jones was publicly reviled and forced to resign from the Old Water Colour Society, as his extra-marital affair with Maria Zambaco reached a dramatic climax with her public attempt to commit suicide by throwing herself into the Regent's Canal. His wife Georgina was forced to flee their house in Fulham for lodgings in Oxford in order to escape the humiliating gossip in London.

Caroline's family would have been fully aware of the crisis as George Howard, and perhaps even more so his wife Rosalind, were the principal confidantes of the Burne-Joneses. On the night of Georgina's departure, Howard stayed talking to Burne-Jones in their house until 1 a.m. Although they were great admirers of his gifts as a painter there is little doubt that the Howards were shocked by his infidelity and sympathised with his wife. Rosalind Howard recorded her admiration for Georgina in her journal:

> her love is the deepest I ever met with. She is centred in her husband, the whole romance of her life is bound up with him from when she was eleven years old – more than romance, every feeling she has. She longs for him. He cannot know what she has endured. Great strength of mind but too absorbed in one object, even if no blight had come on that one object.

If so artistic and cosmopolitan a couple as George and Rosalind Howard were critical of Burne-Jones, how much more scandalised the newly widowed Henrietta Howard would have been by the shameless public acknowledgement of adultery among the group of artists of which young Robert Bateman was a recognised member. By the time the Howards emerged from the shadow of the Dean's death in the early 1870s, any chance of Caroline forming a union with Robert would have vanished.

If the Howards had refused to permit the marriage of Caroline and Robert after 1870, it would provide a plausible explanation of the strange fact that neither of these good-looking, attractive personalities became involved with anyone else until Caroline married Charles Wilbraham in 1876. For her in particular, these six years were crucially important. They were the prime years of her eligibility to become a respected wife and mother. Although age was less decisive for Robert, the consequence of his failure to marry until he was forty-one, and then his choice of a wife older than himself, meant that he missed the opportunity to have children and fulfil one of the most universally respected roles in Victorian life – that of the paterfamilias to a multitude of handsome descendents.

This prohibition would also provide a possible explanation for the unlikely marriage of Caroline to Charles Wilbraham. Ten years earlier, Charles had been angrily rebuffed when Lord Egerton intervened to stop him declaring his love for Beatrix Egerton. If Caroline had been forced by her family to abandon all hope of a life together with Robert, then perhaps their shared suffering was a credible basis for a deep personal bond between them. If they each had lost the one relationship that mattered most to them in the world, a profound empathy may have had the power to overcome the disparity between them. Of course, for their relationship to begin on the basis of a shared experience of lost love, they both had to have reached the crisis point where they accepted that any cherished dreams of fulfilment with their beloveds were utterly lost.

For Charles, that moment arrived with the marriage of Beatrix Egerton to Lionel Arthur Tollemarche on 25 January 1870. Caroline would have to have reached the same state of despairing acceptance of the absolute impossibility of realising her dream of happiness with Robert before a sympathetic rapport between her and Charles had a chance to develop. We can imagine how moved Charles would have been, if confronted by a brave woman crushed by the same relentless forces for no other crime than remaining true to the promises she made to the man she loved.

By 1871 there were signs of Robert trying to gain recognition as an artist among the more respectable sections of society. He still showed work at the Dudley Gallery, but for the first time had an oil painting (unusual for him at that time) on a religious theme shown in the Royal Academy Summer Exhibition at Burlington House in Piccadilly, the time-honoured forum for acknowledged professional artists. The change in medium, subject and location is sufficiently marked and sudden to suggest a conscious intention of distancing himself from the scandal engulfing the Dudley Group.

Although the painting, *The Annunciation*, is lost, Robert's handling of the same subject in the woodcuts for *The Latin Year* suggests a distinctly uncontroversial portrayal of the angel confronting a composed, praying virgin with news of her divine destiny, surrounded by doves, bees and gentle lambs (fig. 69). If this reflects the tone of the oil painting, it does seem a surprising departure from the highly individual, slightly disturbing atmosphere of most of his earlier work. Did this constitute an attempt to redefine himself in the eyes of conventional society, such as that represented by Henrietta Howard, the Dean of Lichfield's widow? If this was his strategy, he repeated it again 1876, when he showed *The Pool of Bethesda*. He continued to show all his work at the RA exclusively until 1881, when he began to exhibit at the Grosvenor. This pattern does suggest that distancing himself from the Dudley and exhibiting at the RA was perceived by Robert as a formula for gaining wider acceptance in respectable society, leading to his complete abandonment of the Dudley in 1874.

The record of his work during these years is strange and suggestive. The two love paintings, *Paolo and Francesca* and *Reading of Love*, which were linked thematically by the highly charged subject of reading of love while experiencing the emotions portrayed in the verses, would be highly revealing if they expressed a deeply felt personal incident, and more so if the object of his love was Caroline. If *Heloise and Abelard* represents the blissful dawning of love between Robert and Caroline, then *Paolo and Francesca* and *Reading of Love* commemorate the momentous experience of re-affirming the survival of their feelings for each other, despite the passage of time and the opposition of the outside world.

Seen in the light of a forbidden liaison, the incident portrayed in the verse from Dante and in *Reading of Love* is critical to an understanding of Robert's state of mind at this moment. The dates of these paintings, 1873 and 1874, mean that any acknowledgement that their mutual love was still alive could not have come at a more appalling moment. By 1873, the indignity of the sale of Biddulph Grange may have ceased to be current tittle-tattle, and the most salacious gossip surrounding Burne-Jones's affair with Maria Zambaco may have subsided a little. However, on the evening of 11 February 1873, the police arrested two men in a public lavatory off Oxford Street and charged them with gross indecency. The two were named as George Roberts, sixty, a stable-man, and Simeon Solomon, thirty-three, an artist. Solomon was an acknowledged associate of Burne-Jones, Rossetti and the poet Swinburne, among many others. He was universally recognised as a leading figure among the young painters at the Dudley Gallery where his name had frequently been linked with Bateman.

The revulsion and venomous condemnation that attached itself to Solomon and those associated with him can be felt in a letter written by Dante Gabriel Rossetti, a long-term friend and mentor of Solomon, to his friend Ford Madox Brown on 19 April:

> Have you heard these horrors about little Solomon? His intimate [William Davies] writes me: He has just escaped the hands of the Law for the second time, accused of the vilest proclivities, and is now in semi-confinement somewhere or other. I have said little about it on account of the family who have suffered bitterly. I hope I shall never see him again. [Burne-] Jones has been most kind and considerate to his friends though sickened to death with the beastly circumstances Poor little devil! What will become of him?

From so dissolute a figure as Rossetti, who had created a cult around his promiscuity by bragging about his pursuit and seduction of 'stunners' (beautiful young girls, ostensibly employed as models), the virulence of this condemnation comes as a shock. His unqualified wish never to see Solomon again gives an insight into how damaging contact with someone accused of these offences would be, even among the scandalously broad-minded artistic fraternity, let alone society at large.

Solomon's other friends also reacted with fear and consternation. Swinburne found it necessary to vacate his rooms in London and flee to Oxford where he wrote on 6 June:

I suppose there is no doubt the poor unhappy little fellow has really been out of his mind and done things amenable to law such as done by a sane man would make it impossible for anyone to keep up acquaintance and not be 'cut' by the rest of the world as an accomplice.

Swinburne ceases even to mention his former friend in correspondence until 15 October 1879, when he describes him in a letter to Edmund Gosse as 'now a thing unmentionable alike to men and women, as equally abhorrent to either – nay, to the very beasts.' This level of moral outrage even from Rossetti and Swinburne gives a fearsome indication of the sanctimonious revulsion that the story would have engendered as it was whispered from ear to ear in the crowded galleries and drawing rooms of fashionable London. In the secluded vestries and chapter houses of the Church of England it would have been beyond comprehension.

The wall of exclusion that came to confront Solomon was so impenetrable that he was unable to sell more than a tiny fragment of his work, or maintain any meaningful relationships with his old friends in the art and intellectual worlds. Gradually, he was pushed to the derelict margins of the community, where he existed in abject poverty as a vagrant, earning a living as a pavement artist or by selling matches, and taking refuge intermittently in St Giles's Workhouse in Seven Dials. He represented a real danger to anyone identified as sharing his degenerate preoccupations with youth, beauty and love.

If Robert was to continue to thrive as an artist and sell his work, he needed to stop submitting work to the Dudley Gallery and to create a new place to work outside London, where he could establish an individual persona in the critics' and the public's minds, distinct from the dangerous 'Dudley people' who included Solomon. If at the identical moment he had just experienced the tumultuous exposure of his and Caroline's feelings for each other through the medium of love poems, how much more desperate would he be to rid himself of any contamination from Solomon. The evidence of the paintings suggests that he and Caroline may have made just such a declaration of their intimacy without gaining the approval of their families – or, worse, have been conducting a clandestine affair.

For Henrietta Howard and the rest of Caroline's family, it was unthinkable that their name and the sacred memory of the Dean might become embroiled, however peripherally, with a criminal offence involving almost satanic sinfulness. The possibility that this danger could be imported into their midst by way of a disreputable artist from a discredited provincial family would have required swift and decisive action.

The immutable formula of emergency measures activated in this situation were tried, tested and universally applied across the spectrum of high society. First, the misguided child or relation would be removed from the influence of the object of their infatuation. This meant being sent as far away as possible, perhaps to stay with a relative in a remote location or, better still, abroad. Next, the interloper was called to an interview or sent a letter leaving him in no doubt that his proposal was utterly unacceptable. Lord Egerton's letter forbidding Charles Wilbraham's approaches to his daughter Beatrix is cruelly characteristic. The third, and perhaps most urgent, rearguard action involved a comprehensive review of all the acceptable potential partners in one's circle of acquaintances and relatives. The purpose of these negotiations, understood by all participants, was to defuse the perilous situation by binding the errant family member safely within the bounds of matrimony, putting him or her out of reach of their pursuer or, at the very worst, into a context where indiscretions could be disguised.

If, in 1873, Caroline was in love with Robert, it seems that the Howards turned for help to a trusted friend, a prominent rector in the Diocese of Lichfield throughout the years of Henry Howard's deanship. Charles Philip Wilbraham was unmarried, morally beyond reproach and from a good family. There was, however, one logistical difficulty with entrusting Caroline to his care: his lifelong parish of Audley lay barely five miles from Biddulph Old Hall, now the home of Robert Bateman, focus of all their anxiety. It would have been impossible to think of her marrying and taking up the semi-public position of rector's wife in the parish next door to the man with whom she had conducted a clandestine or forbidden liaison.

Here, for the first time, there was a credible explanation for Wilbraham's succession of apparently unmotivated decisions at the end of 1873 and the beginning of 1874 – to abandon his lifelong vocation and domestic comfort at Audley for a badly paid living forty miles away at Penkridge, and two years later to marry Caroline Howard in a tiny church in Kent without a single witness from his family.

If separating Robert and Caroline was the objective of his marriage, Charles seemed to be prepared to embrace a heroic level of self-sacrifice to assist Henrietta Howard. He risked enduring an unhappy marriage with a sophisticated woman thirty years his junior who would feel trapped by his willingness to intervene. At the very least, she might have been driven by frustration to ridicule him for the failings of old age – the cantankerousness, complacency, self-absorption and repetition that Lord and Lady Hatherton found so exasperating. But nowhere is there a hint of her having done so, nor of any conflict between them. His continued uxoriousness seems to be his response to her enfolding gentleness and identification with his interests, which others perceived as love. For this to be possible, Caroline must have come to believe that her love for Robert was doomed, and that Charles's motives for coming to her aid were truly born out of respect and identification with her tragic situation.

If our intuition that Robert's work, through most of his active life as a painter, was inspired by his love for Caroline and constituted an encoded record of the critical events of their story, we needed to study the next painting after *Reading of Love*. Did it reflect a change in his state of mind in the aftermath of that ecstatic encounter?

And what was his reaction to her marriage to Charles Wilbraham? The next painting was *The Pool of Bethesda*, which was exhibited in 1876 at the Royal Academy, the year of Caroline's wedding in Milstead. The contrast in colouring, composition and precision of execution between the two pictures is absolute, but the difference between them goes far beyond technique. The worlds that the artist had set out to convey were almost irreconcilable. The first was an evocation of somnolent peace and contentment; the second a parched, barren compilation of rock and masonry against which crippled figures support themselves or struggle to reach a source of relief from pain. No gestures towards surface beauty or prettiness for its own sake disturbs the sad intensity of this work. The plants in the earthenware pots are stunted and dry, and the angel's wings, so often an opportunity for exuberant flamboyance in work of this time, are almost rudimentary, with no real attempt to convey their texture.

If Robert had set out to convey a catastrophic alteration in his perception of the world around him, he could scarcely have produced two contrasting images that achieved his objective so succinctly. But if Caroline was the central creative inspiration of Robert's life, what evidence was there in the painting to suggest that the change in him was brought about by the heart-breaking prospect of her being placed forever beyond his reach, by her marriage to another man? Did the fact that Caroline's marriage was taking place at precisely this moment, in the real world, lead Robert to let out a howl of visualised anguish in his painting *The Pool of Bethesda*?

Although there is always a subjective element in the interpretation of a visual image, the moment we returned to study the painting with these questions in our minds, a new level of understanding suggested itself to us. We looked closely at the two central characters of the composition, the sick man struggling to drag himself through the open door in the centre of the canvas, and the angel descending the steps to trouble the waters and bring healing to the first person entering the water after her. The sick man clearly has no chance of reaching the water before the young man to the side of the canvas who is almost there already and who has the help of a woman. We had always accepted the turbaned and bearded central character as a conventional representation of a Jewish or Middle Eastern man. But for the first time we noticed that the shape of his dark moustache and beard corresponded exactly with photographs of Robert in middle age (fig. 70).

Similarly, when we compared the angel with Robert's portrayal of Heloise, the correlation was striking: a tall, spare figure with a long neck, straight nose, slightly prominent chin, and – most marked – blonde, slightly wavy hair taken severely down from a centre parting and gathered into a chignon or loose bun at the nape of the neck. Suddenly, the narrative of the painting became highly personal to Robert's situation. He is the broken, sick man whose only hope of cure lies with the angelic figure of his beloved Caroline: she possesses the divine power of healing which he is unable to reach and so is condemned to a life of infirmity and pain. The harsh, angular,

Figs. 70, 71. Details from The Pool of Bethesda. *Left: the central bearded character with the small clerical figure behind. Right: detail of the Angel, closely related to Robert's portrayal of Heloise.*

unyielding natural and built structures express the sterile, colourless world that has imprisoned him since her love has been removed. The gentle, pensive angel seems to comprehend his sorrow, but is too bound by the spiritual intensity of her mission to be able to turn aside and engage with his physical struggle (fig. 71).

Before we left the painting, we noticed another component that increased the sense that our reading of it might be correct. Behind the bearded central character is the tiny figure of an elderly man. The painting is ostensibly set in biblical Jerusalem, but this character is dressed in gaiters and a round hat with a broad brim, both traditional elements in the conventional uniform of nineteenth-century clergymen. The tower behind him, albeit given an eastern flavour by the addition of a shallow dome, otherwise looks suspiciously reminiscent of the walled, hilltop site and sturdy tower of Charles Wilbraham's church at Audley. The more we looked at it, the more convinced we became that the emotional power of this picture, which completely transcended the mystic world and pictured poetry of his earlier style, was created out of the depths of Robert's despair at being denied the companionship of Caroline Howard.

However, this apparently desolate moment opened a richly productive new phase in Robert's creative life, centred on his withdrawal into his own solitary world amid the crumbling walls of Biddulph Old Hall. For the sixteen years after his return there in 1873, the house was to represent the fixed point of his existence both physically and emotionally. His paintings from this time are his most deeply felt and accomplished achievements, encompassing *Heloise and Abelard* and *The Raising of Samuel* as well as *The Pool of Bethesda*.

Robert seemed oblivious of the changes outside his reclusive retreat. Ironically, the first of these was Caroline's marriage itself, which liberated her from the authority of her family so that when she emerged after three years as an elegant widow with sufficient means to set up her own household in Mayfair, she could choose her friends and pursue her own private life free of interference. The second change was the effect of his decision to remove himself from the hot-house atmosphere of London and particularly the Dudley Gallery. Gradually, with several of its pivotal figures absent, the identity of the 'Poetry-Without-Grammar School' lost its cohesion, and the louche reputation that had attached itself to them began to fade. Tragically, this was especially true of Simeon Solomon, who disappeared into the impenetrable obscurity of the London underworld and was soon forgotten by all but a handful of relations and loyal friends. Bigoted and cruel though it was, this total ostracism of Solomon was beneficial to Robert in terms of how the public perceived him. By the time he was accepted as a husband for Caroline, the memory of his perceived artistic affinity with Solomon had faded from the public's mind.

Another change that, extraordinarily, seemed to make no impact upon Robert was the seismic shock that hit the art world with the opening of the Grosvenor Gallery in 1877. This transformed Edward Burne-Jones from a despised and almost forgotten figure into the most famous, admired and influential artist of his generation. The gallery building itself created a sensation – in a setting with all the architectural grandeur of a great country house or Italian palazzo, the paintings were spaced widely apart to allow them to be seen individually and give the cumulative effect of a 'palace of art'. But it was the nature of the pictures themselves that shook the foundations of established art appreciation, and brought what had previously been defined as 'advanced art' to the attention of critics and public alike. Their ecstatic reaction launched the whole cult of Aestheticism, the concept that art was justified by its own visual beauty rather than by any moral or intellectual content. This concept was to dominate the last decades of nineteenth-century British cultural life. The critic Sydney Colvin described the revolutionary philosophy underlying these startling images as

> an art that addresses itself directly to the sense of sight: to the emotions and intellect only indirectly, through the medium of the sense of sight ... Perfections of forms and colours – beauty in a word – should be the prime object of pictorial art.

The idea that the first Grosvenor exhibition constituted a fundamental rebirth of British art, through the emergence, apparently from nowhere, of beautiful but unfamiliar works is well caught in the reaction of the young Oscar Wilde:

> Taking a general view of the works exhibited here, we see that this dull land of England, with its short summer, its dreary rains and fogs, its mining districts and factories, and vile deification of machinery, has yet produced very great masters of art, men with subtle sense and love of what is beautiful, original and noble in imagination.

Aestheticism and the Grosvenor Gallery exhibitions involved a complete re-evaluation of the style of painting associated with artists such as G. F. Watts, Dante Gabriel Rossetti and, quintessentially, Edward Burne-Jones and his followers. It is hard to believe that Robert Bateman showed no sign of being aware of the feverish excitement surrounding his former friends. He continued to send his work to the Royal Academy all through this explosion of interest in his type of 'advanced art'. He seemed to be consumed by the single objective of distancing himself from his former Dudley associates and of becoming recognised by the British establishment.

Not until 1881, two years after Charles Wilbraham's death, did he submit his first picture to the Grosvenor Gallery, which from then on showed his work continuously until its closure in 1890. This change must have been influenced by Caroline, whose cousin was married to Lord Wantage, the brother of Sir Coutts Lindsay, the builder and founder of the Grosvenor Gallery.

It was becoming difficult to believe that Caroline was not the mysterious figure who had filled Robert's imagination and canvases with depictions of love and lovers. One thing was certain: we had been unable to find evidence for anyone else. By the autumn of 1881, barely two years after Wilbraham's death, Robert and Caroline were betrothed.

*Fig. 72. The sumptuous classical interior of St Marylebone Parish Church,
where Robert and Caroline were married.*

Chapter 18

A GLAMOROUS MARRIAGE

On 18 October 1883, the marriage was solemnised between Robert Bateman and Caroline Octavia Wilbraham née Howard, at St Marylebone Parish Church. The social cachet of St Marylebone was being enhanced by the daring proposals of its dynamic new rector, Rev. W. Baker, to 'bring it more in harmony with arrangements and decoration suited to the religious demands of the present day' (fig. 72). The scheme sought to enrich the interiors with lavish Aesthetic-style embellishments which caused a great stir in the fashionable world: Mrs Gladstone, the prime minister's wife, laid a commemorative stone to mark the beginning of the work.

As a setting for a wedding ceremony, it is hard to conceive of a greater contrast in scale, style and atmosphere than between St Marylebone and the little church in which Caroline had married for the first time seven years earlier. The contrast was not confined to the building itself. The great church was filled to capacity with aristocratic and honourable Howards, generals, admirals, viscounts and bishops, scarlet uniforms, flashing gems, bustled bottoms and wasp waists, all compressed into a glamorous gaggle, gossiping and gesticulating beneath the soaring pilasters and gilded cornices of the magnificent Neoclassical building.

On Robert's side, the family was there in force: his father James and his mother, his elder brother John with his wife Jessy, and his younger sister Katherine with her barrister husband Ulick Ralph Burke. The service was conducted by an exceptionally well connected close relation of Caroline's. Archibald George Campbell was the husband of her elder sister Charlotte. He was also her first cousin, being the son of her uncle and aunt, John Campbell, Baron Cawdor of Castle Martin, and his wife Caroline Isabella, née Howard. As the newly established choir filled the air with descants, Archibald Campbell greeted her at the altar dressed in a golden cope, where Caroline was given away by Lord Wantage, her wealthy cousin Harriet's husband.

Later, in the vestry, Robert frankly recorded his age as forty-one, whereas Caroline demurely gave hers as 'full', presumably to avoid publicly acknowledging her three-year seniority over the bridegroom. Robert gave his profession as 'Artist' and his home as St Lawrence, Biddulph – the parish church, which suggests that in all the excitement he mistakenly thought he was being asked for his home parish. Caroline gave her address as 14 Upper Berkeley Street, London. The register was countersigned by James Bateman, Robert's father; Lord Wantage; Ulick Ralph Burke, Robert's brother-in-law, and R. G. H. Somerset.

After the wedding the guests made their way to 2 Carlton Gardens, the sumptuous London home of Lord and Lady Wantage who hosted a glittering reception for them. Within a few days Robert and Caroline boarded a boat for Italy, and began what was acknowledged by all who knew them as forty years of blissful happiness. Robert did a series of paintings on this joyful trip, such as *Morning in the Green Cloister, Santa Maria Novella, Florence* and *The Old Market, Milan*, but sadly none of these is known to have survived.

According to Amanda Kavanagh,

> Robert and Caroline spent the first years of their married life at Benthall Hall, Shropshire, where he painted the imposing portrait of his wife which he exhibited at the Grosvenor Gallery in 1886.

So we decided to start our search for them at that lovely old manor house, which had been acquired by the National Trust but was still home to members of the Benthall family. The administrator forwarded one of the house brochures to us, but warned that it contained very little that would help us. The house had been sold by the Benthall family in the early nineteenth century, and bought back in the mid-twentieth century. Very few records were kept in the intervening years during the tenancies granted by the owner Lord Forester.

The Batemans were primarily remembered for creating a Rose Garden, previously called the Pixie Garden, which has now been fully restored. From the brochure we learned that the tenant before them, George Maw, had published a definitive book on crocuses, *The Genus Crocus*, in 1886 while at Benthall. This startled us. From Amanda Kavanagh we had understood that the Batemans had arrived in the first year of their marriage, 1883. However, the administrator corrected us, and insisted that they had not moved in until 1890. Kavanagh had proposed that the background to the portrait of Caroline exhibited in 1886 was 'probably inspired by the view of the Severn from Benthall Edge'. If the Batemans did not move to Benthall Hall until four years after this, it supported our suspicion that the view had, in fact, been inspired by that from Biddulph Old Hall towards Congleton Edge (fig. 73). This gave a fascinating insight into where Robert and Caroline had actually spent the first years of their marriage.

Fig. 73. The view from Biddulph Old Hall towards Congleton Edge.

This discovery was a defining moment in our relationship with Biddulph Old Hall and its involvement with the wonderful love story of Robert Bateman, the mysterious visionary artist, and Caroline Octavia, his complex and beautiful wife. Suddenly we seemed to see them everywhere, watching the setting sun slanting through the glassless windows of the ruins, climbing the tower and gazing over the plain to the Welsh Hills, and walking together past the cascades, waterfalls and still waters of their secret valley. We knew they had been there, laughing, talking and making love, as day by day the huge portrait emerged from the empty canvas in the studio. They did not so much haunt us as simply join us in the house. As they did so we became imbued with the benign intensity of their world.

We returned to the great portrait with a new interest and sought out the article by Richard Dorment published in 2002 in *The New York Review of Books*, which explained the significance of the clothes Caroline was wearing (see fig. 24). Dorment emphasised the extremely precise, clear execution of every detail of the painting, a pronounced characteristic of all Robert's later work in oil after he had ceased to show at the Dudley in 1874:

Immediately striking is the almost Pre-Raphaelite obsession with minute details of dress, accessories and landscape, all the more surprising at the height of the Aesthetic Movement in England when a generally freer handling of paint had superseded the tight linear clarity found here.

He went on to note another unusual aspect of the image that is none the less characteristic of Bateman: the deliberate inclusion of visual references to historic styles of painting:

> Notable too is the homage Bateman pays to the eighteenth-century grand masters, subtly evoked in his wife's costume. This lovingly delineated dress of black silk or crepe, trimmed at the sleeves just below the elbow with flowers of lace and worn with a wrap of antique lace, fills almost half the canvas. Whoever designed it wished to suggest the kind of garments worn by women in the paintings of Gainsborough or Reynolds, just as Renaissance artists used drapery to evoke the classical world . . .

His thesis is that an appreciation of a sitter's clothing is crucial to a proper understanding of the information being communicated, both intentionally and subliminally, to nineteenth-century viewers. In the portrait, that information falls into two distinct categories.

The first is the evocation of the grand portraits of the eighteenth century. In a detailed study of Caroline's dress, he describes the whole ensemble as 'sombre but also fashionable'. He notes her padded bustle, describing it as a 'distant echo both of the mid-Victorian crinoline and of the hooped skirts worn by women in the eighteenth century'. He picks out the short train at the base of her skirt 'such as English women wore in the 1750s' and suggests that 'you find velvet bands, exactly like the one she wears on her right wrist, in portraits by Reynolds and Joseph Wright of Derby'.

The second concerns the clear intention to convey her recent widowhood:

> A contemporary would have seen at once that Mrs Bateman is in the second stage of mourning, between the full black that was customary for at least twenty-one months after the death of a close relative or spouse, and the grey or lilac colour permitted towards the end of a bereavement. In half-mourning, a woman was allowed to alleviate the severity of black with lace and pearls. And indeed we know that Caroline Howard, a granddaughter of the fifth Earl of Carlisle, was the widow of the Rev. Charles Wilbraham when Bateman married her in 1883 . . . Although the portrait was exhibited in 1886, the costume and the urn (a traditional symbol of mourning) suggest that Bateman began it much earlier, perhaps during their engagement . . . This is why the bride wears black, but it is also why she discards the traditional widow's cap, which we know, from many photographs of Queen Victoria taken after the death of Prince Albert, was normally de rigueur for mourning during the whole of the Victorian period.

Dorment adds to the sense that the portrait is a highly orchestrated projection of both the sitter and the artist by suggesting that 'it is more than likely that Mrs Bateman is wearing a dress designed by her artist husband and made by her dress-maker' and defines how this would have been perceived in the mid-1880s:

> The word contemporaries would have used to describe Mrs Bateman's ensemble is 'artistic'. They would have surmised that the circles in which the sitter moved were 'arty' but not bohemian.

The information in the article brought home vividly to us the frightening level of public exposure that exhibiting the ten-foot portrait in the Grosvenor Gallery represented for both Robert and Caroline. The subject and the scale of the image must surely have been conceived by them both as a conscious act of self-promotion, designed to project her likeness, his work and themselves as a couple into the epicentre of fashionable artistic life. In the Grosvenor's West Gallery in 1886, Caroline's picture had to stand comparison with important works including two Burne-Joneses and two pieces by G. F. Watts. Alma-Tadema was there as was Sir William Blake Richmond (with five pictures), Fantin-Latour, Edward Poynter and John Singer Sargeant. Robert's friend Walter Crane showed two pictures and Caroline's cousin, George Howard, showed a small landscape. To make so declamatory a state-ment among figures of this stature, at the height of the craze for Aestheticism that had brought art appreciation to the heart of upper-class cultural and social life, was to invite ruthless critical appraisal. Little wonder they took pains to ensure that the coded messages about Robert as an artist and Caroline as a subject were understood by their illustrious audience.

We came to realise that the whole structure of the composition, with the upper part of the figure silhouetted against naturally rendered foliage and the portion beyond given over to evocative sky and extended landscape, was directly related to the work of Joshua Reynolds. No doubt the intention was to echo Caroline's noble lineage and therefore her natural place at the centre of society. However, as we delved deeper into Reynolds's output, a more personal relationship between Caroline and his work emerged. In 1769 the Howards of Castle Howard had chosen Reynolds to execute a huge full-length portrait of the head of the family, the 5th Earl of Carlisle, set slightly atypically, against grandiose classical architecture but with a characteristic skyscape visible in the background (fig. 74). At almost the same date they had commissioned another large three-quarter-length canvas of the Earl's wife, Margaret Caroline, posing with fashionable informality in front of naturalistic branches and foliage with a landscape of gently rolling hills in the background (fig. 75). The subjects of these flamboyant canvases were Caroline's grandfather and grandmother.

The relationship of both images to Caroline's portrait is marked. The general disposition of the figures within the overall compositions is strikingly similar, and the colouring of the Earl's clothes, predominantly black with embellishments in pale

Fig. 74 (above). James Watson after Sir Joshua Reynolds, Margaret Caroline, Countess of Carlisle, *1773, mezzotint, 45 × 35.2 cm, National Portrait Gallery, London.*

Fig. 75 (above right). Sir Joshua Reynolds, Frederick Howard, 5th Earl of Carlisle, *1769, oil on canvas, 241 × 149.8 cm, Castle Howard Collection.*

grey and silver, is echoed in Caroline's enriched black dress. The trees, foliage and gentle landscape of the Countess's portrait seem directly related to the background of her granddaughter's image, and her upswept hair seems uncannily similar, given the century that separates the two pictures. Caroline never knew her grandparents, who had died some fourteen years before her birth in 1839. Her vision of them must have been formed by seeing the Reynolds portraits on childhood visits to her uncle's palatial home. It would hardly be surprising if these spectacular paintings inspired her as glamorous ideals of the portrait painter's art, and led to the format of Robert's picture.

The question of why, three years into their marriage, they should have elected to make Caroline's mourning – and, by inference, her former husband – central to the message of the painting was perplexing. Dorment's explanation that the painting must have been started during their engagement in about 1882 made sense, but we still had a twinge of unease at their decision to allow her bereavement to dominate society's view of Caroline so long after the event.

Dorment's understanding of Victorian mourning allowed him to pinpoint the date of the painting very precisely. This seemed to raise some slightly uncomfortable questions surrounding the timing of the sequence of events from her first husband's death, through mourning and half-mourning, to her marriage to Robert in 1883. Charles Wilbraham had died in mid-December 1879, so the essential minimum period of twenty-one months would have meant that Caroline remained in deep mourning until October 1881. However, the respectable period of full mourning after the loss of a clerical spouse was longer, two years. If Caroline had observed this convention, and her portrait suggests she was at pains to be seen as a grieving widow, she would not have progressed to the later stage until January 1882. This gave her a total of just nineteen months to complete the second stage of mourning, become engaged and marry Robert on 18 October 1883.

The purpose of these bereavement rituals was to emphasise the sacred solemnity in which marriage was held; their corollary was the period of betrothal, a vital time of patience and self-control in which one demonstrated an appreciation of the irrevocable seriousness of the promises one was about to make. The period between Caroline's emergence from deep mourning and her marriage seems, for the customs of the time, shockingly short. She must have scarcely completed her period of half-mourning and certainly not her time of wearing grey or mauve for her former husband before she was engaged and remarried. Had there been raised eyebrows at the immodest speed with which the daughter of a senior dignitary of the church had abandoned the memory of her respected clerical spouse and embraced a good-looking younger man?

Their London wedding did not suggest that Robert and Caroline made any attempt to downplay their marriage, but if in some circles it had been perceived as a little improper, it might have limited their acceptability in society. And any question of impropriety concerning the speed of their marriage would almost certainly have extended to speculation about the nature of their courtship. To be acceptable there could be no suggestion that this had taken place before Caroline's bereavement or while she was in full mourning. The only time, therefore, when they could have become close would have been after January 1882. So her period of half-mourning must have run concurrently with her betrothal for her marriage in October the next year.

Here the portrait itself, perhaps a little too conveniently, suggests a possible narrative. The extended time together needed to complete so ambitious a piece of work must have provided an opportunity, at the first permissible moment, for the attractive widow to find solace with the gifted artist commissioned to record her sad isolation. Did this, unexpectedly, lead to her renewed zest for life and their marriage a few months later? The decision to use the portrait to remind the Grosvenor Gallery audience of Caroline's status as the widow of an elderly clergyman does suggest they may have had anxieties about the perceived propriety of their own relationship – anxieties they attempted to counter by associating Caroline with the known piety of Rev. Charles Wilbraham.

If, as Richard Dorment logically deduces from Caroline's clothing, the painting was conceived and begun at the time of the couple's engagement in 1882, and simply remained unfinished or unexhibited until 1886, it would reflect the plain truth of her situation at that time. If, however, it was begun at any later date during the ensuing four years, it would represent a much more calculated attempt to dress and present her in a way that recalled her former marriage in order to convey the necessary gravitas to counteract any accusations of 'fastness' in her subsequent relationship with a handsome younger man.

Whatever the reason, there are signs that it might have proved extremely effective in raising both their status and Robert's ability to achieve good prices for his work. By 1890 they finally emerged from the haven of their refuge at Biddulph and took the lease on Benthall Hall, where they began the next phase in their journey through life together.

Chapter 19

BENTHALL, A SHARED SANCTUARY

It was on our third visit to Benthall Hall that we began to understand the profound transformation that the move there represented in the lives of Robert and Caroline Bateman. Unlike our previous visits, there were no parked cars on the lane as we drove up to the house. We arrived at a chained iron gate and realised the hall was closed and we were quite alone.

The moment we turned off the engine the steady rain and green twilight enfolded us in a faintly sinister embrace. Nowhere, not even Biddulph, evoked the strange stillness and disturbing silence of Robert's paintings the way this shrouded lane did. We had come to make a special study of the little church, St Bartholomew's, which was visible beyond an oak lychgate, sunk in thick, deep grasses (fig. 76). We knew from the house brochure that the church had been altered in the middle of Robert's

Fig. 76. Benthall Church, with the Hall in the background.

tenancy in 1893 by the addition of an apsidal westerly extension containing a new staircase and entrance lobby. The windows had been described as highly individual, with stone surrounds culminating in small female heads. A photograph in the leaflet showed the original porch transformed into an eccentric seat within an alcove, with a carved lion's head above it, that apparently gave access to a beehive within the walls of the building. This was in turn surmounted by a somewhat sinister sundial, with a watching eye rendered in mosaic in a recess at its centre and the words 'Out of the strong came forth sweetness' carved over it (fig. 77).

When we got out of the car and walked through the lychgate towards the deserted church, lit by a pale grey sky, the sense of Robert's intense, reclusive personality was overwhelming. By the time we arrived in front of the strange sundial, with its watching eye and open-mouthed lion, we knew it was conceived and executed by Robert. The windows on the curved west wall of the addition were exactly in his unique and quirky spirit. Characteristically, the western extension had an air of slightly wilful originality that included random architectural embellishments for their own sake, without reference to the established character of the building.

To be frank, we had developed a fairly low opinion of Robert's skills as an architect from his work at Biddulph, which was stylistically isolated from the rest of the building and fussily laden with decorative features so poorly built that some had spontaneously collapsed shortly before we moved into the house. At Benthall Church, the western extension and the projection carrying the sundial ignored both

Fig. 77. 'Out of the strong came forth sweetness', Robert's slightly sinister sundial above his quirky integral lion mask beehive.

the texture and the charming simplicity of the original structure of 1667, which was built of faced, whitewashed rubble stone to a severely plain, single-cell design.

In the years immediately before the Batemans' arrival, a small vestry extension had been added in coursed local stone in a modest gothic style, which at least sat comfortably with the texture of the nearby hall. In this context, it seemed surprising that the 1893 work should have been executed in brick, to a design with a strong Italianate flavour, involving many curved elements, embellished with brick dentil courses and round apertures. The decision to reveal the timbers on the little bell tower added a final flourish of sentimentalised inconsistency to what must once have been a simple and dignified little place of worship nestling unpretentiously beside the great house of the village which it served. It was the very shortcomings of the larger-scale architecture, as much as the highly characteristic detailing, that made us feel instinctively that Robert was the guiding creative force behind all the 1893 work.

As ever, the quality of the individual features was excellent. The lion mask was a compelling stylised design conveying strength and ferocity. The female heads on the west windows, although somewhat eroded by exposure to weather, showed great skill, and the face of the sundial itself was elegantly carved. The motto, 'Out of the strong came forth sweetness,' referred to the beehive concealed behind the open mouth of the lion mask. It was beautifully executed in a stylised script with elongated elements on some letters including A, H and N. Robert's trademark of the extended downward stroke on the R was prominent, indicating strongly that he was the sculptor. Recalling Walter Crane's references to Robert's becoming increasingly interested in spheres of creativity beyond painting during his time at Benthall, the link became compelling:

> Besides painting, however, he has worked in a variety of crafts with distinction, and has lately perfected a modelling material of his own invention, which he terms 'plasma Bentellesca' after Benthall Hall in Shropshire – a beautiful sixteenth-century house which was his house for many years, the beauty of which he greatly added to by the gardens he laid out, as well as other improvements.

It was clear that sculpture and modelling became a focus of interest for Robert during these years, which increased the probability that he would have taken a pivotal role in any artistic developments proposed for the little church that stood a few yards from his home.

We hoped that the late Victorian additions designed by Robert held out the possibility of explaining a conundrum. The Benthall Hall booklet gave a great deal of prominence to George Maw as the originator of the documented garden at the hall, whose creation had been praised in 1872 by the influential garden writer, William Robinson, as 'cultivated with no common skill'. It continues:

> The next tenants, Robert Bateman and his wife, lived at Benthall from about 1890 to 1906. Bateman, from a Staffordshire family, was an architect practising in London

and Birmingham and was also a painter of some note. His father was James Bateman, the creator of the famous garden at Biddulph Grange (now in the care of The National Trust). He made some additions and alterations to the church, probably including the girl's heads on the west end and the little statue in the middle of the lily pond (in the garden by the hall). He and his wife laid out the terraces and rockeries. The terrace garden to the west of the house was known as the Pixie Garden in the Batemans' day (now the Rose Garden) and Robert is thought to have built the octagonal dovecote.

This suggested a whole area of Robert's work, as a professional architect, of which we had been completely unaware. When we launched a painstaking search of the architectural profession the mystery began to unravel. We discovered how prominent the name of Bateman had been in the architectural history of nineteenth-century Birmingham. John Jones Bateman (1818–1903) had designed landmark buildings in the city, such as the new Workhouse (1851) and the Unitarian Church of The Messiah in Broad Street. His son Charles went into partnership with his father as Bateman and Bateman. Charles was highly successful and ended up as President of the Birmingham Architectural Association and a leading lecturer in architecture at Birmingham School of Art.

It is not difficult to see how this plethora of creative Batemans had led to confusion. As the years passed, Robert's most enduring legacy to Benthall were his changes to the church and garden, which led to his being remembered as an architect rather than an artist. The true conundrum of Robert's life at Benthall was not that he suddenly began a new career at fifty, but that this obsessive, driven perfectionist metamorphosed, under the influence of this serene place, into a contented country gentleman who enjoyed a leisurely game of bowls and channelled his creative drive into dabbling in a wide range of artistic interests at an amateur level. This was the affable, gifted dilettante encountered by Amanda Kavanagh, who had concentrated her study on his life at Benthall without realising how starkly it contrasted with the solitary visionary of the Biddulph years.

The move to Benthall coincided with the closing of the Grosvenor Gallery in 1890, which marked the effective end of Robert as a professional, exhibited artist. He no longer created images in response to unresolved personal dilemmas and conflicts. He became increasingly fascinated by the means and materials of creation such as new modelling mediums, and revived historic paint recipes such as egg tempera (he was a founder member of The Society of Painters in Tempera in 1901). His interest in refining his techniques grew as the compulsion to express his innermost feelings began to dwindle away. However, it seemed paradoxical that though his disturbed intensity had declined while he was here, we had sensed its distilled essence so strongly by the chained gate to Benthall Hall.

If manor houses define the essence of the romance of England, Benthall Hall, on that sodden May afternoon, dispensed that heady brew at its most intoxicating (fig. 78). All the ingredients were there: the overall scale and grandeur, gently mitigated by the lack of symmetry and the all-embracing ancient texture that united it with the ground beneath it. The great trees, gnarled and magnificent, were planted in the reign of Queen Anne or Queen Victoria, and beyond them a nameless old rose climbed to the eaves, drooping and dishevelled, mingling its scent with the smell of beeswax and musty needlework in the parlour. In front of the rows of gables in the roof, swallows and swifts were soaring and swooping. It did not take much insight to understand how Robert and Caroline would have fallen under the spell of this sublime place.

On our earlier visits, when the house was open, we had not taken in either its extent or its relationship to its setting. Now, as the cows moaned mournfully behind us and the rain finally faded to an almost imperceptible haze, we understood how all this would have represented the fulfilment of the complex romantic yearnings that Robert and Caroline shared, despite the disparity of their families' ranks and positions in society.

Fig. 78. Reticent romance: Benthall hall from the buttercup meadow.

For Robert, who at heart could not have failed to absorb some of his father's and brother's longing for a place among the gentry, the unequivocal identity of Benthall as an historic hall house, the manor which, from time immemorial, had housed the lord or squire of the village, must have added a further source of satisfaction to his longstanding romantic response to all time-worn, ancient buildings. The sense of secret, dreaming reticence would have combined with these characteristics to form a compulsive attraction.

For Caroline there were deep, lifelong ties with Benthall and its surroundings, over and above its beauty. It linked back to her happy childhood and provided the perfect haven in which to find peace and security with the man she loved, after the years of struggle to be together. Benthall was less than nine miles from the little parish of Donnington, which had been held as a subsidiary living by her father the Dean. The Georgian rectory at Donnington had been the family's beloved country retreat. Almost all the children, including Caroline, had been born there, and it was the peaceful place where the Dean had chosen to go in his last illness. He died there and, despite the flamboyant ritual of his funeral and the consecrating of his memorial in the cathedral, it was the place to which his body was quietly returned and buried. Benthall and the lanes and villages around it must have evoked the sunlit, carefree world of her childhood as a pretty, adored younger daughter, securely surrounded by the flock of brothers and sisters who made up her large, privileged family. For Caroline, Benthall held out the magical attraction of coming home to the place where she had always belonged.

The longer we stood gazing at Benthall, the more we came to perceive the fundamental consistency of Robert and Caroline's personalities, despite an apparently abrupt change in the pattern of their daily existence after they moved there. This house represented the final fulfilment of the prime motivating drive of their earlier lives, their longing to be permanently together. The achievement of that aim changed their priorities and led Robert, in particular, to adopt a far less focused, driven approach to his creative life. While from an art history perspective this may seem regrettable, from their own standpoint they were merely continuing to give the stability and development of their relationship priority over every other achievement. All the striving of their lives, even the phase at Biddulph after their marriage when they had set out to promote Robert's work so that he could achieve a sufficiently established artistic and financial position to make him acceptable to her family, had been leading to this place, and this life, which at last resolved some of the external pressures on their relationship and held out the prospect of a secure, loving future.

Where Robert and Caroline differ from the star-crossed lovers of history such as Paolo and Francesca or Heloise and Abelard is that, unlike them, they were ultimately able to overcome the forces ranged against them. Perhaps the most extraordinary quality about their relationship was that its intensity formed a fixed point of contentment at the core of their later lives, sustaining them until their deaths in 1922.

The particular genius of their love was that the interaction of their personalities remained the vibrant focus of their lives even after the reversal of the absent craving and emotional starvation from which it sprang.

As we turned to retrace our steps to the lane, we could not deny a tinge of personal sadness for the approaching end of our ability to share in the galvanising intensity of their love affair. It had moved into a new phase of devoted companionship which could be expressed directly, within the sanctuary of their secluded home, and had no need of public forms of communication through which we could vicariously be part of it.

Fig. 79. Robert, the country squire, with the bowls team and holding the match trophy, in front of his home, Benthall Hall.

Chapter 20

A COUNTRY SQUIRE AND
HIS GOOD LADY

Judging by local records, Robert and Caroline threw themselves with some vigour into the roles of the benevolent country squire (fig. 79) and his good lady. In the early 1890s Robert was elected to the Board of Guardians that oversaw the administration of the local workhouse at Madeley and supported the poor of the parish. His contributions to some of these worthy but convoluted debates have a refreshing humanity and concern for the people under discussion. In January 1892, for example, the Board of Guardians addressed the vexed question of whether to provide the inmates of the workhouse with bread, or the flour with which to make it:

> Mr Mole, relieving officer, asked the Guardians if they intended to give bread instead of flour.
> Mr Bateman, 'What do the poor want?'
> The Officer, 'The majority say bread.'
> Mr Weaver said he should be of the same view, but they should take into consideration 'that one costs 2d and the other 4d'.

The concept of consulting the recipients of charity on their preference was clearly unconventional but it won the day none the less. Robert was an active committee member on the board organising the Brossley Horticultural Show, charmingly reported in the *Wellington Journal* as a

> near miraculous achievement in an area principally associated with smoke (!) because its busy manufactories constantly emit their Stygian fumes, in evidence of the abiding prosperity of the place ... Therefore it must have been a delicious experience to non-residential visitors ... that the district had been made to blossom with such brilliant abundance and give such proof of its full fruition ...

Robert and Caroline played their part in the judging and joined in the dancing to the strains of the Coalbrookdale Band conducted by Sergeant Beardshaw. Robert was the chairman of the Brossley Wood branch of the British and Foreign Bible Society, and suggested scholarships for boys and girls to celebrate Queen Victoria's diamond jubilee.

Robert and Caroline were on friendly terms with the 4th Lord Forrester, owner of a large estate centred on Willey Hall, of which Benthall Hall formed a subsidiary manor. Lord Forrester was an elderly canon of York Minster, who therefore had much in common with Caroline. When he died in June 1894 there was a service in York Minster after which his body was taken to Much Wenlock by train. Robert played a central role in his funeral in Shropshire, as part of the committee who met the coffin at the station and then as one of the pall bearers who bore it during the funeral service at the local church.

Caroline, equally conscientiously, played her part in local life, supporting charities and local institutions, frequently by singing or accompanying concerts in aid of good causes. For example, on 5 January 1901 she presided at one of the tea tables at a concert in aid of the organ fund, chaired by Robert. After tea she accompanied the performers, along with Miss Watkins and Miss Southern, 'their efforts being heartily appreciated'. On 22 June the same year, she and Robert hosted the Mothers' Meeting:

> On Monday, through the kindness of Mr and Mrs Bateman, the members of the Mothers' Meeting, to the number thirty, were entertained to tea at the Hall. After a very enjoyable meal, the members, accompanied by Mr and Mrs Bateman and Mrs Terry [the Vicar's wife], walked for some time in the artistically laid out grounds. Subsequently they returned to the Hall, when Mr Dorbree, lately a member of the original Regiment of the Imperial Light Horse, kindly gave some of his experiences while besieged at Ladysmith.

Census returns and letters from this period make clear that Caroline kept up a regular round of visits to her old friends and relations. In 1891 she was staying with two members of the Monckton family, Mary and Leonora, at Brewood Hall near Penckridge, where she had lived during her marriage to Charles Wilbraham. Her letter to her cousin, George Howard, Earl of Carlisle, in the late 1890s (see fig. 59) was written from Glyngarth Palace, the home of the Bishop of Bangor and his wife, her old friend Alice Monckton. In 1901 she was a guest at Lockinge House, the palatial home of her cousin Lady Wantage. As her letter to George Howard makes clear, she actively encouraged return visits to Benthall by her friends and family. Robert did not always accompany her on these visits, but remained at home 'enjoying his flowers and his painting'. But there is no sense that Caroline feels socially superior or ashamed of him. She never flaunts her connections to impress others, neither does she attempt to downplay them; she is simply natural and loyal to her closest and oldest companions.

This loyalty to those near to her and identification with their interests emerge more and more clearly as core traits in Caroline's nature. They imply a rare blend of personal serenity and innate respect for others, which had the power to resolve conflict within her relationships. She provided an encompassing sense of security to those she loved, through her ability to defer to them willingly without ever losing her dignity or gentle strength of character. This was the alchemy that transformed her marriage of convenience to Charles Wilbraham into a genuine nurturing bond between two starkly contrasted adults.

The same unshakeable loyalty to Robert had brought about not only their eventual union but the gradual fulfilment of his potential as an artist. Later it enabled them to move to Benthall Hall, assume a lifestyle that quietly dissolved the social disparity between them, and integrated him into her world. If the price of embracing Caroline's gift for creating deep, loving relationships was the loss of distracted intensity in his paintings, caused by his loneliness without her, who can blame Robert for paying it?

We went to Benthall again to study the Pixie Garden. This charming confection of informal paths, weaving their way across a mounded site by way of steps and stone-edged beds, has been sensitively restored by The National Trust and constitutes a real embellishment to the setting of Benthall Hall. Our interest in it was heightened by the fact that we clearly had a smaller prototype of it outside our back door at Biddulph. This garden constituted the most successful artistic achievement by Robert that we had been able to discover during his years at Benthall. We did not doubt that he had continued to work on his flower paintings, which were by common consent executed with an almost oriental delicacy. They were, however, lost and have never been recorded as on public exhibition.

The catalogue of the New Gallery, which opened in 1888 and supplanted the Grosvenor after its closure in 1890, showed only one contribution from Robert, *At Romsey Abbey*, dated 1899, despite the fact that Burne-Jones, Crane and most of his former soul-mates transferred there in the early 1890s. Eventually, we were forced to admit that without the dynamic narrative of their thwarted passion for each other, the story of Robert and Caroline's life at Benthall Hall had lost its compulsive intensity. Almost none of Robert's paintings, and certainly not the important ones for which he is remembered, date from these halcyon days after 1890.

The fulfilment that Caroline enabled Robert to achieve encompassed both his hunger to be fully accepted as a gentleman, and his ambition to be a recognised artist whose work was exhibited alongside the idolised modern masters of his day. This process had begun almost immediately after Caroline's widowhood in December 1879. By 1881, Robert had switched from exhibiting at the Royal Academy to the Grosvenor which, at that moment, was at the very peak of its cultural influence. One of the most striking consequences of the cult the gallery generated around its leading artists was that their work reached previously unimaginable prices, particularly when it was perceived as conforming to the refined ideals of the Aesthetic Movement. From its beginnings at the opening of the Grosvenor in 1876, this cult continued to grow. It dominated the art market throughout the 1880s, despite the difficulties that beset the gallery itself in the last years of the decade and its eventual closure in 1890.

An indication of the sensational prices for 'Aesthetic' art was provided by the sale of the collection of Frederick Leyland, a wealthy ship owner, in 1892. A group of 'Illustrations of Boccaccio' by Botticelli, one of the most venerated of fifteenth-century Italian masters, achieved the then staggering sum of £1,300. But this was made to seem trifling in comparison to Burne-Jones's *The Beguiling of Merlin*, which achieved £3,600 guineas later the same day, with the bidding opening at £1,000 guineas.

Although Burne-Jones's position was unique as the acknowledged figurehead of all the purveyors of legendary romance, work by other artists who drew inspiration from broadly comparable sources also saw a dramatic and sustained rise in value throughout the 1880s and early 1890s. This was particularly true of figures such as Walter Crane, who had a history of association with Burne-Jones. By chance we had recently stumbled across evidence of long-term artistic links between Burne-Jones and Robert. We had been shown a small, sinister watercolour of *Little Red Riding Hood* at Mells, a lyrically beautiful manor house in Somerset. It was initialled RB and dated 1866 (fig. 80). The picture was fascinating to us because the architectural setting for the figure was Biddulph Old Hall, and we had never before had any documentary evidence of Robert using it as a home or studio before 1874. Also, the date and its location strongly suggested that the painting was bought by William Graham for his nine-year-old daughter Katherine, who grew up to marry Sir John Horner, the owner of Mells. This probability was effectively confirmed when the current owner of Mells (Katherine's great-grandson) took the picture down in order to show us the back, which had 'R. Bateman' written in chalk, in what he knew to be Katherine Graham's handwriting (fig. 81). Not only was William Graham a friend and patron of Burne-Jones, but the artist had developed a romantic fixation with Katherine that began when he first met her as a little girl in 1865 and lasted all through his life. The close relationship between Burne-Jones and the Grahams was publicly acknowledged throughout the artistic community.

Clearly, Robert had also been part of the circle surrounding this important Pre-Raphaelite patron from its beginning. Whereas in those days the Burne-Jones/Graham connection would have been seen as a liability, by the time Robert had established his name at the Grosvenor Gallery in the early 1880s he must have reaped huge financial advantage from his loyalty to the formerly despised artistic genius, who was now being credited with the most beautiful and profound expressions of the anti-materialist longings of that contradictory age. Those rewards can only have

Fig. 80 (above). Robert Bateman, Little
Red Riding Hood, *1866, watercolour,
private collection.*

*Fig. 81 (right). Katherine Graham's
writing on the reverse confirms that the
painting had belonged to her.*

increased once Burne-Jones became an establishment figure with a peerage in
England and the Legion d'Honneur in France.

This transformation of his earning power must have lain at the heart of Robert
and Caroline's ability to establish themselves in the comfort of Benthall Hall. In
these circumstances, it is difficult to understand his decision to stop exhibiting,
which meant forfeiting the income that had underpinned the move. However, this
is less strange than it appears, for two important reasons.

First, the opening of the New Gallery in 1888 was deliberately intended to
supplant the Grosvenor Gallery, which had got into serious financial difficulties after
the collapse of the marriage of its founder, Sir Coutts Lindsay, and his wealthy wife
Blanche. She withdrew her financial support for the venture after separating from
her husband. Sir Coutts's subsequent commercialisation of the Gallery had upset
not only many of the leading exhibitors, but his two co-directors, Charles Halle and

Comyns Carr. The dispute eventually became public knowledge after Halle and Carr published their differences with Sir Coutts Lindsay in *The Times* on 2 November 1887. They resigned in order to found the New Gallery, which opened the following year, taking Burne-Jones and many of the leading artists with them. The rupture was bitter and artists were forced to take sides.

This presented Robert and Caroline with a dilemma. Her cousin, Harriet, was married to Sir Coutts Lindsay's brother Lord Wantage. So, as family, it was virtually impossible for them to defect to the New Gallery, even after the closure of the Grosvenor in 1890. At the very least, they needed to let a year or two elapse before disloyally patronising Halle and Carr's institution, the opening of which had led directly to the Grosvenor's collapse. This, in itself, might have proved no more than a temporary difficulty had it not been for a far more important, but initially almost imperceptible, change in taste, deep in the bedrock of artistic criticism and evaluation. A new movement emerged that sought to capture the fleeting vividness of immediate first-hand experience. By its very nature it had no place for indirect sources of inspiration such as legends, myths and poems. This new art had its genesis in France and soon became known as Impressionism.

The speed with which Impressionism supplanted the taste for even the most venerated British artists was extraordinary. Burne-Jones, for example, despite the huge sum his *Beguiling of Merlin* had commanded in 1892, found his work being returned unsold from the major galleries by 1895. From then on the decline gathered momentum so that by 1898, the last year of his life, he was recorded complaining to Thomas Rooke, his studio assistant:

> This is the third year now that my things haven't sold. We shall have to finish *Avalon* [The Sleep of King Arthur] and *Car of Love* without any expectation of selling them.

He was utterly baffled that the critics ascribed greater significance to what he saw as semi-abstracted, superficial sketches than to his refined, mystical images. The exquisitely finished surface texture of his work was specifically contrived to entrance the viewer and stimulate a contemplative response, challenging the banality and ugliness of the work-a-day Victorian world. His wife Georgina wrote after his death:

> The doctrine of the excellence of unfinished work was necessarily repugnant to Edward, who was at first incredulous as to its being seriously held by anyone; but as what is called the 'Impressionist' school gained ground it became one of the most disheartening thoughts of his life.

How Robert Bateman must have shared and identified with this bewildered anguish. Within a period of three or four years, the artistic ideals to which he had dedicated his creative energy all his life were increasingly ridiculed as representing a parochial byway, doomed to extinction, while the central tradition of painting thrust exuberantly forward into its modernist future. Little wonder that he withdrew into the sanctuary of his tranquil life at Benthall Hall with Caroline, and ceased even to identify himself as an artist. To do so would have exposed him to incomprehensible disputes with galleries and art critics who regarded his work as irrelevant.

The secret of how Robert made the financial transition from working artist to gentleman of private means lay in the years that preceded the reversal of taste that overtook the art world between 1890 and 1910. Although Burne-Jones had lived to see the ignominy of his work returning unsold, he none the less died an extremely wealthy man, worth £53,493 9s 7d (equal to some £5.5 million in present values). He had earned steadily all his working life through his designs for Morris & Co. as well as his painting, yet this had provided only enough for him to live a comfortable middle-class life, until his dramatic explosion into the fashionable art world at the opening of the Grosvenor Gallery in 1877.

After he established himself at the Grosvenor in 1881, Robert must have shared in the demand for evocative, quasi-mystical, romantic pictures and the high prices they commanded. Of course, neither his celebrity nor his output were comparable to Burne-Jones's, but once Robert got important work exhibited alongside him and the other leading figures at the Grosvenor, he would have begun to benefit by association. If over a period of about fifteen years Burne-Jones became, in present values, a multi-millionaire, it seems highly likely that Robert acquired enough money to take a lease on a rural manor house and invest sufficient capital to live quietly off the income for many years.

If one adds to this the remnants of Caroline's inheritance from Charles Wilbraham and some allowance from her family, the possibility of sustaining an upper-class lifestyle over several years seems highly plausible. Despite this, we were curious to know whether Caroline or Robert had been helped by either of their families to acquire Benthall Hall, or sustain their life there, after Robert had ceased to exhibit as a professional artist.

The 8th Earl of Carlisle died on 23 March 1889, the year before Robert and Caroline moved to Benthall. He was an elderly bachelor with no direct descendents. We wondered if he had made bequests to the Dean's children, his first cousins, after the title and great estates had passed to his only nephew, George Howard. However, when we researched his affairs there was no mention of Caroline. We wondered if the death of Robert's father James in 1897 had brought him an inheritance. We bought a copy of James's will from the probate office and were shocked when we received it. The whole document consisted of a single short paragraph which made no reference to any of his four children or his grandchildren or wider family. It simply left everything to his second wife (his first wife's former lady's maid) and appointed her sole executrix. In view of the vast fortune that James Bateman had been bequeathed by his father and grandfather, his will is worth quoting in full:

The will of me, James Bateman, of Worthing, Esquire. I give and bequeath to my wife, Ann Bateman, all my furniture and articles of household or personal use and ornaments, together with all my money and all my personal estate and effects whatsoever and I appoint her Executrix of my will in witness whereof I hereto set my hand this thirteenth day of April One Thousand Eight Hundred and Ninety Six.

The accompanying sheet recording his death on 27 November 1897, and registering the granting of probate on 23 February 1898, completed the tragic story of James Bateman's decline. At the foot of the page against a section reading 'Gross value of Personal Estate', it records the figure of £273 18s 11d. Immediately below this, the space designated 'Net value of Personal Estate' had the printed '£' sign crossed out and the single word 'Nil' written in ink.

That terse word confirmed the collapse of the fortunes of the Bateman family. It finally exposed the fallacy that Robert Bateman was a gifted artistic dabbler with a secure social position underpinned by his family's huge wealth in mineral extraction, industrial production and landholdings. His father's will made clear that if Robert had married a glamorous figure from the heart of the aristocratic establishment and settled down to a contented life in a sublime English manor house as a country gentleman of private means, he had done so without the support of his progressively impoverished parents. They had been unable to make any contribution to his prosperity, even after their deaths.

Our quest to rescue from obscurity every retrievable fact about the life and work of Robert Bateman, the elusive Pre-Raphaelite artist we had unearthed deep within the historical records of our derelict home, seemed to be coming to its natural conclusion. Despite the implacable forces that were to condemn his work to obscurity, so that not a single painting by him was known to exist by the middle of the twentieth century, the continuance of his happy marriage and his contented adjustment into the role of comfortable country gentleman signalled the end of the dynamic conflicts of his early life and the beginning of the 'happy ever after' phase that defines the end of so many good stories.

Only two areas of Robert's story remained to be followed up. The first was to visit Robert and Caroline's last home at Nunney in Somerset, and the second was to make a concerted effort to see if we could discover the whereabouts of any of the lost paintings and drawings, particularly the ones that had remained with him to the end of his life and may have been passed down privately within his or Caroline's families.

Chapter 21

FOREVER ONE

Nunney was the one place visited by everyone we had met or heard of with a serious interest in Bateman. They had gone there hoping to meet people who would shed light on his life and lost paintings but had all concluded that there was nothing there. Of course this was not entirely true – the churchyard at Whatley, the next village, contains their graves giving the dates of their deaths.

The devotion of their marriage was the most vivid memory of the couple that the inhabitants of Nunney had been able to convey to visitors. Amanda Kavanagh was sufficiently impressed by the frequent repetition of this aspect of their life there to end her article by describing Robert's love for Caroline as the central motivating force of his life and work. The locals were hardly aware of his painting at all. Richard Dorment had described a conversation with an old man in Nunney who stated categorically that Robert was not a painter but purely a sculptor, whose work he remembered. This at least was nearer the mark than the other local references he was able to tap, all of which centred on mutual devotion, rockery gardens and the founding of bowling clubs. Most of these visits had taken place in the late 1980s or early 1990s, so we felt that the likelihood of even these reminiscences still being available was remote.

One problem was the lack of any consistent information about either the date of, or the reason for, Robert and Caroline's move from Benthall Hall to this part of Somerset. Kavanagh guessed that the date was 'probably around 1910'. However, Benthall Hall gave the termination of their lease as 'about 1906', raising the possibility that they might have gone elsewhere for a short while. Caroline would have been about seventy at the time so it seemed probable that the move was triggered by a desire to be near to relatives.

Our first instinct was to search for Howards, as their social prominence usually made them easier to find. By now we had a full family tree of the Howard family, particularly Caroline's immediate relatives and their descendents. We laboriously trawled through census returns of 1891 and 1901 for every household in and around Nunney, but were unable to identify a single relevant Howard in the area who might have prompted them to move there.

The Batemans were no more rewarding. By the early years of the twentieth century both Robert's parents had died, his father at Worthing and his mother at Brightlingsea in Essex, where his eldest brother John lived and remained till his own death in 1910. His other brother, Rowland, retired from missionary work in India in 1902 and took up a post as vicar of Fawley, a little parish near Henley-on-Thames, before moving north in 1906 to become vicar of Biddulph, his old home parish. His son Melville lived with him until he emigrated to Canada in 1904, while his daughter Mary Sybilla lived in London. Robert's younger sister Katharine had been widowed in 1895 and for a time acted as housekeeper to Rowland at Fawley Rectory, before remarrying in 1904 and moving to Fareham in Hampshire. She had two married daughters, Mabel Emma Humphries and Sybil Knatchbull, an unmarried daughter, Hope, and a son Henry. There was no trace of any of them living in the Nunney area before Robert and Caroline's arrival.

Of course, there might have been other reasons for their move. Nunney was a charming little village, clustered round a river with the ruined remains of a medieval castle at its centre. This would certainly have been attractive to Robert, but it did seem a trifle radical, at nearly seventy years of age, to leave a lovely house in which they had lived happily for twenty years in a place with lifelong family links for Caroline to go south to a strange area simply for its picturesque setting. These anomalies had intensified our unease at going there for the sole purpose of making a pilgrimage to their graveside, which would have symbolised the end of our adventure with them. Perhaps this was the reason why several months slipped by before we set out on a blustery January day.

We had almost no information to guide us beyond the name of their house, Nunney Delamere, and the churchyard of St George's, Whatley, where they were reputed to be buried. We had never seen a photograph or description of either, so we went into the village shop to ask for help. The woman serving was very perplexed. Not only did the name Robert Bateman mean nothing to her, but the house Nunney Delamere was not one she could honestly say she had ever heard of. She proffered a booklet written by the local historical society to mark the millennium, entitled *Nunney – The Stone Age*. She was flicking through the pages when I stopped her at a sepia photograph of a tall, elegant old man leading a procession, whom I immediately recognised as Robert (fig. 82). The caption read: 'Robert Bateman leading Nunney's Empire Day walk, 1912.' The accompanying paragraph described Robert as of Rockfield House.

'Now then,' she said, 'Rockfield House – that's a different matter altogether. It's at the top of the village, up Horn Street.'

*Fig. 82. Artistic dandy: Robert leading the Empire Day Parade
at Nunney in pale bowler hat and spats, 1912.*

*Figs. 83, 84. Architectural confusion: Robert's new
entrance front and studio at Nunney Delamere.*

When we arrived at the gates of Rockfield House, we could see that the piece of stone with the house name carved on it was newer that the rest of the gate pier. We were to discover later that Rockfield House was a return to its original name at the time it was built. The change to Nunney Delamere had been instigated by Robert and Caroline, perhaps with the slightly pretentious intention of associating it with the ancient De La Mere family of Nunney Castle in the centre of the village. The house was strange and difficult to comprehend. It did not have any clearly discernible pattern or stylistic unity. However, as we walked up the rising drive towards the porch we were struck by a vivid rush of recognition. The rendered surfaces were embellished with brick detailing that corresponded exactly with the brick patterns on the church, dovecote and garden walls at Benthall Hall.

As the principal facade of a substantial classical building, it was not a cogent or successful design (fig. 83). There was an eccentrically placed circular window below the brick cornice and an offset sash window on the ground floor that broke uncomfortably through a mid-course of brick banding, which in turn collided with an ungainly exterior chimney stack, where it terminated. Otherwise the frontage was a blank expanse of render. The flat-roofed porch was to the right, set back, and saved from actual ugliness by a handsome, severely simple stone door surround and metal fanlight which had almost certainly been part of the original house before it was incorporated into the new structure. As with the church at Benthall, the combination of unresolved architectural elements and elaborate, slightly inappropriate detailing betrayed Robert's hand in the design and his lack of finesse as an architect, compared with his consummate skill as a painter.

We rang the bell and waited anxiously. The door was answered by a small animated woman in her late twenties, who listened to our strange tale with interest but seemed uncertain how to react to our request to see the house. As a tenant, she did not feel she had the authority to show us round, and asked us go across the garden to the cottage attached to the back of the building and ask permission from the owner, Mrs Pomeroy. The view from the garden revealed the true extent of the damage inflicted on this supremely refined, chaste building by the later, gimmicky addition. The harmony of the back facade was achieved through the perfect proportions and precise disposition of its unadorned architectural elements. It was a Regency villa, whose rectangular form was relieved only by a slow curved bay at the centre and shallow, round-headed recesses intended to emphasise the elongated elegance of the ground-floor sash windows (fig. 84). As designers, and lovers of old buildings, we could not help regretting what we regarded as an insensitive addition to the building.

None the less, when we looked carefully at Robert's extension it immediately gave us two crucial pieces of information. Above the ground-floor sash windows were two highly characteristic brick-lined circular recesses containing inscriptions. The first read 'R & C B', and the other the date, 1906 (figs. 85–87). For the first time we could now be certain that Robert and Caroline had not moved in 1910 but well before, in time to have completed and dated their substantial new wing by 1906. Also, since Robert had effectively signed this building there could be little doubt that he had designed not only these alterations but also the church and garden buildings at Benthall which displayed the same highly idiosyncratic brick features.

We made our way past what appeared to be another characteristic Bateman building, a garden pavilion, and on into the rear courtyard, where we knocked on

Figs. 85–87. The garden front of Robert's studio at Nunney Delamere showing his and Caroline's joint initials and the date 1906 in the roundels.

the door of the cottage. No one answered. We could not wait. It was almost 4 o'clock on a late January afternoon and we had not yet been to Whatley churchyard to see the graves, the main purpose of our trip. So we returned to the front door of the main house to ask for Mrs Pomeroy's telephone number.

By the time we reached Whatley church, its tower was silhouetted against a dusky sky. The churchyard was about three feet above the level of the lane, with a stone wall surrounding it. Although it was almost dark we could just make out the shape of the most prominent memorials. We had never seen a picture of Robert and Caroline's graves, but had been told that they were side by side in matching plots. As we began to stumble around the graveyard, our search suddenly seemed to be a desperate undertaking. We had expected the graves to be prominent, commensurate with the Batemans' social standing, so it was dispiriting to find, when we managed to decipher them in the sallow light of our feeble torch, that the pompous edifices with railings and celtic crosses commemorated Edgar Norris, Mary Adelaide Ashby and Charlotte Saunders Shore.

Eventually, we did catch sight of two identical graves, placed side by side. They were unconventional, with both plots defined by what looked like prominent stone kerbs, with pale, lichen-covered crosses laid flat on the ground within them. We knelt on the kerb and shone the torch on to them but they were encrusted with growth. Brian used a credit card to try to scrape the lichen away. He was struggling to decipher the inscriptions and had just managed to read the words 'John —, Aged 8 years' and realised it was neither Robert's nor Caroline's grave when our torch gave out and we had to admit defeat. We were left kneeling on the cold ground in the blackness, bereft. We had to find where they were buried, and go there. It was the culmination of our whole journey into their world.

Suddenly, lights flickered across the bare branches above us, and there was the thump, thump of music as a car roared past down the lane. The silence returned. Slowly we fumbled our way back to the car and set off north to Staffordshire in silence.

It was only a matter of days before we made contact with Anne Pomeroy. The striking thing about my conversation with Anne was her response to Robert's name.

'Oh yes,' she said, immediately. 'I've always been intrigued by him. Fascinating man. My younger son is an artist, actually. Of course he's frightfully snooty about Bateman. He and his friends are all modernists, naturally, but I love his paintings – exquisite in their own way. Peculiarly mesmerising. I find I can look at them for ages and keep finding more in them.'

For a moment my heart stood still.

'You have seen some Batemans . . .' I faltered.

'Oh yes – I have three in my cottage here.'

'Three authenticated Batemans?'

'Yes. They're not originals, of course, I only wish they were. But I wouldn't be without them now. A man in the village organised to get some beautiful coloured prints for me made from books because he knew I was interested.'

I was astonished by Anne's casual familiarity with Robert and his work. The relentless pattern of having to explain our interest in this elusive figure was now so deeply ingrained that it was disconcerting to be greeted with such informed enthusiasm. I asked Anne if she had met other people interested in Bateman, and she replied that one or two had contacted her and visited the house over the years.

'Do come,' she said. 'I think you'll find it's worth a visit. There are almost no actual things of his, but you get what I would call a "feel" for him here. He's definitely left something – a presence. Of course my children think I'm gaga, but I do believe that.'

She promised to liaise with her tenant Clare Johnson, who wanted to be there.

Our next visit to Rockfield House, or Nunney Delamere as we still liked to think of it, bore out Anne Pomeroy's contention that the house retained a distinct aura of Robert and Caroline's personalities. Clare greeted us in the old kitchen and led the way into the hall and then into Robert's studio by way of his new entrance lobby extension. It was heartening to discover how much more successful the extensions were inside the house than out. Both the lobby and the studio were handsome, symmetrical spaces, relating comfortably to the bold classicism of the existing interior.

The studio, in particular, was a long, well-paced space with a fine, central fireplace and long sash windows on to the garden. The quality of the window shutters, dado panelling and bookcases was outstanding. It was a big room and when Clare opened the shutters, the sense of its being virtually unaltered since it was built, and strongly redolent of Robert and Caroline, was intensified by the way it was furnished. Clare was a musician who put on recitals, so it was set out with a fine grand piano and a group of gilt chairs with music stands, with rows of chairs for the audience. It was like a tableau of Edwardian cultural life, silently waiting for the double doors to burst open and usher in a glittering throng of white-waistcoated men and begowned women adorned with pearl chokers and elbow-length gloves. One could almost smell the perfume and cigar smoke, and hear the babble of gossip as the performers tuned their cellos and violas. Caroline's gifts as a singer and pianist were among her most defining characteristics, noted by observers all her life and referenced by Robert when he portrayed Heloise holding a book of music. Only the bare walls betrayed the revolutionary change that had engulfed the world in the century since Robert had conceived this cultivated space as a setting for his art and Caroline's musicality.

It was easy to envisage how Robert's compelling canvases would have contributed a disconcerting twist of originality to the soirées that took place here. As they gazed at them, did the Batemans' more perceptive guests experience a twinge of unease relating these anguished images to the slightly dandified squire whom we had seen leading the 1912 Empire Day parade in white spats and a pale bowler hat? The studio, even without pictures, evoked that man with amazing clarity. Its refinement was derived from classically articulated proportions and fastidious attention to detail. There was no hint here of the agonised, obsessive lover or the distracted visionary which were integral parts of the same personality. In fact, the severe classicism of Rockfield House seemed to emphasise the complexity of Robert's character which always operated on a surface level of unassertive, polite conventionality masking an internalised, imaginative life teeming with gothic dreams and chaotic, intense feelings that generated the mythical world of his paintings.

Presumably his decision to buy Rockfield House was influenced by the change in artistic fashion against all things Victorian that expressed itself in a widespread return to the appreciation of classical buildings. The lack of conviction in the exterior alterations suggests that Robert could not quite make this transition. Rockfield House did indeed retain a strong presence of both Robert and Caroline but, stripped of his paintings, it was a somewhat two-dimensional, polite account of them. It did not bear witness either to her strength of character, in defying the conventions of her family and social class to marry him, nor to his highly individual creative vision, which sprang from a much more intuitive, concealed place than these rational interiors.

Uncannily, as we left Robert's studio and were crossing his entrance hall addition, Anne suddenly stopped and did something that perfectly illuminated this contradiction in Robert's personality. With some difficulty she slid to one side a tall ceramic pot filled with umbrellas and walking canes, to reveal a tiny, exquisitely executed sculpture of an imp or devil, crouching above a baffling cryptic legend incised into the stone skirting of the otherwise austerely classical room (fig. 88). The words

FLIE · SON · TIME FLIES ON

were disturbingly obscure, especially given our uncertainty that the first word even existed as legitimate English. And what could have inspired a childless sixty-four-year-old man to half-conceal this fatherly advice within the fabric of his new

Fig. 88. Impish image and cryptic words in Robert's new hall at Nunney Delamere.

building? The initial rush of delight engendered by the skill and audacity of the piece, followed by a nagging perplexity about the exact intention of its creator, was pure Bateman.

The main hall of the house was a handsome space with a dignified stair, and the area over the studio retained an uncanny sense of having been Robert's private space. Anne told us that when her family came it had been two interconnecting areas which, she felt sure, were his actual painting and sculpting rooms; the grand studio below, she thought, had been for display and entertaining. The main bedroom was a fine room with its slow-curved bay of sash windows. Clare opened one set of shutters to reveal a room in which it was easy to imagine the aristocratic Caroline being at ease, perhaps quietly reading by a flickering fire, or brushing her hair and preparing for dinner. It was a hushed, private place, where that wise woman could contemplate life about her, and compose herself before re-entering the hubbub of the household below.

The other place that produced an unexpected frisson of excitement was the attic, or old servants' rooms. At the top of their own staircase, these retained a palpable sense of another world, untouched for many years. Ever since we first set out on our search for Robert's story, we had always maintained a playful fantasy that, one day, we would find a black trunk in the furthest reaches of a disused garret, hidden beyond backless chairs, rolled-up carpets and piles of china potties. We would wipe a sleeve across the top and reveal the letters RB, with the tail of the R extended. We would persuade the owner to let us break open the trunk. Inside we would find sheaves of exquisite drawings, sketches and bundles of love letters tied in faded ribbon and smelling faintly of eau de cologne.

As we gazed across the servants' rooms at Rockfield House, the parallels were too strong for us not to ask Anne tentatively whether she had found anything up there when she came to the house – no old trunks, for example? She gave us a sweet, knowing smile that told us she understood and empathised with our dream.

'Sadly, no. I only wish we had. But there was one thing here when we arrived that we always thought might be his. It's a sort of bust – the head of an elderly man, made of plaster or something similar.'

It was not, as expected, on a stand in the entrance lobby, because Clare and her husband did not much care for it and had put it out of sight in a cupboard. Anne brought it out for us to see. The moment we saw the sculpture we recognised it as a likeness of Robert in later life (fig. 89). It was animated and craggily modelled in a light material which conveyed a vivid sense of the sitter as a personality. It was by far the most accurate likeness of the older Robert Bateman we had ever come across. When we looked at the base it was signed and dated 'Conrad Dressler 1889'.

We knew that Dressler was a leading sculptor of the late Victorian era, particularly famous for his busts of the artistic luminaries of the age. When we looked into it later, we discovered that in the same year Dressler had exhibited busts of William

Fig. 89. Conrad Dressler, bust of Robert Bateman, 1889, private collection.

Morris, John Ruskin and Algernon Charles Swinburne – further proof that, despite his later obscurity, Robert had at one time held a place beside some of the most influential arbiters of artistic excellence of his day. Anne seemed very pleased, and rather pointedly placed it back on its stand in the hall.

We went through the connecting door into Anne's cottage, where she donned gardening socks and Wellingtons to show us the garden. She was keen to know how it corresponded to other Bateman garden designs we had seen. We told her that the way the spoil from blasting and digging had been mounded up to create an informal area of rockery, dissected by winding paths, was directly comparable to the surviving parts of the gardens at both Biddulph and Benthall. Anne sent us off to look at the more remote parts without her. By some overgrown laurels we stumbled upon an upright stone, carved on one side with an owl. When we pulled the laurel away from it, we found 'RB 1906' carved in a recessed panel along the top (fig. 90).

Figs. 90, 91. Double meaning: two aspects of Robert's personality carved into a single sculpture, 1906, private collection.

The hollow-eyed sculpture gave a strangely compelling sense of the motionless, staring bird dispassionately assessing the onlooker. We were very excited since, apart from the date-stone on our own house, we had never found a piece of carving actually signed by Robert. However, it was not until we moved the stone to get a photograph that the startling individuality and true quality of the sculpture were revealed. On the back the same blank eyes had been used to animate a fabulous grotesque mask contained within a gothic arch (fig. 91). Although it had been damaged over the century since it was made, this had not destroyed its almost oriental delight in the macabre nor the wilful mischief of the hidden, grinning face. Brian and I laughed when we caught sight of it. It was a moment of instant recognition.

This was the Robert Bateman we had come to know at his most endearing – the subversive spirit that juxtaposed a price tag and a tube of oil paint with the fastidious perfection of a trembling bloom; the artist who insisted we acknowledge the anxiety and absurdity concealed behind everything, even the meditative wisdom of the watching owl. We took photographs, and showed them to Anne when we got back to her. She seemed a little taken aback, as if she had not been fully aware of the carving, and certainly not of the reverse face.

The garden pavilion was a stylish structure built facing the house, with an open front divided by four square white columns . Anne felt sure it was by Bateman, as it was furnished with original oak benches suggesting it had served as a pavilion to

Robert's bowling green nearby. Between the two central columns the floor projected forward, ending in a stone beam with a tiny lead mask of a male head, from which water was designed to flow into a square stone basin (fig. 92).

The moment we saw this, we were reminded of a telephone conversation we had had with Colin Cruise, the biographer and acknowledged expert on the life of Simeon Solomon. He was suspicious that one of the pictures illustrated in his book on Solomon, *Love Revealed*, was not by him but quite possibly by Bateman. He had felt compelled to include it because the record of Solomon selling it to one of his patrons, George Powell, was authenticated in a letter. However, he felt that Solomon was quite capable of selling a painting by someone else as his own work if he was short of money – which he frequently was. He had not told us which painting it was, but had set us the puzzle of attempting to identify it and letting him know, to see if we agreed with him.

We had picked an illustration of a painting entitled *Noon*, as we felt that the emphasis on the semi-naked female forms was inconsistent with Solomon, and the organisation of the picture, with foreground figures contained within a strong architectural framework dividing the composition in two, was highly characteristic of Bateman (fig. 93). We also felt the treatment of the group of trees in the background was strikingly similar to that in both *The Dead Knight* and *Women Plucking Mandrakes*. Colin Cruise confirmed that we had chosen correctly.

Another aspect of the image characteristic of Robert's work was the inclusion of statuary and ornamental water as pivotal elements in the overall organisation. The centre of the composition of *Noon* is focused on a statue of Minerva, from beneath which a tiny grotesque mask spouts water into a square basin. It was uncannily

Fig. 92. The highly characteristic square water feature that formed part of the garden pavilion at Nunney Delamere.

Fig. 93. Unsigned painting, Noon, *sold to George Powell by Simeon Solomon, now tentatively reattributed to Robert Bateman, private collection.*

Fig. 94. Robert Bateman, The Four Seasons, *watercolour on gold medium, private collection.*

reminiscent of the water feature Robert had integrated into the garden pavilion at his own home in Nunney (fig. 92).

The water spout only compounded an exciting development that had already led us to feel that the attribution to Robert of *Noon* was increasingly credible. We had gone to a dealer's to see a group of four watercolours depicting the seasons, which were initialled RB (fig. 94). The moment we saw the signature with the square-topped R and extended downward tail, we knew they were Batemans. The delicate modelling of the figures, combined with the exquisitely graded, toning colours set against gilded backgrounds, gave these little pictures an almost jewel- or icon-like intensity. But it was the artist's response to the female forms discernible through the flowing lines of their animated drapery that instantly reminded us of *Noon*.

We were enthralled. This time we made no mistake. We bought them and took them home. Against the fractured textures and red sandstone of Biddulph they acquired an almost wanton richness. With so little work of Robert's having survived, the chance to save them and supply evidence that might allow Colin Cruise to make an informed attribution of another skilful painting to Robert filled us with joy.

Our path back to Anne's cottage led through another garden feature which was strongly reminiscent, not so much of the gardens at Biddulph or Benthall, but of Cooke's and the Batemans' early work at Biddulph Grange. We approached what appeared to be the mouth of a tunnel hewn through an outcrop of rock (fig. 95). The illusion was skilfully maintained through the whole depth of the tunnel, until we opened wooden doors at the end, set in a conventional brick archway, that gave access to a small service courtyard with a range of outbuildings. The whole structure was unmistakably a Bateman confection. It was touching to see Robert still applying the specialised skill with rockwork he had developed in his youth and boyhood, when he worked alongside E. W. Cooke at the Grange and in the Clough walk at Biddulph

Fig. 95. The playful rockwork arch at Nunney Delamere, typical of Cooke's and Robert's work at Biddulph Grange.

Old Hall. The same mischievous delight in illusion and whimsical visual tricks was at work here, at the end of Robert's life, as it had been fifty years before, far away in Staffordshire.

Anne Pomeroy had been a delightfully animated kindred spirit all morning, sharing our interest in every surviving remnant of the Batemans' life at Rockfield House, but by the time we delivered her home she was cold and exhausted. She gamely invited us in but we knew it was time for her to rest, and for us to find the last resting place of Robert and Caroline in the graveyard at Whatley. So we thanked her, made our farewells, and set off.

Try as we might, we had not been able to stop ourselves regarding this visit to the last place with which Robert and Caroline were associated as a private leave-taking. We felt we should bring something, to avoid the emptiness of simply reading the stone and walking away, so were carrying a bunch of Madonna lilies loosely tied with a silk ribbon. We discovered the grave where Robert and Caroline were buried together.

After two long years of searching, in a strange sense we had found them at last (fig. 96). As we anticipated, once we were standing in silence on either side of their burial place, we were unable to do anything but stare at the few bare words on the headstone:

Here lies the body of
ROBERT BATEMAN,
late of Nunney Delamere,
J. P. Salop:
N: August 12th 1842.
Ob: August 11th 1922.

Also of
CAROLINE OCTAVIA HOWARD,
his wife
N: March 20th 1839.
Ob: July 30th 1922.

So few words, and yet how eloquently they conveyed the tragic acceptance that Robert would not be remembered as an artist. The words seemed sad because they were so stilted and inadequate, so unable to convey the truth of the people they sought to commemorate.

Of course, they did not need to do that. The job had already been triumphantly done by Robert, in the language he knew best. His hypnotic paintings were the memorial both to his visionary ability as an artist, and to his lifelong passion for

Caroline. Quietly, one by one, they were emerging from the forgotten places where they had been hidden to bear witness to their creator and his beloved.

Our journey home was unexpectedly buoyant and chatty, imbued with a feeling of something achieved and brought to a satisfactory conclusion. We knew that the outstanding task of attempting to track down at least some of the lost paintings had the potential to ensnare us in a labyrinth of false trails and futile disappointments. It was to avoid getting immersed in that frustration that we had not begun it until we had exhausted the search for Robert and Caroline themselves. Now, the daunting moment had arrived for us to set this final quest in motion. We had no clues to follow, so began by acquiring copies of Robert and Caroline's wills from the Probate Office, to see if any paintings were specifically identified and, if so, who had inherited them. Ninety years after their deaths it seemed a dauntingly vague starting point, but after two years searching for 'The Lost Pre-Raphaelite' and his enigmatic bride we were used to that.

Fig. 96. Robert's and Caroline's headstone marking
their joint grave in Whatley churchyard.

Part 5

THE LOST CHILD

*Fig. 97. Robert's brother, the Indian missionary Rowland Bateman,
astride his camel with his assistant Main Sadik, Lahore 1870.*

Chapter 22

LAST WILL AND TESTAMENT

When Robert's and Caroline's wills arrived from the Probate Office they challenged and perplexed us from the first page. Caroline's will began by identifying her executors as Henry Ulick Burke, of 1 Beaufort Road, Clifton, Bristol, in the County of Gloucester, 'gentleman, nephew of the deceased', and Robert John Howard of Newton Ferrers, Callington, Cornwall, 'Commander Royal Navy'. The appointment of these nephews as executors seemed natural as representatives of the Bateman and Howard families. The difference in their prominence within the will, however, soon became clear.

Robert John Howard received no legacy beyond £100 for fulfilling the role of executor. Henry Ulick Burke was incontestably the prime beneficiary of the whole will. Section 2 read:

> I devise all my share and interest in the freehold mansion house with gardens, lands and outbuildings thereto belonging called 'Nunney Delamere' near Frome aforesaid to my husband, Robert Bateman, for his life, and from after his decease to my said nephew Henry Ulick Burke absolutely.

Section 3 was equally explicit:

> I give all my jewellery, clothes, and personal effects to my said husband, or if he shall predecease me, to my said nephew Henry Ulick Burke, for the purpose of distributing the same in accordance with the memorandum which I shall leave with my will, but I declare that such memorandum shall not form any legal part of my said will.

In other words, Caroline's intention was that, after Robert's death, all her property and personal possessions should pass into the custodianship of Henry Burke.

The next section is the most complex. In it Caroline gave all the residue of her estate (that is, after the earlier bequests) upon trust to my said husband, Robert Bateman, during his lifetime and after his decease upon trust to pay the following legacies all free of duty.

These legacies are all simple money bequests and are comparatively impersonal. They convey no sense that Caroline was passing on beloved family treasures, such as her mother's jewellery or the Dean's beautifully bound books, to her Howard nephews and nieces for safekeeping in the future. After listing small bequests, she concluded by instructing that the net residue was to be paid 'to my said nephew, Henry Ulick Burke absolutely'.

Brian and I were completely disorientated by the content and the intention behind the whole document. Why had Caroline so demonstrably wished to provide handsomely for an obscure nephew of Robert's in preference to her own kith and kin? Why, particularly, was she prepared to place all her most intimate, personal belongings in his care, without any legally valid list of what they were or how they were to be dispersed?

When we turned to Robert's will, it repeated the same instructions almost word for word. Since none of Robert's art or paintings were identified, they must have formed part of the memorandum that remained private, and was to be enacted at Henry Burke's discretion. The final paragraph, revoking all former wills and testamentary writings, ended poignantly with the date of 4 August 1922. It was clear that Robert had to make a new will four days after the heartbreak of losing Caroline, and seven days before his own death. The probate sheet dated 3 November 1922 recorded Robert and Caroline's combined net wealth as £7,930-18s-4d (roughly the equivalent of £820,000 today).

So who was Henry Ulick Burke? How, after all this time following Robert and Caroline, had we scarcely heard the name of the person who played so central a role in their wills? What motivated them to leave their home and their most private possessions and the greater part of their wealth to him after their deaths? What did we actually know about him? Only that he was the son of Robert's sister Katherine. We knew precisely nothing about her except that she had married an Irish lawyer, Ulick Ralph Burke, who had signed the register at Robert and Caroline's wedding.

Henry Burke's address on the probate sheet, 1 Beaufort Road, Clifton, Bristol, was no more than fifteen miles from Robert and Caroline's home at Nunney. If their relationship with Henry had been sufficiently longstanding and close for them to leave him their house and personal belongings, was it to be near him that they had moved south from Benthall Hall in 1905? In these circumstances, Nunney would have represented the perfect location, with its river and pretty cottages, nestled around a historic castle – far enough from Bristol to be peaceful and retiring, but near enough to maintain an ongoing close relationship with their favourite nephew.

At least, for the first time, the wills suggested a credible explanation for the move from Benthall to Nunney.

To discover more about the identity of Henry Ulick Burke we decided to try to find his birth certificate so we could build up the picture of his life story from there. However, no matter how often we checked and re-checked the spelling of his name, the computer steadfastly refused to acknowledge that such a person had ever been born in the British Isles. Eventually, in a last-ditch attempt to preserve our sanity, we moved to another approach. We realised that if Robert and Caroline's reason for moving was to be near him, Henry would have to have been settled in Bristol by 1905–6, so we looked up the census returns for 1891 and 1901, but with no success. But when we checked the census returns for 1911, which had just been made public, Henry's name came up. Within three minutes our information about him increased tenfold.

In 1911 he was living in Bristol, but at a different address, 5 Belgrave Place, Clifton. He was a married man of thirty-seven with a wife called Rose, who was thirty-four, and two children, Katrina, aged seven and Richard, aged three. Henry and Rose had completed eight years of marriage, but had clearly been intrepid travellers: Katrina had been born in a place called Talara in Peru, and Richard in Liverpool in 1908.

The remaining information on Henry was intriguing. His 'personal occupation' was given as Tobacco Manufacturer, his 'position' as Factory Manager, and his 'status' as Employer. His nationality was given as British, but his birthplace was Lahore, India, which instantly explained our failure to locate his birth in the British Isles. Lahore had always been considered a dangerous, lawless area of India. It was not suited to pregnant women or young English children, so Henry's experience must have been a fairly unusual one.

His time in Peru, as a young family man of about thirty, can only have been an altogether more intrepid and hazardous experience. South America, with its Spanish-speaking population and alien culture, was not part of the British Empire, so there were no reassuring cricket clubs, tennis parties or Anglican Church services to maintain the familiar ambiance of home. Henry must have been settled there, however, for his young English wife to be with him when she gave birth to their first child.

Henry was already emerging as an intriguing personality with a flamboyant story to tell. How that tale intertwined with Robert and Caroline, his ostensibly staid and respectable uncle and aunt, we could not imagine. To find out, we needed to know more about his childhood and early life with his mother, Robert's sister, and her husband. The overarching difficulty was that the lives of Henry Burke's family were unrecorded at a public level, except for his father, Ulick Ralph Burke (fig. 98), whose varied and colourful career merited an entry in the *Oxford Dictionary of National Biography*. Apart from naming his parents, however, the dictionary confines itself to a single sentence on his private life: 'On 9th July 1868, he married Katherine (died 1933), daughter of James Bateman; they had a son and two daughters.' Having dealt with the mundane family stuff, the entry dives off into infinitely more galvanising accounts of sewage and Spanish holidays: 'A tour of Spain led Burke, on his return, to bring out in 1872 (the same year as his *Handbook of Sewage Utilisation*) an annotated collection of the proverbs of Don Quixote.'

Luckily we soon discovered a more productive source of information on the family. This took the form of a truly Herculean Victorian publication, in three ponderous volumes, entitled *The Plantagenet Role of the Blood Royal (Exeter Volume)* listing all the descendants of King Edward III (1312–77). By good fortune it had been updated and encompassed Katherine and Ulick Ralph Burke's family:

Mabel Emma Burke: Born 1871. Married, 1901, to John Humphreys. Has issue (not named). Died 1954.

Henry Ulick Burke: Born 4 January 1874. Married, 1902, Rose Ellen Marian Antoinette Uvedale Parry-Okeden. Has issue. Died 2 December 1960.

Hope Katherine Burke: Born 1880. Unmarried. Died 29 June 1960.

Sybil Mary Burke: Born 1882. Married, 1912, Major Wyndham Persse Knatchbull. Has issue. Died 5 August 1957.

The *ODNB* made it clear that the most notable characteristic of Ulick Ralph Burke's career was the relentless transience of his type and place of employment. He was evidently an intelligent, gifted man, a competent lawyer, who had been called to the bar in Dublin in 1870. However, by 1872, he had taken his extended trip through Spain. This enabled him to master the Spanish language and informed his fascination with Spanish culture. Between 1873 and 1878, he practised as a barrister in the High Court at Lahore. He returned to England, and unsuccessfully contested the parliamentary seat of Calne for the Conservatives. He travelled to Brazil in 1882 and published *Business and Pleasure in Brazil* about his experiences. From 1885 to 1889 he practised as a lawyer in Cyprus. In 1890 he returned to Dublin to take a post as Registrar of the Quarter Sessions, where he remained until 1895. He resigned as Registrar in Dublin when he was offered the post of Agent-General to the Peruvian Corporation, a potentially lucrative appointment. He embarked for Lima, but fell victim to dysentery on board ship, and died on 17 July 1895.

Our success with the 1911 census, which had illuminated Henry Ulick Burke as an individual, made us keen to revisit these records again to see if, by any chance, we could establish a link between Henry and Robert Bateman. We set about a diligent and systematic search using all the ten-year census returns from 1881 to 1911.

In 1881 we found Katherine, his mother, staying at a grand establishment near Chester as a guest of the Swettenham family. She was travelling with two of her chil-

Fig. 98. Ulick Ralph Burke, Robert's Irish brother-in-law.

dren, Henry, aged seven, and Hope, a baby of one, accompanied by a nursemaid. The same census showed Robert Bateman at Biddulph Old Hall and Caroline, newly widowed, in her own establishment at 14 Upper Berkeley Street, London. Ten years later, in 1891, we were unable to trace Henry or a single member of his family.

The return for 1901 was a little perplexing. Ulick Ralph had died six years earlier, Henry was nowhere to be found and Hope Burke had begun a career as a nurse at St Mary's Children's Hospital in West Ham, London. The shock came from the discovery that Katherine and her youngest child Sybil, who was by then eighteen, were living at 4 High Street, Long Melford. This proved to be a tiny workman's cottage, part of a terrace of three alongside a pub, the Hare Inn. Although Katherine retained a cook and a maid-of-all-work, none of her neighbours on either side along the road had any servants; they were bricklayers or mat weavers, interspersed here and there by unskilled agricultural labourers. The final strange twist was that Katherine had a visitor on the day of the census, shown as Rose Okeden, the girl whom Henry was to marry the following year, in 1902.

We did not regard this as strange until we followed up the census return for Rose's own family. Her home, Turnworth House, was a fully fledged country mansion at the heart of a landscaped park, just outside Blandford Forum. In addition to game-keepers, gardeners and coachmen, the household numbered ten full-time indoor servants. The house, when we got an image of it, was a massive, playfully castellated confection, with elegant gothic bay windows. The evening of the census, seven of her family were at home, dining in splendour, waited on by their butler, while Rose was aggravating the crush in the workman's cottage by the Hare Inn at Long Melford.

This snapshot was startling. Clearly Katherine's fortunes had fallen on grindingly hard times, presumably as a result of her widowhood six years earlier. This raised so many puzzling questions. Where was Henry? As a man of twenty-seven, was there nothing he could do to rescue his mother and sister from an ignominious descent into poverty? And what about Robert and Caroline, complacently playing the country squire and his lady in their Jacobean country house? If, twenty years later, they were so close to Henry that they were prepared to leave him all their personal belongings, were they not fond enough of his mother, Robert's widowed sister, to provide safe sanctuary for her, away from the alien ambience of the bricklayers, farm labourers and the menacing patrons of the ale house?

This inconsistency between Robert and Caroline's boundless generosity to Henry in their wills, and the complete failure even to refer to his mother or any of his three sisters, was something that had begun to perplex us. While they left Henry most of what they possessed, the wills did not even acknowledge the existence of Katherine, Mabel Emma, Hope or Sybil Burke.

As we pondered all this, one last coincidence caught our attention. Now that we had located Rose Parry-Okeden's family home, Turnworth House, we realised it was no more than fifteen miles away from Nunney. So, in effect, a few years after Henry's marriage in 1902, Robert and Caroline had left Benthall Hall and bought a house midway between Bristol and Turnworth. Of course, we knew that Henry and Rose had been on the other side of the world in Peru in 1904 when Katrina was born, but in the light of Robert and Caroline's wills it seemed uncanny that, in 1906, they should have selected a new house so central to the future workplace of their chosen beneficiary, and his wife's family home.

We felt that we needed to get a clearer picture of Henry's childhood in India, so we set out again to find his birth certificate. We had hoped this would supply an address that might allow us to begin to place him, and his family, in the teeming humanity of nineteenth-century Lahore. We expected that there would be a codified procedure for registering births that we would be able to consult, provided we were sufficiently patient and diligent. So we were surprised, when we consulted the official Indian Archives, to be met by the blank statement that 'There was no compulsory Registration of Births in British India. Hence there is no general availability of Birth Certificates for people born there.'

We felt as if our attempt to discover even the most basic facts about the early life of Henry Burke had vanished into the impenetrable recesses of Imperial India. Then a piece of symmetry in the wider Bateman family story struck us. Lahore had appeared on the periphery of our investigation when, for background information on Robert's family, we had followed his brother Rowland's career from Brighton College, through Oxford and ordination in Durham Cathedral, to his appointment by the Church Missionary Society as an itinerant missionary based at their Lahore station. It seemed probable that the selection of the post of barrister in Lahore by Ulick Ralph Burke would have been influenced by the presence there of Rowland Bateman.

At this stage, we knew almost nothing about Rowland, but we began to wonder if he had played a formative part in Henry's early life. We found an obscure biography by R. Maconachie, *Rowland Bateman – Nineteenth Century Apostle*, published in 1917 by the Church Missionary Society. Sadly, when we searched the index, we found it did not list Henry Ulick Burke, Robert Bateman or Caroline Howard. There was a single entry for Mr Ulick Burke (Ralph) and two for Burke, Mrs Ulick (Katherine). The biography makes clear that Rowland Bateman was already an established figure who had been in the Punjab since 1868, and in Lahore itself since 1870 (fig. 97), when Ulick Ralph and Katherine arrived in 1873.

On 20 December 1871, Rowland began to keep a diary which he maintained regularly until February 1874. Although it has not survived in his archive, it allowed his biographer to give a vivid picture of life in Lahore by quoting extensively from it. Rowland's own words, simple and direct, vividly conveyed the relationship with Christ he experienced through prayer, contemplation, Bible study and interaction with others which was the defining and animating reality of his daily existence. No one was too wretched, ill or poor, no one too hostile or self-important, not to be worth pursuing through burning heat, mockery and physical intimidation if they expressed a flicker of response to his message.

The fact that this fervour was expressed in the simplest terms of overcoming practical difficulties, often with a mischievous sense of humour, made it all the more striking. Rowland described his initial forays into the streets under the leadership of Bishop French:

Fig. 99. Rowland Bateman, the dedicated missionary.

Mr French was always our leader and example. How he did strive for souls! When they jeered at him and pelted him, he would kneel down in the dust and pray for them, when they shouted him down he evinced no resentment, but only a yearning desire that they would listen not to him, but to God.

Rowland's own attempts at street preaching give a sense of the courage and commitment it took to submit himself to this ordeal:

27 December: Out early, preached for two hours. Had some good opportunities and much opposition, which was growing and intensifying when I left. After breakfast, to bazaar again, much opposition, and some enquiry. Some boys from the Musjad hooted us out of town, being evidently sent to insult us.

The skills and knowledge needed to engage in this riotous form of religious debate meant that endless hours of dedicated labour had to be spent becoming completely fluent in all the languages and dialects of the Punjab.

Nothing had prepared us for the dynamic conviction of these Victorian clergymen. Far from lugubriously dispensing well-bred Anglican certainties to a respectful congregation of compliant underlings, they were forced to endure ridicule, abuse, humiliation and intimidating threats, day after day.

Maconachie makes a special point of drawing attention to Rowland's compassion and devotion to the Eurasian population – the despised offspring of casual Anglo-Indian relationships. These people were almost universally illegitimate and shunned by both communities, so they frequently were not able to obtain work, and lapsed into alcoholism and poverty. Rowland's journal for 4 February 1872 records an instance of going to such a case, who had been effectively left to die:

Engaged to preach for Davies (railway chaplain). Just sitting down to prepare when a man came from Shandara to call me to the deathbed-side of a poor Eurasian. Drink had ruined him. He was too far gone to do much for him. His wife was confined yesterday in the next room, and his eldest daughter was attending either parent alternatively – poor child – aged about 5 years.

People exposed to this level of human tragedy on a routine basis could not long remain prudish, and Maconachie acknowledges Rowland's impartial caring for these 'monuments to the moral laxity of Englishmen'.

This, then, was the place in which Rowland Bateman's journal recorded the arrival of Ulick Ralph Burke and his wife Katherine in September 1873. How invaluable must Rowland's knowledge of the language and customs have been as they tried to make sense of clashing cultures and competing gods, of gaudy splendour and squalid death, baked in the ferocious Punjab sun. If this was the world into which Henry Burke was born and lived for the next five years, surely it, and his charismatic Uncle

Rowland, would have left an indelible imprint on his memory and personality which would have lasted the rest of his life.

Since Rowland's biography was written about a missionary, and published by the Church Missionary Society, its prime focus was upon his evangelical work. Ulick and Katherine's arrival in Lahore, in the last week of September 1873, was covered between accounts of his missionary work at Narawal and Madhopur:

> He stayed a few hours with us [Maconachie and his family] in Gurdaspur on the way. But taking as it were only one long cool breath at Dalhousie, he 'rushed through to Lahore' to meet his only sister and help her to settle in her new home there with her husband Mr Ulick Burke, a barrister.

The dates in Rowland's journal place this meeting in the last week of September 1873. Surprisingly, this is is only three months before Henry's birth on 6 January 1874. Katherine was presumably accompanied by Mabel Emma, her first child, who by then would have been three. It seems surprising that Katherine would have risked undertaking the perilous journey to one of the hottest, most inhospitable areas of India while heavily pregnant and caring for a young child.

It also seems odd that Rowland does not record his first meeting with his little niece, who had been born since his departure for India. The journal entry for 10 December 1873 indicates that he was returning from Narawal to Lahore for Christmas, where he remained until 11 February. It is clear that Rowland was keeping his journal right through the crucial weeks before and after Henry Burke's birth on 6 January.

If he recorded these happy family events, Maconachie must have edited them out, although it is hard to see why he should have chosen to do so. Over the next five years, the biography does not once refer to either Henry or Mabel Emma, even though Rowland Bateman must have played a key part in their schooling and education in Lahore, since this was another central preoccupation of his ministry.

The biography covers Rowland's personal life and conveys his reaction to all the important events in his own family, such as his marriage in 1879 to Helen Melvill, and the birth of his three children. The tragic loss of his youngest child is sensitively handled in the form of quotations from letters to trusted friends that demonstrated his wretchedness:

> Our dear little Robin is gone and Oh, what a far reaching blank he has left! Alas, the poor mother, worn with three or four weeks incessant nursing, and now one little life that shared her home has left it. I confess I feel very much crushed, till I look up and try to realise what the welcome is like, which he has already received. Oh dear, I do want help! The natives have found out my loss and come and sit, poor things, with the idea of comforting me, and I can find no words to use that do not choke me in the utterance ... My dear mother's death a few weeks ago was a sore trouble, and this on top of it shows me that what I took for iron within me is clay.

When his wife died the following year, Rowland described his numb state of mind with haunting simplicity: 'I am walking along on deeply shaded ground, and do not yet know, the least, what is before me.' Rowland was evidently prepared and able to express an emotional response to events in his personal life. His biographer considered it important to include them in the narrative of his life story, to give a true portrait of the man. Therefore it seems odd that the birth of the first male child to any of his siblings, arriving in the centre of his world in Lahore, when he was still a bachelor in January 1874, was not sufficiently significant to prompt any written reaction from him then, or at any point in the next five years.

His silence on the subject seemed so unnatural that we began to wonder if Katherine had succeeded in settling down after the birth, or whether she had returned to England with the two children, leaving Ulick Ralph to serve out his term at the High Court in Lahore on his own. The biography makes clear that Rowland and Katherine were close and fond of each other, which adds to the mystery of their failure to interact during her time in India. After his return from the Punjab in 1902, Rowland became rector of a country parish just outside Henley and, as the biography put it, 'his sister, Mrs Burke, was going to share the house with him at Fawley – a great convenience, as she was an excellent manager, whereas R.B. was never a "house-keeper" in any conventional sense.' Katherine's presence at Fawley Rectory may have been presented as a convenience for Rowland, but the evidence of the previous year's census suggests that he had come to her rescue, providing a substantial home for her to live in rather than the workman's cottage in Long Melford.

Rowland's biography presented us with another puzzle. The letters written to his lifelong companions, after his cancer was pronounced incurable, were addressed from Nunney. We realised that he had ended his life in the care of Robert and Caroline, but great trouble had been taken to avoid using their names:

> Later in the year, further advice was taken in Bath, and after consultation held by competent authorities, he was informed that his disease was incurable; malignant trouble had asserted itself and nothing more could be done in a medical way. Removal was advised, as soon as possible, to a permanent resting place for the remaining days of the way-worn but undaunted pilgrim, and this haven of rest was found at the home of his brother, who, with his wife, urged their right to have him with them to the end. Hence, then, in almost ideal surroundings of English scenery, English home life, and the love of his own English folk, did the tireless worker, who had spent so many years under the sun of India, amidst dust and heat, and strange and often unsympathetic neighbours, slowly sink to his rest.

This was a haunting evocation of the peace and serenity of Robert and Caroline's loving home. The author, writing only a year after Rowland's death, had experienced the pervasive atmosphere of loving security that surrounded his friend in the last months of his life, and seemed to be deeply affected by it. It seems strange, then, that he should go to such lengths not to identify Robert or Caroline when expressing the gratitude he obviously felt for the kindness they showed to his friend through his slow, painful decline. It was sadly characteristic of their elusive, secret story that Robert and Caroline should remain ignored and unlisted, even as they willingly extended their mutual devotion to encompass their sick brother.

*Fig. 100. Rowland Bateman at Nunney
near the end of his life.*

Fig. 101. Henry in India, aged about two,
with his bearer, Goolameissei.

Chapter 23

IN SEARCH OF HENRY

It all happened in an instant. Ruth Vilmi had emailed from Finland to say she was going to send some photographs. Brian was at the computer when I heard him murmur, 'That's him,' as a peculiar image filled the screen (fig. 101).

There were words handwritten beneath it that I could not make out.

'What does it say?'

'It says "Henry and Goolameisii, his Indian bearer."'

'Henry!' I exclaimed.

'And Goolameisii – don't forget him!'

The next moment Brian had another image of a slightly older child, with shoulder-length fair hair, with 'Henry' scrawled across the mount. He was a pretty child but his expression had a suggestion of spoilt belligerence. He was sitting in an upholstered Victorian chair with long fringing, holding a hat and riding crop, which gave him an assertive, almost adult, air of assumed authority (fig. 94).

We looked back at the earlier photograph in which the child was younger, perhaps two or three. With his white dress and curly blond hair his prettiness was almost doll-like, but the expression was still detached, with a hint of sulkiness. The bearer's face, by contrast, was aglow with a gentle, inscrutable smile. We kept staring from one to the other of the soft, sepia images. We knew it was Henry Burke, because we knew the bizarre route by which it had come to us was authentic and credible at every step along its path.

It had begun with a routine internet search for background information about his sisters. We had entered 'Mabel Emma Burke' and there was an unexpected response under a heading called 'Write-it'. It was posted by Ruth Vilmi, an English-woman living in Helsinki. The purpose of her website was to display her paintings, plus some watercolours done by her grandmother, Mabel Emma Burke. We posted a blog with a request for information.

Fig. 102. Henry in India at five years of age.

Ruth replied, full of excitement. She remembered her grandmother mentioning the name Biddulph, but had never worked out what the connection was. She confirmed that her grandmother did have a younger brother called Henry, and two sisters – Auntie Hope, whom she remembered well, and Sybil, whom she never met.

Once contact with Ruth was established, things began to move quickly. Her brother had done extensive research into their family history, collecting old photographs and cataloguing them. He confirmed he had several photographs of Henry, including two which had been together on a single page in an ancient album, and inscribed 'Henry in India'. We had given up expecting to find any evidence of Henry's life in India, let alone photographs from the 1870s which actually recorded him as a child. After reading Rowland Bateman's biography, we had become convinced that Henry, his sister and his mother Katherine had returned to England shortly after his birth, since there was no reference to them after Katherine's arrival in Lahore in September 1873. But we had been wrong. These photographs showed that Henry had been there, growing up, over a period of at least five years, from his birth to the end of his father's employment at the High Court in Lahore.

We were interested to know if there were similar pictures of his sister, Mabel Emma, in India. Ruth could only find one picture of Mabel Emma as a child, which was inscribed 'Agnes and Mabel Emma with their governess, Miss Greenslade' (fig. 103). This showed an attractive young woman with the two little girls. The older looks about seven and the younger about three or four. We knew that Agnes was the

Fig. 103. Mabel Emma (centre), Agnes (right) and their governess Miss Greenslade at Brightlingsea Hall, Essex.

name of the only child of John Bateman, Robert's eldest brother, so it appears that at the age of three or four, Mabel Emma was living at her uncle's house, Brightlingsea Hall in Essex, where she shared a governess with her older cousin. She was clearly not arriving in Lahore with her pregnant mother.

This seemed inconsistent. Surely it would have been much safer and more natural for Katherine to stay in England with her little girl till she had had her new baby, and then travel to India, when the danger and trauma of childbirth were behind her, and Mabel Emma was older and less vulnerable. One thing was certain. She did not follow this course, because she is recorded in Rowland's biography as arriving in Lahore in September 1873, in the critical last months of her pregnancy.

So Henry grew up in India, from his birth until his father's return to London in 1879, but he had been completely ignored in Maconachie's biography of Rowland Bateman. The more scraps of information we managed to unearth, the stranger the puzzle seemed to become. We hoped that Ruth, as the living grandchild of Mabel Emma Burke, could shed some light on these formative years of Henry's life. When I rang her, she was fascinated by our story and keen to discuss her family. She was about fifteen when her grandmother died, and had known her well as she lived with her family.

'Did she ever speak about her early life?'

'Yes, sometimes. I suppose, to be truthful, we probably weren't that interested.'

'Did you ever hear her say anything about her childhood in India?'

'No, not that I can remember. Not at all. Was she there? Somehow I had the impression that Henry was there, but that probably only comes from the pictures, which we found after she died. We had never even heard his name before that. We didn't know he existed. We knew Auntie Hope. We liked her. Do you think Gran was out there?'

'I don't know. But we assumed that if Henry was there, the whole family must have been with him.'

There was a pause. Ruth seemed a little perplexed.

'Yes, it makes sense – where else would she have been? But it's strange, I never had the slightest idea that she had ever been in India, and somehow I feel that I would have been told something by her or my mother.'

'She would have been nine years old when they left India and came home to England,' I said.

'Really? Oh, that's extraordinary!' she gasped. 'She would never have forgotten it, would she? The total change, the smells, the weather, the servants, the boat trip home to the cold and drizzle. At that age. What an impression it would have made! But she never said a word about it, ever, as far as I know. She had nothing from there. No beads, no trinkets, nothing in her things after she died. I'm upset now. We should have asked her – but we were only kids, you know.'

We were shaken by what Ruth had told us. We agreed that a boat journey that took a nine-year-old girl from India to the utterly different environment of respectable middle-class England would have been indelibly etched on her memory. Surely it would have been the very thing that she would have retold, to entertain her grandchildren with whom she lived when she was old. Had she stayed in Essex at her uncle's all the time her family were away in Lahore? It seemed hard to believe.

Or had Katherine had Henry out in India and, after a little while, simply gone home without him, leaving him in the care of his Indian bearer? Again, it seemed inconceivable that if she had wanted or needed to go home she would not have taken the baby with her, leaving her husband to pursue his work as a lawyer unhindered by a vulnerable infant. From knowing nothing about Henry Ulick Burke, we were fast becoming swamped in unintelligible facts and images that were threatening to obscure him again, this time in a fog of contradictions.

So when two more images came through from Ruth we were a little apprehensive. Both pictures were later, post-Lahore, but easy to date and just as fascinating as the earlier ones. The first was a group of three children, identified as Mabel, Henry and Hope in ink along the bottom of the mount (fig. 104). Since Hope was born in 1880, and is about three, we can assume that Henry is nine or ten and Mabel Emma fourteen. The poignant anxiety on their faces is intensified by the stiltedness of their

Fig. 104. Henry in his sailor suit with Hope (centre) and Mabel Emma.

Fig. 105. Henry and Rose Parry-Okeden on their wedding day at Turnworth House, November 1902, with Hope Burke and Violet Parry-Okeden as chief bridesmaids.

pose, giving the whole picture an air of acute discomfort. Henry has clearly been ordered to hold little Hope's hand, to add a touch of intimacy to the scene. However, he does it so awkwardly and she ignores it so totally that it emphasises rather than alleviates the complete lack of interaction between the children who stare suspiciously out at the camera.

Henry is recognisable from the Indian photographs, but all trace of girlishness has gone. He is every inch the miniature Victorian male, serious and sombre in his sailor suit, Eton collar and bow tie, with his cropped hair neatly parted and brushed to one side. His fine, straight, completely blond hair is in marked contrast to his sister's, which is thick, curly and dark.

The next photograph portrays the adult Henry on 4 November 1902, the day of his wedding to Rose Parry-Okeden at her family home of Turnworth House in Dorset (fig. 105). He has become a tall, lean, handsome young man. His fair hair is unchanged and, with the addition of a neat blond moustache, is a decisive component of his good looks. His direct gaze gives him an air of quiet self-confidence, but with an edge of hardness. We suspected that Henry was already living in Peru, as he was not listed in the 1901 census and on his marriage certificate he gave his address as Southampton, suggesting he had sailed back for the wedding.

Henry and Rose must have gone back to Peru soon after, as their first child, Katrina, was born at Talara in February 1904. After their return to England a son, Ulick Richard, was born in Liverpool in 1907, and a second son, John Okeden, was born in Bristol in 1912. By then Henry was managing a tobacco factory for W. D. & H. O. Wills in Bristol. We discovered this because the company kept personnel archives on senior executives who were not members of the Wills family. We were told that Henry's file, largely comprising of speeches given at the time of his retirement, was placed in the archive in 1933. The entire Wills archive had been transferred to the Bristol Records Office. We thought the contents sounded too dull to merit a separate journey, so decided to postpone a visit to Bristol until we could tack it on to a more rewarding trip elsewhere. For the moment, we were keen to begin the search for missing Bateman paintings by following the trail of Henry's children. Katrina and Richard were teenagers when their father received his handsome legacy. If Robert and Caroline's intense relationship with Henry encompassed his children, they might have been inclined to keep any paintings for personal reasons, despite their style having become profoundly outdated by the mid-twentieth century.

Of Henry's children, John Okeden had died at eight years old; Katrina and Richard each had one son. We felt that if we could trace either or both of Henry's grandsons, we stood a chance of finding at least one of the lost pictures. John Louis Beauchamp was born in 1930, the son of Guy Louis Beauchamp and Katrina Marian Burke; Jeremy Ulick Burke was born in 1931, the son of Ulick Richard Burke and Cynthia Moya Darling. They would now be about eighty years of age, possibly still alive and able to talk to us directly about their grandfather, who did not die until 1960.

We managed to track down an old address for Jeremy Ulick. When we rang, a quietly spoken woman answered and identified herself as Sheila Ralph. She had bought the house from Jeremy and Prudence Burke, and fortunately remembered them. She thought she had a card with their address on the board in her kitchen.

I heard her walk through and say, 'No, no, I just can't see it, no, that's not it. It's a long time, five years, I'm sure it was here.'

The more she searched, the more tense I became. I had developed an instinct for recognising the moment when a decisive, but deceptively dull, little fact was within reach. Whether she had lost the address or could find it might determine the whole outcome of our pursuit of Henry Burke and Robert's lost work.

Eventually she found it. She read out the address, adding mysteriously, 'Of course, there's no phone number. They're always ex-directory.' That was presumably why we had found them so difficult to trace. That evening we wrote a letter to Jeremy Burke, explaining our interest in his grandfather and the house he had inherited at Nunney. Two days later we received a reply by email which shed new light on Henry's later life:

Dear Mr Daly,

Thank you for your very interesting letter about Nunney Delamere and Robert Bateman.

You are quite correct, Henry Ulick was my Grandfather, and Ulick Richard was my father, who unfortunately died quite young. My understanding is that I was taken to Nunney as a very young child, but have no recollection of that visit. It was a surprise to learn that Nunney was left to my Grandfather, I had no idea, you know much more than I! I am certain that you are aware that Henry's mother was the only daughter of James Bateman of Biddulph Grange and Knypersley Hall. This would explain why he was left Nunney, and named his own daughter Katrina. After my Grandmother died in 1931, Henry remarried and, as far as I am aware, they always lived in hotels after that. I am assuming that any letters, papers and pictures would have been disposed of when leaving Nunney, there being little storage space in an hotel, as in a London flat, where I was brought up. I have no recollection of any references to such relics. I am so sorry not to be able to have far better news for you, as this is absolutely fascinating.

I am wondering if my aunt (Katrina) might have held such documents, as my father was living with her at the time of his death. In this case they may have been passed on to my cousin, his address is 37 George Lane, Marlborough, Wilts. I wish you every success in your fascinating project, and am so sorry that this surviving member of the Burke family is unable to help you. I do not think that my mother will remember anything constructive, she will soon be 102, but I will nevertheless ask her.

Inevitably, the main contents of this email were a sad disappointment to us. It seemed amazingly unlucky that after identifying one of Henry's two grandsons, and finding he had happily survived all the disasters, such as world wars, that had intervened since his birth in 1931, he had no understanding or awareness of Robert's role in his family's fortunes. We had expected to hear that Robert's work had been considered utterly old-fashioned by the mid-twentieth century so had been sold when it was passed to Jeremy's father after Henry's death in 1960. But it seemed strange that it was completely unknown to Jeremy, who would have been thirty at the time. However, the rest of the information helped us move forward, especially the fact that Katrina's son, his cousin John Beauchamp, was alive and well and living in Marlborough.

Jeremy's account of visiting Nunney Delamere as a young child told us that Henry, Rose and their children had moved into the house after they inherited it in 1922, and lived there into the 1930s when Rose died. His life 'in hotels', with his next wife, was a strange twist and not something we could have fully understood from public documentation. The fact that Jeremy's father, Ulick Richard, had died separated from his wife and living with his sister Katrina in 1963, shortly after Henry's death in 1960, did hold out the fascinating possibility that Henry's possessions had all gone to one place, Katrina's house, and were then likely to have passed to her only son, John Beauchamp.

As a formula for preserving a coherent body of art works where it could be retrieved from obscurity, this represented a piece of almost miraculous good fortune. We wrote to John Beauchamp. Ten days later, when we had heard nothing, we contacted Jeremy Burke to ask if he knew of any problems. He emailed us the next day to say that his cousin was suffering with leg ulcers, and he would let us know when he was better. We did not want to burden a sick man with our fixation about past members of his family and their belongings. However, I had John Beauchamp's telephone number on my desk and, disgracefully, it was only a matter of days before I rang it. His wife felt sure John would want to talk to me but he was asleep at that moment as his painkillers made him drowsy. She proposed that I ring back at four o'clock.

So I did, and John answered.

He was quietly spoken, but direct and decisive. He wanted to arrange a meeting but hated the idea that he might still be using a walking frame which, as a 'fit, active chap' he was ashamed of needing.

'The only thing is, I have to say I know almost nothing about your Mr Bateman. I've heard the name spoken about, but more than that I haven't a clue, but I suppose I must know some things that would be of value to you.'

I asked him if he remembered his grandfather.

'Oh, certainly, but it was after he'd sold Nunney, when he was living in hotels. He and Elsie, his second wife, never really settled anywhere. They were either on cruise liners or in hotels. I often met him at one near Bromley. Wonderful place, frightfully grand, you know, with two golf courses. He loved golf.'

'Has anything come down to you?' I asked.

'Precious little. I live in a modern house. There are a few bits, mostly of my mother's – that's how I think of them, but I don't really know where they came from, I suppose it might have been Nunney. Who knows? Anyway, nice to talk to you – let's meet up if you think it's worth it.'

I knew it was, so we made arrangements to meet at his house. As we would be on the road anyway, we decided to make our long postponed visit to the Bristol Records Office the same day.

In the meantime we received a copy of Henry Burke's will from the Probate Office. It was a long, professional, and slightly impersonal document, giving a strong sense of an astute commercial mind being applied to a task with minimal concession given to emotional considerations. It made no reference to any specific personal possessions, such as paintings, furniture, books and papers. Its single non-financial clause gave all his unspecified personal possessions to his second wife. The rest of the will was entirely taken up with financial arrangements which were much more painstaking and precise. The reason for this was evident from the probate document attached to the will, which recorded Henry's death on 22 December 1960 at St Teresa's Nursing Home, Eastbourne, and the gross value of his estate as £102,768 10s 10d, net value £100,399 5s 9d. His address was given as the Mansion Hotel, Eastbourne. His wife Eva Mary was joint executor.

So, despite spending twenty-seven years from his retirement in 1933 either travelling round the world on cruise ships or being waited upon in hotels, Henry Burke had died in 1960 an extremely wealthy man. Whatever else it told us about him, it did not suggest that Henry had kept his uncle's paintings with him to the end of his life, as he roamed from hotel rooms to first-class cabins and back again over almost thirty years.

Henry's arrangements for his children and grandchildren, after his wife's death, are meticulously even-handed and fair. His estate was to be divided between his children Katrina and Ulick Richard, but Richard was to make money available from his share to provide an income for his separated wife and son (Jeremy Ulick). In the event of either of his children predeceasing him, the money was to pass direct to the relevant grandson, provided he had reached twenty-one, or be held in trust until he did so.

The only other, more personalised, paragraph listed a group of small annuities, for their lifetimes, to two of his sisters and two friends:

To my sister Hope Katherine Burke Fifty pounds during her life.
To my sister Mabel Emma Humphries Eighty pounds during her life.
To my friend Alice Lilian Hargraves Thirty-four pounds during her life.
To my friend Millicent Caroline Parry-Okeden Sixteen pounds during her life.

So Henry had made modest provision for two of his three sisters and Alice Hargraves, whom we had never come across. The last annuity was fascinating for two reasons. First, because Millicent is one of only two people named in the will who is not a direct relation, and secondly, because Henry chooses to describe her as 'my friend' rather than 'my sister-in-law', she being the eldest sister of his first wife, Rose Parry-Okeden.

Intriguingly, Millicent alone, of all her family, gave her birthplace as India, and was born in 1874, the same year as Henry. In the light of the central role the Parry-Okedens were to play in Henry's life, was it possible that his friendship with Millicent predated his marriage to her sister by nearly thirty years, and was that why he remembered her, even at the end of his life, and left her a small annuity?

By leaving their estate to Henry, Robert and Caroline must have contributed directly to his ability to end his life as a wealthy man. However, it was looking increasingly as if he had failed to repay them by cherishing his inheritance and safeguarding Robert's reputation. None the less, we still held out great hopes for our meeting with John Beauchamp. We felt certain that something he had, or something he knew, would provide the golden key that would unlock the door to the mystery of Robert and Caroline's wills which would, in turn, set us on a path to the lost paintings.

Fig. 106. Henry Burke in middle age.

Chapter 24

REVELATIONS

On the day of our meeting with John Beauchamp we set off early as we felt that he might only manage a couple of hours in the late morning to talk to us before needing to rest. We had just set off when our phone rang. It was Joyce Beauchamp telling us that John had had a hideous night. As a result he had taken extra medication that meant he would be asleep all day, so our meeting would not be possible.

We had no will to impose ourselves on the Beauchamps, but without them the second leg of our trip was potentially a total waste of time. Was a company personnel file truly going to give us any real insight about Henry, or the lost paintings of Robert Bateman? It seemed wildly unlikely, but as we were on our way we decided to keep to our plan and visit the Bristol Records Office anyway. By the time we had negotiated the labyrinthine complexity of the Bristol traffic system, and been handed a flimsy brown envelope by the archivist, we wondered if our decision had been the right one. We opened the envelope and laid the papers on our desk.

There were three large-scale portrait photographs of Henry, none of which we had ever seen before. He was revealed as a refined, handsome man with a strong, intense presence (fig. 106). A thoughtful sadness persisted through all the images, despite the fact that they were taken years apart. One was part of the cover to a booklet commemorating Henry's farewell dinner from Wills 'upon his retirement after twenty-eight years' service, chaired by Lord Dulverton at the Grand Hotel, Bristol, on 1 May 1933'.

There were also three articles: two obituaries written shortly after his death in 1960, and an earlier editorial piece from the Wills company magazine, published in 1929. They contained much interlocking information, which gradually built up a picture of an amazing life. The searchlight they threw on to the events of Henry's life forced us to accept that we had entirely failed to understand it.

The first began:

Mr Burke joined the BAT [British and American Tobacco Company] in January 1905; after six months' training he spent several months gaining further experience at the Jasmatzi Factory in Dresden, and in the following year was sent to Antwerp as Factory Manager. Two years later, at a moment's notice, he was transferred to Robert Street, Liverpool, to act in a similar capacity. Shortly afterwards he was sent down to Ashton Gate [Bristol] as Deputy Manager to the late Mr Percy Ogden, who was transferred to Head Office in London, when Mr Burke became General Manager for all the BAT interests in Bristol, which included the Bristol Box and Printing Company and the Bristol Tin Case Company.

So Henry began his life in Bristol in January 1905. Henry and Rose had obviously returned from Peru immediately after Katrina was born in February 1904 for him to have got a job and started work in Bristol by January the following year. His short stay in Liverpool explained the birth of Richard Ulick there in 1907. The fact that the company was based in Bristol, and he returned and remained based there for the rest of his working life after a short training phase, made it highly probable that Robert and Caroline's move to Nunney Delamere, in time to sign and date their completed extension in 1906, was driven by a desire to be near Henry and Rose's family.

Henry's meteoric rise from newly recruited trainee to manager of all the BAT company's diverse interests in Bristol indicates that he must have been a highly intelligent, gifted individual with natural leadership qualities. He was evidently very effective as a manager, since he not only sustained his senior position over a period of twenty-five years, but was promoted to overseeing the two prime production units of the company. One of the obituaries focused almost exclusively on his career, and made clear the respect in which he was held and the influence he wielded over the later working lives of those junior to him. It concluded with a vivid word picture, portraying him as a fair but demanding figurehead:

> Those who knew Mr Burke at No. 3 and No. 4 [Factories] had, as Mr Davidson points out, a very great affection for him. They say he was one of the finest men to work with, straightforward, giving a pat on the back for good work done, creating a good working atmosphere, but he was a man's man, and a good disciplinarian, who once he had told you off, forgot all about it.

If there was an element of predictability in this account of Henry's working life, the story told by the other two articles, describing his childhood and young adult years, was startling. Between them they brought his extraordinary experiences into sharp focus:

> I feel sure there must be many of your readers who remember with gratitude and pleasure H.U.B., as he was affectionately known. His early life is like a fairy story,

although perhaps 'fairy' is hardly the right word to use. Many years ago when he was lecturing on his life to a literary society the comment was made, 'This is stranger than fiction.'

Both articles progressed to information about Henry of which we had never caught the vaguest hint. One was straightforward and factual: 'Some of his youth was spent in India and Cyprus, and in his early teens he went from Ireland to Canada.' The other was less concerned with detail but focused on the underlying emotional experience and complex dilemmas confronting a boy with so fragmented and impersonal a childhood:

> His boyhood was lonely, and he spent the greater part in Greece; he eventually ended up at Cranleigh College in Surrey. His father, who was a brilliant barrister and a man of letters, should have had for his motto, 'If you are any good, you will make good.' That is what he said to his son, whom he thought a fool. He bought him, at the tender age of seventeen, a second-class ticket to Canada. H.U.B. went out with a batch of Dr Barnardo's Boys to no job, with very little money in his pocket. Once over there he started off by sweeping a crossing, and the lowest ebb he reached was when he had to sell the buttons off his overcoat for a meal. He then got a job on a farm where the work was very hard and the food very bad, usually bread and onion soup. He stayed in Canada nearly a year, earning at the end the princely sum of four dollars a month. He then went to the States, as far as the railroad took him, and eventually arrived in Wyoming.

Brian and I were stunned. We had arrived at the Record Office expecting to glance through a tedious tribute to a dependable employee. We stopped and sank back in our chairs and slowly removed our glasses. Then we began to read the article again.

The unintentional expression of deep emotional hurt made the beginning of the article almost embarrassing to reread. Although it was ostensibly written by 'a correspondent', no one but Henry himself could have known, or repeated, those events from this painful perspective. When he recounted them many years later they were still too raw and unresolved for him to disguise the rejection he felt they expressed. The lonely years in India and Cyprus must have been spent without Katherine or his sisters, otherwise he would have had no reason to feel isolated.

His only family contact in those bleak years must have been his father, Ulick Ralph Burke, whose perception of him as 'a fool' he had been unable to forget. No one but Henry himself could have described such a cold, judgemental relationship between a father and his only son. How desperately Henry must have sought Ulick Ralph's approval, but it was never to be, because as a teenager he was put on a boat and told that if there was anything in him, he would make good. It is hard to conceive of a more calculated demonstration of indifference to a child than this.

Supposing he failed? Presumably Ulick Ralph would never expect to see his forgotten child again, as indeed he never did. The words that Henry repeats verbatim must have become branded on his memory. 'If there is any good in you – then you will make good' implies that any request for help would be interpreted as a demonstration of innate worthlessness. Could Henry ever have been able to forgive Ulick Ralph for this heartless rejection, or indeed his mother, for acquiescing to the scheme?

There is no suggestion in Henry's account of his agreeing to the emigration, or seeing it as an adventure. He wanted his audience to understand that the hunger and deprivation he experienced in Canada were the result of being deported there by his family with no money, no job and no friends. He was unable to forget the last twist of ignominy, which was being placed among a batch of Dr Barnardo's boys. These were the destitute, unwanted street urchins whom no one cared for; they formed the most deprived and wretched underclass in the gutters of Victorian industrial slums.

These few words were enough to convey the story of an isolated, unloved childhood that ended prematurely with a complete separation from his family, organised by his own parents. The only time he seemed to have experienced anything approaching family life was a period of about five years between his return from India in 1879 and his departure for Cyprus with his father in 1884, when he was ten years old.

Why had Ulick Ralph and Katherine treated Henry as they did? Why had he been kept isolated from his sisters in foreign countries almost from his birth and for long periods later? Why had Ulick Ralph branded him a fool when his later life proved, beyond doubt, that he was a clever and highly capable man? Why had his parents not doted on their tall, handsome, fair-haired boy, the heir to the Burke family name, instead of casting him adrift in North America as a teenager to eke out a living as a crossing sweeper?

I was suddenly certain that Henry's sister, Mabel Emma, had never been in India – no wonder she had no recollections of her return as a nine-year-old. Her mother had returned, leaving her baby in Lahore to begin his lonely childhood in the care of a servant until he was five. Why had she done such an unnatural thing? And why had Ulick Ralph chosen to be accompanied on his later trip to Cyprus by the son he despised? His description of his father as 'a brilliant barrister and man of letters' betrays a hint of hero worship by the solitary little boy, despite being belittled by his father in return.

Suddenly, part of the unremarkable heading at the top of the obituary struck me. It gave Henry's birth as 6 January 1874. I whispered to Brian:

'January 1874 – it's the magic year!'

The crisis. Everyone's moment of truth. Robert Bateman leaving London. Leaving the Dudley. Altering Biddulph – carving the date stone. Charles Wilbraham's move from Audley to Penkridge. *Paolo and Francesca. Reading of Love.* All of it concentrated in the last months of 1873 or early 1874, the exact moment when Henry was born. How on earth did Robert and Caroline have a close enough relationship with Henry to up sticks from their manor house in Shropshire and move to where he was, pretty well as soon as he returned from South America and started work in Bristol in 1905? He was a man of thirty-two by then, who had lived his entire life abroad apart from five years between the ages of five and ten. Why would a couple in their late sixties uproot their whole lives on the basis of a relationship with a nephew whom they had only known as a child over twenty years before? It just wasn't credible. Unless, of course, they had known him since 6 January 1874 . . .

'Hang on a minute!' said Brian in a schoolmasterly tone. 'This is Victorian England. Caroline was the daughter of the Dean of Lichfield. The scandal would have been massive. They could not have stopped it getting out. She would have been an outcast, and never ever have been allowed to marry Robert under any circumstances. Besides, he is always called Henry Ulick Burke, without fail, in every document throughout his life, and Ulick is the Burke family name. It's all too hysterical. Too anachronistic, too soap stars and footballers' wives. It just didn't happen in church families at that level then!'

I knew what he was saying, but I wasn't being glib. I knew we would never find a letter or a document saying, 'My real name is Henry Bateman.' The point was there had been a cover-up – and it had worked. But these were real human beings wrestling with instinctive emotional forces too primal to be contained by the tissue of lies thrown over them to maintain a pretence of respectability. In those obituaries I felt we were confronted by a desperate figure, Ulick Ralph Burke, driven to anger and cruelty by the need to pretend that he felt for Henry what a father would feel for his natural son, when he did not. Ultimately, his frustration got the better of him, and he simply got rid of Henry.

That might not have been sufficient on its own to conclude that Henry was not his son, but once I had seen that date, 1874, it seemed equally clear that Robert and Caroline were unable to suppress the opposite compulsion – to express their love for him. They could not wait to embrace him and move to a place where they could be part of his life. When he appeared back in England, bringing with him the most precious gift a childless couple could imagine, a newborn grandchild, they could not deny their instinct to provide everything they could emotionally and materially to make amends for the years of estrangement. The move to Nunney, and later the bequest of their private possessions and their home to Henry, risked exciting curiosity, even social disgrace, after their death, but they were unable to resist their longing to acknowledge him in deeds, if not in documents.

The account of Henry's early life in America was enthralling. It was the record of a bullied, anxious adolescent discovering the vigour and prowess beginning to develop within himself. He was becoming a potent, powerful young man, resourceful and undaunted by danger, who could take command of the world about him, impose his will upon it, and determine his own fate.

Henry got off the train in Wyoming as a destitute teenager, with no money and no work. He was still a penniless English vagrant, scraping by from meal to meal on the meagre skills he had acquired in Canada as a crossing sweeper and impoverished farm-hand. Almost immediately, he tried to better himself by using his natural aptitude for horsemanship to find work as a jockey. Energetic and wiry, he was soon taken on by the owner of a small ranch, and started to master the skills needed to handle cattle.

After a couple of years he had an amazing piece of luck, which was to transform his prospects:

> Then happened one of the outstanding excitements of his life; there was a local rodeo open to all comers, and H.U.B. won it. The prize was a crocodile-skin saddle, bridle and quirt presented by William Cody – Buffalo Bill. It was a great achievement and Cody then asked him to bring home twenty-five horses for his show.

'Home' meant England, where Buffalo Bill's Wild West Show was causing a sensation in the 1890s. What an amazing transformation in his self-esteem this achievement must have represented for Henry Burke. No longer an outsider, he had proved he could excel in the very skills that were most valued and admired by the remote community around him. What a charismatic figure he must have cut as he clung on to the bucking, flailing animal, his fair hair flying in the wind, and being befriended by the great William Cody when it was over. The saddle and bridle must have been recognised wherever he went by all the ranchers and their awe-struck daughters as emblems of his courage and masculinity.

Cody donated the prizes to these local rodeos in order to find young men with outstanding skills with semi-wild and unbroken horses. These formed the spectacular heart of his Wild West Show. Their transportation across the Atlantic in the hold of ocean liners was a tough and dirty job of vital importance to Cody; he was known to pay handsomely for the service, which made the rodeo competition fierce. Henry's account of his life as a cowboy on his return to the States makes no attempt to glamorise the job:

> He returned to the States, and after various jobs became a fully-fledged cow puncher; this meant being in the saddle for eighteen hours a day, for months on end. It was a very arduous life, and one of the worst conditions was hunger, which was never satisfied.

After delivering a second group of horses to England for Buffalo Bill, Henry did not return to the USA but took a boat to South America and started his life in Peru.

Here he was exposed to a completely different level of risk, which demanded formidable physical endurance to overcome potentially life-threatening dangers. At first he was employed by the huge, British-based Peruvian Corporation, which had wide-ranging rights to extract mineral deposits, establish coffee plantations and build roads and railways. His first task was to transport gold bullion from the coast to the mountainous interior on the backs of mules and llamas. The road over one pass was 18,000 feet high, which caused altitude sickness, and the extreme variation from heat to cold was almost unmanageable. The primitive, insanitary conditions and hostile climate began to undermine his health and he endured a series of alarming fevers and insect attacks that brought him near to death:

> Whilst he was in Peru he had much sickness – scurvy, black water fever, which incidentally caused his deafness, were followed by the attack of a borer beetle. History has it that H.U.B. was one of the few men attacked by this foul creature who did not commit suicide. The beetle bores its way through your body; in H.U.B.'s case, his arm. It took nine months to do this. After two months he began to smell and no human being would or could go near him. His food was put down for him about twenty yards away. It was an unmitigated horror, as you can imagine.

Henry's relentless determination to persevere with his allotted tasks despite appalling conditions built up a picture of a man of extraordinary willpower and resourcefulness, whose instinct for survival never wavered, no matter how desperate his situation:

> His experiences were unending, and one of the worst was when he was attacked by soldier ants. He heard them coming like a gust of wind and knew that the one thing they could not stand was fire, so he made a ring of fire round himself and stood naked for over three hours until they had passed by. There was nothing left but devastation, but his hut was clean as they had eaten all the cockroaches, bugs and centipedes. Not long after that he was stung all over his head by a swarm of bees and went blind. He was in the middle of the jungle and had visions of dying of starvation, but he crawled for hours and eventually came upon a stream. He bathed his eyes until he could see a little and somehow found his way home. Most of this happened whilst he was working in coffee. His underlings were real savages, naked and armed with bows and arrows; some time after he had left that job he heard that the natives had gone berserk and massacred everybody.

Illness forced Henry to leave the Peruvian Corporation in 1900. He went into the oil industry, as deputy manager on the Talara oil fields on the north-west coast, the first wells bored in Peru. There was no fresh water for sixty miles, and they were forced to drink condensed seawater. After his marriage in 1902, he took his wife, Rose, back with him to Talara, where 'there were only two English ladies in the community. Two years later [in 1904] temporary failure of the oil wells, along with bad outbreaks of smallpox and bubonic plague, decided him to return home.'

Brian and I were mesmerised by the ferocious intensity of Henry Burke's experience of life. We felt almost overwhelmed by his flint-hard self-reliance, honed through a lonely childhood and parental rejection, then abject poverty and relentless years in the scalding dust of the prairies. We struggled to keep some sense of a time scale, to stop us merely being absorbed into a *Boys' Own* adventure and lose all sense of continuity between this man and the Henry Burke who worked in Bristol for twenty-eight years and in 1922 inherited a large house from Robert and Caroline Bateman. The article ends with the words: 'He died as he had lived, surrounded by love and affection, a great gentleman.'

A great gentleman indeed! In just one day, Henry had made a mockery of the genteel, sepia-tinted world of posed Victorian photographs. He compelled us to admire the sheer grit and tenacity of his remorseless determination to overcome all obstacles before him and achieve distinction in everything he undertook. He had succeeded triumphantly, ending his days as a wealthy, retired executive, able to provide well for his descendants. Something John Beauchamp said in our telephone conversation, 'I'm afraid you'll find all of us – Henry's descendants – are a pretty dysfunctional family,' came back to me more than once as I thought about Henry's incredible story on the way home.

By the time we reached Biddulph it was dark. The movement-activated lights flicked on as we approached, and the house seemed a little forbidding in the stark electric light. We felt as if we had become complacent and taken its mystery for granted. Unconsciously, we had begun to feel we had solved its riddle, discerned and revealed the strange hieroglyphics time had left on its fractured walls. Suddenly it was inscrutable again – apart, enfolded within its own myth, silently disdaining our conceit for thinking its mystery exhausted. As we gazed at it, a white owl was caught in the glare, passing the pepper-pot dome of the tower. The information we had found that day made it clear that there were strange, sad stories, still secret and hidden, which had their genesis within the walls of Biddulph Old Hall.

I could not help being a little apprehensive of what we might find if we dug deeper into the story of Henry Burke's life. I feared we might find that he had, indeed, died as he had lived, still desperately seeking the love and approval that he had been denied in his lonely, early years, and that the reason for that was intimately bound up with his benefactors, Robert and Caroline Bateman. One thing was beyond doubt: the discovery of Henry's story had changed the whole nature of our search. It was no longer simply about trying to find lost paintings, now it was a need to understand the relationship of this extraordinary personality to Robert and Caroline Bateman, as much for the light it threw upon them as upon himself and his descendants.

*Fig. 107. Henry Burke in later life
after his retirement.*

*Fig. 108. Robert, a tall, slim figure with a moustache and beard,
in the Lime Avenue at Biddulph Grange.*

Chapter 25

DYSFUNCTIONAL FAMILIES

The next clue arrived within days. Ruth Vilmi's brother Monty, who lived in America, had found a picture of Henry as a young man. The photograph was taken on a brief visit to England in 1897 when he was twenty-three. He was exceptionally tall and slim, with a comparatively short body and unusually long legs. This physique was highly distinctive and immediately reminded us of an old photograph of Robert Bateman, taken in the Lime Walk at Biddulph Grange (fig. 108). The match with the tall, thin figure was remarkable. The picture of Henry confirmed the description of his good looks and tall figure, identified as defining characteristics all through his life and passed on to his children and grandchildren. However, there was no hint in Henry's expression of the sad thoughtfulness that united the other pictures we had seen.

The photograph showed a group of five people who apparently made up the amateur cast of *A Poetic Proposal*, a play performed in the lecture hall at Long Melford, Suffolk, in 1897 (fig. 109). Hill House at Long Melford had been given as Ulick Ralph and Katherine's permanent address all through their marriage, regardless of where he was working. The photograph indicates that Katherine must have returned there from Dublin, after her husband's death in 1895. The performers were identified as Mrs Denny Cooke, Mr Sydney Allen, Mr Bennett, Miss Burke (Mabel Emma), and Mr Burke (Henry Ulick). Henry is in the centre of the group and slightly detached from the others. He stands at the back, his stylishly tailored suit and smart cap worn with a panache that makes the others look dowdy. His whole presence exudes a slightly arrogant awareness of a physical magnetism that effortlessly elicits admiration from the world around him. His expression is still boyish, with no hint of the hardness that his face was to betray in the photographs taken at his wedding five years later. It seemed extraordinary to think that a few days earlier, we would have had no understanding of the bizarre background of the cocky lad looking out at us from these photographs.

Fig. 109. Henry with the cast of A Poetic Proposal *in
Long Melford just before his departure for Peru.*

In 1897, Henry had reached one of the high points of his difficult life. He was twenty-three years old and this brief visit to his mother and sisters, two years after his father's death, must have symbolised his triumph over loneliness, mockery and abandonment. His arrival in Long Melford, fully grown, strong, bronzed, confident and self-reliant, can only have created a sensation. His fantastic tales of life on the far side of the world, of riding for days in the blazing heat, roping cattle and winning rodeos, must have represented a bold assertion that he had risen to the challenge posed to him and proved that there was indeed 'good in him'. His family could have had no conception of the hunger, drudgery and loneliness that had underpinned his struggle to escape from the freezing back alleys of Toronto. How laughable he must have found their agitation over the forthcoming production in the village lecture hall, after his long fight against starvation in the lawless New World, where everyone carried guns, and used them! How he must have revelled in the adulation of this world of women and their friends as he was paraded from one house to the next.

It must have been on such a visit to his friend Millicent Parry-Okeden that her sister Rose had met and fallen under the spell of the tall, handsome adventurer. Her infatuation offered Henry the chance to complete the process of overcoming the humiliation of his rejection by joining a richer, grander English family than his own.

Surely it was under the influence of this adulation that Henry took the perilous decision not to return to the United States, where he had been so successful, but to apply instead to the Peruvian Corporation for a job, and travel to South America later in the year.

For the rejected adolescent, there could scarcely be a decision more freighted with personal symbolism. The Peruvian Corporation was the very organisation that had offered his father, Ulick Ralph Burke, a senior position in 1895. To travel to Peru and make good in that company, the one that had selected his father, held out the opportunity for Henry to demonstrate that he had achieved as much as his father, the brilliant barrister and man of letters. Seen in this context, his courage and will to endure sickness and danger in Peru, though no less awe-inspiring, were tinged with an aura of compulsion which had its roots in his unhappy past.

Once having set himself this challenge of 'making good' in Peru, the prospect of returning a failure must have been far more devastating for Henry than anyone else could have realised. How had the Corporation reacted to his prolonged periods of ill-health? Had they waited patiently for him to recover, or had they given his job to someone else? Whatever the reason, by 1900, three years after his arrival, Henry had left the Peruvian Corporation for a speculative oil company. Compared to the solidity of the Peruvian Corporation, with its vast reserves of capital and management structure in London and Dublin, this was a desperate gamble. These were the first oil wells ever drilled in Peru. The aim was to try to tap into the fortunes that were being made by entrepreneurs able to supply the new motor car industry with its lifeblood, petroleum. This previously valueless by-product of refining lamp oil had until then been sold only in tiny quantities, as a stain remover. By 1900, the revolutionary potential of the automobile was understood and production was growing exponentially. Month by month, new manufacturers entered the market across Europe and North America. By 1903, Henry Ford had founded his company and, with the launch of his Model 'T' in 1908, the age of motoring for the masses was born. It irreversibly transformed the lives of ordinary people, and created the first of the giant corporations which were to dominate commercial life throughout the new century.

The corresponding demand for petrol at first created a chronic imbalance between supply and demand, which sent the price of oil rocketing. Sites like the tar pits at Talara, where the oil already broke the surface in small quantities, were the obvious places to sink wells. Once sufficient capital was raised to acquire the site and increase its flow through some rudimentary drilling, the company had a free supply of a substance that could be barrelled up and sold at very high prices. For a time it must have seemed as if they had discovered a source of almost limitless riches, without any of the uncertainty, sweated labour and physical danger of the coffee plantations. However, the lack of understanding of the underlying geology of oil exploitation meant that Henry and his companions were completely unprepared when the oil flow slowed to a trickle and finally dried up in 1903. We were building up a vivid picture of a period of personal crisis for Henry. His troubles intensified until they culminated in his return from Peru with his new family in 1904 and the start of an entirely different, settled way of life, as an executive in a large company.

Our interest in trying to find the trail of the lost Bateman pictures had become part of a wider fascination with the apparently unnatural relationship between the Burke parents and their only son. In the Bristol records, there had been one anomaly that we felt could be crucial to our understanding of Henry's upbringing. Although all the archives indicated that he had accompanied Ralph Ulick on his stay in Cyprus between 1886 and 1889, one account also described him as 'ending up at Cranleigh College'. If this were true, we felt it might have strongly influenced his development and later life by allowing him to test his father's assessment of him as 'a fool' against the independent opinions of the schoolmasters and other boys. We contacted the college and their archivist looked up the early records for us. Henry did attend the school but only during one single year, 1889, by which time he was sixteen years old and back from Cyprus. The fact that he was not at Cranleigh the next year was no surprise, as we already knew that in 1890 his parents had despatched him to Canada. The disturbing implications of this discovery rekindled our sense that we needed to talk to someone who had actually known Henry.

So it was disappointing when John Beauchamp rang with the sad news that he had developed further health problems. In the meantime, he told us that his daughter Jennifer had studied the Burke family history and suggested we make a date to meet her. When I rang Jennifer she opened our telephone conversation with the now-familiar disclaimer that she knew nothing of Robert Bateman or his paintings. She did mention, however, that she owned one family portrait, of the mother of Henry's wife, Rose. I asked Jennifer if she had been close to her grandmother Katrina, and was surprised to discover that they had lived next door to each other.

'I adored her. In a strange way we were companions, after I came to live here. We saw each other practically every day, of course. At first she was next door in the big house, and I was in the cottage, but when she got older she converted the rest of the outbuildings and we lived side by side. We'd often eat together in the evenings, but she ate very little – frankly, she preferred a gin and tonic. Probably how she kept that amazing tall, slim figure that they all had.'

'Did she talk to you about the past?'

'Not a lot, but she did. Especially if there were just the two of us. Actually, she had a wonderful way of talking about the old days. Sort of scandalous, or slightly racy. It's hard to describe but it was exciting, really brought it to life. I loved it!'

'Did she say much about her father, Henry?'

'Occasionally – but she was very fond of her mother's family, the Parry-Okedens. Auntie Vi particularly, and occasionally Auntie Millicent. She had been close to them. Of course, there was a rift with her father after Rose, her mother, died in 1931. She hated Elsie, as she called his second wife – couldn't stand her. Frankly, I don't think there was much contact after they got married.'

We arranged to meet at her house in Westwood, near Bradford-on-Avon. In the meantime, we decided to scan whatever records we could find for more information about Henry's wife Rose, who had effectively shared the bequest of Robert and Caroline's house in Nunney and lived there surrounded by most of their furniture and personal possessions for nine years until her death in 1931. We wondered what Rose's relationship had been with the elderly couple who had moved close to both them in Bristol and her relatives at Turnworth House. Presumably she and her children had managed to establish a sufficiently close relationship with Robert and Caroline to influence their decision to identify Henry as the principal beneficiary of their wills.

The more we looked into it, the more it appeared that Rose Burke's early life had been dominated by the tragic loss of her mother at the time of her birth. Her parents had married in 1871. Her father, Uvedale Edward Parry-Okeden, was a lieutenant in the 10th Hussars and was posted to Lahore a few months after the wedding. Their first child, Millicent, was born in India in 1874. This is the person we had been surprised to encounter in Henry's will, described as his friend. We had speculated that their friendship might have been forged during childhood in India. However, in 1875, Uvedale and Rose Parry-Okeden had a second child, Elinor Violet, who was born in Walsingham in Norfolk; less than two years after that, the ill-fated birth of Rose, again in Walsingham, was followed immediately by her mother's death. The children's father remained based in India until 1879. That year he married Caroline Susan Hambro, and they began a new family, eventually to include seven children.

So the year after Millicent's birth, her mother had returned to England for good. Henry could not have known Millicent in Lahore unless she, like him, had remained behind in India. This raised the intriguing possibility that the two isolated, motherless infants might have been thrown together and formed an intense bond before both returned with their fathers in 1879. Whatever the truth of this, Rose had been raised by a young stepmother with a constantly increasing family of her own. It would be difficult not to feel an outsider, and be acutely aware of the loss of her real mother, whose names she bore.

By the time we arrived at Jennifer Beauchamp's house the following Friday, there seemed every chance that, through her close relationship with her grandmother Katrina, she might be able to help us discover the truth about the contorted human relationships that underlay the astounding surface texture of Henry Burke's life. She lived in an attractive cottage attached to the side of a fine Georgian house, in the centre of the village. She greeted us warmly, but maintained a thoughtful silence as we briefly outlined our discoveries about Robert as an artist. She seemed sceptical about our assertion that the house at Nunney had been inherited by Henry. When we showed her copies of the wills, she became slightly agitated. Despite being a keen researcher into her family's history, she had clearly had no previous knowledge of this connection. She felt that the association with a figure like Bateman was something she should have been made aware of, either by her father John Beauchamp or her grandmother Katrina. Jennifer remembered one conversation when Katrina had referred to an unnamed 'fairly famous artist' who was a distant relation, but she had given no inkling that she had ever seen any of his paintings, let alone that her parents had inherited some of them along with his house. She had talked about the house at Nunney, describing it as grand and comfortable, with three or four staff.

'To be honest, I got the feeling she was still bitter about her father selling it after her mother died and he "ran off with Elsie" as she put it.'

She picked up Robert's will from the table.

'But look at this, 1922. Gran was born in 1904, so she would have been eighteen, grown up, when they moved in after they inherited it. She must have known exactly who Robert Bateman was, and known his paintings – and yet she never said a word to me about it. Even though she must have known how interested I would be, especially when I was doing my research into the family history.'

'Do you think she had forgotten?' I asked.

'I don't believe that. She could be vague about everyday things that didn't interest her, but not something like this. She wasn't shy about letting you know how grand and exotic her friends had been! The romantic artist and his high-born wife would have been right up her street. No, she must have decided not to mention it.'

She searched through a pile of papers and photographs on the kitchen table. There was a photograph of Katrina when she was young – a tall, slender woman in her twenties (fig. 110).

'Her figure never really altered till the day she died. Fantastic really.'

Another photograph had been described by Katrina as Nunney, though Jennifer was unable to confirm this as she had never been there. It was indeed a photograph of the gardens at Rockfield House. They were almost exactly the same as when we had seen them, except that the rockeries and raised beds were less mature and overgrown. The view showed a tall, elegant, older woman in an ankle-length dress on one of the paths near the comparatively new garden pavilion (fig. 111). Her clothes indicated a date around 1918, and her erect bearing and fine hair, drawn back into a loose knot at the nape of her neck, was strongly characteristic of Caroline. So, too, was the handwriting on the back of the image which read, 'With very best wishes for Aug 7th and much love.' It exactly matched the writing on her letter to her cousin,

Fig. 110. Katrina in the late 1920s. She clearly inherited her father's tall and slender figure.

George Howard (fig. 59). For us this was of real interest, as we had never seen a picture of Caroline in later life.

Among the papers was a journal kept by Violet, Rose's sister, over two years round about 1908. It relentlessly recorded the minutiae of every mundane social call, horse ride, tea party and tennis match that made up the life of a well-to-do spinster of that time. Although we all laughed about this, we could not help wondering how her sister, Rose, who was brought up in exactly the same privileged conditions, had managed to adapt to life with the demonically driven Henry Burke in the savage deserts of Peru. Katrina remembered being told by her mother that the family had been forced to return to England within weeks of her birth in 1904. Jennifer found a note she had made during a conversation with her grandmother that the family's return home represented a desperate crisis in their life and marriage. They had returned with, literally, nothing – 'no home, no job, and no money, early in 1904.' What a moment of desolate disillusionment this must have been for the couple.

Fig. 111. Caroline in old age in the garden at Nunney Delamere.

For Henry, it marked the end of his struggle to make good in the New World, for which he had been prepared to undergo unimaginable mental and physical deprivation. For Rose, it must have represented the culmination of a merciless period of education in the harsh realities of the world around her. From the cosseted luxury of Turnworth House, with her days filled with tennis matches and daydreams of her handsome cowboy, she had been catapulted into the searing heat, disease and primitive poverty of Peru, just as the symptoms of her first pregnancy took hold.

Jennifer was still studying her notes when she suddenly said, 'Ah, that's strange. It says here Auntie Vi – that's Violet, Rose Burke's sister – hated Millicent, her other sister. That's what Gran told me. Apparently they never spoke to each other.'

This was fascinating information. Was there the remotest possibility that, after his wife's death, Uvedale Parry-Okeden had been able to return from India with a child of his by another woman, with no birth certificate, whom he had integrated with his younger daughters and his large second family? If at any point Violet and Rose had suspected such a thing, what an insult she would have represented to the memory of their dead mother, and how utterly estranged from their intense relationship she would have been. How 'hated', in a word! Did Henry's lifelong bond with Millicent have its beginnings in the anonymous world of unwanted children, concealed within the unrecorded margins of British India?

Jennifer was gathering up her papers and photographs when she stopped for a moment at the photograph of a little boy of six or seven, posed with a toy horse on wheels (fig. 112). She gazed at it with a gentle smile.

Fig. 112. Katrina's younger brother, John, aged six or seven.

'Gran loved that picture. It always reminds me of her. It was always around some-where in her day. It's her little brother – the one who died, John, his name was. It still seemed to affect her when she talked about him, even as an old lady. I think he was only about eight or nine when he died. Gran always said that her mother was heartbroken.'

Jennifer got up from the table and took us over to the fireplace to look at the portrait of Rose's mother that hung above it (fig. 113). It was titled and dated 'Rose 1877' on the face of the painting, but there was no sign of a signature. The romantic quality of the child-like face with pale luminous skin framed against amber-gold trusses of curly hair was compelling and strongly evocative of the age of the Pre-Raphaelites. It was an ethereal, almost spectral piece, far more than a workaday portrait mechanically setting down a likeness. Its infinitely subtle, graded colouring and merging outlines suggested a figure recorded from a dream or memory, the twilight world of the mind, rather than from the stark daylight of physical reality. It was not hard to see why this haunting vision of her lost mother, who had died in the act of giving life to her and whose name she was destined to perpetuate, had become the most cherished possession of Rose Parry-Okeden as she progressed through her life and became Rose Burke, with children of her own.

Its unique quality might have been designed to imprint upon the mind of a bereaved little girl an idealised image of a gentle mother figure, when she felt she was being pushed aside by the arrival of more and more babies to her father and young stepmother. The cult that Rose had developed around this image had clearly commu-

Fig. 113. Robert Bateman, Rose 1877, *1906–8, oil on canvas, private collection.*
Jennifer Beauchamp's portrait of Rose Burke's mother Rose Lee-Warner, attributed
to Robert Bateman, is the single painting to have remained in the family.

nicated itself to her own daughter. Katrina had kept this single painting with her to
the end of her life, despite retaining almost nothing else belonging to her parents,
and passed it on as a precious inheritance to her granddaughter. Jennifer told us that
it had been done from a photograph, which she showed us (fig. 114).

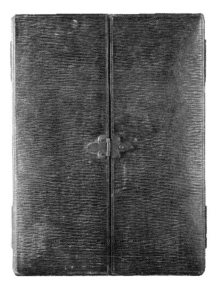

Figs. 114, 115. The case and photograph (with lock of hair) which inspired the painting of Rose some year later.

It was in a wonderful Victorian leather case, and contained a lock of faded blonde hair. Her contention that the painting had been copied from it was clearly correct as the pose was identical. Jennifer went on to outline a longstanding family mystery surrounding the date it had been painted. Apparently this could not have been 1877, as the sitter had died in the first few days of that year, never having recovered from giving birth to Rose (Henry's wife) in late December 1876. She then described another family tradition, passed on to her by her grandmother, that the portrait was unsigned because it had been painted later by an artistic member of the family. Jennifer had always understood this to be one of the Parry-Okedens – but at that stage she had never heard of Robert Bateman. After he moved to Nunney, what could have been more natural than for Robert to use his skills to develop an oil painting from the treasured photograph of Rose's lost mother? Surely this was the one gift that had the power to create an insoluble bond between the Batemans and Henry's wife that would last for the rest of their lives. Jennifer fretted about the risk that the painting might get damaged, and asked if we thought it should be put behind glass. Her pervasive concern for the preservation of this one family heirloom served only to emphasise the sad contrast between its survival and the disappearance of all the other paintings from Nunney.

It was beginning to appear that there might have been a concerted effort to conceal the connection between Henry's family and their benefactors, Robert and Caroline, by dispersing their inheritance. Katrina and Richard certainly did seem to have avoided mentioning the art or the bequest of the house, or indeed Robert and Caroline, to their children. Why? Had they simply forgotten the inheritance, and the people, as the years went by? Or had they understood and acquiesced in a need to obscure the relationship between themselves and Robert Bateman?

It turned out that Amanda Kavanagh, back in 1987 when she was researching her Apollo article, had posed these questions before us. Jennifer showed us a letter that Kavanagh had written to Katrina, having traced her as the daughter of the executor of Robert Bateman's will, to ask if she knew anything about the fate of Robert's work left in his home and studio after his death. She enclosed some images of Robert's work, and emphasised the level of critical recognition his work was achieving in the international art world. She described the portrait of Caroline as 'really wonderful', and claimed it originally hung at Nunney. If Kavanagh was correct, it must have formed an unforgettable component of the interior of Katrina's former home.

Katrina was eighty-two when she received this letter. The most obvious person for her to involve and consult was her granddaughter Jennifer, who lived with her and whose interest in family history would have guaranteed her enthusiasm. But Jennifer had known nothing about it, only finding it among her grandmother's papers after her death, with no pictures attached to it. They had never even discussed it. If Katrina had forgotten the paintings, then the letter with its images and startling re-evaluation of them would surely have jogged her memory. However, she had just put it away and said nothing. Jennifer was unable to tell us even if Katrina had replied to Amanda Kavanagh or not. The obvious way of solving the puzzle was to contact Amanda Kavanagh, and we did so. Although she remembered her correspondence with Katrina, she had no record of any response from her. We also checked the end of the *Apollo* magazine article where Kavanagh had listed her sources. Katrina was not mentioned, nor was there any evidence within the text of information she may have supplied.

In the circumstances, we had little option but to conclude that Katrina had chosen not to reply, and not to mention the letter to Jennifer or anyone else in her family. Considering the possible financial implications for her descendants, and its direct relevance to her own life story, it is hard to see what led her to this decision. Did she feel that responding to the questions it raised would involve delving into something private that she perceived as potentially damaging to herself and her relatives if it were publicly known? It seemed as if the resurrection of Robert, through the recognition of the quality of his work in the late 1980s, had appeared like a ghostly spectre to his living relations, who had buried all trace of the connection between their family and him beneath a conspiracy of silence that even embraced their children. How far this had been deliberate, and what had motivated it, was fast becoming the question at the core of our search.

Fig. 116. The grouped graves of John, Rose, Robert and Caroline in Whatley churchyard.

Chapter 26

CONSPIRACY OF SILENCE

'I was thinking about death,' Brian murmured. 'Well, perhaps graves would be more accurate.'

'Ah. Graves generally, or one in particular?' I said with the forbearing smile of someone preparing to understand.

'The ones in Whatley churchyard,' he said quietly, ignoring my tone.

'Robert and Caroline?' I asked.

'Not exactly. The one I had just scraped with my credit card and realised it wasn't them when the torch ran out. The bit I cleared said John, and the rest of it was covered in lichen except the far end which said died something or other, the month and the day 1920, aged eight years. It seemed irrelevant at the time.'

'You mean – the little boy in the picture?'

'It sounds far-fetched, but it wasn't only that. It was the identical grave next door. I shone my torch on to it and saw one word legible through the mould, and it has come back to me – it was Burke. Of course, it didn't mean a thing then.'

We were both silent for a time.

'Are you sure?' I asked. Brian nodded.

'We'll have to go back.'

The next day Jennifer Beauchamp rang to tell us that she had found Katrina's baptism certificate and would send a copy to us. We mentioned the grave in Whatley churchyard, and told her we intended to go back there. She suggested that we combine the trip to Nunney with a visit to her father, who was a little better and keen to meet us after a long conversation with her. She had shown him the prints of Robert's paintings we had left with her but warned us that he appeared to know nothing at all about them. We rang John Beauchamp and a date was set for the end of the following week.

When the baptism certificate arrived it showed that Katrina was born on 20 February 1904 at Talara, Peru, to Henry and Rose Burke. However, she was baptised

Katrina Marian on 15 May 1904 in the 'City and Port of Valparaiso, Chile, South America, in the British Episcopal Church at this place'. So, less than two months after the birth, the family seem to have left Talara and moved to, or arrived in, the port of Valparaiso. The 'trade or profession' of the father (Henry) was shown as 'gentleman', and the sponsors were Edmund Parry-Okeden, Millicent Parry-Okeden, Hermione Parry-Okeden and Edith Baggs.

For Henry to be back in England in time to start an entirely new career in January 1905, he probably needed to have left Peru by mid-1904. The description of Henry as a gentleman was probably a euphemism to disguise his unemployment after the collapse of the oil company at Talara. The presence of the contingent of Parry-Okedens was a surprise. Presumably they must have gone out to Peru to see that no harm came to Rose during the birth in such a dangerous and primitive place. We guessed that the visit to Valparaiso was a temporary stop on the boat trip taking them back to England; being a large port, it was probably the first place they came to with an Anglican church.

We tried a new line of enquiry by searching the lists of the shipping companies to see if there was any record of the family returning to Britain from South America in the middle months of 1904. We entered the name Henry Ulick Burke, and were stunned by the response. First, we found recorded journeys for Henry and his second wife Elsie in every year between 1933 and the outbreak of war in 1939. There were also earlier records of trips for Imperial Tobacco with the British India Steam Navigation Company, encompassing Tangier, Madras, Port Said and Colombo.

In among the cruises and pleasure trips, however, were one or two critical records of very different voyages, which either endorsed Henry's account of his early life or provided information that illuminated events in a stark new light. It was uncanny to stumble across a list for the SS *Oregon*, part of the Dominion Line, sailing between Portland, Oregon, and Liverpool in 1894. After listing its first-, second- and saloon-class passengers, it records a group of 25 horses in steerage, below the water line, being overseen by a group of eleven roughnecks, defined as farm labourers, led by a twenty-year-old lad: Henry Burke (Cattleman). Somehow, that description, 'cattleman', in conjunction with the image of the stifling, ill-lit bowels of the ship, gives a grimy sense of the menial nature of Henry's work that the word 'cowboy' might completely disguise. He travelled again two years later from New York to Liverpool on the *Luciana*, in marginally better conditions.

However, it was his voyage from New York on the SS *Teutonic*, a ship of the White Star Line, that took us completely by surprise. It arrived in Liverpool on 19 May 1904. His age and other details leave no doubt that this is Henry, especially as his obituaries specified Liverpool as his disembarkation point from Peru. Since Katrina was christened in Chile just four days earlier, it is clear that he was not with his wife for this important family event. This strongly suggests that, under the strain of childbirth and the collapse of the oil company, the relationship between Henry and Rose had broken down and he had returned alone, rather than face the ignominy of travelling back with his traumatised wife. So it was Rose who tactfully gave the profession of her baby's father as 'gentleman', rather than 'none', which might have been more honest at that uncertain moment. Anxiety to have the child baptised, apart from religious orthodoxy, would have been related to the complexities of authenticating the legitimacy of children born in remote areas of the world where no infrastructure for issuing birth certificates was in place.

Had Henry's life continued down the disastrous path it had followed in the first eighteen months of his marriage to Rose, the Parry-Okedens would have had the option of quietly absorbing Katrina into their world at Turnworth House, and providing a good home for her, safe in the knowledge that the documentary evidence defined her absent father as a man of private means. They must have felt that their infatuated daughter had been tricked into marriage by a ruthless fortune hunter, with his fantastic tales of rodeos and Buffalo Bill, gold bullion and oil wells which, within a few months, had proved to be completely worthless.

When Henry landed at Liverpool on 19 May 1904, he was an unemployed, penniless oil worker, from an impoverished family. What can have been in his mind at that bleak moment of defeat as he stood by the rails of the SS *Teutonic*? Who had he been able to turn to, as the unforgettable challenge, 'If there is any good in you, you will make good,' rang in his head only to be answered by the mocking voice of Ulick Ralph, the brilliant barrister, from beyond the grave, 'I rest my case, the boy's a fool'? Could it have been the one couple who, with their aristocratic connections and upper-class lifestyle centred on their ancient manor house at Benthall, had the ability to reassure the Parry-Okedens and broker a reconciliation between Rose and Henry? The people who, the following year, uprooted themselves from their beautiful home in Shropshire, and bought the freehold of a village house in Nunney, near both Henry and the Parry-Okedens – the house which, eighteen years later, they left outright to Henry, including all its contents and all their personal belongings?

By an odd chance, Henry's later career seemed to cast a tantalizing flicker of light on a discovery we had made earlier in our investigations into Robert's work as an artist. We had stumbled on a copy of a skilful but conventional drawing of a house, signed and dated 1889 (fig. 117). The title was recorded as 'The Limes at Wittsbridge'. Initially, our attempts to identify the setting proved fruitless, until we discovered that the title was incorrect and should have read *The Limes at Willsbridge*. This proved to be a village on the outskirts of Bristol that was later absorbed into the city suburbs. The house was demolished in 1960, but had been identified by name in documents and is recognisable from old photographs as the subject of Robert's drawing. It was a late eighteenth-century building that formed a subsidiary part of a substantial property known as Willsbridge Castle, and was built by a former

Fig. 117. Robert Bateman, The Limes at Willsbridge, *1889, pen and ink, private collection.*

owner of the castle for his unmarried sister. By the time Robert made his drawing, the castle was owned by William Sommerville, a prosperous paper manufacturer who owned two factories employing over five hundred men, the principal one in the adjacent village of Bitton. The Sommerville family owned several important local houses, including Bitton Hill House and Bitton Grange. Willsbridge and Bitton were barely six miles from Ashton Gate, the hub of the W. D. & H. O. Wills tobacco empire. The Sommervilles were influential figures at the heart of the industrial community of south Bristol and William Sommerville was a prominent member of the Bristol Chamber of Commerce under the Chairmanship of Sir William Wills.

As chairman of the Wills Company, Sir William dominated local life and was reputedly the second-richest man in England. A prominent JP, he sat as MP for South Bristol between 1894 and 1900, and in 1905 was raised to the peerage as Lord Winterstoke. His greatest achievement was to weld the leading tobacco companies together to form Imperial Tobacco, in order to defend themselves against an attempt by James Buchanan Duke, head of the American Tobacco Company, to gain control of the entire British market after he had bought Ogden's, a major British supplier, in 1901. Eventually, both sides acknowledged the damage being inflicted on their industry by their frenetic rivalry, and a truce was called through the formation of an international conglomerate called British American Tobacco (BAT). Ogden's was absorbed back into the British arm of the operation with its managing director, Percy Ogden, put in overall charge of the core manufacturing base at the Wills factories at Ashton Gate. Percy Ogden held this pivotal post until 1908, when he was replaced by Henry Ulick Burke, who continued to hold it uninterruptedly until he retired in 1933.

Did Henry owe this crucial opportunity, which underpinned his meteoric promotion and successful later life, to a longstanding relationship between William Sommerville and Robert Bateman? Had the Bristol businessman helped an old friend by using his influence with his neighbour Sir William Wills to secure a good position in the BAT empire for an able young man in 1904?

Henry's return from the New World seemed to mark as decisive a turning point in Robert and Caroline's lives as it had in his. Intriguingly, Robert Bateman had inscribed the rock near his lifelong property, Biddulph Old Hall, and his childhood home, Biddulph Grange, with the enigmatic legend, 'Remember this Day 11th June 1904' (see fig. 46), exactly three weeks after Henry's arrival in Liverpool. One of the articles in the Bristol Records Office had described a particular aspect of Henry's return from Peru in 1904 which was blamed on a knee injury that required surgery:

> He had some trouble with his knee, and had an operation without anaesthetic. It was not successful, and he decided to come home and have another operation. Again it was performed without anaesthetic, but it was successful.

Since we know that Henry was penniless at this point, one wonders who met him and financed his second operation. If it was Robert and Caroline, it would explain their presence at Biddulph on 11 June 1904, which was much nearer Liverpool than their home at Benthall Hall, in Shropshire. Biddulph would have provided a quiet place where they could look after him while he convalesced, away from inquisitive servants and neighbours in Benthall. It would have offered the necessary seclusion to consider what was to be done to rebuild from the disasters that had engulfed Henry's marriage and financial affairs. The fact that by January the following year Henry had a new job in Bristol, and Robert and Caroline had moved to Somerset and bought the house they were to leave to him suggests that the date 11 June 1904 might have been the fateful moment when they felt compelled to tell him the truth of their relationship to him, in order to justify the new role they were proposing to assume in his life.

If this was so, it would have been the definitive moment of self-revelation that transformed Robert and Caroline's entire lives. Their son, lost to them at birth, and lost again in America, had been miraculously returned to them. He had been cruelly maltreated by the people in whose care they had placed him but, by a wonderful stroke of good fortune, he had been given back to them at the very moment when he needed them most. They could not deny the compulsion of their parental instincts to claim him as their own and rescue him from destitution.

The day of that unburdening of their souls would indeed be a day they would always remember. Robert had perhaps felt the need to record it, in rock, in the grounds of his childhood home. To access its site he had cut steps into the face of the rock, not only so that his sixty-five-year-old wife could go up to the sacred place, but also so that a handsome young man of thirty, who was recovering from a knee operation, could be there with them, for the first time, as their acknowledged son. Judging by the way Robert and Caroline begin almost immediately to set in motion the process of reorientating their entire lives to centre on Henry, Rose and their family, it is difficult to believe that the 'riddle on the rock' and Henry's return from Peru are not related.

This strange symmetry was on our minds when we arrived at John and Joyce Beauchamp's home in Marlborough. We were still anxious to meet one of Henry's two surviving grandsons, and Katrina's only child, but we no longer approached the meeting with any expectation of stumbling upon a cache of lost Bateman paintings, nor even an explanation of how they were disposed of. It had become clear that neither of Henry's children had conveyed any information about the fate of the paintings, or about Robert and Caroline, to their sons.

Despite his eighty years, John Beauchamp had the distinctive tall, lean figure and refined features that we had seen in so many photographs of Henry. He spoke quietly with a gentle, considered intensity that gave what he said an air of precision and seriousness. After a few enquiries about our journey, he suddenly said,

'As you can see, there is nothing here from my family. Particularly my mother's side. Almost nothing, I'm afraid.'

We asked him about Henry.

After a moment's pause, he said,

'As a child I found him a bit frightening, actually. My first memory of him is sitting on his knee at the wheel of his big car – I don't remember what it was, but I do remember it seemed huge to me at the time – and being told to drive it round the lanes near our house. That was rather typical of him. It should have been fun, but his manner was too distant and detached. It felt like an exam. You felt he was annoyed if he had to intervene and turn the steering wheel.'

'What about all his adventures in America,' I asked. 'Surely they must have been very exciting when you were a boy.'

'Yes,' John replied, quietly, with an air of uncertainty that suggested he had some reservations. 'I did get quite enthusiastic about Buffalo Bill – Bill Cody. I visited his grave years later when I was grown up. My grandfather had two silver or nickel-plated pistols that Cody gave him; he let me hold them, I remember. And we went to his old house in Bristol, where there was a blue plaque saying that Cody had stayed there when he was visiting Grandad. That's been demolished now, I think.'

I asked about the saddle, bridle and quirt that he had won in Wyoming – had Henry passed them on, or the silver pistols?

John shook his head.

'Those are the sort of things I imagined he might have given to you or your cousin,' I said.

'No, I've no idea what happened to any of it. Of course, my mother and Henry hardly saw each other later. She loathed Elsie, his second wife.'

As we talked, the poignant story of John's childhood and adolescence gradually emerged, which had curious echoes of Henry's lonely early years. In 1927 his mother Katrina had married John Louis Beauchamp, the eldest son of a wealthy coal owner, with an extensive landholding based on Norton Hall, a historic house outside Midsomer Norton they had acquired in the middle of the nineteenth century. The Beauchamps were a wealthy and influential family in the south Bristol area. John Louis's grandfather had built over five hundred model houses for his employees, as well as a large Methodist church at Norton Down. According to John, his parents' marriage did not really work from the beginning; he was an only child, and felt lonely and unwanted. He recalled them openly indulging in affairs with other people, to whom he was sometimes introduced. He was frequently sent for holidays with his Auntie Vi, at her house near Shepton Mallett, which had a memorable plum orchard.

John asked Joyce to fetch an old photograph album from the loft. The photographs in the album, predominantly from the interwar years, conveyed a vivid sense of life among a group of good-looking, wealthy young people, which largely consisted of parties, country house visits and foreign travel. John Louis and Katrina Beauchamp were relentlessly stylish and modern, posing in their bags and one-piece bathing costumes, or smoking and sipping cocktails beside their open-topped cars. They were invariably surrounded by glamorous chums, intermittently identified by John as 'a flame' of my father's, or a man who was always around as he was 'besotted with my mother'. The atmosphere of hedonistic pleasure, underpinned by wealth and social exclusivity, was palpable.

It was easy to understand how utterly alien to them Robert's pictures would have been, steeped in a world of historical association and romantic love. The Beauchamps were in the process of discarding both the restrictive morality of Christian monogamy and the fusty Victorian veneration of the past. That would explain Katrina's disdain for the images themselves, and her lack of enthusiasm for keeping them, but not quite the suppression of all knowledge of them and their creator years later.

Was it possible that this was motivated by a less chic instinct, a determination to maintain her social cachet by avoiding any reference to the slightly irregular relationship between her father and his uncle and aunt, which had the potential to raise questions about his (and by implication her own and her son's) legitimacy? In other words, was Katrina aware of a skeleton in the family cupboard, which could under-mine the perception of the grand Burke/Lee-Warner/Parry-Okeden background which had made her eligible to take her place among the Beauchamps of Norton Hall?

One thing had become clear by the time we came to say goodbye to the Beauchamps that day. Katrina had avoided mentioning any connection between herself and Robert and Caroline to her son, either in his childhood or later in life. John acknowledged that he had heard the name Robert Bateman, but from whom and in what context he could not recall.

'The truth is I never ever remember my mother saying anything at all to me about him or the pictures you left with Jennifer. In fact, even now I find it hard to believe that my mother had ever seen any of them in her life.'

As we left Marlborough for Whatley churchyard, Brian and I were only too aware of the power of events from the distant past to resonate and disturb the equilibrium of ordinary lives being lived countless years later, in utterly different conditions. At one level we felt an instinct to stop meddling and let the past keep its secrets. At the same time, we could not overcome the urge to combat what seemed to be an injustice to the reputation of Robert Bateman, which appeared to have been propagated as much by his closest family as by the wider world of art critics and gallery curators. In fact, his relations seemed to have played a key role in frustrating the attempts of influential figures, such as Julian Hartnoll and Amanda Kavanagh, to champion his cause and bring about an informed reassessment of his place in the history of the later Pre-Raphaelite movement. We were beginning to wonder if we had got things out of proportion. Had we attached too much significance to the inheritance of the house and personal possessions, and so overstated the intricate family relationship between the Batemans and the Burkes?

When we reached Whatley, we registered for the first time that the two matched graves were alongside Robert and Caroline's. We crouched down and there, on the kerb, just as Brian had remembered, was the name 'John', then a long section obscured by lichen and, beyond that, just visible, the number '20' and then 'Aged 8 Years'. We had brought a proper scraper this time, and within minutes we had cleared both kerbs. Although they revealed only what Brian had suspected, we were shocked by the strength of our reaction. John Burke, the adored eight-year-old son of Rose, had been buried not only immediately beside her, but at the very feet of Robert and Caro-line's memorial. We were gripped by an uncomfortable sensation of having blundered on to a scene of intensely private love and loss. The graves were grouped together, as near to each other as the sad process of burial would permit (fig. 116). Rose's exact replication of John's grave was an eloquent expression of her longing to be reunited with him.

Just as Robert and Caroline's shared grave showed their longing to be united for all time, and the identical graves of John and Rose, set beside each other, demonstrated a mother's yearning to be reunited with her child, so the closeness of the whole group spoke eloquently of their loving relationship as a family. More specifically, it illuminated Rose's will to identify herself, and her child, with the older couple. By 1920, Robert and Caroline were nearly eighty years old, and in failing health. We can only assume the plot in Whatley churchyard had been reserved for them. It must have been Rose's decision to bring John's body from Bristol, where she was living at the time, and have him buried immediately at the foot of their allocated site, so that he would be near them. Since Robert and Caroline were still alive, this constituted a conscious recognition of the relationship between them. Devastated by John's death, Rose chose the churchyard near the house of her husband's uncle and aunt rather than a grave near to her home in Bristol or the family chapel at Turnworth House.

However, if she was aware of a much closer link between her son and the Batemans, the choice for his grave would have been quite natural. Was Rose symbolically entrusting her little boy to the care of his loving grandparents? Furthermore, if Rose did understand the true relationship between Henry and Robert and Caroline, had she herself acquired the one person she had been longing for, all her life – a devoted, loving mother? Did Caroline come to fill the role of the idealised Rose of her imagination? When, two years later, Robert and Caroline joined John in the churchyard, was this place the focus of three relationships that had transformed her empty life, and filled it with the love she had always craved? The little cluster of graves we were looking down at told their story silently, but with heart-breaking clarity.

The graves made up an L-shape with an empty plot, above Rose's and beside Robert and Caroline's, which had remained unused throughout the succeeding ninety years. We could not suppress the conviction that this patch of earth had been reserved long ago, by Robert and Caroline, for Henry Ulick Burke to be reunited with his wife, his child, and the parents who had longed all their lives to encompass him within the radiance of their love.

That was the story the graves told – the same story that the wills told, and the house told, and the lost paintings told, and retold; the story that Henry, Katrina and Ulick Richard set out to suppress. We now knew that the dry words on Robert and Caroline's headstone had been put there by them, and reflected their priorities. They had chosen to forget everything except Robert's status as a JP and Caroline's exalted Howard connections. But they could not forget the true story, because it was woven into the fabric of all their lives. They had all stood, huddled together in this churchyard, in 1920, when John's little coffin was lowered into its grave. They must have known why it had been brought from their home in Bristol, where he died. They were here again, in the very same spot, two years later, when Robert and Caroline were interred near the child, and again, nine years later, when their wife and mother was placed with them.

In 1933, Henry set out to destroy the route map to this place, and with it the painful narrative of his life. He wanted to be just Henry Ulick Burke, successful businessman, secure in his first-class cabin. No baggage, no traceable past, no shameful memories. For their own reasons, Katrina and Ulick Richard had been equally keen to bury what they knew of the scandalous connection with the Batemans. They had acquiesced in the sale of Nunney Delamere and the disposal of all its contents, especially the paintings, and never referred to them, even to their children.

But Robert and Caroline's deep love for Henry and their grandchildren could not be suppressed. Their compulsion to nurture them and endow them with all their most precious possessions had eventually undermined their descendants' attempts to disown them. It was the sheer power of the love story between Robert and Caroline that had ultimately revealed the truth that lay behind years of attempted evasion and subterfuge. Henry, Rose, baby John, Richard and Katrina, and all their children and grandchildren lay at the very heart of that story, and were created by the passionate intensity of it.

We felt that the relentless series of anomalies that made up the pattern of Henry Burke's extraordinary life, and the repeated evidence of Robert and Caroline's determination to benefit and bond with him and his family, was only explicable if they, and not Ulick Ralph and Katherine Burke, were his parents. It was a bold assertion to make, in the face of the fact that every written document defined Henry as their nephew, including their own wills. It was this that made us send for Katherine's will. When we saw it, it threw a direct light on her reaction to Robert and Caroline's funeral. It was dated 21 August 1922, ten days after Robert's death, strongly suggesting that it was drawn up in direct response to Robert and Caroline's wills, which makes a comparison between the documents especially revealing. The contrast is absolutely clear. Whereas Robert and Caroline identify Henry as the senior executor of their entire estate, Katherine begins, 'I appoint my daughter, Hope Katherine Burke, my Sole Executrix.' Henry dominates the whole of Robert and Caroline's wills, receiving all the really significant bequests. In Katherine's will, although she defines him as her son, he is mentioned only once in a single sentence as part of a series of small individual bequests:

> I give and bequeath the following specific bequests, that is to say: To my daughter
> Sybil Matilda, six silver dessert spoons, six silver dessert forks and six silver teaspoons.
> To my son Henry Ulick Burke – all my family portraits and jewellery set with
> diamonds. I give and bequeath to my said daughter Hope Katherine Burke all the
> rest of my silver and plated goods, pictures, prints, jewellery, furniture and other
> personal and household effects.

Hope is overwhelmingly the main beneficiary of the will, being given the majority, some £3,000, from a trust fund set up at the time of Katherine's marriage, and sharing any residue beyond that figure equally with her sister Sybil. Mabel Emma receives a small annuity.

The most significant feature of Katherine's will, however, is not the small bequest she allocates to Henry, although this would have been distinctly unconventional in a family with a single son and three daughters in 1922. It is the way she organised the business arrangements of her will. These were so irregular that it is hard to believe they were not deliberately intended to undermine Henry's role as head of the family. Henry was six years older than Hope and was a man of business with a responsible management role in a major company. In the early 1920s, to appoint his unmarried sister as sole executrix was so contrary that it must have constituted an intentional rejection of him.

How did Katherine justify this decision? Why wasn't she proud of her son? Why didn't she acknowledge his achievement as a businessman, and use his experience, to administer her affairs after her death, as her brother Robert had just done? Here we come to the heart of the mysterious inconsistency between these two documents, drawn up just over a fortnight apart. Robert's will, though identifying Henry Burke throughout as 'My Nephew', treats him exactly as one would expect a parent to treat his only son. Katherine's, though defining Henry as 'My Son', treats him as one might any ordinary relation. She does not invest him with any authority to dispose of her affairs or belongings, and leaves him just a few individual items, principally some portraits. If these were Burke family portraits, it might constitute some recognition of his role as heir to the family name. And we thought portraits had a far greater chance of surviving for their family associations, as Rose Parry-Okeden's had, than for their artistic quality. Katherine had not died until 1933, so her will would have been activated in the very year Henry was selling Nunney Delamere, getting remarried and beginning his nomadic life in ships and hotels. In those circumstances, we thought it likely that he would have passed the portraits straight on to his only son, Richard Ulick, as Burke family heirlooms. We contacted Richard's son, Jeremy, to ask if he had the portraits but he had never heard of them and had absolutely no recollection of his father or mother ever mentioning them, although he felt sure they would have valued them very highly.

The alternative was that by 'my family portraits' Katherine meant her own family. By the time she made this will in 1922, both her parents and all her brothers had died. If she had a collection of Bateman portraits, leaving them to Henry would have been treating him as the custodian of the Bateman, rather that the Burke, family heirlooms. The only explanation for all these inconsistencies seemed to be that, behind all the subterfuge, an act of expediency had been conceived and carried through, a lifetime earlier, on the far side of the world. At the time, it had appeared simple and easy to manage, but it had slowly grown and asserted its right to be acknowledged, until it had insinuated itself into the entire fabric of the relationships of all those who took part in it.

If we were to reveal the true forgotten world of Robert Bateman we needed to revisit the beginning of his devoted relationship with Caroline. We had to see if we could pick up a faint echo of the startling revelations about their emotional involvement with Henry Burke, in the tumultuous early years of their love affair. If we did, what could it tell us about Robert's life and work?

Part 6

LOST AND FOUND

*Fig. 118. H. H. Armstead's effigy of Henry Howard,
Caroline's father, in Lichfield Cathedral.*

Chapter 27

SCANDALOUS RELATIONS

L ate in the year 1872, the ancient cathedral at Lichfield was host to a mighty
congregation of the social and ecclesiastical establishment of high Victorian
England. The soaring magnificence of the stone vaults and the radiance of the
precious Herckenrode glass were animated by the dancing light of many candles.
They were being carried in procession along the cavernous, arcaded aisles, past atten-
uated stone shafts and acute gothic arches to the south aisle, where the whole devout
pageant came to rest. Before them stood a newly constructed, elaborately canopied
wall niche, which enclosed the white stone effigy of a slightly built, sleeping cleric
of saintly and serious aspect (fig. 118).

The memorial had been designed by one of the greatest architects of the age, Sir
George Gilbert Scott, who was immersed in the momentous task of restoring the
entire historic fabric of the cathedral. This great endeavour had been set in hand by
the subject of the new memorial, Henry Howard, former Dean of Lichfield, some
fourteen years earlier. The superbly sculpted effigy, resting on an altar tomb, dressed
in beautifully rendered loose clerical robes, holding a bible, had been carved by H.
H. Armstead. By 1872, he had established a national reputation through his series
of figures on Scott's great Italianate Foreign Office building in Hyde Park. His fame
had been consolidated by carrying out the huge frieze of famous figures that run
round the base of the Albert Memorial in Kensington.

The sculptor and the architect were there to witness the ceremony of dedication,
being performed by another legendary personality of the British Empire, Bishop
George Augustus Selwyn. Prominent on kneelers, at the very forefront of the throng
of worshippers, was Henrietta Howard, the Dean's widow. She was supported by her
eldest son George Howard, and her large family of ten children and their spouses.
As the chanting of the choir faded into the echoing void above them, Bishop Selwyn
pronounced a blessing over the memorial and led the congregation in a solemn prayer
for the soul of the departed Dean. He went on to contrast the purpose of this memo-

rial with those dedicated to perpetuating the names of great national figures such as kings, soldiers, statesmen or scholars. It was, he said, to commemorate Henry Howard's quiet wisdom in perceiving the futility of the benefits of birth and learning and the fatal pride they engendered within the hearts of men, unless they were subjugated to the service of a purpose higher than the feeding of personal vanity and the gratification of the senses. Dean Howard, he said, had placed his formidable abilities at the service of God, his maker, who, he knew, esteemed the life of the humble widow or abandoned orphan above that of any crowned king or high priest who sought glory before men. Dean Howard had set out on a lifelong pilgrimage to place service to his Lord before all the inclinations and desires of his own nature, and had triumphed in that divinely inspired endeavour.

After a great anthem of celebration by the choir, the procession, followed by Henrietta Howard and the family, made its way across the nave to the great west door. At the heart of this solemn ceremony, walking modestly behind her mother, was Caroline Octavia Howard, a poised and beautiful fair-haired woman of thirty-three, who was known and admired by the great majority of the illustrious congregation.

If our reading of the events of her later life was correct, she was to become pregnant through a clandestine relationship with a man unacceptable to her family, and give birth to an illegitimate son scarcely twelve months after the unveiling of this monument to her father. Her condition, had it become known, would have been perceived as undermining her father's lifelong dedication to upholding the rites of the Christian religion, one of the most sacred of which was the sanctity of marriage. To her mother, the shame and humiliation this would have projected upon her late husband, herself and her children, as a venerated clerical and aristocratic family, would have been impossible even to contemplate. However, through our research, we had concluded that this was the only credible interpretation of the actions and documents defining the end of Caroline's life. What would this disaster have meant for those involved?

For Caroline, the disgrace would have been absolute. To have been discovered in the act of fornication, despite the benefit of her upbringing at the heart of a pious family, would have defined her as a 'fallen woman' for the rest of her life. How absolute her banishment from conventional society would have been would have depended on her reaction to her disgrace. If she were defiant, her actions would be interpreted as stemming from an evil character and she would have been kept completely out of sight by her family. If she were contrite and repentant, she might have slowly gained a measure of acceptance on the margins of social life but would not have been considered acceptable as a marriage partner by any respectable family.

For her mother, Henrietta Howard, the disgrace of her daughter would have drastically limited the number and quality of the people prepared to interact with her socially. This would have severely restricted the prospects of her remaining single children. For the older, married children, their own and their children's positions would depend upon their own achievements, and their willingness to distance themselves from the scandal by never including or referring to their disgraced sister again.

However, once the story became known, the good name and social standing of the whole Howard family would have been damaged by association with sexual irregularity of this kind. Dalliances, mistresses, and even extraneous children, were all semi-acknowledged and accepted, provided the well-bred participants remained within the respectable confines of matrimony. But if Caroline had given birth to a child beyond this safe boundary, she would have been excluded from both marriage and society for the rest of her life.

How was it possible, then, that two years after Henry's birth in January 1874 Caroline married Charles Philip Wilbraham? Of all the people in the world who could not, under any circumstances, contemplate marriage to a woman with a living child born outside the bounds of matrimony, it was a serving Church of England vicar. It was his specific role to uphold the values of family life in his parish, and insist upon the imperative of undergoing the ceremonial solemnising of marriage vows before any sexual contact took place between members of his flock, so as to avoid licentiousness and prevent unwanted children.

Setting an unblemished example in this sphere was central to the respect he commanded in his community. Nothing we had discovered about the life or character of Charles Wilbraham gave us any reason to think that he would have been prepared to contemplate entering into a personal relationship that compromised his core beliefs. In order for Charles Wilbraham to be able, let alone willing, to marry Caroline Howard in 1876, the fact that she had conceived and given birth to a child two years earlier would have to have been totally concealed from him and the outside world at large.

In a society of large complex households, relying upon servants who had access to the most intimate secrets of their employers' lives, to conceal the process of pregnancy and childbirth was dauntingly difficult. Even if the secret was successfully kept at that key moment, the danger would remain throughout the child's life. Some chance or malicious circumstance might arise at any moment to reveal his or her true identity, and ignite both the original scandal and the deceitful measures adopted to conceal it. If an ordained minister of the established church were found to have knowingly played a central role in the process, he would instantly have been debarred from acting as a priest for the rest of his life.

If Caroline was Henry's mother, surely Charles Wilbraham must genuinely not have known it, or he would not have married her in 1876. And yet, as we looked again at the crucial weeks surrounding Henry's birth in late 1873 and early 1874, there was no disguising the fact that Charles Wilbraham, as much as anyone else in our story, had initiated a rush of absolutely fundamental and unprecedented changes in his circumstances.

The decisions and actions he took seemed starkly out of character and were almost impossible to understand in the light of his settled and dutiful life up to that point. We had surmised that his move away from Audley might have been motivated by a desire to help his old friends, the Howards, remove Caroline from the influence of an unacceptable suitor, Robert Bateman. But his reckless discarding of his home, career and whole pattern of life did seem out of proportion with that objective. Had he, in fact, taken part in a much more desperate and serious attempt to cover up a scandal?

To find answers to these questions, we returned to the Bateman family to see if their actions at the moment of Henry's birth suggested anything unusual. If Caroline's marriage to Charles Wilbraham simply represented a determination by the Howard family to end an association of which they did not approve, Robert might well have been devastated and changed his way of life radically, but the rest of the Bateman family would not have been involved or affected. In this case, Robert's own actions at the crucial period – leaving London, ceasing to exhibit at the Dudley, adapting Biddulph to his needs and living a reclusive life there – might simply have been a personal response to his thwarted love for Caroline. On the other hand, if he was about to be exposed as having 'taken advantage' of a refined and cultivated woman from a good family by introducing her to the immoral way of life of his degenerate artistic circle, the whole Bateman family would have been social outcasts. If there was any danger of this, there might be discernible traces of a concerted family plot to conceal the evidence and prevent catastrophe for all concerned.

One thing was certain. If Henry was Robert and Caroline's son, and this had become publicly known in 1873–4, the consequences for the Bateman family would have been draconian even in comparison with the fate of the Howards. The woman in such cases was always given the benefit of at least some mitigating justification, such as having been foolish and misled, or given alcohol or drugs, which led to the man coercing her and taking advantage of her innocence. The man, on the other hand, particularly if he was from a lower social class, was condemned outright as a voracious predator, an uncouth brute, ignorant of the codes of moral or gentlemanly behaviour. If he concealed his rapaciousness beneath a veneer of plausible refinement or silken sophistication, this was considered even more offensive and dangerous.

Surviving records show that neither Robert nor his wider family suffered this kind of public vilification. It follows, therefore, that if Robert was Henry's father, and Caroline was his unmarried mother, the fact must have been concealed by a daring strategy, executed by a tight group of trustworthy individuals, at great personal risk to themselves. To succeed, it would have had to be contained primarily within the family, where everyone had a vested interest in keeping the secret, not only at the moment of crisis, the child's birth, but all through the subsequent years.

Seen from this perspective, the behaviour of several members of Robert's close family in late 1873 did betray signs of following a strangely integrated pattern, perhaps designed to obscure the details of Henry's birth and upbringing from curious outsiders. Henry was to be taken abroad, immediately after he was born, to a remote area of the British Empire where no documentation of his parentage was required, and brought up as the son of Robert's married sister Katherine, and her husband Ulick Ralph Burke, a barrister. Since Katherine already had a young daughter of her own, it was not anticipated that she would settle there and bring the child up, so a location was carefully selected where another reliable member of the family, Robert and Katherine's elder brother Rowland, was involved in missionary work that centred on the care and education of children, especially boys. This would enable the child to be placed in an environment broadly supervised by a trusted relation who would not raise questions about his background, while Ulick Ralph pursued his duties as a lawyer. The ability to keep the process within the strict confines of the family made Lahore the perfect destination.

If these arrangements were driven by panic at the impending birth, one would expect them to be put in place only after the crisis became known in the summer of 1873. If they were activated before that, there would be no reason to suspect that they formed part of a deliberate subterfuge. So we were fascinated to discover that it was only in the middle of 1873 that Ralph Ulick was appointed as a barrister at the High Court in Lahore. He travelled out to take up his post accompanied by his wife, in mid-September – regardless of the fact that she should have been six months pregnant by then. Their arrival was recorded in Rowland Bateman's journal in late September, as was Rowland's journey back to Lahore on 10 December to spend Christmas there. Rowland's biographer made no further mention of Katherine in India, or the birth of a son just after Christmas on 6 January, despite Rowland's presence there.

If the truth was that Katherine had not been pregnant when she arrived, but had simply been present to receive the child and give essential credibility to his birth in Lahore, Rowland would not have compromised his integrity by lying in his journal. Equally, he would not have risked giving a truthful, written record of events, which would expose his brother Robert, and all those trying to help him, to disgrace if it were read by others. As Henry grew up, Rowland must have baptised him and overseen his education. The simple expedient of censoring any mention of him from written records of his work in India was clearly the safest and most honourable course of action.

Maconachie's purpose in writing his book was to pay tribute to Rowland as a towering figure in the story of the Church Missionary Society's work in the Punjab. He would not have dreamed of prying into or exposing a family secret of this kind, even if he had caught wind of it through rumour or gossip. The fact that he failed to list Robert or Caroline in the index, and went to elaborate lengths to avoid mentioning their names as the people who provided a loving and peaceful home for Rowland in his last illness, suggests that he might well have been aware of some impropriety attached to them.

If Caroline gave birth to Henry in the first days of January 1874, the crisis would have appeared in the second half of 1873. Once the pregnancy began to be visible, the first imperative must have been to get her out of sight, among people whose complete goodwill and discretion the Howards could depend on. One particular family had emerged from our research as the lifelong friends and confidants of the Howards – the Moncktons of Stretton Hall near Penkridge in Staffordshire. Although Caroline's mother Henrietta had always been close to General Henry Monckton and his wife Anne, she also retained deep ties with Emma and Anna-Maria Monckton, the General's unmarried sisters, who in the early 1870s lived at Brewood Hall, two miles from Stretton Hall. The particular circumstances of the village of Brewood lay at the heart of the relationship between the Howards and the Moncktons.

Historically, it had been known as the Deanery Manor of Brewood: it always passed into the ownership of each succeeding Dean of Lichfield Cathedral, since the rents formed part of his stipend. In the early nineteenth century, General Monckton had arranged to lease the whole manor from his friend Dean Howard because it adjoined his land at Stretton Hall. Thus, up until the Dean's death in 1868, the Moncktons had held all the land and assets of Brewood as tenants of Caroline's family.

The General had intended Brewood Hall to act as a dower house for his wife after his death, but she never went there. Instead, it was used intermittently by various members of the Monckton family. From the 1860s it was the home of the General's sister Emma Frances Monckton; when she becamse unwell in 1870 her sister Anna-Maria left her home in Bristol to join her as nurse and companion. Emma died in 1872, whereupon her sister returned to her own home at 1 Codrington Place, Clifton, Bristol, where she died five years later.

In 1880 it is recorded that Brewood Hall was let to Sir Thomas Boughey while his own home, Aqualate Hall, was being remodelled. Despite enthusiastic searching by the current Monckton family, there are no records that the house was let between 1872 and 1880. So it seems likely that in the summer of 1873, this quiet, secluded old house that the Howards regarded almost as their own property, stood fully furnished and empty. It was set back behind outbuildings and heavy wooden gates down a tiny rutted lane beyond the village boundary.

The combination of the deep friendship with the Moncktons and lifelong associations with the village must have made this the perfect place for Henrietta Howard to arrange for Caroline to disappear into in the autumn of 1873 without arousing undue curiosity. With her own servants carefully brought from outside the area,

Henrietta Howard could present Caroline's condition as an acute illness for which complete rest and isolation had been prescribed, while Henrietta visited and renewed her relationship with her old friends. It does seem strangely coincidental that Charles Wilbraham should have gone to so much trouble to select this place to move to from Audley in the crucial last months before Henry's birth and a mere two years before his own unexpected marriage to Caroline Howard.

If the first part of the plan to cover up Caroline's pregnancy involved the birth of the baby in a safe, secluded place, followed by smuggling him out to India, once in Lahore the child was effectively given a new identity as the son of Katherine and Ralph Ulick Burke. He then remained conveniently out of sight for the five years' duration of his adoptive father's term of employment in the High Court in Lahore. This period of invisibility was essential to allow any suspicion aroused by Caroline's absence over the last months of 1873 to be dissipated.

At the same time it appeared that a second phase of the strategy was being implemented, centred on the frantic activity of Charles Wilbraham and designed to pave the way for his marriage to Caroline at the first possible opportunity in February 1876. If Charles was a party to the conspiracy this would be the decisive element in the success of the whole cover-up strategy. It would rely upon his publicly acknowledged reputation for absolute honesty and dedicated piety. This had been established by his tireless labour over thirty years to educate and improve the lot of his impoverished parishioners, whose lives were circumscribed by the filth and danger of the ten coal mines around the village of Audley. Presumably, from his arrival in Penkridge in January 1874, just two years before his marriage, he would have been prepared to pronounce himself betrothed to Caroline Howard had anyone challenged her character or moral probity. His moral endorsement of her would move the balance of plausibility overwhelmingly in her favour against any accusation of sexual promiscuity circulating in Brewood, which lay in his new parish of Penkridge.

The problem was that if Charles knew the accusations to be true, why was he prepared to abandon his innate integrity by getting involved in, and lending his authority to, a deceitful attempt to escape the consequences of wrongdoing, as he would have seen it? Surely his honesty was the Achilles' heel in the whole scheme, especially as he was not a member of either the Bateman or Howard families, and therefore not bound into them by bonds of tribal loyalty or self-interest. As a matter of fact, however, it is not strictly true that he had absolutely no family link with the Batemans. Robert's brother John had married the Hon. Jessy Caroline Bootle-Wilbraham in 1865. She was the granddaughter of Edward Bootle-Wilbraham, 1st Lord Skelmersdale, uncle of Charles Wilbraham. So Charles Wilbraham and Jessy Caroline were second cousins. It was only as we struggled to understand why Charles might have allowed himself to become absorbed into a close-knit conspiracy to protect the Bateman name that we remembered this connection between himself and Jessy Caroline.

John's marriage to Jessy Caroline in 1865 had defined the high water mark in the Batemans' fortunes, by establishing him as the brother-in-law of a wealthy aristocrat of his own age, the 2nd Lord Skelmesdale, who had a massive Palladian mansion and estate at Lathom Hall near Ormskirk. What we had not understood, because we had not looked into it earlier, was the absolute contrast between the meandering decline into provincial anonymity of John and Jessy Caroline Bateman, and the focused, driving political ambition that saw her brother Baron Skelmersdale rise to the highest reaches of the aristocracy and achieve appointments at the very heart of power and privilege at court and in parliament.

Edward Bootle-Wilbraham had succeeded his grandfather in 1853, when he was almost seventeen years old. He had entered politics at the first possible opportunity by taking his seat in the House of Lords on his twenty-first birthday, 12 December 1858. From that moment he began a spectacular progress up the political ladder, in the course of which he developed alliances with two of the most powerful professional politicians of the day. Although from the outset of his career he was associated with the Conservatives, centred on Lord Derby and Benjamin Disraeli, in August 1860 he married Lady Alice Villiers, daughter of George Villiers, 4th Earl of Clarendon, the great Liberal foreign secretary of the mid-Victorian age.

In 1866, Lord Skelmersdale received his first important appointment as lord-in-waiting to Queen Victoria. He retained this post until his friend Benjamin Disraeli became leader of the Conservative Party in 1870. Disraeli immediately promoted him to Conservative chief whip in the House of Lords. This was a crucial position of trust for a leader based in the House of Commons who needed to mobilise support among the still powerful and independent peers in the Upper House.

The Conservatives were in opposition, but by 1873 Gladstone's administration was coming to an end and, in early 1874, Disraeli won for the Tories their first absolute majority in the Commons for thirty years. By this time, Lord Skelmersdale had become a key figure, operating at the heart of Disraeli's political inner circle. The same year, he was promoted again to membership of the Privy Council, the government's advisory body to the Queen. Lord Skelmersdale continued to hold these vital liaison roles, between Disraeli, the Queen and the House of Lords, throughout the 1870s. His reward was to be raised to the tip of the aristocratic hierarchy as the 1st Earl of Lathom in 1880, after which he served three terms as Lord Chamberlain of the Queen's Household. This was a position that almost defined the heart of the establishment, where political power coalesced with the ceremonial splendours of the monarchy.

Suddenly, as we came to comprehend the true extent of the Bootle-Wilbraham family's climb into the innermost sanctuary of political power, the potential began to appear for an entirely different dimension to a scandal centred on Robert Bateman and Caroline Howard. The last months of 1873 were the most crucial of Disraeli's career. After six years in opposition, he was preparing to fight a general election which would enable him to establish his stature as a seminal figure in nineteenth-century politics. He was preparing to redefine the old Tory Party as the socially progressive 'One Nation Conservatives' by combining radical legislation, such as his Public Health Act (1875), Education Act (1876), and Employers and Workers Act (which enabled workers to sue employers in the civil courts if they broke legal contracts), with romantic imperial gestures such as the Royal Titles Act (1876), which created Queen Victoria Empress of India.

If in late 1873 or early 1874, when he was on the very threshold of power, a damaging sexual scandal had emerged, implicating Lord Skelmersdale's family, there can be little doubt that Disraeli would have dispensed with the services of his chief whip in the House of Lords, at least until the furore had died down. Even later, he would have been extremely cautious about proposing him for sensitive posts, especially ones involved in projecting the symbolic sanctity of the Queen Empress. If a public scandal involving the Bateman name had threatened to emerge in late 1873, Lord Skelmersdale, Disraeli's ruthless political fixer, would have had no compunction in applying overwhelming pressure on the participants to prevent any damage to the Tory Party's electoral prospects or to his own political career.

In the case of an illegitimate child in his sister's family, he would need to ensure that knowledge of the birth was suppressed, and that the scandal would not reappear later or lay him open to blackmail through his pivotal role close to the centre of power. This could be achieved only by the removal of the baby, as far away as possible, the moment it was born. Then he needed to organise the marriage of the mother to an absolutely trustworthy person of impeccable moral standing, whose willingness to become her husband guaranteed her good character in the eyes of the world. It cannot have taken Lord Skelmersdale and his sister Jessy Caroline Bateman long to realise that they had, within the safe confines of their own family, an unmarried cousin, a venerated clergyman in his mid-sixties, of unblemished character, who fitted the role perfectly.

Their problem must have been to persuade Wilbraham to abuse the sanctity of the Christian marriage bond by committing himself to enter into it dishonestly with someone who was about to give birth to a child fathered by another living man. It is not difficult to imagine the hushed intensity in Charles's study in the vicarage at Audley as the circumstances of Caroline Howard's pregnancy were explained to him by John Bateman and his cousins, Jessy Caroline and Lord Skelmersdale. Charles would have struggled to come to terms with what they were telling him about the daughter of Dean Howard, whose memorial he had just witnessed being dedicated in Lichfield cathedral. How strained the atmosphere must have been, as they outlined the possible repercussions for the family should Disraeli, or Queen Victoria herself, sever their relationship with the Bootle-Wilbrahams. What response could Charles have made to their assertion that the fate of three families – the Howards, the Batemans and the Wilbrahams – hung on his willingness to intervene and avert a catastrophe for them all?

How Charles must have longed for them to leave, and allow him to confront the profound implications their scheme had for the faith in which he had put his trust all his life. He needed to think, and to pray for guidance, before he could respond to so morally complex a dilemma. The only undertaking he could give, if there was any prospect of his doing what they were asking, was to agree to go and speak to Caroline, as one fallible human being to another. He needed to understand the intensity of the forces that had driven her to abandon the virtuous path down which she had been guided by her saintly father.

How agonising his dilemma must have seemed as he knelt alone in his empty church, scouring his conscience for a truthful, valid response to the conflict between the doctrinal clarity of scripture on physical abstinence except within marriage, and the inexhaustible forgiveness and love of Christ for the penitent sinner. How often did he read and re-read St John's account of the woman taken in adultery:

> And the scribes and Pharisees brought unto him a woman taken in adultery; and when they had set her in the midst, They say unto him, Master, this woman was taken in adultery, in the very act. Now Moses in the law commanded us, that such should be stoned: but what sayest thou? This they said, tempting him, that they might have to accuse him. But Jesus stooped down, and with his finger wrote on the ground, as though he heard them not. So when they continued asking him, he lifted up himself, and said unto them, He that is without sin among you, let him first cast a stone at her. And again he stooped down, and wrote on the ground. And they who heard it, being convicted by their own conscience, went out one by one, beginning at the eldest, even unto the last: and Jesus was left alone, and the woman standing in the midst. When Jesus had lifted up himself, and saw none but the woman, he said unto her, Woman, where are those thine accusers? Hath no man condemned thee? She said, No man, Lord. And Jesus said unto her, Neither do I condemn thee: go, and sin no more.

Clearly, there was a refusal to condemn outright the woman taken in adultery – but, equally, there was no attempt to disguise or condone the sin itself.

Charles Wilbraham was not simply being asked to acknowledge his own human frailty, which in itself made him ineligible to pass judgement or punish Caroline. His family were proposing that he take advantage of the fact that she was not married to marry her himself, solely to discredit anyone who discovered the true nature of her condition. The problem was that from Charles's perspective, Caroline Howard's pregnancy demonstrated that she was already conjoined with another man in the eyes of God, which made the passage from St John's Gospel directly relevant to him. Were Charles to marry Caroline and fulfil that commitment physically, he would be complicit in compounding the error of fornication by breaking the sacred bond between her and the child's father and entering into an adulterous relationship with her himself. This made a mockery of the sublime aspiration to absolute mutual faithfulness that lay at the heart of Christian marriage. For a true believer like Charles, it was the sincerity of the intention, not the cynical repetition of a ritualistic formula of words, that legitimised and sanctified Holy Matrimony. And yet, how would the other Charles Wilbraham have responded – the adventurer, the traveller to remote places, the ex-military man of the world, who revelled in the adventure of crossing the scalding passes of Afghanistan and the arctic wastes of Greenland?

As a man, despite all he knew about Caroline's circumstances, it must have been bewitching to be left alone with this tall, pale, beautiful woman to talk privately. He was a clerical bachelor in his mid-sixties, who existed in a world where interaction between the sexes was contained within a rigid framework of repressive formality. Simply to be alone with her, imbued with the radiance of imminent motherhood, in an atmosphere in which all the usual taboos were negated, would have been intoxicating. Her very condition embodied the reality of the relationship between human love and physical desire which the society around them sought to deny. For Charles to talk openly to a wise, gentle woman, bravely facing the condemnation of the whole world outside that room, about the compulsive desires that had impelled her and her lover to give expression to their feelings must have been a deeply revealing and disturbing experience.

Surely he was shocked to discover his own ability to empathise with Caroline's account of the pain of forbidden love, and to recognise echoes of it deep within himself. Did it reawaken the memory of his devotion to Beatrix Egerton, and her father's disdainful rejection of him? How thrillingly new to him those hushed confidential talks must have been, when this beautiful, enigmatic creature opened her broken heart to him and acknowledged her and Robert's inability to contain the urgency of their desires within the confines of their families' wishes. She must have wept bitterly, and prayed with him for forgiveness, both for her lapse from grace and for the shame she had brought on her father's memory.

Charles must have been convinced of her absolute sincerity, or he could never have taken the perilous decision to risk his life and reputation, to save her from disgrace. As their meetings progressed, he must have found greater and greater solace in a relationship that illuminated hidden areas of his own personality, which had remained confined within a shroud of reticence and inhibition all his life. Slowly, the combination of identifying with her obsessive love, cruelly forbidden by others, and the heady intimacy generated by her willingness to acknowledge the nature and intensity of her own deepest feelings must have mesmerised the lonely old parson, until he found himself falling in love with the enthralling, tragic figure fate had put in his path.

Despite her indissoluble bond to Robert Bateman, of which her unborn child was the living witness, Caroline's friendship with Charles also imperceptibly mutated into a spiritual empathy. It was built on mutual respect and kindness, and offered the prospect of a dignified, useful life in the desolate years ahead, when all prospect of being reunited with the man she loved seemed utterly out of reach. However, Charles had to find some way to resolve the conflict between his love for her and his continuing devotion to the service of Christ, before he could take action to save her.

By 5 November 1873, the day he went to dinner at Keele Hall, and left a note for Lord Hatherton proposing himself for the living of Penkridge, he must have succeeded in finding a solution to this dilemma. It was a decision that, at the moment he took it, seemed to offer him a miraculous solution to his mental anguish but, as the years went by and its consequences became more evident, was to test his faith and willpower to the limits of their endurance. In November 1873, I believe that Charles decided to be true to his deepest feelings and marry Caroline, but never to consummate that loving relationship physically, so that in the eyes of the church the relationship could be considered unfulfilled.

Theirs was to be a spiritual union. They were to plight their troth to each other, but they were not to be 'made one flesh', as Caroline had bound herself physically to another man, who was still alive, and had a child by him. Caroline's reputation would be protected by Charles's willingness to marry her, which would have been unthinkable unless her moral standing was beyond reproach. The moment we looked at the events surrounding almost all the central characters of our story in this light, the puzzling anomalies seemed to evaporate. Their actions, no matter how bizarre and outlandish they had seemed before, now formed a comprehensible pattern that told an extraordinary story.

Chapter 28

TRUE LOVE

Our belief is that Robert and Caroline met and fell in love when they were young, as portrayed by Robert in *Heloise and Abelard*. The Howards opposed the marriage, first as a result of the rapid decline of the Bateman family from upper-class society after the enforced sale of Biddulph Grange, and later because of the perceived immorality of Burne-Jones, Simeon Solomon and the Dudley Group artists generally. Neither Robert nor Caroline was prepared to accept this situation and marry anyone else.

By the early 1870s a strange opportunity for them to meet privately was created by Robert's tenancy of Biddulph Old Hall – a remote, secluded, ruined fragment of an ancient house. The highly charged nature of Robert's paintings from this period indicates that they began to meet secretly and became lovers. In the mid months of 1873 Caroline discovered she was pregnant. The religious and social prominence of Dean Howard's family, and the political ambition of the Bootle-Wilbrahams, by now intermarried with the Bateman family, meant that the scandal had the potential to involve pivotal figures in the church, the government and the court.

A plan was developed within the affected families to remove the child to India immediately after the birth, and present it as the son of Katherine and Ulick Ralph Burke. The child was to be left in the care of Robert's missionary brother Rowland in Lahore. Back in England a marriage was proposed between Caroline and Charles Wilbraham, a clergyman thirty years her senior. This required Wilbraham to leave his parish at Audley to put Caroline out of reach of Robert who, in the heat of the crisis, had moved from London to take up permanent residence at Biddulph Old Hall, only five miles away.

The intention was also to remove Charles Wilbraham himself, so that his promise to marry Caroline could be kept from his family and his old parishioners around the period of maximum danger of her disgrace being discovered, when the child was born. The marriage ceremony was unusually modest, with only Caroline's mother and one distant cousin as witnesses, and none of Charles Wilbraham's relations being invited.

For the first time, the marriage itself, and Charles's removal from Audley to Penkridge, became explicable. The strength of Charles's feelings for Caroline outweighed the apparent dislocation of abandoning his parish, his family and friends. It also justified halving his salary and wasting the money he had spent on the advowson of his former living, and starting an entirely new way of life as a married man, at sixty-six, after a lifetime of bachelorhood. By the end of the critical period between 5 November 1873 and February 1874, the major upheaval was complete, and the first danger of exposure had safely passed. For Charles, the emerging possibility of a transformed future with a woman he had come to love must have been an unnerving and exhilarating prospect.

The same weeks must have been equally momentous for Caroline Howard, but in contrast to the frenetic activity of the other participants in the plot – who were uprooting their lives, changing jobs, moving house, sailing to the Punjab, or holding clandestine meetings – hers must have been a time of solitary introspection, as hour after hour, and day after isolated day passed without the opportunity to go outside her room, or meet anyone beyond the confines of her remote refuge.

How focused she must have been upon the child whose presence was growing ever more insistent and familiar to her as the time of its birth approached. What would become of this being, already so inseparable a part of her own identity that she could scarcely imagine her life apart from it? She must have cherished these quiet days, when she could surround her child with security, and guard it from the disapproving people who would brutally take hold of it the moment it was born, and dictate its destiny to safeguard their own status and self-importance. Had she sought reassurance from Charles that the child would be cared for, even if she died? How traumatic the birth must have been, overlaid by her agitated realisation that when the pain and struggle were over, the moment of separation would be at hand. How transfixed Caroline must have been by her beautiful little boy.

She called him Henry, so that his relationship to her and her family would remain with him all his life. Henry was her father's name, Henrietta was her mother's and her elder sister's name. All the boys in her family except one had Henry either as their principal or secondary forename. She had her wish, and he was known as Henry all his life, even though later Ulick, the Irish family name of the Burkes, was added to give credibility to his status as Ulick Ralph and Katherine's only son. In the few days before the separation she must never have let the child out of her sight, and scarcely out of her arms for an instant, knowing what was to come. How harrowing it must have been when eventually Henry was taken from her and carried down the bare oak stairs of the manor house. How desolate she must have been as she stared down from her window to catch a last glimpse of her child as he was bundled into a carriage, and then watched as it rumbled out of sight. How long did she stand there, too numb to move, after the servants pulled the great gates to, and all was still and silent?

Surely, it was this climactic moment of desolation, when the loss of her lover was compounded by the enforced renunciation of her only child, that inspired Robert to identify their story with the parallel tale of Heloise and Abelard. This is the true agenda of the unshown painting that he executed five years later in 1879. It is the emptiness of this separation that his sad Heloise and distracted Abelard know awaits them, even as Robert depicts the blissful awakening of their love for each other. No wonder he kept this eloquent revelation of their secret out of sight.

After a little while, when Caroline was over the birth and her figure had settled down, she returned to her mother's home, Milstead Manor, in Kent. News was discreetly spread to the immediate family that Charles Wilbraham had proposed to her during her stay with the Moncktons, and that she had accepted him. They were engaged as soon as they properly could be, and in early 1876 they were married.

For most Victorians the next imperative would have been to ensure that no trail could ever connect the child back to the mother. Usually this meant the child being placed either in a large orphanage or with a family prepared to ask no questions as long as sufficient money was provided. Had Caroline and Robert followed this strategy, it would almost certainly have been impossible for us to understand the true dynamics of their life stories, or the inspiration behind many of Robert's surviving paintings.

Luckily for us, their feelings for each other were too deep to allow either of them to deny and disclaim Henry completely, the living symbol of their forbidden love. Sending him to India, where he was effectively adopted by Robert's sister and her husband, and looked after by his missionary brother Rowland, meant they were able to retain a line of family communication throughout his early life. Later, it allowed them to be aware of Ulick Ralph and Katherine's attempt to break all ties with him at seventeen years of age. It enabled them to reclaim him, at a critical moment of his life, when he returned from Peru bankrupt and alone in 1904.

One of the most intriguing elements in our strange, compelling tale was the intense relationship that developed between Charles and Caroline Wilbraham over the three years of their short marriage. All the Hatherton papers are consistent in portraying them as a devoted couple, with Charles excessively, or almost obsessively, fond of his wife, and Caroline never giving vent to the slightest impatience with the old parson's irksome repetition of the same stories, or failing to support him in his irrational quarrels with other local dignitaries.

The Hathertons found certain aspects of Charles's behaviour so completely inexplicable that they were forced to ascribe them to gross eccentricity. These centred on his obsessive habit of immersing himself in icy water, in a plunge bath he had constructed behind the vicarage at Penkridge, with complete disregard for the weather or his advancing years. Lord Hatherton had no hesitation in attributing Charles's death to this outlandish practice. Did this fetish for self-inflicted suffering have its roots in the Victorian cult of 'manliness'? Even this explanation was difficult to sustain, however, since Lord and Lady Hatherton, Charles's direct contemporaries, raised in exactly the same class and culture, perceived his icy dips as abnormal lunacy. Was the explanation hidden deep within the ferment of conflicting drives that made up the soul of this complex man?

If our suggestion about Charles and Caroline's relationship was accurate, it had developed out of a series of meetings held to explore the possibility of contracting a pragmatic marriage to cover up a scandal. The candour and intimacy of these meetings had generated a devoted bond between them that imperceptibly acquired the intensity of a love affair. An essential element in the empathy between Charles and Caroline was his identification with her frank acknowledgement of an indissoluble union with Robert Bateman, which she would not deny even though it had been prohibited by her family. Charles had experienced a directly comparable trauma in his own forbidden love for Beatrix Egerton. Neither he nor Caroline would have been available to enter into their marriage if outsiders had not intervened and brought their first great loves to a tragic end.

These were the considerations that had driven Charles to decide never to consummate their marriage. What neither of them had foreseen was that the integrity and mutual respect at the heart of their relationship provided a foundation that enabled it to grow into a powerhouse of sustaining care and platonic devotion, which was recognised by the Hathertons and others who knew them during the years of their marriage. For Caroline to be known and loved for the person she really was, with no pressure to renounce or misrepresent the truth of her feelings for Robert, must have been an ecstatic rediscovery of her self-esteem after the shame and humiliation she had been made to endure. How amazed she must have been that this devout man was prepared to demonstrate his belief in her innate goodness by marrying her, at huge risk to his own good name. Charles's selfless action can only have reaffirmed her trust in the inexhaustible availability of divine compassion, a central tenet of the faith to which he and her father had dedicated their lives. No wonder she responded by enveloping Charles in a nurturing blanket of warmth, companionship and genuine respect.

That respect can only have been increased as, day by day, she witnessed the relentless conflict Charles's commitment to his vow of celibacy ignited within his mind and body. Had he not been physically aware of her as a woman, his self-imposed abstinence would have had a facile, moralistic intention which would have made the dynamics of their relationship quite different. However, from his first hypnotic meetings with her, her gentle wisdom, her real repentance and the appeal of her bodily presence had released a torrent of sensations and responses within Charles which had remained dormant and unexplored all his life. This was love, a love that grew and intensified as they lived together in the rectory, that matured and deepened the more they understood and forgave each other's foibles and weaknesses. It was an inseparable tangle of emotional identification and physical desire which, under normal circumstances, would have found expression in the shared intimacy of sexual intercourse.

Their relationship was a robust human interaction between a passionate, adventurous man with deeply held convictions and a brave woman with sufficient strength of character to defy the conventions of her day in order to be true to the people she loved. No matter how considerate Caroline was, at times the sheer closeness of their bodily contact must have sent a charge of awakened desire crackling between them. Surely, she was wise enough to know that if he was ever overwhelmed by these impulses and gave way to them, he would be betraying his deepest convictions and would eventually project at least some of the blame on to her. Once that fatal line was crossed, the days of their unique love affair would be numbered.

Charles would be trapped within a relationship that he perceived to be inherently sinful, while still functioning as the ordained vicar of Penkridge. He would be faced by the dilemma of abandoning his lifelong vocation to the church or keeping Caroline at a distance in a vain attempt to avoid repetitions of the original offence. Either way, his devoted love for her, his uxoriousness, would soon be replaced by a gradual process of estrangement. The visits to the plunge pool in the vicarage garden were a domestic manifestation of that classic Victorian formula for 'cooling the ardour', and directing one's mind away from 'unhealthy' thoughts – the cold bath!

In an age without antibiotics, the fear of 'the chill' or 'fever' as agents of death was far too widespread to make the taking of cold baths advisable in later life. Lord Hatherton's journal demonstrates that the idea of a man of nearly seventy subjecting himself to this ordeal was considered almost insane. However, the intense psychological pressure under which Charles had placed himself, through his decision to marry and cohabit with a young woman to whom he was strongly attracted while giving a solemn vow not to consummate their relationship, at times called for desperate measures to distract him from the urgency of his instincts. When prayer, reading the scriptures and contemplation proved insufficient to the task, Charles regained his peace of mind by a symbolic act of purification, an icy baptism in his garden pool.

He must have known what he was risking on that winter afternoon of 10 December 1879 when he opened the back door of the rectory at Penkridge. He made his way across the garden to the square tank of water near the thorn hedge and hacked away at the frozen surface of the water. He knew why he was there – to still his compulsion to take physical possession of the woman he had left behind in the drawing room. Before he took off his dressing gown, no doubt he bowed his head and prayed for purity of mind:

> Almighty God, unto whom all hearts be open, all desires known, and from whom no secrets are hid: cleanse the thoughts of my heart by the inspiration of thy Holy Spirit, that I may perfectly love thee, and worthily magnify thy holy name; through Christ our Lord. Amen.

When he stepped, naked, into the ferociously cold water, he would either survive and be granted respite from his tormenting desire, or he would die, perhaps at the very moment of immersion, and bequeath to Caroline the greatest blessing he could bestow – the freedom to be reunited with the true love of her life and the father of her child.

Within two days, inflammation of his lungs had taken hold. How bewildered Caroline must have been as she wept silently by the bedside of her devoted protector and truest friend as his fever raged and he gasped for breath. She knew why he had gone to the pool in the depths of winter when he was already ill, she understood the suppressed intensity of his longing for her. But how could she react? What could she say to him in those few moments of lucidity when he stirred and woke up and they were alone together with all the shared secrets of their lives filling the silent room? Caroline alone must have recognised the mystical selflessness of Charles's final act of love, and remembered it to the last day of her life. Lady Hatherton, in her letter of 18 December, the day after Charles's death, came perilously close to perceiving the truth when she wrote, 'Humanly speaking, he killed himself.' Soon the Wilbrahams arrived and began the bustle and bureaucracy of organising the return of his body to the family fold at Rode Hall, and Caroline and Charles's shared secret world was invaded and dispersed for ever.

It was one of the most poignant moments in our research when we stood in front of the celtic stone cross that marks the last resting place of Charles Philip Wilbraham, alongside the Victorian church of Odd Rode, and read the inscription carved on it:

CHARLES PHILIP WILBRAHAM

BORN AT RODE HALL MARCH 10TH 1810

DIED AT PENKRIDGE DECEMBER 17TH 1879

THE MUCH LOVED VICAR OF AUDLEY FOR 30 YEARS
AND PENKRIDGE FOR 6 YEARS

SUCCESSIVELY RURAL DEAN OF STOKE-UPON-TRENT,
NEWCASTLE AND PENKRIDGE.

We could not help wondering if his family had really understood the true cost Charles had paid in aching self-denial, to be true to his Lord to his very last day on earth, when they added a quotation from the Book of Revelations at the foot of his tombstone:

BE THOU FAITHFUL UNTO DEATH,
AND I WILL GIVE THEE A CROWN OF LIFE.

The failure even to mention Caroline's name was in line with the complete blank in the Wilbraham family archives on the subject of Charles's marriage or of Caroline as a person. Charles's secrecy about his wedding and subsequent married life supported our discoveries about the highly irregular course of events surrounding his move from Audley and the mysterious circumstances of his death. This seemed to be a grossly unjust epitaph for a man who had effectively paid the ultimate price to rescue the shattered life of the person he had come to love.

However, nothing could bear more revealing witness to the hidden agenda behind the marriage of Charles Wilbraham and Caroline Howard than the stark contrast in the reactions of those close to them after Charles's death. The Wilbrahams chose to censor all reference to Caroline from their memorials and records. By contrast, Caroline and her second husband, Robert Bateman, decided to make her former marriage to Charles Wilbraham a defining element of his huge ten-foot portrait of her, dressed as a widow in half-mourning, shown at the Grosvenor Gallery in London in 1886. It appeared that even six years after his death, and three years after their marriage, Robert and Caroline still considered that making reference to her former marriage to Wilbraham had a crucial role to play in how they presented her to the outside world.

As we considered Caroline's portrait from this perspective, we began to wonder whether we were reading it too superficially. Was our interpretation part of the image-obsessed age in which we live, where symbols such as black clothes and prayer books have been exploited for sensational effect so often that their significance is exhausted, and they become mere fashion accessories? Had Robert and Caroline really colluded to employ these sacred elements of the painting simply to promote their own social acceptability? Or were they central to the truth of how Robert saw Caroline? Is the inescapable sadness of Caroline's expression a reflection of her continuing inability to come to terms, morally and emotionally, with what has befallen her?

Abelard and Heloise did not attempt to assert a moral justification for their sexual relationship. Quite the reverse. They accepted the need to commit the rest of their lives to the celibate regime of monastic institutions in order to seek atonement for it. In this context, are Caroline's mourning clothes and the prayer book an acknowledgement of Charles Wilbraham's continuing centrality to Robert and Caroline's internal struggle for absolution? He remains the self-sacrificing agent of their social and spiritual redemption. Is Caroline's dress, which Richard Dorment described as 'very probably designed by her husband', a visual reference to this profound sense of indebtedness? Similarly, is the absence of the widow's cap, normally an essential component of the uniform of bereavement, a signal that she is remarried, therefore technically no longer in mourning for a spouse? It seems more plausible that, rather than attempting to mislead, Robert is doing no more than intuitively delineating the internal dilemmas of the subject before him, a person whose deepest secrets he knows, and identifies with completely.

Despite all her magnificent elegance and composure, is Caroline's portrait the portrayal of a sorrowful penitent, mourning both her fall from grace, and the loss of her only child? One thing is certain. The woman Robert portrays at the outset of their forty-year journey of devotion together is not a conventional, attractive widow on the threshold of a devoted second marriage to a gifted younger man. She is a powerful figure, imbued with an aura of sadness, which she suppresses with gentle dignity but which neither she nor Robert attempt to disguise.

After Charles Wilbraham's death on 17 December 1879, Caroline must have gone through the funeral at Rode Hall in Cheshire, and Christmas a few days later with her friends the Moncktons at Stretton Hall near Penkridge, in a numb haze. Eventually, she must have emerged from three weeks of emotional chaos into a disturbing and utterly transformed personal landscape. If our interpretation of events is correct, Charles's death was the culmination of a year of momentous developments not only for Caroline, but for two other key figures in her life.

For Robert Bateman, 1879 marked the moment when five lonely years of obsessive concentration on his work at last bore fruit, with the completion of two of his finest canvases. One was a deeply personal portrayal of thwarted lovers, *Heloise and Abelard*. The other, entitled *Saul and The Witch of Endor – The Raising of Samuel*, created a sensation when it was shown at the Royal Academy.

The other person at the heart of Caroline's life, for whom the year 1879 was critical, was a handsome, blond little boy of five years old, who had boarded a boat in the sweltering tumult of British India and sailed back to England. No doubt he found it a dank, alien place of regimented formality and domestic orderliness, unlike

Fig. 119 (opposite). Detail of The Artist's Wife *(fig. 24): a powerful figure, imbued with an aura of sadness.*

anything he had experienced in his life. His name was Henry Ulick Burke and, if our reading of his life is correct, his natural mother, Caroline Wilbraham, must have been sorely tempted to follow the instincts of her still aching heart, and go to him at once.

All the accounts of Caroline at this time attest to her sad but calm, gentle demeanour. This must surely have reflected a genuinely sorrowful reaction to the shocking end of her intense, almost tormented, involvement with Charles Wilbraham. None the less, contemporary accounts make clear that Caroline moved decisively to draw an emphatic line under her first marriage by selling all the furniture and contents of the vicarage on 24 March 1880. She had already announced her intention to move to London, which she did in April.

Caroline betrays no apparent will to position herself where she can renew contact with either Robert or Henry. In fact, in the census taken a year later in 1881, the three of them were at different ends of the country. Robert was still alone at Biddulph Old Hall with a single servant. Caroline was at her new home, 14 Upper Berkeley Street, Mayfair, being visited by her mother Henrietta Howard and a retinue of servants. Henry was with Katherine and Hope Burke, visiting the family of Edmund Swettenham at their home Lan-yr-Alyn near Chester.

Robert and Caroline appeared to be maintaining utterly contrasting lifestyles, in starkly different surroundings, at places two hundred miles apart. However, when we looked at the location of Caroline's new house a little more carefully, the opportunity it provided to lay the foundations for her second marriage suddenly came to light. Her house in Upper Berkeley Street lay directly across Hyde Park from Robert's parents' house at 9 Hyde Park Gate South. Although she would not be expected to receive visitors or go out in society during her period of deep mourning, she could take exercise in the park at the end of her street, where she might have chance encounters with anyone.

In these circumstances, the anonymity of London provided opportunity to meet people unnoticed, especially as it was unremarkable for a lady in mourning to be veiled when out in public. We wondered how long it was before Robert and Caroline dared to arrange a clandestine assignation, he with his soft felt hat pulled down over his eyes and she swathed in her crêpe veil. Did they meet secretly on a secluded park bench within days of her arrival in London? Did they, there and then, renew their pledge to remain true to their love and to each other all their lives? We have no way of knowing, but one thing is certain. They must have met at the latest by 1882, to set in motion the process leading to their marriage on 18 October the following year, without contravening the rules of betrothal before matrimony.

This must have been one of the most intense periods of Robert and Caroline's relationship. The months between April 1880 when Caroline left Penkridge, and October 1883 when she and Robert were finally married, must have been a time of radiant, resurgent hope, after six years of resignation in which they had abandoned all thought of a future together. There must have been wonderful letters, love letters, chronicling every step of the journey towards the ritual recognition of the promises they had already given each other years before, promises they had managed to keep, even during Caroline's marriage to Charles. They would never have been able to destroy those letters, either of them. The letters must have been at Nunney, just as the paintings, the sketches and the sculptures were, all telling the same story of passionate, romantic love triumphing over the mundane respectability of a lukewarm, disapproving world.

They must have been there, but they were gone, seemingly without trace, put out of sight, through anxiety or fear, by the very person who had been entrusted with their safe keeping, so that no evidence of his sad role in the story they told could be unearthed and understood by inquisitive busybodies like ourselves.

Despite this, a few random paintings have survived, enough to ensure that the reputation of Robert as a painter could be rescued from oblivion and enough, just enough, to allow him to give a fragmentary account through his work of the compulsive love affair that dominated his life.

It had been a fabulous journey of discovery that had transformed and enriched our lives. How far we had travelled since we glibly dismissed *At Romsey Abbey* – the image of a fair-haired little boy asleep under the protection of Jesus Christ – as mawkish Victorian sentimentality. Now that we had come to perceive the potentially desperate relevance of the subject to Robert and Caroline after Henry's exile in Cyprus and banishment to America, it suggested a starkly truthful visualisation of their deepest anxieties about his wellbeing and anguished prayers for his safety.

However, we could not disguise an ache in our hearts that so many other pieces of the puzzle had been lost. There must have been so many drawings and paintings, delineating the spiritual centre of an infinitely rare, loving relationship. How graphically would they have defined their struggle to mitigate the shame they felt at the hurt inflicted on their child, by their inability to acknowledge and care for him, during his vulnerable formative years. Surely these mislaid images, in which Robert employed his creative imagination and his innate skill as a draughtsman, would have constituted some of his most disturbing and original works of art. The truth and intensity of the relationships that inspired them, married to his idiosyncratic vision, would surely have created a body of work that ensured a place for Robert among the great romantic figures of the nineteenth century, had they survived. The story they illustrated would have generated a legend of enduring mutual devotion that would have inspired new generations of people, longing to put their faith in the indestructible potential of shared human love.

As the end of our quest approached, we became immersed in the process of trying to evaluate the profound impact our involvement with Robert and Caroline's story had had on our perceptions and prejudices about everything, from Pre-Raphaelite painting to cold baths. We were lamenting the fact that, in all our travels, we had never had the luck to stumble across the mythical 'tin trunk in the attic', stored with a treasure trove of sketches and letters that would have allowed them to tell their story in their own words. It was literally while Brian and I were discussing this that the most astonishing event in the whole of our mysterious adventure occurred.

Chapter 29

MOTHER AND CHILD

We were in our office at 4 o'clock on a raw December afternoon, two days
before we closed our business for the Christmas break. We had decided to
make a clean copy of the manuscript of this book to fine-tune and edit it over the
holiday. Brian had been making new copies of some of the early paintings, *Women
Plucking Mandrakes* and *The Dead Knight*. He was just about to print off the images
from the internet when something extraordinary happened. A completely new entry
appeared on the screen under the heading 'Bloomsbury Auctions, New York'. It was
the record of an auction held in America earlier that year which had just been posted:

> Sale NY044, 24 March 2010. Sold for $900.
> Lot No. 71. Robert Bateman (1842–1922). Mother and Child.
> Pen and grey wash. Dated July XX 1880, middle right.
> 10 × 8 in (25.5 × 20.2 cm)
> Provenance: with Christopher Powney, London.

He printed it and held out the sheet of paper. As I leaned forward to take it, the
significance of what he had just read out struck me. A pen-and-wash drawing by
Robert Bateman, entitled *Mother and Child*!

I took the paper but seemed unable to look down at it.

'Don't look so terrified,' said Brian, his face suddenly breaking into an ecstatic
smile. 'Look at it!'

There in my hands was an exquisite, concise image, conveying in a few deft strokes
the intense communion between a handsome, elegant woman in early middle age
and a young boy of five or six years old (fig. 120). The woman enfolds the boy in a
tender embrace, which unmistakably expresses the instinctive, protective love of a
mother for her own child. The economy with which the folds of the woman's clothes
are conveyed belies the precision with which her age and character are incisively
delineated.

Fig. 120. Robert Bateman, Mother and Child, *1880, pen and grey wash, 25.5 × 20.2 cm, private collection.*

The intense, informal intimacy of an unposed, private moment, not contrived for pictorial effect, gave the drawing a powerful truth and immediacy. The woman's soft, flowing clothes and plaited hair indicate that she is at ease in her own home. There is no attempt to idealise either of the figures, so their identity is almost unmistakable in the context of the artist responsible for the drawing and its date. Since the drawing's provenance was provided by Christopher Powney, one of the most prominent London dealers in Old Master drawings during the 1960s and 1970s, we can assume it is beyond doubt, especially as attribution to Bateman at that time held no cachet or monetary advantage in the art market.

The picture was an authenticated Bateman drawing, dated 20 July 1880, entitled *Mother and Child*. This date was almost the earliest moment that Robert, Caroline and Henry were all in Britain, and in a position to meet. Caroline had been widowed in December the previous year and had arrived in London in April 1880. Henry had remained in India until mid-1879, when he returned to England with Ulick Ralph Burke. He would have been six years old in 1880, the same age as the child in the picture, who bears a striking resemblance to the boy in Ruth Vilmi's photographs. In July 1880, Robert was on the threshold of his betrothal and marriage to Caroline Wilbraham, who was forty-one that year, much the age of the woman in the drawing. The informality of the dress, demeanour and setting of the subject convey an intimacy with the unmarried artist that is difficult to explain, unless Caroline is the sitter. Both the title and the clear intention of the drawing to illustrate exactly that maternal relationship meant it could only be a portrayal of Caroline if our account of her life was correct, and she had given birth to a son five or six years earlier.

The drawing addressed itself, with mysterious precision, to the very imponderables surrounding the nature of the relationship uniting these three figures which had been dominating our thoughts. How soon after Caroline's arrival in London did she and Robert meet? Had she sought the first available opportunity to be reunited with Henry after Charles Wilbraham's death and the child's return to England? Had all three of them – father, mother and son – ever been reunited during the four years that Henry was at home before his departure for Cyprus with Ulick Ralph Burke?

As ever with Robert, the exposition of deeply felt, complex emotions, at times quite clumsily realised in other creative mediums, here reaches a sublime level of concise, honest clarity. In this infinitely tender drawing, he uses the recording of an ostensibly commonplace event to capture all the inherent conflict of a fiercely intense, but fleeting, moment of respite from profound inner sadness. In the acutely sensitive way he perceives and responds to the scene before him, Robert betrays the depth of his own emotional identification and involvement with it. It is essentially the record of a moment of supreme fulfilment after years of emptiness and yearning by the mother, and instinctive need by the child. It is a simple sketch, which aspires to the impossible, but because the aspiration is unconscious, and submerged within the driving desire to portray the factual truth of the momentary interaction between all the people taking part in its creation, it comes tantalisingly close to achieving its objective of being a picture of love.

Surely the reason it so nearly attains its elusive ambition is that, at this exact moment in July 1880, it represents three people who have been forced to suppress the yearning to give and receive love in all its forms, as adults, parents and as an unwanted child. It is a picture of love, drawn with love, by Robert, to record the moment of fulfilment of his prophetic injunction 'Carpe Diem' (redeem the day) in his painting *Heloise and Abelard*.

All the youthful hopes and dreams he had sought to recapture in that painting, when everything about him seemed desolate and forlorn, had miraculously been reborn, and burst into dynamic, vivid new life on that summer afternoon in late July 1880, when he watched as Caroline gently wrapped her arms around their son, and gazed down on him. This simple gesture was so pure in its instinctive intent that it was able to reach out and encompass all three of them in an act of spiritual healing. Robert was compelled to record it, so that it could remain with them for ever.

With the discovery of *Mother and Child* we were convinced that the record of a clandestine love story, centred on the birth of a little boy to two beautiful and gifted people, had been revealed through the subtext of Robert Bateman's paintings. Although cryptic clues had been concealed within several pieces of his work, one painting above any other bore witness to the spiritual anguish that underlay the gorgeous surface texture of their tale. Every element of the hidden painting *Heloise and Abelard*, from its identification with the ecstatic despair of the ancient lovers to the symbolic significance of every butterfly and wilted flower, was used by Robert simultaneously to disguise and delineate the forbidden passion between Caroline and himself.

Once we had come to accept this, we could not lay Robert and Caroline's story to rest without revisiting the painting one last time. We needed to decipher Robert's motivation for creating it at so late a date, and who he had intended to be the recipient of its enigmatic message. Since the painting is dated 1879, and Charles Wilbraham only died unexpectedly in mid-December that year, it cannot have been Robert's response to the cataclysmic news of Caroline's renewed availability. At the time he conceived the painting she was powerless to redeem their lost love, by becoming 'forever one' again in any overt or permanent sense. Yet surely only she would have been able to read the covert references and dangerous associations within the image. So what day or event had Robert sought to redeem by including the plea

X : XII : III
Carpe Diem

on the Cupid sundial?

We had discovered that another momentous event in Robert and Caroline's lives had occurred in 1879. A fair-haired five-year-old boy, Henry Burke, had arrived back in England from India. Since he was ostensibly Robert's sister's child, he would have been taken to 9 Hyde Park Gate South, his grandparents' house, where Robert would have seen him, probably for the first time. As the bewildered child stared at him, unaware of any bond between them, Robert must have been overwhelmed by the tragedy of his and Caroline's estrangement from each other and their son. Surely this disquieting encounter in the summer of 1879 was the emotional stimulus for Robert's portrayal of Heloise and Abelard, the devoted lovers brutally torn apart through the conception and birth of a child. Later that year when there did not seem to be any possibility of them ever being reunited, he conceived it as an enduring testimony to the truth of the indissoluble blood link that bound him, Caroline and Henry to each other.

Of course he could not risk showing the picture anywhere and exposing Caroline to the possibility that others might recognise the damning self-portraits and grasp the relevance of them to the narrative of the painting. He painted it for Caroline alone, and gave it to her to cherish secretly for ever.

However, this still did not explain the significance of the date X:XII:III. Was it the actual day for which Robert sought redemption? The X and XII presumably refer to 10 December, but the III deliberately leaves room for doubt. If it refers to 1873, the same decade as the painting was executed, it would mark a day four weeks before the date always given as Henry's, officially unrecorded, birthday in Lahore. This would correspond exactly with the length of time the boat journey from England to India took in the second half of the nineteenth century. Did Robert incorporate this date into his painting to commemorate, for all time, the true day on which his and Caroline's child was born?

If so, the first time the anniversary recurred, after Henry's return from India, would have been his sixth birthday on 10 December 1879 – the day on which, humanly speaking, Charles Wilbraham killed himself.

POSTSCRIPT

Our research into the work of Robert Bateman had left us with one nagging frustration. Nowhere had we uncovered even the vaguest hint or rumour about the fate of Robert's most acclaimed painting *Saul and The Witch of Endor – The Raising of Samuel* which had been hanging in his studio at Nunney Delamere at the time of his death in 1922. The painting had caused a great stir when it was exhibited in 1879, as Walter Crane made clear in his *Reminiscences*:

> His best known picture is perhaps 'The Witch of Endor' which was in the Royal Academy Exhibition. It is a very weird and powerful scene of 'The Raising of Samuel' and is worked out with extraordinary invention and detail.

Since precisely this combination of technical virtuosity and fertile invention had ensured the survival of several of Robert's best paintings, we felt there was a realistic chance that we might track it down.

However, endless scrutiny of sales, auctions and documented private collections had failed to yield even a single lead. In an attempt to gain some idea of what we might be looking for, we decided to investigate the only solid fact available to us – the strange compound title and the Old Testament passage it related to. Saul's consultation of the Witch of Endor is recorded in the 28th chapter of the 1st Book of Samuel. King Saul of Israel has drawn up his forces for battle, but is heavily outnumbered by his enemies, the Philistines:

> When Saul saw the host of the Philistines, he was afraid, and his heart greatly trembled. And when Saul enquired of the Lord, the Lord answered him not, neither by dreams, nor by Urim, nor by prophets.
>
> Then, said Saul unto his servants, seek me a woman that hath a familiar spirit. And his servants said unto him, Behold, there is a woman that hath a familiar spirit at Endor.

The difficulty was that King Saul claimed not to believe in the power of 'familiar spirits' and had passed a law forbidding any consultation of the mediums who contacted them, condemning them as witches perpetuating superstitions incompatible with the worship of the Lord, the true God of Israel. However, the account makes clear that his abandonment of spiritualism is not sincere.

> And Saul disguised himself, and put on other raiment, and he went, and two men with him, and they came to the woman by night, and he said, 'I pray thee, divine unto me by the familiar spirit and bring him up, whom I shall name unto thee.'

> And the woman said unto him, 'Behold thou knowest what Saul has done, how he hath cut off those that have familiar spirits, and the wizards out of the land. Wherefore then layest thou a snare for my life, to cause me to die?'

> Then Saul swore to her by the Lord, saying, 'As the Lord liveth, there shall no punishment happen to thee for this thing.'

> Then said the woman, 'Whom shall I bring up to thee?'

> And he said, 'Bring me Samuel.'

The moment Samuel appears, the woman demonstrates the extent of her second sight.

> And when the woman saw Samuel, she cried out in a loud voice, and the woman spoke to Saul saying, 'Why hast thou deceived me? For thou art Saul!'

The fact that the preamble *Saul and the Witch of Endor* is subservient to the main title *The Raising of Samuel* indicates that it is the psychic's forbidden ability to restore life from beyond the grave that Robert intended to be the subject of the painting. There is an interesting parallel here with Robert's treatment of *The Pool of Bethesda*. The story of the healing pool is included in the New Testament deliberately to contrast Christ's healing power through faith with the ancient Jewish tradition of the troubled water, which had no theological validity. To omit Christ's intervention was essentially to de-Christianise the story and give credence to the earlier superstition, a dangerously radical and unconventional approach to sacred texts in the 1870s.

Equally provocative was the selection of the raising of Samuel as a subject, since it challenged the unique attribute of Christ – his resurrection from death and his ability to confer immortality upon those who placed their faith in him. The Witch of Endor story had always been acknowledged as doctrinally deeply problematic in both the Jewish and Christian religious traditions, since the psychic medium consulted by Saul appears to have the power to resurrect Samuel through her relationship with a familiar spirit (a spirit guide from beyond the grave) without the intervention of either the Jewish god Yahweh or Jesus. What had made Robert deliberately select these highly contentious biblical subjects? Nothing we have discovered about his life – from his illustrations for *The Latin Year*, to his Chairmanship of the Bosely branch of the International Bible Society, and his lifelong relationship with Caroline, a devout believer – suggested he was a religious sceptic.

I suspect that Robert's engagement with these accounts of para-normal happenings deliberately removed from their specifically religious context was part of the wider Pre-Raphaelite return to secular para-normal myths and legends used as allegories of intense personal experience. *The Beguiling of Merlin, Phyllis and Demophoon*, and the many mythical guises in which Rossetti portrayed Jane Morris are a few familiar instances of this practice.

Although until the picture is found it must remain pure speculation, it is tempting to see a relationship between the subject of the painting and Robert's personal situation in the year it was conceived and painted. In 1879 Robert was in the fifth year of his reclusive life at Biddulph. Caroline had been married to Charles Wilbraham three years earlier and lived fifty miles away in Penckridge.

However, if our investigations are correct, a critical development had taken place in the middle of 1879 with the arrival back in England from India of Henry Burke. Robert could hardly have failed to meet the five-year-old boy who was ostensibly his nephew. How would Caroline have reacted to Henry's return and the near certainty that Robert had seen him? Did the compulsion to have news of her child drive her to take the one step absolutely forbidden by everyone who had taken part in the plot to save her from disgrace – did she make contact with Robert, perhaps through an intermediary (the term 'familiar spirit' is derived from the Latin *familiaris*, 'a trusted household servant')? If so, did he perceive her message as an almost miraculous invocation from the one person with the power to release him from his desolate isolation and draw him back into the living world that had forgotten him?

Responding to that contact would have presented Robert with an agonising dilemma. He would have felt compelled to acknowledge the risks Caroline had taken and maintain communication. However, if through desperation he acted rashly, he risked destabilising her marriage and exposing the whole complex web of deception surrounding her pregnancy to outside scrutiny. This had the potential to condemn not only themselves and their families but, crucially, their son to lifelong disgrace and ostracism. We wondered if Robert had hidden his encoded reply within the subject and symbolism of *Heloise and Abelard* – the only other known painting executed by him in the critical year of 1879?

Not long after this tantalising possibility had occurred to us, we unexpectedly stumbled upon the title *Saul and the Witch of Endor* while following up chance information on another lost painting. In 2006 Yale University Press had published a comprehensive list of all the oil paintings by artists born before 1870 held in British and Irish public collections. We were told it listed a small Bateman painting, *The*

Fig. 121. Robert Bateman, The Appleton Thorn, *1880,*
oil on panel, Warrington Museum and Art Gallery.

Appleton Thorn, in a gallery in Warrington (fig. 121). When we visited the gallery to see it, the curator told us that the Yale volume listed a second Bateman, but he could not remember the title. We acquired a copy of the book and were stunned when we read the relevant entry:

> Stoke on Trent. The Potteries Museum and Art Gallery. Saul and the Witch of Endor. List 1997, inv no 151 1954.

The curator at the Stoke Museum at first confirmed that they had the painting, then rang back to say she had been mistaken and that their painting was not by Robert, but by a Samuel Bateman. We went to view it and, sure enough, it was by Samuel Bateman, an oil, approximately 3' 6" × 2' 6", of very mediocre quality, entitled *On the Bosky Backwater* (of the Thames near Henley). A little investigation soon established that Samuel Bateman had been employed as a scenery painter at the Theatre Royal in Hanley, which explained the presence of the painting at the Stoke Museum. It was clearly inscribed on the reverse with the title and a note confirming that it had 'no Inventory Number'.

The Museum insisted that this was the only Bateman they held, and they considered the matter closed. We found this unconvincing, since neither the artist's name, nor the title, nor the absence of an inventory number tallied with our information from an impeccable source.

So we decided to undertake a programme of extremely dull research through the minutes of the Council's Libraries, Museums and Gymnasiums Committee for key years such as 1954 the (the inventory number date given by Yale), 1931–33 (when Nunney Delamere was sold and its contents dispersed) and 1922–3 (the time of Robert's death). Unfortunately, we began with the 1950s and 1930s, so had almost lost the will to live by the time we discovered the following minute, No. 156, for the committee meeting of 2 October 1922:

> The Chief Curator reported that by the Will of the late Mr R. Bateman a large picture had been left to the Corporation, and had been removed to the Hanley Museum upon instruction of the Mayor, Alderman Samuel Sproston.
>
> It was Resolved – That the picture be accepted and that the thanks of the Committee be tendered to the Trustees of the deceased gentleman.

So *Saul and The Witch of Endor* had not been discarded or destroyed. It was willed to the Hanley Museum and Art Gallery in 1922, presumably as part of the private memorandum attached to Robert's Will. It was clearly there in 1954 when it was re-inventorised under its original title and artist's name.

Faced with this evidence, the museum surprisingly revealed that they knew it was a large painting and, in fact, had precise information about its size, which was 6' 6" × 5'. So clearly they must have known that the painting they had shown us, only a quarter of that size, was not *Saul and the Witch of Endor* by Robert Bateman.

We discovered that their handlist had the words 'Longton Case' beside the title, but no one knew the meaning or significance of this. We made a painstaking study of the movements of the paintings of the Hanley Museum since its demolition and the incorporation of its collection into the Potteries Museum and Art Gallery in 1954. Eventually, the Potteries Museum allowed us to audit their handlist, card index and store. The word 'Case' was written on the complete batch of new cards issued in 1954 to cover the old Hanley Museum collection. A case number was then added by hand, unless the paintings were already on display elsewhere, in which case just the location was recorded. The most common sites were the five separate Town Halls that collectively made up the City of Stoke on Trent. On the cards these were indicated by a single word – e.g. Stoke, Hanley, Longton.

So *Saul and the Witch of Endor* had formed part of a collection of paintings in Longton Town Hall until Stoke City Council ordered its demolition in the 1970s. When work began and the roof had been removed, the population of Longton rebelled. They issued the City Council with a legal challenge, which forced them to abandon the demolition and restore the building to good repair. Once this work was complete, many of the portraits of local worthies were again required to grace the fabulously pompous entrance hall and staircase of the Town Hall. However, the huge reception room on the first floor, the Albert Hall, had by this time become a popular venue for pop concerts, etc. Vast Victorian paintings inspired by Old Testament re-incarnations were not thought to contribute anything positive to the atmosphere of liberated youth culture that the organisers were after.

As far as we were able to discover, Robert's painting languished in a council store in the basement of the old housing department until it was demolished. Since then, *Saul and the Witch of Endor*, along with a few other large subject paintings from the Town Halls, have been lost. Despite exhaustive research, we could find no official evidence of Robert's painting being either sold or discarded, although instances of both these processes are recorded in the Council minutes.

We could not rid ourselves of the conviction that *Saul and the Witch of Endor* was leaning against the wall of a forgotten store room, along with an important group of interwar posters by Frank Brangwyn, which were also missing. So we persuaded the Stoke daily, *The Sentinel*, to publish a full-page article, illustrated by a Victorian photograph of Robert Bateman, describing our search for the lost painting.

At the end of the piece the paper gave our contact details and appealed for any information to be sent either to the paper or to us. We had a few responses, but nothing decisive. Then one evening, at about 6.30 p.m., I was finishing off in the office before joining Brian and some friends for a drink when the phone rang. I answered, and was met with a long silence.

Then a voice with a strong Stoke accent said, 'You're looking for a painting?'

I had been thinking of something else and did not instantly understand what he meant, and answered fatuously, 'Am I?'

In the silence that followed I finally caught up and confirmed that I was indeed searching for a painting and quickly ran through the details.

After another silence, the voice said, 'What's in it?'

To my eternal shame I managed again to miss the point completely!

Of course, he wanted to know what reward he could expect for its return, so did not react favourably to my patient explanation that since the painting was lost we did not have any information about exactly what it portrayed, beyond the title.

During the next protracted silence I managed to summon up enough nous to say how anxious I and others were to trace the painting, and how valuable to us any information leading to its rediscovery would be. When he did not respond, I added that although the extent of our anxiety had not yet been quantified in pounds ster-ling, I felt certain that negotiation was likely to be eminently worth his while.

Then he said, 'I've got a van.'

Again, I didn't know how to respond. By now I was so agitated and terrified of messing up again that I remained silent until he said, 'Do you know Chemical Lane, near Bradwall Wood?'

Of course I didn't. I thought of saying yes and giving myself time to find out, but plumped instead for, 'Not really, but I'm sure I could find it,' in the hope that he might give clearer directions.

Our conversation drifted into yet another long silence, which I eventually broke by tentatively asking whether he intended to go there in his van. At this point he hung up.

I ran to find Brian, who remembered that Chemical Lane was on the northern outskirts of Stoke; we passed the end of it when we were heading for the M6. Forty minutes later we were there. The setting was like a cliché from a John Le Carré novel. Huge potholes filled with water, the railway line running down one side behind barbed-wire fencing, sporadic yellow lights, drab warehouses and seedy offices behind padlocked gates – all this combined to exude an Iron Curtain menace that really unnerved us.

The prospect of getting out of the car filled us with fear, but we did drive slowly up and down the whole length of the road four times. There were no vans, and only one man in overalls padlocking the gates of a transport depot. We decided against trying to engage him in a conversation about Pre-Raphaelite art.

The sad dénouement to this tale is that despite several further visits to Chemical Lane we have never heard from my friend on the telephone again. Whether anything will come of it only time will tell, but I do feel instinctively that the man I spoke to had some information about the picture, which suggests that it may have been spirited away rather than discarded during the chaotic destruction and rebuilding of Stoke on Trent in the late twentieth century. If this is true, I believe that Robert and Caroline will lead us to it, when the time is right.

HOWARD FAMILY TREE

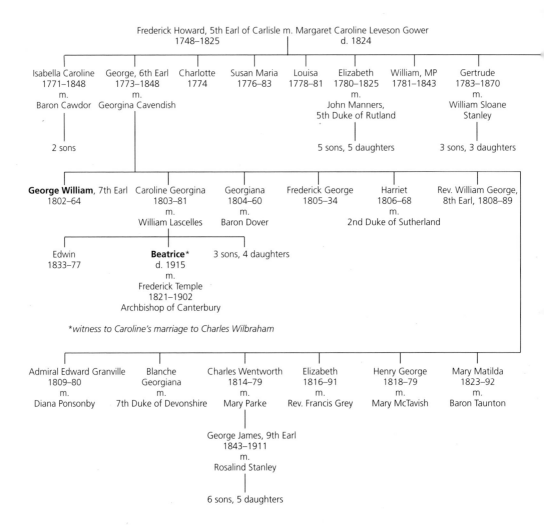

Frederick Howard, 5th Earl of Carlisle m. Margaret Caroline Leveson Gower
1748–1825   d. 1824

Isabella Caroline	George, 6th Earl	Charlotte	Susan Maria	Louisa	Elizabeth	William, MP	Gertrude
1771–1848	1773–1848	1774	1776–83	1778–81	1780–1825	1781–1843	1783–1870
m.	m.				m.		m.
Baron Cawdor	Georgina Cavendish				John Manners,		William Sloane
					5th Duke of Rutland		Stanley
2 sons					5 sons, 5 daughters		3 sons, 3 daughters

George William, 7th Earl	Caroline Georgina	Georgiana	Frederick George	Harriet	Rev. William George,
1802–64	1803–81	1804–60	1805–34	1806–68	8th Earl, 1808–89
	m.	m.		m.	
	William Lascelles	Baron Dover		2nd Duke of Sutherland	

Edwin   **Beatrice***   3 sons, 4 daughters
1833–77   d. 1915
     m.
     Frederick Temple
     1821–1902
     Archbishop of Canterbury

witness to Caroline's marriage to Charles Wilbraham

Admiral Edward Granville	Blanche	Charles Wentworth	Elizabeth	Henry George	Mary Matilda
1809–80	Georgiana	1814–79	1816–91	1818–79	1823–92
m.	m.	m.	m.	m.	m.
Diana Ponsonby	7th Duke of Devonshire	Mary Parke	Rev. Francis Grey	Mary McTavish	Baron Taunton

George James, 9th Earl
1843–1911
m.
Rosalind Stanley

6 sons, 5 daughters

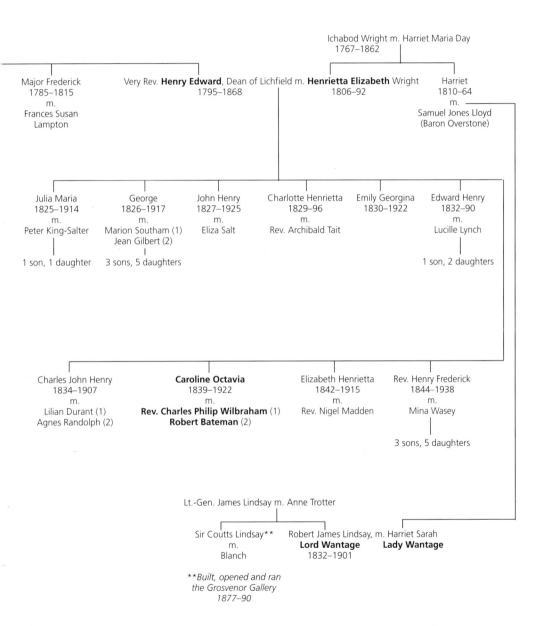

Ichabod Wright m. Harriet Maria Day
1767–1862

Major Frederick
1785–1815
m.
Frances Susan
Lampton

Very Rev. **Henry Edward**, Dean of Lichfield m. **Henrietta Elizabeth** Wright
1795–1868   1806–92

Harriet
1810–64
m.
Samuel Jones Lloyd
(Baron Overstone)

Julia Maria
1825–1914
m.
Peter King-Salter

1 son, 1 daughter

George
1826–1917
m.
Marion Southam (1)
Jean Gilbert (2)

3 sons, 5 daughters

John Henry
1827–1925
m.
Eliza Salt

Charlotte Henrietta
1829–96
m.
Rev. Archibald Tait

Emily Georgina
1830–1922

Edward Henry
1832–90
m.
Lucille Lynch

1 son, 2 daughters

Charles John Henry
1834–1907
m.
Lilian Durant (1)
Agnes Randolph (2)

Caroline Octavia
1839–1922
m.
Rev. Charles Philip Wilbraham (1)
Robert Bateman (2)

Elizabeth Henrietta
1842–1915
m.
Rev. Nigel Madden

Rev. Henry Frederick
1844–1938
m.
Mina Wasey

3 sons, 5 daughters

Lt.-Gen. James Lindsay m. Anne Trotter

Sir Coutts Lindsay**
m.
Blanch

Robert James Lindsay, m. Harriet Sarah
Lord Wantage   **Lady Wantage**
1832–1901

****Built, opened and ran
the Grosvenor Gallery
1877–90**

WILBRAHAM FAMILY TREE

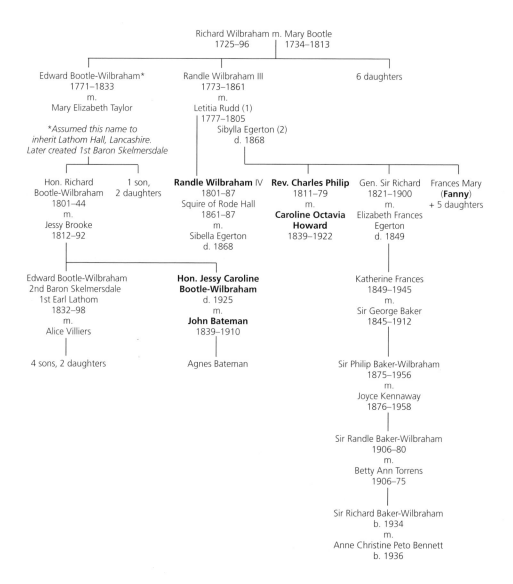

Richard Wilbraham m. Mary Bootle
1725–96 | 1734–1813

Edward Bootle-Wilbraham*
1771–1833
m.
Mary Elizabeth Taylor

*Assumed this name to
inherit Lathom Hall, Lancashire.
Later created 1st Baron Skelmersdale

Randle Wilbraham III
1773–1861
m.
Letitia Rudd (1)
1777–1805
Sibylla Egerton (2)
d. 1868

6 daughters

Hon. Richard
Bootle-Wilbraham
1801–44
m.
Jessy Brooke
1812–92

1 son,
2 daughters

Randle Wilbraham IV
1801–87
Squire of Rode Hall
1861–87
m.
Sibella Egerton
d. 1868

Rev. Charles Philip
1811–79
m.
**Caroline Octavia
Howard**
1839–1922

Gen. Sir Richard
1821–1900
m.
Elizabeth Frances
Egerton
d. 1849

Frances Mary
(**Fanny**)
+ 5 daughters

Edward Bootle-Wilbraham
2nd Baron Skelmersdale
1st Earl Lathom
1832–98
m.
Alice Villiers

4 sons, 2 daughters

**Hon. Jessy Caroline
Bootle-Wilbraham**
d. 1925
m.
John Bateman
1839–1910

Agnes Bateman

Katherine Frances
1849–1945
m.
Sir George Baker
1845–1912

Sir Philip Baker-Wilbraham
1875–1956
m.
Joyce Kennaway
1876–1958

Sir Randle Baker-Wilbraham
1906–80
m.
Betty Ann Torrens
1906–75

Sir Richard Baker-Wilbraham
b. 1934
m.
Anne Christine Peto Bennett
b. 1936

BATEMAN FAMILY TREE

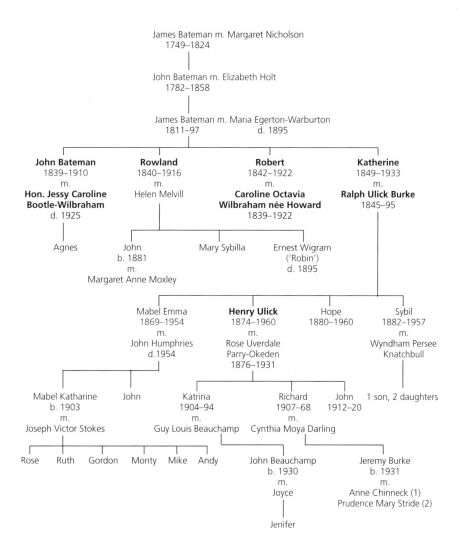

James Bateman m. Margaret Nicholson
1749–1824

John Bateman m. Elizabeth Holt
1782–1858

James Bateman m. Maria Egerton-Warburton
1811–97   d. 1895

John Bateman   Rowland   **Robert**   Katherine
1839–1910   1840–1916   1842–1922   1849–1933
m.   m.   m.   m.
Hon. Jessy Caroline   Helen Melvill   **Caroline Octavia** **Ralph Ulick Burke**
Bootle-Wilbraham   **Wilbraham née Howard** 1845–95
d. 1925   1839–1922

Agnes   John   Mary Sybilla   Ernest Wigram
                           b. 1881   ('Robin')
                           m.   d. 1895
                    Margaret Anne Moxley

                           Mabel Emma   **Henry Ulick**   Hope   Sybil
                           1869–1954   1874–1960   1880–1960   1882–1957
                           m.   m.   m.
                           John Humphries   Rose Uverdale   Wyndham Persee
                           d.1954   Parry-Okeden   Knatchbull
                                                1876–1931

Mabel Katharine   John   Katrina   Richard   John   1 son, 2 daughters
b. 1903   1904–94   1907–68   1912–20
m.   m.   m.
Joseph Victor Stokes   Guy Louis Beauchamp Cynthia Moya Darling

Rose   Ruth   Gordon   Monty   Mike   Andy   John Beauchamp   Jeremy Burke
                                                  b. 1930   b. 1931
                                                  m.   m.
                                                  Joyce   Anne Chinneck (1)
                                                                          Prudence Mary Stride (2)

                                                  Jenifer

PICTURE CREDITS

INDEX